The Palgrave Handbook on Critical Theories of Education

Ali A. Abdi · Greg William Misiaszek
Editors

The Palgrave Handbook on Critical Theories of Education

Editors
Ali A. Abdi
Department of Educational Studies
University of British Columbia
Vancouver, BC, Canada

Greg William Misiaszek
Faculty of Education, Institute
of Educational Theories
Beijing Normal University
Beijing, China

With Contrib. by
Janna M. Popoff
Faculty of Education and Social Work
Thompson Rivers University
Kamloops, BC, Canada

ISBN 978-3-030-86342-5   ISBN 978-3-030-86343-2 (eBook)
https://doi.org/10.1007/978-3-030-86343-2

© The Editor(s) (if applicable) and The Author(s), under exclusive license to Springer Nature Switzerland AG 2022
This work is subject to copyright. All rights are solely and exclusively licensed by the Publisher, whether the whole or part of the material is concerned, specifically the rights of translation, reprinting, reuse of illustrations, recitation, broadcasting, reproduction on microfilms or in any other physical way, and transmission or information storage and retrieval, electronic adaptation, computer software, or by similar or dissimilar methodology now known or hereafter developed.
The use of general descriptive names, registered names, trademarks, service marks, etc. in this publication does not imply, even in the absence of a specific statement, that such names are exempt from the relevant protective laws and regulations and therefore free for general use.
The publisher, the authors, and the editors are safe to assume that the advice and information in this book are believed to be true and accurate at the date of publication. Neither the publisher nor the authors or the editors give a warranty, expressed or implied, with respect to the material contained herein or for any errors or omissions that may have been made. The publisher remains neutral with regard to jurisdictional claims in published maps and institutional affiliations.

Cover illustration: EXTREMEPHOTOGRAPHER/gettyimages

This Palgrave Macmillan imprint is published by the registered company Springer Nature Switzerland AG
The registered company address is: Gewerbestrasse 11, 6330 Cham, Switzerland

Foreword: White Supremacy, White Philosophy, and Rewriting of History

This important book comprehensively embraces and investigates five grounds for critical theories of education—praxis-oriented, fluidity, radical, utopic with countless possible futures, and using bottom-up approaches across nine sections: (i) critical perspectives and philosophies, (ii) critical race theories, (iii) comparative educational approaches and global citizenship, (iv) critical literacies, (v) critical media culture and information studies, (vi) community-engaged learning and research, (vii) sciences and mathematics, (viii) gender and feminism, and (ix) Indigenous and epistemologies of the South. It establishes a matrix for transformative education in the service of a better world and sustainable planet. It aims to decolonize effects of contemporary hegemonic Western-centric systems of education, to critique cultural and cognitive imperialism of neoliberal technocratic regimes of performativity while at the same time fostering critical pedagogy as a means of achieving a world of social justice, sustainability, and community well-being. Frierean critical theories of education are designed to counter forms of oppression and domination that are often hidden from us so that we must unlearn 'epistemologies of the North' to engage in critical work with both kids and adults. 'Epistemologies of the North' is a kind of shorthand for understanding that the conceptual categories accepted as natural, inevitable, and universal in Western education approaches are deeply suspect from the position of women and people of color and seen as embodying power/knowledge cultural assumptions governing politics and history that have constructed white narratives, that is, narratives that privilege white power at the expense of others and disguised as the truth. Critical pedagogy and critical race theory have provided a different set of framework assumptions that question US history, the genocidal origins of the Black slave economy, and the legacy of racial segregation.

A new set of culture wars have irrupted in America heightened by the far-right white supremacist political insurrection and continued police brutality against Black people epitomized in the killing of George Floyd (Samayeen et al., 2020). This is perfectly illustrated by the Black philosopher George Yancy's 'Dear White America' published in the *New York Times* 'The Stone' philosophy column that generated thousands of hate mail. In an interview I conducted with him, Yancy (Peters, 2019) explains his understanding of race as a social construction, a *social* rather than natural kind because there is no external referent and no corresponding reality. The concept is 'ontologically empty,' but it came into existence from Western Europe, 'socially and historically produced and shaped by colonial desire, bad faith, domination, psychological projection, and ontological and epistemic logics that are Manichean in nature, where whiteness has come to constitute what I term the transcendental norm. In short, whiteness, by its very nature, is binary and hierarchical.' Yancy goes on to argue:

> Whiteness is the thesis (that is, it establishes itself as such) and 'racialized' groups that are not white are deemed 'different,' 'deviant,' that is, the antithesis. Despite the fact that race is not a natural kind, it has tremendous *social* ontological power; the concept is a powerful organizing social vector that functions as if it cuts at the very joints of reality. The concept of race constitutes our institutional spaces, our political forms of arrangement, our perceptions, our bodily comportment in space, our organization of lived space and lived experience. In fact, the state itself is a site of racial power. So, let's get one point clear. While the concept of race is unreal qua natural kind, the concept of race has served to create rigid social binaries and used to oppress, to dehumanize, to murder, to render disposable. That is what we mean by racism. Historically, within the context of North America, this is what I mean by white racism. In our contemporary moment, it can be argued that race continues to advantage white people globally, continues to render their lives worth living, and axiologically supreme vis-à-vis people of color.

So much has been achieved through critical race theory and critical pedagogy to conscientize students and teachers alike about the racial dimension of the American Dream and how it rested on a huge generational shift of wealth from the Black to the white population. Under Donald Trump's administration in the last US presidency, the world saw how he ignited, fanned, and legitimated deep systemic racism of US institutions among his white nationalists. As we noted: 'The alt-right protestors sported swastikas, Confederate flags and memorabilia, anti-semitic banners, Trump/Pence signs and carried torches, chanting 'You will not replace us,' 'Blood and soil' and 'Jews will not replace us' (Peters & Besley, 2017). The Black struggle is attacked through an invective against 'cultural Marxists' originating with the European far-right. The Anti-Defamation League (ADL) *With Hate in their Hearts: The State of White Supremacy in the U.S.* (2015) describes 'a dramatic resurgence in the extreme right since 2000 that has led to a significant increase in violence' and noted several worrying trends before Trump was elected, including the fact that white supremacist ideology is dominated by the belief that whites are doomed to extinction by a rising tide of non-whites. The report noted that 'Among domestic extremist movements active in the United States, white supremacists are by far the most violent, committing about 83% of the extremist-related murders in the United States in the past 10 years and being involved in about 52% of the shootouts between extremists and police ...' (ADL, 2015). The historical moment of US white supremacism is not over. Trump is waiting in the wings, having taken over the Republican Party and will be around to contest the next election.

Whiteness works like a drug to distort one's sense of history to protect one from witnessing the mass suffering and slaughter of white capital that pretends to act as neutral arbiter on the question of labor. As George Yancy explains falling in love with philosophy and growing up among it.

> The trap of falling for whiteness is easy and unremarkable. It was an easy addiction, so to speak. Symbolically, it is a process of what Joy James (2004) has called 'mainlining white supremacy.' She writes, 'I likely started off in my preacademic years in incremental dosages, sniffing rather than shooting' (p. 263). It is a powerful metaphor as whiteness involves forms of habituation that masquerade as common sense, as intelligibility itself. And once it takes control, one finds oneself in a state of denial, protesting that nothing is wrong. After all, think about it, the philosophers whom I read were not self-identified as *white*, the encyclopedia did not nominate them as white; they were simply philosophers, 'raceless' human beings, persons. This is how whiteness functions. Whiteness structurally obfuscates its logics, it conceals its racial and racist epistemic assumptions through claims of 'neutrality' and problematic claims of 'universality.' Whiteness vis-à-vis philosophy also attempts to narrate an airtight history that covers over the racially motivated selective processes that undergird the normative and biased dynamics that shape philosophical canonization.

This is what Greg William Misiaszek, Janna M. Popoff, and Ali A. Abdi mean in part when they write of 'Epistemologies of the North'. It immediately calls forth critical pedagogy and critical race theory as an antidote, to question and examine those social categories that are presented as natural and inevitable and simply the way the world is. Yancy's story of becoming a Black philosopher is an important narrative of personal transformation that acknowledges that African American literature became his savior. As Yancy (2020) indicates: 'The dynamic racialized narrativity self-consciously embedded within Morrison's literary work functioned as a template of how I might begin to write philosophy in a way that captured what African American philosopher Cornel West calls the *funk of life* (West & Ritz, 2009, p. 4). I wanted my words on the page *to do* things, to carry the weight, in this case, of historical racist catastrophe.'

In 'White philosophy in/of America' (Peters, 2011), I argued that Rorty and Cavell define American philosophy 'after' Wittgenstein and Heidegger, embracing the *historical* nature of philosophy, culture, and language implied by Wittgenstein's cultural turn to reimagine the American tradition in philosophy both by returning to American philosophers before the analytic fracture and by investigating the Idea of America. Yet I argued in both cases of these leading thinkers American philosophy and the idea of America discussion of race and racism have been notable by their absence. Writing in 2011, I suggested only recently has Black philosophy begun to raise questions about the 'whiteness' of American philosophy, yet even Cornel West who has been responsible for 'black pragmatism' needs to historicize his philosophy further and use it to make links to investigating other forms of racism around the world and, in particular, to extend the notion of global citizenship in a critical fashion to engage with 'colonialist deconstructions and critical reconstructionist possibilities' (Ali A. Abdi), to educate for 'critical race and anti-colonial intersections' (George J. Sefa Dei & Asna Adhami), and to develop 'human rights and transformative justice education in teacher preparation' (Magnus O. Bassey).

Given this history and ideological background, why would it come as a surprise that Republicans are actively trying to block curricula that try to analyze and understand systemic racism. As Gabriel and Goldstein (2021) report.

> From school boards to the halls of Congress, Republicans are mounting an energetic campaign aiming to dictate how historical and modern racism in America are taught, meeting pushback from Democrats and educators in a politically thorny clash that has deep ramifications for how children learn about their country.

Republican senators object to history focusing on systematic racism in American society as a form of 'activist indoctrination'; they object also to the memorialization of the 1921 Race Massacre in Tulsa when white mobs attacked Black citizens burning their homes and leaving 10,000 Black people homeless. Only in 2020 did the shameless episode become part of Oklahoma curriculum.

Republicans are now focused on critical race theory trying to ban it from K-12 public education arguing that students should not be forced to examine the privilege of their whiteness. Texas has already passed a bill preventing the teaching of critical race theory. *The Washington Post* headline 'Texas bill to ban teaching of critical race theory puts teachers on front lines of culture war over how history is taught' explains that critical race theory has become a cultural flashpoint. The Texas bill (H.B.A No.A3979) lays down essential knowledge and skills for the social studies curriculum, specified as follows:

(1) The fundamental moral, political, and intellectual foundations of the American experiment in self-government, as well as the history, qualities, traditions, and features of civic engagement in the United States;
(2) The structure, function, and processes of government institutions at the federal, state, and local levels; and

(3) The founding documents of the United States, including the Declaration of Independence, the United States Constitution, the Federalist Papers (including but not limited to Essays 10 and 51), excerpts from Alexis de Tocqueville's Democracy in America, the first Lincoln-Douglas debate, and the writings of the Founding Fathers of the United States.

The Bill spells out specific areas of prohibition that is worth quoting in some detail:

(1) No teacher shall be compelled by a policy of any state agency ... to discuss current events or widely debated and currently controversial issues of public policy or social affairs;
(2) Teachers who choose to discuss current events or widely debated and currently controversial issues of public policy or social affairs shall, to the best of their ability, strive to explore such issues from diverse and contending perspectives without giving deference to any one perspective;
(3) No school district or teacher shall require, make part of a course, or award course grading or credit including extra credit for, student work for, affiliation with, or service learning in association with any organization engaged in lobbying for legislation at the local, state, or federal level, or in social or public policy advocacy;
(4) No school district or teacher shall require, make part of a course, or award course grading or credit including extra credit for, political activism, lobbying, or efforts to persuade members of the legislative or executive branch to take specific actions by direct communication at the local, state, or federal level, or any practicum or like activity involving social or public policy advocacy;
(5) No teacher, administrator, or other employee in any state agency ... shall be required to engage in training, orientation, or therapy that presents any form of race or sex stereotyping or blame on the basis of race or sex.
(6) No teacher, administrator, or other employee in any state agency ... shall require or make part of a course the following concepts: (i) one race or sex is inherently superior to another race or sex; (ii) an individual, by virtue of his or her race or sex, is inherently racist, sexist, or oppressive, whether consciously or unconsciously; (iii) an individual should be discriminated against or receive adverse treatment solely or partly because of his or her race or sex; (iv) members of one race or sex cannot and should not attempt to treat others without respect to race or sex; (v) an individual's moral character is necessarily determined by his or her race or sex; (vi) an individual, by virtue of his or her race or sex, bears responsibility for actions committed in the past by other members

of the same race or sex; (vii) any individual should feel discomfort, guilt, anguish, or any other form of psychological distress on account of his or her race or sex; or (viii) meritocracy or traits such as a hard work ethic are racist or sexist, or were created by members of a particular race to oppress members of another race.

I mention the Bill in some detail because it indicates the philosophical crux of history and the teaching of history in America in leading Republican states. It is an episode that highlights the stakes and the significance not only of critical race theory and critical pedagogy but also the other historically related elements of this handbook that includes critical literacies, critical media studies, community-engaged learning and research, sciences and mathematics, gender and feminism, and Indigenous and epistemologies of the South.

Only a year after the death of George Floyd, the white racists spurred on by white history are trying to deaden the impact of this progressive education agenda. The battlelines are drawn. This *Handbook on Critical Theories of Education* proves its use and significance *advant la letter*. Even before it has been published, it is the substance of what is to be banned. It is with a heavy heart and in humbleness at this group of world-renowned critical educators and activists that I praise their collective achievement and congratulate them on the essential service they provide.

Michael A. Peters
Distinguished Professor of
Education
Beijing Normal University
Beijing, China

References

Peters, M. A. (2011). White philosophy in/of America. *Pragmatism Today*, http://www.pragmatismtoday.eu/summer2011/Peters.pdf. Also in *Linguistic and Philosophical Investigations*, vol. 10, 2011, p. 7+. Gale Academic OneFile. Accessed 4 June 2021.

Peters, M. A. (2019). Interview with George Yancy, African-American philosopher of critical philosophy of race, *Educational Philosophy and Theory*, 51(7), 663–669. 10.1080/00131857.2018.1498214.

Peters, M. A. & Besley, T. (2017). White supremacism: The tragedy of Charlottesville. *Educational Philosophy and Theory*, 49(14), 1309–1312. 10.1080/00131857.2017.1370896.

Samayeen, N., Wong, A. & McCarthy, C. (2020). Space to breathe: George Floyd, BLM plaza and the monumentalization of divided American Urban landscapes, *Educational Philosophy and Theory*. 10.1080/00131857.2020.1795980.

Yancy, G. (2021). Black disciplinary zones and the exposure of whiteness, *Educational Philosophy and Theory*, 53:3, 217–226. 10.1080/00131857.2020.1830062.

Michael A. Peters *is a Distinguished Professor* of Education at Beijing Normal University and Emeritus Professor at the University of Illinois. He is the Executive Editor of the journal Educational Philosophy and Theory. His interests are in education, philosophy, and social policy, and he is the author of over 100 books, including *The Chinese Dream: Educating the Future* (2019), *Wittgenstein, Education and Rationality* (2020), and *Wittgenstein: Antifoundationalism, Technoscience and Education* (2020).

Contents

Part I General Critical Theoretical Perspectives and Philosophies of Education

1. Critical Theories of Education: An Introduction — 3
   Greg William Misiaszek, Janna M. Popoff, and Ali A. Abdi

2. Critical Theory and the Transformation of Education in the New Millennium — 21
   Douglas Kellner and Steve Gennaro

3. The Philosophy and Politics of Educating Emotions — 47
   Liz Jackson

4. African Philosophies of Education: Colonialist Deconstructions and Critical Anticolonial Reconstructionist Possibilities — 63
   Ali A. Abdi

Part II Critical Race Theories of Education

5. Educating for Critical Race and Anti-Colonial Intersections — 81
   George J. Sefa Dei and Asna Adhami

6. Critical Social Foundations of Education: Advancing Human Rights and Transformative Justice Education in Teacher Preparation — 97
   Magnus O. Bassey

7. Students with Disabilities in British Columbia's (Canada) K to 12 Education System: A Critical Disability and Intersectional Perspective — 113
   Bathseba Opini

Part III Critical International/Global Citizenship Education

8 Contesting Canadian Exceptionalism in the Internationalization of Higher Education: A Critical Perspective 131
Shibao Guo and Yan Guo

9 Global Citizenship Education for Critical Consciousness: Emancipatory Potentials and Entrenched Realities in South Korea 147
Hyungryeol Kim and Sung-Sang Yoo

10 Diversifying Schools with Global and Indigenous Knowledge: Inclusion of Internationally Educated Teachers (IETs) in Schools and Teacher Education Programs 163
Chouaib El Bouhali

11 Rebuilding the Connection Between Politics and Practices of Democratic Education in China: Critical Reflections 181
Wenchao Zhang

12 Teaching Social Justice Amidst Violence: Youth and Enacted Curricula in Canada, Bangladesh, and México 197
Kathy Bickmore and Rim Fathallah

Part IV Critical Pedagogy/Critical Literacy Studies in Education

13 The Indigenous Imaginary and Tertiary Institutions 223
Robert J. Tierney and Robert V. Morgan

14 Critical Education, Social Democratic Education, Revolutionary Marxist Education 243
Dave Hill

15 Critical Perspectives for Educational Leadership and Policy in Higher Education 261
Candace Brunette-Debassige and Melody Viczko

16 Critical Pedagogy in Language and STEM Education: Science, Technology, Engineering, and Mathematics Education 283
Zehlia Babaci-Wilhite

17 Ecopedagogy: Critical Environmental Pedagogies to Disrupt Falsely Touted Sustainable Development 301
Greg William Misiaszek

Part V Critical Media/Information Studies and Education

18 Postdigital Critical Pedagogy 321
    Petar Jandrić and Sarah Hayes

19 Contemporary Critical Library and Information Studies:
    Ethos and Ethics 337
    Toni Samek

20 Critical Methodologies and an Art-Based Method
    of Research in Higher Education Institutions 355
    Janna M. Popoff

21 Rise of a "Managerial Demiurge": Critical Analysis
    of the Digitalization of Education 371
    Juha Suoranta, Marko Teräs, and Hanna Teräs

Part VI Critical Community-Engaged Learning/Research

22 Critical Comprehensive Peace Education: Finding
    a Pedagogical Nexus for Personal, Structural,
    and Cultural Change 393
    Tony Jenkins

23 Showing Up for the Rat Race: Beyond Human Capital
    Models of Higher Education 413
    Alison Taylor

24 The Challenges of Doing Radical Pedagogy in Social
    Movements in South Africa 431
    Salma Ismail

Part VII Critical Perspectives on Science and Mathematics Education

25 Decolonizing Science Education in Africa: Curriculum
    and Pedagogy 449
    Samson Madera Nashon

26 Indigenous Epistemologies and Decolonized Sustainable
    Livelihoods in Africa 465
    Edward Shizha

27 Centering Race, Racism, and Black Learners
    in Mathematics Education: A Critical Race Theory
    Perspective 481
    Julius Davis

28 Mobility of Syrian–Canadian Students and Continuity
    of Math Education: A Comparative Curriculum Mapping
    Approach   497
    Dania Wattar and Emmanuelle Le Pichon

Part VIII Critical Gender/Feminist Studies in Education

29 Transforming Sub-Saharan African
    Universities—Transnational Collaborations
    at the Intersections of Gender as a Viable Pathway?   519
    Philomina Okeke-Ihejirika

30 Revisiting Francophone Sub-Saharan Africa's Eurocentric
    Education System Through a Decolonial Feminist's Lens   537
    Gertrude Mianda

Part IX Critical Indigenous and Southern Epistemologies of
         Education

31 Critical Theory as Lived Meaning: Exploring Anti-Racist
    Practice in Post-Secondary Education   553
    Derek Tannis

32 Critical Adult Education in the (Neo)colonies:
    Racial/Colonial Capitalist and Social Movement
    Ontologies of Land   571
    Dip Kapoor

33 Doing Southern Theory: Shinto, Self-Negation,
    and Comparative Education   589
    Keita Takayama

Index   607

Notes on Contributors

Ali A. Abdi is Professor of social development education at the University of British Columbia. Prior to that was professor of international development education at the University of Alberta, where he was also the founding co-director of the Centre for Global Citizenship Education and Research (CGCER). He is the founding editor of the *Journal of Contemporary Issues in Education* and co-founding editor of *Cultural and Pedagogical Inquiry*. His previous books include *Decolonizing philosophies of education*.

Asna Adhami is a multi-award winning Scholar for her Masters work *In the Spirit of Inclusive Reflection: Reflections of a Cultural Expeditionist*. Asna's unique, Sufi and South Asian heritage-inspired ways of creating content follow traditional principles of 'dil ko dil se raah hoti hai' and interconnection, activating the heart in pedagogy and as praxis on paths to positive transformation, expeditioning into themes of identity, culture, and belonging, inviting introspections and considerations of power and relationships along the way. Her influence on the Canadian institutional landscape is evidenced by her strategic change work as a journalist, scholar, producer, poet, and photographer.

Dr. Zehlia Babaci-Wilhite is an Affiliated Scholar/Lecturer at the University of California, Berkeley in Pedagogy, French, and Applied Linguistics. As an Adjunct Professor at the University of San Francisco and Lecturer at San Jose State University, she teaches Language, Human Rights, and Critical Thinking. She has written numerous articles published in academic journals, chapters for many books, authored two monographs, and edited several books. She is fluent in French, English, Norwegian, and Japanese.

Dr. Magnus O. Bassey is a Professor in the Department of Secondary Education and Youth Services at Queens College, The City University of New York. He is the author of *Western Education and Political Domination in Africa: A Study in Critical and Dialogical Pedagogy; Missionary Rivalry and Educational Expansion in Nigeria, 1885-1945; Malcolm X and African American*

Self-Consciousness. Dr. Bassey has also authored numerous academic articles. His articles have appeared in rigorously peer reviewed journals.

Kathy Bickmore is Professor in Curriculum and Pedagogy and Director of the Comparative International and Development Education Centre and graduate specialization at OISE, University of Toronto. She studies and teaches about young people's lived citizenship and state-funded "regular school" learning opportunities relevant to building and making peace, gender equity, and just democracy, in comparative transnational, Indigenous First Nation, and Canadian communities.

Candace Brunette-Debassige is a Mushkego Cree scholar with French ancestry. She is an Assistant Professor in the Faculty of Education at Western University where her research focuses on the areas of Indigenizing and decolonizing education, Indigenous educational leadership, and critical policy as a decolonial praxis. Beyond her scholarship, Candace brings unique leadership experience to her scholarship including serving as Acting Vice Provost, Special Advisor to the Provost (Indigenous) and Director of Indigenous Services at Western.

Julius Davis, Ed.D. is the University System of Maryland Wilson H. Elkins Associate Professor of Mathematics Education and Director of the Center for Research and Mentoring of Black Male Students and Teachers at Bowie State University. He is the co-editor of the book *Critical Race Theory in Mathematics Education* (2019, Routledge) and co-author of *Black Males Matter: A Blueprint for Creating School and Classroom Environments to Support their Academic and Social Development* (2021, Information Age Publishing).

George J. Sefa Dei was born in Ghana and is today a renowned educator, researcher, and writer who is considered by many as one of Canada's foremost scholars on race and anti-racism studies. He is Professor of Social Justice Education & Director of the Centre for Integrative Anti-Racism Studies at the Ontario Institute for Studies in Education of the University of Toronto (OISE/UT). Professor Dei is the 2015, 2016, 2018–19 Carnegie African Diasporan Fellow. In August of 2012, Professor Dei also received the honorary title of 'Professor Extraordinaire' from the Department of Inclusive Education, University of South Africa [UNISA]. In 2017, he was elected as Fellow of Royal Society of Canada, the most prestigious award for an academic scholar. He also received the 2016 Whitworth Award for Educational Research' from the Canadian Education Association (CEA) awarded to the Canadian scholar whose research and scholarship have helped shaped Canadian national educational policy and practice. He is the 2019 Paulo Freire Democratic Project, Chapman University, United States—'Social Justice Award' winner. Professor Dei has thirty-five (35) books and over seventy (70) refereed journal articles to his credit. In June of 2007, Professor Dei was installed as a traditional chief in Ghana, specifically, as the Gyaasehene of the town of Asokore, Koforidua in the New Juaben Traditional Area of Ghana. His stool name is Nana Adusei Sefa Tweneboah.

Chouaib El Bouhali is a director of Edmonton Institute for Diversity Equity Research and Studies, and a teacher with Edmonton Public Schools. He holds a Ph.D. from the Educational Policy Studies department, University of Alberta. He has also taught courses in education at the University of Alberta. He is co-editor of *Interrogating Models Of Diversity Within A Multicultural Environment* (Palgrave Macmillan, 2019). His research interests include immigrant teachers, critical pedagogy, teacher education, policy analysis, decolonizing education and policy, Southern/Indigenous epistemologies.

Rim Fathallah is a doctoral candidate in Curriculum and Pedagogy and the Comparative International and Development Education graduate specialization at OISE, University of Toronto.

Dr. Steve Gennaro is one of the founding members of the Children, Childhood, and Youth Studies Program at York University and is the author of Selling Youth (2010), co-editor of Youth & Social Media (forthcoming 2021), and co-author of the Googleburg Galaxy (forthcoming 2022). His work explores intersections of media, technology, psychology, and youth identity. He regularly publishes in areas related to the philosophy of technology and education, and critical theories of youth, media, identity, and politics.

Shibao Guo is Professor in the Werklund School of Education at the University of Calgary. He specializes in comparative and international education, citizenship and immigration, and lifelong learning. His latest books include: *Decolonising lifelong learning in the context of transnational migration* (Routledge, 2020), *Immigration, racial and ethnic studies in 150 years of Canada* (Brill|Sense, 2018). He is former president of the Comparative and International Education Society of Canada. Currently, he serves as co-editor of *Canadian Ethnic Studies* and two book series: Spotlight on China and Transnational Migration and Education.

Yan Guo is Professor in the Werklund School of Education at the University of Calgary. Her research interests include critical pedagogy of language learning, diversity in teacher education, immigrant parent engagement, immigrant and refugee children, language policy, and international education. Her previous publications include *Home-school relations: International perspectives* (2018), *Spotlight on China: Changes in education under China's market economy*(2016) and *Spotlight on China: Chinese education in the globalized world*(2016). She is currently co-editing two book series, Transnational Migration and Education and Spotlight on China.

Sarah Hayes is Professor of Higher Education Policy in the Education Observatory at University of Wolverhampton and an Honorary Professor at Aston University, Birmingham, UK. Sarah has also taught at University of Worcester, at a range of international partner institutions and is an external examiner.

Sarah's research, supervision and teaching spans Sociology, Higher Education Policy and technological change. Sarah is an Associate Editor for Postdigital Science and Education (Springer). Personal website: https://researchers.wlv.ac.uk/sarah.hayes.

Dave Hill Marxist political, trade union and education activist, Emeritus Professor at Anglia Ruskin University, with positions at universities in London, Athens and Wuhan, China. Founder/(2003)/Managing Director of the free online academic journal, the *Journal for Critical Education Policy Studies* (www.jceps.com); since 2010, co-founder/ co-organizer of the annual ICCE Conference (International Conference on Critical Education); Editor of the Routledge Studies in Education, Neoliberalism and Marxism.

Salma Ismail Teaches Adult Community Education and Training at all levels. Her research interests include adult learning in informal contexts, namely development projects and social movements and how knowledge is produced in these sites and can lead to social transformation. She publishes in the field of feminist popular education, community- based research, equity, and institutional transformation. Part of an international and national network of popular educators (PEP). Taught literacy in communities and active in community-based movements.

Liz Jackson is Professor in the Department of International Education at the Education University of Hong Kong. She is the Immediate Past President of the Philosophy of Education Society of Australasia and the Former Director of the Comparative Education Research Centre at the University of Hong Kong. Her authored books include *Beyond Virtue: The Politics of Educating Emotions* (Cambridge University Press), *Questioning Allegiance: Resituating Civic Education* (Routledge), and *Contesting Education and Identity in Hong Kong* (Routledge).

Petar Jandrić is Professor at the Zagreb University of Applied Sciences, Croatia, and visiting professor at the University of Wolverhampton, UK. His previous academic affiliations include Croatian Academic and Research Network, National e-Science Centre at the University of Edinburgh, Glasgow School of Art, and Cass School of Education at the University of East London. He is Editor-in-Chief of *Postdigital Science and Education* journal and book series. Personal website: http://petarjandric.com/.

Tony Jenkins, Ph.D. is currently a Lecturer in the Program on Justice and Peace Studies at Georgetown University. Since 2001 he has served as the Managing Director of the International Institute on Peace Education (IIPE) and since 2007 as the Coordinator of the Global Campaign for Peace Education (GCPE). Tony's applied research is focused on examining the impacts and effectiveness of peace education methods and pedagogies in nurturing personal, social and political change and transformation.

Dip Kapoor is Professor, International Development Education & Political Sociology of Adult/Education and is a voluntary research associate for the Center for Research and Development Solidarity, an indigenous-peasant organization in eastern India. His recent collections published by Zed Books include: *Research, Political Engagement and Dispossession: Indigenous, Peasant and Urban Poor Activisms in the Americas and Asia* (2019) and *Against Colonization and Rural Dispossession: Local Resistance in South & East Asia, the Pacific and Africa* (2017).

Douglas Kellner is Distinguished Research Professor of Education at UCLA and is author of many books on social theory, politics, history, philosophy, and culture, including *Herbert Marcuse and the Crisis of Marxism* and six edited volumes of the collected papers of Herbert Marcuse. His work in social theory and cultural studies includes *Media Culture, Guys and Guns Amok: Domestic Terrorism and School Shootings from the Oklahoma City Bombings to the Virginia Tech Massacre*, and *Media Spectacle*. Most recently, he has published two books on *American Nightmare: Donald Trump, Media Spectacle, and Authoritarian Populism*, and *The American Horror Show: Election 2016 and the Ascent of Donald J. Trump*.

Hyungryeol Kim is an Associate Professor in the Department of Ethics Education, College of Education, Seoul National University. She received her Ph.D. at the division of Social Sciences and Comparative Education, International and Comparative Education concentration, from the Graduate School of Education and Information at the University of California, Los Angeles in 2013. Her scholarly interests include civic and citizenship education, political socialization, international comparative education, and youth studies.

Gertrude Mianda is currently Director of the Tubman Institute for Research on Africa and its Diasporas at York University. She is a Full Professor of Gender and Women's Studies program at Glendon Campus and in the School of Gender, Sexuality and Women's Studies, York University. Her research focuses on gender, post-colonialism, decolonization, development, globalization, international migration, and gender-based violence in armed conflict zone in Africa.

Greg William Misiaszek is an Assistant Professor at Beijing Normal University. He also holds various positions including Associate Director, Paulo Freire Institute, UCLA; Executive Editor of *Teaching in Higher Education* journal; and Associate Editor of the *Beijing International Review of Education (BIRE)* journal. His recently published book *Ecopedagogy* (2020, Bloomsbury) discusses critical environmental learning and literacies reinvented from Paulo Freire's work, while his *Educating the Global Environmental Citizen* (2018, Routledge) focuses on citizenships and ecopedagogy.

Professor Robert V. Morgan has a long and distinguished history of involvement and leadership in Aboriginal/Indigenous education and training in

Australia and internationally. He has an indivisible commitment to the principles of Aboriginal sovereignty, social equity, and restorative justice. Professor Morgan serves as Chair of the Board of Aboriginal and Torres Strait Islander Studies and Research at the University of Newcastle, Australia and Chairs the International Council of the World Indigenous People's Conference on Education (WIPCE).

Samson Madera Nashon is the Head of the Department of Curriculum and Pedagogy at the University of British Columbia. His teaching and educational research experiences have convinced him that everyone can, within their locus of control, contribute to educational reform processes. His research focuses on ways of teaching and learning the sciences characterized by understanding the nature of science curriculum and instruction as well as the development of theoretical models that improve the practice of teaching.

Philomina Okeke-Ihejirika is a Full Professor and the Director of University of Alberta's Pan African Collaboration for Excellence. Her nearly three-decade academic career has focused on gender issues among people of Africa descent. Her publication track record reflects extensive knowledge of transnational, post-colonial, and intersectional feminist approaches. She is a Killam scholar, Carnegie fellow, a founding member of the College of Mentors for African Universities, and a collaborating researcher with the United Nations Research Institute for Social Development.

Bathseba Opini is an Assistant Professor in the Faculty of Education, University of British Columbia. Her research interests are in critical disability studies, teaching practices, critical race and antiracism perspectives, international education, and global Indigenous knowledges.

Dr. Emmanuelle Le Pichon is an Assistant Professor at the University of Toronto, Ontario Institute for Studies in Education, head of the *Centre de Recherches en Éducation Franco-Ontarienne*. She has led several projects on the inclusion of minority students in education. Her keen interest in migration policy has led her to conduct research studies on issues related to multilingual education, particularly on the education of newly arrived migrant students in Europe and in Canada.

Janna M. Popoff is a sessional instructor at Thompson Rivers University. Her research interests include art-based methods of data collection and participatory research. She has most recently explored international student experience in China using the photovoice methodology where photographs were used as a data collection tool.

Dr. Toni Samek is Professor at the University of Alberta. Her books include: *Intellectual Freedom and Social Responsibility in American Librarianship 1967 to 1974*; *Librarianship and Human Rights: A twenty-first century guide*; *She Was a Booklegger: Remembering Celeste West*; *Information Ethics, Globalization and Citizenship: Essays on Ideas to Praxis*; and, *Minds Alive: Libraries and*

Archives Now. Toni serves on the Advisory Boards of the Centre for Free Expression and the International Centre for Information Ethics.

Dr. Edward Shizha is a Professor in Youth and Children's Studies at Wilfrid Laurier University in Canada. His research focuses on education and indigenous knowledge systems in Africa and has published 12 books, including *Indigenous discourses on knowledge and development in Africa* (with Ali Abdi, 2014), and several chapters and journal articles which have been extensively cited. Dr. Shizha is the series editor for "Africa in the Global Space" that is published by Peter Lang.

Juha Suoranta is a Professor of Adult Education at Tampere University, Finland. He has worked as Visiting Scholar at the University of Illinois and UCLA, and as Visiting Professor at the University of Minnesota. His research interests are critical pedagogy and public sociology. His latest books are *Rebellious Research* (2014), *C. Wright Mills's Sociological Life* (2017), and *Paulo Freire, A Pedagogue of the Oppressed* (2019).

Keita Takayama is a professor of the Graduate School of Education, Kyoto University, Japan. He spent 11 years teaching at University of New England, Australia before taking up professorship in Kyoto. His research focuses on globalization of education policy and educational research. He was the 2010 recipient of CIES's George Bereday Award.

Derek Tannis is a settler-ally who lives and works in Treaty 6 territory and the Homeland of the Metis. He has worked as an instructor, educational developer, researcher and administrator in post-secondary education. He believes in the role and importance of scholar-practitioner in education, currently working as the Director of Student Engagement and Learning Services at Saskatchewan Polytechnic. He completed his doctorate in Education Policy Studies at the University of Alberta.

Alison Taylor is Professor of Educational Studies at the University of British Columbia, Canada. Her current research, 'The Hard Working Student,' focuses on undergraduate students and their term-time work (see: http://blogs.ubc.ca/hardwork). Her previous research examined community-engaged learning in universities and high school apprenticeship programs. Recent articles appear in the *British Journal of Sociology of Education, Journal of Education and Work*, and *Educational Studies*. She is also the author of *Vocational Education in Canada* (Oxford, 2016).

Dr. Marko Teräs is a Postdoctoral Researcher at Tampere University, Faculty of Social Sciences, Finland. His research focus is critical research of digitalization in education. He is the co-founder of the Critical Applied Research of Digitalization in Education research group (CARDE) and critical EdTech research network (CreditEd). He also supervises master's students in the Master's Degree of Educational Leadership (M.B.A.) at Tampere University of Applied Sciences.

Dr. Hanna Teräs is Principal Lecturer at Tampere University of Applied Sciences. She has over 20 years' experience in teaching, research, and development of technology-assisted learning in higher education in Finnish and Australian universities. Her research interests include digitalization of education, and authentic pedagogies. She is co-founder of the research group Critical Applied Research of Digitalization in Education (CARDE). Currently she leads a Finnish Ministry of Education and Culture funded flagship project in learning analytics.

Robert J. Tierney is Dean Emeritus/Professor Emeritus of the Faculty of Education (University of British Columbia), the former Dean and Honorary Professor of the Faculty of Education and Social Work (University of Sydney) and Distinguished Professor at Beijing Normal University. In US, he served on the faculty of the Universities of Illinois, Arizona, Ohio State, and Harvard. Currently, he is the Editor of the International Encyclopedia or Education and President of the International Literacy Association.

Melody Viczko is a non-Indigenous settler who lives in the traditional territories of the Anishinaabeg, Haudenosaunee, Lunaapeewak and Attawandaron people. She is Associate Professor in Critical Policy Studies in Education at Western University. Her research concerns a critical examination of policy and governance in higher education and is informed by sociomaterial approaches to studying policy using assemblage theory and digital methods. Recent publications relate to internationalization policies, refugee access to higher education and gendered leadership.

Dr. Dania Wattar is a lecturer in the Department of Curriculum, Teaching, and Learning at OISE, University of Toronto. Dani is mathematics teacher and currently works as an academic consultant in Ontario. Her research interest and experience explore curriculum, policy, professional development, equity, supporting multilingual learners, technology, and education in Canada and the Middle East.

Sung-Sang Yoo teaches international and comparative education in education, College of Education, Seoul National University. Holding Ph.D. in education from University of California, Los Angeles, he has participated in the Paulo Freire Institute/UCLA and been involved with the international network of Paulo Freire. His academic interests span from education reform, transformative and alternative schooling, students' human rights to educational aid to developing countries in Sub-Saharan Africa, South and South-eastern Asia, and Latin America.

Wenchao Zhang is a lecturer at the Teachers' College of Beijing Union University in China. Zhang's research includes citizenship and democratic education in China, and ethnographic methodologies. Her most recent research focused on ethnographic approaches in examining the theory and practice of democratic education in two Chinese public schools. Zhang's most recent publications have been on global citizenship education (GCE) within China.

List of Figures

Fig. 12.1	Dimensions of Violence and Peace	215
Fig. 22.1	Mezirow's stages of worldview transformation (a pathway to human agency)	405
Fig. 22.2	Paulo Freire's praxis	406
Fig. 22.3	A pedagogy of relationships	407
Fig. 25.1	Integrated and Transformative Model, Gess-Newsome, 1999	459
Fig. 28.1	Syrian maths books and mapping	504
Fig. 28.2	The website features the multilingual resources as well as the curriculum mapping and the comparative analysis of the programs	505
Fig. 32.1	Contradictions of racial/colonial capitalist accummulation	583

List of Tables

Table 28.1	Reproduction of the synthesis of the Ontarian Curriculum in math, Grades 1–8 (Edugains, n.d.)	500
Table 28.2	Synthesis in Arabic of the Syrian curriculum grades 4–8	503
Table 28.3	Synthesis in English of the Syrian curriculum Grades 4–8	504

PART I

General Critical Theoretical Perspectives and Philosophies of Education

CHAPTER 1

Critical Theories of Education: An Introduction

Greg William Misiaszek, Janna M. Popoff, and Ali A. Abdi

In our conceptualizations of putting this reader together, one major question was the role of education as effecting active transformative change for a better world and sustainable planet. It was main perspective in mind that we invited the contributors to the handbook so as to provide diverse possibilities of using critical theories in the broader social and educational and address this important query. With contemporary, dominant Western-centric systems of education basically reproducing societal contexts in their hegemonic and colonial ways, new critiques of the situation are as important as ever. Indeed, with the classic ethnographic study of Paul Willis (1981) in the United Kingdom, later reconfirmed by Dolby et al. (2004), and the continuities of cultural and cognitive imperialism (Battiste, 1998; Said, 1979) in almost all colonized spaces, the possibilities of critically transformative, decolonizing, and actively developing education are as limited, even absent in more locations across the globe than otherwise (Abdi, 2008, 2020). Therefore, and unfortunately, the

G. W. Misiaszek (✉)
Faculty of Education, Institute of Educational Theories, Beijing Normal University, Beijing, China

J. M. Popoff
Thompson Rivers University (TRU), Kamloops, BC, Canada
e-mail: jpopoff@tru.ca

A. A. Abdi
University of British Columbia (UBC), Vancouver, BC, Canada
e-mail: ali.abdi@ubc.ca

© The Author(s), under exclusive license to Springer Nature Switzerland AG 2022
A. A. Abdi and G. W. Misiaszek (eds.), *The Palgrave Handbook on Critical Theories of Education*, https://doi.org/10.1007/978-3-030-86343-2_1

hopeful goals of education are too frequently subverted to serve and sustain intensifying hegemonic political and economic systems that serve modernist and rationalist technocratic goals that align with the globalization and neoliberalist goals of education as a measurable and outcome-driven commodity. Such education, as has been the case, disregards and devalues, and deliberately counteracts justice, sustainability, and community well-being.

It is with this appreciation of the critical (as interactively and when needed, contrapuntally critiquing the normative locations and contents of the educational) that we also attach this focus to critical pedagogy, that is, teaching and learning contexts grounded upon critical theories with its inherent goals of designing and auctioning the conceptual, theoretical, and the practical into emerging possibilities of social justice praxis. Such praxis shall be globally inclusive and locally contextual (Freire, 1998; Gadotti, 1996), as it could also serve the primacy of planetary sustainability for the human world and beyond the narrowness of anthropocentrism (Freire, 2004; Gadotti, 2008; Misiaszek, 2020). The essence of praxis is using theories as diversely explanatory and analytical lenses to view the world for reflectivity that guides one's actions. Paulo Freire (1992, 2000), arguably the most influential critical philosopher of education for the past 60 or so years, argued that education's vital role is to overcome *limit situations* which are the gaps (or barriers) between current realities and what the world 'should' be. Other critical thinkers of education including Julius Nyerere, the philosopher-statesman and first postcolonial President of Tanzania, forcefully spoke about and planned, with limited success, the problematic, colonial decontextualization of learning projects that excluded the history, experiences, and needs of Indigenous populations (Nyerere, 1968). Such decontextualization created a situation where the critical roles of contextual education in social well-being in precolonial traditional societies, which has been the reality of human life for millennia (Abdi, 2008), were derided and destroyed for the sake of cognitive imperialism and replaced colonial systems of training that actually acted as de-culturing oppressive practices for underdevelopment (Achebe, 2000; Rodney, 1981).

It is with this backdrop and the continuing clashes of monocentric learning systems and ongoing reemergence of critical education and critical pedagogies that currently situate the world's current status of practical hope and its refusal to diminish the utopic possibilities that must sustain our subjectivities which also contextualize one's historical and socio-political positionalities. All of these aspects of immediate, as all mediated by the learning and instructional designs and actions, should be constructed through democratic dialogue and critical literacy to "read the word through a reading of the world" (Freire, 1992, p. 29). It is these possibilities and potential complexities in mind that we hope that this handbook will aid readers in understanding how the deliberate and bold critical*ization* of educational contexts can help them achieve these noble learning and teaching goals, which shall also help them disrupt the type of schooling and education that counters and diminishes such aims. It is important to note that 'education' does not only include schooling and higher forms of learning but also beyond the proverbial classroom walls comprise of non-formal and informal education (i.e., lifelong learning and its public pedagogy continuities). Across its contents, with some not specifically using these terms, the general thematic focus of this handbook aims to highlight the presence of interactive topical situations that, at different emphasis, discuss these and related educational issues.

To be sure, this handbook is far from being all-inclusive in the topics covered, contextuality, epistemological diversity, and theoretical as well as analytical positionalities. This is with the recognition that no book, book series, or even library can provide globally, all-inclusive work of this nature, and there are certainly some important subjective, geographical, and topical omissions, thus making us realize that we could be indirectly silencing some voices and attached critical claims. What we did strive for is providing diversely *deepened* and *widened* perspectives on critical theories through a vast array (in relative terms) of topics and perspectival positionalities. The term 'deepened' here signifies learning and teaching to better understand our world within others' more localized situations and perspectives. As a transformational praxis to end oppressions and domination via actionable bottom-up approaches (Freire, 2000; Gadotti, 1996), deepened understandings are essential for critical analysis of education. As such, critical theories and theoretical frameworks can allow us to better understand perspectives and positionalities which have not been self-experienced, as well as problematizing one's own reflexivity to recognize the limitations of 'knowing' others' lifeworlds. *Widened* perspectives, on the other but related hand, indicate both the diversity of experiences and knowledges which shall be critical theories vital for global and planetary inter-understandings, as well as better understanding of the local through critical comparisons.

Deepened and widened understandings cannot be taken as isolated but are interconnected contextually, historically, and politically. Take for example the contested terrains of globalization which could be, from critical readings and possibilities, undertaken both from above and from below and thus re-termed as pluralized 'globalizations.' As the term 'globalization' itself suggests its widening perspectives (in extensity and intensity formats, see Held & McGrew, 2003), a key critical and continuing question is how the processes of globalizations affect local populations, which calls for deepened understandings at multiple, intersectional sub-global levels. More inclusive and better understood globalizations indeed occur by critically reading the similarities and differences of the processes' effects upon diverse human populations and on Earth overall situation.[1] Such re-doings of globalization can problematize the coloniality that entrenches globalization by applying critical historical de/reconstruction and the introspectively examining the influences of transnational corporations upon curricula within its political, policy, cultural, and related learning deconstructions and reconstructions (Stromquist & Monkman, 2002; Torres, 2009). In addition, critical theories of globalization can be also thought of as anthropocentric analysis of the planetary sphere when understanding environmentalism and environmental pedagogies (Misiaszek, 2020). Globalization is problematized in/directly in many chapters of this handbook.

The importance and reemergence of critical theories after World War II can be exemplified by scholars' (Adorno, 1998; Illich, 1983; Pongratz, 2005) arguments that we must educate for the holocaust to not reoccur and we do not eradicate the human population by using atomic bombs, which were newly invented. Unfortunately, there have been several genocides since the war's end and, although these as the cases of Hiroshima and Nagasaki in 1945, atomic bombs have globally proliferated. Currently, we have too many situations and political circumstances that call for critical pedagogy including, but not limited to, intensifying post-truthism that lacks all truth-seeking, extreme nationalism that systematically distorts 'citizenship' to focus singularly on blaming and suppressing the 'non-citizen,' epistemicide with language and cultural extinctions, increased terrorism at different levels, and potential acceleration to complete environmental devastation. As such, critical theories of education and their analytical as well as practical learning and teaching pedagogies are needed more now than ever to counter these and other forms of oppression and domination that are increasingly complex and systematically hidden, but extensively damaging, even existentially threatening.

FIVE GROUNDINGS OF CRITICAL THEORIES OF EDUCATION

There are five groundings that we conceptually and theoretically considered for the thematic constructions of the book which are the following: praxis-oriented, fluidity, radical, utopic with countless possible futures, and using bottom-up approaches.

We will begin with the second grounding of *fluidity* as we have already discussed praxis as the essential goal for critical theories of education and praxis will be further discussed throughout this introduction. *Fluidity* signifies numerous aspects, but overall fluidity signifies that critical theories cannot be ahistorical with the past as nonconsequential of current and future happenings, nor static for future usages. This coincides with Freire's (1992, 2000) essence of reinvention. Without recognizing fluidity, critical theories become almost sacred, untouchable texts from scholars such as Hegel and Marx. And, possibly no Marxism as Marx could be seen arguably as reinventing, radically in various ways, Hegel's work. As critical theoretical work centers on disrupting unjust hegemonic powers, Freire argued the "key problem was not 'taking power' but 'reinventing power'" (Morrow, 2019, p. 449). The following quote by Raymond Morrow and Carlos Alberto Torres (2019) on reinventions within education helps to explain how we see fluidity a bit more specifically.

> The criteria of adequacy are thus not based on the growth of knowledge, but the capacity to generate diverse contextual "reinventions" that provide validating justifications and reconfigurations of the core concepts. The outcome

is a praxis-oriented program, hence a generative framework of general concepts and questions for informing and motivating transformative pedagogical practices. Thus, the relatively stable core categories become activated pragmatically through their interpretation and translation as social practices in particular "applied" context of learning. (p. 246)

Fluidity of critical theorizing (in education) comes with various cautions, first of which are concerns if specific reinvention of a theory is truly representing its essence rather than superficially touting critical terms and accompanying scholars' names. The following are some key questions. When are (and/or previously has) critical theories (been) used to justify oppressions? For example, sustaining Orientalism as Edward Said (1979) argued that legitimized/es Western scholarship to justify (neo)coloniality. Providing a very current example, how has systematic perversion of critical theories' essence of subjectivity and problematizing, as well as post-modern theorizing, give false authority to intensifying post-truthism (see Peters et al., 2018). An important caution to endlessly problematize is if critical theoretical groundings are Western/Northern and, if so, are they tethered to epistemologies of the Global North—coloniality, patriarchy, and capitalism as Boaventura de Sousa Santos (2014, 2018) argues. As such, is praxis emerging from these inherently oppressive and domineering? This epistemological concern leads to the third grounding of critical work as being innately radical in disrupting oppressions and domination.

The radical nature of critical pedagogies is in disrupting learned ideologies that lead to injustices and planetary sustainability schemes that are fatalistically normalized without any viable alternatives. Many incorrectly view critical theories/pedagogies as 'negative' by shallowly viewing these as only deployed to critique, this over-simplifying the root wordings of the case. However, we argue quite the opposite in that critical work is practically hopeful, even utopic and saturated with viable radical transformations, that even if not easy to attain immediately are nevertheless possible. Critical work in education is intrinsically radical in that it epistemologically disrupts long held and rigid ideological justification of oppressions and forms of domination. In other words, critical work disrupts fatalistic knowledges and ways of 'knowing' the world as innately dehumanizing and Earth overall as unsustainable. Here, we blend in the fourth critical education's grounding of being inherently utopic with countless possible futures.

Social and educational transformation to counter oppressive, domineering systems can only emerge from utopic possibilities of what the world can and should be. These changes are inherently radical as they counter hegemony along with fatalistic ideologies that sustain and justify hegemony. Teaching to disrupt fatalistic ideologies rooted in, and sustained by, oppressions and domination helps students to recognize the world as political and socio-historically constructed and contested—or, as Freire would term it, 'unfinished' (Freire, 1992, 2000). In short, if our histories have constructed the world as it is currently, we have unlimited ability to transform it toward a better world.[2] Critical teaching helps students to dream of possible utopias to determine their action toward achieving their dreams (Freire, 1992). Disrupting/unlearning epistemologies of the North are essential in critical work for liberation and sustainability because Northern groundings have the world as fatalistically 'finished' with hegemony sustained and intensified. Connecting previous arguments with this, Ali Abdi's Chapter 2 "African Philosophies of Education: Colonialist Deconstructions and Critical Reconstructionist Possibilities" provides critiques of being 'critical' is falsely seen as only emergent from the West and the need to problematize many of the iconoclasts of monocentric thought systems and related theorizations including some from those so-called Western luminaries including Hegel. This, of course, is not detached from questioning the essence of critical theories without placing the specific "critical" term upon local/Southern theories, philosophies, and pedagogies.

In contemporary terms, so many designs and dispensations of education are fatalistic and even justify the resulting hegemonic relations and outcomes on such assumptions. The difficulty of having hope is because "hopelessness paralyzes us, immobilizes us," and prevalent banking teaching has students (and teachers) "succumb to fatalism, and then it becomes impossible to muster the strength we absolutely need for a fierce struggle that will re-create the world" (Freire, 1992, p. 8). As the essence of Freire's argument here in *Pedagogy of the Oppressed* (2005), resistance to hegemony needs massification of education to overcome injustices that are normalized within the psychosomatics of the oppressed, who over a long period of time internalize them as 'natural'—an essential grounding of banking education. Without hope and being able to dream for a better world and sustainable planet, oppressions and domination saturate 'realities' without possible goals of justice and sustainability to strive for, thus entrenching hegemony.

We have previously utilized the term 'limitations' not to limit utopic goal-setting (e.g., realizing possibilities of futures) but rather in recognizing of one's own limitations of self-reflexivity to then lessen their reflective restraints. This includes continuous problematizing of one's own epistemological groundings and positionalities in trying to deepen and widen understandings, as well as identifying what needs to be unlearned as epistemologies of the North have become unconscious ideological foundations for too many globally (Santos, 2018). Recognizing Freire's influences on this need in teaching, de Sousa Santos (2018) argued for the "very important reflection on the centrality of listening in the act of [good] teaching" (p. 176).

Limitations of positionality are closely connected with the fifth and final grounding of needing bottom-up approaches for critical educational work for praxis, as well as self-reflectivity of positionalities for all three. Never-ending reading and re-reading of one's own positionalities are essential for authentic and effective self-reflexivity, as well as recognizing and often problematizing positionalities of those being called 'authoritative,' 'expert' voices. In other words, problematizing whose voices are heard, whose voices are not heard, and what are the politics of their non-/selection and de/legitimization. Such problematizing must be realized through the critical understanding of sociohistorical oppressions (e.g., (neo)coloniality, racism, patriarchy, heteronormativity, xenophobia) in order to disrupt them. Successful praxis for social justice can only emerge from bottom-up approaches—from those who are oppressed by the issues at hand and those who continuously strive to better understand oppressions from others' perspectives, with the recognition that absolute understanding will never be fully achieved (i.e., reflectivity of limitations) (Freire, 2005; Gadotti, 1996). Moreover, planetary sustainability, as within critical, Freirean ecopedagogy, includes the recognition of the impossibilities of fully understanding that which is beyond the anthroposphere (humans and human populations, the 'world') and the static laws of Nature returning to equilibrium (see Chapter 17, p. 299; Misiaszek, 2020).

Successful praxis for social justice education also explores how we change the way knowledge is acquired, considered, and actualized. Therefore, engaging with methodologies that are holistic, inclusive, and participatory are areas that research/ers should seek to reflect on. Progressive methodologies such as visual methods of data collection aim to create an environment for participants where they are less objects of a study (i.e., that knowledge is extracted from, and more participants in co-creation of knowledge which is democratic and inclusive). Some prescriptive and oppressive systems of research are predicated on knowledge hierarchies (researcher vs. researched) that need to be challenged and inclusively reconstructed through critical participatory research methods. Changing the role of the research participants from one of passive to active and engaged, and changing the tools of data collection from ones of prescriptive and leading, to ones of co-creation, dialoging, and sharing are important steps toward the emancipation of oppressed people that are often the subjects of Northern conceived designed research studies that more often locate them as exotic, with hegemonic analytical gazes monologically applied. For example, in Janna Popoff's chapter (Chapter 20, p. 353) on visual and creative means of data collection, the method of photography is utilized to engage participants actively in co-creation of knowledge and mitigating the hierarchies of power relations between researcher and research participates.

SUMMARIES OF THE CHAPTERS

This book is separated into the following nine topics of education making up sections: (1) critical perspectives and philosophies, (2) critical race theories, (3) comparative educational approaches and global citizenship, (4) critical literacies, (5) critical media culture and information studies, (6) community-engaged learning and research, (7) sciences and mathematics, (8) gender and feminism, and (9) Indigenous and epistemologies of the South. As stated previously, this is not an all-inclusive list of topics and the chapters are far from including all the aspects and contextualities for each topic. However, these nine topics provide a selection of key current topics important to critical theories of education with the chapters giving the topics' historical foundations, needed discourses, real-world examples, possibilities and challenges, reinventions for today's educational work, and needs for educational futures for socio-environmental justice and planetary sustainability.

Part I: General Critical Theoretical Perspectives and Philosophies of Education

Douglas Kellner and Steve Gennaro compare and contrast critical theories, philosophies of education, and critical media studies throughout their first chapter "Critical Theory and the Transformation of Education in the New Millennium," as well as other fields and disciplines. In very detailed and comprehensive approaches, they deconstruct the histories of critical theories to reconstruct (or possibly better termed as Freirean 'reinventing') education within the current fast-paced world of endless technological advancements. As Kellner and Gennaro stress, it is essential to note that 'advancements' here calls for problematizing their implications upon (de)(neo)coloniality, (anti-)racism, (de)gendering, globalizations, and planetary (un)sustainability, among numerous other (anti-oppressive framings).

The third chapter "The Philosophy and Politics of Educating Emotions" by Liz Jackson analyzes and problematizes the lack of caring for others learnt from 'education for well-being' entrenched by (neo)liberalism and associated over-valued individualism. The need and importance of emotional well-being are unquestionable in education, but its inclusion and viewed importance are eroding through intensifying neoliberalism. Through international, comparative, and feminist lenses, she gives possibilities on how her analysis can provide guidance on students becoming more politically, collectively informed and engaged.

In the fourth chapter, "African Philosophies of Education: Colonialist Deconstructions and Critical Reconstructionist Possibilities," Ali A. Abdi unpacks the dominant Western roots of critical theories and philosophies within education to argue the need of, and hidden influences from, African philosophies. Problematizing the dominance of epistemologies of the North which views Global South as a-philosophical, Abdi provides descriptions and analysis of decolonialized Southern philosophies of education that is essential contextual usage in both the South *and* the North. He utilizes a wide range of diverse Southern scholars including Julius Nyerere, Walter Rodney, Ngugi wa Thiong'o, Chinua Achebe, and Walter Mignolo.

Part II: Critical Race Theories of Education

George J. Sefa Dei (Nana Sefa Atweneboah I) and Asna Adhami argue the need for decolonial, anti-racist, and de-epistemicide scholarship to transform education in their fifth chapter "Educating for critical race and anti-colonial intersections." Paralleling Albert Memmi's (1991) argument that the worst fate forced upon a population is taking away their histories, Dei and Admani argue that critical scholars are aware (or scholars must become critically aware) "of the erasure of our histories and the violences that we and those before us have stood up to, spoken out about and fought against" (Chapter 5, p. 81). Analyzing and deconstructing white supremacy, coloniality, and Southern epistemicide, the authors call for education to de-marginalize socio-historically suppressed authentic voices, histories, epistemologies, and spiritualities for needed praxis for transformation within social justice models.

Magnus O. Bassey argues the need to ground critical teacher pedagogies in "democracy, citizenship, equity, fairness; and is capable of conceptualizing the connection between social justice and education" (Chapter 6, p. 95). However, a majority of teacher preparation courses lack critical dialogue and pragmatic skills for what Freire (1993, 2000) termed as *conscientização*. In his sixth chapter "Critical social foundations of education: Advancing human rights and transformative justice education in teacher preparation," he calls for courses of critical social foundations of education and provides rich descriptions on needed curricula, learning objectives, and pedagogical practices, among other aspects. Bassey argues that these changes are crucial for skilling teaching toward praxis to end violence caused largely from shallow, uncritical, and, too often, false understandings of oppressions.

Critically deconstructing ableism in schooling, Bathseba Opini argues for reconstructing education through contextual, intersectional approaches that disrupt deficient-grounded perspectives within and from schooling and practices from 'solutions' that falsely homogenize populations who have disabilities. Both further marginalizes these populations. Her chapter seven titled "Students with Disabilities in British Columbia's (Canada) K to 12 Education System: A Critical Disability and Intersectional Perspective" focuses on policies and practices in British Columbia; however, the lessons learned from the chapter can be lent and borrowed through other contexts through critical comparative methods.

Part III: Critical International/Global Citizenship Education

Shibao Guo and Yan Guo's eighth chapter entitled "Contesting Canadian Exceptionalism in the Internationalization of Higher Education: A Critical Perspective" analyzes the effects of Canadian educational systems' rhetoric of exceptionalism both internally and externally. The implications that Guo and Guo argue are important not only for the Canadian context, but also other systems touting exceptionalism (e.g., United States, United Kingdom, Australia, Europe) through contextual, critical comparative approaches. The chapter provides critically rich narratives and analysis of Canadian international students' experiences that counter exceptionalism myths.

In recent years, the call for global citizenship education (GCE) has increased tremendously, helped by, but also well beyond, UNESCO's initiatives and influences. GCE's contested terrains that have aligning *and* contrasting goals are analyzed within South Korea by Hyungryeol Kim and Sung-Sang Yoo in their ninth chapter "Global Citizenship Education in a Banking Model?: Emancipatory Potentials and Entrenched Realities of GCED in Korea." Challenging the frequently touted idea that GCE is unproblematically grounded in social justice and sustainability, they critically analyze data of interviewing teachers to reveal that GCE is too often entrenched with neoliberalism.

Chouaib El Bouhali's tenth chapter "Diversifying Schools with Global and Indigenous Knowledge: Inclusion of Internationally Educated Teachers (IETs) in Schools and Teacher Education Programs" critically problematizes what are the framings, depth, and in/exclusionary aspects of when 'multiculturalism' is lauded, as well as the politics of absences in multicultural initiatives. Examining these issues within the Canadian educational system, El Bouhali discusses the possibilities and challenges of utilizing Southern epistemologies within local schools from policy-to-learning spaces through critical theorizing and pedagogies. He disrupts shallow touting of 'being multicultural' without the depth of its Southern essence which includes, in turn, disrupting oppressive Northern epistemologies.

Wenchao Zhang critically analyzes the contested terrain of democracy within China's educational systems in the eleventh chapter "Rebuilding the connection between politics and practices of democratic education in China: Critical reflections." Zhang's analysis is through her extensive qualitative research on teachers and students in China on their understandings and practices of 'democracy' inside and outside classroom walls. She provides in-depth analysis on countering what many outside China and Chinese diasporas see falsely as a contradiction—democracy in China. Zhang gives readers her analysis through various participant quotes, pedagogical influences in China such as from Dewey and Freire, various constructs connected to democracy such as citizenship, and the socio-historical politics of China.

Kathy Bickmore and Rim Fathallah's twelfth chapter, "Teaching Social Difference: Planned and Enacted Curricula in Canada, Bangladesh, and México," draws from a multi-year comparative school-based study on curricula's approaches to social diversity leading toward (or away from) cohesion, tolerance, and peace. The authors compare and contrast curriculum approaches on diversity between the three nations by looking at aspects such as poverty, gender, and relations between settler and indigenous communities. Bickmore and Fathallah unpack various critical aspects of differing value-laden teaching within diverse learning spaces to give possibilities and challenges within, and also beyond, the three nations they focused upon.

Part IV: Critical Pedagogy/Critical Literacy Studies in Education

Robert J. Tierney and Robert V. Morgan's thirteenth chapter entitled "The Indigenous Imaginary and Tertiary Institutions" examines efforts to challenge the domination of Western epistemologies as the only ways of knowing and legitimize all 'scholarship.' They investigate higher education practices that have Indigenous scholarship anchored by western assimilation. Their chapter reveals a polity unwillingness to respect, recognize, and trust Indigenous peoples rather than claims of reconciliation, apologies, and policies. Tierney and Morgan argue that while the rhetoric suggests a repositioning of Indigenous engagements within tertiary institutions in Australia and Canada, the institutional forces reflect a lack of commitment to truly indigenize programs rooted in decolonial Indigenization.

Utilizing Marxist theory, David Hill's fourteenth chapter entitled "Critical Education, Social Democratic Education, Revolutionary Marxist Education" explores critical education within and between relationships of power. He scrutinizes the global assault in this current era of neoconservative/neoliberal/neofascist right-wing authoritarianism. Hill investigates and differentiates between three types of socialism that are integral to his arguments: social democracy, democratic socialism, and revolutionary Marxism. He discusses various educational aspects of pedagogy including curriculum, organization of students, and ownership and control of schooling. Hill concludes with analyses of social democratic reforms and possibilities of replacements of capitalism with socialism through Marxist educators.

Melody Viczko and Candace Brunette-Debassige's fifteenth chapter entitled "Critical Perspectives for Educational Leadership and Policy in Higher Education" explores the field of higher education policy research that is dominated by a concern for administrative processes in the midst of neoliberal reform and priorities. They provide an overview of higher education governance to showcase how leaders in academia come face to face with oppressive structures of (neo)colonial politics and practices in their institutions. Viczko and Brunette-Debassige's work addresses new analytical and critical voicing in Canadian research, policy and practice within academia, and well beyond Canada's borders.

Zehila Babaci-Wilhite's sixteenth chapter entitled "Critical Pedagogy in Language and STEM Education: Science, Technology, Engineering, and Mathematics Education" focuses on the language of teaching STEM subjects 'successfully' within Africa and Asia in comparison with the United States. Babaci-Wilhite argues that the incorporation of language as an art into open and investigative processes, based on inquiry-based approaches that use local languages and cultural references, will improve learning and strengthen educational rights. She concludes by discussing the importance of (inter)national discourse to promote collaborative learning and pedagogical models that expand traditional STEM to include an 'A' for 'Arts'—STEAM.

Greg William Misiaszek argues the importance of teaching ecopedagogy, grounded in the work of Paulo Freire, in his seventeenth chapter entitled "Critical Environmental Pedagogies to Disrupt Falsely Touted Sustainable Development." He delves deeply into investigating how environmental teaching must focus on deepening and widening students' understandings on how our actions affect the rest of Nature and, consequently, upon ourselves—as we (i.e., humans) are *part of* Nature. He puts forth that *unsustainable* violent environmental actions are inseparable to social violence and injustice, as well as devastative to Nature beyond anthropocentric interests. Misiaszek's chapter posits how critical theories are essential within environmental pedagogies, as well as research upon them, for true praxis for planetary sustainability to emerge.

Part V: Critical Media/information Studies and Education

The framings, possibilities, and needs for 'postdigital critical pedagogy' to reinvent (critical) education are discussed by Petar Jandrić and Sarah Hayes in their eighteenth chapter (titled the same as the pedagogy). They argue that the rapid pace of technological innovations and students' use of technologies largely disrupts the effectiveness of continuing traditional teaching, including critical pedagogical teaching, without paradigm-shifting reinvention. This chapter could be read as a radical reinvention of Ivan Illich's (1983) pedagogical and technological warnings in his *Deschooling Society* book. Jandrić and Hayes provide rich descriptions on what are postdigital critical pedagogies throughout their arguments, including giving critical, philosophical foundations of them and numerous examples.

Toni Samek explores deeply critical librarian and other information workers who participate in political movements and discourses to actively engage in the 'global education enterprise.' Samek's nineteenth chapter titled "Contemporary Critical Library and Information Studies: Ethos and Ethics" offers an analysis of critical library and information studies and practices to interrogate their roles of conventional education and advancing of social (in)justice. Samek closes with calls to fight for structural changes within these studies as the politics' global economics upon education are integrally intertwined with the ethical implications of artificial intelligence, networked learning, critical pedagogy, social responsibility, and philosophies of technology.

Aligning with Susan Sontag's arguments in her seminal book *On Photography* (1977), Janna Popoff's twentieth chapter, "Critical Methodologies and an Art-Based Method of Research in Higher Education Institutions," describes how art (more specifically, photography) can critically inform/teach us from the eyes (i.e., self-perspectives) behind the camera (or, those who make the art). Popoff argues the need, possibilities, and challenges of conducting research through art-based critical methodologies to better understand participants' understandings which are often difficult, or even impossible, to fully understand through traditional oral and written means of communications in the research field. She provides rich details and analysis from her research on international students in a university within China.

Juha Suoranta, Marko Teräs, and Hanna Teräs investigate the effects of the COVID-19 pandemic which has caused 'shock effects' worldwide in educational institutions. In their twenty-first chapter "Rise of a 'Managerial Demiurge': Critical Analysis of the Digitalization of Education," they explore the unexpected closures of educational institutions and the different digital solutions in teaching and learning they have resorted to. This rapid move to online has set aside the more profound questions about the role of digitalization in national and international educational policies. In this chapter, Suoranta, Teräs, and Teräs problematize the role of digitalization in the discourses of education's futures.

Part VI: Critical Community-Engaged Learning/Research

Tony Jenkins investigates peace education in his twenty-second chapter entitled "Critical Comprehensive Peace Education: finding a Pedagogical Nexus for Personal, Structural and Cultural Change." He delves into the cognitive imperialism of colonialist pedagogies as impeding on critical and reflexive thinking, social imagination, and possibilities of peace and social justice. The emphasis on reproducing Eurocentric/Western knowledges, ways of knowing, and pedagogies inherently impose a finite set of deterministic social and political values that serve to instill our current world as non-transformable. The chapter develops this critique and explores the possibilities and potential of peace education as a counter-hegemonic force for knowledge decolonization and personal and social liberation. Jenkins explores these possibilities in the tradition of Paulo Freire seeing individuals and societies as 'unfinished' to, in turn, disrupt fatalistic education that justifies and normalizes violence as 'normal' and 'natural.'

In the twenty-third chapter, "Showing up for the rat race: Beyond human capital models of higher education," Allison Taylor addresses questions surrounding the relationship between higher education and graduate work. In particular, Taylor examines how purposes of higher education are framed in terms of preparing graduates for work in a knowledge economy. She explores the contested roles of universities providing information and opportunities for both paid and unpaid work. Taylor focuses her chapter on students' unpaid work that challenges economistic ideas about learning for earning, highlighting instead an expanded role for universities in promoting *meaningful* work.

Salma Ismail's twenty-fourth chapter titled "The Challenges of Doing Radical Pedagogy in Social Movements in South Africa" investigates the practices of radical/popular pedagogies in community contexts by exploring them within poor black communities in South Africa. Radicalness is essential within critical education as it challenges oppressive relations and takes the knowledge of the oppressed as its starting point. Ismail, in part, redefines what radical/popular pedagogies' contributions can be within a neoliberal context of unfolding climate and environmental crisis plus the pandemic which has exacerbated economic and social disasters worldwide.

Part VII: Critical Perspectives on Science and Mathematics Education

Samson Madera Nashon's twenty-fifth chapter, "Decolonizing Science Education in Africa: Curriculum and Pedagogy," focuses on how science curricula and pedagogies are often overly exam-driven, teacher-centered, and entrenched in coloniality, including colonial languages. Such static nature of curriculum and pedagogy is due, in part, to emphasis on grading and 'innovative,' contemporary pedagogies so that, in turn, understanding science through local African contexts and epistemologies is considered time wasting (Sifuna & Otiende, 2006). Nashon highlights ongoing research where specific local contexts in an African setting have been successfully used to develop curricular units that truly engages students in unpacking and understanding scientific phenomena embedded in their local context, thus constructing decolonizing science curricula and pedagogies.

Edward Shizha's twenty-sixth chapter "Indigenous Epistemologies and Decolonizing Sustainable Livelihoods in Africa" explores how the continent's nations continue to mirror colonial education and, thus, argues that Indigenous epistemologies decolonize dominant narratives in curricula. Such education should be reflected through critical approaches anchored by Indigenous worldviews, epistemologies, and ontologies. Shizha seeks to advance decolonization and encourage discourse to reclaim African culture and Indigenous epistemologies meaningfully in higher education.

The twenty-seventh chapter "Centering Race, Racism, and Black Learners in Critical Examinations of Mathematics Education: Forging Ahead to Achieve Liberation" by Julius Davis investigates how STEM knowledge plays a significant role in promoting and advancing global capitalism, gentrification, and international warfare to protect and advance whiteness (Morales-Doyle & Gutstein, 2019). STEM education fields are too frequently falsely viewed and incorrectly operated as race-neutral, culture-free, and objective disciplines. Davis explores and investigates powerful and important themes in of critical race theory to center issues of race, racism, and critical examinations of mathematics education to achieve liberatory outcomes in Black scholarship.

The twenty-eight chapter, "Mobility of Syrian-Canadian Students and Continuity of Math Education: A Comparative Curriculum Mapping Approach" by Dania Wattar and Emmanuelle Le Pichon, delves into the complexities of increased mobility of students which pose new and unique challenges to schools. Watter and Le Pichon argue that welcoming students into Canadian schooling requires a more constructive strategy than which usually occurs. They argue it should include a thorough, critical exploration of students' home country's curricula. They conclude that this approach may help both teachers and parents to understand the different curricula and to rethink how mathematics can be taught in a way that builds on students' cultural and linguistic knowledges and experiences.

Part VIII: Critical Gender/Feminist Studies in Education

The twenty-ninth chapter, "Transforming Sub-Saharan African Universities: Transnational Collaborations at the Intersections of Gender as a Viable Pathway?" by Philomina Okeke, explores the roles that transnational scholarly collaborations, with gender as an entry point, could play in addressing the challenges faced by sub-Saharan African universities as they transit into the twenty-first century. Okeke offers critical reflections on how institutional cultures and systemic inequities in Africa, on the one hand, and global trends in research funding, on the other, might shape future research collaborations. Her chapter is enriched by two decades of researching gender issues in Africa and in new African diasporas, and partnering with funding agencies to undertake capacity building, build research clusters and mentor graduate students and emerging scholars.

The thirtieth chapter, "Revisiting Francophone Sub-Saharan Africa's Eurocentric Education System Through a Decolonial Feminist's Lens" by Gertrude Mianda, explores the contemporary education system in most of Francophone sub-Saharan Africa that continues Eurocentric legacy of Western education and, in turn, disadvantages women. Using a decolonial feminist lens, Miranda critically revisits Francophone sub-Saharan Africa's Eurocentric education systems to bring to light the need for Indigenous education, including its gendered patterns. Miranda argues that, in contrast to the Western Eurocentric education system, African Indigenous education systems did not exclude women from mastering knowledge in diverse domains.

Part IX: Critical Indigenous and Southern Epistemologies of Education

Utilizing phenomenological *and* participatory approaches in his thirty-first chapter, "Critical Theory as Lived Meaning: Exploring Anti-Racist Practice in Post-Secondary Education," Derek Tannis explores essentialness and possibilities of this methodology for anti-racist policy analysis and research. Especially important for this book focused upon critical theories of education, Tannis discusses the innate tensions between critical and phenomenological approaches. While respecting their differences, he argues to also view and utilize their commonalities and intersectionalities within critical race theories and phenomenology toward achieving, what Gayle Salamon (2018) termed as, 'richest possibilities.' He weaves this argument throughout his chapter's poignant narratives and his own self-reflexivity to provide rich stories of such possibilities, as well as their challenges.

Dip Kapoor critically analyzes the ontology of land in thirty-second chapter, "Land Ontologies and Anticolonial Social Movement Learning in the

Neo/Colonies," which advances an anti/decolonial critique of Euro-American materialist ontologies of land, wherein land is construed as private property and a trade-able market commodity. In this chapter, Kapoor explores the main proposition that a materialist ontology of land as a (fictitious) commodity to be bought and sold to the highest bidder to extract surplus at the expense of a resident population has enabled colonization, dispossession, and impoverishment in the (neo) colonies to the present day as "land grabbing." To contrast the materialistic ontologies of land, Kapoor discusses La Via Campesina, a globalizing indigenous and peasant movement network that advances such an epistemology of food and land sovereignty in a counter and/or parallel project to the corporate agro-industrial capitalist agricultural model.

Exploring the possibilities of Shintoism within and between critical theories, Southern/Indigenous theories, decoloniality, and ecofeminism in Japan (and Japanese diasporas) are Keita Takayama's work described in the last, "Southern/Indigenous epistemologies for education: Promises and challenges of Shinto for Japanese education and beyond." Utilizing critical comparative education (CE) methodologies to disrupt Northern CE (aligning with Boaventura de Sousa Santos' (2007, 2018) calls for determining and disrupting *absences* for *emergences* in scholarship), Takayama poses what are/can/should be possibilities of Shintoism that allows, as he cites Taylor (2017), "for transgressive space where children disrupt the nature-culture binary and where children interact with the more-than-human worlds" (InHBPageNumNeeded). Although his chapter is contextualized in Japanese socio-histories and Shintoism, Takayama's arguments have contextual, epistemological significance on education and research upon it, as well as widened implications on justice and planetary sustainability.

Conclusion

Together, the thirty-three chapters should represent a somewhat comprehensive (if never topically totally complete, as we said above) of conceptual, theoretical, and attached practical undertakings and propositions that minimally situate this handbook at the expanding lines of educational and social well-being debates that certainly require more epistemic and epistemological counter-conventional boundary crossing and expansions. To be sure, the rhetorical locating of education, in both global and concerned localized situations, as normatively constructed and accepted, often with dangerously camouflaged horizontal benign*ness*, needs robust critical interventions that unpack the hidden philosophical, curricular, cultural, and linguistic exclusions that marginalize, in all these categories, a majority of the world's population. In situating the term 'marginalize' here, we are using the construct comprehensively in that the majority of educational programs, especially as these are designed and practiced in the so-called postcolonial world (as inherited from colonialism) but also selectively in so-named Western pluralistic democracies, adhere to the continuities of colonialist monocentric, power analysis-averse realities. Here, even when some measured capitalist 'benefits' (credentials, time–space controlled employment, etc.) are drawn from these programs, they do not serve, in critical learning and pedagogy terms, the interests of most people on earth, and certainly not responsive to the emergency ecological sustainability. As such, the boundary expansion and crossing via this work and future one shall continue for critical educational development and critical social well-being.

Notes

1. "Earth" is purposely de-objectified without the article "the" and having an uppercase "E." As well, Nature is capitalized. See Misiaszek, Chapter 17 "Critical Environmental Pedagogy for Disrupting Falsely Touted Sustainable Development."
2. '(Our) Histories' indicates the world's histories throughout its existence, including the endless complexities of and between positive/negative, oppressive/empowering, un/sustainable, de/selected, and de/legitimized histories.

References

Abdi, A. A. (2008). Europe and African thought systems and philosophies of education: 'Re-culturing' the trans-temporal discourses. *Cultural Studies, 22*(2), 309–327. https://doi.org/10.1080/09502380701789216

Abdi, A. A. (2020). Decolonizing knowledge, education and social development: Africanist perspectives. *Beijing International Review of Education, 2*(4), 503–518. https://doi.org/10.1163/25902539-02040006

Achebe, C. (2000). *Home and exile*. Oxford University Press.

Adorno, T. W. (1998). Education after Auschwitz. In T. W. Adorno (Ed.), *Critical models: Interventions and catchwords* (pp. 177–190). Columbia University Press.

Battiste, M. (1998). Enabling the autumn seed: Toward a decolonized approach to aboriginal knowledge, language, and education. *Canadian Journal of Native Education, 22*(1), 16–27.

Dolby, N., Dimitriadis, G., & Willis, P. E. (2004). *Learning to labor in new times*. RoutledgeFalmer.

Freire, P. (1992). *Pedagogy of hope*. Continuum.

Freire, P. (1993). *Pedagogy of the city*. Continuum.

Freire, P. (1998). *Pedagogy of freedom: Ethics, democracy, and civic courage*. Rowman & Littlefield.

Freire, P. (2000). *Pedagogy of the oppressed*. Continuum.

Freire, P. (2004). *Pedagogy of indignation*. Paradigm Publishers.

Freire, P. (2005). *Pedagogy of the oppressed*. Continuum.

Gadotti, M. (1996). *Pedagogy of praxis: A dialectical philosophy of education*. SUNY Press.

Gadotti, M. (2008). *Education for sustainable development: What we need to learn to save the planet*. São Paulo: Instituto Paulo Freire.

Held, D., & McGrew, A. G. (2003). *The global transformations reader: An introduction to the globalization debate* (2nd ed.). Polity Press

Illich, I. (1983). *Deschooling society* (1st Harper Colophon ed.). New York: Harper Colophon.

Memmi, A. (1991). *The colonizer and the colonized* (Expanded ed.). Beacon Press.

Misiaszek, G. W. (2020). *Ecopedagogy: Critical environmental teaching for planetary justice and global sustainable development*. Bloomsbury.

Morales-Doyle, D., & Gutstein, E. R. (2019). Racial capitalism and STEM education in Chicago Public Schools. *Race Ethnicity and Education, 22*(4), 525–544. https://doi.org/10.1080/13613324.2019.1592840

Morrow, R. A. (2019). Paulo Freire and the "logic of reinvention": Power, the State, and education in the global age. In C. A. Torres (Ed.), *Wiley handbook of Paulo Freire* (pp. 445–462). Wiley-Blackwell.

Morrow, R. A., & Torres, C. A. (2019). Rereading Freire and Habermas: Philosophical anthropology and reframing critical pedagogy and educational research in the neoliberal anthropocene. In C. A. Torres (Ed.), *Wiley handbook of Paulo Freire* (pp. 241–274). Wiley-Blackwell.

Nyerere, J. K. (1968). *Freedom and socialism. Uhuru na ujamaa; a selection from writings and speeches, 1965–1967*. Oxford University Press.

Peters, M. A., Rider, S., Hyvönen, M., & Besley, T. (2018). *Post-truth, fake news: Viral modernity & higher education*. Springer.

Pongratz, L. (2005). Critical theory and pedagogy: Theodor W. Adorno and Max Horkheimer's contemporary significance for a critical pedagogy. In G. Fischman, P. McLaren, H. Sunker, & C. Lankshear (Eds.), *Critical theories, radical pedagogies, and global conflicts* (pp. 154–163). Rowman & Littlefield Publishers.

Rodney, W. (1981). *How Europe underdeveloped Africa* (Rev). Howard University Press.

Said, E. W. (1979). *Orientalism*. Vintage Books.

Salamon, G. (2018). What's critical about phenomenology? *Pucta: Journal of Critical Phenomenology, 1*(1), 8–17. Retrieved from http://journals.oregondigital.org/index.php/pjcp/article/view/PJCP.v1i1.2

Santos, B. d. S. (2007). Beyond abyssal thinking: From global lines to ecologies of knowledges. *Review (Fernand Braudel Center), 30*(1), 45–89. Retrieved from http://www.jstor.org/stable/40241677

Santos, B. d. S. (2014). *Epistemologies of the South: Justice against epistemicide*. Paradigm Publishers

Santos, B. d. S. (2018). *The end of the cognitive empire: The coming of age of epistemologies of the South*. Duke University Press.

Sifuna, D. N., & Otiende, J. E. (2006). *An introductory history of education*. Nairobi University Press.

Sontag, S. (1977). *On photography*. Dell Publishing Co.

Stromquist, N. P., & Monkman, K. (2002). *Globalization and education: Integration and contestation across cultures*. Rowman & Littlefield.

Taylor, A. (2017). Beyond stewardship: Common world pedagogies for the Anthropocene. *Environmental Education Research, 23*(10), 1448–1461. https://doi.org/10.1080/13504622.2017.1325452

Torres, C. A. (2009). *Globalizations and education: Collected essays on class, race, gender, and the state*. Teachers College Press.

Willis, P. E. (1981). *Learning to labor: How working class kids get working class jobs* (Morningside). Columbia University Press.

CHAPTER 2

Critical Theory and the Transformation of Education in the New Millennium

Douglas Kellner and Steve Gennaro

It is surely not difficult to see that our time is a time of birth and transition to a new period. The spirit has broken with what was hitherto the world of its existence and imagination and is about to submerge all this in the past; it is at work giving itself a new form. To be sure, the spirit is never at rest but always engaged in ever progressing motion.... the spirit that educates itself matures slowly and quietly toward the new form, dissolving one particle of the edifice of its previous world after the other,.... This gradual crumbling... is interrupted by the break of day that, like lightning, all at once reveals the edifice of the new world. Hegel, *The Phenomenology of Spirit*, 1807.

This article was originally published by Douglas Kellner as "Toward a Critical Theory of Education," *Democracy and Nature*, Vol. 9, No. 1 (March 2003): 51–64. The article has been updated and revised in collaboration with Dr. Steve Gennaro and the co-authorship of this version of the chapter reflects and acknowledges this collaboration.

D. Kellner (✉)
Graduate School of Education and Information Studies, Los Angeles, CA, USA
e-mail: kellner@ucla.edu

S. Gennaro
Department of Humanities, York University, Toronto, ON, Canada
e-mail: sgennaro@yorku.ca

© The Author(s), under exclusive license to Springer Nature Switzerland AG 2022
A. A. Abdi and G. W. Misiaszek (eds.), *The Palgrave Handbook on Critical Theories of Education*, https://doi.org/10.1007/978-3-030-86343-2_2

As the second decade of the second millennium unfolds, against the backdrop of COVID-19, the human species is undergoing one of the most dramatic technological revolutions in history, one that is changing everything from the ways that people work to the ways that they communicate with each other and spend their leisure time. The technological revolution centers on a removal of time and space as the precedents for education and bears witness to online, blended, hybrid, virtual, AI, and even gamified synchronous and asynchronous options for teaching and learning, no longer occupying the periphery of education, but instead now holding steady as normalized educational options. This Great Transformation poses tremendous challenges to educators to rethink their basic tenets, to deploy the emergent technologies in creative and productive ways, and to restructure education to respond constructively and progressively to the technological and social changes now encompassing the globe.[1]

At the same time that technological revolution is underway, important demographic and socio-political changes are taking place throughout the world. COVID-19 has left no corner of the world untouched and has altered all forms of daily living on a global scale. The global explosion of COVID-19 provides a reminder of how earlier conceptualizations and critiques of globalization may not have gone far enough to note the true interconnectedness of all peoples on this globe. Early colonization by imperial European nations brought pandemic and death to large segments of the colonized world, as Europeans imported deadly diseases throughout the colonized world. Ironically, this time the pandemic came from a former colonized part of the globe, so that the COVID-19 pandemic can be seen as revenge of the colonized world, just as the pandemic can be seen as the revenge of nature for slaughtering animals in monstrous conditions of mass production and mechanized killing to feed hungry humans.[2]

In this context, as Gennaro noted in 2010, our definition of globalization needs to be expanded to account for "the movement, interaction, sharing, co-option, and even imposition of economic goods and services, cultures, ideas, ideologies, people's lives and lived experiences, food, plants, animals, labour, medicine, disease, learning, play, practices, and knowledge(s) across time and space(s) previously thought to be impossible or at the very least improbable."[3] Furthermore, the Black Lives Matter movement brought into perspective the very real challenge of providing equitable access to people from diverse races, classes, and backgrounds to the tools and competencies to succeed and participate in an ever more complex and changing digital world despite a structure that has institutionalized and normalized their very oppression.[4]

In this chapter, we propose developing a critical theory of education for democratizing and reconstructing education to meet the challenges of a global and technological society. This involves articulating a metatheory for the philosophy of education and providing a historical genealogy and grounding of key themes of a democratic reconstruction of education which indicates what traditional aspects of education should be overcome and what alternative pedagogies and principles should reconstruct education in the present age. Education has always involved colonization of children, youth, the underclasses, immigrants, and members of the society at large into the values, behavior, labor skills, competitiveness, and submission to authority to serve the needs of white, patriarchal capitalism and to transmit the ideologies that Marx and Engels saw as the "ruling ideas of the ruling class" (1978), and which bell hooks (1994) reminds us also includes the ruling ideas of white men and colonization of the subjects of education into White, Patriarchal Capitalism.

The decolonization of education thus necessarily involves critique of dominant ideologies, pedagogies, and the current organization of education, to be replaced by what Freire calls "the pedagogy of the oppressed" (1970). We will argue that this project includes developing multiple critical literacies as a response to digital technologies and developing critical pedagogies to meet the challenges of globalization, multiculturalism, and institutionalized racism, classism, and sexism, while promoting radical democratization to counter the trend toward the imposition of a neo-liberal business model on education. We will also argue that a democratic and intersectional reconstruction of education needs to build on and synthesize perspectives of classical philosophy of education, Deweyean radical pragmatism, Freirean critical pedagogy, poststructuralism, and various critical theories of gender, race, class, sexuality, ethnicity, disability, indigeneity, and more, while criticizing obsolete idealist, elitist, and antidemocratic aspects of traditional concepts of education.

We are aware that in much of the world hunger, shelter, and basic literacy are necessary requirements for survival, but would argue that in a globalized world it is important to project normative visions for education and social transformation that could be used to criticize and reconstruct education and society in a variety of contexts. Great strides have been made toward basic global education since the introduction of the United Nations Convention on the Rights of the Child in 1989, where UNICEFs millennium goals of extending education to all witnessed a rise in global schooling by across the first 25 years of the UNCRC.[5]

The last decade has witnessed a push from UNCIEF to extend rights of the child to high school access globally, and more recently to push for global access to STEM (Science technology, engineering, and mathematics) programming and job opportunities for girls and girls of color.[6] Our project requires critical awareness that we are reflecting positions of theorists in the overdeveloped world, and that in different parts of the world education will be reconstructed in various ways depending on the exigencies of the system and possibilities for democratic transformation of education and society.[7] Nonetheless, now is the time to reflect on the philosophy of education, to consider what might be constructed as a critical theory of education and radical pedagogy, and to articulate a vision of how education could be reconstructed and democratized in the present age to serve as an instrument of democratic social transformation.

CRITICAL THEORY, CRITIQUE, AND THE SEARCH FOR THE GOOD LIFE

In using the term "critical theory," we are building on the Frankfurt School (Kellner, 1989), but the critical theory that we are anticipating is broader than the version developed by the German-American exiles from World War II. In the context of theorizing and reconstructing education for the contemporary era, we would include the tradition of Freirean critical pedagogy, Deweyean pragmatism, British cultural studies, feminism, critical race theory, and other intersectional theories of oppression and resistance, as well as poststructuralism. Our appropriation of the latter would encompass both the critiques of the subject, reason, and liberal democracy in especially French versions of "post" theory (see Best & Kellner, 1991). Yet we would engage and emphasize the critical theories of gender, race, sexuality, and constructions of subjectivity that have developed from a broad range of theoretical formations over the past years. These themes can enrich critical theory and pedagogy and help with the Deweyean project of democratizing and reconstructing education so that aims of social justice and progressive transformation can inform pedagogy and practice.

We thus use the metatheoretical concept of "critical theory" as a cover concept for this project to signify the critical dimension, the theoretical aspirations, and the political dynamics that will strive to link theory and practice. This conception of "critical" is synoptic and wide-ranging encompassing of "critical" in the Greek sense of the verb *krinein*, which signifies to discern, reflect, and judge, and "theory," in the sense of the Greek noun *theoria* which refers to a way of seeing and contemplation. Greek critique is rooted in everyday life and exemplified in the Socratic practice of examining social life, its institutions, values, and dominant ideas, as well as one's own thought and action.

Critique became central to the Enlightenment project of criticizing authority and legitimating one's intellectual and political positions. The Kantian sense of critique, for example, required putting in question all the ideas of reason, morality, religion, aesthetics, and other dominant ideas to see if they could be well grounded and legitimated. Kantian critique aims at autonomy from prejudice and ill-grounded ideas and requires rigorous reflection on one's presuppositions and basic positions and argumentation to support one's views.

Critical theory also builds on a Hegelian concept of critique (1965 [1807]), as well by criticizing one-sided positions (such as technophobia vs. technophilia) and developing more complex dialectical perspectives that reject and neglect oppressive or false features of a position, while appropriating positive and emancipatory aspects (see Kellner, forthcoming). Critical theory adopts a Hegelian concept of theory by developing holistic theories that attempt to conceptualize the totality of a given field, but that importantly make connections and articulate contradictions, overcoming idealist or reductive theories of society, nature, humanity, or the world.

A critical theory of education also draws on Marxian critique, stressing the importance of critique of ideology and situating analysis of a topic like education within the dominant social relations and system of political economy and society (Marx & Engels, 1978). The Marxian project systematically criticized the assumptions of an established hegemonic discipline, as in Marx's critique of political economy, and constructed an alternative theory and practice to overcome the limitations and oppressive features of established institutions and systems of production. Marxian critique involves radical examination of existing ideologies and practices of education and the need for pedagogical and social transformation to free individuals from the fetters of consumer capitalism and to help make possible a free, more democratic, and human culture and society. Marxian theorists like Gramsci (1971) criticized the ways that Italian education and culture reproduced ideologies of the bourgeoisie and then fascism, and called for a counterhegemonic cultural project that would encompass alternative institutions from schooling to theater to journalism to help construct a socialist and democratic society. Further, as Charles Reitz has demonstrated (2000), Herbert Marcuse carried out sustained criticisms of the existing system of education as a mode of reproducing the existing system of domination and oppression and called for counter-institutions and pedagogies to promote democratic social transformation and the full development of individuals.[8]

Critical theory must also be intersectional, drawing on Patricia Hill Collins and Sirma Bilge (2016) who argue that intersectionality is not a theory, but is also an analytical tool that exposes and makes visible multiple domains of power and oppression and inequity. Hill Collins and Bilge argue that human rights, academia, and technology are sites where intersectionality of critical praxis and critical inquiry occurs. Intersectional approaches, like critical theory, are multilayered, multi-perspectival, and multidimensional and include not only what we see/touch/smell (what our senses reveal), but also what we don't see or cannot see (implicit ideological structures of power). Intersectional approaches require both critical inquiry and critical praxis to better understand power in our society and in our lives. Intersectionality is an approach to exploring social conditions across multiple lawyers and converging spaces, beginning with the unique experiences of the individual and expanding to include how social variables and markers of difference (such as race, class, gender, and age) multiply an individual's privilege or marginalization, and continuing to note how forms of oppression and discrimination (from racism, homophobia, transphobia, etc.) impact individual experiences as they exist inside larger structural forces of history, capitalism, colonialism, misogyny, and more. Hence, the concept indicates that the social conditions of each individual are not experienced equally.

Building on this tradition, we are arguing in a critical Hegelian spirit that classical philosophies of education can aid in the project of reconstructing and democratizing education and society, but that certain idealist, elitist, and oppressive elements of classical and contemporary pedagogy must be rejected and re-visited with an intersectional approach. A critical theory of education has a normative and even utopian dimension, attempting to theorize how education and life construct alternatives to what is. Developing a model of education that promotes the good life and the good society could be aided by normative reflection on classical philosophy of education from the Greeks through John Dewey and critics of classical Western education like Ivan Illich and Paulo Freire. For the Greeks, philosophy signified love of wisdom (*philo-sophia*) and the practice of philosophy involved *Paideia*, the shaping, formation, and development of human beings and citizens (Jaeger, 1965). For the Greeks, it was language and communication that created human beings and philosophical dialogue involved the search for wisdom and the good life. Using the light of reason, the philosopher was to discover concepts for human life and society that would enable the educator to create more fully developed human beings and citizens able to participate in their society.

Thus, for the classical Greek philosophy of education, proper education involved the search for the good life and the good society. Of course, Greek society was built on slavery so only the upper class, and mostly men, could dedicate themselves to education and becoming citizens. In later appropriations of Greek notions of *Paideia*, such as are evident in Werner Jaeger's classical study (1965), the Greek notion of education was idealized and essentialized, leading to idealist notions of culture from the Romantics, Matthew Arnold, to those of current conservative elitists who fetishize idealized aspects of culture, elevate the mind over the body, the superior individual over the masses, and thus undermine democracy, citizenship, and the project of developing a just society.[9]

While the Greeks developed a primarily aristocratic conception of education, for the Romans education was shaped to meet the needs of Empire and to expand a universalized conception of culture and citizenship grounded in Roman ideals that provided the basis for the Western conception of *Humanitas*. For Roman civilization, education involved transmission of basic skills and literacy training for the plebs, more advanced schooling for the administrative class of the imperial society, and a form of classically-oriented tutoring for the patrician class in the codes and manners of Roman aristocracy. Education, then, for the Romans involved *educatio* and *instructio*, in which the teacher was to train children much as the horticulturist cultivated plants and the animal trainer molded animals, even as it aspired to mimic Platonic notions of education within its highest ranks.

Following the Latin roots, the early English conceptions of education involved bringing up and rearing young people from childhood to teach them good manners and habits and to cultivate the qualities of personality and thought. Curiously, the Latin roots of the English terms *education* and *educate* were used to signify the training and discipline of both animals and humans, connotations that lasted into the nineteenth century when more idealized notions of culture gained currency. By the late nineteenth century, both classicist educational conservatives and progressives like Dewey harked back to the Latin term *eductio*, to enrich and legitimate their pedagogical projects. However, as E.D. Hirsch (1988) and Ivan Illich (1981) have both noted, modern progressives made an unfortunate conflation of the term *eductio* (signifying a moving out, emigration, or stretching forth) with the Roman pedagogical term *educo*, which meant either nourishment or training. The result was an idealized version of Western education in which the teachers were to draw out or reduce innate human potentials, a tradition pointing back toward Plato and the Greeks.

The classical ideals of education remain important insofar as they aim at the forming of more developed human beings and what Cicero conceived of as the citizen and "political philosopher." The latter embodied and disseminated humane values and tolerance, and whose wide-ranging knowledge was directed toward the regulation and construction of a public space that accorded with civic values and not toward the ivory tower of theoretical abstraction. To the degree that classical ideals of education articulated a vision of humanity as being that which is capable of transcending itself and reshaping itself and its world is a positive heritage, as is the emphasis on the cultivation of unrealized human potentials, a utopian dimension later brought out by the philosopher Ernst Bloch (1986).

The classical ideals also speak to the ethical duty that any citizen has toward its community and notions of political virtue that would later influence Rousseau and Enlightenment figures. Hence, to the extent that classical education develops pedagogic practices that allow for the greatest release of human potential and cultivation of citizens who will produce a just society, the project counters education contrived to fit students into the existing social system, which reduces schooling to an instrument of social reproduction.

Yet we should recall the elitist and idealist roots of classical education and that *Paideia* and *Humanitas* were used to legitimate slave societies and in the case of the Romans to promote Empire. Indeed, a study of the classical ideals also underlines for us the ways in which previous models of education have been produced within and as discourses of power and domination. Hence, a radically historicist approach to the philosophy of education does not superficially (or mistakenly) draw upon and reproduce theoretical positions that would otherwise prove problematical, but in the spirit of Ernst Bloch and Walter Benjamin's "redemptive criticism" appropriates and reconstructs ideas from the past to produce critical theories of the present and visions of a better future.

Public Education, Democracy, and Pedagogies of the Oppressed

A similar dialectical approach is relevant for reflection on the idealist notion of education encoded in the German *Bildung* tradition, itself connected to an idealized version of Greek *Paideia*, which intended education to shape and form more fully to realize human beings. Both Hegel and Marx shared this tradition, with Hegel stressing the formation and development of spirit as a historical and educational process that properly formed students needed to work through and appropriate tradition as one's own, while criticizing and moving beyond it. Marx, however, was inspired by a vision of socialism as producing more realized many-sided human beings and envisaged in his early writings, a la Schiller, the education of all the senses as an important dimension of becoming a human being (Marx & Engels, 1978, pp. 88ff)—a theoretical position taken up by Marxists like Marcuse.

In their 1848 "Communist Manifesto," Marx and Engels made liberation of the working class from bourgeois education and expanded public education for the working class one of their major demands, offering as a key measure to constructing socialism: "Public education of all children free of charge. Elimination of children's factory labor in its present form. Combination of education with material production, etc. etc." (Marx & Engels, 1978, p. 490). Of course, the infamous "etc. etc." signals the Marxist philosophy of education that was never fully developed, but it is clear that free public education was a key demand of Marxian socialism. Crucially, Marx and Engels wanted to "rescue education from the influence of the ruling class" (1978, p. 487), arguing that education currently reproduces capitalist-bourgeois societies and must be completely reconfigured to produce alternative ones. In the famous "Theses on Feuerbach," the young Marx wrote: "The materialist doctrine that humans are products of circumstances and upbringing, and that, therefore changed humans are products of other circumstances and changed upbringing, forgets that it is humans who change circumstances and that it is essential to educate the educator" (1978, p. 144).

As the twentieth century unfolded, it was John Dewey who developed the most sustained reflections on progressive education, linking education and democracy. Dewey insisted that one could not have a democratic society without education, that everyone should have access to education for democracy to work, and that education was the key to democracy and thus to the good life and good society. Dewey was a proponent of strong democracy, of an egalitarian and participatory democracy, where everyone takes part in social and political life. For Dewey, education was the key to making democracy work since in order to intelligently participate in social and political life, one had to be informed and educated to be able to be a good citizen and competent actor in democratic life.

Dewey, like Rousseau, and even more so, was experimental and pragmatic and saw education as an evolving and experiential process in which one would learn by doing. The term "pragmatism" is associated with Dewey and in one of its meanings signifies that theory should emerge from practice, that education should be practical, aimed at improving everyday life and society, and that by using the method of trial and error, one could learn important life skills and gradually improve democratic society and education.

From similar pedagogical perspectives yet from a different historical location of Brazil in the 1960s and following, often in exile, Paulo Freire argued that the oppressed, the underclasses, have not equally shared or received the benefits of education and they should not expect it as a gift from the ruling classes, but should educate themselves, developing a "pedagogy of the oppressed" (1970). For Freire, emancipatory education involves subverting the Hegelian master/slave dialectic, in which oppressed individuals undertake a transformation from object to subject and thus properly become a subject and more fully developed human beings. Responding to the situation of colonization and oppression, Freire's pedagogy of the oppressed involved a type of decolonization and a consciousness-raising (*conscientizacao*), and allowed the educated the right to thematize issues of study, to engage in dialogue with teachers, and to fully participate in the educational process.

Developing a "pedagogy of the oppressed" requires the creation of learning processes that will help individuals improve themselves and create a better life through social transformation and empowerment, rather than conforming to dominant views and values. Freire is famous for his critique of "banking" education and creation of a dialogical pedagogy. Freire perceived that education is often a form of indoctrination, of enforcing conformity to dominant values, and of social reproduction in which one is tutored into submission and acceptance of an oppressed and subordinate status. Therefore, pedagogy of the oppressed must oppose dominant conceptions of education and schooling and construct more critical and emancipatory pedagogies aiming at radical social transformation.

It is interesting that all the classical philosophers of education that we have discussed, as well as Marx and Freire, assume that education is of central importance to creating better and more fully-realized individuals, as well as a good society, and therefore that philosophy of education is a key aspect of social critique and transformation. Critical philosophies of education provide radical critique of the existing models of education in the so-called Western democracies and provide progressive alternative models, still relevant to our contemporary situation. Many of these philosophies of education, however, work with questionable conceptions of reason, subjectivity, and democracy and neglect the importance of the body, gender, race, sexuality, the natural environment, and other dimensions of human life that some modern theories failed to adequately address.[10] Consequently, the poststructuralist critique of modern theory provides important tools for a critical theory of education in the present age.

Poststructuralist theories emphasize the importance of difference, marginality, heterogeneity, and multiculturalism, calling attention to dimensions of experiences, groups, and voices that have been suppressed in the modern tradition. They develop new critical theories of multicultural otherness and difference, which includes engagement with class, gender, race, sexuality, and other important components of identity and life that many modern pedagogies neglect or ignore. Poststructuralists also call for situated reason and knowledges, stressing the importance of context and the social construction of reality that allows constant reconstruction. A critical poststructuralism also radicalizes the reflexive turn found in some critical modern thinkers, requiring individuals involved in education and politics to reflect upon their own subject-position and biases, privileges, and limitations, forcing theorists to constantly criticize and rethink their own assumptions, positions, subject-positions, and practices, in a constant process of reflection and self-criticism (Best & Kellner, 1991, 1997).

Poststructuralist theories have empowered women, people of color, people identifying as GLBTQ, and others excluded from modern theory and educational institutions. Yet feminist theories of education can also draw upon classical feminism, as well as poststructuralist critique. Mary Wollstonecraft (1988), for example, rethought education after the French revolution as a way to realize the program of the Enlightenment and to make individual freedom, equality, and democracy a reality for men and women. Education in Wollstonecraft's conception involved the restructuring of society, enabling women to participate in business, politics, and cultural life, extending the privileges of education to women (although she tended to neglect the need to educate and uplift working-class men and women). Radicalizing Enlightenment positions, Wollstonecraft argued that women, like men, are human beings who have reason and are thus capable of education. Moreover, she argued that education is the only way for women to better themselves and that if women do not pursue education, they cannot be emancipated, they cannot be participants in society, they cannot be equal to men, and thus, the Enlightenment project cannot be realized.

More recent feminists, influenced by poststructuralism and multiculturalism, like bell hooks (1994), have stressed the importance of gaining agency and voice for oppressed groups and individuals who have traditionally been marginalized in educational practice and social life. Giving a voice within education and society to individuals in oppressed groups marked by race and ethnicity, sexuality, or class articulates well with the perspectives of Paulo Freire, although he himself did not bring in these domains until his later work. Freire's eventual turn toward more inclusive and articulated gender and multicultural perspectives was in part a response to critique from feminists, critical race theory, people identifying as GLBTQ, and other oppressed groups, and in part, the evolution of Freire's thinking marked a development of his theory as he interacted with more groups and individuals.

Reflecting on the term "intersectionality" in a 2020 *Time Magazine* Feature, scholar and activist Kimberlé Crenshaw, who is credited with introducing the term into our collective lexicon three decades ago, defined intersectionality as "a lens, a prism, for seeing the way in which various forms of inequality often operate together and exacerbate each other. We tend to talk about race inequality as separate from inequality based on gender, class, sexuality or immigrant status. What's often missing is how some people are subject to all of these, and the experience is not just the sum of its parts."[11] Crenshaw noted how the main argument inside of academia and in mainstream media positions intersectionality as identity politics. However, for Patricia Hill Collins and Sirma Bilge (2016), limiting intersectionality to a theory of identity is reductionist and largely used to discredit and devalue the components of intersectionality that are most pressing, namely the component of critical praxis in the need to make social inequality visible for all. There is more than just one "intersectionality," as there are multiple politicized localities which individuals occupy—that is they sit in, they rest in, they lay in, they live in, they stay inside of. These localities are occupied, however, in unequal terms and with unequal access which creates the possibilities for alliances of the oppressed across different fields, spaces, identities, and social groupings. Some individuals and groups have more power than others in educational, cultural, and political spaces, and so, an intersectional alliance of the oppressed can fight for equality and justice across racial, gender, class, and regional lines.

Indeed, the issue of privilege and the life-and-death necessity for access to the fundamentals of health, welfare, education, and housing have come to the forefront of discussions in light of the COVID-19 pandemic and Black Lives Matter and other social movements that have created new awareness of oppression and inequality which should inform our struggles for equality, social justice, and the reconstruction of education for the future.

Thus, intersectionality provides a language for inhabitants of multiple localities of oppression and struggle to make visible the politicization of space and the real, lived, and material conditions of the moment. To use intersectionality to explore identity without reducing it, a theory of identity requires locating intersectional dynamics and struggles inside larger philosophical dichotomies of objectivity and subjectivity. Paulo Freire in *Pedagogy of the Oppressed* (1970) argued that one cannot conceive of objectivity without a subjectivity, and that when we talk about oppression, we are speaking about marginalization and the ways in which a society works to provide access to some and deny access to others to basic necessities of life like education and health care. Some of us, like the authors of this piece, based on our privilege, get to be subjects, while others, because of a lack of access and privilege, are subjected to being objectified.

It is indeed this unjust world that we seek to change and that drives education to be an instrument of social transformation and justice. Returning to Freire, an objectified person cannot see the oppression they're living in until they see themselves first as an individual who is living inside of oppression.

Once an individual sees themselves as a subject, that they embody subjectivity and the possibility of resistance and struggle, an individual can perceive him or herself as a person of worth and value and seek to actualize their potentialities for a better life. Only then can they actually see the structures around them, which are actively oppressing them, to which they were previously oblivious. So, one should not conceive of objectivity without first acknowledging their own individual subjectivity and the possibilities of collective subjectivities that provide the possibilities for radical action, and that can bring about social justice and democratic and emancipatory social change.

Building on these perspectives enables a philosophy of education to develop more inclusive philosophical vision and to connect education directly to democratization and the changing of social relations in the direction of equality and social justice. Since social conditions and life are constantly changing, a critical theory of education must be radically historicist, attempting to reconstruct education as social conditions evolve and to create pedagogical alternatives in terms of the needs, problems, and possibilities of specific groups of people in concrete situations. Yet philosophical and normative insight and critique are also needed, driving efforts at reconstructing education and society by visions of what education and human life could be and what are their specific limitations in existing societies.

Hence, a critical theory of education involves conceiving a vision of the democratic transformation of education, and in how radicalizing education could help democratize and create a more just and inclusive society. In this section, we have proposed a comprehensive metatheory that draws on both classical and contemporary philosophies of education to comprehend and reconstruct education. The classical critical theory of the Frankfurt School while rigorously engaging in the critique of ideology always drew on the more progressive elements of the most advanced theories of the day, developing dialectical appropriations, for instance, of Nietzsche, Freud, and Weber (Kellner, 1989). Many other Marxian theorists or groups, by contrast, would just be dismissive and rejecting of these "bourgeois ideologies." In the same spirit, we would argue that a critical theory of education should draw on the radical democratic tradition of John Dewey's pragmatism, Freirean critical pedagogy, and intersectional contemporary critical theories of race, gender, class, and sexuality.

Yet a critical theory of education must be rooted in a critical theory of society that conceptualizes the specific features of actually existing capitalist societies, and their relations of domination and subordination, contradictions and openings for progressive social change, and transformative practices that will create what the theory projects as a better life and society. A critical theory signifies a way of seeing and conceptualizing, a constructing of categories, making connections, mapping, and engaging in the practice of theory-construction, and relating theory to practice.

In the next section, we will accordingly deploy a critical theory framework to suggest some transformations in the situation of youth today and the need to reconstruct education and promote multiple critical literacies appropriate to the novel material conditions, transformations, and subjectivities emerging in the contemporary era. Theorizing important changes in the contemporary moment requires, we would argue, broad-ranging and robust reconstructive theories in order to grasp the changing social and psychological conditions of life in a globalized, high-tech, digitized, multicultural, and highly conflicted world with its intense challenges, problems, and potential. We argue that in this situation of dramatic change, radical transformations of education are necessary to create subjects and practices appropriate to an expanding global society, digitized culture, and world of novel identities, social relations, cultural forms, and social movements and struggles.

Changing Life Conditions, Subjectivities, and Identities

Allan and Carmen Luke have argued (2002) that current educational systems, curricula, and pedagogies were designed for the production of a laboring subject who has become an "endangered species" in the postindustrial economic, social, and cultural system. Modern education was constructed to develop a compliant work force which would gain skills of print literacy and discipline that would enable them to function in modern corporations and a corporate economy based on rational accounting, commercial organization, and discursive communicative practices, supported by manual labor and service jobs. The life trajectory for a laboring modern subject was assumed to be stable and mappable, progressing through K-12 schooling, to universities and perhaps onto professional schools or higher degrees, to well-paying jobs that would themselves offer life-time employment, a stable career, and solid identities.

All of this has changed in a global economy marked by constant restructuring, flux and rapid change, and novel material conditions and subjectivities. Students coming into schools have been shaped by years of television, a variety of music technologies and forms, computer and video games, social networking, and new spheres of multimedia and interactive cyberculture. The university graduating class of 2021 were born in 1999, at the turn of the millennium.[12] They were 5 years old when Mark Zuckerberg launched Facebook, and eight years old when Steve Jobs introduced the world to the iPhone.[13] Moreover, the steady jobs that were waiting for well-disciplined and performing students of the previous generation are disappearing, while new jobs are appearing in the high-tech sector, itself subject to frenzied booms, busts, and restructuring. And this does not even account for what Harry Braverman (1974), following Marx and Engels (1978), called the deskilling effects of technology on the workforce through the division of labor found in the factory system, reducing individuals to the status of machines and objects and providing another example of the alienating effects of the capitalist of labor on the modern individual resulting from expansive transformations in technology and methods of producing.[14] And as COVID-19 has demonstrated, life in a high-tech and global society is much more complicated, fragile, and subject to dramatic disruptions and transformations than was previously perceived.

There is thus a fundamental misfit between youth life-experience and schooling, the expectations of an older generation concerning labor and new work conditions, and the previous print-based and organizational economy and culture in contrast to the new digital culture and global economy. Postmodern theorists have amassed cultural capital theorizing such breaks and ruptures, but have had few positive recommendations on how to restructure institutions like schooling (although there are stacks of books, generally of little worth, on how to succeed in the new economy dating back to the previous millennium). Indeed, in the current conjuncture, advocates of neo-liberal business models for education have used the obviously transformative technological revolution to legitimate technology as the panacea and magic cure for problems of education today and to sell corporate technologies and business models as the solution to educational problems.

One of the major challenges for democratizing education is that it requires acknowledging decolonizing the institutional practices of an education system designed through what Maori scholar Linda Tuhiwai Smith (1999) calls "Imperial Eyes." This requires acknowledging many of the overlapping questions posed by critical theorists of the 1960s and indigenous activists at the time. As Smith (1999, p. 165) notes: "such questions were based on a sense of outrage and injustice about the failure of education, democracy and research to deliver social change for people who were oppressed. These questions related to the relationship between knowledge and power, between research and emancipation, and between lived reality and imposed ideals about the Other."

These questions remain today so that any process of democratizing education needs to draw the consequences for restructuring education and democratizing society from reflection on changing life conditions, experiences, and subjectivities. We need to decolonize and reconstruct education and society in the context of technological revolution and globalization that envisages using technology to democratically promote progressive social and political change without promoting neo-liberal and capitalist agendas. This task is advanced, we believe, by drawing on the radical critique of schooling and proposals for transforming education and learning found in the work of the late Ivan Illich, who was one of the chief educational gurus of the 1970s and a major radical critic of schooling whose work has fallen from view but is still important and should be re-engaged in the present situation.[15]

Ivan Illich's postindustrial model of education contains a radical critique of existing schooling and alternative notions like webs of learning, tools for conviviality, and radically reconstructing education to promote learning, democracy, and social and communal life, thus providing salient alternatives to modern systems (1971, 1973). Illich analyzes in detail how modern schooling prepares students for the modern industrial system and how its "hidden curriculum" promotes conformity, bureaucracy, instrumental rationality, hierarchy, competition, and other features of existing social organization. For Illich, modern systems of schooling are no longer appropriate for postindustrial conditions and require radical restructuring of education and rethinking pedagogy. But unlike many of his contemporaries, Illich had a powerful, explicit, and prescient analysis of the limits and possibilities of technologies and those strange institutions called "schools."

Illich's "learning webs" (1971) and "tools for conviviality" (1973) anticipated the Internet and how it might provide resources, interactivity, and communities that could help revolutionize education. For Illich, science and technology can either serve as instruments of domination or progressive ends. Hence, whereas big systems of computers promote modern bureaucracy and industry, personalized computers made accessible to the public might be constructed to provide tools that can be used to enhance learning. Thus, Illich was aware of how technologies like computers could either enhance or distort education depending on how they were fit into a well-balanced ecology of learning.

Illich provides concrete analyses and a critique of how schooling reproduces the existing social order and is flawed and debased by the defects and horrors of the industrial system. Illich also recognizes that postindustrial society requires certain competencies and that a major challenge is to construct convivial technologies that will improve both education and social life. While he resolutely opposed neo-liberal agendas and was critical of encroaching corporate domination of the Internet and information technologies, Illich's notion of "webs of learning" and "tools of conviviality" can be appropriated for projects of the radical reconstruction of education and learning in the contemporary era.[16] Within this framework, let us consider how the expanding social roles of information and communication technologies require multiple critical literacies and how focusing on the current technological revolution can lead us to rethink learning and reconstruct educational theory and practice.

Expanding Technologies/Multiple Critical Literacies

Prior to COVID-19, schooling in the modern era has been largely organized around the transmission of print literacies and segregated academic knowledges based on a modern division of disciplines into such things as social science, literature, or physical education. The immediate change from classroom learning or school (as a physical entity) to digital spaces around the globe to enforce social distancing and to help combat the spread of COVID-19 in the spring of 2020 though until the writing of this article in spring 2021 has dramatically exposed how the rapidly expanding technologies of information and communication, mutating subjectivities and cultural forms, and the demands of a networked society culture indeed require multiple literacies, more flexible subjects, and inventive skills and capabilities. Theorists such as the Lukes and Kellner suggested solutions to these emerging issues almost two decades ago. For the Luke (2002) and for Kellner (2000, 2002b), the solution was to cultivate in the sphere of education multiple literacies, such as media, computer, and information literacies that will respond to emergent technologies and cultural conditions and empower students to participate in the expanding high-tech culture and networked society.[17]

Hence, the constant development and mutation of information and communication technologies and new forms of culture, economy, and everyday life require a careful rethinking of education and literacy in response to novel challenges that will involve an era of Deweyean experimental education, trial and error, and research and discovery. Yet a critical theory of education will reject pedagogies and literacies that merely aim at the reproduction of existing capitalist societies and creating capabilities aimed primarily at providing cultural capital put in the service of the reproduction of global capitalism. A critical theory of education with a critical intersectional approach could draw on the reconstruction of neo-Marxian, Deweyean, Freirean, and intersectional critical pedagogies of race, gender, and class to attempt to develop Illichian tools and communities of conviviality and genuine learning that would promote democracy, social justice, and cultivate conceptions of the good life and society for all.

This requires teaching traditional literacies as well as multiple forms of computer, information, and communication literacies that will empower students to develop their potentials, create communities of learning, and work toward democratizing society. As Gennaro argued in 2015, in the same fashion that we teach reading, writing, and arithmetic to our kindergarten aged students, we must actively seek to introduce coding with the same importance, enshrined in curriculum, to children as soon as they enter the school system.[18] If young people are to write themselves into existence, they must be literate in the language of the digital culture, which presides over modern subjectivity in current moment. To be sure, digital literacies are necessary, but they need to be articulated with print literacy, in which multiple literacies enable students and citizens to negotiate word, image, graphics, video, and multimedia digitized culture.

In the Hegelian concept of *Geist*, the subject develops through mediations of culture and society in specific historical ways, but encounters contradictions and blockages which are overcome by sublation or Aufhebung, i.e., overcoming obsolete or oppressive conditions that are transcended. In a contemporary version of the Hegelian dialectic, the emergent technologies and conditions of postmodern life are producing novel experiences and subjectivities that come into conflict with schooling, itself based on earlier historical subjectivities and congealed institutions, discourses, and practices, modeled on the industrial factory system (i.e., time-parceled segments, staying immobile at a specific site to perform labor, submitting to the discipline of bosses).

The optimistic Hegelian scenario is that this conflict can be overcome through an Aufhebung that sublates (i.e., negates, preserves, takes to higher stage) the positivities in the conflict and negates the obsolete aspects. Put more concretely: when there are contradictions between, say, a print-based curriculum and evolving subjectivities mediated by multimedia, then resolving the contradiction requires going to a higher level—e.g., restructuring schooling to preserve, for instance, the importance of print-based culture and literacy, while developing new multiple digital literacies.

Hence, restructuring schooling to meet challenges of expanding technologies and emergent social and cultural conditions requires cultivation of multiple literacies, tools, and pedagogies to respond to, mediate, and develop in pedagogically progressive ways the technologies and global conditions that help make possible democratized transformative modes of education and culture. Further, following the calls of some neo-McLuhanites and the digerati, education must be transformed to meet the challenges of technological revolution, yet we must also recognize that a globalized world is fraught with growing inequalities, conflicts, and dangers, so to make education relevant to the contemporary situation it must address these problems.

Indeed, globalization has been creating growing divisions between haves and have nots, and to economic inequality, there now emerge growing information inequalities and gaps in cultural and social capital as well as a growing divide between rich and poor. A transformed democratic education must address these challenges and make education for social justice part of a radical pedagogy, as envisaged by theorists like Marcuse, Illich, and Freire, as well as developing eco-pedagogy to address the environmental crisis raging across the Western United States in a deep freeze as we write in February 2021. Further, to decolonizing education requires constantly questioning biases of class, race, gender, region, and social positioning to create education appropriate for all individuals in one's society.

A radical and decolonizing pedagogy must also engage the difficult issue of overcoming differences, understanding cultures very dissimilar from one's own, and developing a more inconclusive democracy that will incorporate marginalized groups and resolve conflicts between diverse groups and cultures. This requires the three dimensionality of intersectionality articulating the differences between a radical pedagogy that employs an intersectional approach and one that does not in terms of depth, with a multilayered and multi-perspective mode of seeing that grasps alternatives for emancipation and democratization beyond what is immediately visible to us.

This problem of democratizing and decolonizing education is also part of the issue we're having right now in trying to have social discussions around race relations, white privilege, and the structural inequality that exists in the current social moment. A lack of multiple perspectives serves as a significant roadblock to those with privilege acknowledging the systemic injustice experienced by marginalized individuals and groups. When someone is living in a flat, two-dimensional world of privilege, they lack the vision to see a three-dimensional world of inequality and injustice; they can't fathom it because they can't see the complexity and the depth of life experiences that many individuals face as a result of marginalization.

Life is experienced simultaneously in multiple dimensions, and within multiple relationships of power simultaneously that involve economic, politics, culture, and society, all of which are experienced simultaneously in socially constructing our identities that are constantly reconstructed in our social interactions and experiences. This is to say that we are simultaneously gendered, racialized, sexualized, abilitized, culturized, and class-positioned in all of our social interactions and experience. Further, this process is intensified by new technologies, like iPhones, multiple digital devices, and social media, at a pace faster than any moment previous in human history. So how do we engage with this? How do we take this on?

Critical pedagogy is not just about theory or critical inquiry, but it is also about the real lived experiences of the people. Critical pedagogy must examine the material conditions, as informed by theory and as reflected upon by individuals as it actually happens, across many different venues. Crucially, a critical theory seeks to reconstruct education not to fulfill the agenda of capital and the high-tech industries, but to radically democratize education in order to advance the goals of progressive educators like Dewey, Marcuse, Freire, and Illich in cultivating learning that will promote the development of individuality, citizenship and community, social justice, and the strengthening of democratic participation in all modes of life.

Over the past decades, there has been sustained efforts to impose a neo-liberal agenda on education, reorganizing schools on a business model, imposing standardized curriculum, and making testing the goal of pedagogy. This agenda is disastrously wrong and a critical theory of education needs to both critique the neo-liberal restructuring of education and propose alternative conceptions and practices. Globalization and technological revolution have been used to legitimate a radical restructuring of schooling and provide radical educators with openings to propose their own models of pedagogy and reconstruction of education to serve democracy and progressive social change. There is no question but that technological revolution is destabilizing traditional education and creating openings for change. Although one needs to fiercely criticize the neo-liberal model, it is also important to propose alternatives. Thus, one needs to accompany demands for new literacies and a restructuring of education with a program of the democratization of education, as we suggest in our concluding remarks.

Toward a Radical Reconstruction and Democratization of Education

In calling for the democratic reconstruction of education to promote multiple literacies as a response to emergent technologies and globalization, one encounters the problem of the "digital divide." It has been well documented that some communities, or individuals in privileged groups, are exposed to more advanced technologies and given access to more high-tech skills and cultural capital than those in less privileged communities. One way to overcome the divide, and thus a whole new set of inequalities that mirror or supplement modern divides of class, gender, race, and education, is to restructure education so that all students have access to evolving technologies which they can engage with multiple critical literacies, so that education is democratized, and the very learning process and relation between student and teacher are rethought.

The Hegelian Master/Slave dialectic can help characterize relations between students and teachers today in which teachers force their curricula and agendas onto students in a situation in which there may be a mismatch between generational cultural and social experiences and even subjectivities. Educators, students, and citizens must recognize this generational divide and work to overcome conflicts and make differences more productive. That is, many students may be more technologically skilled than teachers and can themselves be important pedagogical resources. We acknowledge know that much of what we've learned about how to use computers we've absorbed from students, and continue to draw upon them both in and out of class to help navigate the new high-tech culture and to devise productive pedagogies and practices for the contemporary era.[19] Democratizing education can be enhanced by more interactive and participatory forms of education and the move to Google Classroom, Microsoft Teams, Zoom, and other technologies in diverse parts of the world for schooling during lockdown and isolation periods in response to the COVID-19 pandemic has illuminated the opportunities for co-constructed learning spaces that technology makes possible—although it also creates problems of access and meeting multiple technological challenges with diverse students and different environments who have differential access to technology, often creating new "digital divides." Building on previous examples such as developing convivial listserves, the collective building of Web-sites, online discussion, and collaborative computer-based research projects; in the current environment, we can use Wikis and shared documents, like Google Docs, to co-create in real time. Blogs and YouTube videos can allow for asynchronous engagement that transcends time and space barriers but still allows for communities of practice. And the aforementioned video conferencing technology has presented the world of online, text-based discussions, with a synchronous alternative where "breakout rooms" can place individuals around the globe into small groups for dialogue instantaneously—providing new opportunities for intercultural communication and for global networks of activism—although different forms of technology and models of pedagogy will be used in different parts of the world.

In addition, a critical theory of education would envisage merging classroom-based Socratic discussion with computer research and projects that would combine oral, written, and multimedia cultural forms in the process of education without privileging one or the other. Some educators still insist that face-to-face dialogue in the classroom is the alpha and omega of good education and while there are times that classroom dialogue is extremely productive, it is a mistake to fetishize face-to-face conversation, books and print media, or new multimedia. We must be careful not to view the educational process through the same lens of nostalgia with which we often view childhood and youth, since nostalgia as a process of memory can act to depoliticize the inhabitants of memory more than it does to liberate the self of future oppression. Rather, the challenge is to draw upon in an experimental and supplemental way all of the dimensions of the traditional educational process into a dialectical conversations with emerging technologies to restructure and democratize education.

Finally, we would suggest that since concrete reconstructions of education will take place in specific local and national contexts, the mix between classroom pedagogy, books and reading print-material, and multimedia and Internet-based education will vary according to locale, age, access to digital technologies, and the needs and interests of students and teachers. The idea behind multiple critical literacies is that diverse and multimodal forms of culture blend in lived experience to form new subjectivities, and the challenge for radical pedagogy is to cultivate subjectivities that seek justice, more harmonious social relations, and transformed relations with the natural world. Ivan Illich called for education to take ecological problems into account (1971, 1973), and as Richard Kahn argues (2010), the extent of current ecological crisis is such that environmental collapse and disaster faces the current generation if ecological issues are not addressed. These ecological issues ring true to heart of the UN sustainable development goals.[20]

A glaring problem with contemporary educational institutions is that they become fixed in monomodal instruction with homogenized lesson plans, curricula, and pedagogy and neglect to address challenging political, cultural, or ecological problems. As Paulo Freire notes: "One cannot expect positive results from an educational or political action program which fails to respect the particular view of the world held by the people. Such a program constitutes cultural invasion…The starting point for organizing the program content of education or political action must be the present, existential, concrete situation, reflecting the aspirations of the people" (1970, p. 85). A *Pedagogy of the Oppressed* is about simultaneous individual and social awakening through action and reflection to seeing the structural domination in our lives, and then working through theory and reflection toward action and praxis, to overcome oppression, and to change the structure and the structural powers at play in our everyday lives.

The development of tools of conviviality and radical pedagogies thus enables teachers and students to break with colonizing and limited models and to engage in Deweyean experimental education. A reconstruction of education could help create subjects better able to negotiate the complexities of emergent forms of everyday life, labor, and culture, as contemporary life becomes more multifaceted and dangerous. More supportive, dialogical, and interactive social relations in learning situations can promote cooperation, democracy, and positive social values, as well as fulfill needs for communication, esteem, and learning.

Whereas modern mass education tended to see life in a linear fashion based on print models and developed pedagogies which broke experience into discrete moments and behavioral bits, critical pedagogies could produce skills that enable individuals to better navigate the multiple realms and challenges of contemporary life. Deweyean education focused on problem solving, goal-seeking projects, and the courage to be experimental, while Freire developed alternative pedagogies and Marcuse and Illich produced oppositional conceptions of education and learning and critiques of schooling. It is this sort of critical spirit and vision to reconstruct education and society that can help produce new pedagogies, tools for learning, and social justice for the present age.

Notes

1. Karl Polanyi saw a "Great Transformation" (1944/2001; 2nd edition) taking place in Europe with the rise of market economies and modern states which create a change in social conditions and relations and all forms of economy, culture, politics, and society; we see another "great transformation" evolving out of revolutions in digital technologies and culture.
2. On the COVID-19 pandemic as the revenge of nature a la the Frankfurt School, see Douglas Kellner, "Trump, Authoritarian Populism, and Covid-19 From a U.S. Perspective," in press and forthcoming from *Cultural Politics*. On the background for the COVID-19 pandemic, see "Wildlife Markets and COVID-19," *Humane Society International*, April 19, 2020 at https://www.hsi.org/wp-content/uploads/2020/04/Wildlife-Markets-and-COVID-19-White-Chapter.pdf (accessed on August 11, 2020). For background on pandemics, viruses and human animal markets, see Quammen (2013).
3. Gennaro, Stephen "Globalization, History, Theory, and Writing" *Society for the History of Childhood and Youth Newsletter*. Winter 2010, No. 16 at http://www.history.vt.edu/Jones/SHCY/Newsletter16/Pedagogy-GennaroArticle.html (accessed November 8, 2016).
4. On youth resistance, Black Lives Matter, and other forces of the Trump resistance who have emerged in recent years, see Kellner and Satchel (2020).
5. A 2020 report from UNICEF, Plan International, and UN Women noted "that the number of out-of-school girls has dropped by 79 million in the last two decades" and that "girls became more likely to be in secondary school than boys in just the last decade." https://www.unicef.org/press-releases/25-years-uneven-progress-despite-gains-education-world-still-violent-highly (accessed February 23, 2021).

6. "Towards an equal future: Reimagining girls' education through STEM" UNICEF, October 6, 2020. https://www.unicef.org/media/84046/file/Reimagining-girls-education-through-stem-2020.pdf (accessed February 23, 2021).
7. Studies reveal that women, minorities, and immigrants now constitute roughly 85% of the growth in the labor force, while these groups represent about 60% of all workers; see Duderstadt (1999–2000, p. 38). In the past decade, the number of Hispanics in the United States increased by 35% and Asians by more than 40%. Since 1991, California has had no single ethnic or racial minority and almost half of the high school students in the state are African-American or Latino. Meanwhile, a "tidal wave" of children of baby boomers are about to enter college; see Atkinson (1999–2000, pp. 49–50). Obviously, we are writing this study from a North American perspective, but would suggest that our arguments have broader reference in an increasingly globalized society marked by a networked economy, increasing migration and multiculturalism, and a proliferating Internet-based cyberculture.
8. On Marcuse and education, see Kellner et al. (2008) and Kellner et al. (2009).
9. Yet Herbert Marcuse radicalized the Greek concept of *Paedeia* and German concept of *Bildung* to reconstruct education as a form of self-development and social transformation; see the sources on Marcuse and education and analyses in note 8 above and in Reitz (2000).
10. For a critique of modern theories of the subject and reason from postmodern perspectives, see Best and Kellner (1991, 1997); for a critique of modern pedagogy neglecting the body, environment, and cosmos, see Kahn (2010).
11. Katy Steinmetz "She Coined the Term 'Intersectionality' Over 30 Years Ago. Here's What It Means to Her Today," *Time Magazine* at https://time.com/5786710/kimberle-crenshaw-intersectionality/
 (accessed February 19, 2021). Kimberlé Crenshaw's (2022) key chapters will be collected in *On Intersectionality: Essential Writings* (forthcoming).
12. "12 Fascinating Facts about the Class of 2021. Back when these freshmen were born, Brady wasn't the G.O.A.T." *Boston University Today* http://www.bu.edu/articles/2017/class-of-2021-facts/ (accessed February 23, 2021).
13. "At last—the full story of how Facebook was founded." *Business Insider*, Nicholas Carlson, March 5, 2010 https://www.businessinsider.com/how-facebook-was-founded-2010-3 (accessed February 23, 2021), and April Montgomery and Ken Mingis, "The evolution of Apple's iPhone. As the iPhone ages, it's important to look at how the now-iconic device has matured since its arrival in 2007." *Computer World*, October 15, 2020 at https://www.computerworld.com/art

icle/2604020/the-evolution-of-apples-iphone.html (accessed February 23, 2021).
14. Shoshana Zuboff (1988, 2020) describes further deskilling and alienation of labor under high-tech capitalism in the contemporary epoch.
15. While reviewing Illich's work for a memorial for him sponsored by the UCLA Paulo Freire Institute, Kellner discovered that much of Illich's work, including his major books, has been preserved on websites; see, for example, http://www.preservenet.com/theory/Illich.html (accessed February 19, 2021).
16. We should note that while we find Illich's work immensely important as a critique and tools for a reconstruction, of education, but reject his notion of "deschooling" and agree with Marcuse that more and better "reschooling" is necessary; on the latter, see Kellner et al. (2008).
17. Kellner and Share (2019) introduced the term "critical media literacy" (CML) to distinguish a form of media literacy that engages the problematic of power and domination and that critically engaged the dimensions of gender, race, class, sexuality, and other domains of oppression and struggle.
18. This was the topic of Gennaro's TEDxYork Proposal; see: "Teach Kids to Code" https://youtu.be/SKLgl58GrqY (accessed February 19, 2021).
19. For examples of how new technology can be used to enhance education, see our Web-sites; Kellner's philosophy of education, technology and society, and cultural studies seminars at UCLA, are accessible at http://www.gseis.ucla.edu/faculty/kellner/Kellner.html), and Gennaro's work on York University's Faculty of Liberal Arts and Professional Studies Arts faculty Professional Development webpage, which he co-authored at https://going-digital.laps.yorku.ca/faculty-resources/ (accessed February 24, 2021).
20. "The 17 Sustainable Development Goals (SDGs), which are an urgent call for action by all countries—developed and developing—in a global partnership. They recognize that ending poverty and other deprivations must go hand-in-hand with strategies that improve health and education, reduce inequality, and spur economic growth—all while tackling climate change and working to preserve our oceans and forests." United Nations Department of Economic and Social Affairs at https://sdgs.un.org/goals (accessed February 23, 2021).

REFERENCES

Best, S., & Kellner, D. (1991). *Postmodern theory: Critical interrogations*. Macmillan and Guilford Press.
Best, S., & Kellner, D. (1997). *The postmodern turn*. Routledge and Guilford Press.
Bloch, E. (1986). *The principle of hope*. MIT Press.
Braverman, H. (1974). *Labor and monopoly capital: The degradation of work in the twentieth century*. Monthly Review Press.
Crenshaw, K. (2022). *On intersectionality: Essential writings*. The New Press.
Freire, P. (1970). *Pedagogy of the oppressed*. Continuum Books.
Gramsci, A. (1971). *Prison notebooks*. International Publishers.
Hegel, G. H. F. (1965 [1807]). *The phenomenology of spirit*. Harper and Row.
Hill Collins, P., & Bilge, S. (2016) *Intersectionality*. Flatiron Books.
Hirsch, E. D. (1988). *Cultural literacy: What every American needs to know*. Vintage.
hooks, b. (1994) *Teaching to transgress: Education as the practice of freedom*. Routledge.
Illich, I. (1971). *Deschooling society*. Harper and Row.
Illich, I. (1973). *Tools for conviviality*. Harper and Row.
Illich, I. (1981). *Shadow work*. Marion Boyars.
Jaeger, W. (1965). *Paideia. The ideals of Greek culture*. Oxford University Press.
Kahn, R. (2010). *Critical pedagogy, ecoliteracy, and planetary crisis: The ecopedagogy movement*. Peter Lang.
Kellner, D. (1989). *Critical theory, Marxism, and modernity*. Polity Press and John Hopkins University Press.
Kellner, D. (2000). New technologies/new literacies: Reconstructing education for the new millennium. *Teaching Education, 11*(3), 245–265.
Kellner, D. (2002a). New life conditions, subjectivities and literacies: Some comments on the Lukes' reconstructive project. *Journal of Early Childhood Literacy, 2*(1), 105–112.
Kellner, D. (2002b). Technological revolution, multiple literacies, and the restructuring of education. In I. Snyder (Ed.), *Silicon literacies* (pp. 154–169). Routledge.
Kellner, D. (forthcoming). *Technology and democracy: Toward a critical theory of digital technologies, Technopolitics, and Technocapitalism*. Springer Publications.
Kellner, D., Lewis, T. E., & Pierce, C. (2008). *On Marcuse: Critique, liberation, and reschooling in the radical pedagogy of Herbert Marcuse* (p. 2008). Brill Publishers.
Kellner, D., Lewis, T. E.., Pierce, C., & Cho, D. (co-editors and contributors) (2009). (2009). *Marcuse's challenge to education*. Rowman and Littlefield Publishers
Kellner, D., & Satchel, R. M. (2020). Resisting youth: From occupy through black lives matter to the Trump resistance. In S. Steinberg & B. Downs (Eds.), *The SAGE handbook of critical pedagogies*, Chapter 107. Sage.
Kellner, D., & Share, J. (2019). *The critical media literacy guide: Engaging media and transforming education*. Brill-Sense Publishers.
Luke, A., & Luke, C. (2002). Adolescence lost/childhood regained: On early intervention and the emergence of the techno-subject. *Journal of Early Childhood Literacy, 1*(1), 91–120.
Marx, K., & Engels, F. (1978). *The Marx-Engels reader*. R. Tucker (Ed.). Norton.
Polanyi, K. (1944/2001). *The great transformation the political and economic origins of our time* (2nd ed.). Beacon Press.

Reitz, C. (2000). *Art, alienation, and the humanities: A critical engagement with Herbert Marcuse.* SUNY Press.

Smith, L. T. (1999). *Decolonizing methodologies—Research and indigenous peoples.* Zed Book Ltd, and Dunedin, University of Otago Press.

Wollstonecraft, M. (1988). *A vindication of the rights of woman.* Norton.

Zuboff, S. (1988). *In the age of the smart machine: The future of work and power.* Basic Books.

Zuboff, S. (2020), *The age of surveillance capitalism: The fight for a human future at the new frontier of power.*

CHAPTER 3

The Philosophy and Politics of Educating Emotions

Liz Jackson

INTRODUCTION

Education for social and emotional well-being has become commonplace in the twenty-first century. Philosophically, such curricula draw primarily on two bodies of knowledge: first, the tradition of virtue ethics, which has unfolded in recent years as approaches to character education; and second, positive psychology, a newer social science movement that has flourished with the promise that 'to feel better is to be better.' These fields have converged with a common purpose, and a shared insight that emotional development is critical to human and societal functioning.

Yet while these approaches have their merits, they also have limitations. Generally, educational approaches to well-being and for related positive affect are deeply rooted in a western liberal individualistic orientation. As such, there is a tendency to ignore the impacts of one's feelings in relation to social justice issues in society. Furthermore, this perspective discounts the way that cultural difference and social positioning in varied local and global contexts also shape expectations and norms related to how one is treated and thus, how they feel. It is therefore not the case that one is simply 'free' to feel however they choose, despite the liberal view undergirding major approaches to emotional learning.

This chapter provides a philosophical examination of emotional virtues education for enhancing social and emotional well-being. First it explores the

L. Jackson (✉)
Education University of Hong Kong, Tai Po, Hong Kong
e-mail: lizjackson@eduhk.hk

© The Author(s), under exclusive license to Springer Nature Switzerland AG 2022
A. A. Abdi and G. W. Misiaszek (eds.), *The Palgrave Handbook on Critical Theories of Education*, https://doi.org/10.1007/978-3-030-86343-2_3

roots of this trend in western psychology and philosophy. Then it suggests a model for education for emotional well-being that is more politically engaged, that frames students as active agents in the social world rather than just 'good' students. This latter view, which I discuss as the 'politics of educating emotions,' uses critical theory perspectives to identify and respond to the limitations of more traditional approaches to educating emotions, contrasting sociological and political insights about education of the self with traditional, western psychological views of the person. Thus, this chapter showcases the value of critical theories of education in developing more just and politically conscientious strategies for educating emotions, and educating for youth well-being, across diverse social contexts.

The Psychology of Emotions in Education

Psychologists traditionally understand emotions to have biological and evolutionary functions, and social and cultural value. They generally aim to decrease dysfunctional emotional states and dispositions and control and reshape them, to be functional and useful. However, toward what ends and aims emotions can and should be 'useful' within society is an important question to raise here. From a psychological view, emotions have always had a major role in education (Jackson, 2020). As Boler notes, emotional education was historically taught in terms of 'mental hygiene' in the United States (1999). The 1909 National Committee on Mental-Hygiene considered 'mental illness' and 'poorly developed personalities of children' as 'the most serious evil of the time' (Boler, 1999, p. 49). Child emotional functioning was the focus of various techniques which regarded mental hygiene as the answer to social challenges. One concern was schooling youth expectations in a society marked by inequality. As one 1938 text notes, 'Either the attitudes must be replaced, or social changes must come about, or the individual must compartmentalize his thinking and submit to permanent dissociation due to the lack of harmony between his beliefs and his actions' (Boler, 1999, p. 51). Early psychological science on education emphasized intervention in relation to mismatched expectations. This is due to the priority toward increasing efficiency in support of a capitalist economic system (Boler, 1999), and the complementary positivist approach to psychology at that time, as a means for controlling and conditioning 'deviant' or undesirable human behavior. In this vein, students were treated like factory workers. Meanwhile, occupational discourse focused not on employee welfare, but on system productivity. Moral and justice considerations, about the benefits of education for young people themselves, were thus bypassed in this way of thinking, as individuals were treated more as factors in economic value. This is reflected in an excerpt from a 1912 New York City Teachers Bulletin :

Comparisons between schools and mercantile establishments:

1. The teacher obviously corresponds to planning department, superintendent, manager of a factory.
2. The elements in the enterprise (the workmen, the raw material, and the finished product) are combined in the pupil. The other elements (tools, etc.) are the text books, charts, and apparatus ... (Boler, 1999, p. 46).

That individuals should improve themselves to function in line with what is good for the social system also undergirds the more recent emotional intelligence (EI) movement (Goleman, 1995). EI is said to consist of traits related to understanding and regulating one's emotions and developing relationships, dispositions, and behaviors that enhance achievement. Vital among these traits are self-awareness, self-regulation, and motivation. EI is believed by proponents to be educable, so people can learn to act in more productive ways, leading to higher achievement. Goleman (1995) also describes EI as equivalent to character and suggests that it is moral to teach it.

'Positive psychologists' today also recommend that people learn to identify and manage their emotions to achieve their goals, develop well-being, and be productive (Allen et al., 2014). Positive psychologists emphasize what can enable an individual to function better and how to cultivate positive emotions and moral virtues associated with functioning, focusing on happiness and joy, gratitude, compassion, and forgiveness, among other traits. Thus, both EI and positive psychology emphasize ideal operation of people within and for educational, social, and occupational systems, through emotional control and self-management.

In relation to positive psychology and EI, curricula have proliferated in the past few decades (Boler, 1999; Ecclestone, 2012). EI has been found in studies to enhance educational outcomes. Likewise, emotional traits highlighted in positive psychology have been found to correlate with markers of academic success. Such findings are more common when EI and related education are integrated into a broad curriculum for social and emotional learning (SEL), to improve caring relationships, cooperation, and safety. Some programs for SEL have been found to enhance social-emotional and academic well-being of students and classrooms, pro-social attitudes, mental health, and academic performance (Brackett & Rivers, 2014). Similarly, positive psychology has been seen to impact young people within a context of community support (Conoley et al., 2014).

However, EI lacks transparent conceptual bases (Jackson, 2020). Some see EI as an incoherent list of items, which 'does not make clear distinctions between emotions and general attitudes, desires, and moods, in so far as it aspires to be a holistic conception' (Kristjánsson, 2018, p. 169). In this context, measuring EI is a challenge. In place of a single model, a variety of perspectives have emerged (Allen et al., 2014; Kristjánsson, 2007). In addition, research designs do not enable studies to trace whether EI specifically provides benefits (Allen et al., 2014). Interventions may give positive results which fade or are ineffective without preconditions, such as being 'embedded within safe, caring, well-managed and cooperative classroom environments, as well as wider settings that provide equitable opportunities for positive participation' (Elias & Moceri, 2014, p. 44). What is measured across studies is also not uniform, owing to diverse definitions and educational aims (Allen et al., 2014).

These challenges make it difficult to evaluate SEL, especially as it is often implemented to respond to specific issues in schools. As Ecclestone (2012, p. 466) observes:

> Promotions and evaluations of [positive thinking] initiatives have tended to reflect the slippery definitions ... eliding conduct disorders, disaffection from formal class teaching, general lack of motivation, poor social skills, emotional difficulties, bad behaviour and lack of 'emotional literacy'. This means that claims about effectiveness and impact seem often to be about simple disciplinary training, such as making students more proactive in their learning, attend regularly, manage their homework...

Interventions may impact students as a kind of training here, which helps achieve immediate, classroom-focused goals, but does not make a deep impact on well-being or align with the interests and concerns of students themselves.

Further, individuals are not all the same in emotional processes and self-regulation strategies (Grubb & McDaniel, 2007; Tian et al., 2014). What works for some may not work for others and may be harmful to them (Jacobs & Gross, 2014). Relatedly, Boler pointed out in 1999 that 'emotional intelligence is based on a universalized portrait of human nature and emotions which entirely neglects significant differences of culture or gender' (pp. 74–75). Given this positivistic orientation toward reducing complex phenomena, apparently to simplify and standardize effective operations, how gender, race, and class impact emotional regulation is not well-known (DeCuir-Gunby & Williams-Johnson, 2014; Pekrun & Linnenbrink-Garcia, 2014). In addition, there are cross-cultural differences related to conceptions and values underlying EI and positive psychology, with people coming from Asian or Global South cultural backgrounds holding divergent views about the nature of the 'self' in society; those working in EI and positive psychology has not responded to the presence of such diversity, or developed frameworks for diverse communities or classrooms (Tian et al., 2014).

Proponents of SEL concede such challenges. Brackett and Rivers (2014) observe that SEL is often applied to ameliorate challenges like bullying or drug use, or used in a piecemeal way, while testing may be the cause of stress (for example), rather than EI. They further note that the firmest foundation for EI is not found within a positivistic approach, which dehumanizes people in order to control and maneuver them into predetermined 'good' instead of 'bad' educational categorizations. Rather, they emphasize the value of self-determination theory in this context, which regards meeting individual needs as prerequisite for flourishing (2014), and thus holds enhancing the environment as integral. Yet here, 'there remains a paucity of research at the mesosystem and macrosystem levels' in positive psychology, hindering the development of 'a sophisticated science of "what works" for children and youth within the context of their schooling' (Gilman et al., 2014).

Emotional intelligence and positive psychology aim to enhance experiences for individuals, to help them succeed in achieving their goals and goals of organizations. But interventions for positive emotional experiences do not necessarily aim at good or moral goals, because they do not include a critical evaluation of goals from a moral view. What tends to be assumed is that academic achievement (or productivity) is good. But teaching for EI or positive psychology can be instrumental, if mental health (or productivity) is sought in negative circumstances (i.e., stressful test-oriented environments). Emotional intelligence or positive psychology approaches may help students achieve goals and engage in pro-social behavior, particularly from an academic or classroom management perspective. But they need not lead to learning or other 'success' in terms defined by students. And they may not lead to more just environments, if students are not also encouraged to reflect on social practices, in the case that prejudice and bias are common at school (Jackson, 2020). As Boler (1999) notes, 'the classroom instances I observed engaged discussion of emotions without attention to political and cultural differences or analyses. Very few of the readings or literature in this area analyze social conflict in terms of social injustice' (p. 103). Students can learn to be emotionally healthy in this case, without being better people, or gaining skills needed to navigate complex social and political environments.

Well-being has become part of the educational agenda in the UK, Canada, and the United States, using positive psychology and EI approaches. Their appeal lies in their positivistic emphasis on being effective and 'what works.' Their use can be seen as moral, if they help young people feel (and be) better, particularly if there is a crisis of well-being. On the other hand, from a systems-level view, such interventions may also be promoted to keep populations working hard, docile, and resilient (Boler, 1999), with worsening prospects and less welfare provision (Ecclestone, 2012). Maxwell and Reichenbach (2007) discuss this as the difference between 'pedagogies of autonomy' and 'pedagogies of control.' While the former is oriented toward the development of young people as social agents, the latter frames students as passive objects to be manipulated for some 'higher', external, predetermined purpose.

There are some responses to such criticisms. In relation to charges that emotional education strategies individualize societal challenges, Kristjánsson writes (2013, p. 65):

the question of what should logically come first, the cultivation of positive personal traits or the creation of positive institutions, is a chicken-or-egg question. The important thing is not to waste time wondering where to start but rather to start somewhere. …it is usually easier to administer personal change … than large-scale political transformation.

Additionally, discourse critiquing psychological approaches as individualistic can dismiss the agency of ordinary people. Psychologists are not necessarily pushing diagnoses for environmental ills. In some cases, people demand diagnoses for possibly environmental challenges, from reluctant practitioners. Here, there is a contrast between seeing mental health and well-being from a psychological versus sociological view; people agentically contribute to, feed into, and respond to positive psychology messaging in significant ways. They are not necessarily brainwashed. Nonetheless, positive psychologists and others emphasizing emotional regulation and SEL focus on one side of the equation, when both individuals and environments matter to functioning, goodness, and justice. In school contexts, a broader view must be developed, as education has social and moral, as well as personal, aims.

The Philosophy of Character: Virtue Ethics

The other theoretical underpinning to character education and emotional virtues education discourse is virtue ethics. Virtue ethics encourages a sense of a moral mean state between deficient and excessive states when it comes to dispositions and emotions (e.g., being brave, rather than cowardly, or rash). For virtue ethicists, a subjective feeling is important in having a virtue. People should not tell the truth only on the rational basis that they know it is judged as right or due to desire to appear good. They should not even do it because they believe (or know) it is good. Rather, they should tell the truth with a subjective feeling related to desiring to be honest. Moral beliefs are thus intrinsically related to feelings and actions. Emotion should not be prioritized over judgment. Rather, a kind of fusion of rationality and emotions should be sought (Jackson, 2020). However, as will be discussed here, from another view, the kind of reasonableness and rationality sought in virtue ethics can be problematic, excluding those not regarded as universal subjects from an individualistic, western view, to the detriment of those persons and societies that think beyond a virtues standpoint.

A virtue ethics approach encourages children and young people to emulate role models and habituate good behaviors, before they internalize being virtuous (Sherman, 1999). It is thought that through emulation and habituation one can become better at acting virtuously and develop a sense of enjoyment in performing virtuous acts (Sreenivasan, 2020). The cultivation of virtue requires continuously developing emotional habits and reflections. At the same time, 'an ethically decent person will see that virtue and practical wisdom are always incomplete, that there are always ways in which virtues can be more fully integrated' (Jacobs, 2017, p. 139).

Virtue ethics is aligned with positive psychology and EI, in that feelings are regarded as central to good life. However, while virtue ethics emphasizes that which makes thought and behavior moral, positive psychology emphasizes what makes feelings and judgments productive (Jackson, 2020). As stated previously, proponents of EI and positive psychology rarely attempt to give moral justifications for cultivating an emotional state or disposition, viewing positive feelings more simply as functional, productive, and healthy. Nonetheless, EI proponents and positive psychologists adopt the language of virtues to describe their views. And despite their different foundations, many educators see virtue ethics and positive psychology going hand in hand, as both focus on the goodness of emotional states and encourage similar strategies for their cultivation.

Virtue ethics undergirds popular strategies for character education and is seen as resonant with how young people morally develop in western societies (e.g., Carr et al., 2017). That is, adults expect young children to form habits and follow elders in moral matters, before they think more deeply and develop independently. Virtue ethics has been incorporated particularly into the work of the Jubilee Centre for Character and Virtues at the University of Birmingham, UK. The center recommends in its publications that students learn to reflect on emotions (Jubilee, 2017). Emotional management is part of reasoning in this view (Harrison et al., 2016). As one Jubilee guide notes, 'developing the virtues involves becoming emotionally skillful … This is a demanding process which begins with an awareness of feelings' (Harrison et al., 2016, p. 135). The guide presents a 'mood map,' which indicates how adrenaline and serotonin interrelate with feelings:

> If I identify that I am in the survival zone and that my adrenaline levels are high, this tells me that … I need to do something to reduce my adrenaline (e.g. mindful breathing) or something to increase my serotonin (e.g. time with good friends, or seeing something funny), or both. By building up a repertoire of activities which I know to affect my emotions in predictable ways, I can start to become more skillful in the way that I experience emotion. (Harrison et al., 2016, p. 135)

Much work in translating virtue ethics into character education is well conceptualized. However, there are some limitations to these approaches and to virtue ethics. First, this framework tends to suggest a universal perspective, as people are implicitly seen as roughly equal or the same. Meanwhile, virtue ethics remains dominated by western, public, and men-authored situations and viewpoints. Yet 'women encounter dilemmas which are not typically part of men's lived experiences' (Berges, 2015, p. 5, e.g., Jackson, 2017, 2019). The

'I' in the extract above has no context, culture, or social position. But character education is meant to benefit the whole school community, and not all students are the same (Suissa, 2015).

Cultural and identity factors are thus absent from the framework. For example, while Miller defends virtues education as it is 'ordinary thinking … to emulate the characters of our moral heroes and saints such as Jesus, Gandhi, or one of our friends or family members' (2014, p. 24), this takes for granted a western cultural context. From cultural views that emphasize disparate and hierarchical social roles and relations (such as Confucianism), it may appear arrogant or inept to emulate saints or relatives or claim the capacity or value in routinely doing so. Global South views which similarly consider community and interpersonal relations as significant over an individualistic sense of self also contradict this apparently ordinary approach to thinking. They would in this context be cast as deviant for not assuming and reflecting the universal, controllable, and discrete sense of self presented here.

Jubilee authors recommend that virtues be contextualized and do not suggest importing their texts to other societies (Harrison et al., 2016). The importance of cultural difference is also acknowledged in some work on virtue ethics (Carr & Steutel, 1999; Kristjánsson, 2007). However, what seems to be dismissed here is that people within a context (even a western classroom) also experience different situations and positions relative to one another in the same instance, while cultural diversity is not an unusual situation. These environmental, social, political, and relational aspects are not foregrounded. The primary emphasis is cultivation and regulation of the singular 'autonomous' self (Berges, 2015; Tessman, 2005). Thus, the notion of civic, communal, or relational virtues become secondary to developing individual inner landscapes.

Examining Nussbaum's (2016) recommendations for people to work through anger demonstrates the limitations of this focus on inner cultivation from a political view. In her (2016) discussion of a woman's response to discovering her friend was raped, Nussbaum considers the woman friend's response, as if it can and should be evaluated apart from the rape, and the extent of rape's wrongness and harmfulness. In this case, Nussbaum claims that feeling vengeful and wanting to lower the status of the rapist is inappropriate (2016), as if all else (i.e., the position of men and women in society) is equal. She argues, ignoring the social context of rape, that preventing future rape is not served by such feelings, such that exercising practical wisdom would apparently encourage the friend to be less angry. Others also prioritize self-cultivation, and this kind of separating of oneself from the social and political world around them, over angry responses to injustice. Fitzgerald (1998) argues that people should follow the Dalai Lama in striving for gratitude when they have been harmed, abused, or oppressed, because anyone can cultivate gratitude, thanking abusers for a 'virtues challenge,' even in cases of harm.

From a more politically oriented view, it is not self-evident that practical wisdom requires such responses. Alternatively, working to maintain a positive attitude in response to these actions may communicate acceptance and tolerance of injustice (Jackson, 2020). Virtue ethics thus tends to err on the side of the status quo, rather than encouraging action against harm or wrongdoing, due to the focus on self-cultivation, and developing as a highly (perhaps overly) reasonable person. Virtue ethics does not encourage 'doing nothing.' But it also does not specifically encourage doing anything, due to the inward turn encouraged, and the implicit framing of character as morally and politically neutral (Suissa, 2015). Here, there is no need to focus on structural injustice in society, against women, people of color, or other minorities. One only needs to 'look within.'

Nussbaum (2016) and Fitzgerald (1998) do strive to distinguish unhealthy acceptance of injustice from healthy and moral responses. Yet given their political and sociological myopia, their accounts overlook how people remain at risk of further damage to themselves through trying to meet social expectations to cultivate emotional virtues. Tessman (2005) describes virtues as 'burdened' in these cases. The burden of virtues is neglected in most psychologically based and philosophically based approaches to educating emotional virtues, because they urge students to work on personal, individual responses to problems, rather than seeing problems as interpersonal, social, or political. As a result, the value of critically responding to social injustice and harm, to address structural injustice in society, is overlooked (Jackson, 2020). Jubilee curricula praise Anne Frank for humility, and Rosa Parks for bravery, largely leaving aside the horrors of the Holocaust and Jim Crow, and how one should confront those social problems, and not only their 'personal feelings' about them (Jubilee Centre, 2014). As Suissa notes, this 'shifts the emphasis away from … collective political movements and the hope and belief they embody that the political system can be radically changed' (2015, p. 115). The political and sociological context of decision-making becomes invisible, given this orientation toward the self.

Such approaches also whitewash history. Nussbaum (2016) cites King, Gandhi, and Mandela as 'not-too-angry' people, to promote her stance. Yet these individuals spoke of and expressed anger. Anyone learning about these cases from Nussbaum would be deceived and disempowered from understanding the conditions under which heroes cultivated themselves, while organizing with others to critically respond to and change society (Jackson, 2020). Such approaches also do not enable young people to understand how virtues may be 'burdened,' and how and why they should take actions against harms and injustices.

Virtue ethicists emphasize that intentionally harmful education and 'efforts at the indoctrination of traits are inimical to' developing practical wisdom (Kristjánsson, 2018, p. 174). Nonetheless, character education which focuses on traits apart from social circumstances and relational issues orients young people toward the status quo, given that traits are first to be habituated and modeled, before being regarded as demanding practical wisdom. In character education, such an approach is thus paternalistic, as young people may be told that others (i.e., teachers, politicians) know better than they do about what they should feel, and what is good for them. Student critical reflection on this topic is not emphasized here.

In relation, texts describing virtue ethics and their cultivation rarely if ever discuss political or social participation in a sustained way (e.g., Arthur, 2019; Harrison & Walker, 2018). As moral worth is associated with 'the extent to which (people) have made the virtues of action and emotion their own,' the value of equal treatment of others is also downplayed (Kristjánsson, 2007, p. 179). Furthermore, any focus on how to treat others around them in a world marked by injustice is significantly overshadowed in virtue ethics by the focus on self-reflection. For example, for Kristjánsson (2018), a major challenge of service learning is that it does not result in 'lasting changes in the emotional make-up' of students (p. 178). Other purposes of service learning—or other challenges, related to service learning as a form of neocolonialism, for example (Nesterova & Jackson, 2016)—are neglected in this account, as the focus is on one's own virtue, not on any form of moral or political action.

The Politics of Educating Emotions

As mentioned previously, global and internal community forms of diversity are overlooked in positive psychology and virtue ethics views undergirding education for emotional well-being across societies. Yet psychologists observe differences in emotional expressions and experiences among men and women and boys and girls. At the same time, there are stereotypes and different associations about gender (and race) and emotions. For example, black women are frequently stereotyped as irrational, emotional, and angry, while angry white men are commonly commended in mainstream media as righteous and justly impassioned (Jackson, 2020). In this context, emotional expressions are expected of people discriminately and judged according to norms which may be the result of differential expectations, or intentional or unconscious bias. This can be experienced by individuals as unequal and discriminatory.

Thus, the politics of educating emotions considers how different people are expected or encouraged to feel and express emotions in social contexts. This approach reflects a critical theoretical perspective as it recognizes that expectations about emotions are educational, as emotional expectations are learned, often informally, inside and outside of schools. One can of course try to ignore or resist emotional stereotypes, and unfair norms and expectations. Yet from a critical view, the stereotypes linger on and continue to unjustly impact social relations, as they express popular, mainstream visions of society and desires for individuals to conform with these visions (Jackson, 2020). From a critical theoretical view, these expectations are also political, as they intersect with views about changing or preserving social orders and cultural norms (for instance, that women or people of color should be meek and pleasant in professional settings).

Emotional expectations particularly differ based on gender. As feminists and critical sociologists and social psychologists trace, such expectations are learned, so they cannot be framed as 'natural' (Jackson, 2020). Ahmed (2010) examines how social and political discourse concerned about women's and ethnic minorities' happiness reinforce sexist and racist social relations. For example, in Rousseau's *Emile* (1762), the girl Sophie's future is as a happy wife who charms others. Her (fictional) parents are quoted, 'We want you to be happy, for our sakes as well as yours, for our happiness depends on yours. A good girl finds her own happiness in the happiness of a good man' (Ahmed, 2010, pp. 57–58). Here, Sophie might feel obliged to conceal unhappiness, while the boy Emile is free to face and deal with unhappiness in other, more external and politically oriented ways (Jackson, 2020). Ahmed finds a similar discourse at work in the stereotype of the 'happy housewife,' who is thought of as happiest while caring for others, and whose foil, the 'feminist killjoy,' ruins others' happiness, by refusing to cultivate happiness when observing and experiencing negative social situations, such as sexism.

Girls and women are expected, in workplaces, schools, and elsewhere, to be happy as caregivers, and seen as happiest when caring (Jackson, 2017, 2019). Such stereotypes, even if related to empirically based generalizations, dismiss diverse women's dispositions, interests, and capacities across fields (such as in areas where caregiving is not primary, such as research); they can also be used to justify gender differences in educational and career opportunities. Such stereotypes furthermore operate in social contexts to encourage or force girls and women to express happiness and interests in caregiving that they do not feel. From a sociological view, this can be seen to alienate them from their own experiences and understandings, rather than simply enhance their 'individual' emotional states (Ahmed, 2010; Jackson, 2019).

While psychologists tend to presume, in EI and positive psychology, that feeling good has social and individual value, and therefore support interventions that lead to personal positive feelings, for the politics of emotions, the relationship of feelings with values is impacted by social roles and norms. The politics of educating emotions also shows how people can be influenced emotionally in problematic ways, to feel anxious, alarmed, disturbed, angry, and afraid, to benefit others or support problematic status quos (Jackson, 2020). These different focuses lead to different diagnoses and solutions. Within education, the politics of emotions approach would part ways with a positive psychologist's view that if students experience emotional challenges, they should work on emotional regulation, to harmonize their emotional processes with the context (e.g., Miller et al., 2014). Here, the politics of emotions considers how feeling expectations are learned by diverse students through relationships with teachers and others. It would also question which children (e.g., boys or girls?), in which situations, are expected or allowed by teachers to be angry or happy or sad, and how expectations may be shaped more by the interests of educators and other stakeholders (parents, school leaders, etc.), than by interests expressed by youth (Jackson, 2020).

The politics of emotions perspective is thus aligned with that the student-led problem-posing education advocated for by Freire (1972), as in the banking conception of education the teacher's view about emotions is all that counts.

An example of this problematic way of thinking is articulated by Boler (1999):

> In this class exercise, each student was asked to mark on a scale on the board how they felt at the moment, from -5 to +5. One girl ... ranks herself at -5 (and indeed in my estimation 'looked' very sad). The teacher responds to this, 'What do we need to know, class?' Before any student had the opportunity to respond, and without asking the girl herself what she needed or wanted, the teacher answered her own question: 'We want to give her space rather than tease her.' It seemed to me that 'what the class needed to know' was what the young girl herself wanted in response to her distress. The teacher's quick conclusion about how to react to an unhappy student is a fairly minor example of setting an arbitrary norm, which might have an adverse effect on the girl. But one can easily imagine other examples of arbitrary impositions of the educator's authority with much harder effects on students. (pp. 100–101)

Within a critical theory of education, people's emotions, and capacities for regulating them, can be impacted by experiences and situations beyond their control, such as poor economic conditions or developmental challenges. In this context, an approach cognizant about the politics of emotion does not focus on promoting personal well-being regardless of social conditions, but questions whether people should be asked or expected to adapt (or blamed for not adapting) to such systems, when systems treat people differently, often ignoring diversity, and actively entrenching discriminately harmful environments (Jackson, 2020). This view thus enables students and educators to critically scrutinize the system, as much as individuals within it. In contrast with mainstream psychological and virtue ethics views, the politics of emotions gives space to attend to possibilities to change social systems and conditions, rather than just control individuals via technologies of self. It also gives space to consider how systems may be harmful (emotionally and otherwise) to students, among others in society. If a situation, like a classroom, is unjust, then bad feelings may be a sign the classroom should change, not the student.

Changing systems, like a classroom or an environment, may seem more challenging and complex to some people, than working to change individuals. It is also difficult (if not impossible) to be scientific (generalizing, validating) about 'what works' in intervening in environments, which are complex, dynamic, and diverse. And it is hard to diagnose a school simply as functional or dysfunctional. Yet individuals are not as simple as they are treated in popular psychologists' formulas, undergirded by positivistic reductionism and politically problematic assumptions that all people are basically the same and equivalent around the world: as if people are not influenced and shaped profoundly by the politics and culture that surrounds them. Given this overly reductive strategy, it is unsurprising that positive psychologists and EI proponents have hardly done away with dysfunctional or unhappy individuals, or eradicated anxiety or depression, through their models. In this context, an educational approach to well-being which is oriented toward social justice should be cognizant about the politics of educating emotions.

SUMMARY AND CONCLUSION

Because emotions are vital to well-being, they have become part of education, for social and emotional learning. Emotional virtues education has noble goals, to enhance personal and social life and flourishing communities. It may also aim to develop 'affective equality,' recognizing as morally and politically problematic emotional experience gaps that correlate with advantage and disadvantage in society. Nobody wants to feel bad. Yet across societies young people grapple with anxiety, depression, fear, anger, unhappiness, and other negative emotional experiences. An obvious solution here is to help them learn to cultivate positive emotions.

Yet there is a risk that education for emotional well-being can exacerbate rather than ameliorate affective inequality, as political attitudes and cultural and other forms of bias structure approaches to social and emotional learning in ways that can reinforce problematic status quos. As expectations about emotional experiences and expressions vary in societies by gender, race, class, and more, diverse students face challenges to cultivating a range of emotional experiences in the classroom. In addition, the traditional western discourses on well-being discourage reactions to negative experiences in the world before personal reflection. Being virtuous, any virtue ethicist will observe, is not to be dogmatic or 'do nothing' when observing challenges. However, a message nonetheless reverberates across social and emotional learning and character education that one's feelings are the main locus of responsibility before anything else. Meanwhile, messages about the importance of acting against negative social and political conditions are in the background, replacing active, critically conscious civic education with apolitical, possibly amoral techniques. Thus, 'pedagogies of emotional control' are employed, while 'pedagogies of autonomy' (Maxwell & Reichenbach, 2007), for acting in relation with diverse others, remain undervalued.

Education should prepare the next generation to live in the world of the present, but also that of the future. Here, it is not wrong to cultivate emotions in line with status quo expectations in part, as young people must learn to be in a community and function within it. However, the problem is when this is done in narrow-minded ways, as the main means of reaction to a status quo that is often harmful, unjust, and problematic. Such a view is thus misaligned with critical approaches to education, ignoring the social and political in favor of positivistic values, of social control, and an education for students to accept the world around them, without critical questioning or deeper personal and social reflection. Looking at curricula around the world from a broad view, civic and citizenship education is being replaced with education for emotional virtues or character education, as what 'works' (Jackson, 2020). Yet such curricula work in a limited, reductive way. They 'work' to discipline and pacify, to make young people manageable and attentive. Yet moral and political questions are evaded given this positivistic standpoint.

From a critical educational view, students should not be discouraged from thinking about and acting in relation to negative, harmful experiences they face and observe around them. Rather, young people should learn to act, and critically respond, not just to feel, in education for emotional well-being. They should be encouraged to think about matters of injustice and communicate and take action alongside others in relation to them. Being a good person in society is not just about having and expressing good feelings. Instead, studying good action, that is collective, social, and critical is important if schools are to cultivate good moral and political beings. Teachers should ensure a better balance between moral and social education to develop young people with good character and behavior. Here, good behavior does not mean sitting still and being obedient, but it involves questioning social injustice and acting in relation to it.

From a critical theoretical view, by neglecting societal causes of so-called personal challenges faced, emotional virtues education which looks inward and places responsibility for emotions on students as individuals also implicitly promotes individualism and self-centeredness. Yet the focus on cultivation of oneself apart from others provides no clear path for learning how to aid others and contribute to society. This is hardly an education for moral development, critical civic-mindedness, or social justice. A more balanced approach, informed by the politics of emotions, can instead empower students to develop themselves in connection with others, as goodness cannot be critically understood or pursued meaningfully in the world without relations.

REFERENCES

Ahmed, S. (2010). *The promise of happiness*. Duke University Press.

Allen, V., MacCann, C., Matthews, G., & Roberts, R. D. (2014). Emotional intelligence in education: From pop to emerging science. In R. Pekrun & L. Linnenbrink-Garcia (Eds.), *International handbook of emotions in education* (pp. 162–182). Routledge.

Arthur, J. (Ed.). (2019). *Virtues in the public sphere*. Routledge.

Berges, S. (2015). *A feminist perspective on virtue ethics*. Palgrave Macmillan.

Boler, M. (1999). *Feeling power: Emotions and education*. Routledge.

Brackett, M. A., & Rivers, S. E. (2014). Transforming students' lives with social and emotional learning. In R. Pekrun & L. Linnenbrink-Garcia (Eds.), *International handbook of emotions in education* (pp. 1368–1388). Routledge.

Carr, D., Arthur, J., & Kristjánsson, K. (2017). Varieties of virtue ethics: Introduction. In D. Carr, J. Arthur, & K. Kristjánsson (Eds.), *Varieties of virtue ethics* (pp. 1–14). Palgrave Macmillan.

Carr, D., & Steutel, J. (1999). The virtue approach to moral education: Pointers, problems and prospects. In D. Carr & J. Steutel (Eds.), *Virtue ethics and moral education* (pp. 241–255). Routledge.

Conoley, C. W., Conoley, J. C., Spaventa-Vancil, K. Z., & Lee, A. N. (2014). Positive psychology in schools: Good ideas are never enough. In M. J. Furlong, R. Gilman, & E. S. Huebner (Eds.), *Handbook of positive psychology in schools*, 2nd ed. Routledge.

Decuir-Gunby, J. T., & Williams-Johnson, M. R. (2014). The influence of culture on emotions: Implications for education. In R. Pekrun & L. Linnenbrink-Garcia (Eds.), *International handbook of emotions in education* (pp. 539–558). Routledge.

Ecclestone, K. (2012). From emotional and psychological well-being to character education: Challenging policy discourses of behavioural science and 'vulnerability.' *Research Papers in Education, 27*(4), 463–480.

Elias, M. J., & Moceri, D. C. (2014). Developing social and emotional aspects of learning: The American experience. *Research Papers in Education, 27*(4), 423–434.

Fitzgerald, P. (1998). Gratitude and justice. *Ethics, 109*, 119–153.

Freire, P. (1972). *Pedagogy of the oppressed*. Continuum.

Gilman, R., Huebner, E. S. & M. J. Furlong. (2014). Toward a science and practice of positive psychology in schools: A conceptual framework. In M. J. Furlong, R. Gilman & E. S. Huebner (Eds.), *Handbook of positive psychology in schools*. Routledge.

Goleman, D. (1995). *Emotional intelligence: Why it can matter more than IQ*. Bantam.

Grubb, W. L., & McDaniel, M. A. (2007). The fakability of Bar-On's Emotional Quotient Inventory Short Form: Catch me if you can. *Human Performance, 20*, 43–59.

Harrison, T., Arthur, J., & Burn, E. (2016). *Character education evaluation handbook for schools*. Jubilee Centre.

Harrison, T., & Walker, D. I. (2018). *The theory and practice of virtue education*. Routledge.

Jackson, L. (2017). Leaning out of higher education: A structural, postcolonial perspective. *Policy Futures in Education, 15*(3), 295–308.

Jackson, L. (2019). The smiling philosopher: Emotional labor, gender, and harassment in conference spaces. *Educational Philosophy and Theory, 51*(7), 684–692.

Jackson, L. (2020). *Beyond virtue: The politics of educating emotion*. Cambridge University Press.

Jacobs, J. (2017). Aristotelian ethical virtues: Naturalism without measure. In D. Carr, J. Arthur, & K. Kristjánsson (Eds.), *Varieties of virtue ethics* (pp. 125–142). Palgrave Macmillan.

Jacobs, S. E., & Gross, J. J. (2014). Emotion regulation in education: Conceptual foundations, current applications, and future directions. In R. Pekrun & L. Linnenbrink-Garcia (Eds.), *International handbook of emotions in education* (pp. 183–202). Routledge.

Jubilee Centre. (2014). *The knightly virtues*. Jubilee Centre.

Jubilee Centre. (2017). *A framework for character education in schools*. Jubilee Centre.

Kristjánsson, K. (2007). *Aristotle, emotions, and education*. Routledge.

Kristjánsson, K. (2013). *Virtues and vices in positive psychology: A philosophical critique*. Cambridge University Press.

Kristjánsson, K. (2018). *Virtuous emotions*. Oxford University Press.

Maxwell, B., & Reichenbach, R. (2007). Educating moral emotion: A praxiological analysis. *Studies in Philosophy and Education, 26*, 147–163.

Miller, C. B. (2014). The real challenge to virtue ethics from psychology. In N. Snow & F. V. Trivigno (Eds.), *The philosophy and psychology of character and happiness* (pp. 15–34). Routledge.

Miller, D. N., Nickerson, A. B., & Jimerson, S. R. (2014). Positive psychological interventions in U.S. schools: A public health approach to internalizing and externalizing problems. In M. J. Furlong, R. Gilman, & E. S. Huebner (Eds.), *Handbook of positive psychology in schools*. Routledge.

Nesterova, Y., & Jackson, L. (2016). Transforming service learning for global citizenship education: Moving from affective-moral to social-political. *Revista Espanola De Educacion Comparada (Spanish Journal of Comparative Education), 28*, 73–90.

Nussbaum, M. C. (2016). *Anger and forgiveness: Resentment, generosity, justice*. Oxford University Press.

Pekrun, R., & Linnenbrink-Garcia, L. (2014). Conclusions and future directions. In R. Pekrun & L. Linnenbrink-Garcia (Eds.), *International handbook of emotions in education* (pp. 659–676). Routledge.

Rousseau, J. J. (1762/1979). *Emile, or on education*, trans. A. Bloom. Basic.

Sherman, N. (1999). Character development and Aristotelian virtue. In D. Carr & J. Steutel (Eds.), *Virtue ethics and moral education* (pp. 35–48). Routledge.

Sreenivasan, G. (2020). *Emotion and virtue*. Princeton University Press.

Suissa, J. (2015). Character education and the disappearance of the political. *Ethics and Education, 10*(1), 105–117.

Tessman, L. (2005). *Burdened virtues: Virtue ethics for liberatory struggles*. Oxford University Press.

Tian, L., Li, Z., Chen, H, Han, M., Wang, D., Huang, S. & Zheng, X. (2014). Applications of positive psychology to schools in China. In M. J. Furlong, R. Gilman & E. S. Huebner (Eds.), *Handbook of positive psychology in schools*. Routledge.

CHAPTER 4

African Philosophies of Education: Colonialist Deconstructions and Critical Anticolonial Reconstructionist Possibilities

Ali A. Abdi

INTRODUCTION

In conceptualizing and theorizing about the conventional (as presented in dominant Western-centric discourses), as well as counter-conventional (as in decolonizing, multicentric perspectives) of philosophy and philosophies of education, we could perhaps and contemporaneously agree on some clustered thought systems, and thereof emerging analytical formations that, in epistemic-contextual terms, inform select social and educational situations. In the more conventional terms, both formalized or otherwise dispensed readings and attached discussions of philosophy are indeed, at least as presented in the Western Canon, credited to early Greece and to its most important thought figures (i.e., Plato and his student Aristotle who were associated with the Athens Academy as founded by the former). To immediately problematize this habit in a more nuanced format, through a habitualized assumption, and straightforwardly staying with general (original), linguistic meaning of philosophy (philosophia as love of wisdom from the Greek word φιλοσοφία), we must be able to argue otherwise. That is, without any historical or related epistemic nationalism, we must safely state 'the love of wisdom' that contextually results from analytical and critical observations and inquiries about our lives and relations as attached and implicated by all social and physical surroundings across the globe. This reality should be at least as old as human

A. A. Abdi (✉)
University of British Columbia, Vancouver, BC, Canada
e-mail: ali.abdi@ubc.ca

© The Author(s), under exclusive license to Springer Nature Switzerland AG 2022
A. A. Abdi and G. W. Misiaszek (eds.), *The Palgrave Handbook on Critical Theories of Education*, https://doi.org/10.1007/978-3-030-86343-2_4

life. While Platonian/Aristoteleian/European philosophical accreditations are about 2500 years old, human life (as counted from the first homo sapiens) is about 300,000 years old.

To perhaps stave off any worries about complexifying my observations here beyond the critical and deconstructive and reconstructive purposes intended, let me affirm that I am not saying that philosophy and its educational packets—as we know and analyze these today—started around the emergence of the first homo sapiens. That might be read as stretching the case too much, too far away, and too thin for the organized ways this area should be comprehended. What I am indicating though, is my continuous, thick argument that this area of knowledge and study is a cultural component and emerges from people's lives, with culture representing the space–time envelops and intersections of individual/groups' understandings, relations, behaviors, and sanctions in given socio-physical contexts. With that in mind, philosophy in so-called classical Greece was not detached from the Greek/European culture, thus sustaining its meanings and valuations in post-Platonic, post-Aristoteleian periods. It was also inherited, via the Latinization of Greek, the rationalization of Eurocentric knowledge and ways of knowing through and post-Enlightenment situations. Across the world, these assumptions about uni-centric philosophies and philosophies of education were undertaken on colonial epistemic projects that were formalized and institutionalized through colonial education (Abdi, 2008, 2013; Nyerere, 1968; Rodney, 1982).

The monocentric fabrications of the philosophical and its attendant philosophies of education as focusing on what education is needed in a given context, why such education and how it should be formulated implemented (Ozmon & Craver, 2012), was what led and sustained these continuous unidimensional belief systems with Africa, and other non-European spaces, constructed as a philosophical. Indeed, as Higgs (2008) noted, the hegemonic colonial discourse that attempted to negate the diversity of knowledges and lived experiences requires a full challenge that accords African populations the needed epistemic and epistemological contexts for liberation and development. It is with the centrality of education (formal or informal) for people to ascertain their situations, analyze their needs and aspirations, and design ways of advancing in select or multiple components of life that also implicates all philosophy as educational. Indeed, the observation attributed to John Dewey that 'all philosophy is a theory/philosophy of education fits well with the ubiquitous presence of the philosophical in both the cultural and attached learning and teaching realms of the person and their community(ies). As such, all socially organized communities, regardless of their geographical or other characteristics, can claim the presence, as well as the practice of, philosophy and philosophies of education as both are so fundamental to critically inquire about and interactively respond to both the prevailing/emergent realities and needs of spatial–temporal mediated life systems and contexts. In terms of educational contexts and analyses, we shall note that philosophy and education, as a constructs and practices, are natural to all human contexts for, as already implicated above, humans are both inquiry-driven and learning beings, which are both fundamental to their continuities and survival.

COLONIALIST DECONSTRUCTIONS OF AFRICAN PHILOSOPHIES AND PHILOSOPHIES OF EDUCATION

Despite the above presented fundamentality of both education and philosophical inquiries for people's lives, the colonialists' deliberate 'de-philosophization' of Africa was not limited to that, but also extended to the educational situation and, so clearly, to African philosophies of education (Abdi, 2008; Achebe, 2000). What should be understood here is the observational looniness of such assumptions which actually pose more dangers that might be initially detected. When we, either out of biased ignorance or for domination or exploitative intentions, cancel the presence and possibilities of education, we can sense and pragmatically notice the denial of historical and current agency. By direct extension, the rescinding of situational initiatives that trigger and drive peoples' advancement and well-being are extensively damaged. Yet, this is precisely what happened to Africans and other subjects of European colonialism, who were perforce exposed to a well-organized psycho-cultural and educational onslaught that derided their cultures, learning systems, pedagogical arrangements, which all served as precursors for, indeed facilitated subsequent political and economic dominations (Abdi, 2013).

To achieve psycho-cultural and educational colonization in the African context therefore, the first steps were to disparage and decommission African educational and social development systems, locating the continent as ahistorical, a-philosophical, uneducated, and deprived of development (Achebe, 2000; Nyerere, 1968; Rodney, 1982). Indeed, these initially presumptive and as we know now, false racist assumptions, which were, nevertheless, realized through colonial education (Kane, 2012 [1963]; wa Thiong'o, 1993), set up and sustained continually damaging psychosomatic impacts. These also extended into intergenerational cognitive colonization schemes that continue to solely elevate Eurocentric and Euro-American-centric ideas, languages, knowledge systems, learning institutions, and related educational desires and valuations. Based on my continuing reading here and as discussed in few previous, related oeuvres (see Abdi, 2008, 2013, 2020), the discrediting of Africa on the historical, educational, and developmental fronts was foundationally attached and carried out through the organized denial of the continent and its peoples' philosophical and educational philosophy achievements. As already implicated here, such denial is, to be precise, nonsensical as it is both counter-rational and counter-reasonable. Yet, these were organized attempts to rescind what has actually defined and formulated, and in primary and fundamental livelihood terms, this ancient land's livelihood and learning dynamisms as well as social development achievements and intentions.

For emphasis at least, and cognizant of this as somewhat already implicated above, the fundamentality of philosophical thinking, analysis, and criticisms must be present in all human contexts, which also makes educational philosophies the sine qua non of human cultural, political, and economic designs and progress. To convey the point as thickly as possible, no social group or other humanly connected entities (whether in larger or smaller community or national spaces, including in family and/or organizational contexts) could have lived or survived over millennia in the African world without conceptualizing and achieving select philosophizing and learning philosophies contexts. Henceforward, it was imperative to add to the extractable learning and teaching thoughts systems that were crucial for the indispensable generation and regeneration of required interdependent ecological and selectively localized vie quotidian existentialities.

Despite these facts, dominant Western philosophy advanced their own ideas as being the totality of philosophy and philosophical thinking as these were created, discovered, and emanated from a universalistic European epistemic center that demands from the rest of the world to draw from it with unquestionable learning and knowledge loyalty. Such loyalty demands strictly following Platonic (Socratic) and Aristotelian intentions (i.e., the so-named classical Greece and Athens) and continued through coinciding Eurocentric thought traditions. Sympathetically, according to such totalizing credit and with analytical amnesia about the rest of the world, the British philosopher Alfred N. Whitehead tried to teach us that all philosophy was, for his own ipso facto, only a footnote to Plato (Ozmon & Craver, 2012). In responding to this shallow and totalizing epistemic crediting and arrogance during the misnamed postcolonial context, Chinua Achebe (1989) marveled, sort of pro-sarcastically, at the non-camouflaged code where for African thinkers and writers, the qualitative validity of their works have had to be sanctioned by contemporary European and Euro-American men [and women] in post-Athenian and currently domineering [sic] centres of power and 'knowledge' (New York, London, Paris). In Achebe's characteristic and blinking-averse format, he notes how he could not decipher the 'cocksurness' (his term) of these still colonialist-minded creatures.

The issue of de-philosophization and its affiliated categories of education and social well-being are directly related to the interchanges of power and knowledge, or in Foucauldian terms, the intersecting and interdependent lines of the two (Foucault, 1980). For me, this affirms the deliberate colonialist historical disempowerment of Africans and others, and which, by direct extension, negated their epistemic and epistemological locations and intentions. Indeed, it was the British historian H.R. Trevor-Roper (1963), who was based at Oxford University (note both the imputed and accrued power statuses of the man and the place, and thus, the knowledge valuation attached to his ideas), who 'affirmed' for his audience the ahistorical nature of Africa. That is the whole place, the whole landmass (i.e., the second biggest continent on earth) and its peoples without any history prior to European colonialism. This should expose the monstrosity of such statements which were, for all practical possibilities, false and useless ethnocentrically racist talk. But that was not the case for Trevor-Roper who was hardly the only inventor of the multitude falsehoods about Africa, from the so-called European thought leaders. The globally celebrated German philosopher G.W.F. Hegel (1965), somehow knew, without setting a foot on Africa and without any contact with one single African, that this ancient continent was devoid of history and historical achievements, representing a darkness-enveloped landmass that was ready to be plundered, taken-advantage-of, and robbed of its resources.

The narrating of these tragically false assumptions about Africa and its peoples need to be told and retold as their impact has represented, at least in knowledge, learning and developmental terms, a systematic onslaught that lowered the onto-existentialities as well as the subjectivities of communities that have not yet recovered from such presumptive if 'believable' (re: the profile of the protagonists) exhortations. To understand the depth of the problem, one need not miss that Hegel was talking about Africa around the advent of nineteenth-century colonialism and certainly had direct impact on the imperial project that pillaged African lands and lives. To show the centrality of Hegel's work to the so-named 'Scramble for Africa' (Pakenham, 2015 [1991]), one can simply refer to his rationale on the wisdom of stealing Africa's resources by Europeans (Hegel, 1965). Africa, as he put it, was an infantile place fit for plunder and pillage by Europe. Interestingly and quite astonishingly, these Hegelian schemes of dehistoricization, plunder, and theft were conveyed in one of his most important works oxymoronly entitled *Reason in History*. At any rate, the point here is not to repeat his diatribe but rather to highlight the colonial rationalist language he mastered to play an intellectual vanguard for the benighted and again massively misnamed *Mission Civilsatrice* (Said, 1993). It is also important and indeed categorically central to my arguments here that such pathologization of Africans, their capacities and life systems minimally shaped so much of the global situations, relationship, and social development contexts we see today.

My arguments should also minimally convey the need to continuously, systematically and as needed, negate and refute item-by-item, the false, racist exhortations with counter-racist humanizing notations and attached perspectival pragmatics. The false assumptions and their attendant destructive impact and outcomes were later perforce advanced through colonial military actions and educational projects, which sustained the schemata of the continent and its peoples' dehistoricizations, de-philosophizations, and de-epistemologizations. Such schemes deliberately destroyed over millennia-thriving primordial, traditional life systems, and almost permamentized, as Nyerere (1968), Rodney (1982), and Achebe (2009 [1958]) cogently analyzed, the now celebrated African poverty and underdevelopment. To critically discern the level of destructiveness that was unleashed on Africa/Africans' corporeal, mental, and wealth contexts (minimally for a clear comprehension for new generations of students and scholars), I revisit Ivan Van Sertima's brilliant, if subjectively difficult, readings on the situation:

> No other disaster with the exception of the Flood (if that biblical legend is true) can equal in dimensions of destructiveness, the cataclysm that shook Africa… .Fast populations were uprooted and displaced, whole generations disappeared, European diseases descended like the plague decimating both people and livestock, cities and towns were abandoned, family networks disintegrated, kingdoms crumbled, the threads of cultural and historical continuity were so torn asunder that henceforward, one could have to talk of two Africas: the one before and the one after the Holocaust. (Van Sertima, 1991, p. 8)

It is indeed with the described magnitude of colonial psycho-cultural, educational, and physical destructiveness that should entice us to not avoid the realities of the case for professional convenience or observational comfort, but rather to deal with it, analyze it and continuously critique all of these headlong. Ongoing comprehensively critical inquiry is needed to psycho-socially, practically, and counter-colonially decommission the damage done to Africa's multiple life references. It is with this in mind that we should reference the still supremely relevant, seminal works of, inter alia, Frantz Fanon (1967, 1968) and Aimé Césaire (1972). Although they were not born in Africa but part of the transatlantic African diaspora (from Martinique in the Caribbean), they read, as much as anyone else, the comprehensiveness of the overall onto-epistemological damages, which they reflected upon, and from there, pointed out active ways to liberate the fundamental particles of people's lives. In Fanon's (1967) terms and connecting well with Albert Memmi's (1991) work who was another excellent colonization scholar, when damages are done to one's fundamental contextual references (in subjective, thought and general worldview situations), the new subjects created become, in psycho-cognitive terms at least, external to their original self. From there, these new subjects normalize their 'naturalized' (minimally in their minds) inferior status vis-à-vis their oppressors.

In comprehensive terms and referencing Nyerere's (1968) excellent analysis, the continuing struggle against the extensive, systematic devaluing of people's lives, which must be confronted tout court, should build more on anti-colonist and liberating philosophy and philosophies of education terrains. Indeed, the depth of internalized inferiority overtime was/is so thick that Freire's construct and possible practice of *conscientization* (*concientazaçao*) could be deployed here as a multistep platform and prospect for onto-epistemological liberation. Nyerere, as a philosopher-statesman (Graham, 1976; Mhina & Abdi, 2009), critically and quite astutely read the long-term impact of colonial education and its attached philosophical assumptions that, as mentioned above, first demeaned the reconstruction of the continent's learning and developmental platforms to counter the longue durée de-patterning of the general perceptions and attached subjective existentialities of generations of Tanzanians and Africans. Indeed, while we might contemporaneously speak about education as a developmental platform (Abdi, 2008; Afful-Broni et al., 2020) that enhances people's lives in personal, professional, institutional, societal situations, or otherwise with observable validity with such assumption (e.g., the usually measurable correspondence between levels of learning and economic viability), Nyerere (1968) clearly saw the damaging nature of colonial education. It minimally imposed an externally problematic and perforce implemented schemes that attempted to alter the situational realities of the colonized, inculcating in the minds of its recipients, enduring clusters of cognitive colonization (wa Thiong'o, 1993, 2009).

Certainly, in all contexts of human history, we continuously thought/think about and established/establish learning systems that were/are ipso facto, essential to our existence and forward movement in civilizational and related matters of life. It is with that fundamental reading of human life, especially as it is attached to historical and contemporary Africa and the lives of Africans, that education as it is perceived, philosophized and constructed, becomes so indispensable for our socio-cultural existentialities (Mandela, 1994; Nyerere, 1968). As Nelson Mandela shared in his autobiography *Long Walk to Freedom* (1994), from elemental individual well-being to social development, the quality as well as the provision of available learning and pedagogical platforms serve as the main drivers of the case and especially so when communalized to all members of the community.

While the constructions of philosophical traditions and the learning operations thereof deduced, span across times-and-spaces, even after the ending of most physical colonialism in Africa in early-to-mid 1960s, the continent and its peoples continue to contend with the derivatives of European Enlightenment-attached modernist thinking and practices (for an interesting read and Euro-centric of modernity, see Huntington, 1971). Modernity would deride, even now, Africa's life systems as irrational, primitively disorganized, and time wise immeasurable. Certainly in partial response to these and other surface assumptions, Nyerere's (1968) anti-colonial educational and social development projects, which were mainly constituted in his *Ujamaa* program (Ujamaa broadly meaning *familyhood* or in extended readings, *villagehood*), aimed to establish a basic platform for Indigenous education and social development projects. These, as sometimes misunderstood, were not against other knowledge systems, but saw the fundamentality of such projects as extendable into the overall social well-being possibilities across Tanzania and potentially elsewhere in Africa.

However, or expectedly, the projects were differently read by opposing interest groups both inside and outside Tanzania. Ujamaa which was negatively depicted by global capitalism and its agents, as McHenry (1994) cogently observed, also faced initially latent opposition from the emerging and individually enterprising comprador class in the late 1960s to early 1970s Tanzania. So with Ujamaa's unfulfilled possibilities for the reconstruction of African philosophies of education, and the factual continuation of colonial education in Tanzania/Africa's curricular, linguistic, and certainly philosophical dimensions, how are we to read the context and respond to it as we enter the third decade of the twenty-first century? For my descriptive, analytical, and critical corners, the redoing of colonial philosophies of education is as urgent as ever. To be sure, and especially for those who might be new or relatively new to African philosophical and educational studies, perhaps a reminder that the continent's slow and, in some places, absent social advancement is not, in absolute categorical terms, natural to Africans and their world. The one human race capabilities (not two races or more, see Cook, 2005), regardless of location and background, are comparable across the board and in global terms. Perhaps a good example of this is to open-mindedly ascertain the achievements of African immigrants in spaces where their initiatives, intelligence, enterprising, and related energies are not impeded by colonial politics and control systems by African dictatorial regimes. This also explains why so many highly educated and capable people are leaving the continent. For those who read and react to Africa from external plateaus, the continent might be seen (in selective terms) via its almost celebrated (if so misplaced) poverty status, complemented by the absence, again selectively, of competitive economies, all occasionally exacerbated by cases of de-development (e.g., destroying the limited institutional viability there via civil wars). While some of these perceptions are not totally out of place, the risk of simplistic, de-historicized readings abound. In critically ascertaining the weight of the counter-dehistoricizing fight, Cabral (1970) noted how the fabrication of ahistorical Africa and its peoples was deliberately connected to the colonial double objective of dehistoricization and the subsequent rehistoricization of Africans as a newly discovered parcel of the natural progression of European history.

Without belaboring the point on the current depressed development situations, which are factually historically connected, we can also practically state, without a thread of hesitancy, that Africa's current development issues are firstly due to the political office longevity schemes of some leaders. This is complemented in quasi-direct terms by the political and policy continuities (the leaders' failure and culpability as well here) of decontextualized and socio-culturally alienating educational systems that continue to disregard and demean the continent's rich knowledge, learning, and pedagogical traditions. Drawing upon Cabral's (1973) seminal points again with prior echoes from Fanon (1968), the rhetoric of national liberation and related anticolonial struggles followed by limited political independence and attempts to create a cohesive developmental community can all be as such, and nothing more than rhetorical and insignificant. That's, unless the postcolonial leadership pragmatizes these into real improvements in the daily living conditions of the people. Alas, the majority of African leadership in the past 60 or so years miserably failed in this, and the masses' developmental aspirations for social advancement are at best of quarterly completion in very few countries. As such, and to reiterate one central objective in this writing, if Africa is to achieve decolonized Africanist philosophical, educational, and development possibilities, African leaders and education policymakers should heed the call for new ways of reviving and reconstructing the continent's rich traditions in these and related domains of life. It is with this call in mind that I now turn to possible ways of reconstructing African philosophies of education for socio-cultural, educational, and overall community well-being.

AFRICAN PHILOSOPHIES OF EDUCATION: CRITICAL RECONSTRUCTIONIST ANALYSES AND POSSIBILITIES

Relying for epistemic and analytical intentions on the preceding arguments, I am able to say, in a straightforwardly manner, that traditional African education was well-conceptualized, well-designed, and well-constructed with communally functional and viable learning pedagogical platforms that were of important historical, cultural, and philosophical foundations, operations and outcomes. As such, precolonial African contexts of education were, perhaps as much as anything else, directly responsive to, and pragmatically implemented within the blocks and actions of critical query situations. In historico-situational terms, these were not dissimilar from the ways we perceive and interact with contemporary educational philosophies. Without that (through a sort of reverse analysis), Africans and other colonized populations across the globe wouldn't have been exposed to Europe's imperial schemes had the former not devised, revised, and advanced important and contextually functioning systems of learning that were built on such philosophies of learning. On the 'sort of reverse analysis' point here, they would have perished long ago, which could have also practicalized the colonialists' false *terrra nullius* thesis about Africa and other places. With this in mind, my direct and sans apologie deployment of the constructs and practices of philosophy and philosophy of education in historical Africa should not represent an extraneous descriptive or analytical puzzle as that is exactly what was happening, calling for necessary modifications and reconstructions and needs on the ground.

A propos then the centrality of the reconstructionist perspective where the intervening purpose here is not to claim a novel need to come up with just new African philosophies of education, but to reassert and re-enliven what was destroyed by the colonial epistemic and epistemological onslaught. This onslaught, which was again designed to damage both the corporeal and cognitive subjectivities of the persona Africana so as to facilitate the colonizing project, encompassed all systems of Indigenous knowledges, educational systems, and the critical queries (philosophical perspectives) attached to those, and to the overall quotidian as well as long-term psycho-cultural locations and formations of people. Indeed, to borrow a few lines from reconstructionist Africana critical theory as a way of countering epistemic apartheid (Rabaka, 2010), while still staying connected to the general intentions of the criticality tradition with ongoing ameliorative intentions and possibilities (Frye, 2020 [1957]), I reaffirm how African traditional societies survived, thrived, and advanced via perspectively querying about their education systems. From there, people suggested and shared potential learning and teaching betterments, and acted upon those, with everything actively and essentially connected to prevailing as well as emerging community needs and aspirations. As such, what we now call the main questions of educational philosophies (i.e., what education, why such education, and how to do it) were categorically and with agentic realities, formulated and selectively undertaken in these traditional societies.

In reaffirming, as many times as opportune, traditional African educational philosophies, were effective to historico-culturally ascertain and appreciate the prevailing contexts for which these were designed, constructed, and utilized. In most cases (with some important exceptions), such educational philosophies and related epistemic as well as learning and teaching platforms were not in conventional written formats. Yet the blocks of knowledge present and operational were systematically and comprehensively preserved in the minds of intellectually well-endowed community members who, as we learned from the trenchant analysis of the late Kenyan philosopher Henry Odera Oruka (1990), were inter-communally recognized for their sagacity, or as he called them, African sage philosophers. To critically comprehend and appreciate such sagacity and the epistemic achievements of African sage philosophers therefore, one need not miss the centrality of all of this in relation to the histories, cultures, and related learning and pedagogical realities as created through, and operationalized via the continent's oral literatures (orature). As such, these systems of knowing, inquiring about, analyzing, and henceforward acting upon critically attained episteme were orality-based-and-expounded philosophies of education. That even when the most comprehensive and systematic writing in the so-called ancient world, as we know that script today and through its millennia formalizations and reformatting, was actually invented in Africa (Ong, 2013 [1982]). That is, through the socio-cultural calligraphic formations and reformations of Egyptian and Nubian kingdoms and dynasties in northeastern Africa.

Indeed, enlarging the potentially assumed confines of the critical in ascertaining the problematic and colonialist interplays or orality-embedded epistemic systems and text-borne knowledge categories, the hegemonic and onto-epistemological supremacist elevation of the latter over the former, established and sustained the extensity of the still impactful mental colonization realities (wa Thiong'o, 1986, 2009). These continue to imprint and sustain so much demerit points on Africans' psycho-political and economic situations and by the needed expansive undertaking of social development projects. As such, the urgency of reviving African philosophies of education to inform and structure both learning and pedagogical systems should be clear. Minimally at the ideational level, followed by structural redrawing of the situation and the multi-focal reconstruction of these philosophies, it is imperative to successfully formulate educational contexts that refrain from alienating people from their cultural, linguistic, and related knowledge and learning needs. What should be practically understood is that this does not mean African schools and institutions of higher education will stop teaching useful knowledge from elsewhere. What it means though is to loudly announce knowledge and education as also emerging from African sources, minds, and achievements. In Sandra Harding's (1998, 2008) cogent analysis, all knowledge, regardless of its current status and composition, is essentially and for all practical intentions, of collective human origin and collaboration. It is within that collective and collaborative reality that African traditional philosophies of education, as emanating from the original space of humanity, contextually and certainly in global terms, must announce their viability and over millennia learning-wise effective mechanisms in the continent's and selectively, in extra-Africa contemporary educational terrains.

As alluded to above, world media readings and simplistic reporting on this ancient continent have Africa as hastily synonymized with interconnected educational, politico-economic, and related progress failures that have become, with more negativities than otherwise, of naturalized status. In more nuanced and generalization-refuting perspective, the continent and its peoples do deal with more than their fair share of human development issues, especially as there are measured through the indices used by the yearly published UNDP Development Report (UNDP, 2020). Perusing the report which is neither perfectly designed as it does not fully account for all the political, economic, and educational situations in the continent, African countries, nevertheless, monopolize the lowest ranks of the available information. Here, perhaps a brief point for now, on the conceptual and practical constructions of development (social development as I have been labeling it for the past little while). The idea of development as it is currently constituted in the social sciences literature is not actually that old; that is in the long history of human life. As policy-into-programmatic terms and intentions, the construct and its practical implications were first presented in a post-World War II speech on an assumed platform of international development by then American President Harry Truman who saw, from his triumphant vantage point, a way of uplifting poor populations via American-centric/Western-centric economic and related advancements (Black, 2002). Interestingly and not unexpectedly, the assumed viability of exported international development did not solve the world's problems, and more often than otherwise, created a uni-directional policy and project perspectives that were more or less only fitted for their Western socio-cultural origins. Somewhat like colonialism, though more benign in its control of people's lives, this modernity predicated progress assumed too much about the well-being needs of Africans and others from afar, thus applying a detached, prejudicial gaze that hardly took into account the actual needs of different populations.

In the analysis of the late Nigerian political economist, Claude Ake, what was termed development (in both economic and political terms) in Western capitals, did not make sense in African terrains, basically and in practical points, thus qualifying itself as non-development and impractical (Ake, 1996, 2000).

Despite such development assumptions and issues and the locational feasibility complexities, the need for human advancement is still an important prospect in the lives of Africans and others. This is important in the sense that Africa and Africans are not detached from the rest of the world, nor located outside the zonal influences and realities of globalization even if in most cases they are systematically marginalized within and around it. It is with such pragmatics that we shall still locate different projects of formal, informal, non-formal education as potentially contributing to people's well-being in these and future times. That, even when we have been speaking extensively about the damages done by colonial education on the bodies and psyches of *dadka Afrikaanka ah* (African people) and other colonized Indigenous populations across the globe. It is indeed with the still intact colonial systems of education in most postcolonial states that we must discuss a new type of social development that could be achieved through the reconstruction of the philosophical, linguistic, curricular and general learning as well as teaching intentions and possibilities of contemporary African learning and teaching systems. In posthumous epistemic and developmental crediting, the seminal works of anticolonial African philosophers including Julius Nyerere and Amilcar Cabral, among others, should, in categorical and postfacto terms, prove the point: Counter-cultural, counter-linguistic, counter-philosophical, and counter-epistemological education, in essence, counter-African onto-existentialities learning and instructional platforms, cannot develop Africa and its peoples.

It is with these irrefutable facts in mind that contemporary and still Western monocentric education with its actual underlying philosophies, policy formulations, and attached practical implications/outcomes cannot and will not establish and sustain acutely needed advancement possibilities in neither Africa's mostly overcrowded urban centers nor in the continent's rural locations. To repeat, with an eye on the pragmatics of the moment and in both psychosocial and material terms, Africans are fully connected to the world and to all its desires and aspirations for better lives, even when they are not economically so endowed. This applies especially to young people, who are the future of the continent and are so more connected via the now ubiquitous internet availability and attached social media platforms, to the rest of the world. The African youth, who are expected to number about 850 million by the year 2050, see/feel, in quotidian terms, the facilities of life, especially in employment and countable wealth parcels, in extra-Africa spaces, which are no longer limited to Europe and North America, but are also present in a number of places in especially Southeast Asia.

While the year 2050 might sound to some as some distant time block, it is actually approaching fast. Even with that potential complicated time–space comprehension, the youth unemployment situation tells a story of economic despair with an estimated 70% of that population exposed to chronic poverty (International Labour Organization, ILO, 2016). Select potential analytical queries to my arguments here could be the following: How about the education, why is that not helpful, and what levels do these youth achieve? Maybe they need more education, could be a suggestive observation. Interestingly and especially in urban centers, a good majority of the young people who are dealing with these difficulty employment situations did not only complete primary and secondary schools but a good number hold tertiary-level credentials. Indeed, the situation is not about the absence of education but more so the relevance of such education, which, as extensively pointed above, is not thought-of, designed and implemented for the needs of Africans. For all practical undertakings, such learning does not only provide decontextualized, de-communal epistemic and training style blocks, but also damages the subjective confidence of its recipients. By extension, it also diminishes the transformative agency of learners by continually elevating, to say de novo, the history, cultures, knowledges, and achievements of the so-called developed world. In parallel terms, such education also directly or otherwise decommissions people's basic ontological and related humanizing as well as close-to-self, and connected-to-community capacities and potential advancement references. As noted by the African Center for Economic Transformation (ACET, 2016), it is with these realities that half of the continent's millions of young people who come out of universities every year remain unemployed.

With the inter-justifying problematics of education and social development in the continent therefore, the reconstruction of Africa's learning and teaching platforms including but not limited to the philosophical as well as the cultural and attached linguistic contexts is important and urgent. Such systematic prospects of reconstruction assure a return, again in Cabralian terms (Cabral, 1970, 1973), to the lost and long-awaited Africanization (as opposed to colonial de-Africanization) of the ways we think about education, conceive the contextual and viability possibilities of such education, and via such deliberations and outcomes, accord a prominent place for African Indigenous Knowledge systems and epistemologies. Again, the process of Africanizing both the learning and knowledge contexts will be emanating from and comprehensively responsive to the whole of African ontologies, cosmo-ecological locations, and communally-benefiting needs, aspirations, and undertakings. It is high time therefore, to speak about the urgent need to Africanize education and its knowledge categories, complemented by the imperative to bring together/query about the multiple, interconnected critical points of the case. Indeed, I agree with Afful-Broni et al. (2020, p. 9) when, with recognitively critical and contemporaneously prescient notations, they write: "put simply, 'Africanization' is a process of making something 'African' in terms of a relation of history, identity, context, politics and the philosophy of practice."

Conclusion

In this work, I have engaged, with broad analytical and critical notations and intentions, a quasi-circular presentation on the fateful knowledge and learning encounters between Africa and its peoples, on the one side, and the dehistoricization as well as the philosophical and epistemological onslaught of European colonialism. Such onslaught was deliberately unleashed to suppress, not just people's basic lives but their educational and social development references as well. As should be gleaned from the chapter, the complexity of the issues that pertain to these historical-into-contemporary contexts and outcomes need to be ascertained with the systematic decommissioning of the Eurocentric deconstructions of Africa's socio-cultural and learning platforms. These platforms included the traditionally embedded philosophical and educational philosophy systems that were foundational to the way Africans thought about, related to, interacted with, impacted and were impacted by their social and physical ecologies, and thrived over millennia. In analytical intermediary terms, I have connected the issues to their epistemic and philosophical trajectories and to select European thought leaders who, in totalizing falsehoods, acted as the de-ethical apologists for the colonial project, thus creating a fabricated image of the continent that was multiply demeaning, and extendedly dehumanizing. To counter these philosophical and educational mythologies which have been perforce pragmatized through colonialism (as most enduring myths become real for willing believers) and with the educational philosophical terrain in 'postcolonial' Africa as still fairly connected to that, I have suggested the need for philosophical and educational philosophies reconstructions for Africanized education and social well-being.

Via the anticolonial constructions of African philosophies of education especially, the main points should be responsive to describing and analyzing the generally major philosophical questions which, although should always be locally formulated, could still have widened global interfaces and connectivity. That is, what systems of learning and teaching do African desire and need in these so-called globally interconnected and networked times. Such primary point should consequence the rational query of why specific categories of education should take precedence over other possibilities, all complemented by the critical methodological question of how such reconstructions should be designed and implemented for inclusive individual and community advancement and wellbeing. Indeed to recall de novo, Amilcar Cabral's timeless analysis, culturally de-sourced peoples cannot achieve development, which should take us back, with the appreciation of the implicated *Sankofa*[1] praxis, to his 'return to the source' prospect (Cabral, 1973) in cultural, philosophical, educational, and social progress counter-colonialist constructions and reconstructions.

---

[1] *Sankofa*, in generalized terms and for my understanding here, is a linguistic/expressive term from the languages of Ghanaian peoples, and serves as an important socio-cultural metaphor to value, indeed to go back and retrieve, what was there before/left behind.

References

Abdi, A. A. (2008). Europe and African thought systems and philosophies of education: 'Re-culturing' the trans-temporal discourses. *Cultural Studies, 22*(2), 309–327.
Abdi, A. A. (2010). Clash of oralities and textualities: The colonization of the communicative space in Sub-Saharan Africa. In D. Kapoor & E. Shizha (Eds.), *Indigenous knowledges and learning in Asia/Pacific and Africa*. Palgrave.
Abdi, A. A. (2013). Decolonizing educational and social development platforms in Africa. *African and Asian Studies, 12*(1–2), 64–82.
Abdi, A. A. (2020). Decolonizing Knowledge, education and social development: Africanist perspectives. *Beijing International Education Research, 2*, 503–518.
Achebe, C. (1989). *Morning yet on creation day*. Heinemann.
Achebe, C. (2000). *Home and exile*. Oxford University Press.
Achebe, C. (2009 [1958]). *Things fall apart*. Anchor Canada.
African Center for Economic Transformation. (ACET) (2016). *Unemployment in Africa: no jobs for 50% of graduates*. http://acetforafrica.org/highlights/unemployment-in-africa-no-jobs-for-50-of-graduates/
Afful-Broni, A., Anamuah-Mensah, J., Raheem, K., & Dei, G. J. S. (2020). *Africanizing the school curriculum: Promoting and inclusive, decolonial education in African contexts*. Myers Education Press.
Ake, C. (1996). *Democracy and development in Africa*. Brookings Institution.
Ake, C. (2000). *The feasibility of democracy in Africa*. Dakar, CODESRIA.
Black, M. (2002). *No-nonsense guide to international development*. Zed Books.
Cabral, A. with Handyside, R. (1970). *Revolution in Guinea: Selected Texts*. Monthly Review Press.
Cabral, A. (1973). *Return to the source: Selected speeches*. Monthly Review Press.
Césaire, A. (1972). *Discourse on colonialism*. Monthly Review Press.
Cook, M. (2005). *A brief history of the human race*. Norton.
Fanon, F. (1967). *Black skin, white masks*. Grove Press.
Fanon, F. (1968). *The wretched of the earth*. Grove Press.
Foucault, M. (1980). *Power/knowledge: Selected interviews and other writings*. Vintage.
Frye, N. (2020 [1957]). *Anatomy of criticism: Four essays*. Princeton University Press.
Graham, J. D. (1976). Review: Julius Nyerere: A contemporary philosopher-statesman. *Africa Today, 23*(4), 67–73.
Harding, S. (1998). *Is science multicultural? Postcolonialisms, feminisms and epistemologies*. Indiana University Press.
Harding, S. (2008). *Sciences from below: Feminisms, postcolonialities and modernities*. Duke University Press.
Hegel, G. W. F. (1965). *Reason in history*. MacMillan.
Higgs, P. (2008). Towards an Indigenous African educational discourse: A philosophical reflection. *International Review of Education, 54*(3–4), 445–458.
Huntington, S. (1971). The change to change: Modernization, development and change. *Comparative Politics, 3*(3), 283–322.
International Labour Organization. (ILO) (2016). *Youth unemployment challenge worsening in Africa*. http://www.ilo.org/addisababa/media-centre/pr/WCMS_514566/lang--en/index.htm
Kane, H. (2012 [1963]). *Ambiguous adventure*. Penguin.

Mandela, N. (1994). *Long walk to freedom: The autobiography of Nelson Mandela*. Little, Brown & Co.

McHenry, D. (1994). *Limited choices: The political struggle for socialism in Tanzania*. Lynne Rienner Publishers.

Memmi, A. (1991). *The colonizer and the colonized*. Beacon Press.

Mhina, C., & Abdi, A. A. (2009). *Mwalimu*'s Mission: Julius Nyerere as (adult) educator and philosopher of community development. In A. Abdi & D. Kapoor (Eds.), *Global perspectives on adult education*. Palgrave Macmillan.

Nyerere, J. (1968). Education for self-reliance. *CrossCurrents, 18*(4), 415–434.

Odera Oruka, H. (1990). *Sage philosophy: Indigenous thinkers and modern debate on African philosophy*. Brill Academic.

Ong, W. (2013 [1982]). *Orality and literature*. Routledge.

Ozmon, H., & Craver, S. (2012). *Philosophical foundations of education* (9th ed.). Pearson.

Pakenham, T. (2015 [1991]). *The scramble for Africa: White man's conquest of the dark continent from 1867–1912*. Harper Perennial.

Rabaka, R. (2010). *Against epistemic apartheid*. Lexington Books.

Rodney, W. (1982). *How Europe underdeveloped Africa*. Howard University Press.

Said, E. (1993). *Culture and imperialism*. Vintage.

Semali, L. (1999). Community as classroom: (RE)valuing Indigenous literacy. In L. Semali & J. Kincheloe (Eds.), *What is Indigenous knowledge? Voices from the academy* (pp. 95–118). Routledge.

Trevor-Roper, H. (1963, November 28). The rise of Christian Europe. *The Listener*, p. 871.

United Nations Development Program. (UNDP) (2020). *Human development report*. UNDP.

Van Sertima, I. (1991). *Blacks in science: Ancient and modern*. Transaction Books.

wa Thiong'o, N. (1986). *Decolonising the mind: The politics of language in African literature*. Heinemann.

wa Thiong'o, N. (1993). *Moving the centre: The struggle for cultural freedoms*. James Currey.

wa Thiong'o, N. (2009). *Re-membering Africa*. East Africa Educational Publishers.

PART II

Critical Race Theories of Education

CHAPTER 5

Educating for Critical Race and Anti-Colonial Intersections

George J. Sefa Dei and Asna Adhami

INTRODUCTION

As we write this chapter, we are over one year into the global coronavirus pandemic on Turtle Island, and likely longer than that in other parts of the world, and probably ours as well. All continents are now affected (CTV, Forani, 2020), over two million people have passed away, almost one hundred million confirmed cases (WHO, 2021), the world has seen many lockdowns, industry upheavals and crash after crash of the capitalistic, credit-based economies, the competition for vaccines, cures, and distribution politics. There is also a consuming debate, counter-visions, and ideas about policing and police reform, defunding and disbandment, renewed again in the aftermath of the police killings in the United States of George Floyd, Breonna Taylor, and other countless other lives, needlessly cut short. In the wake of police incident-related deaths in Canada, including Chantal Moore in Edmunston, Ejaz Choudry in Peel Region, Eishia Hudson in Winnipeg, Regis Korchinski-Paquet in Toronto (Cooke, 2020; Malone et al., 2020), similar conversations are also taking place here. In Toronto, police are finally

G. J. S. Dei (✉) · A. Adhami
Ontario Institute for Studies in Education (OISE), Toronto, ON, Canada
e-mail: george.dei@utoronto.ca

A. Adhami
e-mail: a.adhami@mail.utoronto.ca

© The Author(s), under exclusive license to Springer Nature
Switzerland AG 2022
A. A. Abdi and G. W. Misiaszek (eds.), *The Palgrave Handbook on Critical Theories of Education*, https://doi.org/10.1007/978-3-030-86343-2_5

working toward piloting a project to redirect mental health calls and wellness checks to non-police professionals for response in certain parts of the city (CBC, Toronto Pilot Project, 2021).

We take an anti-colonial approach toward understanding how the past colonialities around the globe, inform the present efforts to attain justice:

> Anti-racism work, now more than ever, requires an integrated, interdisciplinary, and intersectional understanding in order to recognize its global impact, scope, and implications. Anti-racism, thus, has emerged in today's context as a way to theorize, measure, understand, and counter the systemic physical, spiritual, communal, and emotional violences enacted by dominant cultures upon the Black, Indigenous, Racialized and other marginalized communities that they live among and beside. (Dei & Adhami, 2021a, p. 158)

What sometimes is lost—almost always lost except in the hearts and minds of those directly affected by the oppressions—is the historicity of these calls and debates globally, for decades, centuries, and likely millennia. Not only must we look back into both told and untold histories from around the world, it is even more important to implement a broadly informed multicentric approach (Dei, 2016), and we place the many centered views *alongside* one another (Adhami, 2015) in order to facilitate deeper knowing and better application of these learnings, if we want actual change in our communities and related frameworks, such as education, legal, and healthcare. The only way to displace hegemony is to include the rest of us and to remember—and address—the problems of the past so that we may actually progress.

We—as racialized participants in the academy—and indeed citizens in these socially and perpetually unjust globally intersectional societies are all too keenly aware of the erasure of our histories and the violences that we and those before us have stood up to, spoken out about, and fought against. We are aware of the progresses—changes big and small—that came about but were eroded before having a chance to turn the forever tide, by the cyclical processes inherent in supremacies that continually sustain themselves. Among the myriad of upheavals occurring around the world during this time, perhaps one very telling example of the pervasive endurance of coloniality and supremist ideology is the January 6, 2021, Capitol Hill insurrection in the United States. While the systems of safety and security continuously and year over year kept a hyper vigilant attention on Black, Indigenous, Muslim, Asian, and other Racialized peoples and their supporters around the country, other extremists holding majority identities, in this case white and Christian, gained the freedom to flourish en masse and attack their own political infrastructure, while evading the same kinds of fear-inducing labels or responsive policing actions or lasting societal consequences. Such reality and practice are among the reasons we and others remain keenly aware that we must instigate more change as we continue to face and fight the injustices and work to recover the histories, making every effort to ensure these new changes—layered over all those which have come before, last for all future generations.

As anti-colonial scholars, we are also connected to and maintain relationships with our Indigenous heritages, in ways that are relational to lands, spirituality, and community, and we work to integrate these ways of knowing and the many teachings they offer to derive meaning and bring context to our work. We strive to consider beyond the contemporary identity tropes of skin color, ethnicity, national identity, and biological characteristics, which become contested and politicized through colonial displacements, to understand how mechanisms of power can be mobilized to embolden, neutralize, erase, or suppress. The evidence describing the impact of these kinds of colonial impacts on the subjects of its ruptures is long documented by many over decades and centuries. We have referenced only a handful of scholars from the past including Said (1979), Fanon (1961), Freire (1970), Smith (2012), and Césaire (1955), who are among many others who document and demonstrate how Euro-Western hegemonies have oppressed the non-European world. From an Anti-colonial perspective, perhaps one of the most profound implications is that even in cases where sovereignty and freedom are returned to peoples in principle, the menace of supremacist ideologies remains in place, such as in our education systems, for example, as to whose language we work in, and whose science and knowledges are considered valid. In society and everyday life, these ideologies become conveyed subtly in whose battle conquests and religions we center in our societies and observe as holidays, for example. Given the nature of coloniality's supremacist binary tendencies, these ideologies show up in how peoples in these societies—and their beliefs, customs, or traditions—become labeled as good or bad, right or wrong, civil or savage, terrorist or citizen—they show up in who is collectively vilified. It means these same people, by extension, will ignore how global industry exploits land, labor, and climate sovereignty of certain countries, with expansive, invasive projects that offer next-to-nothing wages, with almost complete disregard for local ecologies but then decry human rights abuses or climate pollution and change without any consideration of complicity. In the case of news and journalism, CBC Senior Reporter, Jody Porter (2022, pp. 8–9) describes the damaging impact of this disregard in the context of a growing industry of information dissemination, which values content, technologies, volume, and immediacies over knowledge, accuracy, and responsibility: "Old forms of accountability, of being responsible to one's community through reciprocal relations, are subverted in this dumping ground of data. In the news media's quest for clicks, favor falls on social media accounts with mass followings, so people who are popular on Twitter are coveted as news sources and interview subjects to drive more traffic to the news website. Former U.S. President Donald Trump is only the most extreme example of the damage this can do to public discourse where the person with the loudest voice is given a virtual blow horn." An anti-colonial lens allows us to also extend these analyses of power dynamics in systems predicated on colonial and imperialist dispossession, to deeply understand and reflect on how these endemic values rage on in order to envision strategic educational transformation (Dei, 2006, 2021).

Between us, we locate ourselves as scholars and citizens, we ground in ancestries, experiences, and traditions from other continents, which converge and intersect with those that exist on the lands we presently inhabit. We pool our experiences as Elder, parent, community leader, pedagogue, as daughter, caregiver, journalist, scholar, and artist, as educators, change makers, activists, and of genders, locations, identities from our long journeyed paths. We work to subvert, change, reform, intervene in, and sometimes reinvent how knowledge, education, and information is collected, interpreted, disseminated, hidden, revealed, safe-kept, and used in the systemic continuance of power dynamics in society and institutions. To come from these places is to embody the spirit and the knowledge (Dei, 2013, p. 31), the research, and the history and to make that which we create, healing in essence. We share a clear vision for inclusive social, educational, and community well-being possibilities, that are multiply and simultaneously inter-enriching and brimming with intentions, options, and actions that that can be called upon and deployed for anti-colonial and antiracist emancipation.

While these pandemic times have proven extraordinary in many fathomable and unfathomable ways, we come to this work, also having witnessed many renewals and returns, and with intrinsic hope. Little Bear shares how worldviews shape understanding and engagement:

> In Aboriginal philosophy, existence consists of energy. All things are animate, imbued with spirit, and inconstant motion. In this realm of energy and spirit, interrelationships between all entities are of paramount importance space is a more important referent than time…The idea of all things being in constant motion or flux leads to a holistic and cyclical view of the world. (Little Bear, 2000, p. 1)

We see movements, projects, and programs that serve to uplift, empower, and propel Black and Indigenous peoples all around the world and provide opportunities, mentorships, and avenues that were previously oppressively denied. We have seen the election of President Joe Biden and Vice President Kamala Harris in the United States and their reversal of their predecessor's many problematic, supremacist-informed policies, including the Muslim immigration and travel ban. Some media and other outlets including CNN (Kaur, 2020), Science (Lecoq et al., 2020) reported that worldwide shutdowns since the declaration of a global pandemic had reduced the seismic impact of humans on the planet. Time Magazine (Wagner, 2020) and NBC (Chow, 2020), among others, also pointed to benefits for the climate resulting from a reduction in carbon emissions from restrictions to air, sea, and land travel, while other outlets such as The Guardian (Watts, 2020) point to the planet and nature reclaiming space and time for regeneration and animal population recoveries.

We know restoration is purposeful, at times difficult and unruly, and that healing takes great care and time, so we take inspiration from our peoples and our planet's natural rhythms to work toward empowerment, action, and lasting change. With this understanding, we start with the fundamental premise from Critical Race Theory that racism still exists in all its forms and continues to be endemic in our social systems, and we unpack the decolonial intersections from there.

IN THEORY…RACIALIZING WHITENESS

> Indigenous research is just one aspect of a much broader, transformative project of Indigenous resistance (and decolonization) in all spheres of life. (Dei, 2013, p. 29)

It's a fundamental appreciation for the idea that in a democracy, majority rules, and in such a circumstance, injustice, and imbalance are inherent and intrinsic to any social system created within such structures, unless they heavily manage, monitor and remedy any systemic inequities that may impact that system's minoritized populations. After all, that is the responsibility of having any privilege, to ensure access and benefit to those who may not enjoy the same, the key element being the ability and willingness to share, a plausible, possible ideal. There is also an inherent danger in any democracy which is borne of organized circumstances of coloniality that its every system and institution will carry within it, the ideals and values of supremacy and visible and invisible systemic racism as the very goals of colonialism are to conquer, erase, conform, eradicate, assimilate and exploit for maximum capitalist benefit.

López (2003) outlines many systemic issues that undermine the success of racialized and minority students and educational leaders that emerge directly from the preexisting systemic impediments within founding democratic structures. López demonstrates how prevalent disenfranchising myths of participation, meritocracy, benefit, and equality are active within American structures of governance, conflict, power, and policy, and become replicated in systems and institutions of education, justice, medicine, and more. These myths also continuously feed the obstinate appetites of Eurocentric moncentricizations, totalitarianisms/quasi-totalitarianisms, while serving the exploitive savior ideologies of neoliberal globalization, monoculturalism, unimodal pedagogical hegemonies, and cognitive imperialism, as they work to silence our voices and erase any progress:

> Taken holistically, CRT posits that beliefs in neutrality, democracy, objectivity, and equality "are not just unattainable ideals, they are harmful fictions that obscure the normative supremacy of whiteness in American law and society" (Valdes et al., 2002, p. 3). Notwithstanding, White Americans continue to

believe in these ideals, because a racial reality is, perhaps, too difficult to digest. (López, 2003, p. 85)

When racism operates in covert and overt ways, López (2003) asserts that whether through action or inaction, by presence or absence, it impacts and impedes the success, health, progress, and participation of any who are not defined as 'majority,' while furthermore solidifying impressions and perceptions of blame, failure, irresponsibility, or inabilities squarely onto the disenfranchised.

In the contemporary Western contexts, most present democracies are predicated on Eurocolonial and Christian values and norms. Consequentially As Ard and Knaus (2013, p. 22) also point out, whether in schools, universities, or in societies "[b]asing public policy upon research that relies and adheres to white norms and standards, limits decolonizing methodologies and ignores the large bodies of research that are devalued by traditional academic worldviews."

With such pressures and problems facing us simultaneously as scholars and citizens, decolonizing society and the academy and establishing other narratives, worldviews, and ways of knowing have been the ongoing work of countless activists, scholars, and resistors such as DuBois (1903), Fanon (1961), Friere (1970), Césaire (1955), Said (1979), and Smith (2012). A key element to any decolonizing and critical approach has been the project of speaking back to whiteness, such as in problematizing the neoliberal agendas and their commodifications of knowledge and the consequential resurgence of imperialist Islamophobia, for example, and the violence, and silencing spreading in the aftermath of the tragedies of 9/11, as seen in the works of scholars such as Razack (1998), Mohanty (2004) and Shiva (2004). Mohanty writes:

> [S]ome important sites for feminist, anti-imperialist critique and organising include scrutiny of the militarised US state and cross-border struggles, corporate globalisation, and the economics impacting power relations of gender and sexuality, the growth of a corporate/military nexus in the US academy, the contradictions of national security in the midst of the US Patriot Act, neoliberal agendas and complicit feminisms, US foreign policy, US domestic policy, and the imperial project, to name just the obvious. (2004, p. 71)

Reinstating the value of and restoring the mainstream acceptance of meaning to Indigenous ways of knowing and dismantling systems of supremacy has also been at the forefront of the work of such scholars as Cooper (2012), Coulthard (2010), hooks (1994), Mignolo (2007), and Maldonado-Torres, (2004). In one such intervention, Brayboy (2005, p. 430) extends the interruptions of Critical Legal Studies (CLS) and Critical Race Theory to create Tribal Critical Race Theory (TribalCrit) as a means to center the Indigenous experiences on lands now known as the United States:

CRT was originally developed to address the Civil Rights issues of African American people. As such, it is oriented toward an articulation of race issues along a "black-white" binary (much the way Brown v. Board is), and, until recently, other ethnic/racial groups have not been included in the conversation. As a result, Latino Critical Race Theory (LatCrit) and Asian Critical Race Theory (AsianCrit) have been developed to meet the specific needs of those populations. (2005, p. 429)

Brayboy's innovation provided specific tenets and "a new and more culturally nuanced way of examining the lives and experiences of tribal peoples since contact with Europeans over 500 years ago" (2005, p. 430), addressing important needs for inclusion of diverse perspectives and ways of knowing. These frameworks also consider White supremacy, imperialism, capitalist agendas, assimilation as key impositions on communities, and advocate for the restoration of traditional philosophies and beliefs where stories are seen as legitimate forms of theory and data, which can be mobilized for decolonizing.

The Difference Indigeneities Make

Decolonization and [I]*ndigenizing* my life includes learning and practising my culture; learning my language; speaking my language; fighting ethnocentrism in education, research and writing; battling institutional racism; and the list goes on. Decolonization and [I]ndigenizing is about both knowing and having a critical consciousness about our cultural history. (Absolon, 2011, p. 19)

As we work to decolonize our practices, we work to bring together multiple ways of knowing, centered and as equals, as an active disruption and displacement of hegemony. Little Bear (2000) talks about the importance of relational worldviews, where knowledge is shared as knowledge, and exists in community, with everyone understanding their world and experiences from their own unique location, which is valid, vital, and knowingly contributing to the whole.

Singularity manifests itself in the thinking processes of Western Europeans in concepts such as one true god, one true answer, and one right way. This singularity results in a social structure consisting of specialists. Everyone in the society has to be some kind of specialist, whether it be doctor, lawyer, plumber, or mechanic. Specializations are ranked in terms of prestige. This, in turn, results in a social class structure. Some professions are higher up the ladder, and some are lower down it. In science, singularity manifests itself in terms of an expensive search for the ultimate truth, the ultimate particle out of which all matter is made. And so it goes. (Little Bear, 2000, p. 5)

On the journey of un/re/discovering, Adhami (2015) describes how these themes of love, universality, and relationality as also present in South Asian traditions and Sufi worldviews, also consider, render, and/or view many western, linear paradigms as seemingly incomplete for their neglect of these ways of understanding (inter) connections (Adhami, 2015). As Porter (2022, p. 3) warns, "Any public undertaking that leaves out Indigenous perspectives is destined to lead us to the same harmful place." Adhami's description of these dismissals of traditional knowledges highlights the particular impact of such impositions especially when occurring in smaller minoritized communities, where relationality and solidarity are often—and collectively—mobilized, for example, to counter the displacement and absence of culturally relevant and appropriate scholarly articles, community supports, languages, and histories vis-à-vis the contexts of global coloniality. Dei describes the need for the creation of such 'epistemic communities' as:

> "[A] place for researchers and learners to openly utilize the body, mind, spirit and soul interface in critical dialogues about understanding their communities. It is also a space that nurtures conversations that acknowledges the importance and implications of working with a knowledge base about the society, culture, and nature nexus." (Dei, 2013, p. 32)

Critical reflection tells us that notions of singularity and absoluteness from which distorted notions of objectivity emerge, then insist upon the validity of one worldview and consequently only contribute to notions and practices of supremacy, exemplified within the academy and within other institutions. In these environments, as we know from the past, everything and anything can be weaponized in order to serve the intentions of single or multiple supremacies, even in so-called democracies. Laws can be created to demonize, silence, and assimilate the so-called different, moral panics can be created to get the masses on side, and as (Dei & Adhami, 2021 in press a) wish to note and emphasize, *anything and everything can be weaponized*. Indigenous teachings often center coexistence and peace and other ways to navigate difference and conflict. If we take past racialization in the academy to mean the objectification of non-European, and non-white worldviews, then perhaps now is the time to take back that concept and racialize the academy by repopulating it with knowledge and wisdoms from every part of the world, from all knowledge systems and traditions. Doing that will bring some much needed vibrancy and energy into the institutions and breathe some life into these static spaces known for reference, expertise and teaching. Many have already in the past, and are presently contributing to this process, and we will need to keep up this work until we have displaced the many hegemonies and supremacies, without falling into the polarities that global colonialities posit. Coexistence must prevail.

There is an ever-growing number of intercontextual and interdisciplinary decolonial strategies and actions that are now well documented (Dei, 2017; Smith, 2012) to employ in the academy, and at the same time, these strategies must also be of use and effective in dismantling colonialism in communities and societies. These represent actions of mentorship, of empowerment, of equalizing, and of peace. We take up our positions in the academy, from our given locations and identities, and have previously named key elements of practice that are essential to our stance and how we navigate the present circumstances (Dei & Adhami, 2021b, p. 18 in press b). We share these strategies in solidarity with colleagues and community members who also, especially, address the importance of collective action. What we invite for consideration is: What are the implications for schooling and education, in teaching such things as decolonization, anti-colonialism, and combatting anti-Blackness, when and if steps like the ones we—and others before and alongside us—have suggested become common practice?

In the first place, we insist on the simultaneous restoration of Black, Indigenous, and Racialized voices to conditions of authenticity and primacy, rather than of marginality. This would be transformation whereby scholars and leaders can participate with agency and free of pressure, of performativity, or to maintain a status quo. If we taught about the inherent relationalities of Blackness, Indigeneity, Asian-ness, and other identities as principle elements of our science education, and then incorporate teaching about the impacts and intersections of land dispossessions, labor exploitations, and slaveries on a global landscape, how far might that kind of restorative strategy of voice go toward, for example, reasserting broad, diverse and real notions of Black humanhood and dismantling systemic practices of anti-Black racism and anti-Blackness? What if the global knowledges we learn about span thousands of years, rather than hundreds of years, and were explained by the peoples of the lands rather than those who arrived to exploit them? It is a strategy designed to interrupt—by diverting discourse to be contained within an antiracist framework—any habits that preserve the ongoing narrative, such as those that may erase the connections between settler colonialism and anti-Blackness, and therefore any responsibility to correct that atrocity, by divesting coloniality of its obligations and responsibilities for reparations and amends.

Secondly, as part of this leadership practice, we reiterate our insistence on the multicentric restoration of spirituality and relationality to our institutions, at the very least to the same degree of commonality as any of those of the dominant (Absolon, 2011; Adhami, 2015; Little Bear, 2000). Our spiritualities and Indigenous ways of knowing are imperative and unalienable from our voices and actions. Incorporating our worldviews means doing and seeing things differently, as activating worldviews that center relationality and respect with all sentient and non-sentient beings means that the very essence of the scientific approach will differ greatly. That is, interpreting connection, causation, and consequence are not read the same way they may be in a paradigm that centers dominion, disconnection, observation, and control. That will include spiritual awareness and traditional understandings as nourishment and praxis, all at once. We are talking here about a return to incorporating traditional pedagogies and methodologies such as having Elders in schools, bringing primacy to oral knowledge and traditions on par with written text, while incorporating the multiplatform and multi-context learning that is now taking place, in a very virtual pandemic learning world. In education, like in many other aspects of life, the pandemic has brought us back to many of the basics, creating many instances of isolation, causing introspection while also creating broader opportunities for connecting and understanding connections, especially through the use of multiple kinds of knowledge platforms and technologies.

Thirdly, we continue to engage in and support ongoing efforts to bring back our histories in ways that mitigate further injuries of disconnection and erasure. What if we were to unravel the narratives of colonial conquest and European wars to reframe our teaching practices and focus on multiple contexts of historical and political consciousness and resistance. There are many of these stories across the world, politicized by contexts and constructs of race, religion, nationality, ethnicity, alliances, in African contexts, on Indigenous lands, affecting people in countries now called Pakistan, India, Bangladesh, North-something, and South-something else. This way of approaching education enables a deepening of the discourse that connects Black liberation, Indigenous restoration struggles, and Pakistani/Indian independence, for example, as decolonizing struggles for sovereignty. To restore other versions of relationality. To displace myths of the singularity and single dimensionality imposed upon any one community. An important aspect of this is also to disengage from western frames and lenses, and increase the number of 'trauma-free' representations of peoples and communities (Blake, 2021) as another means to undo the damage caused from the prevalence of distorted colonial narratives and gazes.

Fourth, we look at institutional practicalities, and encourage and advocate for the creation of groups and communities, where working together to accomplish the greater purposes mentioned above. This means working with local communities and the Black, Indigenous, and Racialized educators within our institutions to understand their spiritual, intellectual, emotional, and psychological needs. It requires that we develop strategies for mentorship and support mechanisms to address and overcome barriers. It means that we encourage sustainable practices and success by providing strategies for Black, Indigenous, and Racialized recruitment, retention and promotion, and leadership coaching and training. It requires that we examine and review educational, classroom teaching, and curriculum practices, of workplace equity and implementation strategies on an ongoing basis, to ensure the checks and balances are current and relevant, and state clear goals and outcomes that are accomplishable. These shall also address recourse and accountability at all levels of institutional leadership, and make sure that these measures are backed with financial commitment and support. While this is taking place in our institutions at various levels, and again our pandemic has extended many previously insular communities through global connectivity, we are advocating for a collective paradigm shift in overarching social structures that ensures such strategies and remedies are institutionalized *and* maintained *and* monitored regularly so that they do not fall the way of the tokenized short term programs of the past. We need to commit to this as a global society.

From our perspective here, we suggest an approach that embodies and:

> ...speaks to relationality, interconnectionality and the collaborative approach of multicentric knowledge synthesis that we see in our own and so many world wisdom traditions. We need to be able to exist in academic communities that enable us to *be who we are*, rich with mentors, colleagues and leaders who sustain and foster our healthy engagement and participation in the academy, who reward, privilege and recognize our ways of knowing, learning and teaching, as equal and appropriate, as embodied and entire. (Dei & Adhami, 2021, pp. 21–22, in press b)

We must continue to expand our understandings of how resistance is practiced in all its forms, redefining what is considered 'normal' and challenging objectification of our ways and our bodies in the academy in ways that also serve broader communities (Adhami, 2015; Dei, 2013; Little Bear, 2000). We must empower, uplift, and embolden one another, and resist the colonial temptations to reduce, repress, and overtake one another, simply because coloniality defines success, privilege, reward, and access through tropes of supremacy. Coexistence is possible and valid in its own right, and we must lead with courage, hope, and heart to model it and make it so, for this is an important part of advocacy and an important precursor to all our actions, especially if that means abandoning participation in the politics of a space, and excusing ourselves from becoming our own oppressors.

Defining this kind of location and stance is by no means exhaustive or absolute, rather it is evolving and alive, a living practice. We consider any progress that comes as only one dimension of our society. Such dimension could still be incomplete and susceptible to erosion, especially if its impact and ability to reach, take root, and flourish in entirety are hindered. As has become a common catchphrase during these pandemic times, we are, after all, in this together.

Conclusion

Even with all we know and have learned in the past, we witness the futility and damage from history repeating itself. As in the case of the United States, even with all the checks and balances, the progress spurred by the Civil Rights and equity movements and discourse of mutual respect and coexistence was clawed back in the post-9/11 era, replaced by revitalized demonizing, and an ever-increasing hypervigilant surveillance of Black, Indigenous, Brown, and othered peoples. While that phase directly targeted Muslim and brown bodies, it redeployed the old tried and tested colonial tropes of suspicion and derision enabled by fear, used globally toward Black, Indigenous, and Racialized peoples. In the current climate it continues to feed the rise in populist notions of supremacy as well as propoganda-based fears that have been at the root of American and Eurocolonial injustices for many centuries. And while the fear, surveillance, extreme security measures, and precautions were again meted out on these populations, it was in fact a collection of far right, entitled, white supremacist ideologies that dared attempt to dismantle one of the most visible, self-affirming western democracies of our time, nearly upending it, one January afternoon. Even democracy, after all, is just *that* fragile. As López (2003), among others, points out, this western democracy was questionable at its very inception, in terms of its ability to create fair and equitable societies and communities. So the need for real and lasting change is dire, if we are ever to dream of leaving something for our future generations.

Our critical, anti-colonial insistence calls for:

[T]he subversion of the university/academic space, to uncover the potentialities of being for educational and social transformation. This could require changes in leadership as well as structure, for example, so that the immovable right and space is established – beyond token gestures, and once and for all – for us to *be* as diverse and authentic as who we are. (Dei & Adhami, 2021b, p. 6)

This is an ongoing effort, which calls for the opening up of space, practice, and engagement in ways that are restoratively informed by Indigenous knowledges, cultural practices, and ancestral traditions, so as to create learning spaces infused with ways that engage and uplift participants in a spirit of betterment, evolution, growth, and learning, as our practices of knowledge building, sharing, and keeping have traditionally intended, meant to be devoid of hierarchical preference.

As such, in our work we have long advocated for knowledge practices to encompass and embody international/global citizenship, by reimagining pedagogy and literacy studies, unpacking media and information studies, and broadening and reconnecting perspectives on science, mathematics, history, social justice, and other streams of knowledge in ways that are inclusive of gender/feminist studies and Southern/Indigenous epistemologies. In doing so, we resist the label of critical, as a further marginalization and imposition of structural hierarchy and a colonial binary. We simply add our voices to those among many, as existent on par, not necessarily defined as being in opposition to.

Acknowledgements We honour the important recognition of being situated on the Indigenous Lands of Huron Wendat, Seneca and Mississauga of Credit River, Turtle Island. We sincerely appreciate Indigenous magnanimity and with that we bring humility to all intellectual work. We bring knowledge informed by Earthly teachings from the lands we are situated on and with respect to our Ancestors, Elders, and all who have paved the way for us to be here, in this space, to how we develop our voices as an extension of theirs. We write at a time of heightened Indigenous resistance on Turtle Island and around the world as the struggles for basic human rights and efforts against anti-Indigeneity continue. In the current political climate—of the world remaining in the grips of the COVID-19 pandemic—the disconnect continues to expand between our sincere interests in equality and civil rights and the ongoing, questionable rhetoric of all forms of hate including anti-Blackness, anti-Muslim sentiments, anti-Semitism, and anti-Asian sentiments, to name a few. What remains clear and undeniable are the systemic paradigms, the very values and cultural norms, that entrench injustice in our every institution while purporting to uphold what constitutes civility and fair and decent treatment for all. We stand in solidarity with our friends, colleagues, and partners on the path, of all families and communities, at a time when we are facing a global recurrence of derision, hate, and colonial violence.

REFERENCES

Absolon King, K. (2011). *Kaandossiwin How we come to know.* Fernwood Press.

Adhami, A. (2015), *"In the Spirit of Inclusive Reflection: Reflections of a Cultural Expeditionist"* MAEd thesis, Studies in Lifelong Learning, Mount Saint Vincent University. http://ec.msvu.ca:8080/xmlui/handle/10587/1467. Retrieved January 2021.

Ard, R. L & Knaus, C. B. (2013). From Colonization to R.E.S.P.E.C.T.: How Federal Education Policy Fails Children and Educators of Color. *ECI Interdisciplinary Journal for Legal and Social Policy, 3*(1), Article 2.

Blake, J. (2021, January 24). *We need more 'trauma-free Blackness, 'Here's a start.* CNN.com. https://www.cnn.com/style/article/trauma-free-blackness-culture-queue/index.html. Retrieved January 2021.

Brayboy, B. M. J. (2005). Toward a tribal critical race theory in education. *The Urban Review, 37*(5), 425–446. Published Online: March 14, 2006. https://doi.org/10.1007/s11256-005-0018-y

Césaire, Aimé. [(1955) 1972]. Discourse on colonialism, trans. by Joan Pinkham, *Monthly Review Press*: New York and London. [Originally published as *Discours sur le colonialisme* by Editions Presence Africaine, 1955.] 1–31.

Chow, D. (2020, March 18). *Coronavirus shutdowns have unintended climate benefits: Cleaner air, clearer water: "I think there are some big-picture lessons here that could be very useful,"* one scientist said. NBCNews.com. https://www.nbcnews.com/science/environment/coronavirus-shutdowns-have-unintended-climate-benefits-n1161921. Retrieved January 2021.

Cooke, A. (2020, June 23). Recent deaths prompt questions about police wellness checks. At least 4 people have died during police wellness checks in Canada since April. CBC.ca https://www.cbc.ca/news/canada/nova-scotia/police-wellness-checks-deaths-indigenous-black-1.5622320. Retrieved January 2021.

Cooper, G. (2012). Kaupapa Maori research: Epistemic wilderness as freedom?". *New Zealand Journal of Educational Studies, 47*(2), 64–73.

Coulthard, G. (2010). Place against empire: Understanding Indigenous anticolonialism. *Affinities: A Journal of Radical Theory, Culture, and Action, 4* (2, Fall 2010): 79–83.

Dei, G. & Adhami, A. (2021 in press a). An anti-colonial read of anti-racism in Tanya Golash-Boza (ed.). *A Cultural History of Race in the Modern and Genomic Age (1920 –present)* (Vol. 6, p. 159). London: Bloomsbury. [forthcoming].

Dei, G. & Adhami, A. (2021 in press b). Coming to know and knowing differently: Implications of educational leadership. *Coloniality: Educational Leadership and Research Toward Decoloniality* (pp. 1–30). Educational Administration Quarterly. © The Author(s) 2021 Article reuse guidelines: sagepub.com/journals-per missions. https://doi.org/10.1177/0013161X211036079. journals.sagepub.com/home/eaq

Dei, G. J. S. (2006). Mapping the terrain: Anti-colonial thought and politics of resistance. In G. Dei & A. Kempf (Eds.), *Anti-colonialism and education: The politics of resistance* (pp. 1–24). Sense Publishers.

Dei, G. J. S. [Nana Sefa Atweneboah I]. (2013). Critical perspectives on indigenous research *Socialist Studies/Études socialistes. 9*(1): Spring 2013.

Dei, G. J. S. (2016). *Decolonizing the university: the challenges and possibilities of inclusive education. The Journal of the Society for Socialist Studies / Revue de la Société d'études socialistes, 11*(1,Winter 2016): 23–61.

Dei, J. S. S. (2017). *Reframing blackness and black solidarities through anti-colonial and decolonial prisms*. Springer Publishing.

Dei, G. J. S. (2021, forthcoming). *The Black scholar travelogue in academia*. The Black Scholar Travelogue. New York: Peter Lang Publishing.

Dei, G. J. S. (2021). Foreword. *Curriculum Inquiry, 51*(1), 1–14. https://doi.org/10.1080/03626784.2021.1847533

Du Bois, W. E. B. (1903). *The Souls of Black folk*. Oxford University Press.

Fanon, F. ([1952] 2008). *Black Skin, White Masks*. Trans. R. Philcox. Grove Press.

Fanon, F. ([1961] 2004). *The Wretched of the Earth*. Trans. R. Philcox, Grove Press.

Forani, J. (2020, December 22). *COVID-19 reaches Antarctica, pandemic now on every continent*. CTVNews.ca. https://www.ctvnews.ca/health/coronavirus/covid-19-reaches-antarctica-pandemic-now-on-every-continent-1.5241333. Retrieved January 2021.

Freire, P. ([1970] 2005). *Pedagogy of the Oppressed*. Trans. Myra Bergman Ramos, 30th Anniversary ed., Continuum.

hooks, B. (1994). *Teaching to Transgress: Education as the Practice of Freedom*. Routledge.

Kaur, H. (2020, April 3). *The coronavirus pandemic is making Earth vibrate less*. CNN.com. https://www.cnn.com/2020/04/02/world/coronavirus-earth-seismic-noise-scn-trnd/index.html. Retrieved January 2021.

Lecoq, T., et al. (2020). Global quieting of high-frequency seismic noise due to COVID-19 pandemic lockdown measures. *Science, 369*(6509), 1338–1343. https://doi.org/10.1126/science.abd2438

Little Bear, L. (2000). *Jagged Worldviews Colliding*. Reclaiming Indigenous Voice and Vision by Marie Battiste University of British Columbia 2000.

López, G. R. (2003). The (racially neutral) politics of education: a critical race theory perspective. *Educational Administration Quarterly, 39*(1): 68–94.

Maldonado-Torres, N. (2004). The topology of being and the geopolitics of knowledge: Modernity, empire, coloniality. *City, 8*(1), 29–56.

Malone, G. K., Omstead, M. & Casey, L. (2020, December 21). *Police shootings in 2020: The effect on officers and those they are sworn to protect: 2020 was deadliest year for police shootings in last 4 in Canada, co-author of study says*. CBC.ca. https://www.cbc.ca/news/canada/manitoba/police-shootings-2020-yer-review-1.5849788. Retrieved January 2021.

Mignolo, W. D. (2007). Delinking: The rhetoric of modernity, the logic of coloniality and the grammar of de-coloniality. *Cultural Studies, 21*(2–3), 449–514.

Mohanty, C. T. (2004). Towards an Anti-Imperialist Politics: Reflections of a desi feminist. *South Asian Popular Culture, 2*(1), 69–73. https://doi.org/10.1080/1474668042000210528

Porter, J. (2022). The Awfulization of news: When the real world of technology meets the real world of journalism. In K. Sikri (Ed.), *Humanities Commons*. https://hcommons.org/deposits/item/hc:46087/. https://doi.org/10.17613/jetk-7f85

Razack, S. (1998). *Looking White people in the eye: Gender, race, and culture in courtrooms and classrooms*. University of Toronto Press.

Said, E. W. (2003). A window on the world: Myth and misrepresentation of 'The Orient," *The Guardian*, August 2. http://www.guardian.co.uk/books/2003/aug/02/alqaida.highereducation

Said, E. W. ([1979] 1994). *Orientalism*, 25th Anniversary edn., Vintage Books. Retrieved May 5, 2021.

Shiva, V. (2004, April). Earth democracy: Creating living economies, living democracies, living cultures. *South Asian Popular Culture, 2*(1), 5–18. ISSN 1474-6689 print/ISSN 1474-6697 online © 2004 Taylor & Francis Ltd. http://www.tandf.co.uk/journals. https://doi.org/10.1080/1474668042000210483. Originally retrieved March 5, 2009.

Smith, L. T. (2012). *Decolonizing methodologies. Research and indigenous peoples*. Zed Books. Retrieved April 15, 2021.

Toronto pilot project could remove police from mental health calls—but not in emergencies. (2021, January 21). CBC.ca. https://www.cbc.ca/news/canada/toronto/police-mental-health-crisis-toronto-pilot-1.5882296. Retrieved January 2021.

Wagner, G. (2020, April 1). *Pausing the World to Fight Coronavirus Has Carbon Emissions Down—But True Climate Success Looks Like More Action, Not Less*. Time.com. https://time.com/5813778/coronavirus-climate-success/. Retrieved January 2021.

Watts, J. (2020, April 9) *Climate Crisis: in coronavirus lockdown, nature bounces back, but for how long*? The Guardian.com. https://www.theguardian.com/world/2020/apr/09/climate-crisis-amid-coronavirus-lockdown-nature-bounces-back-but-for-how-long. Retrieved January 2021.

World Health Organization. (2021, January 24). *WHO Coronavirus Disease (COVID-19) Dashboard*. https://covid19.who.int/

CHAPTER 6

Critical Social Foundations of Education: Advancing Human Rights and Transformative Justice Education in Teacher Preparation

Magnus O. Bassey

INTRODUCTION

In a recent poll conducted by the Pew Research Center, 58% of Americans say that the current climate is making race relations worse in the country Horowitz et al., 2019. They also remarked that systemic racism was a problem in the U. S. True to the above polling results, Derek Chauvin, a white Minneapolis police officer tortured George Floyd (a black man) by pressing his knee on George Floyd's neck for almost eight minutes until George lost consciousness and later died in police custody. A similar incident took place in March 2020 in Louisville, Kentucky when police officers entered Breonna Taylor's apartment at night, shot and killed her. In another incident, Ahmaud Arbery was shot and killed by two white men in a pickup truck while he was jogging in a Georgia neighborhood. Again, in Atlanta, Georgia, Rayshard Brooks was fatally shot by a police officer at a Wendy's drive-through lane. We cannot forget Freddie Gray who died in police custody in Baltimore, Maryland in 2015. Similar fate had befallen Trayvon Martin, Michael Brown, Jr., Stephon Clark, Terence Crutcher, Alton Sterling, Philando Castile, Eric Garner, Laquan McDonald, Carlos Ingram-Lopez; and the story goes on (see Feller & Walsh, 2020; Hill et al., 2020; Worland, 2020).

In the United States, people of color and minorities are marginalized and subordinated. The subordination of Black people and minorities, it must be

M. O. Bassey (✉)
Queens College, The City University of New York, New York, NY, USA
e-mail: magnus.bassey@qc.cuny.edu

© The Author(s), under exclusive license to Springer Nature Switzerland AG 2022
A. A. Abdi and G. W. Misiaszek (eds.), *The Palgrave Handbook on Critical Theories of Education*, https://doi.org/10.1007/978-3-030-86343-2_6

pointed out, is not unconnected to the devaluation of Blacks and minorities sustained over centuries through slavery, the Jim Crow laws, and the denial of basic political and economic rights to Blacks. These practices have led to dehumanization of Blacks and minorities in what Freire (1998) calls "a *distortion of the vocation of becoming more fully human*" (p. 26), that has taken, "the character of an inescapable concern" (p. 25), in modern times. Given these circumstances, more and more parents and the general public are looking up to schools for answers to America's race problems. Because schools are charged with the overwhelming responsibility of preparing the next generation of students in the United States, teacher education programs must arm teachers with transformative pedagogy that incorporates human rights and transformative justice education into its curriculum. This chapter will examine the exploratory construct that we should prepare teachers for human rights and transformative justice agenda in American schools because as Bell (1997, p. 12) notes, "The normalization of oppression in everyday life is achieved when we internalize attitudes and roles that support and reinforce systems of domination without question or challenge." According to Tarca (2005), racism in America has changed from institutional bold-faced-fact of daily life to a more subtle form called "aversive," "laissez-faire," or "colorblind" racism. As she puts it, colorblind racism transfers "group-based explanations of disparities between Blacks and Whites to individual-based rationales" (p. 99). Colorblind racism is not only subtle but makes Whites appear to embrace equality for all "while maintaining a belief in the inferiority of Black individuals" (p. 99). Given the pervasiveness and virulence of aversive or laissez-faire racism in American society today, more and more parents and the general public are looking up to schools for answers for America's race problems.

The most significant point to note is that racism is based on shallow and non-justifiable assumptions about race with no biological or genetic basis (Smedley & Smedley, 2005). Racism was socio-historically constructed to justify slavery and colonialism which have extended into current schemes and contexts of marginalization today. Although Cook (2003) in his study of human history over the past 50,000 years came to the conclusion that there is factually only one human race, racism has sustained arbitrary categorization that assures the continuity of privileging racialization schemes in the world because race is a social construct that is used to create inequality. Indeed, over the centuries, racism has been used for domination, exclusion, and control. Smedley and Smedley (2005, p. 24) argue that, "Race is a means of creating and enforcing social order, a lens through which differential opportunity and inequality are structured." Freire (1998) made the point very succinctly that oppressors crave to possess and dominate things, people, and indeed the whole world. As a result, oppressors end up reducing life including humans to "objects" that exist for their profits and plunder. And to cover up their tracks, oppressors create myths in which they present the oppressive world as a given entity that the oppressed must accept passively and adapt to. (Freire, 1998; see also Avinash, 2014).

In this chapter, I want to argue that as a solution to this problem, we should prepare teachers who would be concerned enough to endow their Black and minority students with individual self-worth and their White students with the ethic of concern for others because as Freire and Giroux (1989) have told us, "Educational programs need to provide students with an understanding of how knowledge and power come together in various educational spheres to both enable and silence the voices of different students" (p. ix). In his groundbreaking work, *Education for Critical Consciousness*, Freire (2007, p. 39) argued that there are three levels of consciousness: magical consciousness, naïve consciousness, and critical consciousness. At the level of magical consciousness, the individual accepts life passively and superficially and becomes a victim of magical explanations. At the level of naïve consciousness, an individual identifies his or her place in the world and recognizes that he or she or others are marginalized but is incapable of the type of thoughtfulness necessary for action. At the stage of critical consciousness, a person is able to identify systematic issues of oppression by actively engaging in reflection and action. This state of consciousness is often followed by transformation about individuals and groups of people into specific standards, policies, and attitudes to produce better outcomes. At this level, transformation is the practice of liberation through education where the individual learns of the *self* to be of worth irrespective of circumstances such as illiteracy, poverty, or ignorance (see Goulet, 2007, p. ix). Henceforth, students are not passive recipients of information but active participants in the learning process, and dialogue replaces the giving of information. In this instance, education becomes the act of problematization which gives the individual the ability to confront social, cultural, and political reality. However, Freire (2007) warns that literacy does not involve memorizing sentences, words, and syllables, but rather, the creation and recreation of human reality that adds to the natural world. Similarly, Dewey (1916/1966) defined education as "the principle of continuity through renewal" (p. 2). This means, the creation and recreation of beliefs, ideals, hopes, happiness, misery, and practices (p. 2). However, Dewey affirmed that education is not a matter of quantity or bulk, but of quality (p. 233). He offered a general perspective that provides some frame of reference about proper education and educative experience and argued that education is a necessity of life and educative experience is a means of social continuity of experience through renewal (p. 2). Dewey (1938/1998) highlighted the most important factors in the learning process which include the learner, the values and aims of society, and knowledge base of the subject matter. But he saw some experiences as mis-educative. An experience is mis-educative if it "has the effect of arresting or distorting the growth of further experience" (1938/1998, p. 13). To Dewey, therefore, educative experience is growth which allows for further growth. He pointed out that experiences which are harmful to others or narrow the field of further experience are mis-educative. Martusewicz (2004) argues that "transformations [which] reproduce conditions, e.g., ideologies, attitudes, relationships or practices, or social and economic structures that may be harmful to others" are to be considered mis-educative (p. 4). Similarly, Dewey (1938/1998) pointed out that "growth, or growing as developing, not only physically but intellectually and morally, is one exemplification of the principles of continuity" (p. 28). This means, a man who grows in efficiency as a burglar or as a gangster or as a corrupt politician cannot qualify from the "standpoint of growth as education and education as growth" (p. 29). Dewey likened educative experience to a moving force whose true value can be judged based only on what it moves toward and what it moves into (p. 31). Indeed, Dewey (1938/1998) maintained that growth in and of itself was not enough: we must stress the importance of the direction in which growth takes as well as its final destination (p. 28).

In preparing teachers for human rights and transformative justice agenda, I argue that critical social foundations of education is the only course in the teacher education curriculum that is connected with advancing human rights and transformative justice agenda because it encourages students to think critically about social issues and engages them in meaningful activism to produce social change. Critical social foundations of education not only devotes attention to asynchronous power dynamics and imbalance in the distribution of institutional and systematic power along racial lines, but also it discusses how to dismantle structural racism. It is also about the only course in the teacher education curriculum that encourages students to be involved in concrete struggle for resistance and change. And importantly, critical social foundations of education is the only course in the teacher education course offerings that is capable of introducing the concept of democracy, citizenship, equity, fairness and is capable of conceptualizing the connection between social justice and education. In other words, critical social foundations of education is the construct in teacher education preparation that enables students to navigate power because as Foucault (1980) noted, "The real political task in a society such as ours is to criticize the working of institutions which appear to be both neutral and independent; violence which has always exercised itself obscurely through them will be unmasked, so that we can fight fear" (cited in Rasheed, 2008, p. 4). Indeed, Freire (1998) reminded us some years ago that oppressive regimes are not the natural order of events in the world, but rather, are historically and socially constructed trends that should be changed.

Courses in Teacher Education Programs

Unfortunately, many of the courses in teacher education programs as they are presently constituted are not suited for interrogating public decisions because they are content with citizens' conformist and passive dispositions. Given these shortcomings, I argue that many courses in teacher education cannot endow citizens with the necessary intellectual capacity that would allow them to examine public policies critically as well as allow them to participate in civic transformation effectively. This is to say, most courses in teacher education programs are incapable of awakening students' moral outrage and consciousness to the persistence of subtle racism, exploitation, and psychological oppression. Although some of these courses are necessary for transmitting cultural knowledge, such knowledge alone are insufficient for preparing students for civic citizenship and social justice transformation because they fail to address citizens' civic obligations such as activism. Therefore, as an experiment in civic citizenship, the present teacher education courses are anachronistic constructs which have lost their erstwhile intellectual brilliance and meaning within the larger political agenda in contemporary civic engagement discourse. This chapter argues that a truly transformative agenda of civic citizenship and social justice can be achieved by studying critical social foundations of education that activates civic citizenship of all students, keeps students awake, and encourages them to be active participants in the fight for social change and social justice through social activism such as volunteering, doing charity work, civic missions, political participation, engagement in community affairs, advocacy, debating national policies, and civic values.

Critical social foundations of education also teaches students how to channel their frustrations appropriately in order to initiate change. It also encourages students' involvement in social development projects through collective action as a means of effecting change in their own communities. By enhancing students' capacity for democratic participation, students become active and engaged citizens. And through activism, organization, and mobilization, students are able to transform their communities. It needs to be said also that critical social foundations of education is the only course in the teacher education sequence that is not only suited for introducing the concept of democracy and citizenship but creates the space needed for discussing social justice, democratic citizenship, and social activism. Critical social foundations of education interrogates and addresses issues of gender, race, and class inequalities and challenges dominant assumptions about power, leadership, and democracy thereby establishing community voice in the process of radical transformation (Cuban & Anderson, 2007). Critical social foundations of education allows students to think critically about social issues and provides the space needed for them to work creatively to produce sustained change (see Butin, 2006; Ladson-Billings, 2005, 2009; Mitchell, 2007; Westheimer & Kahne, 2004). This can be done through students' engagement with fieldwork experiences and classroom work focused on social justice, civic citizenship, activism, and the desire to right unjust situations. This way, at the completion of their programs, students graduate with a sense of social justice engagement, responsibility, and an activist vision of community engagement (Butin, 2006).

WHY CRITICAL SOCIAL FOUNDATIONS OF EDUCATION?

Critical social foundations of education is a course in teacher education which critiques domination and discrimination and confronts, contradicts, and corrects inequality in society. Critical social foundations of education is informed by the principles and practices of freedom, equality, and social justice. It encompasses what Butin (2007) described as "the linkage of academic work with community-based engagement within a framework of respect, reciprocity, relevance, and reflection" (p. 1). Its objective is to inculcate in students a sense of self and political consciousness. Critical social foundations of education is the type of education that enables students to question the distribution of power in society: the aim being to transform structural inequalities in order to arrive at a more just society. This means, critical social foundations of education is critical of domination, discrimination, subjugation, and dehumanization of individuals and groups. It demands that public policy be informed by the spirit of equity, social justice, and fairness to all. In critical social foundations classes, students are encouraged to ask questions to uncover the cause of injustice and to envision themselves as agents of change. Critical social foundations of education privileges social justice outcomes over and above mere citizenship objectives because social justice outcomes include not only patriotism to nation but also "allegiance to universal human values, democratic ideals, and human rights and dignity of all people in the world" (Ahmad & Szpara, 2005, p. 10). Critical social foundations of education teaches students to "develop a pedagogical language that emphasizes the importance of being able to identify with others, to empathize with their thoughts and feelings and to develop the capacity for ethical respect" (Giroux, 1993, p. 20). This is because, educators should develop an emancipatory theory of leadership that should begin with the task of "creating a public language that is not only theoretically rigorous, publicly accessible and ethically grounded, but also speaks to a sense of utopian purpose" (Giroux, 1993, p. 24). In this case, Giroux (1993) states that public education should provide students with the principles and practices of democracy that is not devoid of vision or possibilities or struggle. This is the type of pedagogy that would encourage students to be involved in their communities so as to make a difference. In other words, teachers should engage students in pedagogy that would produce engaged citizens. Giroux (2006) makes this point interestingly as follows:

> Educators need to develop a new discourse whose aim is to foster a democratic politics and pedagogy that embody the legacy and principles of social justice, equality, freedom, and rights associated with the democratic concerns of history, space, plurality, power, discourse, identities, morality, and the future. Under such circumstances, pedagogy must be embraced as a moral and political practice, one that both initiates and is the outgrowth of struggles.... (pp. 34–35)

In a very well-researched book chapter, Emenyonu (1988) illustrated the importance of education as an instrument of social reconstruction. However, he maintained that education can mar the social advancement of a nation if it is not properly construed. As an investment in human capital, Emenyonu (1988) argued, the final product of education can determine the nature and quality of life in a given society, but if it is poorly construed, it is bound to produce "weaklings" and people without solid roots. He tells us that, if education at the top is purposeless the learner at the end of the educational process will become a nuisance to the society and a liability even to himself. An educational system must be purposeful so that its products can be functional members of society. According to him, "When an educational process is misconceived, the consequences are socio –economic chaos, political instability, cultural indecorum and moral indiscipline and laxity" (p. 34). Also, if the goals of education are not made particularly clear or are misguided and ambiguous, the students or learners will be unmotivated and schooling will become boring, and to a large extent drudgery (Emenyonu, 1988, p. 34). Similarly, it has been maintained that a free and just society is not self-sustaining. Its citizens must be acquainted with the principles of democracy, social justice, individual rights, and responsibilities (Giroux, 1993).

In critical social foundations of education classes, students are motivated to think critically about social issues and are persuaded to act in creative ways to produce social change. Critical social foundations theorists argue that schools should promote the ideals of democracy and teachers should emphasize democratic ideals and change in their classrooms. Critical social foundations of education focuses on social change and social justice; it encourages students' engagement with civic, social justice issues, and the expansion of community-service programs. It is necessary that students develop commitment to service as well as to systemic changes in society. Students start from the premise that society is not perfects; therefore, it is incumbent on them to uncover the root causes of such imperfections. By understanding society's imperfections, a student's consciousness is raised about issues of society's injustice. In addition to developing social consciousness, students are taught to balance classroom component with social responsibility for the purpose of community change (Mitchell, 2007). During the semester, students are required to spend time in their chosen social justice endeavors or in some form of community political action such as registering voters, participating in community board meetings, serving at soup kitchens, helping at homeless shelters, taking care of the poor, writing letters to editors of newspapers, protest rallies, public meetings, and activism. This way, students acquire civic participation skills which should include, "organizing and conducting public meetings, preparing agendas, writing letters to newspapers and politicians, public speaking, conducting opinion polls, campaigning, utilizing leadership skills, and volunteering" (Ahmad & Szpara, 2005, p. 18). The reasoning here is to produce active, involved, and critical thinking citizens. That is, citizens who can adjust to different questions and different domains of thought. Citizens who are fair-minded about their viewpoints as well as the viewpoints of others. Citizens who would be able to explore and appreciate the adequacy of other people's position. These individuals should be desirous to explore alien and even threatening viewpoints including those that contradict their deeply held assumptions and beliefs. They should be willing to explore, take risks, invent, invest, and create opportunities for others who are less fortunate (Paul, 1990, pp. 18–43). The type of education here would enable an individual to think for him/herself, in what Freire (2007) calls education for critical consciousness. This type of education allows an individual to learn how to analyze questions and problems and how to enter sympathetically into the thinking of others. Those endowed with these types of skills are able to make effective economic, political, and social contributions to their own society, because they can gather, analyze, synthesize, and assimilate information. And most importantly, these skills help people to deal rationally with conflicting points of view and to develop critical thinking abilities (Paul, 1990, pp. 18–43).

Development of Critical Thinking Skills?

In a real sense, critical social foundations theorists maintain that foundations students should develop critical thinking skills through class dialogue,[1] because Freire (1998) argued in *Pedagogy of the Oppressed* that dialogue is a precondition for our humanization. In his notion of "regimes of truth," Foucault (1980) tells us how some discourses operate and work together to reinforce a particular view of the world. Fernandez-Balboa and Marshall (1994), define dialogue as, "an active process of serious continuing discussion which allows people's voices to develop and be heard" (p. 173). They maintain that the advantage of using dialogue is that it is free. Dialogue is also social, inclusive, participatory, normative, propositional, ongoing, transformative, and best of all anticipatory (Fernandez-Balboa & Marshall, 1994). Dialogue in the classroom is advantageous because participants try to influence and direct the future of the events. It is transformative because students construct knowledge by themselves. It improves social relations in the classroom and raises awareness. Through dialogue, individuals can transform and shape their own destinies and remake their own world. The greatest beauty of dialogue is that it promotes self-awareness, self-reflection, and self-criticism (Fernandez-Balboa & Marshall, 1994). In all, dialogue generates reflection because when individuals engage in dialogue, they reflect, concentrate, consider alternatives, listen closely, give careful attention to definitions and meanings, recognize options, and perform serious mental activities more than they would have engaged in otherwise (Lipman et al., 1980). However, "true dialogue cannot exist unless the dialoguers engage in critical thinking" (Freire, 1998, p. 73). As LeCompte and DeMarrais (1992, p. 17) see it, the teaching of "inquiry skills can bring about individual self-awareness… or empowerment, and empowered individuals can… in turn confront oppressive social structures as catalysts for wider change" (see also DeMarrais & LeCompte, 1995). According to Hursh (1992), critical social studies can become a vehicle through which students give voice to their own realities and listen to others because it has been established that when students engage in dialogue in a classroom, they participate actively in the learning process, and a democratic process develops because dialogue is the foundation of a true democracy. Students learn from each other when they are presented with a challenging learning environment through dialogue. As a result, they learn to trust, respect, and care for each other. Fernandez-Balboa and Marshall (1994) maintain that, "Dialogue helps students and teachers relate on a more personal, trusting level and makes the classroom a more humane place in which to learn" (p. 175). Abascal-Hildebrand (1999) informs us that foundations teachers act as public intellectuals because they want their students to use their knowledge and skills to transform social relations in the classroom and to better their society (see also Giroux, 1988). Social foundations teachers encourage dialogue because they want their students to share, communicate, and transform their world. Explaining why foundations scholars teach the praxis of dialogue to their students, Abascal-Hildebrand (1999) states:

> Our interpretative capacities…serve as the means for acting as public intellectuals. Our interpretive capacities enable our understanding of the action dimensions needed for changing public institutions, so it is more possible for all in the community to participate democratically. (p. 5)

Besides, foundations scholars engage their students in active continuing discussions because language is their *house of being*. They engage their students in constant discussions even in their seeming silence because language is the only avenue for understanding their work. Foundations scholars use language because it provides them with the tools to be involved in the democratic process and public discourse (see Abascal-Hildebrand, 1999). Freire (2007, p. 40) argued that "dialogue creates a critical attitude. It is nourished by love, humility, hope, faith, and trust. When the two 'poles' of the dialogue are thus linked by love, hope, and mutual trust, they can join in a critical search for something. Only dialogue truly communicates." Language brings the past into the present, thoughts into action, and from the past and the present one can project the future. However, in their excellent introduction in *Pedagogy, Popular Culture, and Public Life*, Freire and Giroux (1989, pp. vii–xii) warn against any type of education curriculum that takes on "the easy and sometimes sloppy demands of liberal pluralism," because such a curriculum has a tendency to silence, marginalize, and exacerbate forms of cultural containment, conformity, discrimination, and socioeconomic inequality. They argue that education should engage "the power-sensitive relations that articulate between and among different groups." They go on to state that, "We should see schools as places that produce not only subjects but subjectivities," because learning is as much about the acquisition of knowledge as it is about the production of social practices that provide individuals with a sense of identity, self-worth, value, and place. What they mean here is that educators should help students to overcome their voicelessness. Giroux (1988, 1993), for example, advocates for the type of education that is capable of preparing students to be active, critical transformative intellectuals, good community members, and risk-taking citizens. He welcomes learning communities that are capable of producing, "critical citizens capable of exercising civic courage and the moral leadership necessary to promote and advance the language of democracy" (Giroux, 1993, p. 22). According to him, the type of pedagogy that is capable of producing such citizens,

> goes beyond analyzing the structuring principles that inform the form and content of the representation of politics; instead, it focuses on how students and others learn to identify, challenge, and re-write such representations. More specifically, it offers students the opportunity to engage pedagogically the means by which representational practices can be portrayed, taken up, and reworked subjectively so as to produce, reinforce, or resist certain forms of cultural representation and self-definition. (Giroux, 1993, p. 118)

Freire (1998, 2007) tells us that the only way to change the world is for reflection and action to go hand in hand. This is because for objective reality to be transformed, perception must be followed by action. Because of this, Freire and Giroux (1989) maintain that "Educational programs need to provide students with an understanding of how knowledge and power come together in various educational spheres to both enable and silence the voices of different students" (p. ix). In this regard, critical social foundations theorists call for activist vision of social justice engagement in what Giroux (1993) refers to as acts of "resistance and transformation" or representational pedagogy. Giroux (1993) informs us that the dominant culture victimizes some students, whereas representational pedagogy encourages teachers and students to negotiate relationship about teaching and learning so as to enables silenced voices to become active participants in the learning process and in everyday life (Giroux, 1993). Representational pedagogy lends itself to the demands and purposes of democracy because teachers and students engage themselves in the production of knowledge that is transformative, relevant, and emancipatory. Indeed, representational pedagogy is "informed by the principles of freedom, equality and social justice. It is expressed not in moral platitudes but in concrete struggles and practices that find expression in classroom social relations, everyday life, and memories of resistance and struggle" (Giroux, 1993, p. 13). As Kanpol (1994) noted, teachers and students should be involved in cultural politics, that is, challenging dominant oppressive values in our society.

Critical social foundations theorists argue that teachers should incorporate aspects of popular culture and activate voices of those who have been marginalized, silenced, and excluded. Teachers should emphasize cultural relevance and include perspectives from students' point of view. This means, teachers should construct knowledge in relationship to students' strengths, experiences, strategies, goals, struggles, descriptions of reality, and ability of action (see Bassey, 2016, 2020; Freire, 1993, 1998, 2007; Giroux, 1988, 1993; Kanpol, 1994; McLaren, 1994), because learning would be meaningless to students if it does not take into account their lived experiences, their stories, strengths, goals, and visions (Kierkegaard, 1944). The important point here is that educators should take seriously the strengths, experiences, and goals of their students because as Kierkegaard again pointed out: "One must know oneself before knowing anything else. It is only after a man [woman] has understood himself [herself] that life acquires peace and significance" (Kierkegaard, 1959, p. 46). Yes, Pestalozzi told us about two centuries ago that if public education does not take into account an individual's circumstances and family life together with everything else that relates to his/her general well-being, such an education will stunt the individual's intellectual growth (see Nel & Seckinger, 1993, p. 396). Pestalozzi also told us that learning should connect with prior experiences and the personal belief systems of the students. This is how Freire (1993) made a similar point, "school systems should know and value both the class and the knowledge base that students bring to it" (p. 4). The reasoning here is that if learning is not made relevant to students' real-life experiences, such learning can only lead to distortion of the students' objective reality, because as Greene (1978) informed us, "the life of reason develops against a background of perceived realities" (p. 2). Another reason why teachers should make learning relevant to the lives of their students is because learning is likely to occur when students realize that the subject is related to their own backgrounds and experiences. Dewey (1938/1998) made this point as clearly as he could when he noted in his book, *Experience and Education:* "I have taken for granted the soundness of the principle that education in order to accomplish its ends both for the individual learner and for society must be based upon experience – which is always the actual life –experience of some individual" (p. 113).

Conclusion

In this chapter, I have argued that critical social foundations of education conceptualizes the connection between social justice and education and also creates the space needed for discussing social justice, democratic citizenship, and social activism in the classrooms. It does so by "questioning and addressing gender, race, and class inequalities, challenging dominant assumptions about power, leadership, and democracy, and establishing community voice in the process of radical social transformation" (Cuban & Anderson, 2007, p. 146). Critical social foundations of education makes students aware of both institutional and structural barriers to democratic practice and explores the means through which students can negotiate, challenge, and resist dominant control by teaching them how to use school walkouts, marches, and other forms of civil disobedience to make their voices heard in society (Cammarota & Ginwright, 2007).

Another point to note is that there is an organic connection between experience and education. A student's experience derives from the interaction between the student and his or her environment. This means, students are affected in their learning by internal factors and by their environment guided by the principles of interaction and continuity. This is to say that dispositions that students developed from past experiences affect their future experiences (Carver & Enfield, 2006). Additionally, emotional well-being is important in student learning because as individuals we are affected by our environment because we are linked closely to the demands of our daily lives. Also, as members of families, peer groups, and classrooms located within the larger context of schools, neighborhoods, communities, and learners, we are influenced by culture, shared beliefs, values, and norms of our society. (Bassey, 2016, 2020; Coalition for Psychology in Schools and Education, 2015; Gay, 2010; Gehlbach, 2014; Ladson-Billings, 2009). Therefore, it is by understanding the influence of these interacting contexts on learners that teachers can enhance learning effectiveness. This means, teachers must have clear conception of how "cultural backgrounds of students and how differences in values, beliefs, language, and behavioral expectations can influence student behavior, including interpersonal dynamics" (Coalition for Psychology in Schools and Education, 2015, p. 21; see also Gay, 2010; Ladson-Billings, 2005, 2009; Nieto, 2007; Sleeter, 1991). The more teachers understand these facts, the better they will be able to facilitate effective teaching and learning interactions in their classrooms.

By integrating issues of transformative justice, how to dismantle structural racism, fight for freedom and activism into its curriculum, critical social foundations of education creates better understanding among different groups and serves as an important instrument in fighting both institutional and individual racism, thus heralding possibilities of more connected and caring communities.

NOTE

1. Dialogue here includes the virtue of speaking truth to power.

REFERENCES

Abascal-Hildebrand, M. (1999). Narrative and the public intellectual. *Educational Studies, 30*(1), 5–18.

Ahmad, I., & Szpara, M. Y. (2005). Education for democratic citizenship and peace: Proposal for a cosmopolitan model. *Educational Studies, 38*(1), 8–23.

Avinash (2014). Paulo Freire's pedagogy of the oppressed: Book summary. *The Educationist* (Book Review). July 9, 2014. https://www.theeducationist.info/pedagogy-oppressed-critique/. Accessed 25 May 2020.

Bassey, M. O. (2016). Culturally responsive teaching: Implications for social justice. *Education Sciences, 6*(35), 1–6.

Bassey, M. O. (2020). Where is social justice in culturally responsive teaching? *SCIREA Journal of Education,* 5 (3), 59–73. http://www.scirea.org/journal/Education. Accessed 15 January 21.

Bell, L. A. (1997). Theoretical foundations for social justice education. In M. Adams, L. A. Bell, & P. Griffin (Eds.), *Teaching for diversity and social justice: A sourcebook* (pp. 1–15). Routledge.

Butin, D. W. (2006). Disciplining service learning: Institutionalization and the case for community studies. *International Journal of Teaching and Learning in Higher Education, 18*(1), 57–64.

Butin, D. W. (2007). Justice-learning: Service-learning as justice-oriented education. *Equity & Excellence in Education, 40*(2), 1–7.

Cammarota, J., & Ginwright, S. (2007). Today we march, tomorrow we vote: Youth transforming despair into social justice. *The Journal of Educational Foundations, 21*(1–2), 3–8.

Carver, R. L., & Enfield, R. P. (2006). John Dewey's philosophy of education is alive and well. *Education and Culture, 22*(1), 55–67.

Coalition for Psychology in Schools and Education (2015) PRINCIPLE 13 Learning is situated within multiple social contexts.

Coalition for Psychology in Schools and Education. (2015). Top 20 principles from psychology for preK-12 teaching and learning. American Psychological Association. http://www.apa.org/ed/schools/cpse/top-twenty-principles.pdf. Accessed 22 April 2017.

Cook, M. (2003). *A brief history of the human race*. W W Norton & Co Inc.

Cuban, S., & Anderson, J. B. (2007). Where's the justice in service-learning? Institutionalizing service-learning from a social justice perspective at a Jesuit university. *Equity & Excellence in Education, 40*, 144–155.

DeMarrais, K. B., & LeCompte, M. D. (1995). *The way schools work: A sociological analysis of education*. Longman.

Dewey, J. (1916/1966). *Democracy and education*. The Free Press.

Dewey, J. (1938/1998). *Experience and education: The 60th anniversary edition*. Kappa Delta Pi.

Emenyonu, E. N. (1988). Education and the contemporary malaise in Nigeria. In C. E. Nnolim (Ed.), *The role of education in contemporary Africa* (pp. 31–40). Professors World Peace Academy.

Feller, M. & Walsh, S. (2020, June). How you can help get justice for Breonna Taylor's death. *ELLE NAACP.* https://www.elle.com/culture/career-politics/a32477844/breonna-taylor-police-shooting-kentucky/. Accessed 18 June 2020.

Fernandez-Balboa, J. M., & Marshall, J. P. (1994). Dialogical pedagogy in teacher education: Toward an education for democracy. *Journal of Teacher Education, 45*(3), 172–182.

Foucault, M. (1980). *Power/knowledge: Selected interviews and other writings, 1972–1977* (edited by Colin Gordon). Vintage Books.

Freire, P. (2007). *Education for critical consciousness*. Continuum.

Freire, P. (1998). *Pedagogy of the oppressed*. The Continuum Publishing Company.

Freire, P. (1993). *Pedagogy of the city*. Continuum Publishing Company.

Freire, P & Giroux, H. A. (1989). Pedagogy, popular culture, and public life: An introduction. In H. A. Giroux, R. I. Simon, & Contributors (Eds.), *Popular culture: Schooling and everyday life* (pp. vii–xii). Bergin & Garvey.

Gay, G. (2010). *Culturally responsive teaching: Theory, research, and practice* (2nd ed.). Teachers College Press.

Gehlbach, H (2014, 19 November). Creating birds of similar feathers: Leveraging similarities to improve teacher-student relationships and academic achievement. *SES Educational Psychology Lecture Series,* Department of Secondary Education and Youth Services, Queens College, The City University of New York.

Giroux, H. A. (2006). *America on the edge: Henry Giroux on politics, culture, and education*. Palgrave Macmillan.

Giroux, H. A. (1993). *Living dangerously: Multiculturalism and the politics of difference*. Continuum.

Giroux, H. A. (1988). *Teachers as intellectuals: Toward a critical pedagogy of learning*. Bergin & Garvey.

Goulet, D. (2007). Introduction. In P. Freire, *Education for critical consciousness* (pp. vii–xiii).

Greene, M. (1978). *Landscapes of learning*. Teachers College Press.

Hill, Evans et al. (2020). How George Floyd was killed in police custody. *New York Times*. Published May 31, Updated November 5. https://nyti.ms/2XMtUMa. Accessed 1 January 2021.

Horowitz, J. M., Brown, A., & Cox, K. (2019). *Race in America 2019*. Pew Research Center, April 9, 2019. https://www.pewresearch.org/social-trends/2019/04/09/race-in-america-2019/. Accessed 22 July 2020.

Hursh, D. (1992). Multicultural social studies: Schools as public arenas for understanding diversity. *Social Science Record, 29*(1), 31–42.

Kanpol, B. (1994). *Critical pedagogy: An introduction*. Bergin & Garvey.

Kierkegaard, S. (1944). *Concluding unscientific postscript*. Swenson, D. F. & Lowrie, W. (Ed. and Trans.). Princeton University Press.

Kierkegaard, S. (1959). *The journals of Kierkegaard*. Dru, A. (Ed. And Trans.). Harper.

Ladson-Billings, G. (2005). Differing concepts of citizenship: Schools and communities as sites of civic development. In N. Noddings (Ed.), *Educating citizens for global awareness* (pp. 69–80). Teachers College Press.

Ladson-Billings, G. (2009). *The Dreamkeepers: Successful teachers of African American children* (2nd ed.). Jossey-Bass.

LeCompte, M. D., & deMarrais, K. B. (1992). The disempowering of empowerment: Out of the revolution and into the classroom. *Educational Foundations, 6*(3), 5–31.

Lipman, M., Sharp, A. M., & Oscanyan, F. S. (1980). *Philosophy in the classroom*. Temple University Press.

Martusewicz, R. A. (2004). Editor's corner. *Educational Studies, 35*(1), 1–6.

McLaren, P. (1994). *Life in schools: An introduction to critical pedagogy in the foundations of education*. Longman Publishing Group.

Mitchell, T. D. (2007). Critical service-learning as social justice education: A case study of the citizen scholars program. *Equity & Excellence in Education, 40*(2), 101–112.

Nel, J., & Seckinger, D. S. (1993). Johann Heinrich Pestalozzi in the 1990s: Implications for today's multicultural classrooms. *The Educational Forum, 57*(4), 394–401.

Nieto, S. (2007). *Affirming diversity: The sociopolitical context of multicultural education* (5th ed.). Allyn and Bacon.

Paul, R. (1990). *Critical thinking: What every person needs to survive in a rapidly changing world*. Center for Critical Thinking and Moral Critique.

Rasheed, S. (2008). Introduction interdisciplinary approaches to educational reform within Foucaultian framework. *Educational Studies, 44*(1), 3–6.

Sleeter, C. E. (1991). Introduction: Multicultural education and empowerment. In C. E. Sleeter (Ed.), *Empowerment through multicultural education* (pp. 1–23). State University of New York Press.

Smedley, A., & Smedley, B. D. (2005). Race as biology is fiction, racism as a social problem is real. *American Psychologist, 60*(1), 16–26.

Tarca, K. (2005). Colorblind in control: The risk of resisting difference amid demographic change. *Educational Studies, 38*(2), 95–120.

Westheimer, J., & Kahne, J. (2004). What kind of citizen? The politics of educating for democracy. *American Educational Research Journal, 41*(2), 237–269.

Worland, J. (2020). The overdue awakening: Ending centuries of racism requires systemic change. *Time,* June 22–29.

CHAPTER 7

Students with Disabilities in British Columbia's (Canada) K to 12 Education System: A Critical Disability and Intersectional Perspective

Bathseba Opini

INTRODUCTION

The human rights of individuals with disabilities are protected by law in Canada and globally. The United Nations General Assembly adopted the Convention on the Rights of Persons with Disabilities (CRPD) on December 13, 2006. The CRPD seeks to promote, defend, and reinforce the rights of persons with disabilities (Inclusive Education Canada, n.d.). Canada and its provinces ratified the CRPD in 2010 as law. The Canadian Government is expected to use the CRPD framework as a guide to ensure that the needs and rights of individuals with disabilities are met. Article 24 of the CRPD bans discrimination against students with disabilities and advocates removing barriers to participation in education. These are crucial steps to realizing education access for learners with disabilities. The Canadian Human Rights Commission and Canadian Association of Statutory Human Rights Agencies (2017) observe that, "Everyone in Canada has the right to a quality education that opens doors and creates opportunities. But for many people with mental or physical disabilities, Canada's education system must seem like a closed door" (p. 1). Canadians with disabilities still experience systemic barriers to a good quality education. These barriers have negative effects on the educational outcomes, employment, careers, and overall well-being of Canadians with

B. Opini (✉)
University of British Columbia, Vancouver, BC, Canada
e-mail: bathseba.opini@ubc.ca

© The Author(s), under exclusive license to Springer Nature Switzerland AG 2022
A. A. Abdi and G. W. Misiaszek (eds.), *The Palgrave Handbook on Critical Theories of Education*, https://doi.org/10.1007/978-3-030-86343-2_7

disabilities (Canadian Human Rights Commission and Canadian Association of Statutory Human Rights Agencies, 2017).

In the Province of British Columbia (B.C.), laws including the B.C. Human Rights Code and the Canadian Charter of Rights and Freedoms (1982) protect the rights of British Columbians with disabilities. Following the passing of Bill C-81, Accessible Canada Act, in June 21, 2019, (Government of Canada, 2019), the B.C. Government introduced the Accessibility for All British Columbians framework to "reinforce and strengthen the rights of persons with disabilities" (Government of British Columbia, 2019, p. 10). The goal is to ensure full and equal participation in communities, including schools, and build an inclusive province that cares for and protects all its peoples. During the same year, the United Nations' special rapporteur on the rights of persons with disabilities gave B.C. a failing grade for its treatment of students with disabilities (United Nations Human Rights Office, 2019). The report showed that B.C. has no disability-specific legislation and therefore no alignment with the CRPD framework mandate.

Although there have been some gains for persons with disabilities in accessing education in B.C., without proper legislative protections and actions, students with disabilities remain disenfranchised. The struggle for adequate funding, with insufficient teacher and staff training, scarcity of educational assistants, and lack of continuity, contributes to limited access to education, academic underachievement, and limited quality-of-life options for the students. This chapter uses a critical intersectionality approach to highlight the situation of students with disability in K-to-12 schools in British Columbia. Drawing on the province's special needs education policy, available literature, and media information, the chapter shows that learners with disabilities and their families continue to struggle to access education. An intersectional approach to addressing the needs of students with disabilities and their families is critical at all levels in order to realize equity in education. Taking a critical approach allows for highlighting the gaps inherent in the education system as well as suggesting ways of improving access to education and services for students with disabilities and their families.

Intersectionality Framing

Intersectionality, which connects to Black feminist theory and critical race theory, is critical to understanding the complexity of people's identities and experiences of marginalization (Collins, 2003; Crenshaw, 1991). Although attributed to Kimberlé Crenshaw in 1989, earlier works by Black feminists including Sojourner Truth's famous "Ain't I a Woman?" speech delivered to the 1851 Women's Convention in Akron, Ohio (cited by Smith, 2013, p. 3) took an intersectional lens to analyze oppression. Other works by scholars including Patricia Hill Collins; Joyce King; Audre Lorde; Cherríe Moraga; and Gloria Anzaldúa helped advance discussions on intersectionality.

Crenshaw (1989) opined that intersectionality accentuates the multidimensionality of Black women's experiences and how they are shaped by different systems of oppression. "Intersectionality allows for a complex understanding of the ways in which race, gender, class, sexuality, and ability among other dimensions of social, cultural, political, and economic processes intersect to shape everyday experiences and social institutions" (Naples et al., 2019, p. 5; See also Collins, 2000, 2003). Smith (2013) remarked that "... the concept of intersectionality is not an abstract notion but a description of the way multiple oppressions are experienced" (p.1). Therefore, intersectionality attends to multiple identity categories which have meaning, social gravity, and consequences (Artiles, 2013).

The framework has been critiqued as narrowly focusing on issues of identity (Tefera, Powers & Fischman, 2018), using Black women as prototypical intersectional subjects, its ambiguity in terms of its United States-centricity, and definition and coherence with people's experiences with multiple identities (Nash, 2008). It might also be seen as having limited relevance for understanding the perspectives of other groups (Tefera et al., 2018). However, and as Tefera et al. (2018) argued:

> ...this criticism tends to misinterpret the role of identity in intersectional analyses. An intersectional approach is fundamentally oriented toward analyzing the relationships of power and inequality within a social setting and how these shape individual and group identities. That is, our identities are shaped by our experiences in social groups and how we as members of those groups encounter institutionalized social structures ... The fact that intersectional analysis was originally rooted in studies focused on the multiple forms of marginalization that Black women face should not be understood as a limitation. Rather, intersectionality provides a framework to deliberately account for and examine the different ways that intersecting social dynamics affect people within and across groups. (pp. viii–ix; see also Erevelles & Minear, 2010)

Intersectionality framing is applied in research in education, humanities, social sciences, and health sciences to examine power dynamics and people's experiences with intersecting and overlapping systemic and structural forms of oppression and marginalization. In the field of critical disability studies, the framework allows for examining among other questions, able-bodied privileges; manifestations of ableism in the education system; intersections in categories of difference including race, disability, social class, gender, and sexuality; as well as gaining insights about racial inequities in special education (Artiles, 2013, p. 333).

Erevelles and Minear (2010) observed that intersectionality is the "most appropriate analytical intervention expected to accomplish the formidable task of mediating multiple differences" (p. 130). It can be used "to do justice in cases of disadvantage at the intersections of gender, 'race' and disability" (Schiek & Lawson, 2011, p. 2). My use of intersectionality in this chapter heeds Tefera et al.'s (2018) call to trouble "one-dimensional or single-axis analyses that focus on a specific category (e.g., race, class, gender, or ability) or that treat other categories as epiphenomenal more often" (p. viii). It is also to account for "ways race/ethnicity, class, gender, sexuality, religion, citizenship, ability, and age, among other things, shape the structural dynamics of power and inequality in social spaces and individual identities ... [along with] strengthening the synergy between critical inquiry and praxis" (p. viii). Intersectionality analyzes disability as a "socially constructed category that derives meaning and social (in)significance from the historical, cultural, political, and economic structures that frame social life" (Erevelles & Minear, 2010, pp. 131–132). This requires considering interactions between multiple factors and ways in which they connect to restrict access to education, leading to marginalization of students with disabilities in the education system.

Laws and Policies Informing Education of K-to-12 Students with Disabilities in B.C.

This short chapter cannot address all of the laws and policies, which inform the education of learners with disability in B.C., and how they translate into practice, or their implications for learners with disabilities in B.C.'s K-to-12 education system. I will only share a snapshot of the situation of learners with disabilities in B.C.'s K-to-12 education system. The discussion draws inferences from the B.C. School Act, B.C. special needs education policy, available literature, and selected online news reports about special needs education and services in B.C.

B.C. School Act

Neither Canada nor British Columbia has legislation that governs the provision of educational programs for children and youths with disabilities as the United States does with the Individuals with Disabilities Education Act (IDEA). Education in B.C. is governed by the B.C. School Act, which is a provincial statute guiding K-to-12 education. This Act specifies the rights, responsibilities, and duties of parents, students, school personnel, school trustees, Ministry of Education, and the boards of education in providing education (Government of British Columbia, 2021). Section 167 (1) of the Act stipulates that "There must continue to be a ministry of the public service of British Columbia called the Ministry of Education over which the minister must continue to preside and have direction" (Government of British Columbia, 2021). Under Sect. 168 (2 a) the Minister for Education may make orders governing the provision of educational programs for the purpose of carrying out any of the minister's powers, duties, or functions under the School Act. Consequently, the Minister for Education Order relating to students with disabilities—that is, the Special Needs Students Order—defines a student with special needs as a student who has a disability of an intellectual, physical, sensory, emotional, or behavioral nature, has a learning disability or has exceptional gifts or talents (B.C. Ministry of Education, 2021). The order stipulates that:

(1) A board must ensure that a principal, vice principal, or director of instruction offers to consult with a parent of a student with special needs regarding the placement of that student in an educational program.

(2) A board must provide a student with special needs with an educational program in a classroom where that student is integrated with other students who do not have special needs, unless the educational needs of the student with special needs or other students indicate that the educational program for the student with special needs should be provided otherwise.

While important, these stipulations are not specific enough to hold school districts and schools accountable enough in providing education and preparing learners with disabilities to transition to the workplace and independent living. There is no information on how the Ministry assesses or holds school districts accountable when it comes to providing services for students with disabilities.

B.C. Ministry of Education Special Needs Education Policy

The B.C. Ministry of Education special needs education policy is outlined in the Ministry's special education services manual, which was originally developed in 1995 and was revised in 2016. It describes the policies, procedures, and guidelines that support the delivery of special education services in British Columbia's public schools. This document defines special educational needs as:

> ...those characteristics which make it necessary to provide a student undertaking an educational program with resources different from those which are needed by most students. Special educational needs are identified during assessment of a student; they are the basis for determining an appropriate educational program (including necessary resources) for that student. (B.C. Ministry of Education, 2016, p. vi)

The special education services manual serves as a reference regarding legislation, ministry policy, and guidelines to assist school boards in developing programs and services that enable students with special needs to meet the goals of education. Under the B.C. special education policy, "all students should have equitable access to learning, opportunities for achievement, and the pursuit of excellence in all aspects of their educational programs" (B.C. Ministry of Education, 2016, p. 1). The policy enables "students with special needs to have equitable access to learning and opportunities to pursue and achieve the goals of their educational programs" (B.C. Ministry of Education, 2016, p. 1). The manual also summarizes the roles and responsibilities of the Ministry of Education, school districts, schools, parents, and students in the provision of special education services. It discusses the process of developing an Individual Education Plan; different services, which are key to special education including learning assistance programs, counseling services, school psychology programs, speech and language pathology services, physical and occupational therapy services, hospital services, home-based education services, distributed learning services; and the process of funding special education services. The manual outlines the various categories of special needs and the provincial resources program aimed at assisting "districts to meet the educational needs of students in exceptional circumstances". (B.C. Ministry of Education, 2016, p. 91)

In defining inclusion, the policy states:

> British Columbia promotes an inclusive education system in which students with special needs are fully participating members of a community of learners. Inclusion describes the principle that all students are entitled to equitable access to learning, achievement and the pursuit of excellence in all aspects of their educational programs. The practice of inclusion is not necessarily synonymous with full integration in regular classrooms, and goes beyond placement to include meaningful participation and the promotion of interaction with others. (B.C. Ministry of Education, 2016, p. 2)

It remains unclear at times how the ministry's perspectives on inclusion are put into practice. Most of the policy seems to lean toward a medically informed special education model in addressing the needs of learners with disability. Practicing inclusion as a human right pays attention to the United Nations (UN) Convention on the Rights of Persons with Disabilities (CRPD). This calls on state parties to ensure that:

> (i) Persons with disabilities are not excluded from the general education system on the basis of disability, and that children with disabilities are not excluded from free and compulsory primary education, or from secondary education, on the basis of disability.
>
> (ii) Persons with disabilities can access an inclusive, quality, and free primary education and secondary education on an equal basis with others in the communities in which they live.
>
> (iii) Reasonable accommodation of the individual's requirements is provided.
>
> (iv) Persons with disabilities receive the support required, within the general education system, to facilitate their effective education.
>
> (v) Effective individualized support measures are provided in environments that maximize academic and social development, consistent with the goal of full inclusion (UN, 2006).

In the following section, I propose that B.C. special needs policy adopt an intersectional approach to disability.

The Need to Adopt an Intersectional Lens in B.C. Special Needs Education Policy.

Without a doubt, the B.C. School Act and the Ministry of Education special needs education policy recognize the importance of educational services and the significance of education access and participation for students with disabilities. Historically, though, special education and the B.C. special needs education manual have drawn mostly on the medical model of disability. The medical model takes a deficit approach to disability and focuses on impairment as something that needs rehabilitation or treatment, curing and fixing through medical intervention (Degener, 2014; Oliver, 1990). There have been increasing calls for special education to look at the social and human rights models of disability to inform and enrich the field (Baglieri et al., 2011; Connor, 2013).

The social model of disability problematizes disability oppression by drawing attention to the environment as opposed to a person's impairment (Rehabilitation International, 2006). The social model of disability stresses the fact that persons with disabilities are prevented from reaching their full potential as a result of legal, attitudinal, architectural, communications, and other discriminatory barriers which are pervasive in society (Rehabilitation International, 2006). As such, a critical intersectional analysis that pays attention to the intersecting and multiple assumptions and barriers that hinder the rights of persons with disabilities is necessary.

The human rights model recognizes that disability is a natural part of human diversity that must be respected and supported (Disability Advocacy Resource Unit, 2021). Degener (2014) asserts that the model encompasses human rights, civil and political as well as economic, social, and cultural rights. It strives to advance human rights capacity, values impairment as part of human diversity, and acknowledges identity issues. It allows for assessment of prevention policy, when such a policy entails protection of human rights for people with disabilities. The model therefore endeavors to promote equity and social justice. It emphasizes that people with disability have the same rights as everyone else. Impairment must not be used as an excuse to deny or restrict the rights of people with disabilities (Disability Advocacy Resource Unit, 2021).

By drawing on the social and human rights models, special education policy in B.C. and the Ministry of Education would allow for an advanced analysis, recognition, and understanding that learners with disability are rights-holders who can and should determine the course of their lives (Rehabilitation International, 2006). It will also draw needed attention to identifying and addressing limitations imposed by economic, political, legal, architectural, social, and physical structures and environment as infringements on the right of individuals with disability (Rehabilitation International, 2006).

In addition to the B.C. Ministry of Education's special needs policy taking a more expanded, holistic approach to understanding disability, we cannot negate the reality that students with disabilities have other identity markers that reinforce their marginalization and oppression further, including race, class, gender, sexuality, (dis)ability, language abilities, and national origin (see Bešić, 2020). These identity markers are important when discussing special needs education and inclusive education. The one moment the special needs education manual alludes to these intersecting identities is when referencing students with different cultural or linguistic backgrounds (B.C. Ministry of Education, 2016, p. 21). The manual indicates that:

> ... learning another language and new cultural norms, adjusting to a different social and physical setting, or overcoming homesickness or trauma can affect a student's school adjustment and learning. These factors, when combined with a disability or impairment, can significantly undermine school achievement. Assessing and planning for students with special needs becomes more complex when language, cultural or migration factors are involved. Except for cases of obvious disability (e.g., profound intellectual disability, physical or sensory disability), teachers should fully consider cultural, linguistic and/or experiential factors that can affect learning before assuming the presence of a disability or impairment. ... (B.C. Ministry of Education, 2016, p. 21)

These remarks show that different micro and macro forces influence the educational experiences of learners with special needs. Addressing these needs necessitates taking an intersectional lens to understand the experiences, which students bring to class and the context in which they are operating. As such, intersectionality should be the rule not the exception in disability legislation in British Columbia.

I agree with Grant and Zwier (2011) who emphasize employing an intersectional lens for analyzing how the links between disability, race, class, gender migrant background, sexuality, and sexual orientation, shape disabled students' lives as well as those of their families; and the ways in which these connections influence how educational institutions respond to them. For example, wealthy parents of children with disabilities are likely to receive different responses from the school system than poor or racialized parents/families of children who have disabilities. It is not uncommon to hear and read about Indigenous, Black, and other racialized families reporting about experiences of biased and racist interactions with the school system in addition to feeling unwelcome or not being listened to at school. Codjoe (2001) showed that Black students and parents see the school environment as a barrier for Black students' academic success (see also Dei, 2008; Opini, 2019).

Lott (2001) found that teachers' and administrators' beliefs about low-income and working-class parents translated into negative, discouraging, and exclusionary behaviors. These parents received less warm welcome in the schools, their suggestions were less respected and responded to and, as result, were less able to influence their children's education. So, while the B.C. School Act asserts that school leaders must consult with a parent of a student with special needs regarding the placement of that student in an educational program, low-income, working-class parents of children with disabilities would likely be listened to less. Consequently, they will be less able to influence their children's education than wealthier parents of children with disabilities would. There is no accountability for this. When policies and legislation are presented as neutral, there is a failure to recognize how historical and contemporary power and structural hierarchies function in society. Therefore, a few benefit in the path to education access and eventual academic success (see Artiles, 2011). Bešić (2020) states that we ought to recognize that policies are "also tied to the social, financial and cultural capital of particular groups"(p. 119), and these connections have implications for education outcomes that cannot be understated when considering services for students with disabilities. Disability and special needs education services in the B.C. education system ought to be understood in terms of its co-construction with other identities (Hernández-Saca et al., 2018).

Challenges Facing Students with Disabilities and Their Families

Here, I would like to discuss the year 2020 given its unique challenges and particularly the COVID-19 pandemic. COVID-19 exposed the pervasiveness of ableism, racism, classism, and other forms of oppression and the implications for the education system. I looked at the experiences of children and families with disabilities in B.C. schools as were reported in 10 online articles by the Vancouver Sun (5 articles) and CBC News (5 articles). Although CBC is considered a liberal platform and Vancouver Sun conservative, reports on both news outlets discussed very similar challenges.

A common theme which was evident in these news reports was the challenges that students with disabilities and their families experienced. A closer analysis of the reports reveals the effects of interconnections between disability and low income on educational services and learning supports for students with disabilities. The challenges experienced were exacerbated by the COVID-19 pandemic as shown in the news reports and included funding limitations, lack of sensitivity in planning for service continuity, failure of school districts to plan, and communicate with families about services for children with disabilities, continued systemic ableism, and lack of accountability on the part of government and school districts.

In April 2020, *CBC News* journalist Bridgette Watson reported that families of children with complex care and educational needs continued to struggle during the COVID-19 pandemic because of funding problems. Although children over 6 years old in B.C. are allotted $6,000 annually for supports like speech therapy, respite workers, and behavioral interventionists, the families are required to spend that money, within the year in which it is allocated, for particular kinds of services which were specified in the funding. Otherwise, they would lose the funds (Crawford, 2020; Watson, 2020). Many of these services were suspended following the March 2020 COVID-19 lockdown, so some parents were concerned about losing their funding. They were advised by the Ministry to find online solutions to help their kids (Watson, 2020). Little attention was paid to meaningful inclusive instructional planning that pays attention to Universal Design for Learning principles [i.e., multiple means of representation, multiple means of action and expression, and multiple means of engagement; Universal Design for Learning in B.C. (2010)]. These gaps necessitate a rethinking of learning accommodations, adaptations, and modifications as a human right. Most importantly, they are not just symbols for institutions to tolerate disability but rather to be accepting of disability as part of everyday living and the human experience. Moreover, government and school leaders forgot that online services and learning could worsen some students' experiences. For example, as Watson (2020) observed, online learning is not a sustainable solution for children on the autism spectrum due to social and emotional regulation. Specificity and inflexibility on the use of funding are a challenge for families (see also Browne, 2020a, 2020b).

At the beginning of the pandemic, government announcements for funding relief and support were generalized. Later, following activism and advocacy from disability organizations and groups, the federal and provincial governments started providing funds for individuals with disabilities. For instance, the B.C. Government provided $225 per month as short-term emergency relief support funds to assist children and youth with special needs and their families to access critical support during COVID from April through September 2020. Randy Shore from the *Vancouver Sun* reported that this amount was not enough to meet the needs of children with disabilities, and some families had challenges accessing the funds. In responding to the amounts, Autism Community Training (2020) noted:

> … $225 cannot address the needs of isolated, impoverished families supporting very challenging children who are now dependent on their parents 24/7, without access to school, childcare workers, respite or interventionists. This amount has not increased for the last 20 years even though the cost of living in the Greater Vancouver Area in B.C. is the highest in British Columbia and one of the highest in the world. (https://www.actcommunity.ca/why-is-the-res ponse-of-the-B.C.-government-to-children-with-special-needs-so-weak)

While school districts tried to ensure that students continued learning at home through platforms like Google Classroom, Zoom, and Microsoft Teams, most of these were designed for able-bodied students. As such, specialized support for students with disabilities was limited. Cathy Browne from *CBC News* and Glenda Luymes from the *Vancouver Sun* explained that the emotional toll on parents and children was huge (Browne, 2020a, 2020b; Luymes, 2020a, 2020b). Some parents and guardians of children with disabilities experienced enormous fatigue and considered giving up their children to the state/government because of lack of support and services (Browne, 2020a, 2020b). These government organizations are provided money to do what families do (Browne, 2020a, 2020b), so we must ask why that money cannot be given to the families.

The return to school plans for September 2020 also proved challenging. The Ministry of Education indicated that school districts were best placed to share their return-to-school plans concerning the needs of students with disabilities. Winston Szeto, *CBC News,* and Joanne Lee-Young, *Vancouver Sun,* indicated that teachers and disability advocates called on rethinking school cohort models to avoid reinforcing exclusion of students with disabilities from full-time, in-school learning with little success (Lee-Young, 2020; Szeto, 2020). Recommendations like wearing masks were also problematic since some children with disabilities may not be able to do it properly. (Lee-Young, 2020; Szeto, 2020). While the return-to-school plans were under way, school districts failed to communicate effectively about support for special needs students (Luymes, 2020a, 2020b; Szeto, 2020). Some families pointed to gaps in accountability for their children's education and to the fact that students with disabilities were an afterthought in these plans (Autism Community Training, 2020; Browne, 2020a, 2020b; Luymes, 2020a, 2020b). This characterized the provision of education for students with disabilities even before the pandemic (Autism Community Training, 2020; BCED Access, 2020; Luymes, 2020a, 2020b). Families asked the provincial government and school districts to consider planning for smaller class sizes instead of more remote and hybrid learning to better address the learning needs of children with disabilities (Browne, 2020a, 2020b), but with little success. Many ended up signing their children for transitional learning as a wait-and-see approach because they were not clear about what to expect in schools (Luymes, 2020a, 2020b).

In April 2020, Autism Community Training (2020) noted that the B.C. provincial government failed to keep and provide accurate data on how the needs of learners with disabilities were being met during in-person learning in public schools in comparison with independent (private and faith-based) schools in B.C. No doubt this erodes the families' confidence in the ability of the public schools system to serve the needs of the most vulnerable in the province. There are consequences for school choice, including public school student enrollment, and the B.C. Government needs to pay serious attention; otherwise, public education is undermined. The back-and-forth blaming game between school districts and the Ministry of Education is harming the lives and educational experiences of children with disabilities and their families.

Noticeable in the online news reports was only a single intersectional analysis of the challenges, which the students and their families were facing, and that was by Randy Shore from the *Vancouver Sun* in December 2020. While the government and school districts have taken a one-size-fits-all approach to addressing the needs of students with disabilities in B.C. (Luymes, 2020a, 2020b), this does not work for all families. Some are falling through the cracks. Even before the pandemic, families of children with disabilities and who also are Indigenous, Black, racialized, new immigrants and refugees, low-income earners, and single-parent families experienced disproportionate effects and barriers accessing resources to support their children (see Charlesworth, 2020; Shore, 2020). The same is true of the rural–urban divide when accessing special needs education services. Many of these families are struggling and the intersection between disability and other characteristics are real and with quality-of-life implications that must be addressed to promote and support equitable educational access for all learners in B.C.

Conclusion

Using a critical disability and intersectional analysis, this chapter has shown that students with disabilities in B.C. and their families experience oppression and ableism in education. These experiences cannot be detached from the students' geographical and social locations, race, gender, class, sexuality, religion, and other differences. Special needs education policies in B.C. must factor in an understanding of disability through an intersectional lens. Planning for policy and services for students with disabilities needs in B.C. should acknowledge and consider supports that are responsive to the different ways that students with disabilities experience, access, and participate in education. Since the province of B.C. continues to face significant inequity challenges (such as housing, child poverty, and racial inequities), disability cannot be examined without paying attention to these multiple realities and their impact on schooling. Educational transformations aimed at addressing challenges for students with disabilities in B.C. and across Canada cannot happen meaningfully without examining the intersecting ways ableist privilege happens and is supported by societal structures and systems.

With these marginalizing realities, educators and leaders in schools and school districts should examine their understanding and enactment of inclusive education using an intersectional approach to disrupt the normative practices and perceptions about disability. COVID-19 has exposed more the "exclusionary inclusive educational practices" common in schools and driving government planning and funding models. The recent reports referenced above paint a picture of current practices reinforcing inequities and rendering students with disabilities and special needs education as an afterthought in educational policies and eventual service planning and provisions.

References

Artiles, A. J. (2011). Toward an interdisciplinary understanding of educational equity and difference: The case of the racialization of ability. *Educational Researcher, 40*, 431–445.

Artiles, A. J. (2013). Untangling the racialization of disabilities: An intersectionality critique across disability models1. *Du Bois Review: Social Science Research on Race, 10*(2), 329–347.

Autism Community Training (2020, April 27). Why is the response of the BC Government to children with special needs so weak? Retrieved January 22, 2021, from https://www.actcommunity.ca/why-is-the-response-of-the-bc-government-to-children-with-special-needs-so-weak

Baglieri, S., Valle, J. W., Connor, D. J., & Gallagher, D. J. (2011). Disability studies in education: The need for a plurality of perspectives on disability. *Remedial and Special Education, 32*(4), 267–278.

BCED Access. (2020). 2019/20 Exclusion Tracker Final Report: July 22, 2020. Retrieved January 22, 2021, from https://bcedaccess.com/wp-content/uploads/2020/07/Exclusion-Tracker-Report-July-22-2020.pdf

Bešić, E. (2020). Intersectionality: A pathway towards inclusive education?. *Prospects, 49*(3), 111–122. https://doi.org/10.1007/s11125-020-09461-6.pdf

British Columbia Ministry of Education. (2016). *Special education services: A manual of policies, procedures and guidelines* Retrieved January 22, 2021, fromhttps://www2.gov.B.C.ca/assets/gov/education/administration/kindergarten-to-grade-12/inclusive/special_ed_policy_manual.pdf

British Columbia Ministry of Education. (2021). *School Act Ministerial Orders*. Retrieved January 22, 2021, from https://www2.gov.bc.ca/gov/content/education-training/k-12/administration/legislation-policy/manual-of-school-law/school-act-ministerial-orders

Browne, C. (2020a, June 28). Desperate families of kids with complex needs consider surrendering their children to the province. *CBC News*. Retrieved January 22, 2021, from https://www.cbc.ca/news/canada/british-columbia/complex-care-ministry-of-children-family-development-1.5627552

Browne, C. (2020b, September 21). Parents of children with complex needs feel abandoned as B.C. students return to school. CBC News. Retrieved January 22, 2021, from https://www.cbc.ca/news/canada/british-columbia/parents-of-children-complex-needs-feel-abandoned-1.5733489

Canadian Human Rights Commission and Canadian Association of Statutory Human Rights Agencies. (2017). *Left Out: Challenges faced by persons with disabilities in Canada's schools*. Retrieved January 22, 2021, from https://www.chrc-ccdp.gc.ca/eng/content/left-out-challenges-faced-persons-disabilities-canadas-schools

Charlesworth, J. (2020, December). *Left out: Children and youth with special needs in the pandemic. Representative for children and youth*. Retrieved January 22, 2021, from https://rcybc.ca/wp-content/uploads/2020/12/CYSN_Report.pdf

Codjoe, H. M. (2001). Fighting a public enemy of Black academic achievement: The persistence of racism and the schooling experiences of Black students in Canada. *Race Ethnicity and Education, 4*(4), 343–375.

Collins, P. H. (2000). *Black feminist thought: Knowledge, consciousness, and the politics of empowerment* (2nd ed.). Routledge.

Collins, P. H. (2003). Some group matters: Intersectionality, situated standpoints, and Black feminist thought'. In T. L. Lott & J. P. Pittman (Eds.), *A companion to African-American philosophy* (pp. 205–229). Blackwell.

Connor, D. J. (2013). Who "owns" dis/ability? The work of critical special educators as insider outsiders. *Theory and Research in Social Education, 41*(4), 494–513.

Crawford, T. (2020, April 9). COVID-19: Relief fund set up for B.C. children with special needs. *Vancouver Sun*. Retrieved January 22, 2021, from https://vancouversun.com/news/covid-19-relief-fund-set-up-for-b-c-children-with-special-needs

Crenshaw, K. (1989). Demarginalizing the intersection of race and sex: A Black feminist critique of antidiscrimination doctrine, feminist theory and antiracist politics. *University of Chicago Legal Forum, 1989*, 139–167.

Crenshaw, K. (1991). Mapping the margins: Intersectionality, identity politics, and violence against women of color. *Stanford Law Review, 43*(6), 1241–1299.

Degener, T. (2014). A human rights model for disability. In P. Blanck & E. Flynn (Eds.), *Routledge handbook of disability law and human rights* (pp. 31–50). Routledge.

Dei, S. G. J. (2008). Schooling as community: Race, schooling, and the education of African youth. *Journal of Black Studies, 38*(3), 346–366.

Disability Advocacy Resource Unit. (2021, March 16). *How does the human rights model differ from the social model?* Retrieved March 3, 2021, from https://www.daru.org.au/lesson/how-does-the-human-rights-model-differ-from-the-social-model

Erevelles, N., & Minear, A. (2010). Unspeakable offenses: Untangling race and disability in discourses of intersectionality. *Journal of Literary & Cultural Disability Studies, 4*(2), 127–146.

Government of British Columbia. (2019). British Columbia framework for accessibility legislation. Retrieved March 3, 2021, from https://www2.gov.bc.ca/assets/gov/government/about-the-bc-government/accessible-bc/disability-consultation/2019-consultation/framework-for-accessibility-legislation.pdf#:~:text=Accessibility%20for%20all%20British%20Columbians,that%20are%20available%20to%20all

Government of British Columbia. (2021, January 20). *School Act: Revised statues of British Columbia, 1996*. Retrieved March 3, 2021, from https://www2.gov.bc.ca/assets/gov/education/administration/legislation-policy/legislation/schoollaw/revisedstatutescontents.pdf

Grant, C. A., & Zwier, E. (2011). Intersectionality and student outcomes: Sharpening the struggle against racism, sexism, classism, ableism, heterosexism, nationalism, and linguistic, religious, and geographical discrimination in teaching and learning. *Multicultural Perspectives, 13*(4), 181–188.

Hernández-Saca, D. I., Gutmann Kahn, L., & Cannon, M. A. (2018). Intersectionality dis/ability research: How dis/ability research in education engages intersectionality to uncover the multidimensional construction of dis/abled experiences. *Review of Research in Education, 42*(1), 286–311.

Inclusive Education Canada. (n.d.). *Right to education*. https://inclusiveeducation.ca/learn/right-to-education/

Lee-Young (2020, July 31). Parents and educators ask how B.C.'s learning groups will manage education assistants. Vancouver Sun. Retrieved March 3, 2021, from https://vancouversun.com/news/local-news/parents-and-educators-ask-how-b-c-s-learning-groups-will-manage-education-assistants

Lott, B. (2001). Low-income parents and the public schools. *Journal of Social Issues, 57*(2), 247–259.

Luymes, G. (2020a, August 21). Parents of child with autism in 'agony' over back-to-school plan. *Vancouver Sun* Retrieved March 3, 2021, from https://vancouversun.com/news/parents-of-child-with-autism-in-agony-over-back-to-school-plan

Luymes, G. (2020b, September 4). 'This isn't The Hunger Games': B.C. parents of autistic kids say back-to-school concerns not addressed. *Vancouver Sun*. Retrieved March 3, 2021, from https://vancouversun.com/news/local-news/this-isntthe-hunger-games-b-c-parents-of-autistic-kids-say-back-to-school-concerns-not-add ressed

Naples, N. A., Mauldin, L., & Dillaway, H. (2019). From the guest editors: Gender, disability, and intersectionality. *Gender & Society, 33*(1), 5–18.

Nash, J. C. (2008). Re-thinking intersectionality. *Feminist Review, 89*(1), 1–15.

Oliver, M. (1990). *The politics of disablement*. MacMillan.

Opini, B. (2019). Inclusive education as exclusive practice: One parent's experience advocating for children with Fetal Alcohol Spectrum Disorders within the school system. *Exceptionality Education International, 29*(2), 72–90.

Rehabilitation International (2006). *UN Convention on the human rights of people with disabilities: Ad hoc committee seventh session – Daily summaries*. Retrieved March 3, 2021, from https://www.un.org/esa/socdev/enable/rights/ahc7summary.htm

Schiek, D., & Lawson, A. (2011). *European Union non-discrimination law and intersectionality: Investigating the Triangle of racial, gender and disability discrimination*. Ashgate.

Shore, R. (2020, December 4). COVID-19: Pandemic has hit special needs kids hard, advocate's report says. *Vancouver Sun*. Retrieved March 3, 2021, from https://vancouversun.com/news/covid-19-pandemic-has-hit-special-needs-kids-hard-advocates-report-says

Smith, S. (2013). Black feminism and intersectionality. *International Socialist Review, 91*(11), 1–16.

Szeto, W. (2020, August 5). Concern that cohort system in B.C. schools will neglect special needs students, substitute teachers. *CBC News*. Retrieved March 3, 2021, from https://www.cbc.ca/news/canada/british-columbia/disabilities-advocate-substitute-teachers-cohort-1.5674500

Tefera, A. A., Powers, J. M., & Fischman, G. E. (2018). Intersectionality in education: A conceptual aspiration and research imperative. *Review of Research in Education, 42*(1), vii–xvii. https://doi.org/10.3102/0091732X18768504

United Nations Human Rights Office. (2019, April 2012). *End of Mission Statement by the United Nations Special Rapporteur on the rights of persons with disabilities, Ms. Catalina Devandas-Aguilar, on her visit to Canada*. Retrieved March 3, 2021, from https://www.ohchr.org/en/NewsEvents/Pages/DisplayNews.aspx?NewsID=24481&LangID=E

Universal Design for Learning in B.C. (2010). Retrieved March 3, 2021, from https://www.setbc.org/Download/LearningCentre/Access/bcudl_review6_small.pdf

Watson, B. (2020, April, 3). B.C. mothers of children with autism plead for more government help during COVID-19 pandemic. *CBC News*. Retrieved March 3, 2021, from https://www.cbc.ca/news/canada/british-columbia/special-needs-children-covid19-1.5520971

PART III

Critical International/Global Citizenship Education

CHAPTER 8

Contesting Canadian Exceptionalism in the Internationalization of Higher Education: A Critical Perspective

Shibao Guo and Yan Guo

Fueled by globalization, the internationalization of higher education in Canada is happening at a rapid pace. One manifestation of such development is the increasing enrollment of international students. As its marketing strategy to attract top international students, Canada adopts a discourse of Canadian exceptionalism to promote itself as an immigrant country and a land of opportunities with a vast territory and rich resources. More specifically, EduCanada (2021) identifies a list of reasons for international students to study in Canada, including outstanding quality of education, high standard of living, safety, clean environment, wide-open spaces, low tuition fees, and affordable living expenses. Canadian exceptionalism is also evident in its rhetoric about Canada's multiculturalism policies which present the country as an open and culturally diverse nation. Canadian exceptionalism as a social imaginary also constructs Canada different from its southern neighbor as a peaceful and tolerant country without racism.

In this chapter, we contest the discourse of Canadian exceptionalism as a myth in contrast to the actual policies and practices of the internationalization of Canadian higher education. In particular, we focus on the perspectives and lived experiences of international students as they adapt to a

S. Guo (✉) · Y. Guo
University of Calgary, Calgary, AB, Canada
e-mail: guos@ucalgary.ca

Y. Guo
e-mail: yanguo@ucalgary.ca

© The Author(s), under exclusive license to Springer Nature Switzerland AG 2022
A. A. Abdi and G. W. Misiaszek (eds.), *The Palgrave Handbook on Critical Theories of Education*, https://doi.org/10.1007/978-3-030-86343-2_8

new educational system in Canada. To be more specific, we analyze how internationalization policies at a university in Western Canada were interpreted and experienced by international students. Based on policy analysis and interviews with international students, our findings reveal that international students have multiple understandings of internationalization and view internationalization as a positive experience for academic and personal growth. Findings also indicated several persistent problems, including a neoliberal approach that treats internationalization as revenue generating and branding strategy, limited internationalization of the curriculum, difficulty in making friends with local students, and racial discrimination. The findings have important implications, not only for Canada but also to countries which share similar contexts and challenges, for providing appropriate levels of support for international students and building an internationally inclusive campus, where cross-cultural learning is encouraged and global citizenship are nurtured.

Rationales of Internationalization

As a contested term, internationalization can mean many different things to different people. For some people, it means a series of international activities (e.g., academic mobility of students and faculty), international linkages and partnerships, and new international academic programs and research initiatives, while for others it means the delivery of education to other countries through satellite programs (Guo & Chase, 2011; Knight, 2004). De Wit et al. (2015) define internationalization as "the intentional process of integrating an international, intercultural or global dimension into the purpose, functions and delivery of post-secondary education, in order to enhance the quality of education and research for all students and staff, and to make a meaningful contribution to society" (p. 29). This definition places a focus on intentionality and broadens internationalization from mobility to include curriculum and learning outcomes. Another term that is often used interchangeably with internationalization is globalization. There is a general consensus among scholars that internationalization is not globalization. They are seen as related, but at the same time very different processes. According to Knight (2003), "internationalization is changing the world of education and globalization is changing the world of internationalization" (p. 3).

Having defined the term, it is necessary to understand the rationales of internationalization. De Wit et al. (2015) named four key rationales for internationalization: political, economic, sociocultural, and academic. In the twentieth century, and in particular after the Second World War, there was an increased focus on international cooperation and exchange in higher education. Although peace and mutual understanding were the declared driving rationales, "national security and foreign policy were the real reasons" behind the expansion of internationalization (de Wit & Merkx, 2012, p. 49). From the second half of the 1990s onwards, the principle driving force for internationalization has shifted from political to economic. International students and international activities were used by many institutions in Australia, the United Kingdom, and the United States as revenue generation (Kelly, 2000; Teichler, 2010). In addition to international student recruitment, preparing graduates for the global competitive labor market and attracting top talent for the knowledge economy have become important pillars of the internationalization of higher education over the past decade (de Wit et al., 2015). Socioculturally, internationalization was based on the hope that international mobility could enhance mutual understanding (Khoo, 2011). Academically, internationalization was perceived as a means to improve "the quality of teaching and learning and prepare students to live and work in a globalized world" (de Wit et al., 2015, p. 28). It has been promoted as a way to achieve international academic standards for branding purposes and foster international collaboration in research and knowledge production.

Unlike European priorities that were driven by economic and political considerations (Elliott, 1998), the rationales for the internationalization of Canadian higher education focused on sociocultural and academic aspects: preparing graduates who are internationally knowledgeable and interculturally competent global citizens and enhancing scholarship for interdependence between Canadian and international students in addition to generating income for universities (Knight, 2000). Knight also found the three rationales for having international students at Canadian institutions were to "integrate domestic and international students in and out of the classroom, to increase the institutions' profiles and contacts in target countries, and third, to generate revenue for the institution" (Knight, 2000, p. 53).

INTERNATIONALIZATION OF THE CURRICULUM

Internationalization of the curriculum aims to incorporate "international, intercultural, and/or global dimensions into the content of the curriculum as well as the learning outcomes, assessment tasks, teaching methods, and support services of a program of study" (Leask, 2009, p. 209). Three approaches are often used by faculty members to internationalize the content of the curriculum, namely, the add-on approach, the curricula infusion approach, and the transformation approach (Bond, 2003). The add-on approach, as the name implies, often involves adding on a reading or an assignment to the existing course content and leaves the main body of the course untouched and unquestioned. This is the easiest approach with a narrow focus and limited impact. The second is perhaps the most widely used approach infusing the curriculum with international content in the selection of course materials and integration of student experience into learning activities. It requires much more preparation on the part of the faculty member and often involves the broader participation of faculty and students. The transformation approach is more difficult to undertake, but has the potential to change people. This approach, Bond argues, enables students to move between two or more worldviews and requires a shift in the way we understand the world. When it is realized, it yields genuine reform in the curriculum.

The second component in internationalization of the curriculum involves internationalizing teaching strategies and classroom experiences which best support the learning objectives of an internationalized curriculum. Unfortunately, literature documenting such practices remains nearly nonexistent (Bond, 2003). Drawing from other studies that are relevant to internationalization of the curriculum, Bond offers the following observations. She suggests that it is important for faculty members to develop a classroom climate of respect and trust; communicate to students what is important in a course; get to know your students; respect and value students' knowledge and experience; and use contextualized and cooperative learning strategies to enhance participations. She emphasizes the importance of collaborating with colleagues and using campus resources to ensure effective practices. She also reminds us that students with international and intercultural experience are untapped resources. She further cautions us not to separate international students from other students. Finally, Bond argues, there is no predetermined starting point for internationalizing the curriculum, nor any single way to internationalize the curriculum. We have to take into consideration the context, including class size, subject matter, and the international and intercultural experiences of participants. Furthermore, in the process of internationalizing the curriculum, faculty members play a significant role in determining its success.

THE IDENTITY CRISIS OF INTERNATIONALIZATION

Reflecting on the internationalization over the last decade, internationalization has suffered from an identity crisis. As Knight (2014) lamented, "internationalization has become a catch-all phrase used to describe anything and everything remotely linked to the global, intercultural or international dimensions of higher education and is thus losing its way" (p. 76). In response to this identity crisis of internationalization, Knight calls for an examination of the fundamental values underpinning internationalization.

One identity crisis related to the fundamental values underpinning internationalization pertains to the economic approach as a principle driving force of internationalization. The literature on the internationalization of higher education presents two major discourses: market-driven (i.e., related to fostering economic performance and competiveness) and ethically driven (i.e., related to charitable concerns for enhancing the quality of life of disadvantaged students) discourses (Khoo, 2011). Financial crises are driving profit-seeking policies of internationalization in higher education in many countries. Critics highlight the exploitation of international students as being treated like "cash cows." As such, internationalization is seen as a reflection of "a complex, chaotic and unpredictable *edubusiness*, whose prioritization of the financial 'bottom line' has supplanted clear normative educational and, indeed, overtly ideological intents" (Luke, 2010, p. 44). With respect to the second discourse, internationalization is believed to have the ethical responsibility to engage with alternative agendas such as human rights and building a global civil society (Kaldor, 2003). Recent literature, driven by critical scholars such as Abdi and Shultz (2008) and Andreotti (2013), also indicates that concepts expressed in internationalization policies and initiatives such as governments' and institutions' social responsibility, transnational mobility of students, and students' interculturality that are associated with global citizenship have come to combine both market and ethical influences to enhance students' learning.

Second, critical scholars question internationalization as the dominant global imaginary and its colonial myth of Western ontological and epistemological supremacy (Guo et al., 2021; Ng, 2012; Stein & Andreotti, 2016). As Stein and Andreotti note, the dominant global imaginary of Western supremacy is produced and reproduced not only by and in the West, but also by many across the globe. Duplicating Western policies without consideration of the local context in many universities in Asia raises the question of "whether internationalization becomes recolonization in the postmodern era" (Ng, 2012, p. 451). To illustrate with an example, Guo et al. (2021) interrogate the unidirectional orientation of internationalization as understood and practiced in Chinese higher education as "Westernization" and "Englishization." In the context of China, the internalization of the superiority of Western sources of knowledge has become a crucial element of a hidden curriculum. In this process, the domination of English is closely associated with the superiority of Western knowledge. As Yang (2016) reminded us, Westernization is not new. Since China's encounters with the West in the nineteenth century, repeated defeats led China to feel disadvantaged in its relations with the West. So the West came to China with enormous prestige. Furthermore, the use of English as a medium of instruction (EMI) promotes the hegemony of English as a global language in China (Guo & Beckett, 2007). As such, the need to internationalize the university is interpreted to mean to "Englishize" the university and their programs (Rose & McKinley, 2018). Marginson (2006, p. 25) made a similar point in arguing that the English language universities "exercise a special power, expressed as cultural colonization" and the displacement of the intellectual traditions other languages support. As a symbol of internationalization, English has become a gatekeeper for internationalization; only those with high scores in IELTS and TOEFL are selected for studying abroad. Hence, the "Englishization-equals-internationalization ideology" is pervasive in the Chinese education policy, curricula, and use of EMI (Guo et al., 2021). In light of this, the authors call for an approach to de-Westernize the ideological underpinnings of colonial relations of rule and Eurocentric tendencies influencing the current ideological moorings of internationalization and practices of Chinese higher education.

THE CANADIAN CONTEXT

In 2014, the Government of Canada (2014) launched its first federal international education strategy, with a vision to "become the twenty-first century leader in international education in order to attract top talent and prepare our citizens for the global marketplace, thereby providing key building blocks for our future prosperity" (p. 6). With a neoliberal agenda driven by economic motives, international education was identified as one of the 22 priority sectors to help Canada enhance its economic prosperity and global competitiveness in a knowledge-based economy. As part of the international education strategy, attracting international students at all levels of education became the top priority with a goal to double the number of international students by 2022 (from the level of 2011). In fact, Canada's federal policy on internationalization has always had a strong focus on international students as a market. Since the 1980s, Canadian universities have been utilizing the revenue from international student tuition to ameliorate financial shortfalls resulting from marked declines in government funding for higher education (Cudmore, 2005; Knight, 2008).

The 2014 strategy reinforced the narrative of international students as a source of revenue for universities and for the country, stating that "international students in Canada provide immediate and significant economic benefits to Canadians in every region of the country" (Government of Canada, 2014, p. 7). Citing a commissioned study by Kunin (2012), it reported that in 2012 international students' tuition, books, accommodation, meals, transportation, and discretionary spending was estimated to be about $8.4 billion per year, which in turn generated more than $455 million in government tax revenues. Furthermore, international students are also seen as "a future source of skilled labour" which is critical to ensuring Canada's national prosperity in an increasingly competitive global environment (Government of Canada, 2014, p. 12). It is evident that internationalization is primarily seen in terms of its economic benefits to Canada.

As a result of its aggressive promotion, Canada's international student population has tripled over the past decade to 642,000 in 2019 which ranked Canada the third most popular destination after the US and Australia (El-Assal, 2020). The five countries from which the largest number of international students came in descending order of number were: India, China, South Korea, France, and Vietnam. Yet, when international students arrive on Canadian campuses, they face a number of challenges including isolation, alienation, marginalization, and low self-esteem. In the following section, we will examine how international students experience the internationalization of higher education in Canada.

Contesting Canadian Exceptionalism in the Internationalization of Higher Education

In responding to Knight's (2014) call for scholars and institutions to rethink the fundamental values of internationalization, in this section, we contest the discourse of Canadian exceptionalism in the internationalization of Canadian higher education. We focus on internationalization at one university and international students' experiences of internationalization at this institution in Western Canada. The university launched its International Strategy in 2013, in which internationalization formed one of the priorities in the university's long-term strategic policy visions. A key target of internationalization goals was to increase the number of international students on campus to 10% of the undergraduate population by 2016. In the following discussion, we analyze how internationalization policies and practices at this university were interpreted and experienced by international students. Based on interviews with 26 international students from nine countries, our study shows that international students have multiple understandings of internationalization. Their views of internationalization and lived experiences contest the mythical narrative of Canadian exceptionalism in higher education.

Multiple Understandings of Internationalization

Our findings demonstrate international students' multiple understandings of internationalization. In the interviews, most participants referred to internationalization as the increasing enrollment of international students in Canadian institutions of higher education and their international experiences. International students reported the challenge and difficulty of defining internationalization. The fact that they had mixed understandings of internationalization is not necessarily a problem, considering that the literature applies different definitions. In general, they referred to internationalization as student mobility and research collaborations between institutions. One student from China commented, "To me, it means coming to Canada to study" (Yumi). For many participants, there was a direct link between their understanding of internationalization and their personal experiences of studying in Canada. For some participants, internationalization offered an opportunity for them to develop a global vision. These aspects of internationalization identified by the participants were similar to academic and sociocultural principles of internationalization discussed by Knight (2004) and de Wit et al. (2015). But for others, internationalization was about particular ways of thinking about the world or about westernization as illustrated by one student from Taiwan.

Most participants felt internationalization had a positive effect on them in offering opportunities for development of research interests, independence in learning, and personal growth. The participants enjoyed acquiring information, research training, hands-on experience, and analytical skill. Most participants reported they enjoyed the academic freedom in Canada. For example, all four Chinese students in computer science said they had more choices in their course selection from software, hardware, and network, three parts that were separated in China. Mike was one of the undergraduate students sponsored by the China Scholarship Council (CSC). As a fourth year student, he was doing a required final project and noted that studying in

Canada, particularly learning how to do a literature review, helped him develop his research interest. He also commented on the development of independence in learning as an international student.

Other students illustrated the development of their hands-on ability by having more opportunities to conduct experiments in the lab and making equipment themselves. For example, Kimo in Geography noted: "If we need to use tubes [in the lab], we need to buy pipes, cut and assemble them." Most students reported that they not only developed a strong sense of independence in learning but also increased their self-confidence and developed stronger communication skills. For example, James, a Chinese student in Geophysics, noted his positive character change from being shy to not being afraid to talk to new people. Other students commented they matured as a result of their independent life experiences in another culture, such as learning how to budget for grocery shopping and learning how to cook. Similarly, Krystal from China in Computer Science noted her growing maturity and her open-mindedness as a result of her international experience.

Internationalization, Revenue Generation, and Branding

In this study, international students critiqued the university's goal of internationalization for revenue generating and branding purposes. Access to international mobility is often limited to students who have earned scholarships. Most participants of our study primarily represent two groups of elites in the source country, the socioeconomic elite who are mostly self-funded and the educated elite who are funded by government scholarships. Participants in this study reported that the average international student at the university paid $21,932 CAD in tuition fees—a number that was three times higher than what domestic students paid. On average, international students spent about $40,000 on tuition and living expenses together annually. In light of this, most participants perceived that the university used international students for revenue generation, an "internationalization as marketization model" critiqued by Luke (2010, p. 49). This is in part due to declining government funding for higher education that has formed the context for the internationalization of universities in many Western countries (Marginson, 2006). For example, between 2000/01 and 2012/13, the proportion of university revenues from provincial governments was decreased from 43 to 40% in Canada (CAUT, 2015). Many of the Chinese students in the study represented the educated elite, receiving scholarships from the China Scholarship Council. They had a grade point average above 85% in all academic subjects at their domestic university in China and passed the interview in English. In some cases, they represented the brightest students from their home universities. Given this context, some participants critiqued the university's desire to capitalize on their talents and use international students to raise its profile nationally and internationally. This aligns with one of the university's rationales for internationalization: to position the university as a global intellectual hub and to increase international presence and impact. Khoo (2011) suggests that financial pressures push universities toward marketized, competitive, and unethical interpretations of internationalization whereas ethical development policies and programs for mutual learning and benefit are eroded. Most participants in this study were critical about the university's tendency to view international students as "cash cows" (Stein & Andreotti, 2016) and its emphasis on raising revenue and branding purposes ahead of the care and education of international students.

Little Internationalization of the Curriculum

At the policy level, the university emphasized the internationalization of the curriculum as illustrated in its 2013 International Strategy. In practice, however, international students reported that they felt there were few teaching and learning resources that were related to their experiences as noted by Jane in Education from China who stated, "I don't see there are many materials on my international experience. They [instructors] seldom talk about things happening in China. I think only in X course I experienced a lot because the instructor is from a similar background" (Jane, Education, China). Similarly, Alice, an international student from Brazil who studied film commented that in the courses that she took, mostly American and European film history was taught, but Brazil was only mentioned in passing. Even when there were some teaching and learning resources that were related to their experiences, these resources appeared to portray their countries as backward. Amy in English mentioned that in her drama course, she was shocked to see how Korean surgery was portrayed in a video shown by the instructor. Mery was also critical that Iran was portrayed as both backward and violent in students' discussion in class.

Students' experiences show the contradictions between the internationalization of the curriculum across policy and practice. At the policy level, internationalization of the curriculum aims for "the incorporation of international, intercultural, and/or global dimensions into the content of the curriculum as well as the learning outcomes, assessment tasks, teaching methods, and support services of a program of study" (Leask, 2009, p. 209). In practice, from the international students' perspectives, the internationalization of the curriculum is limited. For example, our findings revealed that students rarely encountered materials that reflected their experiences, and when they did, the materials tended to be dated or skewed. As Haigh (2009) argues, "today, although many classes emerge as a cosmopolitan mix, curricula remain Western" (p. 272). Some students felt that the effect of this lack of international content may be negative, in that it reinforces prejudices and stereotypes. These findings provide evidence for Leask's (2015) critique that "one common misconception about internationalization of the curriculum is that the recruitment of international students will result in an internationalized curriculum for all students" (Leask, 2015, p. 11).

Difficulty in Developing Friendships with Local Students

One of the goals of the internationalization policy at this university is to increase international representation among the study body on campus. For some time, it was a commonly held belief that increasing the diversity of the student body would lead to understanding and friendships between international and local students (Leask, 2015). Unfortunately, this is not something that happens naturally. When international students came to the Canadian campus, particularly for those from Asia and the Middle East, they indicated that they were not well-received and often felt alienated. The international students in this study reported that it was difficult for them to make friends with local students. Lily, a student from China who spent four years in Canada pursuing her undergraduate degree, stated that while she could develop working relationships with her classmates over one semester, it was difficult to become friends with them. She explained that university students in China usually stay in the same cohort for four years, attending the same courses together each semester, making it easier to become friends with classmates. In Canada, however, as the students are different in each class, she noted that it was difficult to be in touch with the same classmates consistently, making it difficult to develop friendships with local students. Lily added another reason, explaining that "local students don't have patience. They don't want to understand international students" Liwang concurred. Similarly, she noted a lack of understanding among local students in that they "never experience what we experience, learning a different culture and language."

A few students identified their low English language proficiency as the main reason for difficulties in becoming friends with local students. Other students indicated that even without language issues, it was still difficult to make friends with local students. One student who studied in English major noted the lack of opportunity for her to interact with local students: "I don't even see any Canadian around me except in class…after class they just leave, not much opportunity to talk to them" (Amy, English, South Korea). Many students mentioned that they did not share the same interests. For example, Tyler, an indigenous American from Alaska, reported he enjoys going to the Native Centre at the university whereas his Canadian peers like to play hockey. Alex, a Chinese student in Engineering, said some local students like to go to the bar and he does not like the pub environment. Another reason why it was difficult for them to make friends with host university students was related to dealing with different life styles. James in Geophysics from China was surprised by the amount of partying and drinking involved in undergraduate life. He did not partake in his roommates' usual activities and suggested this could be one of the reasons he felt excluded from friendship. He further expressed discontent dealing with a roommate who did not cleanup, which was another barrier to friendship.

The above discussion reveals that many factors influence engagement between international and domestic students, including linguistic, academic, and social factors. The participants in our study reported English language and communication challenges as major obstacles to forming meaningful relationships with students of the host society. Difficulty with English language is also reported in other studies (Aune et al., 2011; Scott et al., 2015). In addition to language barrier, many international students felt there is a lack of common interests or different life styles between them and local students. The international students in this study also reported there is a lack of opportunities for interaction between these two groups. Similarly, Zhang and Brunton's (2007) study also found that 55% of the 140 Chinese students they surveyed in New Zealand "were dissatisfied with the availability of opportunities to make New Zealand friends" (p. 132). Sometimes, the international students in this study also sensed unwillingness from local students to connect. This study shows that the mere presence of international students on campus does not necessarily lead to interactions and intercultural understanding between local and international students.

Racism and Racial Discrimination

At the policy level, most institutional internationalization efforts tend to neutralize existing racial hierarchies in the realm of education and beyond (Stein et al., 2016). In reality, some international students in this study had to deal with deep-rooted racism from their peers and people in the local community in the form of verbal attacks, including swearing and being told to return to their home country. Feelings of hurt were exacerbated in classrooms where international students felt excluded or ignored by other students, as illustrated by Liwang who felt she was left out of students' study groups because of who she is. Lily, on the other hand, felt even though she was physically included by other students in study groups, her ideas were ignored due to her English accent. To Krystal in Computer Science, people in Canada appear to be friendly, but may discriminate against other people based on race. She stated, "I actually feel that on the surface, people here will not discriminate against you; they are very friendly. If you have any difficulty, they will help you. But there is deep-rooted racism." Mery, an international student from Iran, had to deal with racism in the local community. She was ridiculed because of the hijab she was wearing in part-time employment. From her perspective, the choice to wear a hijab remains poorly understood in Canada, partly due to Islamophobia, dislike of or prejudice against Islam or Muslims. Mery stated that it is important to guard against equating difference in dress with cultural backwardness, similar to Zine's argument (Zine, 2000).

This finding is consistent with results of Lee and Rice's (2007) and Brown and Jones' (2013) studies. Lee and Rice, in their study of the experiences of international students at a US university, found that students from Asia, Africa, South America, and the Middle East experienced neo-racism in the form of verbal insults and direct confrontation. Brown and Jones, in their study of international graduate students at a university in the UK, found that one third of 153 surveyed experienced racism, including verbal assaults. The limited receptiveness of the local community may contribute to the sense of alienation among international students. More recently, since the outbreak of COVID-19, racism and ethnic discrimination resurfaces and proliferates in many countries on the globe. In Canada, for example, there has been a surge in racism and xenophobia during the global pandemic toward Asian international students, particularly those of Chinese descent (Guo & Guo, 2021). De Wit et al. (2015, p. 29) identified the main purpose for internationalization as "to enhance the quality of education and research for all students and staff, and to make a meaningful contribution to society." It seems that from our findings, the university is not doing enough to enhance the quality of education and research for all students. Universities appear as unprepared as international students in handling the current cross-cultural encounters.

Conclusion

In this chapter, we contest the discourse of Canadian exceptionalism in the internationalization of Canadian higher education by exploring the perspectives and lived experiences of international students in Canada. Contrary to the rhetoric that Canada is an open, welcoming, and racism-free society, students' actual experiences testify that the Canadian exceptionalist discourse is a myth. The results of the study reveal several discrepancies between internationalization policies and practices at the institutional level and the lived experiences of international students. In its current approach to internalizing Canadian higher education, several persistent problems are identified. One pertains to treating internationalization as business opportunities and marketing strategies. Second, in internationalization of the curriculum, the current practice privileges Eurocentric perspectives as some international students did not see teaching materials that reflected their experiences. Third, despite a false narrative of Canada as a culturally tolerant nation, students' experiences reveal difficulties of integrating into the Canadian academic environment with challenges ranging from making friends with domestic students to racial discrimination. Although there is an interest in bringing in international students to internationalize Canadian campuses, in reality there has been a lack of support to help international students successfully integrate into Canadian academic environments.

From these findings, we beg the following questions: Are we too complacent? Is Canada truly exceptional? What are the limits of the discourse of Canadian exceptionalism? With respect to internationalization, what changes need to be made to maximize the learning experience of international student in Canada? The findings suggest that we must engage in critical deep reflections as to how we treat our international students. We argue for more ethically oriented policies and practices of internationalization in higher education as opposed to profit-seeking orientation. First, host institutions need to be cognizant of how they put the internationalized curriculum into action.

An internationalized curriculum demands that educators view international students not only as knowledge consumers but also as knowledge producers. This means that the knowledge and linguistic resources that international students bring need to be valued, and the internationalized curriculum needs to connect to international students' lived experiences. The findings also have important implications for host institutions in providing appropriate levels of support to help international students with their transition and adaptation. Support for international students has to move beyond the usual one-time welcome orientation. It is important to combine students' academic needs with their social and cultural needs. Furthermore, urgent actions need to be taken to eliminate racism and racial discrimination on Canadian campus and to recognize and embrace cultural differences and diversity. It is important to note that integrating international students requires collective efforts of university administrators, faculty, staff, and students in building an internationally inclusive campus, where cross-cultural learning is encouraged. If institutions of higher education are serious about internationalizing their campuses, it is essential that they provide necessary support to assist international students with their transition and integration. Like Canada, many countries in the world (e.g., Australia, Japan, UK, US) are experiencing increasing enrollment of international students who also encounter numerous challenges similar to those reported in this chapter in adapting to new academic environment in their host societies. While many universities and colleges are searching for solution to help international students with their adaptation, it is hoped that lessons learned from the Canadian experience will serve as catalyst for other countries to examine exceptionalism from their own contexts so that positive changes can take place.

REFERENCES

Abdi, A. A., & Shultz, L. (2008). Continuities of racism and inclusive citizenship: Framing global citizenship and human rights education. In A. A. Abdi & S. Guo (Eds.), *Education and social development: Global issues and analyses* (pp. 25–36). Sense Publishers.

Aune, R. K., Hendreickson, B., & Rosen, D. R. (2011). An analysis of friendship networks, social connectedness, homesickness, and satisfaction levels of international students. *International Journal of Intercultural Relations, 35*(3), 281–295.

Andreotti, V. D. O. (Ed.). (2013). *The political economy of global citizenship education.* Routledge.

Bond, S. (2003). *Untapped resources, internationalization of the curriculum and classroom experience: A selected literature review.* Canadian Bureau for International Education.

Brown, L., & Jones, I. (2013). Encounters with racism and the international student experience. *Studies in Higher Education, 38*(7), 1–16.

Canadian Association of University Teachers (CAUT). (2015). *CAUT Education Review.* Retrieved March 30, 2021 from https://www.caut.ca/docs/default-source/education-review/caut---education-review-(spring-2015).pdf?sfvrsn=8

Cudmore, G. (2005). Globalization, internationalization, and the recruitment of international students in higher education, and in the Ontario Colleges of Applied Arts and Technology. *The Canadian Journal of Higher Education, 35*(1), 37–60.

de Wit, H., Hunter, F., Howard, L., & Egron-Polak, E. (2015). *Internationalization of higher education*. Brussels: European Union Parliament Policy Department B: Structural and Cohesion Policies. Retrieved March 30, 2021.

de Wit, H., & Merkx, G. (2012). The history of internationalisation of higher education. In D. Deardorff, H. de Wit, J. Heyl, & T. Adams (Eds.), *The SAGE handbook of international higher education* (pp. 43–59). SAGE.

EduCanada. (2021). Top reasons to study in Canada. Retrieved March 30, 2021 from https://www.educanada.ca/why-canada-pourquoi/reasons-raisons.aspx?lang=eng

El-Assal, K. (2020). 642,000 international students: Canada now ranks 3rd globally in foreign student attraction. *CIC News: The Voice of Canadian Immigration*. Retrieved March 30, 2021 from https://www.cicnews.com/2020/02/642000-international-students-canada-now-ranks-3rd-globally-in-foreign-student-attraction-0213763.html#gs.g781rr

Elliott, D. (1998). Internationalization in British higher education: Policy perspectives. In S. Peter (Ed.), *The globalization of higher education* (pp. 32–43). Society for Research into Higher Education & Open University Press.

Government of Canada. (2014). Canada's international education strategy: Harnessing our knowledge advantage to drive innovation and prosperity. Ottawa, ON: Government of Canada. Retrieved March 30, 2021 from https://www.international.gc.ca/global-markets-marches-mondiaux/assets/pdfs/overview-apercu-eng.pdf

Guo, S., & Chase, M. (2011). Internationalisation of higher education: Integrating international students into Canadian academic environment. *Teaching in Higher Education, 16*(3), 305–318.

Guo, S., & Guo, Y. (2021). Combating racism and xenophobia in Canada: Toward pandemic anti-racism education in post-COVID-19. *Beijing Review of International Education, 3*(2), 187–211. Retrieved March 30, 2021 from https://doi.org/10.1163/25902539-03020004

Guo, Y., & Beckett, G. H. (2007). The hegemony of English as a global language: Reclaiming local knowledge and culture in China. *Convergence, 40*(1–2), 117–132.

Guo, Y., Guo, S., Yochim, L., & Liu, X. (2021). Internationalization of Chinese higher education: Is it Westernization? *Journal of Studies in International Education*, 1–18, https://doi.org/10.1177/1028315321990745

Haigh, M. (2009). Fostering cross-cultural empathy with non-Western curricular structures. *Journal of Studies in International Education, 13*(2), 271–284.

Kaldor, M. (2003). *Global civil society – an answer to war?* Polity.

Kelly, P. (2000). Internationalizing the curriculum: For profit or planet? In S. Inayatullah & J. Gidley (Eds.), *The university in transformation: Global perspectives on the futures on the university* (pp. 162–172). Greenwood Publishing.

Khoo, S. M. (2011). Ethical globalisation or privileged internationalisation? Exploring global citizenship and internationalisation in Irish and Canadian universities. *Globalisation, Societies and Education, 9*(3–4), 337–353.

Knight, J. (2000). *Process and promise: The AUCC report on internationalization at Canadian universities*. Association of Universities and Colleges of Canada.

Knight, J. (2003). Updating definition of internationalisation. *International Higher Education, 33*, 2–3. https://doi.org/10.6017/ihe.2003.33.7391

Knight, J. (2004). Internationalization remodeled: Definition, approaches, and rationales. *Journal of Studies in International Education, 8*(1), 5–31.

Knight, J. (2008). The role of cross-border education in the debate on education as a public good and private commodity. *Journal of Asian Public Policy, 1*(2), 174–187.

Knight, J. (2014). Is internationalisation of higher education having an identity crisis? In A. Maldonado-Maldonado & M. R. Bassett (Eds.), *The forefront of international higher education: A Festschrift in Honor of Philip G. Altbach* (pp. 75–87). Springer Netherlands.

Kunin, R. (2012). *Economic impact of international education in Canada—An update: Final report*. Retrieved March 30, 2021 from http://www.international.gc.ca/education/assets/pdfs/economic_impact_en.pdf

Leask, B. (2009). Using formal and informal curricula to improve interactions between home and international students. *Journal of Studies in International Education, 13*(2), 205–221.

Leask, B. (2015). *Internationalizing the curriculum*. Routledge.

Lee, J. J., & Rice, C. (2007). Welcome to America? International student perceptions of discrimination. *Higher Education, 53*(3), 381–409.

Luke, A. (2010). Educating the 'other' standpoint and internationalization of higher education. In V. Carpentier & E. Unterhaler (Eds.), *Global inequalities in higher education: Whose interests are you serving?* (pp. 1–25). Palgrave/Macmillan.

Marginson, S. (2006). Dynamics of national and global competition in higher education. *Higher Education, 52*(1), 1–39.

Ng, S. W. (2012). Rethinking the mission of internationalization of higher education in the Asia-Pacific region. *Compare: A Journal of Comparative and International Education, 42*(3), 439–459.

Rose, H., & McKinley, J. (2018). Japan's English-medium instruction initiatives and the globalization of higher education. *High Education, 75*, 111–129.

Scott, C., Safdar, S, Trilokekar, R., Masri, A. (2015). International students as 'ideal immigrants' in Canada: A disconnect between policy makers' assumptions and the lived experiences of international students. *Comparative and International Education, 43*(3), Article 5.

Stein, S., & Andreotti, V. D. O. (2016). Cash, charity, or competition: International students and the global imaginary. *Higher Education, 72*, 225–239.

Stein, S., Andreotti, V., Bruce, J., & Suša, R. (2016). Towards different conversations about the internationalization of higher education. *Comparative and International Education, 45*(1), Article 2. Retrieved March 30, 2021 from: http://ir.lib.uwo.ca/cie-eci/vol45/iss1/2

Teichler, U. (2010). Internationalising higher education: Debates and changes in Europe. In D. Mattheou (Ed.), *Changing educational landscapes. Educational policies, schooling systems and higher education – a comparative perspective* (pp. 263–283). Springer.

Yang, R. (2016). Internationalization of higher education in China: An overview. In S. Guo & Y. Guo (Eds.), *Spotlight on China: Chinese education in the globalized world* (pp. 35–49). Sense Publishers.

Zhang, Z., & Brunton, M. (2007). Differences in living and learning: Chinese international students in New Zealand. *Journal of Studies in International Education, 11*, 124–140.

Zine, J. (2000). Redefining resistance: Towards an Islamic subculture in schools. *Race Ethnicity and Education, 3*(3), 293–316.

CHAPTER 9

Global Citizenship Education for Critical Consciousness: Emancipatory Potentials and Entrenched Realities in South Korea

Hyungryeol Kim and Sung-Sang Yoo

INTRODUCTION

Paulo Freire proposed that education should be freedom as it is the only way to break free from oppression, where the poor and powerless are deprived of the ability to choose a course of actions toward happiness (Freire, 1996). Drawing our attention to the contrast between banking education and problem-posing education, Freire (1970b) contended that students are conceived as an empty vessel to be filled by the teacher and the teacher must comply with legal standards established by the preexisting norms in the former model, whereas the latter model counterposes the banking concept with a paradigm whereby students and the teacher are dialoguing and problematizing together. In so doing, he added that the role of the teacher-educator should be to develop the capacity for critical thinking by the oppressed—of themselves and communities, and ultimately societies they take part in—so that one can perceive, analyze, and transform an oppressive reality into an emancipatory one (Freire, 1970b). In this sense, Freire's critique of banking education and the pivotal

H. Kim (✉)
Department of Ethics
Education, College of Education, Seoul National University, Seoul, South Korea
e-mail: ksyhr70@snu.ac.kr

S.-S. Yoo
Department of
Education, College of Education, Seoul National University, Seoul, South Korea
e-mail: sungsang@snu.ac.kr

concepts of his education for emancipation are mainly associated with critical global citizenship education (hereafter GCE), in which students and teachers are encouraged to dialogically engage in the process of developing critical consciousness of power relations and seeking to destabilize the unjust status quo (Bosio, 2020; Torres, 2017; Torres & Bosio, 2020).

Guided by Freire's rejection of oppressive elements of the educational system and alternative emancipatory vision of education, this study takes a case of GCE in South Korea (hereafter Korea) to explore teachers' perceptions and experiences of GCE. As GCE has been initiated in Korea in part for serving the government's political agenda of positioning itself to be a leading nation of GCE in the global community (Cho & Mosselson, 2018), Korea is a notable case for the study of state-centric and neoliberal tensions in GCE. In this context, many previous studies on GCE in Korea have employed the lens of critical GCE and critically deconstructed the nation's official GCE discourses, as appeared in policy documents, curricular, and textbooks. In comparison, there has been scant attention paid to the actualization of GCE in a concrete setting, that is, its "*place of enunciation*" in Lacanian terms (Žižek, 1997), wherein the goals of GCE are being realized at a specific time and place (for exceptions, see, Y. Kim, 2019; Pak & Lee, 2018). Based on the assumption that what teachers experience and believe about GCE are key to understanding the concrete practice of GCE in schools as its place of enunciation, especially in countries like Korea where an explicit national model for GCE is absent or vague (Gill & Niens, 2014), this study conducts in-depth, semi-structured interviews with 10 Korean teachers who have implemented GCE across schools. On the basis of such interview data, we then identified emergent themes concerning the emancipatory potentials of GCE in Korea as well as the "empirical realities" entrenched within Korea's educational system that hinder teachers from realizing GCE's full emancipatory potentials. By presenting potentials and obstacles that Korean teachers confront when they aim to expand students' emancipation toward critical consciousness in and through GCE, this study argues why emancipatory conceptions of GCE are vital to reframe the purpose of education and protect the future of critical democracy.

Particularities and Varieties of GCE

A large body of longitudinal cross-national research has indicated that while the construction of national citizenship continues to be a key component of formal education, many countries have increasingly incorporated the teaching of global citizenship in their educational systems (e.g., Meyer et al., 2010). Behind this worldwide trend is the instrumental need of the nation-state to compete in a global society and the role of international organizations in the diffusion of a global education agenda, which is often labeled under the overall umbrella of GCE. While GCE constitutes a worldwide phenomenon in such ways, detailed case studies of single and a small number of countries have also shown that GCE takes different forms in different societies (Rapoport, 2015). For instance, in countries such as the United States (Rapoport, 2010) and China (Law, 2007; Rose, 2015) that valorizes nationalism as central forces in the globalizing world, GCE is found to be pressed into service to reinforce nationalistic discourses on national global competitiveness in a rapidly changing international environment. In Latin American countries like Argentina and Cost Rica, the primary aim of GCE is often related to the strengthening of economic and cultural ties with the United States through acquiring English proficiency and engaging with Americans and US culture (Suarez, 2008). As Goren and Yemini (2017b) succinctly noted in their systematic review of empirical studies on GCE, GCE appears to be universally adopted across countries but operationalized differently in light of its instrumental benefits for each country.

These diverse local manifestations of GCE have led to the development of various typologies by the academic critics, which allow scholars and policymakers to classify the ways GCE is perceived and interpreted. Dill (2013), for example, made a distinction between two approaches to GCE from which clearly different goals can be inferred; a *global competencies* approach, which aims to offer learners with knowledge and skills necessary to compete in a global free market, and a *global consciousness* approach, which aims to offer learners with global orientations, empathy, and cultural sensitivity. In a similar vein, Andreotti (2006) identified two main approaches to GCE, i.e., a *soft* approach and a *critical* approach; while the primary aim of soft GCE is to promote an understanding of the globalizing world and cultural tolerance, critical GCE encourages learners to reflect critically on and engage with global issues and to strive for change. Likewise, in efforts to highlight the binary at work in the way GCE is practiced, Camicia and Franklin (2011) distinguished between a *neoliberal* approach and a *critical democratic* approach; in the former approach, the emphasis is given to the values of the global free market for structuring institutions and human relations, whereas the latter approach emphasizes the principles of social justice, diversity, and equality, and thereby counters neoliberal GCE. Extending these categorizations, Chung and Park (2016) proposed three categories of GCE, i.e., *competency-based*, *moral*, and *critical* GCE. No matter how they are labeled, these typologies serve as competing forces in the struggle to identify the content and practical implications of GCE.

Criticism of GCE

Admittedly, these efforts to classify a variety of approaches to GCE have been made with a view to deconstructing neoliberal and Western-centric assumptions that are embedded in the core of certain type of GCE (Goren & Yemini, 2017b). In their ideology critique of GCE, Pais and Costa (2020) explicated that the enactment of GCE into schools and higher education institutions seems to be thwarted by neoliberalism, marked by a market rationality and the idea of an entrepreneurial citizen (Burbules & Torres, 2000; Torres, 1998), which is contrary to the official discourse of GCE as pronounced in the international community. After its eventual triumph in the world economy, neoliberalism has made major inroads into non-commodified public spheres, and education has been no exception to this invasion (Torres & Van Heertum, 2010). A series of trends, including but not limited to the advents of private management of schools and higher education institutions (Kandiko, 2010), exemplifies the triumph of the neoliberal agenda in education around the world. Underlying this neoliberal educational frame is the idea that the purpose of education is to help students become more competitive, entrepreneurial, and individualistic so that they can fit in and succeed in a *given* market system rather than to open educational spaces for working for a more just and humane world (Jorgenson & Shultz, 2012). With such ascendancy of neoliberalism in education worldwide, the crucial functions of the market solution—privatization and standardization—have increasingly supplanted the notion of democratic participation in education as a public good (Giroux, 2013), and GCE have also been framed within this neoliberal agenda across national boundaries. Recent studies from various countries have shown that neoliberal values are undeniably pervasive in GCE curricular and textbooks, as, for example, narratives in textbooks give too much weight to the merits of competition and trade in a global free market (Yoon & Choi, 2017) and conceptualize citizens as those who can proactively participate in a global economy driven by capitalism and technology (Alviar-Martin & Baildon, 2016).

Along these lines, the Western imperial worldview embedded in GCE discourses has also received much criticism. In analyzing the official social studies curriculum of one US state, Georgia, Reidel, and Beck (2016) found that its GCE discourses are framed within a fallacious construction of the contemporary world and reinforce or even exacerbate preexisting cultural stereotypes. Cho and Mosselson (2018)'s analysis of GCE-related teacher handbooks and curricular published by government organizations in Korea also produced a similar finding. The authors found that in GCE materials in Korea, the term "helping" countries are used as synonymous with Western leaders and the term "needing help" is mainly associated with passivity and poverty, contributing to the perpetuation of the sociocultural and economic superiority of Western countries. In the same vein, some scholars criticized and challenged a latent imperial assumption behind certain GCE discourses associated with the world society perspective (e.g., Buckner & Russell, 2013; Meyer et al., 2010), contending that discourses of this sort have usually been made based on an analysis of the processes whereby the oft-touted Western ideals (e.g., democracy, human rights, global citizenship, and multiculturalism) are imported to non-Western contexts and of the resulting change in educational systems themselves (Steiner-Khamsi, 2006; Vickers, 2020).

CRITICAL GCE IN FREIREAN THOUGHT

In denunciating neoliberal and Western-centric conceptions of GCE, scholars whose interest is in critical GCE have paid a special attention to Paulo Freire's notion of "conscientization," i.e., critical consciousness. Freire conceived conscientization as the highest value of education, where it refers to the process in which humans become more aware of the sources of their oppression (Freire, 1970a). Since the oppressed are disadvantaged in this respect, as Freire understood, education is the only way to emancipate the oppressed from domination by raising their critical consciousness. Later, in his groundbreaking work, Pedagogy of the Oppressed, Freire (1970b) added that emancipation means becoming critically aware of social injustices and global issues that maintain these injustices. More specifically, he explicated that education as emancipation constitutes being able to "read the world" and to "rewrite the world" (Freire, 1970a). By reading the world, one can acquire a capacity to critically analyze the global systems of power and their positions within the power systems (Freire, 1970b; Torres, 2014), and this capacity also includes what Freire (1994) termed "denunciations" and "annunciations." Whereas the concept of denunciations is related to the development of critical consciousness about the globe that denounces social injustices in the world, the concept of annunciations refers to the awareness of all people's humanity, dignity, and their potential. In other words, when one is able to become critically aware of the world through denunciations and annunciations, one is ready to rewrite the world (Torres & Bosio, 2020).

As discussed in the introduction, contrary to this emancipatory vision of education, Freire (1970b) posited that formal education, as practiced in schools and universities around the world, was an instrument of oppression rather than an instrument of emancipation. Freire termed this degraded form of formal education as banking education, as the more students attempted to receive and store knowledge deposited in them, the less they can attain critical consciousness stemming from "intervening in reality as makers and transformers of the world" (Freire, 1970b). In so doing, Freire (1970b) advocated problem-posing education as a counter-force to banking education, wherein the teacher and students can dialogically engage in the process of developing critical consciousness and challenging an oppressive social order. In such ways, problem-posing education can create a space in which the teacher and students can educate themselves and each other. For this reason, the role of the teacher is key to problem-posing education in a Freirian sense, as one must be ready to respect students' knowledge as valuable as one's own as well as to enter into the reality of students' daily lives rather than to deposit "superior knowledge" to be passively digested, memorized, and repeated into them (Blackburn, 2000).

Inspired by Freire's critique of banking education and the revolutionary character of the concepts of conscientization and dialogue, critical GCE, as it is seen as a way of empowering students to critically reflect upon global issues and contribute to a more socially just and humane world, can trace its origin to Freirean thought. In this respect, many GCE scholars have made clear that their "preferred" approach is a critical one and argued that GCE should be grounded in problem-posing education (e.g., Bosio, 2020; Torres, 2017; Torres & Bosio, 2020). By challenging students with critical questions and encouraging them to bring their lived knowledge and experiences to classrooms, critical GCE can promote students' emancipation toward critical consciousness and ultimately help them advance social justice, environmental justice, and sustainability for all communities.

GCE in Korea

Since the United Nation's Secretary-General Ban Ki-Moon articulated "fostering global citizenship" as one of the international community's priorities in the Global Education First Initiative (GEFI) in 2012, there has been a growing interest in GCE worldwide. Korea has been no exception to this worldwide trend and has taken a leadership role in diffusing and implementing GCE (Sim, 2016). In Korea's educational landscape, GCE has been a major policy concern in recent years, and the central government has played a key role in undertaking diverse GCE initiatives. For instance, the central government initiated the "GCE Lead Teacher (LT) Program" since 2015 that provides selected teachers nationwide with knowledge and skills necessary for teaching GCE across schools (Pak et al., 2018). This typical "state-led" model of GCE in Korea has often been criticized for its hidden motive, as it may take an instrumentalist view toward GCE which aims to cultivate human capital with global competencies and ultimately serve the interest of political and economic elites and neoliberal agenda (Choi & Kim, 2020; Kim, 2019, 2020; Pak & Lee, 2018). At the same time, the Western imperial worldview prevalent in Korea's GCE teaching materials and textbooks has also been the focus of academic criticism (Cho & Mosselson, 2018). At stake here is the tension between soft versus critical GCE, as identified by Andreotti (2006), one focused on economic progressivism and Western supremacy and another one focused on social justice and critical democracy. This tension inherent in GCE discourses was also adequately captured by Camicia and Franklin (2011, p. 321), as they argued that "students are being prepared to participate as global citizens, but the meaning of this citizenship is complicated by a tension and blending between neoliberal and critical democratic discourses."

Participants, Data Collection, and Analysis

As we used purposeful and snowball sampling to recruit participants, 10 in-service teachers, those who have had experiences in teaching GCE in schools in the past 5 years, were volunteered to participate in the study. Among these 10 participants, 7 were identified as female, and 3 identified as male. All participants had obtained bachelor's and/or graduate degrees and worked in primary, middle, and high schools that serve more or less advantaged student populations in the Seoul metropolitan area. Their teaching experiences range from 5 to 17 years, and the majority of participants are in their early- or mid-thirties.

We collected the individual interview data from 10 teachers who have had experiences in teaching GCE and were willing to share their perceptions and experiences regarding GCE. The interviews were conducted at mutually convenient times in January 2021 via Zoom to prevent the spread of COVID-19 in the face of the global pandemic and lasted from 50 to 80 min. Interviews were audio-recorded per participants' permission and conducted in Korean by a native Korean speaker researcher. All audio-recorded interview data were transcribed verbatim in Korean, and selected quotes from these interviews were later translated into English by a native English speaker for publication.

Utilizing the in-depth, semi-structured interview data, we first developed various codes and connecting codes with similar meanings as analytical units (Miles & Huberman, 1994). Then, drawing upon the finalized pattern codings, we identified emergent themes concerning emancipatory potentials of GCE in Korea as well as the "empirical realities" entrenched within Korea's educational system that hinder teachers from realizing GCE's full emancipatory potentials.

POTENTIALS AND CONSTRAINTS OF GCE IN KOREAN SCHOOLS

Emancipatory potentials of GCE

The majority of the participants in our study perceived that the value of GCE lies in its emancipatory potentials, which promote new ways of understanding and critical engagement with the world. These new ways of understanding and critical engagement include: (1) an understanding of how the local conditions of our everyday practices are embedded in global contexts (i.e., global interconnectedness), (2) an understanding that a global citizen's responsibility is not limited to a particular area, but extended to a universal one (i.e., global ethical responsibility), (3) a critical reflection upon values such as empathy, solidarity, and respect for differences and diversity, and (4) an willingness to engage in the democratic process for transforming the current situation into a more just and humane one. Furthermore, in practicing GCE in their classrooms, our participants stated that they themselves achieved a greater sense of belonging and responsibility toward a global community and began to formulate their own agenda for change. One female teacher in her mid-thirties, for instance, shared the following anecdote:

> Since I taught GCE, I feel like I am changing into a different person. One day, I discussed environmental issues in my GCE class, and asked students how much water is needed to make a jean. Then, students asked me again, "how

many jeans do you have?" I had to confess that I have a lot of jeans. Students lamented, "What a shame! You've wasted a lot of water!" I told my students that afterwards we all, including myself, should be more careful about the environmental cost of making jeans and do our best to change this process. As much as I prepare for teaching GCE in classes, I feel obligated to a global community and believe that my individual action can do make a difference (Participant 1).

Additionally, in light of the predominance of neoliberalism in Korea's educational landscape, teachers in the study also advocated a "logic of compensation" (Pais & Costa, 2020, p. 6), whereby emancipatory discourses and practices in GCE can compensate for the overriding influence of neoliberalism in education. As discussed above, at the center of the neoliberal educational frame is the idea that education should prepare students to become more competitive, entrepreneurial, and individualistic in a free market system, and its outcome is often assessed by whether they acquire enough quantified and objective knowledge in a standardized test. This is what Giroux (2010) labeled as a "business model in education," in which students are conceived as consumers and schooling as a personal investment for accumulating human capital. In the face of such increasing influence of the market-driven scenarios in education, some Korean teachers stated that they have practiced GCE in schools with the hope that it can serve as an "antidote" to the neoliberal educational frame. As mentioned by one male teacher who works in a public primary school and one female teacher who works in an international high school:

> When I became a teacher in the 2010s, students took a nationwide standardized test on a regular basis, and I believed that my primary mission as a teacher was to boost their test scores in the test. This was especially so because the primary school I worked for was located in a disadvantaged area and notorious for poor educational outcomes. I even asked myself, "did I something wrong? If I were to adopt better teaching techniques, were my students able to get better scores?" Since I taught GCE, however, I increasingly became aware that getting good scores in the standardized test should not be the primary goal of teaching and learning, and this realization made me ponder my role as a teacher. When I found noticeable differences in my students' perspectives of social justice and sustainability as my GCE classes have progressed, I feel rewarded and fulfilled as a teacher. I hope teaching GCE can function as a counterforce to Korea's 'teaching-to-the test' ideology. (Participant 4)

> My students focus too much on good grades and college readiness. This is understandable given the emphasis placed on the measurement of their performance and GPA in the current educational system. One day, I asked my students what they ultimately wish to do after graduating college. They answered that they want to be professionals, like a medical doctor, judge, and lawyer. I further asked why they prefer these jobs, and their answer was so impressive. They

believed that these jobs would lead them to a comfortable and luxurious life. By practicing GCE, I hope I can let my students realize that there are more important values in our lives. I also want to let them know that we can lay the foundation for a more just and sustainable world for everyone. (Participant 10)

As such, by encouraging students to reflect upon and critically engage with global phenomena, the teachers in our study do their best to realize the emancipatory potentials of GCE in schools. In this process, they also saw positive changes inside themselves and envisaged GCE as an opportunity to counteract the pernicious influence of neoliberal practices in Korea's educational system. These findings imply that Korean teachers have emerged to implement GCE as a form of problem-posing education in a Freirian sense, where students and the teacher problematize together and develop critical consciousness in efforts to transform the world into a better place.

"Empirical Realities" Entrenched within the Educational System

When attempting to enact GCE as a form of problem-posing education, however, the Korean teachers in our study encountered a variety of barriers and constraints in their classrooms and schools. Accordingly, the result often seems to be a reproduction of the same system that the teachers seek to transform to the detriment of the emancipatory potentials of GCE. We term these barriers and constraints that hinder the Korean teachers from realizing GCE's full emancipatory potentials as "empirical realities" entrenched within Korea's educational system (Pais & Costa, 2020, p. 7). These empirical realities include (1) the eminent subordination of learning to the college entrance examination, (2) the general (mis-)perception that GCE comes attached to a privileged social background, and (3) the ideological tension surrounding different agendas for GCE.

As discussed above, our teacher participants asserted that GCE is the path that contemporary education should follow if one agrees that the purpose of education is to transform the world into a better place. Given Korea's "education fever" and craze for elite universities (Seth, 2002); however, the teachers were simultaneously anxious that teaching about GCE-related contents in their classrooms may have little to do with students' college entrance. Therefore, against the background of the overheated competitive college prep environment in Korea, the teachers, particularly those who teach in high schools, had no choice but to link GCE to their students' exam preparation. These types of pressure were depicted as follows:

At times, students and their parents in my school seem to be enthusiastic about GCE, as they believe that participating in GCE-related extracurricular activities would increase the chances of getting accepted to elite universities. As comprehensive student records screening has become the norm for entrance at most major universities in Korea, with extracurricular activities like clubs, volunteering and career building counted as major factors, many high schools began to offer GCE programs to help their students build extracurriculars and make a stronger application for college admission. In recent years, it is believed that having a global orientation is a prerequisite for prestigious university admission. (Participant 8)

The first time when I introduced GCE-related activities in this school, some parents had serious reservations about its utility. Thus, I had to explain to them that engaging in such activities would be a great chance to strengthen their children's application for college admission. Only then they became supportive of my GCE initiatives. At any rate, all that matter in the current educational climate is college entrance, so I have to conform to it. (Participant 9)

Another obstacle that the Korean teachers confronted is the general (mis-) perception that GCE comes attached to a privileged social background. While the official GCE discourses define global citizenship as a way of transcending the boundaries created by each nation-state and sharing a sense of belonging to a larger community, it is often perceived as an exclusive concept that only privileges a very particular group of people (e.g., an well-educated elite) (Iftekhar & Misiaszek, 2019). In the same vein, GCE is often perceived as an exclusive property of "high-end" international schools that serve students from well-off families (Goren & Yemini, 2017a), as only these schools have abundant resources that can afford extravagant GCE activities such as traveling abroad and visiting overseas universities. Indeed, these perceptions seem to highlight neoliberal aspects of GCE, construing international mindedness and global competencies as pedagogically attractive ideas that benefit privileged families and schools. In our study, the teachers who work in disadvantaged school settings indicated that similar perceptions were pervasive in Korean schools as well, eroding the emancipatory orientation of GCE in the favor of the neoliberal one. For instance, one male teacher working in a disadvantaged school setting stated that a stereotyped view of GCE as "a commodified brand for the privileged few" was so widely held by his colleague teachers as such:

As I shared my experiences as a GCE Lead Teacher and vision for GCE with my colleague teachers, one asked me, "is it possible to implement GCE in this school? Isn't it a program tailored to the needs of *Gangnam* [one of the most affluent neighborhoods in Seoul] kids who have had many international experiences?" Even more, the school principal told me that as students in this school cannot afford expensive extra-curricular activities like overseas field trips, he did not want to launch GCE programs this year. (Participant 6)

Finally, the Korean teachers involved in our study acknowledged that GCE is not implemented in an ideological vacuum; it rather occurs within a wider society that is sharply divided by partisanship and political dissent. As a result, the problem arose when the teachers tried a variety of pedagogical endeavors in GCE classes, with a view to changing students' perspectives of global phenomena that hide unequal power relations and maintain the unjust status quo, but faced strong antagonism from "conservative" school leaders who are against the transformative nature of GCE. More specifically, the teachers added that those in a leadership position in Korean schools tend to conceive GCE as the strictly individualistic goal of passing the course or achieving special education records, not as the actualization of a collectively motivated goal of transforming the world in a more just and humane one. Given such ideological tension surrounding different agendas for GCE, a teacher working in a public high school shared the following anecdote:

> A few months ago, I organized a special GCE lecture by inviting a guest speaker in my school. The theme of the lecture was global citizenship and the future of democracy, and the guest speaker was an activist well-known for his liberal orientation. However, the vice principal opposed the idea of inviting the guest speaker, arguing that he did not want to implicate our school in political turmoil. In Korea, those in school administration tend to have a strong conservative inclination, and conceive GCE as a left-wing, subversive, and radical idea for social change. In the face of his opposition, I had to cancel the special lecture. Afterwards, the vice principal requested me to organize GCE activities that would "look good and fit comfortably" in students' school records. (Participant 3)

Why We Need Emancipatory Conceptions of GCE

Drawing a parallel between the mission of GCE in today's globalizing world and Freire's notion of critical consciousness, this study shed light on the potentials and obstacles that Korean teachers confront when they aim to implement GCE as a form of problem-posing education in concrete school settings. Our in-depth, semi-structured interviews demonstrated that the Korean teachers did their best to realize the emancipatory potentials of GCE by encouraging students to critically reflect upon global phenomena and bring about a change toward more equitable, just and sustainable world. In so doing, they began to conceive both themselves and students as the loci of transformation as well as to see that GCE can perform a key role in counteracting the pernicious influence of neoliberal practices in Korea's educational system. While GCE is posited by Korean teachers as such an emancipatory enterprise for a better world, the present study also identified some objective realities that constrain the successful fulfillment of GCE's potentials in Korea's educational landscape: (1) the eminent subordination of education to the needs of college readiness, (2) the general (mis-)perception that GCE comes attached to a privileged social background, and (3) the ideological tension surrounding different agendas for GCE. Altogether, this study adds to the previous GCE literature that has criticized the prevalence of neoliberal ethos, the lack of critical perspectives, and the socioeconomic aspect of GCE gap across families and schools in Korea (e.g., Cho & Mosselson, 2018; Kim, 2019; Sim, 2016) and other countries (e.g., Alviar-Martin & Baildon, 2016; Goren & Yemini, 2017a; Swanson & Pashby, 2016). While GCE has the potential to transform an oppressive reality into an emancipatory one, the result often turns out to be a reproduction of the same system that it seeks to transform, thereby making it a temporary venture for maintaining the status quo.

In this sense, this study's findings remind us of Freire's central claim that education should be freedom, as it is the only way to break free from oppression. As Freire (1970b) noted in his *Pedagogy of the Oppressed*, "Any system which deliberately tried to discourage critical consciousness is guilty of oppressive violence. Any school which does not foster students' capacity for critical inquiry is guilty of violent oppression." (p. 74) Now that we observe the unrelenting predominance of neoliberal and neoconservative politics and policies that reframe the purpose of education from "critical thinking and action" to "job training" (Macrine, 2020), we, critical educators, must engage in a collective struggle against oppressive elements of any kind in education and wider society. As the illumination of hope can exist even during the darkest of times, teachers are in a unique position to revitalize the emancipatory power of education and eventually to reconstruct critical democracy in and through GCE. We await future research that would explore the teacher's central role and agency in achieving GCE's full emancipatory potentials in other sociocultural contexts.

References

Alviar-Martin, T., & Baildon, M. (2016). Context and curriculum in two global cities: A study of discourses of citizenship in Hong Kong and Singapore. *Education Policy Analysis, 24*(56), 1–27.

Andreotti, V. O. d. (2006). Soft versus critical global citizenship education. *Policy and Practice: A Development Education Review*, 3, 40–51.

Blackburn, J. (2000). Understanding Paulo Freire: Reflections on the origins, concepts, and possible pitfalls of his educational approach. *Community Development Journal, 35*(1), 3–15.

Bosio, E. (2020). Towards an ethical global citizenship education curriculum framework in the modern university. In D. Bourn (Ed.), *Bloomsbury handbook for global education and learning* (pp. 187–206). Bloomsbury.

Buckner, E., & Russell, S. G. (2013). Portraying the global: Cross-national trends in textbooks' portrayal of globalization and global citizenship. *International Studies Quarterly, 57*(4), 738–750.

Burbules, N. C., & Torres, C. A. (2000). *Globalization and education: Critical perspectives*. Routledge.

Camicia, S. P., & Franklin, B. M. (2011). What type of global community and citizenship? Tangled discourses of neoliberalism and critical democracy in curriculum and its reform. *Globalisation, Societies and Education, 9*(3–4), 311–322.

Cho, H. S., & Mosselson, J. (2018). Neoliberal practices amidst social justice orientations: Global citizenship education in South Korea. *Compare: A Journal of Comparative and International Education, 48*(6), 861–878.

Choi, Y., & Kim, Y. (2020). Deconstructing neoliberalism in global citizenship discourses: An analysis of Korean social studies textbooks. *Critical Studies in Education, 61*(4), 464–479.

Chung, B. G., & Park, I. (2016). A review of the differences between ESD and GCED in SDGs: Focusing on the concepts of global citizenship education. *Journal of International Cooperation in Education, 18*(2), 17–35.

Dill, J. S. (2013). *The Longing and Limits of Global Citizenship Education: The Moral Pedagogy of Schooling in a Cosmopolitan Age*. Routledge.

Freire, P. (1970a). Cultural action and conscientization. *Harvard Educational Review, 40*(3), 452–477.

Freire, P. (1970b). *Pedagogy of the Oppressed*. Herder and Herder.

Freire, P. (1994). *Pedagogy of Hope*. Continuum.

Freire, P. (1996). *Pedagogia da Autonomia*. Paz e Terra.

Gill, S., & Niens, U. (2014). Education as humanisation: A theoretical review on the role of dialogic pedagogy in peacebuilding education. *Compare: A Journal of Comparative and International Education, 44*(1), 10–31.

Giroux, H. A. (2010). *Bare pedagogy and the scourge of neoliberalism: Rethinking higher education as a democratic public sphere*. Paper presented at the Educational Forum.

Giroux, H. A. (2013). Can democratic education survive in a neoliberal society. In C. Reitz (Ed.), *Crisis and Commonwealth: Marcuse, Marx, McLaren* (pp. 137–152). Lexington Book.

Goren, H., & Yemini, M. (2017). The global citizenship education gap: Teacher perceptions of the relationship between global citizenship education and students' socio-economic status. *Teaching and Teacher Education, 67*, 9–22.

Goren, H., & Yemini, M. (2017). Global citizenship education redefined–A systematic review of empirical studies on global citizenship education. *International Journal of Educational Research, 82*, 170–183.

Iftekhar, S. N., & Misiaszek, G. W. (2019). Critically countering appropriations of global citizenship education in the Indian context: Hard, gated and unmentionable. In *Exploring the Complexities in Global Citizenship Education* (pp. 191–214). Routledge.

Jorgenson, S., & Shultz, L. (2012). Global Citizenship Education (GCE) in postsecondary institutions: What is protected and what is hidden under the umbrella of GCE. *Journal of Global Citizenship & Equity Educaiton, 2*(1).

Kandiko, C. B. (2010). Neoliberalism in higher education: A comparative approach. *International Journal of Arts and Sciences, 3*(14), 153–175.

Kim, H. (2020). Negotiating the global and national in citizenship education: Historical legacies and its complicated neighbor in South Korea. In L. I. Misiaszek (Ed.), *Exploring the complexities in global citizenship education: Hard spaces, methodologies, and ethics* (pp. 178–190). Routledge.

Kim, Y. (2019). Global citizenship education in South Korea: Ideologies, inequalities, and teacher voices. *Globalisation, Societies and Education, 17*(2), 177–193.

Law, W. W. (2007). Globalisation, city development and citizenship education in China's Shanghai. *International Journal of Educational Development, 27*(1), 18–38.

Macrine, S. L. (2020). Introduction. In *Critical pedagogy in uncertain times: Hope and possibilities* (3rd ed., pp. 3–15): Springer.

Meyer, J. W., Bromley, P., & Ramirez, F. O. (2010). Human rights in social science textbooks: Cross-national analyses, 1970–2008. *Sociology of Education, 83*(2), 111–134.

Miles, M. B., & Huberman, M. A. (1994). *Qualitative data analysis: An expanded sourcebook*. SAGE.

Pais, A., & Costa, M. (2020). An ideology critique of global citizenship education. *Critical Studies in Education, 61*(1), 1–16.

Pak, S.-Y., Choe, Y., Kown, O.-W., Lee, C., & Park, A. (2018). *GCED Teacher Training Module Examples and Assessment Tool Suggestions Based on GCED Lead Teacher Program in the Republic of Korea: A UNESCO Research Report*. Bangkok: UNESCO.

Pak, S.-Y., & Lee, M. (2018). 'Hit the ground running': Delineating the problems and potentials in State-led Global Citizenship Education (GCE) through teacher practices in South Korea. *British Journal of Educational Studies, 66*(4), 515–535.

Rapoport, A. (2010). We cannot teach what we don't know: Indiana teachers talk about global citizenship education. *Education, Citizenship and Social Justice, 5*(3), 179–190.

Rapoport, A. (2015). Global aspects of citizenship education: Challenges and perspectives. In B. Maguth & J. Hilbum (Eds.), *The state of global education: Learning with the world and its people* (pp. 27–40). Routledge.

Reidel, M., & Beck, S. (2016). Forcing the world to fit pre-existing prejudices: Why and how global education has failed in the State of Georgia. 교과교육학연구, *20*(3), 196–207.

Rose, C. (2015). Going global? National versus post-national citizenship education in contemporary Chinese and Japanese social studies curricular. In E. Vickers & K. Kumar (Eds.), *Constructing Modern Asian Citizenship* (pp. 83–104). Routledge.

Seth, M. J. (2002). *Education fever*. University of Hawaii Press.

Sim, H. R. (2016). Global citizenship education in South Korea through civil society organizations: Its status and limitations. *Asian Journal of Education, 17*, 107–129.

Steiner-Khamsi, G. (2006). The economics of policy borrowing and lending: A study of late adopters. *Oxford Review of Education, 32*(5), 665–678.

Suarez, D. F. (2008). Rewriting citizenship? Civic education in Costa Rica and Argentina. *Comparative Education, 44*(4), 485–503.

Swanson, D. M., & Pashby, K. (2016). Towards a critical global citizenship?: A comparative analysis of GC education discourses in Scotland and Alberta. *Journal of Research in Curriculum and Instruction, 20*(3), 184–195.

Torres, C. A. (1998). Democracy, education, and multiculturalism: Dilemmas of citizenship in a global world. *Comparative Education Review, 42*(4), 421–447.

Torres, C. A. (2014). *First Freire: Early writings in social justice education*. Teachers College Press.

Torres, C. A. (2017). *Theoretical and empirical foundations of critical global citizenship education*: Taylor & Francis.

Torres, C. A., & Bosio, E. (2020). Global citizenship education at the crossroads: Globalization, global commons, common good, and critical consciousness. *PROSPECTS, 48*(3), 99–113.

Torres, C. A., & Van Heertum, R. (2010). Educational reform in the U.S. over the past 30 years: Great expectations and the fading American dream. In C. A. Torres, R. Van Heertum, & L. Olmos (Eds.), *Educating the global citizen: Globalization, educational reform, and the politics of equity and inclusion* (pp. 3–27). Bentham Science Publishers.

Vickers, E. (2020). Critiquing coloniality, 'epistemic violence' and western hegemony in comparative education – the dangers of ahistoricism and positionality. *Comparative Education, 56*(2), 165–189.

Yoon, N., & Choi, Y. (2017). The portrayal of globalization in economics textbooks of the 2009 revised curriculum: Critical discourse analysis. *Theory and Research in Citizenship Education, 49*(1), 41–67.

Žižek, S. (1997). *The Plague of Fantasies*. Verson.

CHAPTER 10

Diversifying Schools with Global and Indigenous Knowledge: Inclusion of Internationally Educated Teachers (IETs) in Schools and Teacher Education Programs

Chouaib El Bouhali

INTRODUCTION

Contemporary policies and systems of education are situated within dominant discourses of mono-epistemic learning rationalities, neoliberal capitalism, and colonialism (Abdi, 2020; Giroux, 2015), which reduce educators to technicians and diminish substantive meanings of democracy, inclusion, and equity. Critical pedagogy questions these hegemonies in education and society and provides critical agency and awareness to understand and change forces of degradation and dehumanization. In this sense, McLaren (1998) explains that critical pedagogy is "equipped to provide both intellectual and moral resistance to oppression" (p. 29), and critical educators have to assume their responsibility in the reproduction of inequality and injustice. In this pedagogy, educators reflect, resist, and transform the status quo for freedom and justice. Based on his understanding of Freire's critical thought, Giroux (2015) states that "Critical pedagogy attempts to understand how power works through the production, distribution, and consumption of knowledge within particular institutional contexts and seeks to constitute students as informed subjects and social agents" (p. 717). This affirms the relationship between pedagogy, knowledge, and power in relationships, and the role of decolonizing critical

C. El Bouhali (✉)
Edmonton Institute for Diversity Equity Research and Studies (EIDERAS), University of Alberta, Edmonton, AB, Canada
e-mail: elbouhal@ualberta.ca

pedagogy to open up avenues for re-centering and decolonizing production of knowledge and formulation of policies as well.

To sustain robust economic growth, the countries that belong to the Organization for Economic Co-operation and Development (OECD) compete and use their best marketing tools and migration policies to attract the best talented and highly skilled workers in the world. In this attractiveness for talented migrants, Canada is ranked fifth, after Australia, Sweden, Switzerland, and New Zealand (OECD, 2019). This form of global mobility of professionals or brain drain should have negative impact on the countries of origin as they keep losing significant human capital resources of their economy. On the other hand, ethnic-cultural diversity increases in the North host countries with less planning and allocation of resources that assist newcomers in their successful settlement and full participation. In such contexts, the foreign credentials (education, qualifications, and experience) and knowledge of the skilled migrants get invalidated and devalued which impede their access to professional jobs and to regain their social status (Maitra & Guo, 2019).

In this chapter, the discussion aims at humanizing policies that determine the certification of immigrant teachers and decolonizing the epistemologies in teacher education programs and school classrooms. The fact of integrating internationally educated and trained (IETs) into K-12 education systems and diversifying teacher education programs and schools with global and Indigenous knowledges is to disrupt and shift the Western neoliberal understanding of standardized teaching that constructs generic teachers with generic skills and competences. This concept of standardization of education limits meanings of diversity and equity in classrooms (Mayer et al., 2008) and disregards multiplicities of knowledge and context. Including immigrants with their global epistemologies generates new insights and promotes constructive dialogues that go beyond superficial multiculturalism as a traditional framework of integrating immigrants. In this analysis of including the IETs, I use critical pedagogy to understand the marginalization of immigrant teachers in Canada. I consider it as an act of dehumanization that is "a result of unjust order that engenders violence in the oppressors, which in turn dehumanizes the oppressed" (Freire, 1970, p. 44). This dehumanization is caused by "injustice, exploitation, oppression, and the violence of the oppressors; it is affirmed by the yearning of the oppressed for freedom and justice, and by their struggle to recover their lost humanity" (p. 44). Freire (1970) wanted the oppressed to be engaged in a liberation process and to not "remain passive in the face of the oppressor's violence" (p. 37). Additionally, the struggle of making foreign credentials recognized is a struggle for epistemic decolonization, humanization, and emancipation and for making subaltern voices heard. It seeks to raise the critical consciousness and awareness of both the settler and the immigrant and engage in a creative and dialectical epistemological process that results in social change and meaningful inclusion of skilled immigrants.

Mapping the Field of IETs

Immigration plays a major role in the social and economic prosperity of many developed countries; however, it becomes a mechanism of deskilling racialized immigrants and engendering more social inequalities. Canada is using a point system to select the best educated and experienced immigrants in the world. To be considered for permanent residence, skilled immigrants must meet the requirements of the Federal Skilled Worker Program and get assessed in their work experience, language, and education (Government of Canada, 2021). After their arrival, the skilled immigrants have to obtain a license from regulatory authorities to practice their profession. However, they encounter issues of getting their foreign credentials recognized which forces them to engage in lifelong learning and to do menial jobs to survive (Maitra & Guo, 2019; Marom, 2016). Moreover, Maitra and Guo (2019) further argue that racial stratification and racism based on a colonial history are other factors that prevent skilled immigrants from a successful integration into the labor market. Immigrants and refugees are disadvantaged when they seek professional jobs because of the lack of networking and resources (Kariwo, 2019). Similarly in education systems, Schmidt (2010) asserts that: "the Canadian teaching profession's tendency toward exclusion of non-Whites, immigrants, and linguistic minorities" (p. 238). Seen in this light, colonial policy and knowledge in North countries become a patriarchal and racialized framework to mis/interpret immigrants who are moving from the global South with their global epistemologies and worldviews. Despite their years of work experience and education, talented immigrant teachers are seen as inferior and deficient and are rejected from Western public education that is breaking its promise of democracy and equity, as articulated by Marom (2016), "ETs' diverse knowledge and teaching practices were not considered in the credential evaluation process and were not deemed valuable in the recertification program" (p. 92). Internationally educated teachers (IETs) are considered skilled immigrants who go through multiple assessments of their credentials before and after their immigration to Canada. Unlike other professions, immigrant teachers are not visible in schools which are formal organizations that construct knowledge, values, and attitudes of children who are the future citizens. In Canada, teaching is considered the largest profession and education affects lives of every immigrant family and community (Schmidt, 2010). However, in a pluralist society, schools remain homogenous and generic in their teaching practices, epistemology and ontology as argued by Mayer et al. (2008):

> We challenge the construction of the generic teacher where teachers' knowledge and professional practice are assumed to be static commodities that can be objectified, represented by standards, and measured as visible outcomes, transmitted with new economies of scale and efficiency to culturally, linguistically and experientially generic trainees across and irrespective of local histories and sites, and reassembled and deployed in generic schools, regardless of the diverse

industrial, ideological and cultural conditions where teachers actually live and work. (p. 96)

Simply, generic forms of schools and teacher education programs underline uniformity and static ways of learning. In this model, teaching becomes oppressive as it is irrelevant to its ethno-cultural diverse context and confined in a parochial nationalism. In a study by Villegas and Clewell (1998), it has been noted the racial and ethnic imbalance of student population and teaching force and the increasing need of teachers of color to diversify schools and meet the diverse needs of students.

The underrepresentation of IETs in public education systems is happening at the time when the ethnical and cultural diversity of Canadian student population is increasing. As other immigrants, the IETs bring with them an epistemic richness because of their multilingual abilities and their years of education and experience in teaching. They can be role models and cultural liaisons which could contribute in the school achievement of immigrant and refugee students (Schmidt & Janusch, 2016). This rejection of IETs poses questions of: What are IETs missing to be teachers again in Canada? Or is it the unwillingness of the local structures, cultures, and policies to accommodate them?

The literature on IETs shows the marginality that these teachers experience; it is because of the roadblocks of bureaucracy and the structural obstacles they encounter in their teaching recertification (Brigham, 2011; Marom, 2017; Pollock, 2010; Schmidt & Block, 2010; Walsh et al., 2011), and because of the systemic discrimination and racism (Mojab, 1999; Schmidt, 2016). Further, the IETs are marginalized because of the local policies that are standardized and are not equitable to help the inclusion of these immigrant teachers (El Bouhali, 2019a). This reveals a refusal of cultural and racial diversity in the Canadian school systems that favor teachers with the dominant characteristics (white, Canadian-born, monolingual English speaking) (Schmidt, 2016). The foreign credentials of IETs who immigrate from the South represent their history and a non-Western knowledge and worldview (El Bouhali, 2019a). In some contexts, this regime of credentials is used to achieve recognition and privilege; on the other hand, it can be a means of rejection and erosion of others' knowledge and culture. In fact, the skilled immigrants are assessed through systems and policies that are designed for Canadian-born population (Guo & Shan, 2013) and that are distorted by the myth of meritocracy (Cho, 2010). In this way, the regulatory authorities function as a gatekeeper to local schools and other professions, as they have the power not only to certify teachers, but to legitimize the kind of knowledge and pedagogy that are required for the teaching profession as well.

The IETs' foreign credentials confront complexities to be recognized because these newcomers are required to be tested several times for their language, education, and experience. They go through a politics of triage (El

Bouhali, 2019b; Shohamy, 2007) in which government resources are minimized and immigrants are categorized: Some are given conditional access while others are left to the fierce forces of the market. Triage systems block immigrants from access to educational institutions. It is also found that testing of the IETs' language proficiency makes them feel unsecured and mistreated (Marom, 2016, 2017). The use of language tests is to standardize language homogeneity, to determine prestige, and to reject diversity, as argued by Shohamy (2007). In addition, the foreign English language accent and use by immigrant teachers are treated with hostility (Schmidt, 2010). This explains the raciolinguistic ideologies that are used to rationalize linguistic deficiency of foreign users of English (Flores & Rosa, 2015). With this emphasis on perfect use of colonial languages, Pennycook (2007) asserts that Eurocentrism and colonialism marginalize other foreign languages and cultures. This creates a context where difference can be viewed as deficit (Cummins, 2003; Ghosh & Abdi, 2004) and that preserves social and systemic privileges for dominant groups. Accordingly, IETs become unfit to local education systems, though their foreign education and professional experience. This raises ethical questions on decision makers and the goals of immigration policies of Canada that do not secure full and equitable participation of skilled immigrants. Recently, to bolster the economic growth, the federal government has decided to bring 1.2 million immigrants over the next three years (CBC, October 2020); however, it does not state the funding and resources that need to be allocated for their settlement and successful integration.

Decolonizing Critical Pedagogy

In education, critical pedagogy is a humanizing, anti-colonial, and anti-oppressive project as it connects social justice and democracy to the field of education. Critical pedagogy helps to comprehend power in relations and it has a tendency to liberate both the oppressed and the oppressor. In this sense, Freire (1970) affirms that education should be based on the co-creation of knowledge that is a democratic practice that seeks the liberation (from fear) and emancipation of all students. Because of their co-ownership of knowledge, they become engaged in the learning process and they apply their critical reading of the word and the world. In this model of critical education, students are no longer empty vessels that teachers used to fill up with information. They are empowered and have agency that leads to full humanity of everyone. The process of this anti-oppressive education liberates the teacher and the student and sets up inclusive dialogues and constructive conversations that transform distorted realities. In this pedagogy, teachers and intellectuals are committed social agents as they seek to address inequitable conditions.

Exploring the issue of the IETs and skilled immigrants in Canada requires considering its multiple dimensions and nuances. It involves understanding the multilayer meanings given to the fact of marginalizing some to the benefit of others and to the fact that immigrants should accept to be inferior to locals. In the context of IETs, decolonizing critical pedagogy is constructive as it helps to approach the main issue of these immigrant teachers who want to access local schools with open minds and to reason from their perspectives. In academic research, critical thought disrupts the "traditional binaries and dichotomies (i.e., humans/nature; mind/body, etc.) and hierarchical notions (i.e., elitism, privilege) of the world" (Darder, 2015, p. 67). As well, decolonizing critical pedagogy uncovers power in research and knowledge that conceptualize institutions of immigration, citizenship, and democracy, as described by Darder (2015), the interests of the wealthy and powerful control theories of schooling and society. In immigrant-receiving countries, it is observed that democracy is not benefiting everyone; and resources have been invested enough to highlight the value of diversity, but it has not been done enough to demonstrate the importance of inclusion (Bergan, 2018).

The struggle of the IETs and other skilled immigrants to get their foreign credentials recognized and to assert themselves in the Western societies has connections to the Eurocentric ways of producing knowledge and making policies. They are forced to go for lifelong learning and to go through "therapy" for their foreign use of English/French. The context of this struggle is hegemonic, in the Gramscian sense, as it maintains material and power inequalities and exerts dominance over minority groups. This reality is for the advantage of those who are in the center of the privilege and who exercise an epistemic coercion on immigrants as holders of foreign credentials and global epistemologies. The dehumanization of non-Western others and assertion of Western domination have been maintained by some Western knowledge producers, as stated by Darder (2015) that: "[Colonial] studies work to undermine the social and material conditions of the oppressed, often leaving them marginalized, exploited, disempowered, and excluded from participation in decision-making about their own lives and from the benefits enjoyed freely by the wealthy and privileged" (p. 70). Similarly, the policies and practices of immigration and settlement in Canada deepen the social and economic inequalities and create an "abyssal line" between newcomers and the mainstream population. This line generates an ontological and epistemological division between immigrants and aboriginals on one hand and settlers who represent the dominant culture on the other hand. Boaventura de Souza Santos (2019) uses the concept of "abyssal line" to explain the continuous global exploitation of the North countries to the populations of the South. This colonial manipulation of human resources from the South countries continues to be manifested in the attitudes and policies that determine the lives of immigrants and refugees in the host countries. Skilled immigrants are brought to be placed at the discretion of employers and to fill gaps in local markets. In this way, they are stripped of their knowledge, culture, and agency.

The construction of the other as a sub or non-human being who does not possess knowledge, history, and education is based on the intersection between the rational Western epistemic project and the colonial political project (Santos, 2019). The global South has been subjected to colonialism that legitimizes the epistemologies of the North and the unequal status quo in the world. It is essential to note that: "Colonialism did not end with the independence of the European colonies" (Santos, 2019, pp. 118–119). In fact, the colonial project is continuous and takes other forms. It benefits North hegemonies of capitalism and patriarchy that seek exploitation and misrecognition of non-Eurocentric alterity and that modern science is the only valid knowledge (Santos, 2019). European rationalism has worked for the project of colonialism that suppresses other ways of life, education, and knowledge production. In this meaning, Ali Abdi (2009) points out that: "the rationality of European enlightenment could not disentangle itself from the cruel deeds of the colonial master" (p. 273). Rationalism as a Eurocentric civilizational paradigm has been negating non-Western epistemologies and degrading other humans in the world. It has established globally an "epistemic arrogance that assumes the knowledge supremacy of the West over others" (Abdi, 2018, p. 14). Therefore, capitalism, colonialism, and patriarchy function in totality for exploitation, inequality, and exclusion; however, the resistance of oppressed groups against these forms of domination is fragmented and vulnerable (Santos, 2019).

Epistemic Decolonization

Despite this fragmentation in combating the colonial capitalist project, Santos (2019) contends that the South epistemologies that emanate from the struggles against oppression provide an alternative thinking that opens new spaces of diverse ways of knowledge. These ways of knowledge refuse the claim that modern science is the only valid form of knowledge and the division of science and arts. Global and Indigenous epistemologies provide a critical understanding of Western actions and policies that marginalize the lives of immigrant professionals. They go beyond the abyssal line and dichotomies of modern domination that create humans/sub-humans, settler/immigrant, and local/foreigner. The global and Indigenous epistemologies are anti-colonial and anti-racist as they provide a humanizing form of interpretation that recognizes and de-objectifies rejected immigrants and foreigners, and in which everyone is fully human. Thus, non-Western forms of knowledge generate a persistent struggle against capitalism, colonialism, and patriarchy.

Epistemic decolonization is a critical approach that aims at decolonizing teacher education programs, school policies, and regulatory bodies that authorize the material and social oppression of immigrant teachers and their ways of knowledge. It ends control of knowledge and unequal relations of power within schools and universities. In this sense, Santos and Meneses (2019) define epistemic decolonization as:

> Being also a process of ontological and epistemological restitution, decolonization is based on the acknowledgement of silenced knowledges and on

the reconstruction of humanity. Decolonization processes are witness to the numerous alternatives to modern hegemonic thinking. (p. xxii)

Including other epistemologies and silenced knowledges in the education systems is an act of emancipation and humanization. A social justice and betterment in the situation of the IETs could happen if there is a way to an epistemic decolonization and to an epistemological and social "reptura", in the Frierian language, with the unequal systems and forms of the bureaucratization of the mind (Horton & Freire, 1990). An open discussion is required on the recognition of foreign credentials, valuing immigrants with their global South epistemologies, and scrutinizing underrepresentation of immigrant teachers in Western education systems. Epistemic decolonization sets up a critical dialogue that helps to move beyond models of Ethnocentrism and monoculturalism, as suggested by Abdi (2009), that there is a need for a multicentric platform of world epistemologies. South and Indigenous epistemologies lead this project of epistemic decolonization as they include and reconcile different forms of knowing and being. Santos and Meneses (2019) argue:

> Instead of polarization or the dogmatism of absolute opposition, so frequent in academic disputes, the epistemologies of the South choose to build bridges between comfort zones and discomfort zones and between the familiar and the alien in the fields of struggle against oppression. (p. xviii)

It is also important to note that, "the continuities of the globally dominant unicentricism did not and could not silence the counter logocentric realities of people's actualities" (Abdi, 2009, p. 273). With this mind, there is a possibility of an alternative thinking and praxis that can decolonize oppressive narratives and unlearn the hierarchies of Western knowledge. Further, the epistemologies of the South are humanizing as they center the human being, seek multiple polarization of knowledge, and enable immigrants and racialized people to represent the world in their views and their understandings. As articulated by Freire, "respecting the knowledge of the people for me is a political attitude" (Horton & Freire, 1990, p. 101), this principle is a part of the free society that critical pedagogy scholars are advocating for.

Interestingly, epistemic decolonization can be manifested in the way newcomers are treated and are accommodated with their differences. In education, epistemic decolonization can be achieved when teacher education programs and local school systems include immigrant teachers and their global and Indigenous knowledges. In this meaning, Biles et al. (2011) emphasize: "flexibility to adapt our social, economic, and cultural practices to accommodate newcomers as well as a willingness to accept difference and to appreciate the benefits of immigration and diversity" (p. 2). This commitment of recognizing immigrants' qualifications and differences provides a framework for critical engagement and negotiation of common and shared values and benefits. In this interactive model of diversity, the epistemologies of the South and epistemologies of the North create a humanizing and dialectical amalgamation that appreciates the non-Eurocentric ways of knowledge.

Diversifying Teaching Force

The discourses and promises of diversity and multiculturalism that are emptied of meaning fail to recognize IETs' foreign credentials and integrate them in education systems. It is said that Canada is a land of opportunities that hosts everyone with different abilities, cultures, ethnicities, and ontologies; conversely, the unequal power in relations and colonial epistemic constructions make racialized minorities and Indigenous people vulnerable and exposed to racial, socio-economic, and cultural forms of domination and oppression. Banks (2001) explains these material and non-material inequalities when stating that "Institutionalized discrimination and racism are manifest by the significant gaps in the incomes, education, and health of minority and majority groups in many nation-states. Ethnic, racial, and religious minorities are also the victims of violence in many nation-states" (p. 6). Hence, the language of diversity that is void of substantive actions of including immigrant professionals becomes a serious impediment to social justice and equity. It is crucial to note that the mobility of people is a vital source of diversity; however, Western immigration and citizenship policies break their promises of inclusion and justice for immigrants and refugees (Shiza, 2019). To resist forced assimilation and acculturation and because of their frustration with racism and discrimination of the dominant groups, immigrants voluntarily construct and join ethnic enclaves or ghettos that offer them social and cultural solidarity (Shiza, 2019). In this sense, ethnic enclaves generate a mechanism that provides immigrants and newcomers with the social and cultural capital they need for their social and economic uplifting. Chan (2019) affirms that in absence of willingness to be open in discussing issues of meaningful inclusion and employment equity, diversity becomes a "majestic mirage" (p. 114) in a myth of multiculturalism that promotes ethnic and cultural hierarchies (Shiza, 2019). Locally, straw man policies of employment equity and diversity are for the advantage of some groups who are overrepresented in institutions; whereas, the same policies reject and damage the careers of immigrants with foreign credentials (Chan, 2019). Internationally, IETs and skilled immigrants are commodified as their business values are emphasized in the global marketplace. In this line, Abu Laban and Gabriel (2002) point out that "globalization has resulted in a selling of diversity, whereby the skills, talents, ethnic backgrounds of men and women are commodified, marketed, and billed as trade-enhancing" (p. 12). Indeed, a selling of diversity is a dehumanizing act to IETs and professional immigrants as they are deskilled in the welcoming countries that do not design corresponding policies and structures to these talents and are also impassive to racist anti-immigrant ideologies.

Because of their differences and their South epistemologies and worldviews, the IETs with other Indigenous educators are able to meaningfully contribute to the diversification of the teaching staff and teacher education programs. According to Ladson-Billing (2005): "Scholars of color have the potential to blaze new epistemological and methodological grounds. Their work may push them to break down some old paradigms and create new forms of knowledge" (p. 233). In other words, minority scholars can disrupt hegemonic structures and suggest alternative thinking and knowledge that result in social and cognitive justice. Educators from racialized communities hold epistemologies that stem from their struggle and their advocacy for justice and human freedom, which is a liberation of the oppressed and the oppressors at the same time (Freire, 1970).

In North American education, Banks (2001) explains that it is irrelevant to continue applying an assimilationist Eurocentric ideology that is failing certain communities, and its aim has been (200 "to educate students so they would fit into a mythical Anglo-Saxon Protestant conception of the "good citizen"" (p. 6). This hegemonic approach widens the growing cultural gap between an increasingly diverse students and predominantly white educators. Communities of color receive education in a context that is diverse and multicultural; yet, this education is considered in crisis because of students' disengagement and their high rates of dropping out (Sleeter, 2001). Minority students, therefore, lack the dominant language and culture capital that they need to access the society's privileges and opportunities. With this, they become marginalized in their ethnic communities and excluded from the mainstream culture as well (Banks, 2001). From a social justice perspective, education should uplift individuals and communities; in this line, Abdi and Shultz (2008) inform us that education is a "tool for social change with a focus on disrupting the structures and continuities of the ongoing colonizing process of constructing white, and later, other superiorities that are enacted as privilege based on skinned color or other perceived capacities" (p. 29).

In education, there are still debates on whose knowledge should be taught, and there are pressures of market-driven politics that de-value public goods and services (Apple, 2008). Public education has been in the risk of losing its democratic promise of equalizing the playing field for everyone and in which people are not underprivileged because of their markers of difference: race, class, and gender (Carlson & Gause, 2008). In this vein, Apple (2008) points out that "the market has been less responsive to particular groups than others" (p. 34), and race has had a significant presence in plans of market and education. This indicates that it is an exclusion of racialized people and their epistemologies as well, as argued by Abdi and Guo (2008) that postcolonial countries reject "indigenous linguistic, cultural and overall worldview" of other societies (p. 5). Therefore, public education is perpetuating interests of dominant groups and reproducing societal equalities in which immigrants and Indigenous communities are isolated subjectivities.

As discussed earlier, the teaching force of Canadian public schools is homogenous and functions in a context that is ignoring the diverse ways of knowledge of students and their communities. Similarly, teacher education programs highlight standardized ways of teaching and generic teachers who do not consider students' various knowledges in their planning and delivery of school programs (Kelly et al., 2009). In doing so, higher education becomes a milieu that is plagued by corporate models that seek to silence democratic engaged scholarship (Rwiza & El Bouhali, 2018) and maintain one-sidedness in its policy and practice. This institutionalized monoculturalism is a tacit eradication of others' epistemologies and cultures as it is blind and arrogant to the intellectual diversity of students, which is another form of forced assimilation. Banks (2001) explains one of the effects of this monoculturalism on student teachers by arguing that, "the monocultural experiences and the privileged racial and class status of many White college students in teacher education programs is their tendency to view themselves as noncultural and nonethnic beings who are colorblind and raceless" (p. 9). Future teachers are serving a politics of race/color blindness that is limiting educational and life opportunities for racialized minority students. Another effect of monoculturalism that aims at cultivating solid national identifications by stripping students of their ethno-cultural backgrounds is to make them ashamed of their families' languages and beliefs (Banks, 2001). When educators deliberately and unintentionally use the race-neutral lenses to see their students, they are exacerbating the existing inequalities and systemic racism. In fact, educators should respond to the needs of their students and recognize their ways of knowledge and histories, which is a pragmatic and contextualized form of education (Abdi, 2008). They should reject apolitical practice of education and empower students to be active citizens in society. In this regard, Shultz et al. (2009) note: "teacher education programs cannot continue to ignore the fact that student bodies represent multiple knowledge systems. In public school classrooms across this continent, increasingly those knowledge systems are representative of African, Asian, and Indigenous intellectual traditions and not of the European Western tradition" (p. 336). With this in mind, teacher education programs and schools ought to underpin the critical connection of knowledge to the place and to the humans which is a basic human right that fosters meanings of social justice and human dignity. In this model, educators are equipped with skills to teach culturally diverse student populations and relate to their backgrounds. They co-construct contextualized knowledge that helps students to make sense of the influence of race, ethnicity, class, and gender on the production of knowledge (Banks, 2001). Educators could create safe places to discuss issues of their community and to facilitate critical dialogues on differences and race relations, as contended by Sleeter (2008) that, "Well-constructed teacher education programs can guide teachers in learning to build bridges among diverse students and dialog across differences" (p. 216).

It is important to recognize that there is a connection between knowledge construction, school systems, and teacher education programs. In this complex diverse population of students, there is no room for teachers who are not global in their perspective and who are not accommodating of other ways of knowing. In this context, Villegas (2012) asserts:

> Teachers who lack an awareness or who are dysconscious of the multiple social positions they inhabit as individuals and how such positioning influences their understanding of self and the world (including how they see students) are not likely to acknowledge, let alone understand, the complex and intersecting identities of their students—an insight critical to developing the unified teaching approach needed to teach today's students. (p. 290)

In other words, in the contemporary systems of education, teachers are required to understand and interact with the different identities of their students. A diverse teaching force is a democratic project that seeks not just the inclusion of IETs and their epistemologies, but it is an applicable sense of equity that meets the educational needs of all students and provides them with a learning environment in which they experience the value of learning and living together. In this regard, Ladson-Billing (2005) argues that:

> The point of creating a more diverse teaching force and a more diverse set of teacher educators is to ensure that all students, including White students, experience a more accurate picture of what it means to live and work in a multicultural and democratic society. (p. 231)

Including IETs into public education systems is an act that gives meaning to democracy, employment equity, and critical pedagogy that should have positive effects on students and society in general. In this meaning, Kirova (2008) suggests that provincial ministries of education need to incorporate:

> marginalized voices into the privileged domain and to reinvest in employment equity such that the presence and concerns of minorities are introduced into the classroom by losing the visible-minority gap. In other words, a commitment to ensuring that non-Christian, non-White, non-native English-or French speaking teachers are well represented in the public school system is critical for providing nodal points of immediate cross-cultural and multi-ethnic identification for students outside the so-called Canadian majority. (p. 119)

This equitable representation and presence of immigrant teachers in local education systems help minority students to identify themselves with role models that should open up possibilities of social transformation and change that is the main purpose of democratic and fair systems of education.

Conclusion

Immigrant teachers are rendered absent subjects from the education affairs of their children and ethnic communities, as they are considered as unfit to be a part of knowledge production and distribution. In this politics of absences,

Santos and Meneses (2019) argue that the epistemologies of the South: "must transform absent subjects into present subjects as a primary condition for identifying and validating knowledges capable of reinventing social emancipation and liberation" (p. xx). This affirms the critical role of others' epistemologies and its connection to social justice.

Using a colonizing critical pedagogy, I have argued for a meaningful integration of IETs as skilled immigrants and for an epistemic diversity and inclusion in teacher education programs and K-12 public education systems. This liberating praxis is humanizing for both who suffer from subordination and those who formulate policies for schools and higher education. It has been noted that there is a need for global and Indigenous epistemologies and epistemic decolonization to reconcile different forms of knowing and being and to equalize power within educational institutions. Because of the increasingly diverse students and the homogenous teaching force, a diversification of knowledges and teachers within teacher education programs and school classrooms would be beneficial for students' academic achievements and social equity. Western education is under the sway of neoliberal standardized teaching and generic teachers who are unable to understand and meet the intellectual and social needs of diverse students and contribute to the enhancement of their education. Including IETs and recognizing foreign credentials go beyond superficial meanings of multiculturalism and emptied meaning of diversity. In fact, allowing immigrant and Indigenous teachers to public schools establishes forms of epistemic reconciliation and resiliency, and it disrupts colonial Eurocentric thinking and practice that seek to erode the epistemologies and ontologies of non-Western others.

The implication of this chapter is that there is a need for critical pedagogy and epistemic decolonization to understand the suffering of marginalized communities in Western societies and to raise the critical consciousness of both the oppressed and oppressors. The anti-colonial critical analysis of the situation of IETs helps to challenge the generic policies and practices that are indifferent to teachers with foreign credentials and to construct global knowledge as a humanizing process of collaboration and negotiation. Decolonizing critical pedagogy requests educators and public intellectuals to be engaged social agents who critically reflect and act to transform their world and to be participant in the deconstruction of social and cognitive inequalities. Through praxis, humans are creative beings who are able to create history, produce knowledge and ideas for social institutions, and cultivate continuous transformation (Freire, 1970).

Colonialism, capitalism, and patriarchy as modern forms of domination and major constituents of North epistemologies have applied epistemicide to suppress South and Indigenous knowledge systems (Santos & Meneses, 2019). Eurocentric epistemology and policy are colonial frameworks that perpetuate discriminatory structures that do not recognize foreign credentials and non-Western ways of knowledge. However, decolonizing global and Indigenous epistemologies that have germinated from social resistance and struggles of oppressed people provide an equitable alternative way of thinking and knowledge that are post-abyssal and post-Eurocentric (Santos, 2019). Anti-colonial and anti-capitalist knowledges construct channels of dialogue and reciprocity between what is local and what is foreigner and render visible of a critical global teacher with world epistemologies that would be able to engage with complex educational contexts and respond positively to different needs of marginalized students and communities.

REFERENCES

Abdi, A. (2008). From 'education for all to education for none': Somalia in the 'careless' global village. In A. Abdi & S. Guo (Eds.), *Education and social development: Global issues and analyses* (pp. 181–194). Brill.

Abdi, A. (2009). Recentering the philosophical foundations of knowledge: The case of Africa with a special focus on the global role of teachers. *Alberta Journal of Educational Research, 55*(3), 269–283.

Abdi, A. (2018). The contradictions of international education and international development. In L. Shultz & T. Pillay (Eds.), *Global citizenship, common wealth and uncommon citizenships* (pp. 9–21). Brill.

Abdi, A. (2020). *Critical theorizations of education*. Brill.

Abdi, A., & Guo, S. (2008). Education and social development. In A. Abdi & S. Guo (Eds.), *Education and social development: Global issues and analysis* (pp. 3–12). Sense Publishers.

Abdi, A., & Shultz, L. (2008). Continuities of racism and inclusive citizenship. In A. Abdi & S. Guo (Eds.), *Education and social development: Global issues and analysis* (pp. 25–36). Sense Publishers.

Abu-Laban, Y., & Gabriel, C. (2002). *Selling diversity: Immigration, multiculturalism, employment equity, and globalization*. Broadview.

Apple, A. (2008). Schooling, markets, race, and an audit culture. In D. Carlson & C. P. Gause (Eds.), *Keeping the promise: Essays on leadership, democracy, and education* (pp. 27–44). Peter Lang.

Banks, J. (2001). Citizenship education and diversity: Implications for teacher education. *Journal of Teacher Education, 52*(1), 5–16.

Bergan, S. (2018). Democracy, knowledge and inclusion versus post-truth politics—Reaffirming the principles of higher education. In *Higher education for diversity, social inclusion and community: A democratic imperative* (pp. 19–28). Council of Europe Publishing.

Biles, J., Burstein, M., Frideres, J., Tolley, E., & Vineberg, R. (Eds.), (2011). *Integration and inclusion of newcomers and minorities across Canada*. Queen's School, Policy-Metropolis.

Brigham, S. (2011). Internationally educated female teachers' transformative lifelong learning experiences: Rethinking the immigrant experience through an arts-informed group process. *Journal of Adult and Continuing Education, 17*(2), 36–50.

Carlson, D., & Gause, C. P. (2008). Introduction. In D. Carlson, & C. P. Gause (Eds.), *Keeping the promise: Essays on leadership, democracy, and education*. Peter Lang.

CBC. (2020, October). *Federal government plans to bring in more than 1.2M immigrants in next 3 years.* https://www.cbc.ca/news/politics/mendicino-immigration-pandemicrefugees-1.5782642

Chan, J. (2019). Employment equity for whom? Deconstructing the Canadian paradigm. In M. Kariwo, N. Asadi, & C. El Bouhali (Eds.), *Interrogating models of diversity within a multicultural environment* (pp. 97–116). Palgrave Macmillan.

Cho, C. L. (2010). "Qualifying" as teacher: Immigrant teacher candidates' counterstories. *Canadian Journal of Educational Administration and Policy*, 100, 1–22.

Cummins, J. (2003). Challenging the construction of difference as deficit: Where are identity, intellect, imagination, and power in the new regime of truth? In P. P. Trifonas (Ed.), *Pedagogies of difference: Rethinking education for social change* (pp. 9–38). Routledge Falmer.

Darder, A. (2015). Decolonizing interpretive research: A critical bicultural methodology for social change. *The International Education Comparative Perspectives*, 14(2), 63–77.

El Bouhali, C. (2019a). Internationally educated teachers in Canada: Caught between Scylla and Charybdis. In M. Kariwo, N. Asadi, & C. El Bouhali (Eds.), *Interrogating models of diversity within a multicultural environment* (pp. 157–196). Palgrave Macmillan.

El Bouhali, C. (2019b). *Is there a glass ceiling for internationally educated teachers in Alberta? A critical interpretive analysis.* Doctoral dissertation. https://era.library.ualberta.ca/items/cdafd30c-cb43-456e-a78a-805afd72c497

Flores, N., & Rosa, J. (2015). Undoing appropriateness: Raciolinguistic ideologies and language diversity in education. *Harvard Education Review*, 85(2), 149–171.

Freire, P. (1970). *Pedagogy of the oppressed.* Continuum.

Ghosh, R., & Abdi, A. (2004). *Education and the politics of difference: Canadian perspectives.* Canadian Scholars' Press.

Giroux, H. (2015). Neoliberalism's war on higher education and the role of public intellectuals. Límite. *Revista Interdisciplinaria de Filosofía y Psicología*, 10(34), 5–16.

Government of Canada. (2021). *Eligibility to apply as a federal skilled worker (express entry).* https://www.canada.ca/en/immigration-refugees-citizenship/services/immigrate-canada/express-entry/eligibility/federal-skilled-workers.html#minimum

Guo, S., & Shan, H. (2013). The politics of recognition: Critical discourse analysis of recent PLAR policies for immigrant professionals in Canada. *International Journal of Lifelong Education*, 32(4), 464–480.

Horton, M., & Freire, P. (1990). *We make the road by walking: Conversation on education and social change.* Temple University Press.

Kariwo, M. (2019). Introduction. In M. Kariwo, N. Asadi, & C. El Bouhali (Eds.), *Interrogating models of diversity within a multicultural environment.* Palgrave Macmillan.

Kelly, J., Shultz, L., & Weber-Pillwax, C. (2009). Expanding knowledge systems in teacher education: Introduction. *The Alberta Journal of Educational Research*, 55(3), 263–268.

Kirova, A. (2008). Critical and emerging discourses in multicultural education literature: A review. *Canadian Ethnic Studies*, 40(1), 101–124.

Ladson-Billing, G. (2005). Is the team all right? Diversity and teacher diversity. *Journal of Teacher Education*, 56(3), 229–234.

Maitra, S., & Guo, S. (2019). Theorising decolonisation in the context of lifelong learning and transnational migration: Anti-colonial and anti-racist perspectives. *International Journal of Lifelong Education, 38*(1), 5–19.

Marom, L. (2016). *From experienced teachers to newcomers to the profession: The capital conversion of internationally educated teachers in Canada.* Doctoral dissertation. https://open.library.ubc.ca/cIRcle/collections/ubctheses/24/items/1.0300018

Marom, L. (2017). Mapping the field: Examining the recertification of internationally educated teachers. *Canadian Journal of Education/Revue canadienne de l'éducation, 40*(3), 157–190.

Mayer, D., Luke, C., & Luke, A. (2008). Teachers, national regulation and cosmopolitanism. In A. M. Phelan & J. Sumsion (Eds.), *Critical readings in teacher education: Provoking absences* (pp. 79–98). Sense Publishers.

McLaren, P. (1998). *Life in schools: An introduction to critical pedagogy in the foundations of education.* Longman.

Mojab, S. (1999). De-skilling immigrant women. *Canadian Woman Studies/les Cahiers De La Femme, 19*(3), 123–128.

Organization for Economic Development and Cooperation (OECD). (2019). *Migration policy debates.* OECD Publications Service. https://www.oecd.org/els/mig/migration-policy-debates-19.pdf

Pennycook, A. (2007). The myth of English as an international language. In S. Makoni & A. Pennycook (Eds.), *Disinventing and reconstituting languages* (pp. 90–115). Multilingual Matters.

Pollock, K. (2010). Marginalization and the occasional teacher workforce in Ontario: The case of internationally educated teachers (IETs). *Canadian Journal of Educational Administration and Policy, 100.*

Rwiza, G., & El Bouhali, C. (2018). The scholarship of engagement: Moving higher education from isolated islands to an inclusive space. In L.Shultz & T. Pillay (Eds.), *Global citizenship, common wealth and uncommon citizenships* (pp. 57–75). Brill Sense.

Santos, B. (2019). Toward an aesthetics of the epistemologies of the South: Manifesto in twenty two theses. In B. Santos & M. Meneses (Eds.), *Knowledges born in the struggle: Constructing the epistemologies of the global South.* Routledge.

Santos, B., & Meneses, M. (2019). Introduction. Knowledges born in the struggle: Constructing the epistemologies of the global South. In B. Santos & M. Meneses. (Eds.), *Knowledges born in the struggle: Constructing the epistemologies of the global South* (pp. xvii–xliii). Routledge.

Schmidt, C. (2010). Systemic discrimination as a barrier for immigrant teachers. *Diaspora, Indigenous, and Minority Education: Studies of Migration, Integration, Equity, and Cultural Survival, 4*(4), 235–252.

Schmidt, C., & Block, L. A. (2010). Without and within: The implications of employment and ethnocultural equity policies for internationally educated teachers. *Canadian Journal of Educational Administration and Policy, 100,* 1–23.

Schmidt, C. (2016). Herculean efforts are not enough: Diversifying the teaching profession and the need for systemic change. *Intercultural Education, 26*(6), 584–592.

Schmidt, C., & Janusch, S. (2016). The contributions of internationally educated teachers in Canada: Reconciling what counts with what matters. In C. Schmidt & J. Schneider (Eds.), *Diversifying the teaching force in transnational contexts: Critical perspectives* (pp. 137–151). Brill Sense.

Shiza, E. (2019). Transnationalism and ethnic enclaves among immigrants: Resistance to Canadianization? In M. Kariwo, N. Asadi, & C. El Bouhali (Eds.), *Interrogating models of diversity within a multicultural environment* (pp. 117–138). Palgrave Macmillan.

Shohamy, E. (2007). Language tests as language policy tools. *Assessment in Education, 14*(1), 117–130.

Sleeter, C. (2008). An invitation to support diverse students through teacher education. *Journal of Teacher Education, 59*(3), 212–219.

Sleeter, C. E. (2001). Preparing teachers for culturally diverse schools: Research and the overwhelming presence of Whiteness. *Journal of Teacher Education, 52*, 94–106.

Villegas, A. M. (2012). Collaboration between multicultural and special teacher educators: Pulling together the threads in the conversation. *Journal of Teacher Education, 63*(4), 286–290.

Villegas, A. M., & Clewell, B. (1998). Increasing the number of teachers of color for urban schools. *Education and Urban Society, 31*(1), 42–61.

Walsh, S., Brigham, S., & Wang, Y. (2011). Internationally educated female teachers in the neoliberal context: Their labour market and teacher certification experiences in Canada. *Teaching and Teacher Education, 27*(3), 657–665.

CHAPTER 11

Rebuilding the Connection Between Politics and Practices of Democratic Education in China: Critical Reflections

Wenchao Zhang

In a chilly teaching hall of a Chinese public school during my research on democratic education, a teenager boy expressed his idea of democracy to me seriously.

Politics: In this chapter, the meaning of politics tries to keep in line with that the Chinese translation used in practice, to present the phenomenon of democratic education in China genuinely. As the Chinese translation of politics, the word 政治, is mentioned in a high frequency when explaining democratic education. 政治 is originally a loan word, so its meaning changed after being used in the context of China. Integrated with Chinese culture, the main meaning of 政治 is related to the governmental politics. In Xinhua Dictionary, 政治 is explained as activities about national life and international relations that are organized by classes, parties, social organizations and individuals, it is a manifestation of economy ("政", 2020). While in oral communication, the definition of 政治 is more ambiguous, which frequently refers to the process of governance, political system and ideologies. To present this, in this chapter, politics mainly refers to governmental politics. Only in the citation of Freire's argument that education is political, politics means influences and the power of relations.

W. Zhang (✉)
Beijing Union University, Beijing, China
e-mail: sftwenchao@buu.edu.cn

© The Author(s), under exclusive license to Springer Nature Switzerland AG 2022
A. A. Abdi and G. W. Misiaszek (eds.), *The Palgrave Handbook on Critical Theories of Education*, https://doi.org/10.1007/978-3-030-86343-2_11

> I think the word democracy in the expression of Chinese democracy should be replaced, just call it something else. ……as it has huge difference in comparison with western democracy. (Xiuzi, student)

His assertive answer and solemn face contradicted with a lovely happy song coming out from a piano which was open to all the students and staff, and at the same time was mentioned dozens of times as a symbol of the school's democratic culture.

Similar to this boy's reflections, although democracy has been explicitly written into more national documents in China, especially in the Core values of Socialism, many people still cast their doubts on the connotation and practice of Chinese democracy. Chinese democracy is often criticized and condemned as its different understanding and practice through many discussions within China or internationally. However, should/could democracy be all the same across the world and neglect its local issue or culture? As the influence of globalization increases, ideas and ideologies all over the world, particularly those from powerful western countries, are transmitted to more societies in the global market, which largely challenges the values of local culture and shakes people's cultural identity. China is immensely involved in the global market, although China has become increasing powerful and plays a dominant role in the world, it is also highly and promptly influenced by diverse culture and ideologies, especially those from western countries.

Particularly influenced by neoliberalism, more Chinese people including educators and students show their misgivings and doubts on Chinese culture and Chinese democracy. Given this context, how could citizenship education be carried out in China to face these challenges? In such an unprecedented epoch when countries become more connected to each other, how could citizenship education balance between enhancing the students' cultural identity and preparing students for this increasingly interdependent globe?

To reflect on these questions and seek solutions, this chapter adopts lenses of critical pedagogy to reflect on practices of democratic education in mainland China. Focusing on specific practices in China, this chapter will analyze ways and possibilities that could ease the tensions. This chapter is mainly based on my research on the exploration of democratic education in China. Focusing on the implementation of Chinese democratic education, a four-year ethnographic study on democratic education was carried out in two Chinese public schools, which aimed to understand the comprehension and practice of democratic education within the context of mainland China.

Repositioning Democratic Education in China

In the twentieth century, when democracy was imported to transform the aftermath of World War One in China, the idea of democratic education was frequently adopted to cultivate informed citizens in the new environment. Although the connotation and advocated values of democracy have been changed constantly, improving students' democratic consciousness and ability is frequently mentioned as a teaching target in the curriculum system. To realize this target, content about democracy is a scattering in topics of patriotism, governmental politics, democratic revolution and so forth in different subject courses. For example, in the subject of history, the Chinese democratic revolution is introduced as a critical condition before the new regime came into power in 1949. In the curriculum of Morality and Rule of law, the curriculum of Ideology and Politics, democracy is explained as part of the political system, with its historical trajectory in China and specific ways of citizen participation. These relevant learning materials comprehensively present the model of Chinese democracy, which echoes with the target of improving students' democratic literacy officially written in the national curriculum standards (The Ministry of Education of the People's Republic of China, 2011, 2017).

In contrast with the positive advocacy of democracy reflected in the documents and textbooks, people's attitude about democratic education is not as simple as it shows from policies. Many people show their doubts and hesitation in practice. In the process of conducting my research about democratic education, many Chinese educators including practitioners and scholars have been suggesting to me to change my research topic on democratic education in China. Without providing much reasonable reasons, such dialogue often ended in open and mysterious ways, leaving me feeling confused and doubting the value of my research. If I am feeling this way, it is easy to imagine the shadow cast on students when this phenomenon happens to them. In different national documents, the clear emphasis on democracy has shown support on the practice of democratic education, but why do people seem to be confined within an invisible boundary in terms of this topic?

From the perspective of critical pedagogy, the challenge and reflection on such unquestionable and self-evident thoughts could contribute to better understanding and develop a critical view about connections below the surface (Scherr, 2005). With an attempt of breaking up the potential illusions as Apple and Au (2009), the following section would present and analyze problems emerging from the practice to lay the foundation for repositioning the practice of democratic education in China.

THE AVOIDANCE OF POLITICS IN DEMOCRATIC EDUCATION

The contradiction between people's act on democratic education and the general advocacy in documents and policies did not stop outside the research school. Although both schools advocate for a democratic school culture, some staff still show their hesitation and particular concern when talking about this topic .

> PINMING (teacher): Your talk (about democratic education) today is different. As the material you gave me discusses a lot about democracy in [governmental] politics, my first thought about your research is sensitive.

Realizing my research would focus on education rather than directly about governmental politics, this teacher showed a big relief, which enabled our discussion to continue. Such phenomenon of avoiding talking governmental politics in democratic education is common. In many Chinese literature, democratic education is applied as a pure educational theory to promote the quality of teaching and learning on various subject courses. Even for the research on John Dewey's theory, the political and ideological foundation is largely neglected in China.

Furthermore, some people conceive democratic education is isolated from [governmental] politics and works as an independent topic of education.

> YUANBING (teacher): [When talking about the meaning of democracy in democratic education.] What I want to emphasize here is the meaning of democracy we discussed here is democracy in daily life, democracy at work. It is not democracy in political system. I think they are two different things. ...... democracy in politics should be another totally different topic.

By staying away from governmental politics, people attempted to keep democratic education as a neutral area in education and reduced the impact from dispute on ideologies and political systems. However, as Freire (1972) argued that education can never be apolitical, the practice of education is no longer neutral, it constantly receives various influences from different spheres. The impact from ideologies and political system is a critical aspect. The ignorance of ideological and political foundation actually cannot break up their connection with democratic education.

In the face of this phenomenon, I would place some important critical questions for discussion. How could people develop such ideas and what restricts people's mind from building connections between democracy in education and in governmental politics? How could people keep citing Dewey's theory, but totally ignore his ideal of political system and ideologies intertwined in all his propositions? In next section, I would explore possible reasons from the aspect of relevant history and the aspect of contemporary practice.

Historical Reasons and the Conventional Thinking

As the most influential theory and the one which introduced democratic education into China, Chinese literature about John Dewey's theory could generally reflect an overall situation of democratic education in the Chinese context. This section will review the research trajectory of John Dewey's theory in China to explore possible reasons for this phenomenon.

Drawn from history, Dewey's theory is not separated from governmental politics for the duration of time in China. In 1920s, when Dewey visited China, he began to exercise great influence, his theory was still adopted as a combination of democracy, politics and education (Allsup, 2012; Yang & Frick, 2015; Zhang, 2010). At that time, his political proposition of liberalism corresponded with the aspiration of some critical Chinese progressives who hoped to apply liberal democracy to reform China. Within a context when the western political thoughts started to prevail in China, Dewey delivered more than two hundred speeches about social and political philosophy, composed 23 papers about China (Zhang, 2019) and was able to participate in the "New Education Reform Movement (新教育改革运动)" (Feng, 1998; Su, 1995; Zhang, 2019). In accordance with Dewey's argument that the concept of democracy should be readjusted according to particular context, democracy was then understood and translated as the "populism" (平民主义) in Chinese which implies the emphasis on the equality between people (Chuankao, 2009) and the power of the masses. With this background, the practice of democratic education was carried out to support this political idea. Dewey's students and devotees, represented by Tao Xingzhi carried out a great deal of educational reform to realize this target in education. The attention was paid to popular education and teacher education, with the emphasis on people's equal rights of receiving education, and the endeavor to eliminate public illiteracy, all aimed to support the transformation of politics. The difference between Dewey's work and the way Chinese scholars used his work could be recognized. But this is also in line with Dewey's proposition about China. In his middle work, Dewey argued that the act of democracy should be carefully considered upon certain social context, and China could only be saved from its internal transformation rather than the simple imitation of western philosophies (Dewey, 1983). The different activity on democratic education showed a contextual comprehension on Dewey's theory, but the intimate relationship between democratic education and politics ran through this period.

However, since the 1950s, the research on Dewey's theory and democratic education was nearly ceased for the reason of political conflict. Due to the complicated history of the national transformation and the international conflict in the Cold War, Dewey received severe criticisms and strong objection from the aspect of political ideology. Elaborated from the divergence between Dewey's thoughts and the political ideology at that time, the fixed orthodox Marxism, some severe criticism claimed that Dewey was anti-Marxist and reactionary (Su, 1995). The negative comments on John Dewey, such as the "biggest obstacle for establishing the people's education" (Cao, 1950), "the one who induces students to an evil road" (Teng, 1957) was mainly due to its ideology of capitalism, prevented educators from researching his theory, and the relevant topic at that time.

Around 1980s, the situation transformed again. Aligned with the change of the international climate and the adjustment on the political ideology within China, research on Dewey's theory and democratic education recovered again.

In contrast to the former stage when Dewey's thoughts were criticized for its different ideological foundation, academics resumed to seek the compatibility of Dewey's thoughts with the context of China and the political background. But with the impact of the whole evolution, the concentration on Dewey's theory was directed to his propositions particular about education, namely "learning by doing", "education has no end beyond itself" and the "children-centred activity or techniques" (Dewey, 1916). The focus on democratic education in China was then changed from supporting the construction of a democratic society to reform and improve the practice of education itself.

Since then, despite of the revival of researching on Dewey's theory and democratic education, the conceptions and relevant theories are gradually separated from politics. The political and ideological connotation is deliberately and carefully avoided in either the discourse of theory or the discussion of practice. In addition, based on the essential contested feature of democracy (Gallie, 1964) and all the global controversies about democracy, people seem to have gradually gained the conventional thinking that it is easy and safe not to get involved in the issue of political democracy, which echoes with the behavior of teacher PINMING and YUANBING shown above. Such behavior shows an interesting conundrum that people who support democracy or democratic education avoid in-depth discussion on democracy. However, it does not make sense, as the act of avoidance is a political act itself.

The Lack of Comprehension on Democracy

Another factor emerged as the second reason to explain the phenomenon of avoiding politics.

> RESEARCHER: Why do you think democracy is conceived as a sensitive topic? Have you ever considered about this question?
>
> ZINUO (teacher): I think the reason is not we are not allowed to talk about it, but we are not able to provide a reasonable idea or make any reasonable judgement. In this circumstances, we would just avoid this topic. It does not matter if we don't talk about it.
>
> LINYI (teacher): This is a quite big topic, it is related to the history of our country, right? [I think] it might related to the relationship between Communism and democracy. It seems democracy has become a sign of Western capitalism. So it is definite sensitive when talking about it.

As teacher ZINUO admitted, lacking enough comprehension of democracy gives rise to the lack of interest in talking and participating in democracy. While as these two factors have mutual influence on each other, it could lead to a vicious spiral that the less people engage in this topic, the less they understand. As teacher LINYI mentioned in the quote, many people have misunderstood democracy as an equal of liberal democracy in the face of the challenge of other variants of democracy in the tide of globalization.

In terms of the conventional thinking, people hope to get rid of the influence of political ideology in the research of education. Nonetheless, does the split between democratic education and politics really avoid the influence of politics? In the trend of eliminating politics from democratic education in China, it could be recognized that political ideology and climate played a decisive role in this process, which just proved the intimate relationship between politics and democratic education. As Freire (1972) stated, there is no such thing as a neutral educational process. In fact, the practice of democratic education in China is never far away from governmental politics, and it cannot be detoured from it.

History and Features of Chinese Democracy

After the disclosure of the Cold War, the international situation transformed dramatically. Chinese democracy has been constantly constructed. Especially after entering the twenty-first century, the emphasis on Chinese democracy is constantly embodied in a series of national conferences and documents. In the process of democratization, all the historical events and the indigenous Chinese cultures keep shaping the structure of Chinese democracy which gains a set of unique features. Understanding the history and features of Chinese democracy would be helpful for clarifying people's misunderstanding of democracy and reflecting on the rationality of the conventional thinking.

Democracy is not an original Chinese concept, the earliest introduction of democracy was interpreted by western missionaries. 民主, the current Chinese interpretation of democracy was initially picked up by an American missionary, W. A. P. Martin, when translating the book of Element of International Law into Chinese in 1864. At that time, the word 民主 was used for the interpretation of three concepts including president, republican and democracy (Wang, 2006). Despite of its ambiguity and the difference from the original meaning of democracy, 民主 managed to present relevant concepts and features of democracy in western countries, precisely liberal democracy. Hence, from its first appearance in China, 民主 had showed its confusing and elastic meaning.

It was not until the end of nineteenth century when the Chinese imperial system was destroyed by a series of domestic revolution and the exotic invasion that democracy started to get extensive attention in China. Chinese scholars commonly perceive that democratic systems in western countries were established proactively as a result of the economic prosperity and certain social revolutions, while the reform in China was initially coerced by the invasion of exotic powers (Lin, 2012). As the previous social structure was destroyed and the traditional bureaucrat system collapsed, individuals were passively and vulnerably pushed into the process of this big reform (Wang, 2004). Because of hundreds of years' passive governance, people lacked the awareness of freedom and rights despite the massive social transformation. With the collapse of the traditional empire, the emperor no longer had the power, but the authority failed to go directly into the hand of individuals and was transferred to some unofficial regional regimes that were set up right after the empire fell (Lin, 2012). The society changed dramatically, but people's living philosophy still stayed the same. Individuals were not capable of participating in certain democratic procedures, so the preliminary endeavor on liberal democracy, specifically on organizing elections and running the parliament failed successively.

This history proved that the modernization of political system cannot be independent from certain social context, history and culture (Lin & Zhao, 2015). Under this certain social background, in order to assist the mass to firstly get the power, the pursuit of democracy in China diverted its path from seeking for individuals' rights to striving for obtaining the power for the whole community people. The emphasis on the collective power corresponded with the ideology of Marxism which was then chosen as the basis to construct the system of contemporary Chinese democracy since the 1940s.

In the democratic evolution in China, the Chinese translation of democracy, 民主, mainly gains the connotation in the sphere of governmental politics and is understood as a particular type of political system and a process of governance. Among a set of specific rules of Chinese democracy, participation lies as a central and basic principle. In the practice of democratic education, democracy is generally conceived as critical participation in school life. Considering this context, here to explore democratic education in China, I adopt the definition of thick democracy which emphasizes participation and social justice rather than just the electoral procedure (Zyngier et al., 2015). In accordance with Dewey's argument, democracy here is conceived as more than a form of government, but as a mode of associated living, of conjoint communicated experience (Dewey, 1916) especially in the field of education.

The Main Mechanism of Chinese Democracy

In China, the development of democracy started in the sphere of governmental politics, and the word democracy is most frequently used in the same area. Understanding Chinese political system is important for the exploration of Chinese democracy and democratic education. Based on the dilapidated condition of the whole country after the turmoil of the war and the theoretical emphasis on human's sociality in Marxism (1970), China proposed people's democracy which aims to accomplish human beings' freedom and development throughout the prosperity of the whole community (Lin, 2016). For the realization of this political conception, the mechanism of both politics and economy has been constructed after a few decades' exploration.

In the terrain of politics, the system of People's Congress works as a main mechanism. As a hierarchical election and opinion collection system, people's congress is constituted by different levels' congresses from the lowest county level to the highest national level. Electorates could directly participate in the election by voting for the delegates on the lowest level of the congress. And other levels of congresses are formed by the delegates that are orderly elected by its lower congress. The elected delegation obtains the legislation power to formulate regional laws and regulations, the executive power to supervise the work of government, and their most important deputy is to gather electorates' opinions and report them to the congress and the government as the important reference on decision-making (Congress, 2010). Albeit the role of delegate in this system and the role of representative in liberal democracy both signify a level of representation, they are designed with different functions (Pitkin, 1967). Instead of working independently after being elected as representatives in liberal democracy, delegates are required to work faithfully in accordance with their constituents' interests. By gathering and considering people's opinions, this mechanism aims to ensure people's participation of various forms throughout the process of governance.

Another mechanism underpinning people's democracy is the Chinese People's Political Consultative Conference (CPPCC). Consisting of the invitees from democratic parties, various organizations, ethnic minorities, people without party affiliation and people with different career background, this mechanism aims to understand the public opinions from diverse perspectives and provide more chances for people's participation in politics. In practice, it also works as an assistant mechanism for the people's congress. Every year, the national people's congress and the CPPCC on the national level would be organized in the capital city, Beijing, to discuss the significant issues in diverse areas for the whole country. CPPCC is always inaugurated a few days earlier than the national people's congress, so the important issues could be first discussed and questioned through CPPCC. Important opinions or proposals would be reported to the national congress as the critical reference before making the final decisions. The combination of CPPCC and the national people's congress have become the well-known "Two Conferences (两会)".

In correspondence with Marxism's emphasis on economy in the framework of democracy, China developed a particular economic system to support the realization of Chinese democracy. Following the propositions of Marxism-Leninism and practices in Soviet Union, a highly centralized planned economic system has been applied since 1940s. Although in the first several years this system helped the whole country settle down and promoted the economic stability after the chaos, the excessive interfere soon led to inappropriate resource distribution and hardship on people's living, so a significant economic reform was put in place from 1978 (Shen & Yang, 2018). Subsequently, the socialist market economy (社会主义市场经济) was created which maintains to have the market played its basic function of deploying resources under the macro-regulation and control by the State (Xi, 2007). Specifically, the socialist market economy asserts to jointly develop multiple economic elements with the economy of public ownership as the main body (Xi, 2007). In this structure, the employment of public ownership economy aims to ensure the equality, and the permission for other economic forms provides more freedom.

Within the structure built up by these big mechanisms, experiments on other forms of practice are continuing carried out across the country. In accordance with various occasions, activities such as informal democratic consultation, public hearing have been designed to involve people's participation on specific issues. Such exploration has been supplementing and improving the whole practical structure.

Enriching the Connotation of Chinese Democracy with Chinese Culture

Politics would not make any difference if it does not have any positive interaction with the local culture (Harrison & Huntington, 2002). To improve the efficiency and compatibility in practice, Chinese democracy also absorbs elements from the indigenous culture along its evolution.

As a high-frequency concept in national policies, the people-oriented thought (以人为本) is often applied to emphasize the sovereignty of people. But in correspondence with the collectivism culture, here people refer to the whole collective of people rather than individuals. In ancient China, this thought is often proposed to instruct the emperor and governor to pay attention on the interest of the mass. In the pre-Qin period before 221 B.C., a famous political saying first proposed this idea as the following: the populace is the foundation of a country, when the foundation is firm, the country could be stable (民为邦本, 本固邦宁.) (Ruan, 1980). In different times of Confucian philosophy, this thought is explained as: the populace is the most important element in a country; the country comes next; the emperor is of slight importance (民为贵, 社稷次之, 君为轻.) (Zhu, 1992) or the emperor is the boat, the people are the water; the water can uphold a boat, it also can overthrow a boat (君者, 舟也; 庶人者, 水也.水则载舟, 水则覆舟.) (Zhang, 1995). From the original thought, the contemporary people-oriented thought absorbs the emphasis on the ability and power of people, while criticizes the emperor possesses the absolute power and transfers the sovereignty to the people. When deliberating this idea, some scholars adjust the metaphor and assert the people could not only be "the water", but also "the boat" and even "the helmsman" who should be vested in the sovereignty of the country (Wang, 2006). In practice, this traditional cultural thought has already been weaved into the democratic mechanism. The highlight of people's participation of different modes, the collection of people's opinions for decision-making all reflect this idea.

Harmony (和) is another thought extracted from the traditional Chinese culture to enrich the connotation of Chinese democracy. Simultaneously developed by Confucianism, Buddhism and Taoism, this thought is always applied as a fundamental logic when settling the disputes and solving the personal or social problems in Chinese history. In an early traceable text in the Commentary of Zuo (左传), a Confucian classic, the harmony thought is explained with a metaphor:

Sir Jing asked: Is there any difference between [being] the same and harmony?

Yanzi answered: Yes, there is. Harmony is like cooking a meat dish. It needs to be prepared with water, heat, fish sauce, salt and plum, and then cooked with fire. The cook would mix these condiments to make the dish taste good. If it tastes too plain, then the cook would add more condiments. If it tastes too heavy, the cook would reduce some condiments. Such mixture could make a gentleman feel peaceful after eating the dish. This is just like the relationship between the monarch and the ministers. For those when the monarch thinks good, the minister could point out their drawbacks, which could make some improvement. For those that the monarch thinks not good, the ministers could point out the good part. In this way, the governance would be nice and peaceful, the populace would not have the intention to combat and fight. (Guo, 2016)

As implied in this text, harmony is not a single thing or opinion, it is a mixture of difference. By accepting difference, it at the same time stresses the need to coordinate divergence to reach agreement. In the later Confucian classics, this thought was iteratively discussed in various texts: in practicing the rules of propriety, it is harmony that is prized (礼之用，和为贵.). The man of noble character seeks harmony in diversity, the man of vile character aims at uniformity but not harmony (君子和而不同，小人同而不和.).[1] The advantageous climate is not as important as favorable geographical position, the favorable geographical position is not as important as the harmony among people (天时不如地利，地利不如人和.). In Taoism, the Tai Chi diagram also indicates this thought. The two parts yin and yang constitute a circle, which indicates the two contradictive parts could co-exist. Each of them determines and highly influences the existence of the other part (Liu, 2020). In Buddhism, the harmony thought is both manifested as pursuing a harmony of mind in individuals' life and cultivating harmony (Dong, 2007).

Generally speaking, the harmony thought stresses that different parts of the entirety are highly influential on each other and depend on each other, so it is important to coordinate them to reach harmony and cultivate a peaceful atmosphere. Rooted in all these traditional Chinese philosophies, the harmony thought has been applied as a fundamental logic when settling the disputes and solving the personal or social problems in Chinese history. In the 1930s, during the war against Japan, this thought was applied for regional governance by the Communist Party of China (CPC). Aiming at widely absorb opinions on different sides to save the country and protect the populace during the war, the "Triangular Organization" Regime was invented of which the governmental staff and public representatives were made up of three groups. One-third of the group was made up of the CPC members who represented the interest of the proletariat and poor peasants, one-third was the left progressivists representing the interest of petty bourgeoisie, while the remaining one-third was constituted by the middle bourgeoisie and the landlord class who endorsed democratic reform (Lin, 2019; Wu et al., 2019). In that special period, this regime managed to improve the wisdom of the government and won support from more communities. This attempt laid the foundation for the routinization of CPPCC and the further exploration on the mode of consultative democracy.

In summary, the construction of Chinese democracy is based on a fusion of ideologies and cultures and gains a series of features from the historical events and the indigenous culture.

DIGGING INTO THE ROOT, REBUILDING THE CONNECTIONS

After several decades' exploration, the political system of Chinese democracy is becoming more comprehensive and mature. In comparison to the chaotic situation of the preliminary attempt in the mid-twentieth century, the current system encourages people's engagement and provides a supportive basis for its implementation in the terrain of education. In this context, the conventional thinking of avoiding governmental politics is no longer compatible with present needs, and even become a hindrance for the practice of democratic education.

In both of the schools researched, in correspondence with the phenomenon reflected in the literature, most practitioners only take the educational theory as the reference for the practice of democratic education. A set of principles absorbed from educational theories especially from John Dewey's theory are applied as the manifestation of democratic education. However, as democracy in China is originally and still mainly working as a concept in political system, the avoidance of talking politics basically ignores a critical root of democratic education.

In addition, as such educational principles are built up on certain understanding of democracy, simple imitation on these principles may lead to inappropriate application in a different context and may cause more problems unconsciously. For example, as the most cited theory of democratic education in the school researched, Dewey's arguments on education work as the educational embodiment of his ideal democracy. Being developed with a comprehensive meaning from diverse perspectives including the aspect of society, ethics, politics, economics and even religious, the ultimate goal of Dewey's theory is to improve the practice of liberal democracy in a capitalist society. Merely avoiding talking about the political elements cannot erase the influence of its political foundation, and may lead to more confusions and contradictions in practice.

Indicating the political foundation in Dewey's theory does not mean I intend to request educators to stop researching or learning from Dewey again. This chapter just wants to remind people that the connotation of democracy including its political aspect lays the foundation for the implementation of democratic education and needs more attention. Based on a clear understanding of democracy in China, different theories of democratic education could be applied in a more appropriate way.

In fact, although most practitioners do not relate the exploration of democratic education with Chinese democracy in governmental politics, features and principles of Chinese democracy have been implicitly adopted to translate the theoretical principles into practice. For example, in both research schools, an activity of raising suggestions for the school management has been carried out for years.

> YANRAN (student): [In Central City Middle School,] students could propose their own doubts or suggestions about school management [by writing a proposal]. The student council would first help deal with these proposals. We would form feedback working groups for each proposal to enhance it with a more reasonable solution and prepare for the formal discussion with leaders…… Every year around the time of student council's campaign, a formal proposal conference would be organized publicly based on the interaction between the proposer, the student council and school leaders…… Proposals would be discussed between different stakeholders in this conference……School leaders of different departments would participate in this discussion…… if they agree with the suggestions, they would put it into practice. If not, they would provide some reasonable answers.

In Sunflower Middle School, a similar activity, the "Good Idea" is carried out annually.

> YUANBING (teacher/ school leader): In our school, students have the autonomy and many opportunities to raise their suggestions. For example, every year we organize an activity called Good Idea…… Students' opinions could be raised and collected through this activity. Their opinions will be considered by school leaders to see if they can be implemented. If cannot, the feedback will be given to students.

Observing carefully, this activity mirrors the mechanism of people's congress and CPPCC. Students are encouraged to report their own opinions, and the final decision would be made by a central committee. At the same time, harmonious thought and consultative democracy are integrated in different procedures to promote a friendly negotiating atmosphere.

As Freire positioned education is inherently political, and the neglect of the political background cannot remove the political influence at all. If, in a certain period of time, avoiding politics could help maintain the freedom of doing research on democratic education, this conventional thinking has suppressed people's freedom on understanding democracy and put negative restrictions on schooling currently.

Conclusion

From the perspective of critical pedagogy, democracy in education emphasizes different stakeholders' participation in the process of decision-making including students, teachers and government to realize people's emancipation. In schools, the practitioners indeed try hard to provide more opportunities for students' participation, a series of arrangements allows students to communicate with adults and cooperate to solve problems at school. For example, activities mentioned above encourage students to express their ideas and participate in the process of school management. This enables students to experience that they are not just followers or listeners, they are members and could be active participants who can control their campus life. However, the avoidance of talking about governmental politics does not support this proposition, it actually prevents students' and teachers' participation in such topic which leads to the opposite of schools' democratic goal in this aspect. In addition, this is inconformity with the requirement of Chinese political system either. Promoting participation and maintaining social justice are two mains aspects in the political system of Chinese democracy as well. If such content can only be learned in class rather than being discussed in practice, in Freire's position, this could be called the banking method of education as it does not involve people's participation in a dialogue which allowed everyone to engage in the process of creating knowledge (Kohan, 2018; Taylor, 1993).

In practice, there are a few Chinese teachers who are not concerned to relate democratic education with Chinese democracy in political system. All these teachers obtain one feature in common, that they understand Chinese political system quite well. They understand the history of Chinese democracy and are capable of explaining the relationship between democracy in political system and in education. This echoes with the phenomenon that many teachers showed a lack of comprehension of Chinese democracy in the political system.

In conclusion, the reestablishment of an explicit relationship between democracy in politics and democratic education is demanding in China. This would be helpful for both educators and students to understand and practice of democratic education more comprehensively. While the preparation for constructing this connection is to enhance educators' political literacy especially about the Chinese political system, on the basis of that, they would feel easier about connecting the two themes. At the same time, this would assist them in obtaining more references for the comprehension and practice of democratic education.

Building up a clear connection with relative politics, students would be able to develop a deeper understanding on both the advantages and drawbacks of Chinese democracy in the school activities, which would enhance their cultural confidence and culture identity. Simultaneously, the ability of engaging in democracy and the rational way of analyzing democracy would allow them to gain in practice and would enable them to better understand and respect the divergence among various ideologies.

Note

1. In this citation, gender issues are recognized as only man is mentioned in this philosophy. But this problem originates from Confucius himself.

References

Allsup, R. E. (2012). Music education and human flourishing: A meditation on democratic origins. *British Journal of Music Education, 29*(2), 171–179.

Apple, M. W., & Au, W. (2009). Politics, theory, and reality in critical pedagogy. In *International handbook of comparative education* (pp. 991–1007). Springer.

Cao, F. (1950). 杜威批判引论 (上篇) [Critiques on John Dewey (Part 1)]. 人民教育, 6, 21–28.

Chuankao, W. (2009). 杜威来华与"五四"之后的教育界——以陶行知的杜威思想受容为中心 [The field of education after the May fourth Revolution and Dewey's visit to China: Centering on Tao Xingzhi's acceptance of Dewey's thoughts]. 社会科学研究, 6, 142–153.

Dewey, J. (1916). *Democracy and education: An introduction to the philosophy of education*. Macmillan.

Dewey, J. (1983). Federalism in China. In J. A. Boydston (Eds.), *The middle works of John Dewey: 1899–1924*. Southern Illinois University Press.

Dong, Q. (2007). 汉传佛教的和谐伦理思想研究 [Research on Chinese Buddhism and the ethical thought of the harmony thought]. 道德与文明, 6, 24–28.

Feng, W. (1998). 民国时期小学课程改革浅探 [Exploration on the primary school curriculum during the Republic of China era]. 安徽教育学院学报 (哲学社会科学版), 1, 79–83.

Freire, P. (1972). *Pedagogy of the oppressed* (M. B. Ramos, Trans.). Herder.

Gallie, W. B. (1964). *Philosophy and the historical understanding* (Vol. 16). Schocken Books.

Guo, D. (2016). 左传 [The commentary of Zuo]. 中华书局.

Harrison, L. E., & Huntington, S. P. (2002). 文化的重要作用 [Culture matters]. 新华出版社.

Kohan, W. O. (2018). Paulo Freire and philosophy for children: A critical dialogue. *Studies in Philosophy and Education, 37*, 615–629.

Lin, P. (2019). 协商民主的发展进程：从协商建国到协商治国 [The evolution of consultative democracy: From the country establishment to country management on the basis of consultative democracy]. 行政与法, 11, 1–7.

Lin, S. (2012). 建构民主——中国的理论，战略与议程 [Constructing democracy: China's theory, strategy and agenda]. Fudan University Publishing House.

Lin, S. (2016). 论人民民主 [Discussing people's democracy]. Shanghai People's Publishing House.

Lin, S., & Zhao, Y. (2015). 中国协商民主的逻辑 [The logic of Chinese consultative democracy]. Shanghai People's Publishing House.

Liu, J. (2020). "和合" 思想的基本内涵与实践意义 [The connotation and practical meaning of the harmony thought]. 湖南省社会主义学院学报, 21(1), 66–68.

Marx, K. (1970). *Critique of Hegel's philosophy of right*. Cambridge University Press.

Ministry of Education of the People's Republic of China. (2011). *Compulsory education curriculum standards of morality and society*. Beijing Normal University Publishing Group.

Ministry of Education of the People's Republic of China. (2017). *High school curriculum standards of ideology and politics*. People's Education Press.

Pitkin, H. F. (1967). *The concept of representation*. University of California Press.

Ruan, Y. (1980). 十三经注疏 [Thirteen classics explanatory notes and commentaries]. 中华书局.

Scherr, A. (2005). Social subjectivity and mutual recognition as basic terms of a critical theory of education. In *Critical theories, radical pedagogies, and global conflicts* (pp. 145–153). Rowman & Littlefield.

Shen, W., & Yang, R. (2018). 从理论突破到体制创新: 中国特色的社会主义与市场经济融合发展研究 [From the theoretical breakthrough to the institutional innovation: Research on the integration of Chinese socialism and market economy]. 现代财经 (天津财经大学学报), *11*, 2.

Standing Committee of the Eleventh National People's Congress. (2010). 中华人民共和国全国人民代表大会和地方各级人民代表大会代表法 [Act on the national delegates and other delegates on the regional level of people's congress]. 中国人大网. http://www.npc.gov.cn/wxzl/gongbao/2010-12/09/content_1614028.htm

Su, Z. (1995). A critical evaluation of John Dewey's influence on Chinese education. *American Journal of Education*, *103*(3), 302–325.

Taylor, P. V. (1993). *The texts of Paulo Freire*. Open University Press.

Teng, D. (1957). 批判杜威关于道德教育的理论 [Criticizing Dewey's thought about moral education]. 河北天津师范学院学报, *1*, 1–11.

Wang, D. (2004). 马克思主义学说与今日中国 [Marxism and the current China]. 云南大学学报: 社会科学版, *3*(1), 3–6.

Wang, R. (2006). 庶民的胜利——中国民主话语考论 [The triumph of the grassroot people: Discussion on Chinese democracy]. 中国法学, *3*, 30–45.

Wu, D., Liu, L., & Mao, Z. (2019). 中国社会主义协商民主: 逻辑基础与实践路径 [Chinese socialist consultative democracy: The logical foundation and practical path]. 赤峰学院学报 (汉文哲学社会科学版), *40*(12), 17–20.

Xi, J. (2007). 科学发展观百科辞典 [Dictionary of scientific outlook on development]. 上海辞书出版社.

Yang, J. Z., & Frick, W. C. (2015). When Confucius encounters John Dewey: A brief historical and philosophical analysis of Dewey's visit to China. *International Education*, *44*(2), 7.

Zhang, H. (2010). Cultivating an inclusive individuality: Critical reflections on the idea of quality education in contemporary China. *Frontiers of Education in China*, *5*(2), 222–237.

Zhang, H. (2019). 论杜威与中国教育改革 [Discussion on Dewey and educational reform in China]. 华东师范大学学报 (教育科学版), *37*(2), 18–28.

Zhang, J. (1995). 荀子译注 [Explanations about Xunzi]. 上海古籍出版社..

Zheng (政). (2020). *Dictionary Xinhua dictionary* (12th ed.). The Commercial Press.

Zhu, X. (1992). 孟子集注 [Explanations about Mengzi]. 齐鲁书社.

Zyngier, D., Traverso, M. D., & Murriello, A. (2015). 'Democracy will not fall from the sky'. A comparative study of teacher education students' perceptions of democracy in two neo-liberal societies: Argentina and Australia. *Research in Comparative and International Education*, *10*, 275–299.

CHAPTER 12

Teaching Social Justice Amidst Violence: Youth and Enacted Curricula in Canada, Bangladesh, and México

Kathy Bickmore and Rim Fathallah

This chapter articulates, and applies to education, a theoretical perspective on the dimensions of social conflict, violence, and just peace. Violence is a key indicator and form of injustice. Education may (but often does not) address the dimensions and causes of destructive conflict, to contribute to building just peace. Drawing from a five-year research project with youth and teacher participants in three or four urban public schools in each of Mexico, Bangladesh, and Canada, the chapter highlights the direct (physical) and systemic (injustice-based) violence that these young people routinely endured. This lived experience of violence was linked to participants' marginalized social-economic class, ethnocultural and gender identities. These countries differ widely in their cultures and levels of violence, yet none are divided or war-torn societies: The study focuses on the "ordinary" social conflict and violence that may be obscured or ignored in some research on education in war zones. The chapter also illustrates and discusses, based on examples of participating teachers' work, how schooling might contribute to disrupting ordinary violence—informing young people's agency to mitigate or transform those problems. The chapter argues that education for justice requires

K. Bickmore (✉) · R. Fathallah
Ontario Institute for Studies in Education (OISE), University of Toronto, Toronto, ON, Canada
e-mail: k.bickmore@utoronto.ca

R. Fathallah
e-mail: rim.fathallah@mail.utoronto.ca

© The Author(s), under exclusive license to Springer Nature Switzerland AG 2022
A. A. Abdi and G. W. Misiaszek (eds.), *The Palgrave Handbook on Critical Theories of Education*, https://doi.org/10.1007/978-3-030-86343-2_12

confronting violence and facilitating students' development of peacebuilding agency. However, education that addresses only symptoms (not causes) of violence or that only holds individual students responsible—without introducing them to mediating institutions, civil society actors, social movements, and governance processes to transform the causes of that violence—is inadequate. Learning about collective democratic factors and actors is key to building potential bridges across difference and remedies for the justice conflicts that underlie customary violence.

THEORETICAL FRAMEWORK: DIMENSIONS OF SYSTEMIC VIOLENCE AND JUST PEACE (IN) EDUCATION

Social conflicts refer to competing interests and disagreements among groups that may be expressed in constructive (resolution or transformation) and/or destructive (violent) ways. Violence, on the other hand, is direct (intentional physical hurt) and/or indirect (systemic injustice) harm (Galtung, 1969, 1990). Indirect conflict and violence have cultural (systems of belief legitimizing inequity, fractured social ties, and violence) and/or social-structural (systemically inequitable distribution of power and resources) dimensions: each reinforces the other (also Ross, 2007). In contexts of systemically unequal power, some forms of direct physical violence, such as gendered or criminal "gang" aggression, are so normalized as to seem "invisible" and inevitable (Bourgois, 2009).

The opposite of violence is justice-building transformation to build systemic peace. Political theorist Nancy Fraser's (2004, 2005) articulation of the "content" of justice—(social-structural) redistribution of economic resources plus (cultural) recognition of plural identities—is parallel to Galtung and Ross' theories of sustainable peace. Fraser also articulates a third dimension of justice, (political) representation, referring to the "processes" by which diverse people are enabled to participate and to get heard in nonviolent confrontation to transform social conflicts, in the globalized context of multilevel institutions and rules for decision-making. Together, these three interacting dimensions of justice constitute a strong foundation for building sustainable (just) peace: participation in dialogic processes transforming social conflicts, cultural expression of identity-based inclusion and rejection of bias, and political-economic redistribution of resources for social-structural equity.

Putting together these intersecting factors enables us to discern the potentially transformable *conflicts underlying* patterns of *harm*, and thereby to shed light on the ways education might contribute to building toward just peace in the context of globalized systemic violence (also Bellino et al., 2017; Lopes Cardozo et al., 2016). Alternative ways of handling social conflicts (and their sometimes-violent symptoms) range from narrow control-based interventions aimed at securitization (peace*keeping*), through participatory democratic processes of mutual dialogue, negotiation, and problem-solving to resolve evident disputes and their causes (peace*making*), toward multidimensional systemic approaches (peace*building*, also called transitional justice and conflict transformation) that (re-)create inclusive processes in order to collectively address and redress cultural and social-structural injustice and other social conflicts (Galtung, 1976; Lederach, 2003). People and communities develop (narrow or wider) repertoires of options for addressing social conflicts:

> Violence, clearly, is resourcelessness; it is the brutal response of those who see force as their only approach to conflict. Nonviolence, in contrast, is resourcefulness; it is the cultivation of and the reliance on a broad range of approaches to conflict resolution. (Franklin, 2006, p. 261)

Globalized systemic causes of resourcelessness may have heartbreaking consequences in very particular local neighborhoods (and their schools). Examples include ecological disasters caused by transnational business out-sourcing such as factories or chemical plants, shipping, or pipelines (Nixon, 2011). Citing urban activist Butterfly GoPaul and sociologist Julius Haag, a recent news analysis shows a concentration of mutually reinforcing systemic and physical violence in particular unfortunate neighborhoods:

> So many Toronto locations where gun violence has been historically rampant have also been 'hot zones' for the COVID-19 pandemic. The same long-standing systemic and structural symptoms of poverty and inequities that have led to worse outcomes with the virus are the major root causes of gun violence. … Violence is concentrated in places that [Haag concurs], 'have also faced other forms of systemic structural disadvantage, a lack of sustained investment in community programs and initiatives, and these also tend to be the neighborhoods that suffer the most from aggressive policing.' (Ngabo, 2021, p. IN4)

In the conceptual diagram below, the triangle's points refer to the three intersecting dimensions of conflict underlying (just) peace and (unjust) violence. Participation, at the top, refers to direct or representative engagement in social conflict-handling processes. Inclusion and equity, at the bottom, are the indirect dimensions of (in)justice conflicts that would be redressed and transformed in a comprehensive systemic peacebuilding process. The outer (yellow) triangle represents the violence that surrounds many human societies. The inner (blue) triangle represents systemic democratic (just) peace—the processes by which conflicts and dimensions of injustice (identity-based exclusion and/or resource and status inequity) are collectively transformed into dynamic, just relations.

Extending Galtung's notions of peacekeeping (securitization) and peacemaking (negotiation) to make visible the actions for addressing indirect (as well as direct) dimensions of conflict, the middle (green) triangle represents a range of options and strategies to handle conflicts, in order to resist and replace violence. Closest to the yellow (violent) edge of the green zone, imposed regulatory interventions (comparable to peacekeeping) aim to stop particular outbreaks of violence such as military attacks or child abuse, while not probing causes or challenging injustices at the roots of violence. These approaches "affirm" existing social-cultural hierarchies (Fraser, 2008), yet can temporarily mitigate or stop episodes of un-peace. Examples include worker protection regulations (that do not challenge the wage structure) or policing to control criminal violence (that disproportionately repress certain types of people rather than addressing systemic incentives). Closer to the blue (systemic peace) edge of the green zone (comparable to peacemaking and other problem-solving processes), conflict mediating actions represent restorative and transitional justice efforts to reverse and "transform" historic and contemporary systemic harm at the roots of destructive conflict. This green zone is the crucial arena of democratic citizenship—where people act with local and distant others, through multidimensional social-institutional processes, to handle and transform injustices and other social conflicts.

This chapter applies the above theories to education, to make sense of the dimensions of making, building, and teaching peace in schools (also Bickmore, 2017; Carbajal & Fierro, 2019; Cremin & Guilherme, 2016). Of course, young people learn "feet first" as well as "head first" (McCauley, 2002). That is, models, practices, and discursive understandings for handling conflicts are embedded in daily social learning in each lived context (Bandura, 1986), and explicit school curriculum may ignore, contradict, inform, or supplement what diverse young people learn from their experiences. Schools may contribute (or not) to peacebuilding, by creating opportunities for young citizens to develop repertoires of capabilities, motivations, and understandings for democratic peacebuilding citizenship agency that recognize, challenge, and build upon their lived understandings and concerns about conflicts.

The provision, structure, and curriculum of school education—such as legitimating (or challenging) chauvinism or inequality, or (ir)relevance to communities' histories of relative deprivation—may reinforce *or* resist direct and indirect violence. Many educational responses to conflict are relatively passive, working within the status quo (Davies, 2011). For instance, educative forms of peacekeeping (Bickmore, 2005) teach students to internalize self-regulation and "governmentality" (Foucault, 2003), to supplement direct coercion. Such lessons emphasize individual values, morals, and compliant behavior, without facilitating inclusive peace*making* (problem-solving) that would examine each participant's point of view on their own needs or causes of the conflicts. In contrast, comprehensive "justice-sensitive" peacebuilding education (Davies, 2017) would both mitigate direct violence by addressing dimensions, causes, and consequences of conflicts in a participatory manner and creating preconditions for democratic transformation to redress societal fracture and injustice. For instance, pedagogical inquiry about particular institutions' contributions to injustices, or encounters with multiple perspectives about difficult histories, would actively seek to disrupt enmity or abuse of power.

On one hand, when school experiences create opportunities for students to acquire and practice language, concepts, and skills for recognizing, communicating, and deliberating about the causes and consequences of destructive conflicts, it may facilitate their development of agency applicable to transformative peacebuilding. On the other hand, school curriculum may over-emphasize the responsibilities of (even victimized) individuals for handling conflicts properly, at the expense of enabling and inspiring them to probe and resist social-structural, cultural, and political factors that constrain their agency and reinforce un-peace. Discourses over-emphasizing individual responsibility let the powerful off the hook and divert attention from how socially structured interactions actually work:

> The discourse of personal responsibility fails to acknowledge the many ways that some middle-class and rich people behave irresponsibly. It assumes a misleading ideal that each person can be independent of others and internalize the costs of their own actions. It ignores how the institutional relations in which we act render us deeply interdependent. (Young, 2011, p. 4)

In contrast to prevailing personal responsibility approaches, transformative agency for peacebuilding requires critical recognition of the indirect social-economic, cultural (including gender), and political dimensions of social conflicts—awareness of how people may make demands for state and transnational policy change, in order to alleviate the systemic causes of direct violence and other harm.

This chapter illustrates this framework in relation to students' understandings and capabilities, and the implicit and explicit curriculum-in-use reported by themselves and their teachers in focus groups in México, Bangladesh, and Canada.

Research Design and Methodology

This chapter is drawn from a multiyear international research project that involved youth and teacher participants in 3–4 schools in each of Mexico, Bangladesh, and Canada—countries that are not war zones or divided societies, but located very differently on the Global Peace Index (IEP, 2016, 2017). Out of 163 countries: Canada was 8 (peaceful), Bangladesh 83 (medium), Mexico 140 (violent). The sites were ordinary curriculum practices in ordinary public schools in economically marginalized areas experiencing too much violence—not special justice ed programming, but rather the potential spaces for just peace transformative learning within these ordinary settings.

The research methodology is inspired by culturally "elicitive" conflict transformation education (Lederach, 1995): Its focus was not on any explicit or self-contained program of peace or citizenship education (prescription), but on the understandings and concerns selected young people narrated based on their life experiences, compared with the ordinary curriculum-in-use described by the youth and by participating teachers in the same classrooms. The study was designed to facilitate participants' articulation and participatory dialogue about the lived social conflicts experienced by marginalized youth in each context, and upon the ways their daily schooling did and did not show potential to develop their citizen agency for transforming those conflicts.

The *cases* are purposively selected urban public schools in economically marginalized neighborhoods suffering from direct violence—in one Ontario, Canada city (3 schools, grades 5–8), two Bangladesh cities (2 boys' and 2 girls' schools, grades 6–9), and one Guanajuato, Mexico city (2 elementary schools grades 5–6, and 2 lower secondary schools grades 7–9), in 2014–2017. *Participants* included 81 Mexican, 36 Bangladeshi and 81 Canadian youth (age 10–15), and 21 Mexican, 16 Bangladeshi, and 17 Canadian teachers who taught those young people. Beyond location in violent communities, the criterion for including schools, teacher, and student participants was just that they needed to be interested enough in violence-reduction education to choose to participate, during compensated school hours, in the focus group workshops.

Within each case, multiple *student focus group* workshops per school each elicited 4–6 students' understandings and concerns about various social conflict and violence problems they experienced, and what they believed citizens could do about these problems. After briefly describing their understandings of the conflicts represented or elicited by a set of 10–12 image prompts (locally relevant cartoons and photos), the young people selected two problems they considered to be of particular concern, and worked like reporters, discussing the "who-what-where-why-how and now what" of each of those conflicts—the stakeholders affected, what they thought had caused or exacerbated the problems, and what they thought authorities or ordinary citizens could do about those problems. Students also mentioned how their experienced school curricula had (and had not) addressed those concerns and offered suggestions for teachers.

A series of *teacher focus group* discussions in each school, a few months apart, began with their examples of what and how they had been teaching, that they viewed as relevant to peace and/or citizenship. One school in Mexico, GTO4, was able to hold only two teacher focus group sessions. One school in Canada (ON2A) was similarly cut off by staffing changes after two teacher focus group sessions, but we were able to start over there with new groups of teachers and students (ON2B, not reported separately in this paper). The data collection process in Bangladesh, conducted by Ahmed Salehin Kaderi (2018) under the first author's supervision, was shorter, including just two student focus groups and (pre and post) two meetings with the teacher focus group in each school.

Teachers helped to recruit sets of student volunteers in their schools to represent the diversity of each school's population in relevant grades. Teachers previewed the image prompts to be used with students to improve local comprehensibility and relevance. After completing student focus groups in each school, the research team presented to teacher focus groups (draft, anonymized summary) results of their students' focus groups, to invite teachers' reflections on how their teaching responded to students' understandings and concerns and to elicit further teaching examples. Later teacher focus group sessions were animated by the research team's summary analyses of official curriculum guideline documents in each jurisdiction, prompting further joint reflection about potential intersections or (mis-)fit between peacebuilding goals and the curricular spaces available within teachers' work contexts. In keeping with a commitment to democratic research process, student and teacher focus group processes were flexibly semi-structured, designed to be educative and to invite participants to voice and pursue their own concerns (Mason & Delandshere, 2010).

Contexts: Living with Violence

In the communities where we conducted this research, all the foregoing dimensions of violence were pervasive and apparent. There was wide economic inequality between wealthy and poor neighborhoods and schools; the school research sites were situated in poor and working-class areas suffering from high levels of criminal and intimate violence. To a significant degree in the Canadian schools, and to an even higher degree in Mexico and Bangladesh, students and some teachers expressed considerable concern and discouragement about pervasive physical violence in communities and homes and (especially in Mexico and Canada) inside schools. Gender-based violence and harassment were very pervasive and a major concern in all three settings, especially Bangladesh and Mexico. Bangladeshi students described sexual harassment as "an everyday normal experience." Only in the Bangladesh schools, (male) students also reported that teachers frequently hit them (although corporal punishment had become illegal).

In the Canadian schools, many students were aware of help lines, domestic violence shelters, and welfare options. In the Mexican and some Bangladeshi schools, some students knew about the government child protection agency and welfare programs, but did not show awareness of other violence mitigation institutions (such as those available to the Canadian students). Most teachers in all participating schools showed evident compassion and offered extra support to students. So, severe violence and fear were omnipresent (to varying degrees) in these contexts. Especially in Bangladesh and Mexico, young people knew of very few ways to get assistance. Schools were sometimes safer than outside and sometimes offered protection.

Young People's Perspectives and Peacebuilding-Relevant Education in Their Schools

Student focus group participants from all three **Canadian** schools, in especially violent marginalized neighborhoods in an otherwise fairly peaceful big city, described direct experience with physical violence. Inside the school, a girl described being choked by a peer; a boy spoke of a friend sexually abused at school; students described a lot of bullying. Teachers confirmed frequent violence, especially during recess. In ON3, students in all focus groups described pervasive ongoing peer aggression: a girl (East Asian heritage) sobbed about it during one focus group session. A boy (African heritage) in another focus group also showed tears about being bullied, saying bitterly, "There is no peace in the classroom whatsoever." Students told of a memorial for a murdered girl in front of the school, a teacher at their school accused of child abuse, a lock-down when they hid from a building invader. ON3, in an especially high-poverty community, distributed food supplies to needy students' families—confidentially, due to stigma against those facing economic scarcity.

Students in all three schools, especially ON2 and ON3, described their neighborhoods as unsafe, with pervasive abuse and violence, as well as frequent surveillance and stops by police; a few mentioned racist treatment by police. Their relatives had been shot or brutalized—two by police, another by a community member, a recent stabbing at the library. Several students also had been targeted by indirect (bias-based) violence, such as Muslims called terrorists, homophobic slurs, and racist "jokes." Most students frequently encountered poor and homelessness people on the street, some of their parents/guardians were out of work. Several students' families had immigrated to Canada to escape war, finding that they had not left all insecurities behind. In sum, these Canadian participants witnessed and suffered from substantial direct and indirect violence, including some by government representatives (police)—often targeting female gender, ethnocultural or religious minoritized identities, and/or lower social-economic class locations—inside and beyond their schools.

The most common school staff response to overt conflict (sensitive issues, escalating disputes, bias-based slurs, or aggression) was avoidance. Teacher participants were aware of violence in their students' lives, for example telling of students who were being abused at home, but shared that they did not know how to respond. All teacher focus groups named conflict issues in which they did intervene, also types of conflict (such as gender-based and homophobic bias and aggression) in which they did *not* intervene and that they chose not to speak about with students in class. Some said they felt unqualified to address sensitive justice issues or escalated conflicts, or (in one school) to effectively work with a particular ethnocultural minority population they blamed for much aggression. Other teachers named time-constraining curricular mandates or unsupportive administrations as impediments to addressing differences and conflicts as learning opportunities.

Some participating educators occasionally addressed aggression incidents among students, class disruption, or discriminatory language incidents, afterward through facilitated classroom "conversation." Two teachers created student conflict scenarios, based on past episodes, for class discussion. An administrator held a weekly meeting with students to discuss violent incident experiences. Several teachers also facilitated occasional culture-of-peace activities on social relations and community belonging, such as: community circle sharing, lessons on self-esteem and forgiveness, mindfulness meditation, and making beaded bracelets symbolizing values students wanted to carry into adulthood. Students in all the schools' focus groups said they needed more in-depth and extended educational help, to become able to handle peer conflicts and bias-based aggression. School and system policy officially disallowed physical violence and identity-based slurs, but did not always support teachers' peacekeeping, nor encourage pro-active, planned peacemaking and peacebuilding education.

At the same time, participating teachers did teach several capability elements of peacemaking and just peacebuilding, embedded in subject area lessons. All participating teachers led some class discussions. However, two teachers said they had stopped holding most discussions because they didn't know how to keep some students from getting loud or hostile to peers. Similarly, some focus group students lamented that their class discussion experiences involved aggression and exclusion. All participating teachers in the three Canadian schools taught oral and written (first and second) language lessons that included elements of conflict analysis and resolution, such as discerning alternate points of view—applied to conflicts in fiction stories, news articles, or NGO and UN-related websites. Classes practiced creative and communicative expression through arts, graphic representation, mapping, media literacy, and multimedia productions. These building-block lessons for peacemaking participation often did not explicitly address social difference or cultural (bias and inclusion) dimensions of conflicts.

Teachers and students, in focus groups, described a few learning activities examining complex and justice-oriented social conflicts. Typically, teachers created space for such inquiry without directly "teaching" conflicts, by asking each student or small group to choose an issue for an independent project presentation. One class set of "social justice" project issues included diverse topics of indigenous land, pollution, education of girls in the developing world, and bullying. In another class, students each selected a "conflict" on which to collect information and write a report. Students' choices were apparently limited by their pre-existing knowledge (including awareness of alternate information search resources), which could tend to reinforce mainstream discourses (Vibert & Shields, 2003). In their focus group, some of those students lamented not having studied issues closer to their own lives—they previously had assumed that "conflict" mostly meant wars. In all three schools, participating teachers' enacted curriculum emphasized that individuals could "make a difference"—lessons on exemplary leaders such as Malala Yousafzai, Nelson Mandela, and Terry Fox, who had confronted problems far away in time or place.

Very few participating Canadian teachers or students articulated a sense of confidence to learn or implement peacemaking dialogue processes with which they might autonomously co-create resolutions to their own disputes or to take tangible action regarding problems of injustice. Although virtually all student participants *demonstrated* excellent discussion skills *in the (research) focus groups*—listening attentively, participating readily, responding constructively to peers' alternate viewpoints, articulating emotions and perspectives on justice issues—many said that they wanted more opportunity to learn and practice conflict dialogue, resolution, and justice-building processes in school lessons.

Students in both **Bangladesh** communities, especially girls, suffered considerable direct aggression and insecurity. They described peer exclusion, bullying, and especially gender-based harassment as "an everyday normal experience," mentioning girls who had stopped attending school because of gender-based aggression. Beyond pervasive gender-based and domestic violence, in the B2 city, the most challenging direct violence threats occurred during periodic polarized election campaigns. During election polarization, strikes, blockades, and street violence, boys and girls sometimes could not even get to school. Poverty was an extreme challenge, experienced close up, especially in the B1 schools' community. Peer aggression seemed more prevalent in the neighborhoods than inside the controlled environments of participating schools. Unlike other jurisdictions, Bangladesh students also reported direct violence perpetrated by adults in their schools (although caning was officially illegal). Many students also complained of a corrupt power structure—for instance, asserting that relatives had found it impossible to get a decent job without bribing somebody.

Students expressed discouragement that, even if they complained of abuse, "the police will not help us." Girls confirmed: "Our teachers teach us … to just be mindful and careful of ourselves. They also teach us … never to say anything angrily even if somebody verbally harasses you. They also teach us to go straight home from school…" A student at another school (B2F) reiterated this narrative, adding that wrong attitudes were "influenced by foreign cultures in the media." Thus, teachers, and often students themselves, supported curtailing female students' mobility (thus their access to economic, social, and political participation) in exchange for insecure partial peace. To address conflicts which they understood as misbehavior, teachers said, "We threaten them with punishment." However, students mentioned that teachers and a headmaster in the same school (B1F) took action to protect girls who were harassed or exploited. So, physical violence was exacerbated by cultural violence (especially sexism and sometimes corruption in institutional hierarchies), which together in turn exacerbated political-economic exclusion by constraining females' mobility. Some educators in participating schools had tried to protect girls from exploitation, yet they also taught self-regulation in which girls were denied freedom and assigned primary responsibility for protecting themselves.

Teachers did teach some elements of peacebuilding, in lessons across the official curriculum, apparently because of (more than despite) the Bangladeshi requirement to follow the textbooks. At the same time, these lessons tended to be univocal—presentation of the government's preferred narrative, acknowledging social conflicts but usually without opening space for alternative voices or perspectives. A frequent pedagogical approach to building inclusive community identity, described by teachers and students, was to present stories and poetry about exemplary individuals, especially in Bangla language and Moral Education classes. These personified various moral qualities, such as taking individual responsibility to help fellow citizens, support for human rights (at least tolerance), economic development initiative, and patriotism. A social studies teacher (B1F) described a lesson "about qualities of great women who made differences in Bangladesh." In an English lesson, students were to, "Find a person in your locality who has succeeded in the face of difficulties and write about her/him." Focus group students recalled such arts and stories as positive ways to "help us to change the mentality against this discrimination" (B1F). Participants suggested that individual attitude change was a prerequisite to social justice.

Bangladeshi curriculum-in-use acknowledged a range of social conflicts—including systemic problems of injustice, social exclusion, and discrimination—and offered a few opportunities for student perspective-taking (giving ideas and opinions). However, high-stakes examinations as well as social hierarchies limited the time available, the breadth of viewpoints recognized, and the depth of analysis. A teacher reflected: "I do not think we are well prepared to our approach our students with discussions around our various social and political problems. ... I teach my students only about passing the exams" (B1F). A student described a one-correct-answer approach: "Our teachers teach us what we should and should not do in various situations" (B2F). Another student critiqued the irrelevance of textbook approaches to conflicts: "There are problems and solutions [in our textbook] and there is a description of the problems. Everything is given correctly there. But we read these only to write in the exams. But these are never utilized in real life" (B2M).

There was no indication that peacemaking or dialogue capabilities (such as active listening, dialogue, negotiation, reflexivity, problem-solving) were taught explicitly in participating Bangladesh schools. However, a few teachers in multiple schools (and a student in one focus group) did describe lessons in which students took and juxtaposed perspectives, playing the roles of characters with different viewpoints in skits. Further, English textbook tasks required students to explain and take stands on issues such as overpopulation, healthcare funding, and the claim that "massive burning of the world's coal reserves may lead to worldwide ecological disaster." Similarly, a social studies textbook: "Initiate a debate regarding the dependent economic relationship of Bangladesh with developed and developing countries." Also, the Moral Education text: "Discuss the negative impacts of Eve-teasing and snatching [gender-based harassment and kidnapping], and consider preventive measures from the Islamic perspective;" and "Give your opinion regarding distribution of income in the capitalist economy." Teachers and exams evidently expected "correct" answers to such questions, affirming current government policy, whether or not applied in practice. Thus, the Bangladesh curriculum-in-use offered fairly numerous, albeit constrained, opportunities for students to analyze some individual, social-structural and cultural dimensions of several social conflicts—potentially complementing the more diverse lived understandings and capabilities that students demonstrated in focus group discussions.

As in other jurisdictions, nearly all students in all Bangladesh focus groups demonstrated conflict communication capability: articulating and explaining points of view, listening respectfully, engaging in responsive exchange (including disagreement and building upon ideas) with peers. Their analyses of various social conflicts were not comprehensive, but included direct participants (wants and needs motivating parties' actions) and some indirect (cultural recognition and social-structural equity) dimensions.

Similarly, many Bangladeshi students showed comprehension, and some hope as well as passion for contributing to social change. They showed outrage that (B1M),

> There is one class of people in Bangladesh who are hugely rich, and there is another class of people who are extremely poor. These poor people are constantly deprived of their basic rights. And, even the government is not playing any leading roles to solve this problem... Common people should create organizations and protests to make... various parts of the government aware of the real scenario.

Students in one city had participated in school-sanctioned symbolic protest actions—a rally against *hartal* strikes and a human chain to protest political violence. Yet, peers acknowledged, "Some people who want to do something [about political economy conflicts] are scared, and many of them are corrupt themselves" (B2M). Several student focus group participants expressed distrust of their government. "They will arrest us whenever we say anything against the government." Presumably, this fear (as well as the selection of participants by adults in the school) influenced some students to not voice some critiques in their focus groups. Yet, other voices in the same focus groups did describe electoral corruption, repression, and hopelessness about potential dissent: "I cannot raise my voice, staying in Bangladesh. The government has killed many."

Over all, the prevailing curriculum-in-use we encountered in the participating Bangladesh school focus groups—implicitly in patterns of post-incident conflict management and explicitly in classroom lessons—reflected steep hierarchies in which those with less power (including students inside school) were often punished or harmed without significant opportunity to present their points of view or to participate in repairing or solving problems. Educative peacekeeping lessons emphasized compliance and self-regulation within a dominant moral-political code.

At the same time, the research surfaced some apparent opportunities for learning and practicing several elements of justice-sensitive peacebuilding. There were lessons about cultural and social-economic inclusion, especially the immorality of gender-based aggression and the value of sharing material aids with the poor. Not least, there were rare opportunities for students to voice, even rarely to debate, their own or others' perspectives on a few issues. As in the other jurisdictions, the least common curricular opportunities were in the realm of democratic participation representation: to encounter or hear from specific civil society or governance institutions or other policy actors, and to autonomously generate or deliberate about options for actually taking democratic action to transform social conflicts. In sum, participating Bangladesh students showed capability and commitment to democratic peacebuilding citizenship, and their curriculum-in-use offered several infrequent and constrained, but tangible, opportunities for students to expand their horizons of social analysis and capabilities for some forms of peacebuilding engagement.

Although **México** is not in the usual sense a war zone, young people participating in this research lived in a culture of normalized severe direct and indirect violence, pervasive securitization including unreliable and corrupt armed police, and little awareness of or access to public infrastructure institutions that could mitigate these difficulties. Many teachers and students voiced high hopes for public education as the primary—or only—avenue for achieving social success and building peace.

Young people in all the participating Mexican schools reported substantial experience with direct physical violence—especially gender-based domestic violence in their own and relatives' homes, gender-based harassment, fighting and bullying inside and outside of school, armed violence among competing gangs in the community, and two named episodes of teacher violence toward students in school (GTO1). For instance, a girl lamented that, "In my neighborhood there are gangs that are always fighting;" a boy in another group shared, "Sometimes my father hits my mother" (GTO3). Many students told of beatings, gunfire, killings, and insecurity in or near their homes, in environments they had to traverse to get to school. They also recognized indirect harms: "amid more delinquency, there's less opportunity to work because of the insecurity." Girls' opportunities to go anywhere were severely constrained by community violence (GTO1). An intermediate teacher said, "I have had students who know a lot about weapons, including I have had students who want to become drug dealers" (GTO4). An elementary teacher elaborated:

"At present the children are living through constant situations of relatives dead or injured in their families or neighborhoods. Sometimes there is helplessness among them. They can't go out because of stray bullets … they don't see a future" (GTO2).

Participating Mexican youth also described living with pervasive systemic (indirect) violence—especially, enormous social-economic inequality, poverty, and hunger; abandonment by parents migrating northward for work; illegal drug trafficking; discrimination especially against women, people from indigenous and rural communities, and their own poor neighborhood; systemic inequality between the global north and south; pollution; and the corruption and ineffectiveness of various governing authorities to mitigate the causes or consequences of such problems. Some students missed school when they had nothing to eat (GTO4). Pedagogical equipment was scarce in school, because "the neighborhood is an insecure context and things get stolen easily" (GTO2). The youth reported heavy police and even military presence in their communities: few considered this be contributing to their insecurity. An intermediate teacher's students had told her, in a lesson about authority, about frequent police abuse: "[police] mooch bribes, they search them, they rob them; they found a marker and scratched it across the face of one student" (GTO4). Students were unable to name any neighbors, social movements, institutions, or leaders that took action to mitigate or resolve such conflicts (e.g. GTO3).

Teachers were required to keep records of student indiscipline including violent behavior, and to refer students for strict punishment including school exclusion, without school-provided opportunities for conflict resolution dialogue. Students and teachers in all schools described how teachers counseled students to refrain from aggressive and destructive behavior—after incidents of fighting, bullying, or local gang activity, and sometimes as planned self-regulation lessons, "so that they will understand that acting rudely is not acceptable" (GTO2). In these educative peacekeeping instances, students were being taught compliant citizenship for passive peace. The repertoires of potential responses to aggression students voiced in focus groups were often limited to avoidance (staying home, hiding, not getting involved) and force (reporting to police, despite their explicit distrust).

A few teachers facilitated peacemaking dialogue between individuals or in class groups, to facilitate problem-solving after episodes of interpersonal conflict escalation. Sometimes, teachers invited students to suggest solutions to a problem a peer was experiencing (also GTO4). An elementary teacher led a class discussion after a boy had been excluded from peers' soccer team (GTO3). An intermediate teacher confronted students who had laughed at a girl who cried after they had hit her: "Even so, this girl had taunted a peer in recent days. I prohibited the group from laughing at her. They did a reflection to not mock the girl, and the girl did a reflection to not mock anybody" (GTO1). Such peacemaking interventions addressed multiple points of view and facilitated a measure of active citizenship engagement in handling some conflicts, perhaps occasionally provoking reflexivity or deliberation.

The elementary Civics-Ethics textbook—a course created through a recent policy change—guided teachers to elicit self-expression: sharing, reflective class discussion, creative (drawing, interpreting images, brainstorming) and critical thinking (analyzing information, explaining opinions), about aspects of their local social environment. A teacher illustrated how other enacted curriculum also could touch students' lives: after her history lesson about Mexican leader Francisco (Pancho) Villa becoming engaged in the Revolution after his sister had been raped, one student disclosed that her father was in prison for raping her sisters (GTO1). In another teacher's lesson on "responsibility," students used a values education questionnaire to conduct interviews with family members regarding problems in the neighborhood.

All the participating Mexican teachers emphasized explicit *values education*. Participating teachers' most vocalized teaching priority in all four schools was "respect," followed by responsibility (fulfilling obligations). Other values articulated included: honesty, self-control, cooperation, *convivencia* (peaceful coexistence), tolerance of difference, caring for the environment, reciprocity, solidarity, peer dialogue, non-discrimination, and equality. Teachers often blamed students' disrespectfulness and aggression on their inadequate home lives. Elementary science lessons on caring for self and others included nourishment (nutrition, bulimia, anorexia), hygiene, and living things. Participating teachers showed evident awareness and care in relation to their students' serious life challenges—sometimes confidentially helping individuals to access shoes, uniforms, scholarship assistance or dental care, or encouraging students to share snacks and learning materials with needy peers.

Teachers in all four schools described lessons on recognizing gender, ability, and cultural differences. Intermediate teachers had student teams collect information about diverse languages and dialects, especially indigenous languages, within and beyond México. Teachers taught about valuing Mexico's indigenous heritage—telling the focus group they hoped this would reduce students' stigma and mistreatment of indigenous peers. Rarer intermediate lessons linked diversity with globalization, such as examining a community's adaptations to Japanese residents working for Japanese companies there. Similarly, elementary Civics lessons taught about gender equity and that gender-based violence was illegal. One elementary teacher organized a class "debate," allowing three boys to argue their view that women who were beaten at home had done something to deserve it—while voicing, and encouraging the other students to present, their view opposing gender-based violence. Thus, many lessons advocated passive tolerance, but students had some opportunities to consider their own experiences and viewpoints in relation to cultural bias dimensions of conflict and violence.

All participating Mexican teachers frequently implemented teamwork pedagogies in various subject areas, sometimes guiding heterogeneous groups to recognize one another's strengths and the value of working together cooperatively. In conjunction with a science lesson on human body systems (circulatory, digestive, etc.), a teacher constructed a game about valuing peers' diverse appearances and abilities: She concluded with the analogy that students in a group were like systems of the body, each one different but working together for the good of the whole (GTO3). In other science units about health and the environment, students worked together on projects designed to benefit their community, such as developing a public display about reusing water for plants and bathing. Students described getting together to clean-up abandoned (brownfield) land and collecting money to pay people for clean-up work (GTO4). These are examples of schoolwork practicing small, non-disruptive episodes of participatory citizenship—little analysis of underlying social conflicts, nor dissent linked to governance or social movements, but opportunities to experience inclusion and taking some action together to improve their communities' lives.

In a typical conflict analysis pedagogy described, teachers presented "cases" of conflict (from textbooks, poetry, news, videos, comic strips, or images) to build students' capabilities and inclinations for peacemaking and citizenship. The class would read a story or view a film clip, asking students to identify the motives, feelings, and concerns of each character about a problem, then to express their own opinions about the characters' action choices. Often, teachers invited students to express themselves through the arts—such as acting out characters' points of view, and then showing, "what would you have done in this situation?" Orally or in letter-writing assignments, students were invited to justify their opinions about problems experienced in the community. In Civics-Ethics, students prepared and held class debates on topics such as the pros and cons of transgenic foods and the merits of urban vs. rural areas. In a history and Spanish project, students created a play about Plutarco Elias, a Mexican politician who opposed Catholicism (leading to the Cristero War), to investigate, "why he acted without considering the people" (GTO3). Many teachers guided students to analyze some causes and consequences of individual decisions to migrate—emphasizing empathy for children whose parents and relatives had left home to work in North America (GTO3). A history unit examined the roles of various people (including displaced indigenous people and workers) in founding this city, examining how they handled problems and disagreements (GTO2). Another teacher engaged students in comparing an historical case (Porfirio Diaz) to a contemporary Mexican Zapatista revolutionary leader, Comandante Marcos (GTO2). In these activities, students would have had experiences encountering conflicting perspectives, thinking for themselves, and engaging dialogically with others with whom they agreed and disagreed.

A few classes talked about poverty, hunger, and deprivation (lived by many of the students) rooted in social conflict over scarce resources and employment. In one school, a teacher mentioned in the focus group a local heritage of peacebuilding citizenship—the community had formerly mobilized to support the poor through public cafeterias (GTO2)—but none mentioned presenting such information to students. A teacher shared a lesson alluding to stigma against Mesoamerican indigenous peoples living in poverty: She had told her class that, as Mexicans, they should be proud to be "descendants of brave people" (GTO3). Focus groups with teachers and students elicited almost no examples in which students would encounter actors in their own civil society, social institutions, or system of governance (especially beyond the local).

A predominant narrative reiterated by several teachers and students in all the schools was that access to schooling, staying in school, working, and studying hard would help individuals to overcome adversity and violence including poverty. Some asserted directly that those who prospered had worked harder than those who did not. This suggests an implicit curriculum that evades institutional and political causes and tends to blame those victimized by resource-based conflicts like poverty or migration.

As in the other jurisdictions, virtually all students in all Mexican focus groups demonstrated to research team facilitators their clear and enthusiastic conflict communication capability: articulating and explaining points of view, listening and engaging respectfully with peers' contrasting ideas. Similarly, they capably identified direct and some indirect participants (desires, needs, and context factors motivating parties' actions) in various conflicts, and recognized cultural diversity and bias including gender and indigeneity dynamics, and social-structural equity factors. Like participating students elsewhere, they felt that their understandings of intertwined difference and conflict matters were shallow, and that they wanted more in-depth opportunities in school to develop further their conflict understandings and capabilities for peacebuilding participation.

Cross-Case Discussion

Severe direct and systemic violence was a prominent feature of student research participants' lived citizenship, in all three cases (significantly in the Canadian city communities, more in the Bangladeshi city communities, and even more in the Mexican city communities). These young citizens demonstrated remarkable resourcefulness in navigating and comprehending some multidimensional social conflicts—economic, cultural, and political/participatory—that underlay the violence surrounding them. Collectively in focus groups, they were always able to articulate the contrasting perspectives and desires of multiple direct actors in and contributing to the escalation of those problems. In describing the conflicts they selected as especially important in their experience, participating young people, and many of their teachers, also capably identified indirect factors—economic distribution and access to tangible resources, and cultural reinforcement of narratives, biases, and beliefs—shaping and escalating the conflicts. Thus, these young people and teachers understood that patterns of social conflict underlay and exacerbated patterns of direct as well as systemic harm suffered in their daily lives. In a vicious cycle, through such mechanisms as repressive securitization, stigma, and constrained mobility, those daily patterns of direct violence in turn further exacerbated systemic harm, including discrimination and severely limited access to resources for well-being. In sum, confirming Galtung's diagnosis, violence—even outside war zones—is a crucial and underappreciated instance of injustice, as well as a risk factor that intensifies injustice.

So, participating young people in all three jurisdictions understood, largely based on lived experience, a great deal about many of the direct and systemic social conflicts around them, including some of their cultural (identity, learning beliefs) and economic (resource control) causes. That's important: a necessary, although not sufficient, ingredient for peacebuilding citizenship action. Some decades ago, Merelman (1990) theorized why this might be so: through social learning embedded in their lives in local escalated conflict zones, these non-affluent young people developed and practices sophisticated repertoires for recognizing, navigating, and talking about such social conflicts. Merelman illustrated, on a small scale, how some children from conflictual contexts were better able, compared to some children from peaceful contexts, to do things like put conflict escalation events in order and to identify contrasting viewpoints. Some of the school lessons that participants talked about had apparently expanded these horizons of knowledge—describing and discussing some of these problems, although rarely probing multiple perspectives about their causes or anatomy (actors, factors) as social conflicts.

However, as Fraser (2004) and Lederach (2003) explain, in addition to understanding the "what" of injustices (systemic roots of violence), people need to understand the "how"—the official and unofficial *processes* of direct participation and (government and transnational) political representation through which people participate in creating, reproducing, and—crucially—transforming social injustice conflicts. Although not designed as free-standing peace education programming, the enacted mainstream public school curricula participants described in focus groups also merited Ross' (2010) critique: They paid very scant attention to questions or mechanisms of power or political process. The young people in these Mexican, Bangladeshi, and Canadian schools demonstrated understanding of problems, but not of the actors, actions, mechanisms, or processes (that is, the politics) by which people did or might engage collectively in trying to transform or solve them. Presumably as a result of this close-up understanding of problems but not of any actors inventing or deliberating solutions, many of these young people expressed discouragement and distrust of governing authorities.

The understanding most absent from the peacebuilding-relevant capabilities that most participating students showed us—*and*, not incidentally, from the enacted *school lessons* that they and their teachers described—is represented by the green zone in the triangle diagram (Fig. 12.1). This middle zone, between violence (depicted in yellow) and perfect peace (blue), is the space for citizenship—action in the context of collective community—in the imperfect real world. Conflict regulation actions in the yellow-green area include regulatory interventions to mitigate the harms of violence through peacekeeping, coercive

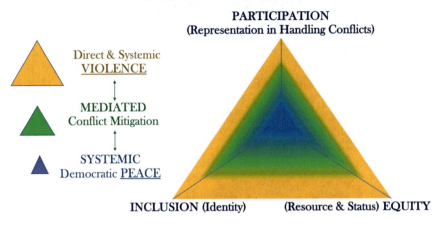

Fig. 12.1 Dimensions of Violence and Peace

rules and punishment, cultural sanction, or self-regulation, while assuming or actively reinforcing existing social-political hierarchies. Further along toward systemic peacebuilding in the blue-green area, conflict mediation and transformation involve a wider range of democratic actors and actions such as civil society, dissenting social movements, mediating institutions, and deliberated transitional justice remedies for injustices at the roots of enduring systemic and direct violence. Although none of the three systems was a perfect democracy, all three societies surely would have had, to some extent, such collective democratic actors and actions. Unfortunately, virtually none of the participating youth had really encountered these actors, inside school or in their marginalized communities. Students in all focus groups were aware of surface symptoms of democratic actions such as "protest" demonstrations, and of historical actors who had fomented revolutionary change, but not of who had organized these actions, how, with whom, nor toward whom (that is, what particular policy actors/actions those protests were intended to influence). It was impossible for them to feel confident in their own capacities to contribute to building just peace without such encounter with citizenship actors. Did these school curricula contribute to primary ignorance? Few of the young people, nor equally their teachers, showed awareness that their education was missing this active democratic citizenship dimension.

Of course, there were interesting differences as well as similarities among the cases. Bangladeshi and Mexican participants showed clear awareness of how physical violence in interpersonal life and broad society, such as gender-based abuse and harassment, was exacerbated by cultural violence such as sexism. The participant-described examples of Bangladeshi curriculum-in-use that participants communicated a moral justice perspective, by describing as normative problems many examples and kinds of destructive cultural and social-structural conflict practices, such as gender-based harassment and dowry exchange, poverty, and transnational colonial exploitation. As remedies, the curriculum encouraged individual desistance from bad behavior, compliance with moral strictures, and patriotic support for the nation in the face of external enemies. Mexican curriculum-in-use that was shared also denounced cultural bias, such as discrimination against indigenous people and people with different (dis)abilities, and economic mal-distribution such as poverty and lack of clean water. As remedies, the curriculum communicated the neoliberal values of respecting and complying with authority, self-regulation, working hard, and staying in school. Participating Canadian youth and teachers, in contrast, tended to describe cultural biases and social-structural harms as primarily occurring to others at a distance in time or space: for instance, colonial oppression of Indigenous First Nation Canadians by earlier European settlers, gender oppression impeding girls' schooling in Afghanistan, or racist apartheid in South Africa. As remedies, the reported curriculum communicated a curious mix of nationalism (aren't we fortunate to be Canadians today, where we have rights and these problems are largely solved) and a more self-confident version of neoliberalism, in which "one person can make a difference" to help others. Lessons in all the jurisdictions mentioned pollution, with anti-pollution remedies largely limited to self-regulation and occasional clean-up campaigns. Although they taught some (univocal, rarely multi-perspective) analysis of some injustice, apparently none of these sets of curriculum taught much about community or larger-scale mediating institutions, civil society actors, or democratic political processes for building just peace. This constitutes a gap that public schooling ought to be able to fill.

All participating teachers evidently implemented some pedagogies in which students practiced interpersonal-scale communication, critical reflection, and cooperation. Especially in the Canadian sample, substantially in the Mexican sample, and somewhat in the Bangladeshi sample, focus group evidence indicates that participating teachers' students had opportunities to consider, listen, express, and occasionally even debate their viewpoints about various conflictual (and less often, controversial) questions, orally and in writing. Only one or two participating teachers in each of Canada and Mexico said they had explicitly taught any particular process or principles for communicating constructively and persuasively about conflict, in small-scale peer disputes or in larger-group dialogue or decision-making deliberation, although a number of students in each focus group context advised that they would like to have such learning opportunities. Participating Mexican teachers implemented the most (semi-) autonomous student groupwork pedagogy, Canadian teachers some, and Bangladeshi teachers little. Only in Mexico did a few teachers explain how they explicitly prepared and guided students to cooperate in an equitable and inclusive manner, taking diversities into account. Only in Bangladesh did all (mandated) teaching texts in social studies, moral education, and language include creative expression such as poetry. A few Bangladeshi and many Canadian and Mexican teachers also engaged their students in creative self-expression through drama skits, visual arts, or (in Mexico) music. These are democracy-relevant capabilities, that could be extended and strengthened to facilitate encounters with democratic actors and application to larger-scale participation and representation dimensions of building just peace.

In every focus group in all three cases, the young people selected to participate showed enthusiastic interest in probing and discussing various locally relevant conflicts, and many of them said that they would like more such opportunities in school. They also demonstrated clear communicative capabilities in the focus group workshops—in the ways they spoke, listened, agreed and disagreed, and built upon one another's ideas to develop collective understanding—even though they told us that they felt they needed far more in-depth opportunities to practice such in-depth inquiry, thoughtful dialogue, and deliberation in school. Many of the youth showed passion and commitment to participate in learning difficult knowledge about injustice and violence, and in acting to make their worlds better, even though they showed little awareness of other people (much less groups) who had participated in such democratizing citizenship. Clearly, these young people were resourceful in the face of daunting violence. From the shining exceptional lessons shared by teachers in their focus groups, it is clear that ordinary public schooling could do considerably more to equip and support youth for more effective democratic peacebuilding citizenship participation.

Acknowledgements The authors gratefully acknowledge the Haudenosaunee, Huron-Wendat, Mississauga First Nations, and other original occupants of the territory where we live in southern Ontario, Canada. The Dish with One Spoon Covenant is a living agreement for all groups to share and care for this land and its ecology.

References

Bandura, A. (1986). *Social foundations of thought and action*. Prentice-Hall.

Bellino, M., Paulson, J., & Anderson Worden, E. (2017). Working through difficult pasts: Toward thick democracy and transitional justice in education. *Comparative Education, 53*(3), 313–332. https://doi.org/10.1080/03050068.2017.1337956

Bickmore, K. (2005). Foundations for peacebuilding and discursive peacekeeping: Infusion and exclusion of conflict in Canadian public school curricula. *Journal of Peace Education, 2*(2), 161–181.

Bickmore, K. (2017). Conflict, peace-building, and education: Rethinking pedagogies in divided societies, Latin America, and around the world. In K. Bickmore, R. Hayhoe, C. Manion, K. Mundy, & R. Read (Eds.), *Comparative and international education: Issues for teachers* (Second, revised and expanded ed., pp. 268–299). Canadian Scholars Press.

Bourgois, P. (2009). Recognizing invisible violence: A 30-year ethnographic retrospective. In B. Rylko-Bauer, L. Whiteford, & P. Farmer (Eds.), *Global health in times of violence* (pp. 17–40). School for Advanced Research Press.

Carbajal, P., & Fierro, M. (2019). *Convivencia Escolar: Una revisión del concepto* (Vol. 18).

Cremin, H., & Guilherme, A. (2016). Violence in schools: Perspectives (and hope) from Galtung and Buber. *Educational Philosophy and Theory, 48*(11), 1123–1137.

Davies, L. (2011). Can education interrupt fragility? Toward the resilient citizen and the adaptable state. In K. Mundy & S. Dryden-Peterson (Eds.), *Educating children in conflict zones: Research, policy and practice for systemic change—A tribute to Jackie Kirk* (pp. 33–48). Teachers College Press.

Davies, L. (2017). Justice-sensitive education: The implications of transitional justice mechanisms for teaching and learning. *Comparative Education, 53*(3), 333–350. https://doi.org/10.1080/03050068.2017.1317999

Foucault, M. (2003). Technologies of the self. In P. Rabinow & N. Rose (Eds.), *The essential Foucault: Selections from the essential works of Foucault 1954–1984* (pp. 145–169). The New Press.

Franklin, U. (2006). Stormy weather: Reflections on violence as an environment. *The Ursula Franklin reader: Pacifism as a map* (pp. 257–262). Between the Lines.

Fraser, N. (2004). Recognition, redistribution and representation in capitalist global society [Nancy Fraser interviewed by H. Dahl, P. Stoltz, & R. Willig]. *Acta Sociologica, 47*(4), 374–382. https://doi.org/10.1177/0001699304048671

Fraser, N. (2005). Reframing justice in a globalizing world. *New Left Review, 36*, 1–19.

Fraser, N. (2008). Abnormal justice. *Critical Inquiry, 34*(3), 393–422.

Galtung, J. (1969). Violence, peace, and peace research. *Journal of Peace Research, 6*(3), 167–192.

Galtung, J. (1976). Three approaches to peace: Peacekeeping, peacemaking, peace-building. In J. Galtung (Ed.), *Peace, war and defense: Essays in peace research* (Vol. 2, pp. 297–298). Christian Ejlers

Galtung, J. (1990). Cultural violence. *Journal of Peace Research, 27*(3), 291–305.

IEP, Institute for Economics and Peace. (2016). *Global peace index 2016: Ten years of measuring peace*. http://www.economicsandpeace.org.

IEP, Institute for Economics and Peace. (2017). *Positive peace report 2017: Tracking peace transitions through a systems thinking approach*. http://www.visionofhumanity.org/reports, http://www.economicsandpeace.org.

Kaderi, A. S. (2018). *Peacebuilding citizenship education in a Muslim-majority context: Challenges and opportunities in Bangladeshi Public Schools*. Ph.D., University of Toronto.

Lederach, J. P. (1995). *Preparing for peace: Conflict transformation across cultures*. Syracuse University Press.

Lederach, J. P. (2003). *The little book of conflict transformation*. Good Books.

Lopes Cardozo, M., Higgins, S., & Le Mat, M. (2016). *Youth Agency and Peacebuilding: An Analysis of the Role of Formal and Non-Formal Education Synthesis Report on Findings from Myanmar, Pakistan, South Africa and Uganda*. Retrieved from University of Amsterdam. https://educationanddevelopment.files.wordpress.com/2016/06/youth-agency-synthesis-report-final16.pdf

Mason, T., & Delandshere, G. (2010). Citizens not research subjects: Toward a more democratic civic education inquiry methodology. *Interamerican Journal of Education for Democracy/Revista Interamericana De Educación Para La Democracia, 3*(1), 5–26.

McCauley, C. (2002). Head first versus feet first in peace education. In G. Salomon & B. Nevo (Eds.), *Peace education: The concept, principles, and practices around the world* (pp. 247–258). Lawrence Erlbaum Associates.

Merelman, R. (1990). The role of conflict in children's political learning. In O. Ichilov (Ed.), *Political socialization, citizenship education, and democracy* (pp. 47–65). Teachers College Press.

Nixon, R. (2011). Introduction. In *Slow violence and the environmentalism of the poor* (pp. 1–44). Harvard University Press.

Ngabo, G. (2021, June 5). The hyper-local toll of Toronto gun violence, Crime reporter analysis. *Toronto Star*, pp. IN1, IN4-5. www.thestar.com

Ross, M. H. (2007). *Cultural contestation in ethnic conflict*. Cambridge University Press.

Ross, M. H. (2010). Peace education and political science. In G. Salomon, & E. Cairns (Eds.), *Handbook of peace education* (pp. 121–133). Psychology Press/Taylor & Francis.

Vibert, A., & Shields, C. (2003). Approaches to student engagement: Does ideology matter? *McGill Journal of Education, 38*(2), 221–240.

Young, I. M. (2011). *Responsibility for justice*. Oxford University Press.

PART IV

Critical Pedagogy/Critical Literacy Studies in Education

CHAPTER 13

The Indigenous Imaginary and Tertiary Institutions

Robert J. Tierney and Robert V. Morgan

For Indigenous communities in colonized countries, education has been used as a weapon to silence their cultural practices, eradicate their ways of knowing, and forge their assimilation and subservience. Under the guise of protection, Indigenous children have been extracted from their communities, and Indigenous education has been supplanted with western curricula, teaching practices, learning outcomes, and pathways. In her discussion of Indigenous education prior to colonization, Joanne Archibald (1995), from the Stó:lō Nation and Professor Emerita at the University of British Columbia, commented that the western dismissal and mischaracterization of First Nations education have been used to justify assimilation, including residential schools. In contrast to such false and disparaging accounts, she recounts how Indigenous education was based upon principles (spiritual, physical, emotional, and economic) and methods that are holistic and experiential; individualized; and carefully sequential and systematic—with the support of the family and community, especially elders. Drawing upon a case study of the Stó:lō Nation of British Columbia, she stated:

R. J. Tierney (✉)
University of British Columbia, Vancouver, BC, Canada
e-mail: rob.tierney@ubc.ca

R. V. Morgan
University of Newcastle, Callaghan, NSW, Australia

© The Author(s), under exclusive license to Springer Nature Switzerland AG 2022
A. A. Abdi and G. W. Misiaszek (eds.), *The Palgrave Handbook on Critical Theories of Education*, https://doi.org/10.1007/978-3-030-86343-2_13

> ...educational expectations and the roles of all villagers were clearly defined and structured. Goals reflected the values of sharing, cooperation, and respect for the environment, oneself, and others. The curriculum content included training in cultural, historical, environmental, and physical (body) knowledge. Community members and the environment became teaching resources, individual empowerment in and responsibility for education created a lifelong learning process.... The educational process was not static; it allowed for adaptation to environmental change and outside cultural influences. These changes were controlled and directed by the Stó:lō people until the arrival of the missionaries. (Archibald, 1995, p. 292)

Similar colonizing forces were enlisted in other countries and perpetuated by a false deficit view of Indigenous culture and ways of knowing. As Australian Aboriginal author Bruce Pascoe (2014) lamented in the conclusion of his book, *Dark Emu*, Australian Aboriginal ways of knowing were destroyed, displaced, and hidden by the British colonialists:

> It seems improbable that a country can continue to hide from the actuality of its history in order to validate the fact that having said sorry, we refuse to say thanks. Should we ever decide to say thanks, the next step on a nation's moral agenda is to ensure that every Australian acknowledges the history and insists that, as we are all Australians, we should have the opportunity to share the education, health and employment of that country on equal terms. To deny Aboriginal and Torres Strait Islanders agricultural and spiritual achievement is the single greatest impediment to the intercultural understanding and perhaps, to Australian moral wellbeing and economic prosperity. (pp. 228–229)

In the last fifty years, momentum for change has been gathering globally and within nations. Globally, the United Nations (UN) has produced a different imaginary through a number of declarations that have challenged current Indigenous circumstances with regard to human rights and freedoms. The UN declaration of Education for All, ratified in 1990, proclaimed education as a basic right for all anchored in respect for culture. It outlines the "responsibility to respect and build upon their collective cultural, linguistic and spiritual heritage, to promote the education of others, to further the cause of social justice, to achieve environmental protection, to be tolerant towards social, political and religious systems which differ from their own" (United Nations, "Article 1," 1990). In a similar vein, the pursuit of cultural ways of knowing is consistent with the UN Declaration of Human Rights for Indigenous Persons (2006), which declares Indigenous persons' right to self-determination (Article 3); their right to establish and control Indigenous education systems tied to language and culture (Article 14); and Indigenous rights relative to traditional knowledge (Article 31). Befittingly, Indigenous considerations have also infiltrated discussions pertaining to global ecology matters.[1] The UN has made clear the importance of the support and revitalization of languages and local knowledge in the interest of the planet's ecology and in the potential for addressing environmental disasters.

Furthermore, comparisons afforded by international benchmarking have exposed the shameful disparities between Indigenous and non-Indigenous populations. In Canada and Australia, for example, comparisons between Indigenous and non-Indigenous communities suggest major failures as well as the systemic oppression of Indigenous populations (in terms such as education, health, and other indicators of wellbeing, including income and incarceration rates). Consequently, governments have been forced to reconsider their Indigenous engagements—instigating policies that have provided incentives and sometimes mandates for change. These initiatives have led to quite mixed and often questionable results, as many seem to remain tethered to a colonial, assimilative sensibility rather than aligned with Indigenous tenets of respect, recognition, reciprocity, and relevancy. (Indeed, governments seem to be states of upheaval, as social movements including Black Lives Matter and the Uluru Statement, along with commitments to Reconciliation, have drawn attention to systems and practices that perpetuate racism and inequities.) The 2021 Australia Day comments offered by Australian Prime Minister Scott Morrison that seemed to commiserate with the British convicts arriving with the First Fleet—without acknowledging the genocide and continuing dismissive, assimilative practices against Aborigines—represent the lag in progress on addressing these matters.[2] They portend the reluctance of current political leadership to reconcile with past genocide and pursue a different course with respect to Aboriginal rights, freedoms, and equality.

As a means of illustration, consider the circumstances of Indigenous developments in Australia at the tertiary level for Australian Aboriginal and Torres Strait Islanders beginning with some historic background and then focused upon recent developments using one of Australia's premier and first university as a case study.

Australian Indigenous Developments

For Australian Aboriginal and Torres Strait Islander communities, the effects of westernization immediately followed the arrival of the British on the eastern shores in 1770. Befitting the imposing nature of western science, a botanist on board James Cook's ship was quick to take samples of the land—labeling and categorizing the plant life as well as the places and animals that they encountered. In conjunction with their imperialistic claim to Australia as a British colony, they declared Australia as Terra Nullius—"land belonging to no one;" unoccupied; and uninhabited—despite the presence of Aboriginal communities with sophisticated systems of governance and flourishing societies. The western colonization of Australia occurred almost immediately thereafter, with the subsequent arrival of a fleet of British soldiers and convicts. Their approach to colonization involved a combination of efforts to exterminate or assimilate

Aboriginal communities, displacing the importance of Aboriginal knowledge, literacies, and languages. The colonists did so with little regard for the ecology of a country where Aboriginal peoples had thrived for at least 50,000 years.[3]

For political reasons, the colonists and settlers kept the world ignorant of Aboriginal communities—and their resistance to colonial rule—as they proceeded to proselytize, assimilate, annihilate, subordinate, and enact the forced removal of Aboriginal peoples from their lands (Willmot, 1987). Behind the British flag and under the banner of religion, they separated children from their communities to reeducate them in western traditions, thereby displacing or silencing Aboriginal practices. Their approach to colonization blatantly refrained from intercultural relationship-building; instead, they pursued the extermination of the Aboriginal culture (Rizvi, 2021) and by their ignorance devastating the lands that Aboriginal communities tilled and harvested with crops (Pascoe, 2014). As Morgan et al. (in press) note, the ongoing British occupation has altered a society that was rich in literacies, with hundreds of languages, to a present population (now a fraction of its size prior to colonization) that has very few remaining languages and traditions.[4] Colonizing forces privileged anglophone knowledge and practices while taking control of or eliminating or erasing others (Hong, 2008). Essentially, the colony was intended to serve the interests of the empire (Connell, 2019; Nozaki, 2009). Nowadays, despite recognition of Australia's multiculturalism, populism related to nationalism—together with monolingualism and xenophobic tendencies—seems to serve as continuing justifications for dismissing Aboriginal cultural practices and opposing Indigenous sovereignty, or "sui generis," along with culturally reciprocal forms of Indigenizing education (Rigney et al., 2015).

If engagement in tertiary education is enlisted as a proxy for the advancement of Australian Aboriginals and Torres Strait Islanders, the results to date are dismal and alarming. Despite the investments and vocal support for social inclusion and diversity, the Australian government and Australian universities seem to be falling short in achieving social inclusion targets. By retaining restrictive forms of gatekeeping and maintaining forms of enculturation, they seem dominated by approaches that keep Aboriginal and Torres Strait Islander students excluded, marginalized, or assimilated. An interrogation of the data on Aboriginal and Torres Strait Islanders' participation suggests that the methods to address and improve the educational experiences and learning outcomes of Aboriginal and Torres Strait Islander students are perpetuating a form of western status quo (resulting in a disproportionately low percentage of Aboriginal and Torres Strait Islander students completing high school, performing well on national and international tests, and being awarded places in universities). Viewed through a prism of access, participation, and success at the tertiary level, the participation of Aboriginal and Torres Strait Islander students falls significantly below the percentage of Aboriginal and Torres Strait Islander people in the general population (i.e., participation at the tertiary level is 1%, compared with 4% of the general population); additionally, the graduation rates fall significantly below those for non-Indigenous students. According to the government-commissioned report, *Review of Higher Education Access and Outcomes for Aboriginal and Torres Strait Islander People* (IHER, 2012), tertiary institutions in Australia are failing and remain far behind those in countries such as United States, Canada, and New Zealand—despite years of funding universities to increase enrolments and support for Aboriginal and Torres Strait Islanders. As the report's authors commented:

> Despite significant progress in recent decades, Aboriginal and Torres Strait Islander people remain significantly underrepresented in Australian universities. The important milestones in Aboriginal and Torres Strait Islander higher education, such as the first Aboriginal or Torres Strait Islander student to receive a degree from an Australian university or the graduation of the first Aboriginal or Torres Strait Islander doctor, came nearly a century after other countries with similar colonial histories, such as the United States, Canada and New Zealand.
>
> The Panel believes that this disadvantage comes at a cost not only to Aboriginal and Torres Strait Islander people, but also to the nation in terms of opportunities lost. (IHER, 2012, p. 4)

Taken together, the situation in Australian tertiary institutions befits the mantra of assimilation and non-recognition of Australian Aboriginal and Torres Strait Islander sovereignty in the interests of perpetuating the social reproduction of western privilege for those of Anglo-Saxon heritage. When confronting university administrators at the executive level with the possibility of complicity with social reproduction, the responses have been flaccid suggesting the acceptability of their privileged traditions and the reasonableness of placing reputation of the university ahead of social responsibility and cultural responsiveness using arguments for objectivity and culturally free approaches as rational, preferred, and legal defensibility to justify their complicity. Indeed, the strategy taken by most Australian universities is consistent with a view that universities will identify and serve the needs of those exceptional Aboriginal students who perform well on traditional high school tests of western knowledge and provide some support for them to perform well at university without a substantial respect or regard for building upon their background of experiences or cultural knowledge.

The positioning of Indigenous knowledge ignores its vital role in Aboriginal people's lives. Marie Battiste (1998), from the Potlotek First Nations in Nova Scotia, has suggested that in Canada, as in Australia, the notion that Eurocentric knowledge and concepts are better and should be considered universal is a form of cognitive imperialism. Educational tests mask their Eurocentric features behind labels such as "culturally-free" or "unbiased." Students from diverse backgrounds who are identified as falling behind may find themselves receiving a narrower curriculum, caught in a corrupt cycle of prescribed learning (often devoid of cultural considerations). This positioning of Indigenous knowledge ignores its vital role in Aboriginal people's lives. As Australian Aboriginal leader Bob Morgan (2019) noted, being an Australian Aboriginal is akin to being an Indigenous stranger in one's own land—reflective of a "guest paradigm" in which colonizers advance scholarly venues, educational systems, and cultural norms with which non-westerners and Indigenous people are expected to align. As a 2017 report by the Australian House of Representatives Standing Committee on Indigenous Affairs poignantly declared, Aboriginal and Torres Strait Islanders do not feel

> ... (a) sense of belonging when at school. This is because they attend schools that do not accept the relevance of, or acknowledge, understand or celebrate their culture, which results in children not feeling culturally safe. (House of Representatives Standing Committee on Indigenous Affairs, 2017, p. 43)

Unfortunately, if you examine the circumstances more closely tertiary institutions often have pursued approaches that have been directed at relegating Indigenous engagements to a minor or aligned with the status of a stepchild or outlier while maintaining the status quo of a western primacy. Take if you will the record of the University of Sydney, which dates backs over 150 years.

The University of Sydney

Founded in 1850, the University of Sydney was Australia's first established university and is one of the historic "sandstones," or elite Group of Eight (Go8), universities. The University is located on the traditional lands of the Gadigal people of the Eora Nation. Traditionally these lands were regarded as a site for exchanges among Aboriginal communities around the water springs in the area. It was also a burial site for Aboriginal people, usually in trees positioned alongside of what is now the University of Sydney's main quadrangle and Great Hall. Notably, it is situated on the edge of what is now the downtown of Sydney, adjacent to Redfern, Newtown, and Glebe—suburbs that include the largest urban Aboriginal population that flowed to the city from various rural and interstate clans.

The University of Sydney claims of commitment to Aboriginal and Torres Strait Islanders might be supported by its role in the matriculation of one of Australia's first Aboriginal graduates (Charles Perkins, who graduated from the university in 1966) and the launching in 1989 of one the first Aboriginal and Torres Islander centers at an Australian university (the Koori Center). But recent reviews of their commitment suggest limited progress in terms of accessibility and Aboriginal and Torres Strait Islander participation as students, staff, or faculty hires. If their approaches to Indigenous ways of knowing are examined, their programs seem anemic and subordinative. Their interfacing with Aboriginal and Torres Strait Islander society seems detached and patronizing.

Despite claims of significant increases, the overall percentage of Aboriginal- and Torres Strait Islander-enrolled students remains close to 1% across the university, statistically comparable with the national average enrollment for tertiary institutions but well below the overall 4% of Aboriginal and Torres Strait Islander people in the nation (The University of Sydney, 2017, 2020; Tierney et al., 2010a, 2010b). For example, in its 2021–2024 strategy report, *One Sydney, Many People*, the University of Sydney (2020) acknowledged that it "has a lower proportion of Aboriginal and Torres Strait Islander students (0.9%) than the Australian sector (average 1.72%). The University is currently placed 7th amongst its Group of Eight (Go8) peers in Aboriginal and Torres Strait Islander student participation" (p. 14).

The data in terms of participation across faculties are also quite troubling. The enrollment pattern at the University of Sydney suggests that faculties in the Health Sciences and Education account for many more Aboriginal and Torres Strait Islander enrollees than other faculties. The number of Aboriginal and Torres Strait Islander students enrolled in agricultural, dentistry, nursing, pharmacy, science, and engineering are very limited. And, regardless of the faculty, it is striking how few Aboriginal and Torres Strait Islander students have been enrolled in research degrees (0.06% of the total number of students enrolled, with the majority of faculties with either one or no Aboriginal or Torres Strait Islander enrollees). Adding to this bleakness, the University focuses a significant amount of research on Aboriginal matters—conducted predominately by non-Aboriginal scholars.

As one might predict, there is a strong correlation between Aboriginal student participation and staffing. The percentage of Aboriginal and Torres Strait Islander staff across faculties as administrators and other personnel is very low. Indeed, there is a chronic shortage of general and academic staff that identify as Aboriginal, despite targeted employment pursuits (including the hiring of an Aboriginal Deputy Vice Chancellor). While University enrollment is approximately 50,000 students (2:1 in terms of the proportion of undergraduate to postgraduate students), the total number of academics over the past ten years has been approximately 3000–3500, and the number of general staff has been approximately 3500–4000 (The University of Sydney, 2015). The number of those academic and general staff who are Indigenous has remained at approximately 1%. According to the University's 2016 Annual Report, the number of Aboriginal and Torres Strait Islander employed within the University was 84 (65.39 full-time equivalent positions), with 21 targeted positions that would increase the number of Aboriginal and Torres Strait Islander overall to slightly more than 1% (The University of Sydney, 2017, p. 28). While a number of universities seem to be on the verge of enacting plans for significant hiring, the number of Aboriginal and Torres Strait Islander staff has failed to be realized. As the *One Sydney, Many People* strategic plan acknowledged: "Aboriginal and Torres Strait Islander staff, both professional and academic, are under-represented at the University, with only 1.2 percent of staff identifying as Aboriginal and/or Torres Strait Islander" (The University of Sydney, 2020, p. 15).

Indigenous Ways of Knowing at the University of Sydney
Alongside undertaking various reviews of their support services and programs for Aboriginal and Torres Strait Islander participants, the University of Sydney has proffered various strategies. However, an analysis of these initiatives suggests that the strategies have historically had and continue to have a reverence for mainstream Australia, aligned with western traditions rather than being respectful of or relevant to Aboriginal and Torres Strait Islander culture and ways of knowing. Despite widely-touted Indigenous strategic initiatives, the University of Sydney's approach has been tempered in terms of its acknowledgment and support of Indigenous communities and ways of knowing. It might be viewed as more "talk" and "show" than "walk" and "empowerment."

For example, in 2012 the University initiated the Wingara Mura-Bunga Barrabugu Strategy (The University of Sydney, 2020; see also The University of Sydney, 2019). This program touts the University's ambitions to support diversity, but in a fashion that suggests a new narrative for all Australians without regard for the existing Aboriginal and Torres Strait Islander culture. It is as if there exists a new convenience that excludes and displaces Aboriginal and Torres Strait Islanders in service to a broader cultural milieu of diversity—one that is actually assimilative and subordinating. Despite more Aboriginal course offerings and an integration of Aboriginal matters into coursework, Aboriginal culture remains secondary and dominated by an overall allegiance to western traditions.

More recently, the University's 2020 strategic plan for 2021–2024 entitled, *One Sydney, Many People*, outlines a number of initiatives that suggest an enhanced and renewed commitment to addressing the shortcomings of the University's pursuits to date. It promises a stronger commitment to integrating Aboriginal perspectives, ways of knowing and practices in a fashion that the University refers to as "authentic," with dedicated offerings as well as pathways and access points for Aboriginal and Torres Strait Islanders. Yet, in conjunction with these goals, the University has pursued campus-wide initiatives that are intended to heighten cultural understandings pertaining to a broad vision of diversity. As its National Centre for Cultural Competence (the NCCC, a joint venture between the University and the Australian government for $AU 5.6 million) states:

> We develop knowledge and build capacity in cultural competence across a range of social domains. The NCCC has initially prioritized the growth of student, staff and community cultural competence. Our broader perspective is forming national and international partnerships, initiating dialogues and implementing initiatives to improve educational, economic, cultural and social outcomes throughout society. (NCCC, 2021)

Essentially, it is as if a banner of "cultural competence" instantiates a vision of culture that overshadows Indigenous considerations, reconciliation, and advancement. The University of Sydney's approach seems aligned with a western image of multiculturalism that shapes the image of "others." Indeed, the University of Sydney's motto, "Sidere mens eadem mutato," reflects the singularity of this orientation. Its many translations are all tied to a single model of the mind—namely, "the stars change, the mind remains the same;" "the constellation is changed, the disposition is the same;" or "the same learning under new stars" (The University of Sydney, 2021).

For Aboriginal and Torres Strait Islander students, Indigenous concerns seem to be relegated to the study of Aboriginality rather than being on an equal footing or substantially integrated into all studies. For instance, you might expect to see an expanded set of course offerings on Aboriginal matters in many degree programs, such as the Indigenous Studies degree within the Faculty of Arts and Social Sciences (see: Faculty of Arts and Social Sciences).[5] Indeed, there will likely be the addition of units within areas targeted for early adoption of the strategy (e.g., Music, Science, and Law). But it remains to be seen if these developments will exist as parallel and somewhat separate, or viewed as equal to the pre-existing western traditions of teaching, research, and service pursuits. The rhetoric of the *One Sydney, Many People* strategy remains ambiguous:

> We recognize that the exchange of knowledge, teaching and learning occurred on the Countries and places across the nation predating that of higher education institutions anywhere in the world. By expanding upon the representation of Aboriginal and Torres Strait Islander Peoples' knowledges, skills and understanding we honour the founding knowledge of the custodians of the land upon which the University's campuses are situated. (The University of Sydney, 2020, p. 16)

> ...

> As part of One Sydney, Many People, we will support curriculum owners to embed Aboriginal and Torres Strait Islander values, culture and teachings across all faculties and schools. A range of models will be employed to facilitate innovative and culturally quality-assured representation of Aboriginal and Torres Strait Islander knowledges in curriculum, programs and courses. To ensure the successful delivery of these knowledges we will support development opportunities for teaching and research staff to be equipped to deliver Indigenous content appropriately and with an understanding of the ethical and other requirements of working with Aboriginal and Torres Strait Islander communities and students. We will commence this work with the Faculty of Science, The University of Sydney Law School and Sydney Conservatorium of Music. (University of Sydney, 2020, p. 16)

It is notable that the umbrella notions of "one" and "many" are enlisted in a fashion befitting the Australian government's educational initiatives. That is, although the diversity of Australia, with over 400 language groups enrolled in schools, is acknowledged, the approach is streamed toward a largely monolingual education (Morgan et al., in press). In the University plan there is little mention of Aboriginal Languages, nor are there statements that would suggest building substantial connections to Aboriginal ways of knowing.

Engagements with Aboriginal Communities at the University of Sydney
The pivoting away from and failure to address Aboriginal and Torres Strait Islander considerations more fully and in a transformative manner befit the sidelining of engagement with the broader Aboriginal and Torres Strait Islander community. The University of Sydney has positioned itself alongside of these communities instead of being actively engaged with them. Despite the location of the University in the largest urban populations of Aboriginal and Torres Strait Islanders in Australia, only a few programs are engaged with those communities. Apart from programs offering community-based fieldwork, the University remains largely separate from Aboriginal communities—failing to engage in substantial partnerships let alone oversight involving Aboriginal community representatives. No one denies that for universities to move forward, the cultural mix of institutions needs to change. But such a need extends to the communities within which universities are located or are intended to serve.

Even for those faculties that may already have embraced community engagements, the path is not straightforward. This was illustrated well in a 2012 study sponsored by the Australian Council of Deans of Education, which looked at the preparation of Aboriginal and Torres Strait Islander teachers across Australia (Lambert & Burnett, 2012; Patton et al., 2012). While this research suggests success in attracting Indigenous students to teacher education programs, it also—with few exceptions—points to a failure to address a range of Indigenous issues in these programs, as well as a failure to address Indigenous teachers' experiences of racism upon entering the profession. Across the various teacher education programs in Australia, Aboriginal and Torres Strait Islander failure levels are aggregated at approximately 70%.[6] While the University of Sydney teacher education program has had more success in terms of graduation rates of Aboriginal students, many of the students in the program have felt as though they did not belong and express a sense of alienation alongside those they perceive to be their privileged "white" students. Many of them struggle to meet the demands of a university that seems fitted to the life of those full-time students who have few other commitments and easy access to resources that enable them to invest fully in teacher preparation (Chambers, 2012).

The interface of these failings with the broader circumstances of Aboriginal and Torres Strait Islanders throughout Australia should not be dismissed. For example, teacher education programs might aspire to prepare teachers with the disposition, talents, and knowledge to make schools places that are "culturally safe" (Papps & Ramsden, 1996) and bridge between the communities and their students. However, most surveys of teachers suggest that they lack the knowledge and strategies to accommodate the Indigenous students they encounter, whether they are teaching these students in urban or remote settings (Luke et al., 2012). As a number of Indigenous scholars stress, without more substantial development of teachers' understandings of the communities that they serve, they will likely fall back to mainstream and "white"-informed practices (Phillips, 2011; Phillips et al., 2007; Prior, 2009; Smith, 1999, 2005, 2015).

The University of Sydney and many other tertiary institutions seem tethered to their allegiances to western traditions and a view of their exclusivity and superiority. The predisposition to partially integrate Aboriginal matters and ways of knowing seems to treat them as objects of study rather than key vehicles and lenses for a world conceived of as equal. Tertiary institutions seem to be having difficulty bridging from creating centers devoted to Indigenous support to more university-wide, transformational change. The adoption of the Indigenous commitments and units of study seem isolated and, in some cases, seem to default to a generic, uniform approach to diversity. The integration of some elements, in other words, is often overshadowed by an overall assimilative orientation (i.e., a reverence for western ways of knowing and a subordination of Indigenous elements and focus).

Indeed, the status quo in most Australian universities for Aboriginal and Torres Strait Islander outreach appears based upon a reverence for a western mainstream. At the point of recruitment, there is a focus upon the use of traditional measures of performance without regard for non-western cultural engagements. In terms of what counts as participation, there appears to be a bias toward a westernized mainstream curricula and a monolingualism tied to English—befitting what Morgan et al. (in press) described as a generally muffled background of xenophobia. There is a tendency to underscore the genuineness and authenticity of the approach while refraining from elevating Aboriginal ways of knowing to equal status. Aboriginal matters remain at the discretion of traditional forces within the university. One should be careful not to equate signage and spaces, especially dedicated museum space, with significant change or equal footing for Aboriginal matters (see Fordham & Schwab, 2007; Rigney, 2011; Rigney & Hattam, 2018).

Moving Forward

The privileged position of Western epistemologies is deeply embedded within a number of western universities. It is supported by a number of internal and external support systems that block, mute, or fuse change in ways that ensure the reproduction of western domination. This should not be surprising, given the stakes and the shifts required to change. Epistemological accommodation involves wrestling with issues as formidable as re-naturalization, the revitalization of language, the re-establishment of organic pursuits, an awareness and respect for cultural ways of knowing, and the repeated leveraging of a future educated by the past (but not stuck in it). Epistemological change requires all parties to commit to interrogating, challenging, and perhaps shifting their values, practices, and privileges.

In the New Zealand context, for example, despite Maori leaders being able to leverage changes to ensure and advance some foundational rights and protocols (stemming from the Treaty of Waitangi, first signed by the British and Maori chiefs in 1840), Maori efforts at tertiary institutions have often confronted opposing forces, fear, and a failure to recognize the forms of aspirational, transformative change being pursued. Unfortunately, the past privilege of mainstream circumstances often impedes progress and results in forms of obstructionism or compromised approaches. Indigenous engagements have faltered due to tertiary institutions' efforts to wed their colonizing pasts with an imaginary, decolonized future. Sometimes universities position approaches in ways that maintain the status quo. As Sharon Stein (2017) notes, universities perpetuate a form of subordination of Indigenous engagements, which enables

> ... the rest of the institution to largely continue reproducing the status quo. By granting conditional inclusion without also substantively redistributing resources, decentering whiteness, or shifting other disciplines' curricula, universities largely left in place existing institutional hierarchies of knowledge and indeed of humanity (Ferguson, 2012). Today these interdisciplinary fields consistently face de-/underfunding, forced consolidation, or even termination.... (Stein, 2017, p. S36)

One would hope that universities were politically independent—not shaped by the same hierarchical forces that are aligned with colonization. Indeed, in the United States, Canada, New Zealand, and some other countries (e.g., Norway, India, and China), a number of independent Indigenous tertiary institutions have been established with a strong commitment to connecting with local communities. For these independent universities—disillusioned by the sense of alienation and removal experienced at mainstream western insitutions—connections with community have been shown as key to their sustainability and the realization of educational pursuits that resonate with cultural pratices and ways of knowing (Barnhardt, 1991).

Various forms of affiliatons have also been shown to be key. For example, some programs act akin to satellite programs within Indigenous communities, maintaining connections to other universities to enable the completion of programs and provide a fuller set of offerings. These affiliations can be mutually benficial by supporting transactions across institutions that are respectful and affording fusings that are synergistic. Other affiliations have involved graduate study collaborations in which Indigenous faculty come together to support various cohorts from different universities. In New Zealand, this model was the basis for the successful pursuit of 500 Maori doctorates in 5 years. In Canada, it served as the basis for the SAGE initiative across British Columbian universities. Some universities have also established centers devoted to supporting Indigenous students and initiatives, with strong ties and mandated commitments to the communities that they serve (e.g., First Nations House of Learning at the University of British Columbia, or the Wollotuka Institute at the University of Newcastle). Although still dependent upon the good will of tertiary institutions, such centers have served as vital links and leaders in their communities.

Closing

The advancement of Indigenous developments in tertiary institutions are not minor shifts, nor are they straightforward—especially given the extent to which faculty may have privileged western norms and be ignorant of Indigenous matters. Without an orientation and set of values and understandings tied to cultural mores, the path forward continues to be challenging. Wittingly or unwittingly, the education system seems complicit in perpetuating these circumstances, especially through its adoption of certain curricula and assessment methods and the hierarchy it continues to impose. It seems most troubling that educators at the top of this institutional hierarchy (i.e., at universities) are partners in this.

Despite revering intellectual freedom and political independence, universities are not blameless. Historically, most western universities, touted as temples of learning, represent denominational allegiances. They espouse forms of education and scholarship dominated by European colonizing forces have an interest in re-socializing diverse populations in that image, and commodify or claim discovery of the knowledge of others. For Indigenous societies, educational institutions represent the vestiges of oppression, displacement, and assimilation that Indigenous educators and southern scholars have decried (e.g., Alfred, 2004; Barnhardt, 1991; Archibald & Hare, 2017; Ottmann, 2017). It is a colonial history of exclusion that has existed for at least six centuries (Stein, 2017). It is how education is used to advance the empire. As Willinsky (1998) postulated, it is to "make the whole of the world coherent for the West by bringing all we knew of it within the imperial order of things" (Willinsky, 1998, p. 11).

There might be a shift to a rhetoric of recognition, but the policies and practices of many colonizing nations fall short of transformative change befitting full recognition. In Australia, the government offered an apology, but still fails to recognize Aboriginal sovereignty. In Canada, the government has declared respect for Aboriginal rights of recognition and an education that builds upon their language and culture, yet with few exceptions, western education tenets remain dominant in such Indigenous education. Oftentimes developments seem to ebb and flow—as if governments and the tertiary institutions in colonizing countries shift back and forth from an embrace of the possibilities to reluctance, again not willing to fully recognize Indigenous peoples, their ways of knowing or their rights. When measured against what Indigenous scholars refer to the 4 Rs—respect, relevance, reciprocity, and responsibility—mainstream tertiary institutions fail on what they consider to be key tenets.

As past analyses indicate, Indigenous students often experience a sense of estrangement in mainstream Eurocentric tertiary institutions. They report experiencing a lack of respect, verging on racism; a failure to find content relevant to their experiences within their community; and a lack of regard for Indigenous ways of knowing (ACIL Allen Consulting, 2014; Anderson, 2011; Campbell et al., 2012; House of Representatives Standing Committee on Indigenous Affairs, 2017). There seems to be a loss of community connections, and little recognition of Indigenous autonomy—let alone a balanced approach to teaching and learning wherein Indigenous interests are given equal status. It is as if despite a clear articulation of the importance of connections to community and the relevance of Indigenous ways of knowing, mainstream universities remain anchored in an assimilative orientation rather than an accommodative transformation. As Battiste (1998) stated almost 25 years ago:

> The modern context of Eurocentrism is seriously endangering Indigenous knowledge and heritage. Rapid economic development guided by Eurocentric theories has subordinated the strategy of sustainable development. Eurocentric laws have denied equal protection of the law to Indigenous knowledge and heritage. Transforming any of the entrenched Eurocentric contexts will be difficult; yet such a transformation is a prerequisite to obtaining respect for Indigenous worldviews. The challenge of protecting Indigenous knowledge and heritage requires the transformation of all these interdependent areas. This is a huge undertaking that will require concerted , comprehensive effort. It will require many generations working together with persistence. It will take vision, trust, and tolerance, which can be manifested by skilled diplomacy, strategic agreements, and deliberate commitments by all parties. Creating these transformations and respecting Indigenous knowledge and heritage is an intimidating task but a necessary goal for the end of colonialism and for the construction of postcolonial global and national orders. (Battiste, 1998, pp. 289–290)

While the rhetoric suggests a repositioning of Indigenous engagements within tertiary institutions (e.g., across institutions in Australia and Canada), institutional forces reflect a lack of commitment to Indigenous programs rooted in decolonial Indigenization. As Gaudry and Lorenz (2018) note, based upon interviews with Indigenous Canadian faculty members and allies, while they might envision a reorientation based upon a "dual university structure," tertiary institutions and non-Indigenous faculty seem more interested in much more modest models that increase inclusion of some content and more Indigenous enrollees. It is, as Morgan (2019) noted in Australia and Kuokkanen (2007) described for Canada, a discourse that befits a view of Indigenous staff and students as guests: "The academy represents itself as a welcoming host, but not without conditions. Indigenous epistemes are unconditionally welcome only to a handful of marginal spaces that are insignificant to the academy at large" (Kuokkanen, 2007, p. 131).

Notes

1. At various other UN gatherings on issues of diversity and ecology, such as the 1992 UN Conference on Environment and Development (and the UN Convention on Biological Diversity), there has been recognition of the importance of the Indigenous knowledge and their relationship with the land.
2. According to *The Sydney Morning Herald*, Morrison commented: "When those 12 ships turned up in Sydney all those years ago, it wasn't a particularly flash day for the people on those vessels either" (Harris & Nicolussi, 2021, para. 5). Such commemoration in defense of Australia Day diverges with the view held by many that this moment represents an Invasion.
3. Based upon research at a number of archeological sites (e.g., Nauwalabila I in the Northern Territory), it is generally believed that there is evidence of Aboriginal communities and culture dating as far back as 65,000 years.
4. This is a consequence of schooling, which has also become increasingly disconnected from Aboriginal lives. Nevertheless, recent research suggests that the stability of populations, the development of rich narrative cultures, and culture-specific mechanisms of intergenerational transmission have combined to make Australian Aboriginal people the custodians of the world's oldest orally-transmitted memories. These include recording, for instance, late-Holocene inundations of the continental shelf that occurred about 10,000 years ago (Nunn & Reid, 2016), a narrative feat of human memory probably unparalleled on other continents.
5. The Aboriginal studies degree includes a focus upon, as they state:

   - *Contemporary and traditional Indigenous Australian cultures, cosmologies, and societies.*
   - *The centrality of Indigenous cultural integrity, cultural wellbeing, and cultural expression.*
   - *How and why contemporary Indigenous cultures continue to flourish despite the impacts of colonisation, dispossession, and the trauma of assimilation.*
   - *The various phases and critical issues in Aboriginal and Torres Strait Islander history, politics, and cultural development.*

- *Connecting traditional and contemporary Indigenous knowledge and narratives to a range of key disciplinary issues.*
- *The students can choose to focus upon.*
- *Traditional and contemporary Indigenous Australia and the sustenance of cultural traditions.*
- *The history of colonization and its social, legal, and environmental legacies.*
- *The national and international resurgence of Indigenous cultures during the late twentieth century.*
- *Language revitalization and the importance of language in the sustenance of Aboriginal cultural wellbeing and integrity.*

Aboriginal creative expression in art, literature, film, music and performance, and critical curatorial and market issues.

6. In their review of teacher education as well as their survey of some 33 teacher education programs, Lambert and Burnett (2012) reported a history of shortcomings relative to Aboriginal teachers, the programs to support them, the failure to integrate Aboriginal understandings into the curriculum and the difficulties (verging on racism) preservice teachers encounter in their programs. As they noted:

> Aboriginal and Torres Strait Islander teachers are significantly underrepresented in Australia, making up less than 1% of teachers in schools. Although the need to increase the numbers of Indigenous teachers has been highlighted for many years, nationally, little has changed since the 1980s when Hughes and Willmot (1992) called for 1000 Indigenous teachers by 1990. (Lambert & Burnett, 2012, p. 1)

REFERENCES

ACIL Allen Consulting. (2014). *Evaluation of the Aboriginal and Torres Strait Islander education action plan 2010–2014.* http://www.ec.edu.au/site/DefaultSite/filesystem/documents/ATSI%20documents/ATSI%202010-2014%20Final%20Evaluation%20Report/1Final_Evaluation_ATSIEAP_ACILAllenConsulting.pdf

Alfred, T. (2004). Warrior scholarship: Seeing the university as a ground of contention. In D. A. Mihesuah & A. C. Wilson (Eds.), *Indigenizing the academy transforming scholarship and empowering communities* (pp. 88–99). University of Nebraska Press.

Anderson, C. (2011). Impediments to education success for Indigenous students. In N. Purdie, G. Milgate, & H. R. Bell (Eds.), *Two way teaching and learning: Toward cultural reflective and relevant education* (Chapter 6). ACER Press. https://research.acer.edu.au/indigenous_education/38

Archibald, J. (1995). Locally developed Native studies curriculum: An historical and philosophical rationale. In M. Battiste & J. Barman (Eds.), *First Nations education in Canada: The circle unfolds* (pp. 288–312). University of British Columbia Press.

Archibald, J., & Hare, J. (Eds.), (2017). *Knowing, sharing, doing: Celebrating successes in K-12 Aboriginal education in British Columbia*. British Columbia Principals and Vice Principals Association.

Barnhardt, R. (1991). Higher education in the fourth world: Indigenous people take control. *Canadian Journal of Native Education, 18*(2), 1–20.

Battiste, M. A. (1998). Enabling the autumn seed: Toward a decolonized approach to Aboriginal knowledge, language and education. *Canadian Journal of Native Education, 22*(1), 16–27.

Campbell, P., Kelly, P., & Harrison, L. (2012). *The problem of Aboriginal marginalisation: Education, labour markets and social and emotional well-being* (Working Paper No. 31). Alfred Deakin Research Institute. http://hdl.handle.net/10536/DRO/DU:30051878

Chambers, B. (2012, July 23). *What do we already know about our students?* Conference presentation. Faculty Learning and Teaching Forum on Social Inclusion, The University of Sydney.

Connell, R. (2019). *The good university: What universities actually do and why it's time for radical change*. Zed Books.

Faculty of Arts and Social Sciences. *Indigenous studies* [webpage]. The University of Sydney. https://www.sydney.edu.au/handbooks/arts/subject_areas_im/indigenous_studies.shtml. Accessed 9 June 2021.

Ferguson, R. A. (2012). *The reorder of things: The university and its pedagogies of minority difference*. University of Minnesota Press.

Fordham, A. M., & Schwab, R. G. (2007). *Education, training and Indigenous futures: CAEPR Policy Research 1990–2007*. Center for Aboriginal Economic Policy Research. The Australian National University. http://www.curriculum.edu.au/verve/_resources/Education_Training_and_Indigenous_FuturesCAEPR_Policy_Research_1990-2007.pdf

Gaudry, A., & Lorenz, D. (2018). Indigenization as inclusion, reconciliation, and decolonization: Navigating the different visions for indigenizing the Canadian academy. *AlterNative: An International Journal of Indigenous Peoples, 14*(3), 218–227. https://doi.org/10.1177/1177180118785382

Harris, R., & Nicolussi, C. (2021, January 21). 'Wasn't a particularly flash day': PM lashed over Australia Day convicts comment. *The Sydney Morning Herald*. https://www.smh.com.au/politics/federal/wasn-t-a-particularly-flash-day-pm-lashed-over-australia-day-convicts-comment-20210121-p56vx7.html#:~:text=Prime%20Minister%20Scott%20Morrison%27s%20comment%20that%20January%2026%2C,and%20the%20Greens.%20Scott%20Morrison%27s%20Australia%20Day%20

Hong, G. K. (2008). "The future of our worlds": Black feminism and the politics of knowledge in the university under globalization. *Meridians: Feminism, Race, Transnationalism, 8*(2), 95–115.

House of Representatives Standing Committee on Indigenous Affairs. (2017). *The power of education: From surviving to thriving: Educational opportunities for Aboriginal and Torres Strait Islander students*. Commonwealth of Australia. https://www.aph.gov.au/Parliamentary_Business/Committees/House/Indigenous_Affairs/EducationalOpportunities/Final_Report

Hughes, P., & Willmot, E. (1992). A thousand Aboriginal teachers by 1990. In J. Sherwood (Ed.), *Aboriginal education: Issues and innovations* (pp. 45–49). Creative Research.

IHER. (2012). *Review of Higher Education Access and Outcomes for Aboriginal and Torres Strait Islander People: Final Report*. Australian Government Department of Industry, Science, Energy and Resources. http://www.innovation.gov.au/TertiaryEducation/HigherEducation/ReviewofIHER/Pages/default.aspx

Kuokkanen, R. J. (2007). *Reshaping the university: Responsibility, Indigenous epistemes, and the logic of the gift*. The University of British Columbia Press.

Lambert, J., & Burnett, B. (2012). Retention and graduation of Aboriginal and Torres Strait Islander students in initial teacher education: A review of the literature. In M. Simons & T. Aspland (Eds.), *Proceedings of the 2012 Annual Australian Teacher Education Association (ATEA) Conference* (pp. 1–10). Australian Teacher Education Association (ATEA). https://eprints.qut.edu.au/58067/

Luke, A., Shield, P. G., Théroux, P., Tones, M., & Villegas, M. (2012). Knowing and teaching the Indigenous other: Teachers' engagement with Aboriginal and Torres Strait Islander cultures. Unpublished manuscript. http://eprints.qut.edu.au/53510/

Morgan, A., Reid, N., & Freebody, P. (In press). Literacy and linguistic diversity in Australia. In L. Verhoeven, S. Nag, C. Perfetti, & K. Pugh (Eds.), *Global variation in literacy development*. Cambridge University Press.

Morgan, B. (2019). Beyond the guest paradigm: Eurocentric education and Aboriginal Peoples in NSW. In E. A. McKinley & L. T. Smith (Eds.), *Handbook of Indigenous education* (pp. 111–128). Springer. https://doi.org/10.1007/978-981-10-3899-0_60

National Centre for Cultural Competence (NCCC). (2021). *Developing and integrating cultural competence*. The University of Sydney. Accessed 9 June 2021.

Nozaki, Y. (2009). Orientalism, the west and non-west binary, and postcolonial perspectives in cross-cultural research and education. In M. W. Apple, W. Au, & L. A. Gandin (Eds.), *The Routledge international handbook of critical education* (pp. 482–490). Routledge.

Nunn, P. D., & Reid, N. J. (2016). Aboriginal memories of inundation of the Australian coast dating from more than 7000 years ago. *Australian Geographer, 47*(1), 11–47. https://doi.org/10.1080/00049182.2015.1077539

Ottmann J. (2017). Canada's Indigenous peoples' access to post-secondary education: The spirit of the 'New Buffalo.' In J. Frawley, S. Larkin, & J. A. Smith (Eds.), *Indigenous pathways, transitions and participation in higher education: From policy to practice* (pp. 95–117). Springer. https://doi.org/10.1007/978-981-10-4062-7_7

Papps, E., & Ramsden, I. (1996). Cultural safety in nursing: The New Zealand experience. *International Journal for Quality in Health Care, 8*(5), 491–497. https://doi.org/10.1093/intqhc/8.5.491

Pascoe, B. (2014). *Dark emu: Aboriginal Australia and the birth of agriculture*. Magabala Books Aboriginal Corporation.

Patton, W., Hong, A. L., Lampert, J., Burnett, B., & Anderson, J. (2012). *Report into the retention and graduation of Aboriginal and Torres Strait Islander students enrolled in initial teacher education*. Australian Council of Deans of Education and the More Aboriginal and Torres Strait Islander Teachers Initiative (MATSITI). https://www.acde.edu.au

Phillips, J. (2011). *Resisting contradictions: Non-Indigenous pre-service teacher responses to critical Indigenous studies*. Doctoral thesis. Queensland University of Technology, Brisbane. https://eprints.qut.edu.au/46071/

Phillips, S., Phillips, J., Whatman, S., & McLaughlin, J. (2007). Introduction: Issues in (re)contesting Indigenous knowledges and Indigenous studies. *The Australian Journal of Indigenous Education, 36*(S1), 1–6. https://doi.org/10.1017/S13260 11100004634

Prior, D. (2009). Decolonising research agendas: Claiming voice and power in academia. In J. Frawley, M. Nolan, & N. White (Eds.), *Indigenous issues in Australian universities: Research, teaching, support* (pp. 66–74). Charles Darwin University Press.

Rigney, D., Bignall, S., & Hemming, S. (2015). Negotiating Indigenous modernity: Kungun Ngarrindjeri Yunnan—Listen to Ngarrindjeri speak. *AlterNative: An International Journal of Indigenous Peoples, 11*(4), 334–349. https://doi.org/10.1177/117718011501100402

Rigney, L. (2011). Action for Aboriginal social inclusion: Mobility, quality teaching and growing an Aboriginal workforce. In D. Bottrell & S. Goodwin (Eds.), *Schools, communities and social inclusion*. Palgrave Macmillan.

Rigney, L., & Hattam, R. J. (2018, April 13–17). *Toward a decolonizing culturally responsive pedagogy?* Conference presentation. American Educational Research Association Annual Meeting.

Rizvi, F. (2021, April 26). *Creating dynamic cultures in education post-Covid-19*. Dean's Lecture Series Presentation. University of Melbourne Graduate School of Education. https://www.youtube.com/watch?v=wMWkxUElfKM

Smith, G. H. (2015). *Transforming research: The Indigenous struggle for social, cultural, and economic justice within and through education*. Paper presented at the Annual meeting of the American Educational Research Association. Retrieved June, 2015, from http://www.aera.net/EventsMeetings/AnnualMeeting/PreviousAnnualMeetings/2015AnnualMeeting/2015AnnualMeetingWebcasts/TransformingResearchTheIndigenousStruggleforSocial,Cultural,andEconomicJusticeWithinandThroughEducation/tabid/15952/Default.aspx

Smith, L. T. (1999). *Decolonizing methodologies*. Otago University Press.

Smith, L. T. (2005). On tricky ground: Researching the native in the age of uncertainty. In N. K. Denzin & Y. S. Lincoln (Eds.), *The Sage handbook of qualitative research* (pp. 85–108). Sage.

Stein, S. (2017). The persistent challenges of addressing epistemic dominance in higher education: Considering the case of curriculum internationalization. *Comparative Education Review, 61*(S1), S25–S50. https://doi.org/10.1086/690456

The University of Sydney. (2015). *Statistics report: Staff 2015*. http://sydney.edu.au/staff/planning/statistics/staff/staff.php?yr=2015&type=1&fac=u

The University of Sydney. (2017). *Annual Report 2016*. https://ses.library.usyd.edu.au/handle/2123/16782

The University of Sydney. (2019, November 19). *Summer school inspires next generation of Indigenous teens* [online newsletter article]. https://www.sydney.edu.au/news-opinion/news/2019/11/25/summer-school-inspires-next-generation-of-indigenous-teens.html

The University of Sydney. (2020). *One Sydney, many people: Strategy 2021–2024*. https://www.sydney.edu.au/content/dam/corporate/documents/about-us/values-and-visions/one-sydney-many-people-digital.pdf

The University of Sydney. (2021). *Our motto and coat of arms*. https://www.sydney.edu.au/about-us/our-story/our-motto-and-coat-of-arms.html

Tierney, R., Peck, C., Llewellyn, G., Taylor, R., Sharma, M., Mooney, J., Blanchard, M., Payne, T., & Paynter, S. (2010a). *Indigenous Data Overview Report: A Resource to Inform Planning at Various Levels Within the University.* The University of Sydney.

Tierney, R., Peck, C., Llewellyn, G., Taylor, R., Sharma, M., Mooney, J., Blanchard, M., Payne, T., & Paynter, S. (2010b). *Indigenous participation, engagement, education and research strategy.* Senior Executive Indigenous Education Review Working Group, The University of Sydney.

United Nations. (1990). *World declaration on education for all: Meeting basic learning needs.* Retrieved March 12, 2018, from http://www.un-documents.net/jomtien.htm

United Nations. (2006). *United Nations declaration on the rights of Indigenous peoples.* Retrieved February 26, 2018, from https://www.un.org/development/desa/indigenouspeoples/declaration-on-the-rights-of-indigenous-peoples.html

Willinsky, J. (1998). *Learning to divide the world: Education at empire's end.* University of Minnesota Press.

Willmot, E. (1987). *Pemulwuy: The rainbow warrior.* Bantam Books.

CHAPTER 14

Critical Education, Social Democratic Education, Revolutionary Marxist Education

Dave Hill

CREEPING FASCISM: CRITICAL, SOCIALIST AND MARXIST EDUCATION AND EDUCATORS UNDER ATTACK

Critical Education, questioning power relationships throughout society and proposing/working for egalitarian alternatives are under global assault in this current era of neoconservative/neoliberal/neo-fascist right-wing authoritarianism. Capitalist individuals, think tanks, organizations and governments are seeking to dilute, expel or criminalize socialist, Marxist, anti-nationalist education, particularly in schools' and universities' curricula- and activity. Currently and historically, the neo-conservatives and neo-/actual Fascists also target LGBT, feminist and anti-racist writing, teaching and thought (Faulkner et al., 2021; Hill, 2019a).

However, in this current, early twenty-first century era, critical education, questioning power relationships throughout society and proposing/working for egalitarian alternatives, are under spectacular assault in this current era of neoconservative/neoliberal/neo-fascist right-wing authoritarianism. This is/has been so from Trump's USA, and, in many states of the USA, in post-Trump USA, to Johnson's England and Wales, to Bolsonaro's Brazil, to Erdogan's Turkey, to the Law and Justice Party government in Poland, to Modi's India, to Orban's Hungary and to the Ukraine. In each, powerful forces are seeking to dilute, expel or criminalize socialist, Marxist, anti-nationalist education—particularly in the schools' and universities' curricula-

D. Hill (✉)
Anglia Ruskin University, Chelmsford and Cambridge, UK

© The Author(s), under exclusive license to Springer Nature Switzerland AG 2022
A. A. Abdi and G. W. Misiaszek (eds.), *The Palgrave Handbook on Critical Theories of Education*, https://doi.org/10.1007/978-3-030-86343-2_14

and activity. One of the most notable is the policy of the Bolsonaro quasi-/would-be Fascist government in Brazil, promising during his 2018 election campaign to 'enter the education ministry with a flamethrower to remove Paulo Freire' (Woods, 2020).

The iron fist of Capital and its structures severely limit resistant 'agency', punishing, restricting, illegalizing, dismissing, for example, trade union and Left political activists and, their Left, anti-capitalist beliefs. As one example, in September 2020, schools in England were told by the Department (Ministry) for Education not to use material from anti-capitalist groups, with anti-Capitalism categorized as an 'extreme political stance' equivalent to endorsing illegal activity (Busby, 2020). As left-wing Labour MP John McDonnell responded: 'On this basis it will be illegal to refer to large tracts of British history and politics including the history of British socialism, the Labour Party and trade unionism, all of which have at different times advocated the abolition of capitalism' (Busby, 2020). As another example, in Poland, the possession of Marx's *Capital* is punishable with three-year imprisonment (Stańczyk, 2021). In Turkey, many leftists and Marxist educators were dismissed and lost social and public rights, including their passports, following the failed July 2016 coup (in which they were not involved) against President Erdogan, and currently, in 2021, governments in both Greece and Turkey are attempting to assert further control over universities.

While it is true that the ideological apparatuses of the state (Althusser, 1971) (such as Ministries of Education and school and university governing bodies) have, in their ideological and their repressive functions, to varying degrees, sought to marginalize, contain, vilify, destroy Marxist (and, indeed Left social democratic programs such as those of Jeremy Corbyn and Bernie Sanders) at this current juncture we are witnessing, suffering from an intensification of ideological repression. The harassment and dismissals of Marxist educators and activists are ratcheting up in country after country.

Three Types of Socialist Education, Three Types of Critical Education

In this chapter, I am not discussing conservative-technicist or liberal pluralist/'neutrality in the classroom' versions of critical education. Instead, I critically analyze three types of Left critical education.

'Centrist' social democrats want to *reform* education (to make it a bit fairer, a bit more meritocratic, with some positive discrimination).

More Left, democratic socialists, or 'left social democrats/ left reformists', such as Jeremy Corbyn and Bernie Sanders, also want to reform education to make education—but to make it *much* fairer, with pronounced positive discrimination to help 'under-achieving groups'.

Revolutionary Marxists, that is to say, Marxists who wish to replace Capitalism with socialism, want an education critical of Capitalism, an education for social, political and economic *transform*ation, into a socialist economy and society. My own writing, much of which is online at http://www.ieps.org.uk/ publications/online-papers-dave-hill/, is from a Revolutionary Marxist political and also from a Classical Marxist theoretical perspective, that is, referring to Marx and Engels, not just their interpreters). I argue for a Marxist education policy (e.g., Edwards et al., 2018; Hill, 2010, 2015, 2019a, 2019b, 2019c), focusing on Marxist education, differentiating it from other versions of Critical Education.

Centrist' Social Democrats and Left Social Democrats/Democratic Socialists and Education

Social democrats have advanced policies intended to make the system more 'meritocratic', with 'equal opportunities' policies involving positive discrimination for under-represented groups (in particular, the poorer sections of the working class and particular ethnic groups), with academic and scholastic advancement and future positions in the labor market purportedly resulting from 'effort plus ability', that is, merit. For entry, however, into what is a grossly unequal society.

Traditional social democratic education systems are those such as in Sweden and Finland, and the reforms of the Wilson Labour government in England and Wales in the 1960s and 70s. Wilson widely (if not universally in the state system—private schools remained outside the state system)—established comprehensive/common schooling, and grants to help children from poorer families (such as me, and such as my grandson) ('Education Maintenance Grants') stay on at school and also, to go to university. (There were no university tuition fees for 'domestic' students until 1998.) Policies such as smaller class sizes for the lower attainers, and residential education centers and 'cultural trips' were widespread, from all of which I benefited and recall, as a school student, a teacher, and as a local councillor. At the post-school level, free adult education was ubiquitous for leisure as well as vocational 'further education', and the Open University was set up in 1969 whereby people from working-class backgrounds who had left school at the minimum school-leaving age, or at the age of 18/19, could study for a degree (primarily by distance learning), free of fees, while still at work.

At various stages in various countries, all types of socialists attempted, at various times, to make the schooling curriculum more inclusive and 'relevant' to different communities and classes. The Community Schools movement, particularly strong in England between the 1970s and the 1990s, attempted to make schools more central to local communities, by developing Community Schools—to 'lessen the distance' between schools and their working-class communities. The 'Community Schools' Movement, 'seeks to obliterate the boundary between school and community, to turn the community into a school and the school into a community' (Halsey, 1972, p. 79). As did the much overlooked 'Hargreaves Report' into secondary education in the Inner London Education Authority (ILEA, 1984, summarized in Doe, 1984).

However, sociologists of education over the last 70 years, and communists and socialists since before then (see Simon e.g., 1978); Floud et al. (1957) and, more recently, Stephen Ball (2003), Jean Anyon (2011) and Diane Reay (2018), have pointed out the enduring myth of meritocracy in schooling systems. Marxist reproduction theorists from early Soviet writers Bukharin and Preobrazhensky (1922/1969) to contemporary Marxist theorists such as Glenn Rikowski (*passim*) and Dave Hill (*passim*) drawing to an extent on Althusser (1971), Bowles and Gintis (1976), Bourdieu and Passeron (e.g., 1977), have for many decades pointed out that the education system is purposefully and intentionally rigged in favor of the elite capitalist class, in favor of class reproduction.

Marxist theorists (and activists), together with social democratic theorists and activists also agree that within the working class, the 'middle class' strata secure 'positional advantage'—the 'better schools and universities' (better grades/exam results), compared to the 'working class', the less advantaged, poorer strata of the working class, within which particular racialized ethnic and gendered groups achieve less than others and are subjected to far greater levels of oppression and discipline—racism, sexism, homophobia—than other groups.

Such social democratic reforms, though usually focusing on pedagogy and curriculum, have been advanced by Critical Pedagogues, such as Henry Giroux (e.g., 1983, 2001), and also by what I consider to be 'Marxian' educators' such as the very influential Michael W. Apple (e.g., 2006), and his co-thinkers such as Ken McGrew (e.g., 2011). These can be considered to be democratic socialist, wishing teachers to be committed to anti-racist, social justice teaching, and to developing teachers as 'transformative intellectuals' seeking a fairer society. Such Left social democrats, or democratic socialists, want *substantial* reform (of the wider economic, penal, political, welfare systems, and in education, more equal chances—provision, funding, attainment).

Foley et al. (2015) point out that 'critical pedagogy has entered the mainstream in the United States, with over 7000 titles alone which address the topic offered on the major book retailer Amazon.com'. Drawing from Gramsci and the Frankfurt School, and seeking to apply Freire, critical pedagogues seek to transform consciousness and teach for social justice. As compared with more Structuralist neo-Marxists, Culturalist neo-Marxists, such as proponents and writers on Critical Pedagogy see greater space for the autonomy of individuals, groups and institutions/organizations (such as teachers, schools, Local Authorities) to engage in resistant practices, anti-hegemonic praxis. Critical Pedagogy has been praised and practiced widely.

However, McLaren, for example (2000) notes that Critical Pedagogy (as opposed to his own Revolutionary—that is, Marxist—Critical Pedagogy),

> … at least in classrooms throughout the United States) (is) little more than liberalism refurbished with some lexical help from Freire (as in words like *praxis* and *dialogue*) and basically is used to camouflage existing capitalist social

relations under a plethora of eirenic proclamations and classroom strategies. (McLaren, 2000, p. xxv, For similar critique, see also; Gonzalez & Rikowski, 2019; McLaren, 2016; Stańczyk, 2021)

This is not at all, to demean the efforts of those millions of teachers and educators globally attempting to work for a critical citizenry and for social justice in classrooms and seminar rooms/lecture theaters and online, nor the compilers of the various compendia/edited collections on Critical Pedagogy.

What Critical pedagogues such as Giroux, and 'Marxian' educators such as Apple do *not* want is Marxist revolution, the replacement of Capitalism and Capitalist education by socialism. (For a discussion between Revolutionary anti-capitalist Marxist Educators and 'Marxian' or left reformist/Educators, see; Banfield (2015), Farahmandpur (2004), Hill (2009), Kelsh and Hill (2006), McLaren (2010, 2013), Rikowski (2006, 2019); on the one hand and Apple (2006), and McGrew (2011) on the other). Anyon (2011) labels Revolutionary Marxists as 'traditional Marxist' and left social democrats such as Michael W. Apple as 'neo-Marxist'.

Classical Marxists critique neo-Marxisms, though like Marx, Lenin, Luxemburg, welcome reforms, without being reformist (see, e.g., Hill, 2021; Lenin, 1902/1999; Luxemburg, 1899/1999). To return to an earlier—and important—argument, it is not just the Capitalist state apparatuses (and those apparatuses supporting the capitalist state, such as the media) that discipline the working class—it is also the economic warfare, the brute force and power of the Capitalist Class in the domain of labor, employment, wage suppression and repression, immiseration. This is one instance of where Classical Marxist analysis is in disagreement with neo-Marxist analyses. Where the barrel of the gun ordered by the capitalist class crushes the relative autonomy of resistance. Where Overdetermination is trumped by Economic Determination.

My critique of the neo-Marxist Althusser (Hill, 2001) was of Althusser's formulation that *Economic Determination in the Last Instance* means, 'in the last "overdetermined" analysis' (Althusser, 1962). Although Althusser did admit 'economic determination in the last instance', he added the important—and in my view, negating, qualification that, in overdetermined form, '*its bell never tolled*' (my italics). The analysis I am presenting here is that the bell of economic determination is indeed now tolling.

FIVE ASPECTS OF MARXIST EDUCATION

Revolutionary Marxists, that is, Marxists who are anti-capitalist and wish to see Capitalism replaced by socialism, want an education system that is not only 'free' (from fees) from early childhood through life, but is a system with well-trained/educated teachers who are well-paid and valued in society, with a Marxist school and higher/university education curriculum that exposes Capitalism and inequalities, argues for socialism and values solidaristic as opposed to competitive individualistic school activities. In a Marxist education system, all schools and universities, including private ones, would be brought under local accountable democratic control. There would be no private schools or colleges/universities, no possibility for the wealthy to purchase educational advantage for their children.

The Questions Marxist Educators Ask

In schools, colleges, universities, many radical and Marxist critical educators try, in addition to seeking dramatic increases in funding, to affect five aspects of learning and teaching, asking questions about (at least) five aspects of education. These relate to: (i) Curriculum and Assessment, (ii) Pedagogy, (iii) Organizational Culture within the School/Institution, (iv) Organization of The Education System and of Students, that is, comprehensive schooling or selective schooling and (v) Ownership and Control of Schools/Colleges/Universities.

These questions are common to many types of radical educator, from liberals to social democrats and democratic socialists, not simply Marxists. Below, therefore, I add what is *specifically Marxist* about these five aspects of education policy and praxis (see Hill, 2019a, 2019b, 2019c).

(i) Curriculum and Assessment

A first question Marxist and other critical educators ask is what should be in the *curriculum*? A related question is, 'who should decide?' Should the curriculum be a curriculum for conformity—to create conformist and dutiful workers and citizens, devoid of 'deep critique' (of existing society for example). Should it be 'a white, male, middle class curriculum', uninfluenced by decolonization theory, Black Lives Matter, Extinction Rebellion and feminisms? Or, as Marxists propose and practice, should it be a curriculum for reform and revolution, where curriculum areas/subjects (or cross-disciplinary projects/themes) focus on inequalities, resistance, transformation, the collective good, not on individualistic consumerism, on environmentalism not capitalist ecocide. Thus, geography would include a focus on social geography, science on the social implications of science, and history and literature and the arts would encompass (white/black, male/female) working-class history and novels/plays exposing ('race', gender, social class, for example) injustice and promoting socialism and communism. The curriculum would be decolonized and revolutionized. It would be anti-racist, anti-sexist, environmentalist, Marxist. (It would also develop subject-specific concepts, skills, knowledge.)

Marxist educators, indeed critical educators in general, can, with students, look at the curriculum and ask, 'What do you/ we think should be in the curriculum that is currently absent?' 'Who benefits and who loses from this curriculum'? What 'messages' come from this curriculum, about, for example, power, protest, individualism, collectivity/collectivism, Black Lives Matter, Generation X and environmentalism, sexism and misogyny, sexuality and class oppression and exploitation. Where Marxists and Revolutionary Critical Educators (McLaren, 2010, 2013) differ from more social democratic, democratic socialist and liberal critical educators are in the emphasis placed on resistance, activism and socialist transformation—and on social class analysis.

Regarding Assessment, what is assessed is usually what teachers focus on. It can be restricted to subject knowledge and skills, or it can assess more widely. The (social democratic) Hargreaves Report about schooling in the left-dominated Inner London Education Authority (Doe, 1984; ILEA, 1984), for example, proposed that indices of pupil achievement include not only exam results but also pupils' achievements in areas such as problem-solving, personal and social skills, and motivation and commitment. Furthermore, it recommended that pupils/students be given a real say in school policies such as the curriculum and exams.

Elsewhere (e.g., Edwards et al., 2018) I set out a Manifesto for Teacher Education, partly drawing on an attempt I developed and led as a Marxist teacher education course leader. Many of these proposals are supported by other reform and social justice groups. But taken together, they offer a sustained challenge to neoliberal/neoconservative, pre-/proto/quasi fascist Capitalism.

(ii) Pedagogy

Many Marxist (and other critical) educators question the overwhelming teacher-centered *pedagogy*, the pattern of teaching and learning relationships and interaction, what Freire termed 'the banking model' of education. Instead, using Freirean perspectives and praxis, they try to use democratic participative pedagogy which can break down, to some extent, patterns of domination and submission and is a pedagogy that listens to children's, students' and local communities' voices. This is a pedagogy that bases teaching and learning on the concerns and issues in everyday life, in life as experienced by the learners. Furthermore, it is a collaboration between teachers and students, teachers and pupils. Here, learning is collaborative, not individualistic and competitive. It is a pedagogic system—pattern of learning and teaching relationships—that is collective, collaborative, mutually supportive.

In addition to 'democratic participative collaborative pedagogy', Critical Marxist educators use different types of pedagogy in teaching, to engage in non-hierarchical, democratic, participative, teaching and research. Vygotsky (e.g., 1934), as a Marxist, was inspired by Marx's *dialectic* in that it rejects top-down and bottom-up accounts of the learning process—these unidirectional models originate in class-based societal relations which Marxists reject.

In England, pedagogy in primary (elementary) school teaching has become removed, to an extent, from the control of teachers. Following the 1998 National Literacy Strategy (NLS) (DfEE, 1998), a specific teaching and learning strategy was advised—and was surveilled and inspected for more than a decade, its prescriptions still felt. Across the subject curriculum, lessons followed a standard four-part pattern—introduction, lecture/explanation/teacher teaching, pupil/student discussion/work, plenary. No room for Freirean, Vygotskyan, or liberal-progressive child-centered teaching and learning, no room for the 'dead cat flying through the window' syndrome, whereby teachers and pupils/students could seize upon a happening event, to explore. And no room for extended group interdisciplinary focus and analysis of a particular problem or social event, the type of school-teaching and teaching as a teacher educator that I engaged in between the late 1960s and the late 1980s. Instead, 'there is no time'—the curriculum is full (of content designed by conservative think-tanks, advisers and Ministers) (Hill, 1994, 1997; Jones, 2003).

To return to questions of pedagogy, of course, critiques of over-dominant teacher-centered pedagogy are not restricted to Marxist educators. They are also made by liberal-progressive, child/student-centered educators, anarchist educators and by some conservative educators, concerned about teaching effectiveness and preparation for the workplace. And, following Gramsci, Marxist teachers, by virtue of their social and ideological *role* in actually teaching, in actually carrying out the role of teacher, should maintain an authoritative stance where appropriate. There is room for class teaching and lectures as well as dialogic and discussion-based learning, and learning based on an individual's or a community's needs.

Marxist educators differ between themselves (as do conservative educators) on the degree to which education is or should be proselytizing, for example, praising 'the revolution', and the degree to which it is/should be 'critical'—(including 'auto-critique') criticizing/critiquing not just Capitalism and inequality, but also the current and alternative ideologies, policies and praxis. There is a spectrum across different times and places from authoritarian to democratic pedagogy, from some Communist states in particular periods, to some insurgent movements.

My own Classical Marxist theoretical analysis and Revolutionary Marxist praxis, developing from a huge personal and a theorized awareness of class inequality and resistance, attempts a synthesis of Vygotskyan, Freirean and Gramscian pedagogy. My own early praxis as a young schoolteacher (at Stockwell Manor Comprehensive School in Brixton in Inner London) took place during the relatively liberal-progressive, child-centered period of education in England of the late 1960s and early 1970s—before Labour Prime Minister James Callaghan's Ruskin College speech of 1976 started the process of yanking back education into fulfilling primarily economic and vocational aims, a process carried out to fruition and completion following the Thatcher and Major governments of 1979–1987. This was also a time of socialist teaching and curriculum development in some state schools, at a time when there was no national curriculum, schools and teachers were able to develop their/our own curricula. The sheer hatred expressed by Conservative party/politicians, and media of both liberal-progressive and attempts at socialist egalitarian critical education is described in books by Ken Jones (1989, 2003), and in my own writing, (such as Hill, 1997), which detail Conservative politicians' reactions to and sheer venom directed at liberal child-progressive as well as at social democratic and socialist education, and their determination to crush them all. Conservative legislation—the 1988 Education Reform Act, and its introduction of a compulsory and rigidly surveilled/inspected National Curriculum for schools, and national curriculum for teacher training of 1991/1992 saw the removal of many left teachers and teacher educators from their posts. I was one of many teacher educators dismissed/'made redundant' following the removal of most sociological, political and psychological aspects of teacher education courses through these revised teacher education criteria of 1991/1992, their removal being justified on grounds of 'the need to prioritise the practical over the theoretical' (Hill, 1994, 1997, 2003).

(iii) Organizational Culture Within the School/University/Institution

A third question for education relates to the social relations and power relations between management and shop-floor education workers, that is, between the school/university head, principal, director and the teachers and lecturers (and ancillary staff). It also concerns the 'hidden curriculum' of head teacher/Principal—teacher–pupil/student relationships, demands and expectations.

Is the school culture democratic and collegiate, or is it dictatorial and authoritarian? Prior to the diversification of state education into City Technology Colleges, Academies, teachers and head teachers were employed by local education authorities, the democratically elected local councils. There were *national* pay scales, no individual pay bargaining and seeking Performance Related Pay, and no head teachers earning far more than the Prime Minister, as is the case with some head teachers of Academies and Directors of Academy Chains. As with other sectors of the quasi and part-state provision, with New Public Managerialism, the difference in pay and emoluments between those at the top and the shop-floor workers such as teacher and lecturers has ballooned.

Globally, and in the UK, where neoliberalism has triumphed in education, common results have been increased casualization of academic labor, increased proletarianization, increased pay and conditions differentials within education sectors, cuts in the wages/salaries (as well as in 'the social wage' of state benefits and rights), payment by results/performance-related pay, cuts to school and further and higher education budgets, increased intensification of labor, with larger classes, decreased autonomy for school and college teachers over curriculum and pedagogy, being subject to the surveillance and rigors of 'new public managerialism', increased levels of monitoring and report-writing, and accompanying increased levels of stress, increased concern with timekeeping and tighter and more punitive discipline codes. There is also the curtailment of trade union rights and attacks on trade unions as organizations that defend and promote working-class interests.

This is a far cry from the occasional more collegiate approach to school democracy and management of the more 'progressive', and in some schools, more socialist management. In my own experience of a First/Infant school of the mid-1980s, the whole teaching staff would sit round in a circle to discuss school policy, such as reading schemes, the head teacher would act more as a chairperson than a dictator. Under neoliberalism, the Portuguese (left-wing) revolution of 1974 legally instituted collegial and democratic management of schools in Portugal, whereby school staffs elected their head teachers, 'president of the directive council' (Castanheira & Costa, 2011) (with candidates for head teacher, often running on party tickets). This lasted until 2008, when the Portuguese government 'recognised' 'the need to develop strong leadership in the management body of a school by replacing the collegial body executive council for a single person body – a director' (Castanheira & Costa, 2011, p. 210).

The managerialist school culture is also a far cry from a key feature of the Hargreaves Report for London's schools (ILEA, 1984) which was to give pupils a say in the running of the school, with, for example, school councils (made up of elected representatives from the student body, plus a degree of teacher involvement) having powers not just over trivia, such as lavatories, food and litter, but also on issues such as school hours, extra-curricular activities, as well as (as previously mentioned) in relation to the curriculum and assessment, the curriculum and exams, to give pupils/students experience of democratic procedures.

Part of the ongoing de-critiquing and de-professionalization of teachers, and their reducing levels of pay, is the proletarianization of teachers—and, increasingly of the burgeoning precariat teaching in universities, has been an increased level of identification by teachers and their main unions such as the National Education Union in England and Wales, and 'education professionals' with the working-class movement, workers' struggle and industrial action. That is, by increased working-class consciousness. The National Education Union (NEU), and the Universities and Colleges Union (UCU) have been two trade unions in England and Wales fighting the current Conservative government(s) most successfully over various issues, such as not opening schools until safer from Covid.

(iv) Organization of Students and of the Education System Itself

A fourth question in education that critical and Marxist educators can and should ask is about *organization of the students*. How should children of different social classes, gender, and ethnic backgrounds be organized within classrooms, within institutions such as schools and universities, and within national education systems?

Marxists prefer and work for what in Britain is called 'comprehensive schools' and in India 'the common school'. Socialists of various types argue that school should be a microcosm of society, that each school should contain a mixture of children/students from the different social classes and social class strata, and a mix of attainment levels. That is, children/students should not be divided by selection into 'high achievers' and 'low achievers', or by social class, by wealth. No moneyed or relatively well-off sections of the population should be able to buy educational advantage, and thereby disadvantage others.

Under the academic results based 'league table' competitive marketization of schools children/students as young as four years old are 'ability grouped' by able or by 'stream'/class. This is very different from the mixed ability organization of many schools in the 1960s–1980s, and very different from the proposals of the Hargreaves Report into Secondary Education in the Inner London Education Authority (ILEA, 1984, summarized, respectively, in Doe, 1984).

(v) Ownership, Control and Management of Schools/Colleges/Universities

A fifth question Revolutionary Marxists pose is 'who should own, control and govern schools, further education (vocational) colleges and universities?' Should it be 'the people'? Local councils/municipalities? Speculators, carpet salesmen and Hedge Funds? Churches and Mosques?

Revolutionary Marxist educators (and others, of course) believe that schools, colleges and universities should be run democratically, with education workers and students, as well as elected representatives of local communities, having powers in and over those education institutions, within a secular, democratic national framework. There should be no private control of schools, colleges or universities, either by private companies/shareholders, religious organizations or private individuals. Commodification and marketization in education must end (Rikowski, 2019). Thus, there should be no 'Academies' in England, no 'Charter Schools', whether 'not-for-profit' or 'for profit' in the USA. Currently, summer 2021, three quarters of all state-funded 'Secondary' (High) schools in England, and a third of state-funded 'Primary'/(Elementary) schools are managed and run by private academy chains. (For attempts to address these various aspects of education, in developing a socialist policy for education, see, Edwards et al., 2018; Ford, 2016; Hill, 2010, 2013, 2015, 2019a; Hill et al., 2016).

What Is Specifically Marxist About These Policy Proposals?

What defines Marxists is *firstly*, the belief that <u>reforms are not sustainable under Capitalism</u>, they are stripped away when there are the (recurrent and systemic) crises of capital, such as the 1930s, 1970s, and currently, post 2008, and as they are likely to be post-Covid-19 (e.g., with pay cuts, union rights, social budgets under renewed threat).

The *second* difference is an understanding of the <u>salience of class</u> as compared with other forms of structural oppression and discrimination and inequality. Marxists go further than criticizing (and acting against) social discrimination, oppressions, for example, of sexism, homophobia, racism, into economic rights and into the recognition that full economic rights cannot be achieved under a capitalist economic system, but only under a socialist or communist system. Formal and informal curricula should teach Marxist analysis of society, its class-based nature—in theoretical terms, the Labour-Capital Relation. The aim is to develop class consciousness, or, as Marx put it, the working class as a 'class for itself', not simply a 'class in itself' (Marx, 1852/1999). What Gramsci called 'good sense', as opposed to 'common sense' (Gramsci, 1971/2000).

The *third* point of difference between Marxist and non-Marxist socialists is that in order to replace Capitalism, Marxists have to actually work to organize for that movement, for that action. Thus, a duty as a Revolutionary Marxist teacher is as an *activist*, and a recognition that political organization, program development, intervention are necessary. What is needed is a revolution to replace, to get rid of, the capitalist economic system.

These are three points of difference between Marxists and other socialists, between what is Marxist and what is not (Hill, 2019a, 2019b, 2019c).

The Task and Role of Marxist Educators

The role of organic Marxist public intellectuals is crucial. Marxist public intellectuals—such as the 'political' shop steward, or union organizer, the member of a socialist/Marxist party or group, the teacher, the teacher educator, the youth worker—intellectualize social, political, cultural, economic matters from the standpoint, to repeat, of what Gramsci (1971/2000) termed 'good sense', from a class—conscious perspective, or, to refer to a Classical Marxist injunction from *The Communist Manifesto* (Marx & Engels, 1848/2010), that the key political task facing communists is 'the formation of the proletariat into a class', that is, a 'class *for* itself', a class aware of itself as a class in the Capital–Labour relation (Marx, 1847/1999). Herein lies Marxists' pedagogical importance, of party, organization, leaflets, newspapers, booklets, books and social media; here, as well as in the classroom in conversation and in rhetorical speeches, we carry out the role of socialist analysis, of revolutionary pedagogy, of connecting the here and now of a rent strike, a pro-immigrant rally, an anti-austerity march, a picket line of a zero-hours contract employer, an occupation of a tax avoiding multinational company owned shop: here is essential Marxist pedagogical praxis.

> 1. to expose and contest the ways and extent to which the capitalist class itself, through its economic power, and through its power over fiscal and economic policy of the governments that serve them, suppresses and represses both the direct wage as wage instead of capitalist profit for example as the proportion of national income, and 'scaling back'/ underfunding/ cutting the social wage (welfare and social support systems and public health and education and social care)- and through its brute power to suppress trade unions and to dismiss workers;

2. to explain and develop consciousness, critical Marxist understanding, of the Labour-Capital Relation- that Capitalism is the exploitation of the labour power of workers through the theft of the surplus value produced by workers, stolen from them by capitalists (and by the capitalist state organisations) in the form of profit;

3. to expose and organise and teach against the actual and the symbolic violence by the capitalist state and class against the ('raced' and gendered) working class;

4. to expose and contest the ways and extent to which the capitalist state and its apparatuses perpetuate and reproduce their power, that of their class, through the ideological and repressive apparatuses of the state (such as the media, the schooling, further education and university systems, the electoralist parliamentary system);

5. in particular the way they do this through demeaning and deriding the 'cultural capital' and knowledges of the ('raced' and gendered) working class through what Pierre Bourdieu termed 'cultural arbitrary' and 'symbolic violence'

6. argue for, propagate, organise, agitate for and implement democratic Marxist egalitarian change and policy in the wider society and economy- throughout society-not just within the classroom walls.

Conclusion

This chapter is intended as a guide to Marxist educational/pedagogical activist praxis. I have tried to set out the differences between Marxist analysis and policy for Education, distinguishing Revolutionary anti-Capitalist Marxist theory, analysis and policy from non-Marxist Critical Pedagogy, such as that of Henry Giroux, and from 'Centrist' as well as 'Left'; social democracy, such as the 'Marxian' analysis of Michael W. Apple. Within the broader polity, this Marxist critique is also applied to left social democrats such as Bernie Sanders and Jeremy Corbyn.

The chapter poses questions which implicitly ask the reader to pause and critique their own situatedness, their own praxis, in regard to the curriculum, critical education, critical pedagogies, their public pedagogy and social and political analysis of education in general. In particular to the overall, if contested, repressive and differentiating, divisive, socially and economically reproductive role of Capitalist Education.

Using Marxist theory in general, and Marxist educational theory in particular, the chapter points the way, identifying some of the key parameters, areas of policy, in which Marxist educators can and do engage in public pedagogy and activism within education institutions.

References

Althusser, L. (1962). *Contradiction and overdetermination.* https://www.marxists.org/reference/archive/althusser/1962/appendix.htm

Althusser, L. (1971). Ideology and ideological state apparatuses. In L. Althusser (Ed.), *Lenin and philosophy and other essays.* New Left Books. https://www.marxists.org/reference/archive/althusser/1970/ideology.htm

Anyon, J. (2011). *Marx and education.* Routledge.

Apple, M. (2006). Review essay: Rhetoric and reality in critical educational studies in the United States. *British Journal of Sociology of Education, 27*(5), 679–687.

Ball, S. J. (2003). *Class strategies and the educational market: The middle classes and social advantage.* RoutledgeFalmer.

Banfield, G. (2015). Marx and education: Working with the revolutionary educator. *Journal for Critical Education Policy Studies, 13*(3). http://www.jceps.com/archives/2792

Bourdieu, P., & Passeron, J. (1977). *Reproduction in education, society and culture.* Sage.

Bowles, S., & Gintis, H. (1976). *Schooling in capitalist America.* Routledge and Kegan Paul.

Bukharin, N., & Preobrazhensky, Y. (1922/1969). *The ABC of communism.* Penguin Books. https://www.marxists.org/archive/bukharin/works/1920/abc

Busby, M. (2020, September 27). Schools in England told not to use material from anti-capitalist groups. *The Guardian.* https://www.theguardian.com/education/2020/sep/27/uk-schools-told-not-to-use-anti-capitalist-material-in-teaching

Castanheira, P., & Costa, J. A. (2011). From a collegially elected council to a director: The evolution of Portuguese school management. *Procedia Social and Behavioral Sciences, 15,* 2007–2011. www.sciencedirect

Department for Education and Employment (DfEE). (1998). *The national literacy strategy: Framework for teaching.* HMSO.

Doe, B. (1984, March 23). Improving London's schools. *Times Educational Supplement.*

Edwards, G., Hill, D., & Boxley, S. (2018). Critical teacher education for economic, environmental and social justice. *Journal for Critical Education Policy Studies, 16*(3). http://www.jceps.com/archives/49021

Farahmandpur, R. (2004). Essay review: A Marxist critique of Michael Apple's neo-Marxist approach to educational reform. *Journal for Critical Education Policy Studies, 2*(1). http://www.jceps.com/wp-content/uploads/PDFs/02-1-4.pdf

Faulkner, N., Hearse, P., Hannah, S., Fortune, R., & Fortune, N. (2021). *System crash: An activist guide to the coming democratic revolution: Chapter 6 the new fascism.* https://www.anticapitalistresistance.org/post/the-new-Fascism

Floud, J., Halsey, A. H., & Martin, F. M. (1957). *Social class and educational opportunity.* Heinemann.

Foley, J. A., Morris, D., Gounari, P., & Agostinone-Wilson, F. (2015). Critical education, critical pedagogies, Marxist education in the United States. *Journal for Critical Education Policy Studies, 13*(3). http://www.jceps.com/archives/2758

Ford, D. (2016). *Communist study: Education for the commons.* Lexington Books.

Giroux, H. (1983). Theories of reproduction and resistance in the new sociology of education: A critical analysis. *Harvard Education Review, 55*(3),

257–293. https://www.academia.edu/3638580/Theories_of_Resistance_and_Reproduction_in_the_New_Sociology_of_Education

Giroux, H. (2001). *Theory and resistance in education: Towards a pedagogy for the opposition*. Bergin and Garvey.

Gonzalez, A. O., & Rikowski, G. (2019). Interview with Glenn Rikowski on Marxism, critical pedagogy and inclusive education: Discussions for a revolutionary discourse. *Revista Izquierdas, 45*(1), 260–276. https://www.aacademica.org/aldo.ocampo.gonzalez/9.pdf

Gramsci, A. (1971/2000). *Selections from the prison notebooks*. International Publishers Co. https://www.marxists.org/archive/gramsci/prison_notebooks/selections.htm

Halsey, A. H. (1972). *Educational priority volume 1: EPA problems and policies*. HMSO.

Hill, D. (1994). Teacher education and training: A left critique. *Forum (For Promoting 3-19 Comprehensive Education), 6*(3), 74–76. http://www.wwwords.co.uk/forum/content/pdfs/36/Forum_36_3.pdf

Hill, D. (1997). Equality in primary schooling: The policy context, intentions and effects of the conservative 'reforms'. In M. Cole, D. Hill, & Shan, S. (Eds.), *Promoting equality in primary schools*. Cassell. http://www.ieps.org.uk/publications/online-papers-dave-hill/

Hill, D. (2001). State theory and the neo-liberal reconstruction of schooling and teacher education: A structuralist neo-Marxist critique of postmodernist, quasi-postmodernist, and culturalist neo-Marxist theory. *The British Journal of Sociology of Education, 22*(1), 137–157. http://www.ieps.org.uk/media/1162/brit-jnl-sociol-of-educ-22-1-2001-dave-hill-state-theory-article.pdf

Hill, D. (2003). *Brief autobiography of a Bolshie Dismissed*. http://www.ieps.org.uk.cwc.net/bolsharticle.pdf

Hill, D. (2009). Culturalist and materialist explanations of class and 'race': Critical race theory, equivalence/parallelist theory, and Marxist theory. *Cultural Logic: An Electronic Journal of Marxist Theory & Practice, 12*, 1–52. https://ojs.library.ubc.ca/index.php/clogic/article/view/191552/188664

Hill, D. (2010). *A socialist manifesto for education*. Institute for Education Policy Studies. http://www.ieps.org.uk/media/1003/socialistmanifestofored.pdf

Hill, D. (2013). *Marxist essays on neoliberalism, class, 'race', capitalism, socialism and education*. The Institute for Education Policy Studies.

Hill, D. (2015). A socialist education policy. *Forum for Promoting 3-19 Comprehensive Education*. http://www.wwwords.co.uk/rss/abstract.asp?j=forum&aid=6224

Hill, D. (2019a). Marxist education and teacher education against capitalism in neoliberal/neoconservative/neofascist/times. *Cadernos do GPOSSHE On-line*, 2018 Estadual do Ceará Fortaleza, Brazil (Grupo de Pesquisa Ontologia do Ser Social, História, Educação e Emancipação Humana). https://revistas.uece.br/index.php/CadernosdoGPOSSHE/article/view/1524/1275?fbclid=IwAR349OKt6lL5HRD1SiJK-6Iv7EwlQLoJpbNlVQqrjvH-LW89JHT5fAeXdFA

Hill, D. (2019b). Marxism and teacher education. In M. Peters (Ed.), *Encyclopedia of teacher education* (pp. 1–6). Springer Singapore.

Hill, D. (2019c). Marxist public policy principles: Schooling and teacher education training. In P. Vittoria & D. Hill with I. Accioly (Eds.), *O Bella Ciao; Critical education as resistance against populism, sexism and racism*. Educazione Aperta. http://educazioneaperta.it/

Hill, D. (2021). *Excluding/including the ('raced' and gendered working class: Neoliberal, neoconservative/neofascist schooling and education in Covid times: A classical Marxist critical analysis and activist programme* [Excluyendo/ Incluyendo la Clases de Trabajo ('Raced' y de Genero): Escuela y Educacion Neoliberal/ Neoconservador/ NeoFascista en Tiempos Covidos: Un Programa de Activis y Analisis Critico Clasico Marxista]. Centro de Estudios Latinoamericanos de Educación Inclusiva (CELEI), Chile

Hill, D., Cole, M., & Williams. C. (1997). Equality and primary teacher education. In M. Cole, D. Hill, & S. Shan (Eds.), *Promoting equality in primary schools*. Cassell. http://www.ieps.org.uk/publications/online-papers-dave-hill/

Hill, D., Lewis, C., Maisuria, A., Yarker, P., & Hill, J. (2016) Conservative education policy reloaded: Policy, ideology and impacts in England. *Journal for Critical Education Policy Studies, 14*(3). http://www.jceps.com/wp-content/uploads/2016/12/14-3-1-1.pdf

Inner London Education Authority (ILEA). (1984). *Improving secondary schools—A summary of the Hargreaves report*. ILEA.

Jones, K. (1989). *Right turn: The conservative revolution in education*. Hutchinson Radius.

Jones, K. (2003). *Education in Britain, 1944 to the present*. Polity.

Kelsh, D., & Hill, D. (2006). The culturalization of class and the occluding of class consciousness: The knowledge industry in/of education. *Journal for Critical Education Policy Studies, 4*(1). http://www.jceps.com/?pageID=article&articleID=59

Lenin, V. I. (1902/1999). *What is to be done? Burning questions of our movement.* https://www.marxists.org/archive/lenin/works/1901/witbd/

Luxemburg, R. (1899/1999). *Reform or revolution: Party, vanguard, programme and organisation*. https://www.marxists.org/archive/luxemburg/1900/reform-revolution/

Marx, K. (1847/1999). *The poverty of philosophy*. https://www.marxists.org/archive/marx/works/1847/poverty-philosophy/

Marx, K. (1852/1999). *The eighteenth Brumaire of Louis Bonaparte*. https://www.marxists.org/archive/marx/works/1852/18th-brumaire/

Marx, K., & Engels, F. (1848/2010). *The Communist Manifesto*. Marxist Internet Archive. https://www.marxists.org/archive/marx/works/download/pdf/Manifesto.pdf

McGrew, K. (2011). On being holier-than-thou: A critique of Curry Malott's "Pseudo-Marxism and the reformist retreat from revolution". *Journal for Critical Education Policy Studies, 9*(1). http://www.jceps.com/index.php?pageID=article&articleID=222

McLaren, P. (2000). *Che Guevara, Paulo Freire and the pedagogy of revolution*. Rowman & Littlefield.

McLaren, P. (2010). Revolutionary critical pedagogy. *Interactions: UCLA Journal of Education and Information Studies, 6*(2). http://escholarship.org/uc/item/7qj2b570

McLaren, P. (2013). Critical pedagogy against capitalist education—A socialist alternative. *Global Education Magazine*. http://www.globaleducationmagazine.com/critical-pedagogy-againstcapitalist-schooling-socialist-alternative-interview-peter-mclaren/

McLaren, P. (2016). Revolutionary critical pedagogy: Staking a claim against the macrostructural unconscious. *Critical Education, 7*(8), 1–43. https://ices.library.ubc.ca/index.php/criticaled/article/view/186144

Reay, D. (2018). *Miseducation: Inequality, education and the working classes*. The Policy Press.

Rikowski, G. (2006). In Retro Glide. *Journal for Critical Education Policy Studies, 4*(2). http://www.jceps.com/?pageID=article&articleID=81

Rikowski, G. (2019, July). Education crises as crises for capital. *Theory in Action, 12*(3), 128–172. https://rikowski.wordpress.com/2019/08/25/education-crises-as-crises-for-capital-2/

Simon, B. (1978). *The politics of education reform, 1920–1940*. Lawrence and Wishart.

Stańczyk, P. (2021). The critique of the critical critique of critical pedagogy: Freire, Suchodolski and the materialist pedagogy of emancipation. *Critical Education, 12*(4), 1–24. http://ojs.library.ubc.ca/index.php/criticaled/article/view/186502

Vygotsky, L. S. (1934). *Thinking and speech*. https://www.marxists.org/archive/vygotsky/works/words/Thinking-and-Speech.pdf

Woods, A. (2020, July 2). *Why is the Brazilian right afraid of Paulo Freire?* Open Democracy. https://www.opendemocracy.net/en/democraciaabierta/why-is-the-brazilian-right-afraid-of-paulo-freire/

CHAPTER 15

Critical Perspectives for Educational Leadership and Policy in Higher Education

Candace Brunette-Debassige and Melody Viczko

Speaking to the assumed neutrality and the dominance of whiteness in the neoliberal university, Handel Kashope Wright (2019) spoke of the experiences of Black scholars in the academy and noted Stuart Hall's call for critical engagement, stating, "the university is a critical institution or it is nothing". In his work entitled *Positioning Blackness, Necessarily, Awkwardly, in the Canadian Academy,* Wright acknowledges Hall's call for engagements beyond the university, but also argues for the importance of reorienting the work of faculty and administrators within the neoliberal academic communities toward *the political*, "hence to recognize that there is crucial work to be done in making institutions of higher learning more diverse and equitable, in imbricating academic and intellectual work, in doing what we might call academic activism" (para. 5). This is challenging work, when neoliberal policy agendas assume "common sense" logics that permeate the conditions of higher education (Brown, 2015). Wright's concern is for the necessity of including critical anti-racist theorizing into critiques of neoliberalism in the university, particularly in relation to what it means to be a Black scholar in the academy. In this chapter, we acknowledge and align with Wright's critiques, recognizing that the conditions for depoliticizing the university are driven by complex matrixes

C. Brunette-Debassige · M. Viczko (✉)
Western University, London, ON, Canada
e-mail: mviczko@uwo.ca

C. Brunette-Debassige
e-mail: cbrune2@uwo.ca

© The Author(s), under exclusive license to Springer Nature Switzerland AG 2022
A. A. Abdi and G. W. Misiaszek (eds.), *The Palgrave Handbook on Critical Theories of Education,* https://doi.org/10.1007/978-3-030-86343-2_15

of power rooted in global capitalism, colonialism and white supremacy, and hetero-patriarchy (Andreotti et al., 2015; Grande, 2015). We examine the call for the university as a critical institution to consider the politics by which faculty and administrators engage in the neoliberal institution of higher education, considering the opportunities for refusal and resistance. We begin from the stance that any engagement with the notion of a critical institution must emerge from acknowledging the dimensions of coloniality and its modernistic assumptions in contemporary higher education contexts, as Andreotti et al. (2015) detail as "universal reason and history, teleological, logocentric, dialectical and anthropocentric thinking, and objectification and commodification of nature and the Cartesian self" (p. 23). We discuss what it means to work as faculty and administrators that engage the institution as critical through the enactment of Indigenous refusal and the notion of resistance against common sense administrative logics. Drawing on decolonial and postcolonial theorizing, as well as critical feminist scholarship, we conceptualize the notions of Indigenous refusal and of resistance and draw on our own experiences as academics and scholars doing administrative and leadership work in higher education. In the conclusion, we discuss the contributions of criticality and the urgent need for faculty and administrators to acknowledge that while criticality can be messy and feel disruptive to hegemonic norms, criticality offers generative perspectives that can lead to transforming the education system in meaningful ways.

LOCATING OURSELVES WITHIN EDUCATIONAL INSTITUTIONS

We write this chapter as gendered and raced bodies who are committed to naming the locations of power in academic spaces of the white colonial eliteness of higher education halls. We have taken care in our work not to speak as one voice and so we name ourselves as we write to locate the voices with which we speak.

Waban Geesis nintishnikaas. My name is Candace Brunette-Debassige. I am a Mushkego-ininew iskwew originally from Peetabeck (Treaty 9). As an Indigenous woman, I recognize my complex "intersectional Indigeneity" (Clark, 2016), I am a cis-gender Indigenous woman with mixed Cree, French and Métis lineage who has benefited from a certain degree of "white passing" privilege. While I was born and raised in small town northern Ontario, my connection to my Cree identity, culture and community belonging has been dramatically shaped, regulated and governed by ongoing settler colonial systems of power steeped in white supremacy and hetero-patriarchy. Currently, I live and work in London Ontario Canada lands of the Anishnawbek, Haudenosaunee and Lenapewak people. I have been working in Indigenous education at the K-12 and post-secondary levels for nearly twenty years. For five years, I served as the Director of Indigenous student services at my university. After the release of the Truth and Reconciliation Commission of Canada in 2015, I was called to take on a Special Advisor to the Provost

Indigenous Initiatives role and later served as the Acting Vice Provost Indigenous Initiatives. Today, I am an Assistant Professor in the Faculty of Education with keen interests in critical Indigenous policy and leadership studies. As an Indigenous scholar and leader, I draw from my embodied experiences studying and struggling to change the Euro-Westernized academy from within and advance Indigenous educational sovereignty.

And I am Melody Viczko, a cis-gender non-Indigenous woman, a first-generation university graduate from a working-class family. I work and live in the traditional territories of the Anishanaabeg, Haudenosaunee and Lenapewak People in London, Ontario. I am not from this territory, having moved here for work from the territories of Treaty 6, traditional lands of the Cree, Dene, Nakota, Saulteaux and Ojibwe, and the homeland of the Métis Nation. My family's relationship to the land in Treaty 6 territories is bound in our farming history and I recognize the privilege from which I benefit by my family occupying space on these lands. My experiences as an educator, administrator, researcher and scholar are because of both my experiences of privilege and marginalization in education institutions. In my work as a scholar in the area of critical policy studies, I toil as a gendered white woman that reflects on my background as a first-generation scholar with a deep care for the effects of policy on women as they continue to labor for their place in higher education, as Jones and Maguire (2020) assert, "this is where our loyalties sit—this emotional investment in our work is both classed and gendered within academic women from working-class backgrounds" (p. 49).

UNVEILING THE UNIVERSITY ADMINISTRATION

In this chapter, we situate an urgency for Hall's valuing of criticality, and the assertion of a critical institution within which we call for all university actors, especially administrators complicit in maintaining the university system of power, to acknowledge and interrogate its deeper allegiances to global capitalism, colonialism, white supremacy, hetero-patriarchy and nationalism embedded within the neoliberal university. Andreotti et al. (2015) fetter the modern university's life support system to these deeper roots and common sense understandings modernity. Furthermore, they assert that, "efforts to name and disrupt the university's life support system often get dismissed [by administration] as violent, unproductive and uncivil" (p. 26). Leigh Patel (2015) exposes the relationship between settler colonialism and whiteness in higher education in the United States. In her essay on *Desiring Diversity and Backlash*, Patel (2015) reveals how white settler entitlement built on notions of white property becomes threatened and lashes out against Indigenous and Black bodies in diversity work in the United States. At its core, she argues, "education is and represents property, and more specifically in the US, white property" (p. 658). Patel draws on settler colonial and critical race theories to show how the academy's underlying logic "trains people to see each other, the land and knowledge as property, to be in constant insatiable competition for limited resources" (p. 72). In Canada, settler colonialism operates similarly as an ongoing structure (Wolfe, 2006) and in education as a metaphorizing process (Tuck & Yang, 2012) inextricably tied to the extraction and ownership of Indigenous lands, resources and knowledges. These logics have been imposed on Indigenous People through settler colonial nation state laws and policies reinforced through educational aims that serve to appropriate Indigenous lands and knowledges and erase and eliminate Indigenous People voices in society through education. In this paper, we assert universities as Westernized institutions of knowledge production and dissemination that have long served to advance global imperial colonial networks of European domination, acting as key sites of authority (Grosfoguel, 2016) that uphold the stranglehold of white colonial patriarchal and capitalist interests and systems of power (Grande, 2015; Malott, 2010). Furthermore, relationships among the various stakeholder groups in higher education have been formed and forged through these global imperial colonial networks of Euro-Western domination, creating categorizations and hierarchies that stifle meaningful engagements beyond economic and Euro-centric knowledge production. Higher education around the world has long been used as a tool for maintaining dominant systems of power and excluding marginalized groups and voices. For Indigenous People in Canada, education has acted as a primary tool of assimilation and cultural genocide (TRC, 2015) used to rationalize settler colonial aims and control Indigenous People and lands. We argue therefore that it is dire to not only interrogate the underlying matrices of power that fuel the academy, but also to expose how settler colonial logics often shape common sense understandings of authority and control in administration and policy today.

Not only do universities play a central role in asserting an empire of knowledges entrenched in enduring settler colonial interests and ideologies, universities have entangled pasts connected to the dispossession of Indigenous land (Nash, 2019; Patel, 2015). In a known Canadian university context, institutions continue to be uniquely positioned under settler colonial jurisdiction-specific acts and charters tied to ongoing settler white property rights. Operating under a bicameral governance system, Canadian universities exercise rights to operate as both a public institution and corporation; its policies and administrative hierarchies further these interests by decoupling decision-making where academic decisions are forwarded to the Senate, and corporate fiscal decisions are despatched to the Board of Governors (BOG) (Jones et al., 2001). While academic freedom offers individual faculty members protection to teach, research and share ideas that may be controversial and even challenge authority, the academy continues to be less capable of protecting collective Indigenous rights under its white liberal academic norms. In both Senate and BOG governance contexts, Indigenous People and other marginalized voices continue to be chronically underrepresented under a veil of colonial discourses that espouse "democratic" and "collegial governance" ideals. These academic governance systems are difficult for Indigenous individuals and collectives to penetrate and continue to exclude these voices in academic decision-making processes, thereby reproducing dominant orders that subject different bodies.

Connecting Managerialist Logics to Neoliberal Ideologies in Higher Education

Within this academic administrative context, the clutch of power is often practiced through common sense approaches and underlying managerialist ideologies that can be tied to colonial discourses including "civilizing the profession; promoting hierarchies of knowledge; and sustaining interconnections between neoliberal educational policies and global colonialism" (Shahjahan, 2011, p. 182). As Indigenous and other equity and diversity work continues to be institutionalized, we have observed an impetus toward measuring new policies, noting the ways in which "managerialism reflects a particular formation of masculinity that is competitive, ritualistic, unreflexive and false" (Ozga & Walker, 1999, p. 107). Situated within rationalist notions of increasing measurability, quantifiability and predictability, measuring progress is often situated within evidence-based regimes rooted in colonial vestiges of educational policy, research and neoliberal reform (Shahjahan, 2011). Shahjahan (2014) articulates neoliberalism as the continual encroachment of material developments that privilege market principles, privatization and human capital development and logic developments that perpetuate inequitable materialities. In this way, neoliberalism is a form of colonial domination within higher education as it draws upon its institutional rights including ability to hold land property, accumulate associated resources and compete in growing global imperial markets.

Feminist scholar, Jill Blackmore (2020) also notes the progression of the higher education from "state welfarism (a caring state) to state-managed capitalism (individual responsibility for self-care)" (p. 1332), illustrating the effects of neoliberal policies on higher education to privilege the economy, "as if it is distinct from society and human rights" (p. 1332). Importantly she critiques the responses from university institutions to address racial, gender and ethnic disparities through policies that aim at equity because they miss the mark: their aim is to increase production in the capitalist institution, not to shape universities as socially inclusive. As she states, "equity becomes an institutional asset, a brand, rather than a matter of rights and an ethical practice of care" (p. 1332). The field of higher education is dominated by a concern for administrative processes in the midst of neoliberal reform and priorities. Olssen and Peters (2005) identify the radical cultural shift in higher education toward measurements and performance metrics, stating, "The ascendency of neoliberalism and the associated discourses of 'new public management', during the 1980s and 1990s has produced a fundamental shift [whereby]...the traditional professional culture of open intellectual enquiry and debate has been replaced with institutional stress on performativity" (p. 313). Admittedly, the concern on performances and its metrics makes sense when administrators are overburdened with new managerialism ideals that push higher education institutions toward priorities that stress corporate governance models as though they are self-managing institutions. Governance relations have changed under new managerialism, including league tables to rank research and teaching and creating audit culture technologies for measuring performance (Blackmore et al., 2010; Wright & Øberg, 2017). For example, in 2019, The Times Higher Education developed the Impact Rankings that assess universities against the United Nations' Sustainable Development Goals (SDG) in areas such as "peace, justice and strong institutions" (Times Higher Education, 2021). The focus on performance works to shift the governing relations within university institutions toward metrics-based practices aimed at making visible the efficiencies and accountabilities present in global knowledge economy driven institutions, all of which have been inequitable (Blackmore, 2010). As Blackmore et al. (2010) state, "Managerialism, marketisation, privatisation and diversification have changed universities' roles in relation to states, individuals, economies and communities" (p. 6).

Moreover, the continuation of colonial ideologies in educational policy and leadership, reinforce widely assumed paternalistic relationships between settler institutions and Indigenous People and other marginalized groups. Considering this complex ongoing reality, we assert an urgent need for critical and decolonial approaches to understand enact educational policy and leadership that can transform the system. This assertion is borne out of our experiences working and doing research in higher education and aligns with Samier's (2017) critiques of the field of educational administration that is premised on problematic assumptions that limit epistemological perspectives to those dominated by Western ideals of managerialism: "a progressivist view of educational development predicated upon Western models; the reassertion of good administration instead of leadership, which is derived from the neoliberal managerialism movement; assuming stable nation state conditions instead of the political realities of many countries undergoing significant transitions, destabilisations and disintegrations; and universalist assumptions about the configuration of social institutions that politically, culturally and legally reflect Western bias" (p. 269).

THE NATURE OF POWER RELATIONS IN ADMINISTRATIVE PRACTICE

The need for criticality connects to the fact that the university is an ongoing site of power relations that has been dominated by epistemic whiteness, patriarchal and colonial perspectives. While there are increasing pockets of support for marginalized and Indigenous groups in Canada, power dynamics continue to play out in ongoing structures of power. Moreover, there is a chronic lack of understanding of power relations, and a lack of appreciation even resistance of criticality in administrative theory and practice. In the field of organizational change and leadership studies, Colleen Capper (2019) identified a critical "epistemological unconsciousness" among scholars (and we argue leaders) who claim to be "equity" or "social justice" minded. In this research, Capper exposes a tendency toward maintaining structural functionalist and interpretivist epistemologies in organizational change and leadership research where hierarchal and individual leader-centric accounts prevail along with normative understandings on the nature of change and knowledge. As a result, social justice and equity leadership research often claim to be addressing the needs of marginalized groups, yet they continue to keep allegiance to maintaining the administrative structures "ontology of hierarchy" (Malott, 2010) and epistemic dominances that condition injustices in the first place.

Similar tendencies of self-proclaimed equity and diversity research work in education have been critiqued by Tuck and Yang (2018) who craft together the complexities of understanding, using and materializing the principle and commitments to social justice in education practice. As Tuck and Yang articulate, "how justice and injustice materializes, matters" (p. 6). Their review of the multiple meanings and realities of social justice as it is infused in education research is insightful in laying out the ways in which social justice thinking separates spaces for education projects that challenge dominant ways of being in education. and they note how they have done similar critiques of , Acknowledging eclectic contributions from fields such as social sciences and law, Tuck and Yang suggest that social justice is a space to mark distinctions between mainstreamed positivist and developmental approaches to thinking about education work and "other" ways, as "a way to signal to ourselves and to one another this epistemological and political difference" (p. 5). We call attention to how Tuck and Yang frame how the notion of social justice can be considered in education work:

> Social justice education— whether or not we continue to use those words to define it— is the crux of the future of our field. Social justice is not the other of the field of education, it is the field. There is no future of the field of education without the contributions of people who are doing their work under the rising sign of social justice. There is no legitimacy to the field of education if it cannot meaningfully attend to social contexts, historical and contemporary structures of settler colonialism, white supremacy, and antiblackness. Social justice is not the catchall; it is the all. (Tuck & Yang, 2018, p. 5)

The notion that social justice *is the field* in education may then be extrapolated to leadership in higher education spaces. Feminist and Indigenous scholars in educational leadership have argued that leadership is about social justice (Blackmore, 2021; Blackmore & Sachs, 2007; Ottmann, 2009; Shields, 2012; Shultz & Viczko, 2016). Yet leadership in higher education has come to be structured around the neoliberal decisions of "building a corporate university that is able to respond to market principles, economic ideology driven policies and practices, alliance with the big business and industry" (Shultz & Viczko,

2016, p. 1). Theories of social justice that examine the distribution of benefits and burdens in society can inform leadership practice in a way that focuses decision-making on "social justice as the field" in education. Postcolonial, decolonial, and anti-oppression theorists lead the way to explore "how justice must also overcome and reconcile the historical, social and material legacies of colonial practices based on imperialism, patriarchy and racism that continue to exert organizing strength" (p. 2) in higher education institutions. Davies (2005) suggests we may "rethink our vision of life and reconsider 'the terms of our existence'" (p. 13) in higher education institutions, in order to shift away from techno-rational points of view, arguing that "existential questions" offer the boundaries in which to reconstruct our subjectivity.

Admittedly, the concerns with neoliberal pressures make sense when administrators are overburdened with new managerialism ideals that push higher education institutions toward priorities that stress corporate governance models as though they are self-managing institutions separating social justice from larger systems of power and internal micropolitics (Ryan & Armstrong, 2016). However, the calls among scholars for criticality in university policy and administrative practice continue to be echoed even though they are often refuted by administrators based on their assumption that criticality is at best "lofty idealistic" "impractical" or at worst "uncollegial" and "divisive" thereby reducing these voices to simply a play of "identity politics" (e.g., subtext of this discursive move is to blame the individual versus making the system and its actors accountable to change). In the neoliberal market-driven conditions in which economic and political decision-making are pursed from "social costs" of higher education (p. 3), Giroux (2013) argues the university exists in conditions of depoliticization, "removing social relations from configurations of power" (p. 3), whereby emotional and personal vocabularies are substituted for political ones (Brown, 2006). In the context of the depoliticization that occurs, Giroux argues that resistance to capitalist ideals becomes near impossible, rendering students in university institutions bereft of the conditions for a social imagination that can "translate private troubles into public concerns" (p. 3). Higher education has a long history of oppression "in terms of race, gender, class, sexuality, religion and ability" (Shahjahan, 2014, p. 227). Under these conditions, some scholars call for a university that enacts itself as critical institution or it risks dying altogether (Giroux, 2013), while others, from different decolonial perspectives, note the necessary dismantling of systems of power resulting from historical foundations of colonialism, whiteness and patriarchy that continue on in higher education today (Andreotti et al., 2015; Gaudry & Lorenz, 2018; Grande, 2018a, ; Stein, 2019; Tuck & Yang, 2012). Regardless of the various debates in the degree of reform and dismantling, scholars continue to stress the need and value for questioning normalized hegemonies embedded in institutional structures and practices and resisting them in order to transform the university to be more inclusive of Indigenous and marginalized people and knowledges. Sharon Stein (2019) challenges universities to interrogate how colonial relations shape underlying theories of change. She marks three levels of change at play in higher education: minor, major and beyond reform, and advocates for engaging strategically across different theories of change and increasing stamina to hold tensions for divergent perspectives. Nonetheless, in an academic setting that naturalizes administrative "ontology of hierarchy" (Malott, 2010) and authority, critical questioning is all too often received as threats to positional power. Nonetheless, critical scholars have argued for perspectives that challenge normative tendencies in higher education policy and administration and lean into the messiness and epistemological questioning of these underlying administrative logics.

Refusal and resistance are themes that have been taken up in academic scholarship aimed at examining the ways in which faculty and administrators may counter the hegemonic practices of managerialism that perpetuate conditions of colonial institutions of higher education. The perspectives are varied and diffuse. Refusal and resistance have been taken up in higher education scholarship to interrogate the politics of the neoliberal and neocolonial university through multi-modal research (Brown & Strega, 2005; Metcalfe, 2018). Literature has also documented how Indigenous resistance emerges in relation to Western colonial research practices (Bubar & Martinez, 2017; Grande, 2018a, b; Johnston, et al., 2018; Simpson, 2014), in research related to capitalist ideals (Giroux, 2013); in student movements against neoliberal reform that make way for the privatization and corporatization of universities (Amsler, 2011); and in the areas of teaching (and learning) (Gibbs & Lehtonen, 2020).

In her work about the resistance of equity workers who lead diversity policy work in higher education institutions in the United Kingdom, Sara Ahmed (2018) speaks about how racialized members of equity and diversity committees in higher education are seen as "disagreeable" in their difficult work of having to speak about, point to, and name the transgressions carried out in the name of "doing diversity work". Those who are tasked with making complaints and are then deemed problems in institutions for their work. In these conditions, Ahmed illustrates, "the word race might be used because it does more. The word race carries a complaint; race as refusal of the smile of diversity....a complaint seem to amplify what makes you not fit". Sandy Grande (2018a, b) and Eve Tuck (2018) call for "refusing the university" as an Indigenous praxis necessary to advance Indigenous futurity in research releasing Indigenous People from the shackles of colonial and patriarchal strangleholds. In another article, Brent Debassige and Candace Brunette-Debassige (2018) position Indigenizing leadership in universities as "willful" work (Ahmed, 2014)—the will, they draw from Ahmed to argue "has been historically used to define a problem and has acted as a pedagogic tool to characterize someone as not conforming to the dominant European hetero-patriarchal system" (p. 123). They further assert that as Indigenous administrators drawing on Indigenous ways of knowing and being in their leadership, they have observed how Indigenous People often get automatically positioned as a problem because they are received by the administration, when they object to normative rules, as a threat to the settler colonial status quo.

McGranahan (2016) argues that refusal is not the same as resistance, though they are genealogically linked, referring to Lila Abu-Lughod's (1990) foundational piece in which she theorized "the nature and forms of domination" (McGranahan, 2016, p. 320) involved in refusals. The idea of refusal allows for a complexity that includes political action aimed at structures and systems, including decolonization and self-determination, both at and beyond the level of the state. Also, as McGranahan notes, Sherry Ortner (1995) speaks about the ways in which refusals are enacted on those who resist, as in a "bizarre refusal" to academic research that reveals resistance to political dominance. Those who aim at or speak to resistance to power become silenced in the refusal to acknowledge research that aims at understanding embedded ways of knowing.

Shahjahan (2011, 2014) theorizes resistance as an analytical form in tackling and changing systemic oppression in higher education institutions. Shahjahan (2014) argues that discourses of resistance permeate educational spaces yet remain under-theorized in higher education as they are often taken up as descriptive rather than analytical tools. He proposes, resistance to neoliberal conditions possible in higher education by drawing on David Jeffress' (2008) book *Postcolonial resistance: Culture, liberation and transformation* to examine four modes of resistance: (1) resistance as rewriting and undermining colonial narratives; (2) resistance as subversion; (3) resistance as opposition; and (4) resistance as transformation. Shahjahan acknowledges limitations of how resistance has been conceived and suggests the fourth mode of transformational resistance remains marginal, yet necessary, in how scholars working within neoliberal higher education have taken up critiques. He argues that transformational resistance may lead to "new ways of being, knowing and doing within increasingly neoliberalized HE contexts" (p. 230) that focus on the rights and responsibilities academic faculty and administration possess to make shifts in neoliberal institutional cultures of performativity. The notion of resistance offered by Shahjahan is not wholly new, but the linking of resistance to decolonial aims may center epistemological challenges to the academy, as a way of resisting the colonization of our imagination and thinking in higher education systems (Abdi, 2016). As McNish and Spooner (2018) note, universities have not fully given up their potential to disrupt hierarchy and inequity, whereby alternate ways of knowing and being exist.

While addressing different institutional realities and conditions, each of these scholars shares an appeal against an assumed rationality in academic administration and decision-making underpinned by a concern for the complex hegemonies prevalent in the structural and cultural aspects of academic institutions. Scholars call for an embracing of a criticality in administrative policy and leadership theory and practice. We turn next to sites of possibility we see in our own professional experiences as scholar, researcher and administrator.

Indigenous Refusal

In my (Candace's) doctoral research focusing on Indigenous women administrators' experiences enacting Indigenous policies in Canadian universities (Brunette-Debassige, 2021), Indigenous women leaders interviewed underscored their need to enact a criticality through "Indigenous refusals" (Grande, 2018a, b; Simpson, 2014; Tuck & Yang, 2014b). Indigenous refusals therefore emerged as a necessary leadership and policy enactment disposition that helped Indigenous People collectively advance Indigenous educational sovereignty and move institutions toward deeper levels of Indigenization (Gaudry & Lorenz, 2018). Tuck and Yang (2014b) describe Indigenous refusal as

> the stance that pushes us to limit settler territorialization of Indigenous/Native community knowledge, and expand the space for other forms of knowledge, thought-worlds to live. Refusal makes space for recognition, and for reciprocity. Refusal turns the gaze back upon power, specifically colonial modalities of knowing persons as bodies to be differentially counted, violated, saved and put to work. (p. 817)

In this study, Indigenous women administrators talked about the need to enact Indigenous refusal in similar ways such as asserting limits in their work, interrupting settler colonial status quo in practice and pushing back against hegemonic norms embedded in the administrative academy. The need to enact Indigenous refusals emerged in relation to settler colonial power relations. Participants recounted refusing the administrative academy in numerous ways including: refusing to ascribe to reconciliation discourses that tended toward performing Indigenization and "institutional speech acts" (Ahmed, 2006); refusing tokenistic approaches to Indigenous community engagement; and refusing cooptation of Indigenous projects by refusing what Graham Smith (2003) describes as "politics of distraction" where settler colonial needs attempt to invade Indigenous administrators' time, focus and attention.

One participant in the study explained the ongoing critical self-reflexivity required to enact Indigenous refusals in this way: "So you have to pick your battles: Okay I'll let that one go, this one, I'm going to stand. You have to be conscious all the time" (Pimahamowi Pisim).

Another participant described the critical assessment involved before enacting Indigenous refusals as a careful weighing out of risks and benefits, an ethical process of asking herself, "is it a hill worth dying on?" (Athiki Pisim). Opawahcikianasis another participant in this doctoral work explained her assessment process as weighing out "on a scale of 1 to 10; how significant is this particular issue?" Asking herself "should I say something or hold my peace".

While Indigenous women's stories of enacting Indigenous refusals in the administrative academy show some discretion, they often underscored deeper Indigenous ethical accountabilities to the Indigenous collective and land in their decision-making processes. This finding points to underlying aims of enacting Indigenous refusal and their connections to Indigenous ethics.

At the same time, many Indigenous women involved in this study recounted the dangers of enacting Indigenous refusals in the academy, underscoring the ongoing systems of settler colonial, hetero-patriarchal and capitalistic power within which they operated. Therefore, despite an influx of Indigenous senior leadership positions emerging in Canadian universities since the release of the TRC (Smith, 2019), this research highlighted how Indigenous women administrators continued to struggle operating within a normative Euro-Western administrative context. From this "contentious ground" (Ottmann, 2013), Indigenous women administrators highlighted how they were sometimes problematized and casted in gendered and colonial ways for enacting Indigenous refusals. As a result, several participants talked explicitly with me about their concerns of being labeled "difficult", "resistant", "militant", and "activist" in their leadership. Activism in leadership was deemed a dirty word. For example, one participant described being problematized by a colleague at her university:

> I have a colleague. She slips and—I don't know if she thought I realized, but she made a comment like, 'You know you're so great to work with.' She was praising me, only to come to the fact that – 'I don't understand when some people say you're so difficult to work with.' And I was like, interesting. (Niski Pisim)

Another participant admitted that she tried to dispel troubling colonial stereotypes often imposed on Indigenous administrators by actively creating collaborative relationships: "I try to create trust with certain people who automatically assume that I'm going to be the big militant" (Thithikopiwi Pisim). And yet another participant admitted she had become so concerned about being labeled an activist at her university that she literally changed the way she dressed to avoid negative associations and messages. The unseen dimension of participants' worrying about what to wear and how they might be misperceived in racial and colonial ways, I argue contributes to an emotional labor—the management of one's feelings and expressions as requirement of administration work.

In this research, I argue that the common sense academic administrative norms operationalize through an epistemic dominance based in structural functionalist and interpretivist approaches to organizational change and leadership. These dominant epistemologies hinge on including Indigenous administrators through "conditional inclusion" (Stein, 2019) that preserve the university's hierarchal and authority system, not necessarily work toward "decolonial Indigenization" (Gaudry & Lorenz, 2018) which aim to reposition Indigenous communities and Indigenous nations in decision-making positions of power.

While Indigenous women administrators described struggling to work in academic administrative settings, some participants practiced Indigenous refusals in more nuanced and subtle ways as a strategic diplomatic intervention and survival mechanism. In this sense, participants enacted Indigenous refusals in multiple ways—explicitly, discretely and strategically working with the collective—demonstrating that Indigenous refusals were taken up in complex and nuanced ways in leadership practices. Indeed, participants shared common stories of struggle, resistance and strategic astuteness in the face of ongoing settler colonial power.

Interestingly, some participants in this doctoral study pointed to the protection they felt that academic freedom offered some administrators when refusing. The knowing that administrators could return to their academic appointments should they be removed from administration, allowed some participants to speak more freely and challenge hegemonic colonial norms.

Furthermore, several participants commonly described a need to engage in ongoing critical self-reflexivity around their practice of Indigenous refusals. They described a need to examine and evaluate, on an ongoing, case-by-case basis, the needs and implications of enacting Indigenous refusals. They also identified a need to reflect on their own complex intersectional positionalities and relational dynamics, and to examine ethical implications of their leadership practices and decision-making in relation to decolonial aims, and attempt to elevate Indigenous voices and agency in education. Their insights, I assert, offer critical direction for decolonial approaches in educational leadership theory and practice as well as leadership training in the context of Indigenization movements in future.

From this study, I assert that Indigenous refusals are directly related to settler colonial power dynamics in the academy; they are a (re)action to unequal power relations or dominant hegemonic norms that have gone unquestioned, which are situated within ongoing settler colonial academic contexts. At the same time, Indigenous refusals were generative as they often interrupted settler common sense (Simpson, 2014; Tuck & Yang, 2018) and shifted projects and practices toward advancing Indigenous educational sovereignty. Indigenous refusals are therefore, not simply resistance for resistance sake. Indigenous refusals have purpose, their aim is to assert Indigenous collective autonomy in decision-making and make space for Indigenous ways of knowing and being in dominant whitestream educational settings. While Indigenous women administrators shared many stories of enacting Indigenous refusals, they also highlighted consequences they endured in terms of being casted in negative ways for daring to do so.

TEACHING POLICY AS RESISTANCE

In my (Melody) teaching in critical policy studies in education/higher education, I aim at including opportunities to interrogate relevant and contemporary pressing policies that influence governance in public (education) institutions. In an article examining the effects of neoliberal government policies and discourses on the spaces for intellectual engagements in higher education, over 15 years ago, Davies (2005) wrote about how neoliberal agendas co-opt the desires and values of faculty, administrators and students. (Note: I am indebted to Shahjahan [2014] for introducing me to Davies' text and am excited for the questions she asks that can frame critical policy studies courses.) Davies beckons for an intellectual engagement to awaken our constitution even as we are neoliberal subjects, asking, "What is it we long for, then, in universities? And what part does neoliberalism play in shaping our longing, or in counteracting it, even obliterating it? What kind of social fabric is it that neoliberalism envisages?" (p. 3). Reflecting on Davies' queries and more recent literature that locates our work as "neoliberal academics" (Ball, 2016, p. 258), I am arguing here for a response within our teaching in the neoliberal university to consider how we may engage in processes that ask how we can decolonize our own institutional practices. By decolonize, I mean to become aware of the totalizing force of our own institutional policies as they shape what we come to think and know about ourselves as we live in university institutions. We have much to learn from writers such as Ngugi wa Thiong'o (2007) who remind us that language matters in coming to shape which knowledges are valued and legitimized, including our own existence. Here I argue that we can learn from decolonizing scholars to consider how to decolonize policy discourses within our own institutions and to seek opportunities in teaching within higher education policy courses to rethink the oppressive policies that constitute our neoliberal subjectivity as students and scholars. As Davies (2005) suggests, "It is not a choice between compliance and resistance, between colonizing and being colonized, between taking up the master narratives and resisting them. It is in our own existence, the terms of our existence, that we need to begin the work, together, of decomposing those elements of our world that make us, and our students, vulnerable to the latest discourse and that inhibit conscience and limit consciousness" (Davies, 2005, p. 13).

In both researching and working in higher education, there is opportunity to examine powerful policy discourses shaping our institutional work, both as we constitute them and are subjected to them. In the Canadian province of Ontario, the Conservative-party government (2019) announced its plans to be a "national leader" by tying 60% of provincial funding for post-secondary institutions to their performance by the 2024–2025 academic year. Performance-based funding (PBF) is an approach to transfers of public funding from government to university institutions that is based on a system of metrics by which university institutional output is measured in order to calculate the work that is being produced and how funding will be provided from government to support this work. In Ontario, the move to PBF was noted in the provincial government's 2019 budget, in which the Strategic Mandate Agreements, set up as bi-lateral agreements between the provincial government and universities and colleges, established performance indicators that include measures tied to funding. These include graduate employment earning, experiential learning, skills and competencies, graduate employment rates, graduation rates, research funding and output, funding from the private sectors, as well as locally determined metrics as identified by each institution.

As a reform steeped in the new managerialism principles of efficiencies and productivity tied to the labor market, shifts towards PBF as a means of rationing public funds to public education institutions demonstrate a modern manifestation of neoliberal ideals in higher education. The connections to neoliberal rationalities have been well engaged. PBF faces sharp critiques from countries where such policies have had detrimental effects on the teaching, research and service mandates. Spooner (2020) expertly crafts critique of PBF in the Canadian context, drawing attention to surveys conducted with UK academic and international researchers that show how PBF initiatives have diminished policy efforts at institutions to address issues of equity and diversity. The focus in PBF on student graduation and employment rates, along with experiential learning and skills, is located in the global shift of policy agendas towards building twenty-first-century skills, as supported by the global institutions such as the OECD and UNESCO. Yet, these globalized discourses may take on totalizing, dominating effects in constituting the lifeworld (Amsler, 2008) of those of us who work and learn in higher education institutions. The focus on skill and competency development that can be measured to support PBF initiatives needs to be named as neoliberal agenda that homogenize and reduce knowledges into measurable categories, as experiences in higher education institutions are deeply intertwined with student subjectivity and privilege (Viczko et al., 2019).

Yet, as a critical policy studies scholar, my work entails critique of reforms in higher education with concern for understanding how such reforms change governing within institutions. In a review of the encroachment of neoliberal policies in English universities and the struggles of faculty and staff to resist such advancement, Amsler (2008) queried how students and academics have become "so ill-equipped" to respond to impending neoliberal policies while others have been able to "undertake bold experiments in political resistance" (p. 67). Amsler suggests a multitude of narratives provide insights about how neoliberal logics displace critical perspectives, as a "colonization of the cultural lifeworld by systems of industry, finance, and governance; or an enclosure by corporate power" (p. 67). In teaching about critical policy studies, we might ask how different policies support others in their enactment, but also the tensions that emerge as they co-exist within institutional practices. How do governing practices shift away from institutional commitments to justice in institutional practices when authoritarian policies are mandated? Archer (2007) speaks of the tensions in the discourses of diversity, such as "choice", "social mobility" and "student diversity" as they are appropriated by neoliberal ideals. Such discourses can be brought for interrogation into policy studies classes to examine how these policies rub up against pervasive institutional commitments for Indigenization and decolonization on campuses? Also, how do PBF policies perpetuate the colonial hierarchies of dominant and subjugated knowledges, as choice and social mobility are tied to limited means of measuring student skills and employment as they are attached only to the needs of the labor market/knowledge economy?

What does it mean for an institution to think and act critically in an era of PBF reforms? Resistance requires acknowledging the process as a form of oppression that reinforces imperial logics of hierarchies of knowledge systems. We need resistances to cease the assault of neoliberal policies that determine us all to be only "homo economicus" (Brown, 2015) but while that occurs (and takes time to do), as we build the capacities for resistance within against the oppression of PBF, we may begin to consider how we interrogate the data that forms the premise of measuring performance. PBF is a clear manifestation of the colonial state's reach into HE, as a means of ownership of what knowledges count enough to be measured. As a matter of sovereignty, who owns the data about us that determines our successes and contributions? Whose performance counts in our institutions and who owns the knowledge upon which that success is measured? D'Ignazio and Klein (2020) argue for forms of data feminism that begin by interrogating how power operates in the world through data we collect, asking who stands to be most impacted by the data? Furthermore, important questions are raised about Indigenous data sovereignty in higher education, including data ownership, usage and storage (Carroll et al., 2020; Wilks et al., 2018), especially considering a resistance to data that erases Indigenous outcomes associated with Indigenous ways of knowing. What if metrics we collect through PBF became powerful spaces for resistance, in thinking about: what do we do with the data? How do we respond to metrics? In what ways can we consider that we can resist the determinist ways in which such neoliberal measures oppress our ways of being and learning, colonizing the very visions we have ourselves as students, faculty and researchers? How are those most implicated in the data delivered justice through our engagements with it?

Shahjahan's (2014) position that transformational resistance is necessary to lead to "new ways of being, knowing and doing within increasingly neoliberalized HE contexts" (p. 230) requires that academic faculty and administration resist neoliberal institutional cultures of performativity, including the narrow metrics in tenure and promotion, and publication in so called "top-tier" journals, supervising students within narrow terms of what time is needed to complete a degree, etc. But transformational resistance may also take the form of our own teaching as critical policy and leadership scholars, to provide spaces for students to query what happens in our own institutions, how we are continually perpetual neoliberal subjects for measurement and performativity. Resistance is not easy, but Grande reminds us that for Marcuse, "refusal should not be confused with 'passive withdrawal or retreat' but rather understood as an active instantiation of a 'radically different mode-of-being and mode-of-doing'" (p. 58). The naming and locating of the logics of the colonial institution can take various forms, including resistance in our classrooms to transform our relationship to our institutions.

Conclusion

Considering the university's complex lineage and ongoing structures, we argue that the university is not innately critical, in fact if unchecked we assert that the institution will succumb to its hegemonic white colonial nature. Moreover, the notion of a critical university relies on the courageous commitments of social actors to engage in critical thinking and praxis and thereby be willing to ask difficult questions and even at times, enact Indigenous refusal and of resistance in their work. Drawing on Maori scholars Linda T. Smith and Graham H. Smith (2018), we understand criticality through the "need to have a good understanding of the historical, social, cultural, economic, and political relations of inequality, privilege and colonialism and an understanding of how these relations get produced and reproduced" (p. 22) and moreover to have the courage to exercise our limited power through praxis that aims to question and interrupt dominant systems of power. We further position the utility of Indigenous refusal and resistance as agentic dispositions helping preserve and (re)shape an ongoing critical institution—preserving the university's role as both critic and ethical and political conscience of society. While we recognize that common sense administrative tendencies tend toward masking politics through so-called neutrality and apolitical positions, we acknowledge higher education as an ongoing field of practice forever shaped by political actors.

Furthermore, Smith and Smith (2018) also call for the need to continually return to evaluating transformative decolonial work, that inherently involves commitments to self-reflecting. Sandy Grande (2015) similarly stresses the vital importance of continuing to be critical in leadership when she identifies three repeating and overlapping steps necessary in educational leadership: (1) being aware of existing power dynamics; (2) working to make these power dynamics transparent; and (3) making an honest attempt to negotiate power dynamics and structures of power. Grande offers important considerations for Indigenous People who take a critical approach to leadership, that they are not necessarily simply assimilating within the colonial institutions of the academy, but their actions as leaders offer moments of negotiating power, and survival in the educational system. Much work has yet to be done in the praxis of non-Indigenous leaders who seek to decolonize the university system, as well, to learn from scholars who theorize decolonial engagement in HE and from Indigenous scholars and leaders. In writing together, we have pointed to divergence and alignment as we consider the moments of both possibility and incoherence for allyship and commitments to criticality, as we forge spaces for solidarities and co-resistance. The politics of Indigenous refusals and resistance are tenuous and require a commitment toward shared understandings of what it means to work and learn, indeed to be, in a critical university institution. Grande's (2018a,b) call for *justice as refusal* is one that we should not miss, in our work as scholars and administrators, considering the possibilities such resistance may open.

REFERENCES

Abdi, A. A. (2016). The location of the public intellectual: Historical and contemporary analyses. In L. Shultz & M. Viczko (Eds.), *Assembling and governing the higher education institution: Democracy, social justice and leadership in global higher education* (pp. 113–130). Palgrave Macmillan.

Abu-Lughod, L. (1990). The romance of resistance: Tracing transformations of power through Bedouin women. *American Ethnologist, 17*(1), 41–55. http://www.jstor.org/stable/645251

Ahmed, S. (2006). The nonperformativity of antiracism. *Meridians, 7*(1), 104–126. https://www.jstor.org/stable/40338719

Ahmed, S. (2014). *Willful subjects*. Durham & London, UK: Duke University Press.

Ahmed, S. (2018, June 23). *No! refusal, resignation and complaint*. Lecture presented by Sara Ahmed at Colonial Repercussions conference, Berlin. https://feministkilljoys.com/2018/06/28/refusal-resignation-and-complaint/

Amsler, S. (2008). Pedagogy against "dis-utopia": From conscientization to the education of desire. In H. F. Dahms (Ed.) *No social science without critical theory (Current perspectives in social theory, Volume 25)* (pp. 291–325). London, UK: Emerald Group. Retrieved from http://eprints.lincoln.ac.uk/5679/1/Pedagogy_against_disutopia_Amsler_Nov_2007.pdf

Amsler, S. (2011). Beyond all reason: Spaces of hope in the struggle for England's universities. *Representations, 116*(1), 62–87. https://www.jstor.org/stable/10.1525/rep.2011.116.1.62

Andreotti, V., Stein, S., Ahenakew, C., & Hunt, D. (2015). Mapping interpretations of decolonization in the context of higher education. *Decolonization: Indigeneity, Education & Society, 4*(1), 21–40. https://decolonialfuturesnet.files.wordpress.com/2018/02/mapping-decolonization-he.pdf

Archer, L. (2007). Diversity, equality and higher education: A critical reflection on the ab/uses of equity discourse within widening participation. *Teaching in Higher Education, 12*(5–6), 635–653. https://doi.org/10.1080/13562510701595325

Ball, S. J. (2015). Living the neoliberal university. *European Journal of Education, 50*(3), 258–261.

Ball, S. J. (2016). Subjectivity as a site of struggle: Refusing neoliberalism? *British Journal of Sociology of Education, 37*(8), 1129–1146.

Blackmore, J., & Sachs, J. (2007). Managing the self: The consuming passions of performing and reforming leadership. In *Performing and reforming leaders: Gender, educational restructuring, and organizational change* (pp. 149–171). Albany, NY: SUNY Press.

Blackmore, J. (2010). Research assessment: A calculative technology governing quality, accountability and equity. In J. Blackmore, M. Brennan, & L. Zipin (Eds.), *Re-positioning university governance and academic work* (pp. 67–83). https://doi-org.proxy1.lib.uwo.ca/10.1163/9789460911743_006

Blackmore, J. (2020). The carelessness of entrepreneurial universities in a world risk society: A feminist reflection on the impact of Covid-19 in Australia. *Higher Education Research & Development, 39*(7), 1332–1336. https://doi.org/10.1080/07294360.2020.1825348

Blackmore, J. (2021). Governing knowledge in the entrepreneurial university: A feminist account of structural, cultural and political epistemic injustice. *Critical Studies in Education*, 1–17. https://doi.org/10.1080/17508487.2020.1858912

Blackmore, J., Brennan, M., & Zipin, L. (2010). Repositioning university governance and academic work: An overview. In J. Blackmore, M. Brennan & L. Zipin (Eds.), *Re-positioning university governance and academic work* (pp. 1–16). https://doi-org.proxy1.lib.uwo.ca/10.1163/9789460911743_002

Brown, W. (2006). *Regulating aversion: Tolerance in the age of identity and empire*. Princeton University Press.

Brown, W. (2015). *Undoing the demos: Neoliberalism's stealth revolution*. Zone.

Brunette-Debassige, C. (2021). *Trickiness of settler colonialism: Indigenous women administrators' experiences enacting Indigenous policies in Canadian universities*. PhD unpublished dissertation.

Bubar, R., & Martinez, D. E. (2017). Trickster as resistance: Impacts of neoliberalism on Indigenous research and Indigenous methodologies. In *Qualitative inquiry in neoliberal times* (1st ed., Vol. 1, pp. 136–150). Routledge. https://doi.org/10.4324/9781315397788-10

Capper, C. (2019). *Organizational theory for equity and diversity: Leading integrated, socially just education*. Routledge.

Carroll, S., et al. (2020). The CARE principles for Indigenous data governance. *Data Science Journal, 19*(43), 1–12. https://doi.org/10.5334/dsj-2020-043

Clark, N. (2016). Red intersectionality and violence-informed witnessing praxis with Indigenous girls. *Girlhood Studies, 9*(2), 46–64. https://doi.org/10.3167/ghs.2016.090205

Davies, B. (2005). The (im)possibility of intellectual work in neoliberal regimes. *Discourse: Studies in the Cultural Politics of Education, 26*(1), 1–14. https://doi.org/10.1080/01596300500039310

Debassige, A., & Brunette-Debassige, C. (2018). Indigenizing work as "willful work": Toward Indigenous transgressive leadership in Canadian universities. *Cultural and Pedagogical Inquiry, 10*(2), 119–138. https://journals.library.ualberta.ca/cpi/index.php/cpi/article/view/29449/21460

D'Ignazio, C., & Klein, L. F. (2020). *Data feminism*. Cambridge, MA: MIT Press.

Gaudry, A., & Lorenz, D. (2018). Indigenization as inclusion, reconciliation, and decolonization: Navigating the different visions for indigenizing the Canadian Academy. *AlterNative: An International Journal of Indigenous Peoples, 14*(3), 218–227.

Gibbs, J., & Lehtonen, A. (2020). *Teaching to resistance and refusal: Feminist pedagogical engagements in the UK higher education classroom*. https://maifeminism.com/teaching-to-resistance-and-refusal-feminist-pedagogical-engagements-in-the-uk-higher-education-classroom

Giroux, H. (2013). *Public intellectuals against the neoliberal university*. https://truthout.org/articles/public-intellectuals-against-the-neoliberal-university

Grande, S. (2015). *Red pedagogy: Native American social and political thought*. New York, NY: Rowman & Littlefield.

Grande, S. (2018a). Refusing the settler society of the spectacle. In E. A. McKinley & L. T. Smith (Eds.), *Handbook of Indigenous education* (pp. 1–27). SpringerLink.

Grande, S. (2018b). Refusing the university. In E. Tuck & K. W. Yang (Eds.), *Toward what justice? Describing diverse dreams of justice in education* (pp. 47–65). Routledge. https://doi.org/10.4324/9781351240932

Grosfoguel, R. (2016). The dilemmas of ethnic studies in the United States. In R. Grosfoguel, R. Hernandez, & E. Rosen Velasquex (Eds.), *Decolonizing the Westernized university: Interventions in philosophy of education from within and without* (pp. 27–37). London, UK: Lexington Books.

Johnston, R., McGregor, D., & Restoule, JP. (2018). Relationships, respect, relevance, reciprocity, and responsibility: Taking up Indigenous research approaches. In D. McGregor, J. P. Restoule, & R. Johnston, (Eds). *Indigenous research: Theories, practices, and relationships*. (pp. 1–21). Canadian Scholars.

Jones, G. A., Shanahan, T., & Goyan, P. (2001). University governance in Canadian higher education. *Tertiary Education and Management, 7*(2), 135–148.

Jones, L., & Maguire, M. (2020). Investing ourselves: The role of space and place in being a working-class female academic. *Discourse: Studies in the Cultural Politics of Education, 42*(1), 45–59. https://doi.org/10.1080/01596306.2020.1767937

Malott, C. (2010). *Policy and research in education: A critical pedagogy for educational leadership*. Peter Lang.

McGranahan, C. (2016). Theorizing refusal: An introduction. *Cultural Anthropology, 31*(3), 319–325. https://doi.org/10.14506/ca31.3.01

Metcalfe, A. (2018). Thinking in place: Picturing the knowledge university as a politics of refusal. *Research in Education, 104*(1), 43–55. https://doi.org/10.1177/0034523718806932

Nash, M. A. (2019). Entangled pasts: Land-grant colleges and American Indian dispossession. *History of Education Quarterly, 59*(4), 437–467. https://doi.org/10.1017/heq.2019.31

Olssen, M., & Peters, M. (2005). Neoliberalism, higher education and the knowledge economy: From the free market to knowledge capitalism. *Journal of Education Policy, 20*(3), 313–345. https://doi.org/10.1080/02680930500108718

Ortner, S. (1995). Resistance and the problem of ethnographic refusal. *Comparative Studies in Society and History, 37*(1), 173–193. https://doi.org/10.1017/S001041750001 9587.

Ottmann, J. (2009). Leadership for social justice: A Canadian perspective. *Journal of Research on Leadership Education, 4*(1), 1–9. https://doi.org/10.1177/194277510900400105

Ottmann, J. (2013). Indigenizing the academy: Confronting 'contentious ground.' In K. Anderson & M. Hanrahan (Eds.), *Morning watch* [A special 40th anniversary edition]. http://www.mun.ca/educ/faculty/mwatch/vol40/winter2013/indigenizingAcademy.pdf

Ozga, J., & Walker, L. (1999). In the company of men. In R. Moodley & S. Whitehead (Eds.), *Transforming managers: Engendering change in the public sector* (pp. 256–270). Routledge.

Patel, L. (2015). Desiring diversity and backlash: White property rights in higher education. *Urban Revolution, 47*(4), 657–675.

Ryan, J., & Armstrong, D. (2016). *Working (with/out) the system: Educational leadership, micropolitics and social justice*. Charlotte, NC: Information Age Publishing.

Samier, E. (2017). Towards a postcolonial and decolonising educational administration history. *Journal of Educational Administration and History, 49*(4), 264–282. https://doi.org/10.1080/00220620.2017.1343288

Shahjahan, R. (2011). Engaging the faces of 'resistance' and social change from decolonizing perspectives: Toward transforming neoliberal higher education. *Journal of Curriculum Theorizing, 27*(3), 273–286.

Shahjahan, R. (2014). From 'no' to 'yes': Postcolonial perspectives on resistance to neoliberal higher education. *Discourse: Studies in the Cultural Politics of Education, 35*(2), 219–232. https://doi.org/10.1080/01596306.2012.745732

Shields, C. (2012). *Transformative leadership in education: Equitable change in an uncertain and complex world*. New York, NY: Routledge.

Shultz, L., & Viczko, M. (2016). Global social justice, democracy and leadership of higher education. In L. Shultz & M. Viczko (Eds.), *Assembling and governing the higher education institution: Democracy, social justice and leadership in global higher education* (pp. 1–7). Palgrave Macmillan.

Simpson, A. (2014). *Mohawk interruptus: Political life across the borders of settler states*. Duke University Press.

Smith, G. H. (2003). *Indigenous struggle for the transformation of education and school*. Keynote Address at the Alaskan Federation of Native (AFN) Convention, Anchorage, Alaska, U.S. http://www.ankn.uaf.edu/curriculum/Articles/GrahamSmith/

Smith, L., & Smith, G. (2018). Doing Indigenous work: Decolonizing and transforming the academy. In E. A. McKinley & L. T. Smith (Eds.), *Handbook of Indigenous education* (pp. 1–27). SpringerLink. https://www.springer.com/gp/book/9789811038983

Smith, M. (2019). *The diversity gap in 2019: Canadian universities*. (Infographic series on U15 Presidents' Leadership Teams or Cabinets, U15 Deans, U15 Leadership Pipeline, Equity Diversity Intersectionality Decoloniality.) https://uofaawa.wordpress.com/awa-diversity-gap-campaign/

Spooner, M. (2018). Qualitative research and global audit culture: The politics of productivity, accountability and possibility. In N. Denzin & Y. S. Lincoln (Eds.), *The SAGE handbook of qualitative research* (5th ed., pp. 894–914). Sage.

Spooner, M. (2020). *The plain truth about performance-based funding*. Retrieved from https://www.caut.ca/bulletin/2020/03/commentary-plain-truth-about-performance-based-funding.

Stein, S. (2019). Navigating different theories of change for higher education in volatile times. *Educational Studies (Ames), 55*(6), 667–688. https://doi.org/10.1080/00131946.2019.1666717

Times Higher Education. (2021). *Times Higher Education World University Rankings: Impact rankings 2021*. https://www.timeshighereducation.com/impactrankings#!/page/0/length/25/sort_by/rank/sort_order/asc/cols/undefined

Truth and Reconciliation Commission of Canada (TRC). (2015). *Honouring the truth, reconciling for the future: Summary of the final report of the truth and reconciliation commission of Canada*. (Electronic monograph in PDF format). http://www.trc.ca/assets/pdf/Executive_Summary_English_Web.pdf

Tuck, E. (2018). Biting the university that feeds us. In M. Spooner & J. McNinch (Eds.), *Dissident knowledge in higher education* (pp. 149–168). University of Regina Press.

Tuck, E., & Yang, K. W. (2012). Decolonization is not a metaphor. *Decolonization: Indigeneity, Education & Society, 1*(1), 1–40.

Tuck, E., & Yang, K. W. (2014a). R-Words: Refusing research. In D. Paris & M. T. Winn (Eds.), *Humanizing research: Decolonizing qualitative inquiry with youth and communities* (pp. 223–247). Sage.

Tuck, E., & Yang, K. W. (2014b). Unbecoming claims: Pedagogies of refusal in qualitative research. *Qualitative Inquiry, 20*(6), 811–818.

Tuck, E., & Yang, K. W. (2018). Born under the rising sun of social justice. In E. Tuck & K.W. Yang (Eds.), *Toward what justice? Describing diverse dreams of justice in education* (pp. 1-17). New York, NY: Routledge.

Viczko, M., Lorusso, J. & McKechnie, S. (2019). The 'problem' of the skills gap agenda in post-secondary education policies. *Canadian Journal of Educational Administration and Policy, 191*, 118–130.

wa Thiong'o, N. (2007). *Decolonising the mind: The politics of language in African literature.* Heinemann.

Wilks, J., Kennedy, G., Drew, N., & Wilson, K. (2018). Indigenous data sovereignty in higher education. *Australian Universities' Review, 60*(2), 4–14.

Wolfe, P. (2006). Settler colonialism and the elimination of the native. *Journal of Genocide Research, 8*(4), 387–409. https://doi.org/10.1080/14623520601056240

Wright, H. K. (2019). *Positioning blackness, necessarily, awkwardly, in the Canadian academy.* https://www.ideas-idees.ca/blog/positioning-blackness-necessarily-awkwardly-canadian-academy

Wright, S., & Øberg, J. (2017). Universities in the competition state: Lessons from Denmark. In S. Wright & C. Shore (Eds.), *Death of the public university?: Uncertain futures for higher education in the knowledge economy* (pp. 69–89). New York, NY: Berghahn Books.

CHAPTER 16

Critical Pedagogy in Language and STEM Education: Science, Technology, Engineering, and Mathematics Education

Zehlia Babaci-Wilhite

INTRODUCTION

Critical thinking in Science, Technology, Engineering, and Mathematics (STEM) pedagogy with a focus on languages and cultural diversity provides a better understanding of the learning skills required for success in STEM by adding the A for Arts (STEAM). Furthermore, the climate crisis is the most acute crisis directly related to Science and Technology. Therefore, I will introduce a critical eco-pedagogical model (Misiaszek, 2018) that expands the traditional STEM methods to Environment that includes the A for arts. I will argue that the incorporation of critical pedagogy (Abdi, 2019) into an open and investigative process, based on the inquiry-based approach, provides a source of new thinking which will improve and strengthen educational rights. This model is particularly important in educational systems that utilize cross-cultural critical thinking in an asymmetrical global development of the past century which has left us with a critically vulnerable euro-global system.

Language, culture, and art in instruction must be viewed via the importance of national and international environmental discourse, which aims at promoting collaborative learning as well as a cross-cultural pedagogical model that expands the traditional STEM to STEAM. This model will include the introduction of cross-cultural critical thinking education into the classroom as well as international collaboration across STEM subjects which I link to

Z. Babaci-Wilhite (✉)
University of California, Berkeley, CA, USA
e-mail: z.b.wilhite@berkeley.edu

© The Author(s), under exclusive license to Springer Nature Switzerland AG 2022
A. A. Abdi and G. W. Misiaszek (eds.), *The Palgrave Handbook on Critical Theories of Education*, https://doi.org/10.1007/978-3-030-86343-2_16

language and the Art-Science divide. This model is grounded in both local and global challenges, as well as a cross-cultural educational system that could include a plethora of knowledge within the cultural and linguistic rights framework in education. This critical eco-pedagogical model of teaching gives our environment and human rights its rightful place in a cross-cultural pedagogical curriculum. Teaching in a classroom is a very practical activity. The curriculum should aim at furthering true openness to knowledge in order to achieve critical pedagogy. It is important to impart knowledge in ways that inspires freethinking and empowers students to critical thinking. Having students memorize information by heart should not be the basis for a curriculum. "Liberating education consists in acts of cognition, not transferrals of information" (Freire, 1993 [1970], p. 60). Every society should liberate its educational system, not by transferring knowledge but by inspiring people to think of ways to achieve a better life. Even though education encompasses much more than schooling, schooling is nonetheless central to knowledge acquisition and primary schooling was formally accepted as a human right more that 50 years ago.

STEM Subjects, Linguistic Rights, and the Art-Science Divide

The teaching of STEM subjects represents a model of education that divides the Art-Science, thus not satisfying human rights criteria for education. I will argue that the incorporation of the arts into an open and investigative process—based upon the inquiry-based approach—using cultural references will improve learning and strengthen human rights in STEM. This model is particularly important in educational systems that today uses languages and culture in their instruction, disregarding local languages and local knowledge. In contrast to conventional approaches to education, I argue that teaching is more effective when it is based in local languages and culture that includes the arts. Therefore, the introduction of a cross-cultural critical eco-pedagogical model that expands the traditional STEM method to include local language and culture linked to the arts is crucial (Babaci-Wilhite, 2023).

The importance of national and international efforts aimed at promoting collaborative learning through the introduction of virtual and digital narratives into the classroom as well as an international collaboration across the Art-Science divide should be visible. These narratives could be grounded in both local and global cultures (Misiaszek, 2020) and include a diversity of knowledge within the human rights framework of education. The Universal Declaration of Human Rights (1948) represents one of the great advances of global civilization (Alfredsson & Eide, 1999). However, education in many developing countries today is decontextualized, in that it is not conducted in local languages and does not promote cross-cultural critical thinking, thus limiting intellectual inquiry. I have argued in recent publications (Babaci-Wilhite, 2012, 2014, 2015) that the contextualization of education and the use of local languages of instruction should be considered a right in education. Article 26 of the United Nations Declaration of Human Rights (1948) states that

> Everyone has the right to education. Education shall be free...Education shall be directed to...the development of human personality and to the strengthening of human rights and fundamental freedom (Preamble).

The globalization trends for language in education outlined above, in which local curricula is decontextualized is in contravention with the tenets of the rights-based approach to language in education. This approach is based upon the premise that the use of a local curriculum should be regarded as a right in education (Babaci-Wilhite, 2020). However, it says very little about the nature and quality of education. Rights in education imply that rights are not ensured unless the education offered is of high quality. The UN calls for a mainstreaming of human rights to encourage the government's responsibility to insure the rights-based approach. The rights-based framework includes the principle that every human being is entitled to a decent education and gives priority to the intrinsic importance of education, implying that governments need to mobilize the resources to offer quality education. Katarina Tomasevski (2006) advocates that education should prepare learners for participation stating, "it should teach the young that all human beings – themselves included – have rights" (p. 33).

Education has the potential to empower students if the method of teaching provides both intellectual nourishment and a personal sense of self-respect. This in turn would bring greater self-confidence to both teachers and learners. I agree with Ingrid Robeyns (2006) who writes that in order for a government to ensure everyone the full benefit of an education, and they must provide not only a well-developed curriculum, along with sufficient teaching materials, but that teachers must also be well-trained and, importantly, well-paid. Education is fundamental in developing human capability and creating individual opportunity in today's world. Crucial to quality in education is the incorporation of the United Nations Development Programme (UNDP) principles of "Common Understanding": indivisibility, equality, participation, and inclusion (UNDP, 2006, pp. 17–18). These principals are an intimate part of the social, political, cultural, religious, and artistic life of people (Bostad, 2013; Geo-JaJa, 2013) and support the argument that the safeguard of a culture's original language should be considered a Human Right (Babaci-Wilhite, 2015; Skutnabb-Kangas, 2000). UNESCO's convention on the Protection and Promotion of the Diversity of Cultural Expressions emphasizes the importance of linguistic diversity as part of cultural diversity (2005) and that this should apply to the educational sector. In an increasingly interdependent world, it is important to facilitate the mastery of all subject matter (Spreen & Vally, 2006; Babaci-Wilhite & Geo-JaJa, 2014). The linguistic and cultural policies within education should, for all countries, be context-sensitive and permit countries to remain partners in the global society. In this chapter, collaborative learning is viewed as a way to start the implementation of new ideas in education, which should be regarded as a process intended to enhance new ways of learning.

Many scholars argue that the lack of African and Asian countries using local languages and knowledge in school has been a detriment to children (Babaci-Wilhite, 2015; Brock-Utne, 2012; Majhanovich, 2014; Nyerere, 1968; Prah, 2005). According to Joseph Ki-Zerbo (1990), a historian from Burkina Faso, these points about cultural learning and local needs have not been adequately addressed in Africa. Ki-Zerbo (1990) claims that for African societies, education lost its functional role and that African countries are adopting the standards of the world without the inclusion of local languages and local culture in education (Babaci-Wilhite & Mchombo, 2019; Okonkwo, 2014).

In Tanzania, South Africa, Nigeria, Malawi, and elsewhere in Africa as well as Malaysia, Sri-Lanka, and India (see Brock-Utne, 2012; Babaci-Wilhite, 2013; Majhanovich, 2014; Mchombo, 2016), reforms and policies connecting local cultures to education have been neglected. According to Samoff (2007, p. 60) "effective education reform requires agendas and initiatives with strong local roots." In other words, local knowledge, also referred to as indigenous knowledge should be included in the curriculum (Spreen & Vally, 2006; Babaci-Wilhite & Geo-JaJa, 2014; Odora Hoppers, 2002; Semali & Khanjan, 2012). This knowledge should be conveyed in local languages, which is critical to the preservation and development of local knowledge. Storytelling is a way to safeguard local and indigenous knowledge, which can then be shared through contemporary digital media. Digital storytelling also allows for the Arts to be brought into the classroom via written text and images that are composed of the screen for twenty-first-century literacy students (Vu et al., 2021).

Furthermore, I argue that arts will contribute to student's participation and will foster teamwork as well as collaboration for innovation and creativity in the field of STEAM subjects in the classroom and will provide accessibility as well as enhance understanding. This chapter draws on examples in the United States wherein workshops provided a model of how arts can be a tool for bringing to light questions on diversity and power-relations between non-dominant (minorities) and dominant cultures through what Inga Bostad calls "an investigative pedagogy" (Sath㳠Peder's Grant, 2016). The method used in the workshop involves engaging two sets of students, one from Norway and the other from the United States both of whom illustrate the creative use of Arts to establish collegiality and collaboration.

Critical Pedagogy Through Cross-Cultural Virtual Exchange

In most educational models today, the knowledge and information taught in school curricula are decontextualized. An educated person is expected to master facts, propositions, models, and cognitive skills that are separate from any particular context in which they were learned. Stanton Wortham and Kara Jackson (2012) argue that the many approaches to education we know of today differ in how well they increase a learner's knowledge. Some approaches emphasize the typical learner as a passive recipient of information. Others encourage the learner to be more proactive in their education, to pursue inquiry, ask questions, and discuss with teachers and peers.

Traditional education involves the transmission of isolated bodies of knowledge. Schools can survive as institutions given how both this form of stable knowledge and a particular reasoning of a scientific culture come to underly it. They, thus, allegedly bring value to other contexts, those then outside of the school where the knowledge learned might also be applied. Therefore, because the context of an "unscientific" way does not appear to be integral to a given knowledge or skill, isolated bodies of knowledge often hold little meaning for anyone outside the community. This means that the knowledge learned here is less useful outside the classroom given the decontextualized, insular nature of the knowledge being passed on; there is generally little opportunity for students to question the claims on which the knowledge is based.

Globalization creates great convenience of aims through the links it creates between production, communication, and technology, primarily through the use of English. But something is lost in this great cultural leveling. In contrast, STEAM learners gain a better understanding of the concepts they are studying when they are taught in their local instead of a foreign language (Babaci-Wilhite, 2016; Brock-Utne, 2016). To develop conceptual knowledge, students need help in linking scientific concepts to their everyday environmental and cultural experiences and thereby assimilate new and unfamiliar scientific words and concepts so as to learn how to use concepts in context (Bravo et al., 2008).

Lucia Bigozzi et al. (2002) establish that the main difference between a deep and lasting learning and a learning that is purely oral and superficial is that the former approach offers the ability to justify the data learned. Berit Haug (2014) argues that when Norwegian students were asked to explain how their newly learned knowledge serves them, none were able to respond, since the students had developed no capacity for inquiry. She states that students needed further clarification and explanation to develop a higher level of conceptual knowledge. This shows that knowing definitions and being able to use science concepts in short answers is but one of the first steps to be taken in moving toward developing a greater conceptual understanding of this world (Bravo et al., 2008). In order for learners to develop a stronger conceptual understanding of their field of study, teachers must include enough time for inquiry-based discussion about their empirical findings and how they connect to established science.

Through a Pre-Service Teacher Collaboration integrating Technology, Culture, and Human Rights, at the University of California, Berkeley (USA) in collaboration with the University of Tromsd the Norwegian Center for Human Rights (Norway) I developed with Jabari Mahiri, Kirsten Stien, Inga Bostad, Lanette Jimerson, and Lisbeth Rngsbakk, a significant conceptual framework and novel pedagogical competencies needed to effectively integrate innovative technologies, diverse cultures, and human rights perspectives into comprehensive designs of learning experiences for middle and high school students (Sath泪 Peder's Grant, 2016). The project was aimed at enhancing teaching competence through critical thinking within education and explore how to best prepare teachers to be most effective in designing and implementing instruction for their students. The aim was to meet the challenges of a world of rapid technological change in the domains of information access where learning tools have been made, none being largely available through digital devices. It offers an original alternative to most approaches orienting instruction set out to prepare new teachers to become professional practitioners.

Beyond teaching students what amounts to content knowledge of particular disciplines, this new exigency is to systematically develop student abilities to think creatively, critically, and comprehensively while understanding how to access, research, and utilize traditional disciplinary knowledge in conjunction with continually emerging digital sources of knowledge (Mahiri, 2011). These are skills students need in order to understand how to work toward solutions of problems actually rooted in complex local and global problems, each of which we referred to as twenty-first-century skills to be learned if understood through twenty-first-century literacies. We engaged better-equipped students with academic knowledge, technical competence, and research skills, each of which is needed for them to critically address the challenges of a rapidly changing and increasingly complex, inter-connected world. This model of learning allowed for accessing, researching, and utilizing traditional disciplinary knowledge. Furthermore, it facilitated understanding of emerging knowledge sources by working toward solutions for complex global challenges. We believe that the kind of education teachers need must be framed by an ideology of global awareness that must be translated into a systematic method of investigative pedagogy in order to guide their delivery of learning in schools. This is true insofar as we do not want students to give answers alone as we want them to find the right kinds of questions relating to not just the science itself but to their own existence, language, and approaches to the world (Sath泪 Peder's Grant, 2016).

Through virtual intellectual exchanges, we focused on increased understanding of diverse cultural perspectives, conjoined with the power of human rights perspectives, all made to inspire and engage both the pre-service teachers and their future students in rigorous learning. Importantly, development of competencies in using appropriate technologies was central to the success of collaborations between the University of Tromsd the University of California at Berkeley's pre-service teachers. This project has been innovative in how it intricately links technology, diverse cultures, cross-cultural communication, and human rights perspectives as being interdependent. In attempting to improve learning and make it more relevant to real-world issues and challenges, we have explored and documented viable roles for digital technology in the actual process of learning for both teachers and students. It has enabled cross-cultural and cross-continental communication between collaborating partners. This project has enhanced our understanding of a significant issue across societies: how to best prepare teachers to be effective in preparing their students to meet the challenges of a changing world. We believe this model offers an original alternative to most approaches used to prepare new teachers for becoming professional practitioners, since it attempts to improve learning by making it more relevant to real-world issues and challenges. This collaboration has brought us to a collaborative model based on how we may further explore and document viable roles for digital technology. This has thus acknowledged the importance of cross-cultural and cross-continental communication, which facilitate the development of a new phase producing digital stories. To summarize the outcomes, we made a short video illustrating our collaborative process, one including workshops, virtual meetings, and our mini-conference (Sath沮 Peder's Grant, 2016).

One of the workshops addresses the integration of arts into STEAM teaching with the purpose of promoting creativity and innovation as well as understanding the power-relations between dominant and non-dominant languages in teaching and learning at all levels in education. This change in focus from STEM to STEAM needs a strong emphasis on interdisciplinary collaboration. We have provided tools and strategies for organizing and managing interdisciplinary learning and teaching based on a team collaboration of pre-service students, researchers, and artists.

Arts Activities to Increase Inclusivity, Collegiality, and Collaboration

Arts in an academic context or in any other area that involves group dynamics or collaborative interaction can serve as an insight into process, if not "the scientific method," as such. This is especially true when dealing with the need to overcome cultural or linguistic barriers. Since the Arts by their very nature appear as cross-disciplinary and thus universally neutral, they can be utilized in a variety of ways. One method used in our workshop has illustrated the creative use of the Arts in order to further produce results of improved learning and increased knowledge by virtue of collegiality and collaboration on the parts of both teachers and students. I outline below the methodology used in our workshop.

The students were divided into groups consisting of equal numbers; and each student was given a sheet of paper and drawing materials. They were instructed to make a random mark/figure on the paper. At ten-minute intervals, the drawings were passed to the student on the right; that student then added her/his symbol to the previous students work as they saw fit. The drawings were passed sequentially in this manner at ten-minute intervals until the drawing with all the additional inputs arrived at its originator. The originator then had twenty minutes to complete the drawing by incorporating the additions in a manner that they deemed appropriate. In order to level the playing field, the first round of drawing was done with the *non-dominant hand* while the finishing work was done with the *dominant hand*. In this activity, the hand could be replaced by the language used, thereby serving to make students understand the power relation implicit anytime a student uses a different language other than the local one.

After completion, there was a period of discussion and commentary on the exercise. This was followed by a display of the finished artwork. This activity had many consequences, since there was no set of guidelines as to how each person made their additions. It is most noteworthy that no guidance gave space as well as agency for creativity. Some students attempted to compliment others' drawings; while some used the new drawing as a starting point for another's directions; and some students were relatively neutral in their approach. Moreover, students became aware of differences in perception and approaches by their collaborators. Finishing the work(s) allowed the originator of each piece to express ownership on what will have begun as a common undertaking, while recognizing the unique and isolated contributions of collaborators sharing in the elaboration of an enterprise all could prize.

In the discussion, students noticed the flexibility and creativity of their peers, just as they were pleased with the results both in the actual finished work and the collaborative exercise, that is, the process. This activity reflects upon how the arts can be a tool for bringing to light questions on diversity, as well as power-relations between non-dominant and dominant cultures through an investigative pedagogy.

Theory of Inquiry to Rethink STEM and Arts Subjects in Curricula

In my previous work, I have argued that a new model of teaching and learning based on the Seeds of Science/Roots of Reading (S/R), a science curriculum model developed by the Lawrence Hall of Science and the Graduate School of Education at UC-Berkeley, has been shown to improve the learning process. The model has been adapted to the cultural context of each country acknowledging the local languages and evaluations have shown that students exposed to this approach made significant learning improvements based on measures of science understanding, science vocabulary, and science writing (Pearson et al.,

2010). Science inquiry implies that learners search for evidence in order to make and revise explanations using critical thinking in efforts to learn about the natural world (Babaci-Wilhite, 2017).

Academic approaches to literacy tend to regard literacy as an end unto itself, ignoring structures that undercut disciplinary learning, comprehension, critical literacy, and strategic reading. The inquiry-based approach goes beyond this superficial conceptualization of literacy, drawing heavily on the work of several educational theorists. David Pearson (2007) and Jacqueline Barbers's approach (2005) to the role of language and literacy in the learning of science emphasizes the importance of the theory of inquiry, which John Dewey (1939 [2007]) defines as a development of ideas. Furthermore, Dewey (ibid.) argues that the theory of inquiry is one of the most essential skills that can help clarify the learning process and develop skills for inquiry in the context of decision-making. Jabari Mahiri and Jeremiah Sims (2016, p. 57) argue that, through a critical pedagogical approach, students would "develop competency in STEM and identify connections to STEM."

In line with the philosophy of Paulo Freire's (1970), inclusive education through the integration of formal and non-formal knowledge, teaching should give value to local knowledge in non-"western" contexts rather than oppressing it. Freire's theory has implications for the language used in schools, especially in societies with vulnerable communities. Given that inquiry-based learning leads to better results, it makes sense that a localized language of a type with which students are familiar with would facilitate a better understanding of a scientific process. Science is intimately connected to the lives of a people and their native language should be a part of their method of learning. Language plays a critical role in cognitive learning and in the development of critical thinking (Ngugi, 1986 [1994]). Drawing on scholars who address imagination and reimagining communities, we argue that acknowledging local knowledge and localized languages in educating for science literacy, as well as emphasizing inquiry-based learning leads to improved teaching and learning. This can make a positive contribution to achieving quality education in STEM subjects because it acknowledges the importance of language and culture—and thus the arts.

Improving STEM learning can be addressed by beginning with the effort to improve literacy, which facilitates inquiry. Barber (2005) argues that inquiry is curiosity-driven and involves a great deal of reading. An in-depth inquiry calls upon critical and logical thinking that allows readers to correctly interpet the information gathered. Therefore, Pearson and Barber's approach to improving literacy by emphasizing inquiry as a real-world approach can lead to better results for both students and science itself. Pearson and Barber's teaching model, in which students learn scientific concepts while they are taught how to read, write, and discuss (Pearson et al., 2010), involves students searching for evidence to support their ideas. Through firsthand (hands-on) and secondhand (text) investigations, students also engage in critical thinking to learn how to create explanations based upon the evidence found. This teaching model addresses the ways that reading, writing, and discourse can be used as tools to support inquiry-based learning. It also addresses the benefit of reading, writing, and discussion when they are part of an inquiry-based science. This has greater potential of improvements in the teaching and learning of science and students gain a deeper understanding of their subject where language plays a key role in quality education. Furthermore, each positive outcome in the student's course of development reveals the complex web of activities needed to bring about the change. These principles of learning address the connections between early, intermediate, and long-term outcomes and the expectations about how and why the proposed interventions bring them about (Cervetti et al., 2007). This inquiry-based approach aims for a deep, conceptual understanding, an implementation of a program of planning and evaluation, and a shared cross-disciplinary understanding of the long-term goals. It also aims to understand how they would be reached, as well as what can be used to measure progress along the way. This approach requires teachers to be clear about their long-term goals, identify measurable indicators of success, and to be knowledgeable about practices that meet linguistic needs, such as using graphic representations of abstract concepts (Pearson & Hiebert, 2013). The approach puts an emphasis on literacy through texts, routines for reading, word-level skills, vocabulary, and comprehension instruction. It corrects a serious problem in much of STEM teaching today, which results from bringing universal scientific principles to students through non-local contextualization and non-local examples.

A model with an emphasis on critical cultural contextualization through the arts and the local language of instruction has great potential for improving STEM learning (Babaci-Wilhite, 2016). Such a model of instruction leads to meeting the expectations of higher goals in literacy and science by providing students with clear instruction, opportunities for practice and greater independence through their increased literacy in order to understand and communicate about the natural world. In the classroom, the teacher needs contextualized materials and teachers' guides that describe when to introduce different modes of learning such as doing, talking, reading, and writing. These guides also include detailed information on scientific subjects, instructional suggestions, and clear guidelines for what can be expected in a student's progress as they gain knowledge of specific scientific concepts that serve to create a meaningful picture of their world. By using a Multi-Modal Approach made up of different learning modalities (doing, talking, reading, and writing), students gain an understanding of basic concepts by carrying out experiments, reading about them, and by writing about their newly gained knowledge. For instance, students in coastal areas might read about shorelines, then investigate sand, gather evidence from sand, and write a text about its properties, the whole of which leads to an understanding of the original source of the sand. Learners discuss their work (in their language), eventually forming expert groups focusing on particular sand samples. They read about shorelines, then do, talk, read again, all followed by doing more, further talking, writing to develop this, then talk again, and finish what they will have begun to write (Barber, 2005). Again, multiple modalities provide opportunities for learners to apply, deepen, and extend their knowledge of the learned concepts (Pearson & Hiebert, 2013). Furthermore, learners engage in discourse, both written and oral, with the goal of communicating their evidence-based explanations. Secondarily, they then carry-out a re-evaluation of their explanations and revise them based on their research. This is in opposition to the usual approach that simply adds literacy tasks onto a science curriculum, without connecting those additional tasks directly to the advancement of the understanding from the initial investigation and does not provide explicit instruction on how to read and write science texts (Pearson et al., 2010). Recent studies have shown that learners exposed to such models made significantly greater gains in measures of scientific understanding, vocabulary, and writing (Cervetti et al., 2012). A model that links firsthand experiences, discussions, and writing to the ideas and language in informational texts not only fosters development of core science knowledge and literacy skills, but is also crucial to improving STEM literacy, where the local contexts of everyday life contrast sharply with the North American and European contexts (Afflerbach et al., 2008). This approach resolves the problems of teaching and learning science associated with poorly trained teachers as well as inadequate teaching aids and facilities. A major challenge in STEM education is how to support teachers in understanding and enacting inquiry-based instruction.

The S/R model links firsthand experiences, discussions, and writing to the ideas and language in informational texts to foster development of core science knowledge and literacy skills (Afflerbach et al., 2008; Cervetti et al., 2007). The model would address how reading and writing can be used as tools to support inquiry-based science in Zanzibar and how to support their implementation in today's complicated curricular landscape in Zanzibar using a digital device. The computer has been the digital device that has been used in education to facilitate learning. However, it is revealing to note that developing countries are facing a massive infrastructure deficit. Despite robust growth over the last decade, many people in emerging markets and developing economies still do not have access to reliable and safe basic services (World Bank, 2014) that are regarded as commonplace in the industrialized world in order to improve policy and practice (Arnove, 2003, p. 6). However, the main digital device used in classrooms is no longer a computer. In 2012, the US Department of Education and the Federal Communications Commission encouraged the development of digital textbooks and digital learning in K-12 public education. According to Pew Research Internet Project (PRIP), the rise of E-Reading (2012) has increased and 50% of US adults own a tablet computer and/or an e-book reader. One in five Americans now listens to audiobooks (Perrin, 2019).

In the African context, with no books and no support materials in teaching and learning, tablets can be very useful and adaptable. The implementation costs for e-textbooks on iPad tablets are higher than new print textbooks due to costs including Wi-Fi infrastructure, the training of teachers and administrators on how to use the technology, and annual publisher fees to continue using e-textbooks. Advances in technology have long been changing the way scholars work in terms of teaching and administrative duties; however, the trend is now growing globally. In most African countries, with high demands in literacy and technology, the use of tablets has a huge potential to improve teaching and learning particularly during the pandemic, as long as the content is contextualized. Its application can be a major step in correcting violations of children's rights in education caused by the aforementioned learning environment, particularly with regards to the lack of trained teachers and support materials. This will contribute to a solid curriculum grounded in thorough teacher preparation and quality support materials. An application of the S/R model has the potential to contribute to a realization of science learning that ensures every child's rights to quality education.

Reimagining the Value of Languages and Knowledge Through Arts

Pearson et al. (2010) point out the connection between word knowledge and conceptual knowledge by emphasizing that when science words are taught as concepts applied in a particular context to other science words and concepts, word knowledge is consistent with conceptual knowledge. Since this practice of a method of education that is based on contextualization by using the local language of instruction, it leads to a rethinking of all aspects of education, both formal and informal education in and out of school. Education must therefore acknowledge culture through the arts. This includes the non-material aspects of life such as language, together with social and historical identities. Education should address both the needs of the local people and the country in which they live in, just as with any life-long learning process.

Education using non-localized languages and concepts cannot transmit a society's values and knowledge from one generation to the next; on the contrary, education has involved a deliberate attempt to change those values while replacing traditional knowledge by the knowledge from an alien or foreign society (Geo-JaJa, 2013). To motivate the mind, one has to take into consideration variations that indubitably exist in different societies, differences in knowledge, and different ways of teaching; in other words, variations used to achieve quality education. If education is conceived of as imparting knowledge about the world, then schooling should be regarded as only one aspect of education, since it does not cover all forms of knowledge, whether it yields formal or informal varieties of education. According to Freire (1993 [1970]), much of the knowledge that forms the basis for schooling has its origins in another place and another time: "Knowledge emerges only through invention and re-invention" (Freire, 1993 [1970], p. 53). Students who catch on to this form of learning are more likely to succeed in school, even if they might actually have less knowledge, in the broad sense of the word, compared to those who do not attend school. However, education is most often equated with schooling, which does not take into account the knowledge gained outside the classroom. Therefore, it is time to think of what is actually out there, outside the classroom in order to rethink the value of local knowledge.

Evidence from countries around the world demonstrates that the best way to learn science is through use of the local language. Paraphrasing Wolff (2006), "Language is not everything in education, but without language, everything is nothing in education." Acknowledging this insight means that local languages are important in order to both convey higher levels of knowledge and function as bridges to languages of wider communication. Having several languages within one classroom gives us the opportunity to explore the benefits of bilingualism and multilingualism. As, Ngugi wrote to me in a personal correspondence (March 26, 2017), "Multilingualism is the oxygen of culture - and monolingualism, the carbon monoxide of culture."

Globalization creates great convenience through the links it creates between production, communication, and technology, primarily through the use of English. But something is lost in this great cultural leveling. In contrast, STEM learners gain a better understanding of the concepts they are studying when they are taught in their local language instead of a foreign language (Brock-Utne, 2012; Mchombo, 2016). To develop conceptual knowledge, students need help in linking scientific concepts to their everyday environmental and cultural experiences to assimilate new and unfamiliar science words and concepts, and to learn how to use concepts in context (Bravo et al., 2008).

Bigozzi et al. (2002) considered that the main difference between a deep and lasting learning and a learning that is purely oral and superficial is that the former approach offers the ability to justify the data learned. Haug (2014) argues that when Norwegian students were asked to explain how their newly learned knowledge serves them, none were able to respond since the students had not developed a capacity for inquiry.

According to Samoff (2007, p. 60) "effective education reform requires agendas and initiatives with strong local roots." Local, or as it is more precisely known, indigenous knowledge, should be included in the curriculum. Storytelling is a way to safeguard local or indigenous knowledge, which can then be shared, among other means, through contemporary digital media. Digital storytelling is one among a number of means allowing for the arts to be brought into the classroom via written text and images that are composed for the screen for twenty-first-century students subject to learning through improved approaches to literacy and language acquisition. Inspired by DIGICOM, a professional program to train in-service teachers in the use of digital storytelling, in collaboration with colleagues (Mark Warschauer and Viet Vu) at the University of California, Irvine while teaching a course on twenty-first-century literacies), and as part of a twenty-first-century model of education. We implemented digital storytelling where I added human rights perspectives into the curriculum in order to develop critical thinking skills with letting others expressing themselves as Voltaire said, "I disagree with your ideas but I will fight for your right to express them" (My own translation: *Je ne suis pas d accord avec vos idees mais je me battrais pour que vous puissiez les exprimer*). Local knowledge and languages are being severely strained through globalization, which is a shorthand way of describing the spread and connectedness of production, communication, and technologies around the world. Appadurai (1990, p. 17) argues that "The critical point is that both sides of the coin of global cultural process today are products of the infinitely varied mutual contest of sameness and difference on a stage characterised by radical disjunctures between different sorts of global flows and the uncertain landscapes created in and through these disjunctures." Therefore, adding the A for arts in STEM will bring local contexts and language to those of a global variety which will lead to cross-cultural critical thinking.

Conclusion

In this chapter, I have reviewed the importance of rethinking a curriculum grounded in local context through a localized language helping to facilitate the integration of the arts into STEM, thereby adding something of essential import that makes for more than some air of science's "method(s)" alone, as "STEAM." I have argued that this would improve learning and thus satisfy our global yearning for Human Rights as dignifying, respected, honored, and commonplace. Such an approach emphasizes the importance of indigenous concepts articulated in their natural environment.

Education is more than just schooling; therefore, science cannot be taught without contextualized inquiry. When STEM content is addressed through a combination of inquiry and literacy activities, students learn how to activate, read, write, and talk STEM simultaneously. These literacy activities support the acquisition of STEM concepts and inquiry skills at once inside and outside of the classroom. Furthermore, recent studies discussed in this chapter emphasize the connection between word knowledge and conceptual understanding. Therefore, the synergy between STEM and literacy rests upon the understanding that an active level of word knowledge in STEM (understanding of words as they are situated within a network of other words and ideas) can be described as conceptual knowledge.

The frameworks applied for word knowledge and link making are effective in terms of enhancing conceptual learning actively engaged in making the links. It appears clear that, in order to enable inquiry, language facilitates the learning process, just as it supports students in attending to their preparation for engaging with the world in a greater variety of ways. Such a model, which represents an opportunity to apply a well-tested inquiry-based science model to the teaching of science, leads to improved STEM literacy, scientific knowledge, and personal efficacy of applications for students, which brings about greater professional efficacy for teachers who venture to include it in their delivery of knowledge as a form of freedom(s).

This renewed pedagogy would examine the whole inquiry cycle in different stages, including the pedagogy of digital literacy and how this could be planned for so as to utilize it in teaching. Collaboration could strengthen the teaching of STEAM subjects and allow teachers to engage learners in discussions that build upon evidence collected through investigation. This process makes them more aware of what to seek and research in learners' responses, not forgetting how to act upon these very salient elements of any language in contexts attending to what may better promote conceptual understanding. This then contributes to human rights in education as it improves teachers' and learners' confidence in their skills with respect to STEM; it facilitates their ability to apply knowledge to projects in their community. Drawing language and cultural perspectives into educational models makes both teaching and learning more accessible in classrooms in context(s). I believe that collaborative projects which include the arts' activities offer an original alternative to preparing new teachers for becoming professional practitioners. It can help students to access and understand diversity in dominant and non-dominant languages.

A model that embraces and builds upon STEM and integrates visual arts through technology and films—especially considering the connection between word knowledge and conceptual knowledge through Human Rights in everyday perceptions of scientific phenomenal—is the way forward for STEM-STEAM education.

REFERENCES

Abdi, A. A. (2019). Critical teachings of comparative and international education. In M. A. Peters (Ed.), *Encyclopedia of teacher education*. Springer Nature. https://doi.org/10.1007/978-981-13-1179-62

Afflerbach, P., Pearson, P. D., & Paris, S. G. (2008). Clarifying differences between reading skills and reading strategies. *Research Based Classroom Practice, 61*(5), 364–373.

Alfredsson, G., & Eide, A. (Eds.). (1999). *The universal declaration of human rights: A common standard of achievement*. Martinus Nijhoff Publishers.

Appadurai, A. (1990). Disjuncture and difference in the global culture economy. *Theory, Culture & Society, 7*(2), 295–310. https://doi.org/10.1177/026327690007002017

Arnove, R. F. (2003). Introduction: Reframing comparative education. The dialectic of the global and the local. In A. Robert & C. Torres (Eds.), *Comparative education: The dialectic of the global and the local* (pp. 1–22). Rowman & Littlefield.

Babaci-Wilhite, Z. (2012). A right based approach to Zanzibar's language-in-education policy. Special Issue on right based approach and globalization in education. *World Study of Education, 13*(2), 17–33.

Babaci-Wilhite, Z. (2013). An analysis of debates on the use of a global or local language in education: Tanzania and Malaysia. In D. B. Napier & S. Majhanovich (Eds.), *Education, dominance and identity* (pp. 121–133). Sense Publishers.

Babaci-Wilhite, Z. (2014). *Local language as a human right in education: Comparative cases from Africa*. Vol. 36 of the series: Comparative and international education: A diversity of voices. Sense Publishers.

Babaci-Wilhite, Z. (2015). Zanzibar's curriculum reform: Implications for children's educational rights. *Prospects, UNESCO's Quarterly Review of Comparative Education*. Springer. https://doi.org/10.1007/s11125-015-9341-6

Babaci-Wilhite, Z. (Ed.). (2016). *Human rights in language and STEM education: Science, technology, engineering and mathematics*. Sense Publishers.

Babaci-Wilhite, Z. (2017). A rights-based approach to science literacy using local languages: Contextualizing inquiry-based learning in Africa. *International Review of Education, 63*, 381–401.

Babaci-Wilhite, Z. (2020). Linguistic and cultural rights in STEAM: Science, technology, engineering, arts & mathematics. In J. Abidogun & T. Falola (Eds.), *The Palgrave handbook of African education and Indigenous knowledge* (pp. 631–649). Palgrave.

Babaci-Wilhite, Z. (2023). Improving critical thinking in STEM for girls: A contextualized education integrating the arts and human rights. In R. Arnove, C. A. Torres, & L. Misiaszek (Eds), *Comparative education: The dialectic of the global and the local* (5th ed.). Rowman & Littlefield.

Babaci-Wilhite, Z., & Geo-JaJa, M. A. (2014). Localization of instruction as a right in education: Tanzania and Nigeria language-in education's policies. In Z. Babaci-Wilhite (Ed.), *Giving space to African voices: Right in local languages and local curriculum* (pp. 3–21). Sense Publishers.

Babaci-Wilhite, Z., & Mchombo S. (2019). Language and culture in global literacy. In Z. Babaci-Wilhite (Ed.), *Learning critical thinking in 21st century literacies for multidisciplinary courses*. Cognella.

Barber, J. (2005). *The seeds of science/roots of reading inquiry framework*. http://scienceandliteracy.org/sites/scienceandliteracy.org/files/biblio/barber_inquirycycle_pdf_54088.pdf

Bigozzi, L., Biggeri, A., & Boschi, F. (2002). Children "scientists" know the reasons why and they are "poets" too: Non-randomized controlled trial to evaluate the effectiveness of a strategy aimed at improving the learning of scientific concepts. *European Journal of Psychology of Education, XVII*(4), 343–362.

Bostad, I. (2013). Right to education—For all? The quest for a new humanism in globalization. *World Studies in Education, 14*(1), 7–16.

Bravo, M. A., Cervetti, G. N., Hiebert, E. H., & Pearson, D. P. (2008). From passive to active control of science vocabulary. In *The 56th yearbook of the National Reading Conference* (pp. 122–135). National Reading Conference.

Brock-Utne, B. (2012). Language policy and science: Could some African countries learn from Asian countries? *International Review of Education*. https://doi.org/10.1007/s11159-012-9308-2

Brock-Utne, B. (2016). English as the language of science and technology. In Z. Babaci-Wilhite (Ed.), *Human rights, language in STEM education* (pp. 111–128). Sense Publishers and Springer.

Cervetti, G. N., Pearson, P. D., Barber, J., Hiebert, E. H., & Bravo, M. A. (2007). *Integrating literacy and science the research we have, the research we need*.

Cervetti, G. N., Barber, J., Dorph, R., Pearson, P. D., & Goldschmidt, P. G. (2012). The impact of an integrated approach to science and literacy in elementary school classrooms. *Journal of Research in Science Teaching, 49*(5), 631–659.

Dewey, J. (1939, Reprinted in 2007). *Logic: The theory of inquiry*. Henry Holt and Company.
Freire, P. (1970, Reprinted in 1993). *Pedagogy of the oppressed*. Penguin Books.
Geo-JaJa, M. A. (2013). Education localization for optimizing globalization's opportunities. In S. Majhanovich & M. A. Geo-JaJa (Eds.), *Economics, aid and education: Implications for development*. Sense Publishers.
Haug, B. S. (2014). Inquiry-based science: Turning teachable moments into learnable moments. *Journal of Science Teacher Education, 25*, 79–96. https://doi.org/10.1007/s10972-013-9375-7
Ki-Zerbo, J. (1990). *Educate or perish: Africa impasse and prospects*. BREDA with WCARO (UNESCO-UNICEF, Western-Africa).
Mahiri, J. (2011). *Digital tools in urban schools: Mediating a remix of learning*. University of Michigan Press.
Mahiri, J., & Sims, J. (2016). Engineering equity: A critical pedagogical approach to language and curriculum change for African American males in STEM. In Z. Babaci-Wilhite (Ed.), *Human rights, language in STEM education* (pp. 55–71). Sense Publishers and Springer.
Majhanovich, S. (2014). Neo-liberalism, globalization, language policy and practice issues in the Asia-Pacific region. *Asia Pacific Journal of Education, 34*(2), 168–183. https://doi.org/10.1080/02188791.2013.875650
Mchombo, S. (2016). Language, scientific knowledge, and the "context of learning" in African education. In Z. Babaci-Wilhite (Ed.), *Human rights, language in STEM education* (pp. 129–150). Sense Publishers and Springer.
Misiaszek, G. W. (2018). *Educating the global environmental citizen: Understanding ecopedagogy in local and global contexts*. Routledge. https://doi.org/10.4324/9781315204345
Misiaszek, L. I. (Ed.). (2020). *Exploring the complexities in global citizenship education: Hard spaces, methodologies, and ethics*. Routledge.
Ngugi wa Thiong'o, J. (1986, Republished in 1994). *Decolonising the mind: The politics of language in African literature*. James Curry.
Nyerere, J. K. (1967, Reprinted in 1968). Education for self-reliance. In *Essays on socialism* (pp. 44–75). Oxford University Press.
Odora Hoppers, C. (Ed.). (2002). Stories of the hunt—Who is writing them? In *Indigenous knowledge and the integration of knowledge systems. Towards a philosophy of articulation* (pp. 237–257). New Africa Education.
Okonkwo, J. I. (2014). Appropriate language in education: The strategy for national development in Nigeria. In Z. Babaci-Wilhite (Ed.), *Giving space to African voices: Right in local languages and local curriculum* (Vol. 33, pp. 131–146). Sense Publishers.
Pearson, P. D. (2007). An endangered species act for literacy education. *Journal of Literacy Research, 39*(2), 145–162.
Pearson, P. D., Moje, E., & Greenleaf, C. (2010). Literacy and science: Each in the service of the other. *Science, 328*, 459–463. https://doi.org/10.1126/science.1182595
Pearson, P. D., & Hiebert, E. H. (2013). Understanding the common core state standards. In L. Morrow, T. Shanahan, & K. K. Wixson (Eds.), *Teaching with the common core standards for English language arts: What educators need to know* (Book 1: Grades PreK-2; Book 2: Grades 3–5, pp. 1–21). Guilford Press.

Perrin, A. (2019). *One-in-five Americans now listen to audiobooks*. Retrieved January 2020, from https://www.pewresearch.org/fact-tank/2019/09/25/one-in-five-americans-now-listen-to-audiobooks/
Pew Research Center's Internet & American Life Reading Habits Survey. (2012, April 4). *The rise of e-reading*. libraries.pewinternet.org
Prah, K. K. (2005). Language of instruction for education, development and African emancipation. In B. Brock-Utne & R. K. Hopson (Eds.), *Languages of instruction for African emancipation: Focus on postcolonial contexts and considerations* (pp. 23–87). CASAS and Mkuki na Nyota.
Robeyns, I. (2006). Three models of education rights: Rights, capabilities and human capital. *Theory and Research in Education, 4*(1), 69–84.
Samoff, J. (2003, Re-edited 2007). Institutionalizing international influence. In R. F. Arnove & C. A. Torres (Eds.), *Comparative education: The dialectic of the global and the local* (pp. 52–91). Rowman & Littlefield Publishers.
Sath沮 Peder's Grant. (2016). *A University of California, Berkeley based project in collaboration with the University of Tromsd the Norwegian Center for Human Rights (Norway)*. In the video made by Vu, Babaci-Wilhite, Mahiri, Bostad, and Rngsbakk. https://www.youtube.com/watch?v=2Y9BiAJf8Gs&feature=youtu.be
Semali, L., & Khanjan, M. (2012). Science education in Tanzania: Challenges and policy responses. *International Journal of Educational Research, 53*, 225–239.
Skutnabb-Kangas, T. (2000). *Linguistic genocide in education or worldwide diversity and human rights?* Lawrence Erlbaum Associates.
Spreen, C. A., & Vally, S. (2006). Education rights, education policies and inequality in South Africa. *International Journal of Educational Development, 26*(4), 352–362.
Tomasevski, K. (2006). *Human rights obligation in education: The 4-A scheme*. Enfield Publishing & Distribution Company.
UNDP. (2006). *Human development report*. United Nations.
UNESCO. (2005). *Convention on the protection and promotion of the diversity of cultural expressions*. UNESCO.
United Nations. (1948). *The Universal Declaration on Human Rights*. Adopted by the General Assembly on 10 December 1948. United Nations.
Vu, V., Prado, Y., Yim, S., & Ngoc Le, P. (2021). Digital storytelling for academic literary. In Z. Babaci-Wilhite (Ed.), *Learning critical thinking in 21st century literacies for multidisciplinary courses*. Cognella.
Wolff, H. (2006). *Optimizing learning and education in Africa—The language factor: A stock-taking research on mother tongue and bilingual education in sub-Saharan Africa* (pp. 26–55). Association for the Development of Education in Africa (ADEA): UNESCO Institute for Education—Deutsche Gesellschaft technische Zusammenarbeit. ADEA 2006 Biennial Meeting (Libreville, Gabon, March 27–31, 2006).
World Bank. (2014). *Global infrastructure facility*. Retrieved June 1, 2021, from https://www.worldbank.org/en/topic/publicprivatepartnerships/brief/global-infrastructure-facility-backup
Wortham, S., & Jackson, K. (2012). Relational education: Applying Gergen's work to educational research and practice. *Psychological Studies, 57*(2), 164–171.

CHAPTER 17

Ecopedagogy: Critical Environmental Pedagogies to Disrupt Falsely Touted Sustainable Development

Greg William Misiaszek

INTRODUCTION

This chapter problematizes the need for critical-based environmental pedagogies to deepen and widen students' understandings of the politics of environmentalism and development grounded in sustainability within the world (i.e., all humans, human population) as *part of* Earth (i.e., all of Nature).[1,2] Sustainability emphasized here is globally holistic *and* planetarily balanced with the rest of Nature. Pedagogical deconstruction of the politics of environmental violence, especially systematically hidden politics, is essential to understand the deeper reasons why environmental violence occurs. Human acts of environmental violence would not occur without benefiting some person(s)/population(s). For example, deep-ocean oil drilling would be senseless unless there were benefits because it leads to numerous socio-environmental injustice and planetary unsustainability issues. In this chapter, I argue the need for, and discuss the grounding tenets of, *ecopedagogy* for teaching critical literacy to read who benefits from environmentally violent acts, who suffers from them, and how does the acts affect Nature both anthropocentrically and planetarily (i.e., human-centric *and* beyond humans)—*ecopedagogical literacy*.

G. W. Misiaszek (✉)
Faculty of Education, Institute of Educational Theories, Beijing Normal University, Beijing, China

© The Author(s), under exclusive license to Springer Nature Switzerland AG 2022
A. A. Abdi and G. W. Misiaszek (eds.), *The Palgrave Handbook on Critical Theories of Education*, https://doi.org/10.1007/978-3-030-86343-2_17

Ecopedagogical reading problematizes how coinciding and contrasting framings of 'development' result in differing populations benefiting or suffering, and (un)sustainability globally and planetarily (Misiaszek, 2015, 2020d). Reading 'sustainability' critically questions at what level do we sustain and is the level determined by justice, laws of Nature, and/or oppressive 'development' framings? Such questioning leads to asking what would be the socio-environmental outcome if the lower socio-economic 90%+ of the population had the lifestyles of the top 10%? Without question, it would lead to total environmental devastation. The top 10% can only accomplish such unsustainable 'lifestyles' on the backs of the masses. Ecopedagogy is an essential element of social justice pedagogies because environmentally violent actions are inherently political and most often benefit the few powerful while negatively affecting the vast powerless masses, aligning with unjust hierarchical power structures stemming from hegemony.

This chapter does not give enough space to delve into all aspects of ecopedagogies, as well as its practices, theories, and methodologies to (un)teach 'development' and 'sustainable development.' What will be focused upon key critical-based needs for environmental pedagogies with primary focus on Freirean-based ecopedagogy. I will first briefly give a brief overview of ecopedagogy and then discuss some of the key aspects.

Ecopedagogy

Ecopedagogies are critical, transformative environmental pedagogies that center praxis to end unsustainable environmental violence,[3] guided by deepened and widened understandings of our world within Earth. Although plural in framing, ecopedagogies emerged from Paulo Freire's popular education models of Latin America and his direct work on ecopedagogy in his later work (Gadotti, 2008b; Gutiérrez & Prado, 2008; Misiaszek, 2012; Misiaszek & Torres, 2019). Due to this chapter's rather short word-length constraints, I will not delve deeply into defining Freirean groundings within ecopedagogy, but rather I will discuss how and why his work and reinventions of his work are essential for teaching environmentalism and sustainable development.

Below is my definition of ecopedagogy.

> Ecopedagogy is essentially literacy education for reading and rereading human acts of environmental violence with its roots in popular education, as they are reinventions of the pedagogies of the Brazilian pedagogue and philosopher Paulo Freire. Ecopedagogies are grounded in critical thinking and transformability, with the ultimate goal being to construct learning with increased social and environmental justice. Rooted in critical theories and originating from popular education models of Latin America, ecopedagogy is centered on better understanding the connections between human acts of environmental violence and social violence that cause injustices/oppressions, domination over the rest of Nature, and planetary unsustainability. [Better understanding is] through the aspect of deepening and widening understandings from different perspectives,

ranging from the Self to local, to national, to global, to the planetary (Misiaszek, 2018). With this widening there is the aspect of environmental well-being—of not just ourselves and our communities, but of all of human populations together and Earth overall —which, as explained by Neera M. Singh (2019), calls for an extension of NIMBY to NIABY worldwide and NOPE that has a planetary scope. (Misiaszek, 2020c, pp. 16–17)[4]

Ecopedagogical literacy is for deepening and widening understandings of environmental violence to determine necessary transformative action emergent from critical theorizing (i.e., praxis), rather than environmental pedagogies that focus on students gaining environmental knowledges quantitatively (Misiaszek, 2012, 2015).

> Ecopedagogical work is both deepening and widening understandings for praxis toward balance with the rest of Earth and socio-environmental peace for the world. Reading the world locally to globally, as part of Earth-as part of the planetary sphere-is the essence of ecopedagogical work. Ecopedagogical work should widen our world as part of Earth, with our actions in the name of 'development' problematized within the planetary sphere. Such planetary perspectives are widened from critical global perspectives in which we act for socio-environmental justice for all the world-inclusive of all human beings. But it also includes the need for deepened understandings of locally contextualized perspectives. (Misiaszek, 2020c)

How (in)(non)formal education sustains, intensifies, or counters world-Earth unsustainability is essential to continuously (re-)read. Ecopedagogical reading must happen through socio-historical and local-to-global-to-planetary lenses, as well as knowledges we have of Earth beyond our world (i.e., facts and 'laws' of Nature that are not subjectively mendable by humans). Local-to-global ecopedagogical reading problematizes how socio-historical oppressions (e.g., coloniality, racism, patriarchy, neoliberalism, globalization *from above*, non-/citizenship othering, heteronormativity) have created, sustained, and intensified socio-environmental ills and planetary unsustainability. Critical pedagogies, such as ecopedagogues, have the goal of ending oppressions by centering the understanding unjust struggles from those who suffer from them (Gadotti, 1996).

As emphasized here, ecopedagogical literacy is not only for reading to better understand socio-environmental ills but for transformative praxis to end them. Ecopedagogues teach through problem-posing societies' structures for praxis with deepened and widened reflectivity on possibly actions for socio-environmental transformation within the anthroposphere. Social and environmental violence's inherently inseparability highlights the need for teaching to disrupt *distancing* that justifies environmental violence and planetary unsustainability. Distancing (e.g., geographically, time-wise, othering) of environmental violence's causes and effects from one's self and community is too-often ideologically taught to falsely justify injustices and unsustainable development. Teaching for de-distancing innately grounds ecopedagogical work for unlearning ideological "reasoning" for unsustainable environmental violence (Misiaszek, 2012, 2020c).

Differing from Other Environmental Pedagogies

Environmental pedagogies (e.g., environmental education [EE], education for sustainable development [ESD], ecopedagogy) are often publicly viewed as interchangeable; however, the essence of each and the politics of specific approaches to them are essential. Environmental teaching is inherently political with differing processes, goals, and practices, which form contested terrains of teaching socio-environmental justice, sustainable development, and/or planetary sustainability. EE models have historically been critiqued for overlooking oppressive social issues caused by environmentally harmful acts (McKeown & Hopkins, 2003). ESD models emerged largely to focus teaching on how environmental issues affect societies to better understand how actions for development can minimize the negative environmental outcomes—"'sustainable' 'development.'"

The critical deconstruction of politics grounding ecopedagogies does not only define ecopedagogical research but also is part of ecopedagogical spaces. In other words, problematizing what is learned from environmental pedagogies and *pedagogies on the environment*[5] must be critically deconstructed to truly understand their ideological foundations. This includes problematizing how do the politics of both pedagogies positively and/or negatively affect subjectivity within our world *with* the rest of Nature's non-subjectivity (i.e., non-reflectivity due to the lack cognitive abilities of everything outside of human beings). Environmental pedagogues that teach for environmental violence *a*politically fail to teach why they happen in order to benefit, frequently, only a few while many other suffer and Nature is destroyed.

The simplification of answering this question and the separating social and environmental oppressions in learning space are political pedagogical tools to rationalize injustices and unsustainability. As discussed previously, environmental justice is inseparable from social justice, environmental violence inseparable from social violence, and planetary sustainability is inseparable from peace; however, many pedagogies often distance these inherent connections. Shallow teaching through apoliticization and distancing happens in various ways, including placing environmental devastation into a single disciplinary and a single, often dominant, epistemological framing (Misiaszek, 2012). By disrupting environmental pedagogies that impede deconstructing the politics of unsustainable environmental violence, ecopedagogical reinventions allow for students to determine what is needed to be done to disrupt the violence itself.

Planetary Widening

Ecopedagogy might be initially viewed as being anthropocentric by focusing on politics within our world; however, it is planetary because its widened perspectives of how our politic affects the rest of Nature affecting 'us' (anthropocentrically) and beyond humans' interests (non-anthropocentrically). It is humans' actions for socio-environmental (in)justice that determine (un)sustainability within the planetary sphere, including the world. Nature has the essence of being balanced with only humans as reflective entities that challenge this equilibrium. In short, human actions disrupt and challenge such balance (i.e., sustainability). Humans are also the source of justice and injustice for the world-Earth, as the rest of Nature cannot offer (in)justice without being able to be reflective (Warren, 2000)—or as Freire (2000) argued, absent of histories and cognition to act upon one's own dream (i.e., utopia and education arguments). For example, a wolf attacking a child due to hunger, or a typhoon destroying a town. Although both are tragic, the wolf and typhoon do not happen through reflectivity but due to survival and atmospheric air pressure systems returning to equilibrium.

Ecopedagogical planetarization of teaching problematizes knowledges and epistemologies that have our world within or outside of Earth as factors in determining actions for development. This includes too-often conceptualized goals of modernity the reside outside the concerns for the rest of Nature that, in turn, leads to 'development' framings without possibilities of planetary sustainability (Misiaszek, 2020e). Many critical scholars have argued this including Ivan Illich (1983) who, in his book <u>Deschooling Society,</u> argued that *contemporary man* has increasingly viewed himself outside Nature's control as opposed to *classical man* who sometimes acted against Nature but recognized there would be consequences. A key question is how can environmental pedagogies counter entrenching ideologies of Illich's contemporary (wo)man?

Outside the anthropocentric sphere, *laws of Nature*'s truths are static with our (i.e., humans') perspectives as incomplete and politically subjective. Incompleteness stems from us not knowing all the complexities of Nature holistically, although we are, or should be, continuously trying to better understand all of Nature. Ecopedagogical work problematizes the politics of socio-environmental oppressions from the subjective historically constructed world upon Earth's objective laws of Nature. This includes problematizing how is learning the static laws of Nature disrupted by falsely taught ideologies that the laws are fluid and mendable within humans' subjectivity. In addition, self-reflectivity of the limitations of knowing the rest of Nature is also essential, with contemporary (wo)man too-often lacking such cognitive processing, especially with current intensification of post-truthism (a topic discussed more later).

*d/D*EVELOPMENT

'Development' is too infrequently debated critically within and between contexts but is touted without critical reflection as rationalizing the need for socio-environmental actions. Ecopedagogical literacy centers the mapping of what defines 'development' as inherently political, socio-historical, and socio-environmentally dependent. 'Sustainability' is often brought into the argument to limit such actions; however, it is often overshadowed by economic development, especially within neoliberal globalization that normalizes world-Earth distancing. Examples of neoliberal world-Earth distancing occur whenever economic profit is overly valued above considering, if at all, the environmental devastation caused by the profiteering that only benefits specific population(s). A more specific example would be Northern mining operations within the Global South which do not care about the environmental effects upon the local populations but profit for the (trans-international) corporation with only a fraction of economic benefits received by the local mining population(s). In this example, *D*evelopment distances environmental effects in all decision-making and thus 'world-Earth distancing is occurring.' Together, understanding 'sustainable development' is crucial to guiding action but only when it is taught and read critically, within a biocentric framing which is locally-to-globally-to-planetarily contextualized.

As ecopedagogical learning spaces are Freirean, teacher(s) and students democratically learn and teach together to understand ESD's contested terrain of empowering and oppressive outcomes. There are various tenets of Freirean-based dialogue within these spaces. Ecopedagogical spaces are also inevitably full of conflict, with coinciding and contrasting thoughts of 'good' or 'bad' development, must be safe so students can have Freirean, *authentic dialogue* without feeling threatened. Coinciding with Freirean pedagogy, dialogue within ecopedagogical spaces counter ideologies that are viewed as ahistorical, apolitical, and epistemologically singular. It is essential to note that Freirean dialogue in learning spaces called for the end of teachers' authoritarianism but not their authority, an important distinction, in which the former grounds banking education but not the latter (Freire, 1997, 2000).

Ecopedagogical tools problematize the politics of environmental violence that causes social oppressions within the world and Earth's unsustainability. This includes ecopedagogical reading of the politics of 'development' and 'sustainable development', as well as actions emergent from them. The crucial question of teaching for "progress" is how the *goal(s)* are defined that are inherently better than the current situation(s) to teach toward. Ecopedagogical reading of the connections between human populations and the rest of the planet, to determine the connections between 'development,' 'livelihood,', and overall well-being to counter environmental violence that is inseparable to social violence/injustice (and vice versa) (Gadotti, 2008a, 2008b; Gadotti & Torres, 2009; Kahn, 2010; Misiaszek, 2011, 2018, 2020c, 2020d). In how we teach the concepts and possible actions toward "development" (or progress), teachers must problematize what (un)sustainable, (anti-environmental), and socio-environmental (un)just action are we ideologically promoting.

Disrupting development singularly framed and measured by hierarchical upward positioning compared to others and increased accumulation is a key goal ecopedagogy (Misiaszek, 2018, 2020d). Although such logic can be very much problematized, it is problematizing the defining masters by their slaves (a la Hegel), or by the numbers of people "beneath" them (false 'success,' a la Freire [2000]), in which liberation emerges from the "slaves" recognizing their own bottom-up power. Banking education, including shallow environmental pedagogies, systematically suppresses such power. This includes teaching toward oppression by ideologically framing labor and natural resource usage for *D*evelopment to benefit the "masters" rather than *d*evelopment for themselves, humans overall, and planetary sustainability. The passage below briefly define *d/D*evelopment differences:

> ...lowercased development and uppercased *D*evelopment indicate, respectively, empowering versus oppressive, holistic versus hegemonic, just versus unjust, sustainable versus unsustainable, and many other opposing framings of who is included within "development" and framings of *d/D*evelopment goals. There are no absolute origins or framings differentiating *d/D*evelopment, but rather the essence and outcomes of their framings. (Misiaszek, 2020c)

Pinpointing, understanding, and then countering environmental violence for *D*evelopment masked as *d*evelopment perverting education as the masking tool is a goal of ecopedagogical literacy (Misiaszek, 2018, 2020c, 2020d). Teaching to disrupt *D*evelopment as *d*evelopment is an ecopedagogical foundation, as well as disrupting sustainability ideologies, models, and baselines that lead to *D*evelopment rather than *d*evelopment.

GLOBALIZATIONS: DECOLONIALITY OR NEOCOLONIALITY

To teach deepened understandings of sustainable development and globalization, ecopedagogues must problem-pose how, as a global society, do we determine what to sustain and at what level of sustainability? In short, what are the baselines of 'sustainability' that is locally-to-globally-to-planetarily *d*evelopment and sustainable—a balance of being locally contextual, globally holistic, and planetarily aligned with the laws of Nature? Currently, are baselines determined through local and/or global lenses, as well as are they determined anthropocentrically or planetarity? I argue that making this determination through global lenses creates a deficit-framed determination of sustainability because global demands on local societies are almost always impossible and they structurally "export" socio-environmental ills (from the 'globalizers' to the 'globalized'), thus creating distanced local societies unsustainable (Misiaszek, 2020d). Reproductive environmental pedagogies instilled upon the globalized are essential for sustaining/intensifying globalizers' hegemony because such teaching avoids problematizing socio-environmental harmful effects from *D*evelopment. These are effects from globalization from above; however, 'globalization' is best conceptualized as plural.

I utilize the plural term of globalization*s*, as Carlos Alberto Torres (2009) has framed, to indicate that processes of globalizations can be either empowering or disempowering (e.g., globalizer/globalized, from below/from above) and thus demand rigorous, contextual analysis to better understand who/what[6] are negatively or positively affected. Reading how the contested terrain of globalizations affects local societies both currently and historically is essential to better understand the multilayered dynamics of unsustainable environmental violence.

There are various reasons for needing the analysis of processes of globalization (mis)guiding sustainable *d*/*D*evelopment and (anti-)environmentalism. One of the most obvious reasons is that environmental ills do not respect geo-political borders, especially the term's "-political" part. Countering the myth that globalization and education research is through only macro-lenses, micro analysis through local lenses on how globalizations' affects local communities is central. Distancing socio-environmental effects upon far away local populations is aligned with Giddens (1990) famous defining of globalization in which he centers global "link[ing]" effects upon "distant localities... many miles away and vice versa."[7] The need to understand the commonalities and differences between what diverse populations view as socio-environmental *d*evelopment is essential with the recognition that environmental issues are almost always never contained locally and are often globally far-reaching in their effect.

As discussed previously, histography is an essential part of ecopedagogical work and disrupting coloniality for decolonial praxis cannot be absent from this work. What is necessary in analyzing globalization within a "postcolonial" world is how its processes can counter colonial-structured education oppressions rather than often sustaining such oppressions arising from neocoloniality (Abdi, 2008). Ecopedagogy inherently counters globalizations from above, which can be fittingly termed as *neocoloniality*, through acts of unsustainable environmental violence.

There are innumerable socio-historical aspects of oppressions from colonializations and globalizations that can be characterized as neocolonial with *D*evelopment ideologies purposely taught as *d*evelopment. Teaching to better determine the oppressive and empowering framings of development is largely through analyzing histories of defining *d*/*D*evelopment, as well as false ideological teaching to veil *d*evelopment for oppressive *D*evelopment to continue without protest. In short ([EPAT 2020—PT], neocolonial global governance purposely discourages possibilities of localized democratic participation [Dale, 2005]).

Although impossible to fully know, understanding histories of colonialism that had led to socio-environmental injustices for the (neo)colonialized and planetary unsustainability are unceasing ecopedagogical goals. Key to this goal is dismissing the myth that the world has been wiped clean from coloniality's thick residue (Grosfoguel, 2008). Without decoloniality, environmental pedagogies become/remain tools to sustain (neo)coloniality and coinciding Development (Misiaszek, 2020c, 2020d).

Epistemological (Re)reading and (Un)learning

Ecopedagogues utilize the work of post-/de-colonial scholars such as de Sousa Santos (2007, 2016, 2018) and Raewyn Connell (2007, 2013) on epistemologies of the South that inherently counter pedagogies and associated research based on epistemologies of the North. Ecopedagogical literacy includes reading what epistemologies are socio-environmental "knowledges" being taught through, including the socio-historical grounding of the ways of knowing as Boaventura de Sousa Santos (2018) differentiates between those of the South and North (Misiaszek, 2019). Processes of legitimizing knowledges and ways of knowing Earth, paralleling globalizations' contested terrain, can be inside, outside and/or between epistemologies of the South and those of the North. The innate hegemonic dominance of epistemologies of the North negates epistemological diversity, which de Sousa Santos (2018) termed *epistemicide*, thus countering diverse epistemological teaching, reading, and praxis (a.k.a., *ecologies of knowledges*). Reworded in my own terminology in this chapter, ecopedagogical work needs to de-distance (or legitimize) epistemologies of the South to counter epistemologies of the North.

Ecopedagogical deconstruction of the politics of epistemological (de)legitimization is essential to understand how specific knowing leads toward socio-environmental injustices and unsustainability due, in part, to how anthropocentrism, world-Earth distancing, and Development are shaped and reinforced. These influences are not absent in academic scholarship as disciplinary foundations must be epistemologically problematized for what de Sousa Santos (2018) argued as disciplinary *absences* for needed disciplinary *emergences* to materialize in transformational and often radical ways. This chapter does not provide the space to elaborate upon the complexities between epistemologies of the South/North; but below de Sousa Santos (2018) described epistemologies of the North—grounded in coloniality, patriarchy, and capitalism—from epistemological perspectives of the South:

> From the standpoint of the epistemologies of the South, the epistemologies of the North have contributed crucially to converting the scientific knowledge developed in the global North into the hegemonic way of representing the world as one's own and of transforming it according to one's own needs and aspirations. In this way, scientific knowledge, combined with superior economic and military power, granted the global North the imperial domination of the world in the modern era up to our very days. (2018, p. 6)

De Sousa Santos (2018) argues that epistemologies of the South exist to counter epistemologies of the North to sustain/intensify coloniality, patriarchy, and capitalism. Such epistemological analysis coincides with Edward Said's (1979) Orientalism, and arguments from decoloniality scholars such as Albert Memmi and Franz Fanon.

De Sousa Santos directly argued that epistemological hegemony, leading to epistemicide, cannot lead to environmentalism or sustainability in the following quote:

> Nature, turned by the epistemologies of the North into an infinitely available resource, has no inner logic but that of being exploited to its exhaustion. For the first time in human history, capitalism is on the verge of touching the limits of nature. (Santos, 2016, p. 19)

Traditional sociological goals are to deepen and widen our understandings of the anthroposphere. However, ecopedagogical work bends and stretches the sociology beyond anthropocentricism that, in turn, challenges its foundation(s) (such as capitalism above) which cannot be done within the absences from epistemologies of the North. Because humans are *part* of Earth, true sustainability cannot singularly lie within our own understandings from interactions both with one another as social beings and us with the rest of Nature, but also outside of our world and cognitive reflectivity. It is important to note ecopedagogical literacy must be through ecologies of knowledges for deepened and widened self-reflectivity, because reading must not only strengthen previously held epistemological foundations but also challenge them. And, sometimes needing to unlearn them. With global dominance, this means that reflectivity is most frequently bounded by epistemologies of the North that, as argued previously, cannot lead to environmental justice or sustainable *d*evelopment due to the entrenchment of coloniality, patriarchy, and capitalism.

Economics: Justice and Sustainability, Versus Neoliberalism

Ecopedagogical work must deconstruct local-to-global economics to determine praxis for economics saturated with goals for socio-environmental justice, *d*evelopment, and Earth's well-being beyond anthropocentricism. Economics also form a contested terrain of models; however, ecopedagogues are inherently the nemeses to neoliberal economics—capitalism on steroids. Roger Dale (2018) argued that "[a]t base, the 'global' does not represent the universal human interest, but the interests of capitalism; it represents particular local and parochial interests which have been globalized through the scope of its reach" (p. 68). Streeck et al. (2016) exemplify this by arguing that the West has:

de-coupl[ed] the fate of the rich from that of the poor; *the plunder[ed] of the public economy*, which had once been both an indispensable counterweight and a supportive infrastructure to capitalism, through fiscal consolidation and the privatization of public services (Bowman, 2014); systemic de-moralization; and international anarchy. (p. 167)

Neoliberalism only centers the Self's private sphere to, in turn, devalue all of the public spheres, including the vastest sphere of Earth holistically (Postma, 2006).

For example, neoliberal-grounded environmental pedagogies (an oxymoron) solely problematize socio-environmental ills upon economics to sustain and intensify hegemony without concerns that ground ecopedagogies. It is important to note that teachers are often uncritically unaware of neoliberal ideologies being instilled by them, coinciding with arguments of deeply engrained epistemologies of the North to be taken as apolitical and without alternatives. Neoliberalism continues to exist by having environmental teaching that blocks critical questioning its ideology, hiding who really benefits, suppresses knowledge on the vastness of suffering, and instilling that there are no alternatives to neoliberalism or neoliberal-framed _D_evelopment. Neoliberalism innately distances 'us' from one another and from the rest of Nature (i.e., world-Earth distancing). Ecopedagogues teach to problematize and critically reading what is "development" and "livelihood" including and beyond the realm of economics, to better understand the environmental burden that those who "have" place upon the "have-nots." and upon the rest of Nature. Teaching through rigorous theorizing of otherness and oppressions emergent from 'development' ideologies is essential to disrupt normalized neoliberal-grounded livelihood and _D_evelopment.

Ecopedagogical lessons for _d_evelopment must include the discussions within and between private and public spheres, as well as a continuum of citizenship spheres from local to planetary. This includes juxtaposition problem-posing of livelihood as dis/commented with framings of _d_/_D_evelopment. Neoliberalism's infatuation of the private sphere, the public sphere, traditionally defined as the relationship between citizens and the State, negatively, as a non-private sphere, devalues both in priority and in action (Capella, 2000; Postma, 2006). Livelihood framings construct our developments' goals, with specific focus on neoliberalism, through our roles and responsibilities as citizens (from local-to-planetary spheres) within private and public spheres. Citizenships is the topic of the next section.

CITIZENSHIPS: LOCAL-TO-PLANETARY

Histories of citizenship have created solidarity with populations, but too commonly it's through othering of "non-citizens" initializing and continuing public education ideological training aligning non-/citizens with socio-historical oppressions. Ecopedagogical work problematizes how can constructs of citizenship both deepen our understandings and solidarity for one another beyond the traditional framings of citizenship and for the rest of Nature.

I (2012, 2015, 2018) have argued that citizenships' plurality is essential, indicating local-to-global-and-planetary citizenship spheres.

> The inclusion of citizenship is not singular; it could be framed as inclusive of different degrees of civil connectedness between planetary, global, and nation-state citizenships. Such incorporations are necessary for social-environmental well-being to exist. (Gutiérrez & Prado, 1989; Misiaszek, 2015, p. 281)

Solidarity is a core aspect of citizenship, and looking at the concept of livelihood through various spheres leads to an expanded view of progress and what should be sustained through multiple levels, from local to planetary. Moacir Gadotti defined planetary citizenship as "an expression that was adopted to express a group of principles, values, attitudes and habits that reveal a new perception of Earth as a single community" (2008a, p. 8). Planetary citizenship highlights the need for ecologies of knowledges, as epistemologies of the North objectify and commodify Nature for profit within systems of capitalism. Education for *D*evelopment is development for only, at the very most, those considered as 'fellow citizens' without concern of deemed non-citizens' de-*d*evelopment or, even less, the devastation of nature (purposely lower-cased).

Planetary citizenship helps us to acknowledge that focusing on justice and peace only within the anthroposphere is problematic, thus objectifying the rest of Nature and separating 'us' as the sole determining factor. This previous sentence is actually impossible due to social-environmental inseparably as argues throughout this chapter, as peace within the anthroposphere is impossible without planetary peace/sustainability. For such planetary solidarity, we must teach through epistemologies, disciplines, perspectives, and fields that are often ignored, as well as ecopedagogically reading why such ignorance is systematically constructed. Examples of largely dismissed 'items' within many environmental pedagogies include the following important aspects within ecopedagogies: the 'residue' of the philosophies, ecolinguistical analysis on how we utter all that is non-human (e.g., 'who'/'what', 'Earth'/'the earth'), epistemologies of the South that counter the objectification of Nature, and an overly humanizing characterization of Nature (e.g., conserving only esthetically pleasing animals and environments rather than see the values of diverse ecosystems).

Post-Truthism

The increased rise of post-truthism within environmental public pedagogy is one of ecopedagogues' greatest threats needing to be countered. Post-truth*ism* centers false 'truths' solely emergent from specific ideologies not grounded in truth-seeking, without listening to authentic others' truths, perspectives, and realities, or within the known laws of Nature. Critically reading how post-truth*ism* constructs socio-environmental knowledges and associated framings of development that deceptively touts opinioned-falsities as truths, is increasingly essential as post-truthism seems to be spreading at expediential rates. This leads to the following key concern: how can critical, authentic dialogue occur in the post-truth era? Post-truthism obliterates any baseline of agreed upon facts for dialogue to exist, critical or otherwise. Ecopedagogical spaces that center critical, authentic dialogue is the enemy of post-truthism.

Post-truth falsifies *D*evelopment as benefiting the masses and planetary sustainability as unimportant at best and absolute denial at worse, too-often saturated with conspiracy theories. From epistemological hubris of the North, post-truth*ism* has intensified with false lessons that opinions from our subjective world will alter the laws of Nature which have outcomes absent of any subjectivity (Misiaszek, 2020a). Ideological opinions replace facts in post-truth*ism* to reject 'truths' that counters self-determined benefits within a specific ideology(ies) that oppose plural, multicultural understandings, and ignore or manipulate all other epistemologies that are self-contradictory. Within the realm of environmentalism, post-truthism often goes a step(s) further by blaming diversity and environmentally sound actions as causes of 'our' oppressions, rather than the actual culprit—unsustainable environmental violence.

Post-truth epistemologies strengthen ideological opinions rather than authentic pursuits for truths. Thus, epistemological framings emergent from post-truth*ism* pervert world-Earth (mis)understandings confined to closed, ideologically singular ones. Post-truth*ism* increasingly twists our understandings of nature to one's ideological opinions to, quite literally, breaking them (i.e., outside of Apple's [2004] defined *basic rules* as opposed to selectable *preference rules*). In addition, persons (un)consciously utilizing post-truth*ism* either ignore incompleteness of knowledges as they discuss their opinions as truths or call upon incompleteness to ignore scientific truths that oppose their opinions.

Ecopedagogical work is essential to countering post-truth populism that falsely reconstructs truths and truth-seeking to coincide with *D*evelopment. Such reconstructions are systematic, most frequently unknown by the those believing but systematically constructed for ideological coherence through instilling ignorance. Teaching to read the politics of such systematic ideological perversion that manipulates socio-environmental truths is an ecopedagogical goal; post-truthism is a sounding alarm of needing ecopedagogy with truths being entirely disregarded for ignorant, blinded devotion that will only lead to total environmental devastation.

CONCLUSION

Several scholars have argued that the Second World War marked two defining moments that emphasized the need of critical pedagogy to counter the blind following of authoritarianism that led to Nazism and the horrific Holocaust, and the first time the human race could blow the world entirely up with the invention of the atomic bomb (Pongratz, 2005). Scholars have also discussed this time in history as screaming the need for a Kuhnian paradigm shift toward peace education (Harris & Morrison, 2003). Although differing in contexts, untethered environmental violence is unquestionably leading us toward a bleak, fatalistic future in which the recognition of needing radical change and critical education for it may take place beyond the tipping point. Hopefully not. I (Misiaszek, 2020b, 2020f) have written that COVID-19 has provided us lessons on the devastative results when the rest of Nature is ignored due to politics of being 'inconvenient' to current social systems, especially guided by neoliberalism (e.g., shutdowns disrupt capitalism, health systems guided by humanistic concerns and medical knowledges rather than the market, solidarity of wearing masks to protect the most vulnerable prioritized rather than mask-wearing as an individualistic choice linked to 'freedom'); however, if these lessons are widely learned remains largely to be seen. My arguments of needing Freirean-based ecopedagogy here in this chapter can be critiqued but needing environmental pedagogies for transformative action is an indisputable certainty.

NOTES

1. "Education" and "pedagogy(ies)" include schooling (i.e., formal education), but also non-formal and informal (i.e., public pedagogies) education.
2. The article "the" will not be used with "Earth" to not linguistically objectify Earth and will be upper-case. Coinciding with "Earth," N̲ature will be upper-cased.
3. "Sustainable" here is important because there are continuums of environmental violence (e.g., from turning on a computer to mountain top removal [MTR] for mining).
4. NIMBY: Not In My Backyard; NIABY: Not In Anybody's Backyard.
5. My own work on *environmental pedagogies* separates them that have goals of "being environmental" and *pedagogies on the environment* that teaches on the environment, but the goals can be either environmental or not (education, in both models, must include and be well beyond schooling, with in/non/formal pedagogies).
6. The terms "who/what" is given to signify a biocentric framing of contextualizing globalization which does not only include human but also all other life beings and the non-organic natural world (e.g., landscapes, seascapes).
7. Globalization as "the intensification of worldwide social relations which link distant localities in such a way that local happenings are shaped by events occurring many miles away and vice versa" (Giddens, 1990, p. 64).

REFERENCES

Abdi, A. A. (2008). De-subjecting subject populations: Historico-actual problems and educational possibilities. In A. A. Abdi & L. Shultz (Eds.), *Educating for human rights and global citizenship* (pp. 65–80). State University of New York Press.
Apple, M. W. (2004). *Ideology and curriculum* (3rd ed.). Routledge.
Bowman, A. (2014). *The end of the experiment? From competition to the foundational economy*. Manchester University Press.
Capella, J.-R. (2000). Globalization, a fading citizenship. In N. C. Burbules & C. A. Torres (Eds.), *Globalization and education: Critical perspectives* (pp. 227–252). Routledge.
Connell, R. (2007). *Southern theory: The global dynamics of knowledge in social science*. Polity.
Connell, R. (2013). Using southern theory: Decolonizing social thought in theory, research and application. *Planning Theory, 13*(2), 210–223. https://doi.org/10.1177/1473095213499216
Dale, R. (2005). Globalisation, knowledge economy and comparative education. *Comparative Education, 41*(2), 117–149. http://www.informaworld.com/smpp/content~content=a772749155
Dale, R. (2018, September). Framing post-SDG prospects for 'education for development'. *Global Comparative Education: Journal of the World Council of Comparative Education Societies (WCCES), 2*(2), 62–75.
Freire, P. (1997). *Pedagogy of the heart*. Continuum.
Freire, P. (2000). *Pedagogy of the oppressed*. Continuum.
Gadotti, M. (1996). *Pedagogy of praxis: A dialectical philosophy of education*. SUNY Press.
Gadotti, M. (2008a). *Education for sustainability: A critical contribution to the decade of education for sustainable development*. University of São Paulo, Paulo Freire Institute.
Gadotti, M. (2008b). *Education for sustainable development: What we need to learn to save the planet*. Instituto Paulo Freire.
Gadotti, M., & Torres, C. A. (2009). Paulo Freire: Education for development. *Development and Change, 40*(6), 1255–1267. https://doi.org/10.1111/j.1467-7660.2009.01606.x
Giddens, A. (1990). *The consequences of modernity*. Stanford University Press.
Grosfoguel, R. (2008). Decolonizing political-economy and postcolonial studies: Transmodernity, border thinking, and global coloniality. *Revista Crítica de Ciências Sociais, 2008*(80), 115–147.
Gutiérrez, F., & Prado, C. (1989). *Ecopedagogia e cidadania planetária* [Ecopedagogy and planetarian citizenship]. Cortez.
Gutiérrez, F., & Prado, C. (2008). *Ecopedagogia e cidadania planetária*. Instituto Paulo Freire.
Harris, I. M., & Morrison, M. L. (2003). *Peace education* (2nd ed.). McFarland.
Illich, I. (1983). *Deschooling society* (1st Harper Colophon ed.). Harper Colophon.
Kahn, R. (2010). *Critical pedagogy, ecoliteracy, and planetary crisis: The ecopedagogy movement* (Vol. 359). Peter Lang.
McKeown, R., & Hopkins, C. (2003). EE ESD: Defusing the worry. *Environmental Education Research, 9*(1), 117–128. http://www.informaworld.com/10.1080/13504620303469

Misiaszek, G. W. (2011). *Ecopedagogy in the age of globalization: Educators' perspectives of environmental education programs in the Americas which incorporate social justice models*. Ph.D., University of California, Los Angeles, Dissertations & Theses: Full Text. https://search.proquest.com/openview/d2d5c04ffc0e8d63441b3a9797643b07/1?pq-origsite=gscholar&cbl=18750&diss=y (Publication No. AAT 3483199).

Misiaszek, G. W. (2012). Transformative environmental education within social justice models: Lessons from comparing adult ecopedagogy within North and South America. In D. N. Aspin, J. Chapman, K. Evans, & R. Bagnall (Eds.), *Second international handbook of lifelong learning* (Vol. 26, pp. 423–440). Springer.

Misiaszek, G. W. (2015). Ecopedagogy and citizenship in the age of globalisation: Connections between environmental and global citizenship education to save the planet. *European Journal of Education, 50*(3), 280–292. https://doi.org/10.1111/ejed.12138

Misiaszek, G. W. (2018). *Educating the global environmental citizen: Understanding ecopedagogy in local and global contexts*. Routledge.

Misiaszek, G. W. (2019). The end of the cognitive empire: The coming of age of epistemologies of the South by Boaventura de Sousa Santos. *Comparative Education Review, 63*(3), 452–454. https://doi.org/10.1086/704137

Misiaszek, G. W. (2020a). Countering post-truths through ecopedagogical literacies: Teaching to critically read "development" and "sustainable development." *Educational Philosophy and Theory, 52*(7), 747–758. https://doi.org/10.1080/00131857.2019.1680362

Misiaszek, G. W. (2020b). COVID-19 foreshadowing Earth's environmental tipping point: Education's transformation needed to avoid the ledge. *Educational Philosophy and Theory, Add* (with "Reimagining the new pedagogical possibilities for universities post-Covid-19" by Peters, Michael A.; Rizvi, Fazal; McCulloch, Gary; Gibbs, Paul; Gorur, Radhika; Hong, Moon Hwang; Yoonjung, Zipin; Lew, Brennan, Marie; Robertson, Susan; Quay, John; Malbon, Justin; Taglietti, Danilo; Barnett, Ronald; Chengbing, Wang; McLaren, Peter; Apple, Rima; Papastephanou, Marianna; Burbules, Nick; Jackson, Liz; Jalote, Pankaj; Kalantzis, Mary; Cope, Bill; Fataar, Aslam; Conroy, James; Misiaszek, Greg William; Biesta, Gert; Jandrić, Petar; Choo, Susanne; Apple, Michael; Stone, Lynda; Tierney, Rob; Tesar, Marek; Besley, Tina & Misiaszek, Lauren), 31–32. https://doi.org/10.1080/00131857.2020.1777655

Misiaszek, G. W. (2020c). *Ecopedagogy: Critical environmental teaching for planetary justice and global sustainable development*. Bloomsbury.

Misiaszek, G. W. (2020d). Ecopedagogy: Teaching critical literacies of 'development', 'sustainability', and 'sustainable development.' *Teaching in Higher Education, 25*(5), 615–632. https://doi.org/10.1080/13562517.2019.1586668

Misiaszek, G. W. (2020e). Locating and diversifying modernity: Deconstructing knowledges to counter development for a few. In M. A. Peters, T. Besley, P. Jandrić, & X. Zhu (Eds.), *Knowledge socialism: The rise of peer production: Collegiality, collaboration, and collective intelligence* (pp. 253–276). Springer Nature.

Misiaszek, G. W. (2020f). Will we learn from COVID-19? Ecopedagogical calling (un)heard. *Knowledge Cultures, 8*(3), 28–33. https://doi.org/10.22381/KC8320204

Misiaszek, G. W., & Torres, C. A. (2019). Ecopedagogy: The missing chapter of pedagogy of the oppressed. In C. A. Torres (Ed.), *Wiley handbook of Paulo Freire* (pp. 463–488). Wiley-Blackwell.

Pongratz, L. (2005). Critical theory and pedagogy: Theodor W. Adorno and Max Horkheimer's contemporary significance for a critical pedagogy. In G. Fischman, P. McLaren, H. Sunker, & C. Lankshear (Eds.), *Critical theories, radical pedagogies, and global conflicts* (pp. 154–163). Rowman & Littlefield Publishers.

Postma, D. W. (2006). *Why care for nature? In search of an ethical framework for environmental responsibility and education*. Springer.

Said, E. W. (1979). *Orientalism*. Vintage Books.

Santos, B. d. S. (2007). Beyond abyssal thinking: From global lines to ecologies of knowledges. *Review (Fernand Braudel Center), 30*(1), 45–89. http://www.jstor.org/stable/40241677

Santos, B. d. S. (2016). Epistemologies of the South and the future. *From the European South: A Transdisciplinary Journal of Postcolonial Humanities, 1,* 17–29.

Santos, B. d. S. (2018). *The end of the cognitive empire: The coming of age of epistemologies of the South*. Duke University Press.

Singh, N. M. (2019). Environmental justice, degrowth and post-capitalist futures. *Ecological Economics, 163,* 138–142. https://doi.org/10.1016/j.ecolecon.2019.05.014

Streeck, W., Calhoun, C., Toynbee, P., & Etzioni, A. (2016). Does capitalism have a future? *Socio-Economic Review, 14*(1), 163–183. https://doi.org/10.1093/ser/mwv037

Torres, C. A. (2009). *Chapter 1: Globalizations and education: Collected essays on class, race, gender, and the state*. Teachers College Press.

Warren, K. J. (2000). *Ecofeminist philosophy: A Western perspective on what it is and why it matters*. Rowman & Littlefield Publications.

PART V

Critical Media/Information Studies and Education

CHAPTER 18

Postdigital Critical Pedagogy

Petar Jandrić and Sarah Hayes

INTRODUCTION: LIVING IN THE WORLD OF COMBINED CRISES

2020 was a year to remember—and, for most of us, a year we would also like to forget. But forgetting is not an option; the world will never return to its pre-pandemic condition. As the Covid-19 crisis has shaken the fundamentals of our societies and global order, the world has experienced a crisis comparable to wars, earthquakes, and other large-scale natural and human-made disasters. Some of us, including co-authors of this chapter Petar and Sarah, have experienced a combination of several immediate crises. Living in Zagreb, Croatia, Petar experienced a strong earthquake in the middle of the first wave of lockdowns. In a recent article, Jandrić analyzed some implications of such combined crises.

> In the midst of unprecedented lockdown measures, Zagreb was hit by the strongest earthquake in 140 years—and its citizens were equally unprepared for both. To add insult to injury, recommended responses to these disasters are

P. Jandrić (✉)
Zagreb University of Applied Sciences, Zagreb, Croatia
e-mail: pjandric@tvz.hr

P. Jandrić · S. Hayes
University of Wolverhampton, Wolverhampton, UK
e-mail: sarah.hayes@wlv.ac.uk

© The Author(s), under exclusive license to Springer Nature Switzerland AG 2022
A. A. Abdi and G. W. Misiaszek (eds.), *The Palgrave Handbook on Critical Theories of Education*, https://doi.org/10.1007/978-3-030-86343-2_18

directly opposed—the virus is avoided by staying at home, while (the consequences of) the earthquake are avoided by going out. Faced with the invisible threat of the virus and the visible threat of being buried alive, no-one has returned to their flats. (Jandrić, 2020, p. 34)

Such situations reveal the contradictions arising through the 'lived experiences' of a pandemic. What is advised in government policy discourse, or reported through varying accounts across the global media, is also 'lived' in an individual 'postdigital positionality' (Hayes, 2021). Each of us meets the pandemic personally and environmentally, via a complex intersectionality of our biological, social, and technological circumstances. Living in the United Kingdom, Sarah Hayes did not have to navigate the devastation and trauma of an earthquake. She does though live close to the River Severn which floods dangerously and persistently, this time during lockdown, and requiring many to evacuate their homes. In a collection of testimonies Jandrić and Hayes edited in Spring 2020, she described her ongoing, complex family caring responsibilities that require emergency travel at short notice, levels of personal care she has no training for, and decisions that may conflict with the broader guidance on staying at home:

We have since all been residing, working, supervising, researching, studying and caring for vulnerable and elderly family members… in these oddest of circumstances. Life has never felt more postdigital, when I haven't visited campus since February and even a family funeral was held via a webcast. Yet simultaneously, we have family members who cannot use the Internet and are more isolated than ever, including a father with dementia and a sister who has been mentally unwell since her teens. I think of them, as I leave my computer windows for a moment, to open physical windows, and I hear the sound of applause for carers. I reflect on a testimony I have just read, that caused me to wonder, in this time of crisis: does the digital network now support the social, or does the social now support the digital? (Jandrić, Hayes, et al., 2020, p. 1217)

Either way, this is a question that critical pedagogy can both input into and draw new energy from. While it is fair to say that 2020 was a year of unprecedented crises and combinations thereof, it is also fair to say that these crises are far from new. Pandemics and earthquakes are regular historical events. Most of us are not used to them merely because the timespan between pandemics and differences are longer than a human lifetime so we have not personally experienced them before. But some pockets of the world have experienced very similar crises, such as the measles epidemic in Congo and Samoa, very recently. Also, many parts of the world, such as California and Japan, suffer from permanent earthquakes and other parts of the world regularly experience wildfires and floods. There are considerable challenges too, in gaining consensus about what constitutes 'building back better' (Matthewman & Goode, 2020, p. 92). Furthermore, pandemics and earthquakes are not the only crises we experience. Mere months before the pandemic, Greta Thunberg poignantly made the point that the whole world is in a much deeper environmental crisis, which is also much more consequential for the long-term survival of humankind (Jandrić, Jaldemark, et al., 2020). Living at the intersections of all these (and more) crises, therefore, we need to ask: What is different this time? And what is the role of critical pedagogy in these developments?

We now live in the age of the Anthropocene, where human actions have significant impact on the planet as a whole. Globalization turns local epidemics into global pandemics. Climate change does not stop at the borders of 'responsible' countries. While the economically rich obviously have more means for alleviating consequences of pandemics and global warming than poor countries, they may also be much more responsible for their arrival—and arguably should therefore be much more responsible for their prevention. Of course, that does not happen easily. We are all used to garbage being taken out of our sight and colonial powers are used to having their dirty industry in Third World countries. This paradigm, which served the rich so well for centuries, has finally arrived at an end. The role of critical pedagogy in confronting this task is manifold, yet in this chapter we will focus on the recent and radically developing field of biodigital studies of education.

CRITICAL PEDAGOGY IN THE POSTDIGITAL CONDITION

Critical pedagogy arose from the works of Paulo Freire, Ivan Illich, and others, in the mid-twentieth century. Freire wrote *Pedagogy of the Oppressed* (1972) in the late 1960s. This was the world of wired phones and one-way television and radio. Freire's words were written on a typewriter; proofs went through snail mail. Computers were used in isolated army and university labs. Oil was cheap and cars were much fewer than today. The world's population was 3.683 billion (compared to today's 7.840 billion). It is hardly a surprise, therefore, that Freire seriously took up the question of the environment only at the very end of his life. Rumor has it that his last book, which was never completed because of his sudden death, was about ecopedagogies (Misiaszek & Torres, 2019). Like Prometheus, Freire fought both lovingly and mercilessly against the evils of his day—poverty, inequality, racism.

Freire's Epimethean brother Ivan Illich, the 'bad boy' of the critical pedagogy movement, felt the same problems as Freire. But Illich also had an incredible foresight for times to come. He predicted the advent of the Internet, he seriously understood the natural limits to the capitalist paradigm of constant growth, and he developed a sophisticated, if weird, relationship to science (and especially medicine). However forward-looking, Illich was not a technical man. As a Catholic priest, and a deep (although never open) anarchist, Illich was just too advanced for his times. At worst, he was ridiculed and laughed at; at best, he was seen as a utopian thinker.

Freire and Illich had been the two main influences on the twentieth-century critical pedagogy (for more about their relationship to technology, see Jandrić & Ford, 2020). As people like Henry Giroux, Peter McLaren, Shirley

Steinberg, Ira Shor, Donaldo Macedo, and others, have taken their message first to North America and then to the rest of the world, critical pedagogy has worked well. A major practical departure from Freire and Illich happened with the popularity of postmodernism and identity politics in the 1980s, but this was soon addressed by Peter McLaren's 'return to Marxism' (McLaren & Jandrić, 2020). Another major development from Freire and Illich happened with Elizabeth Ellsworth's poignant feminist critique in 'Why does it not feel empowering?' (1989). Perhaps the most striking critique of critical pedagogy, at least in our generation, seems to be caused by the typical leftist tendency of the movement's fragmentation. As critical pedagogy has slowly entered the mainstream, many could not resist the siren call of jobs, positions, and privileges. Some of the first-generation critical pedagogues have created developed cults of their own personality, their 'schools' and 'disciples'—in total contrast to the ethos of critical pedagogy, you can be either with them or against them. Yet all communities have similar problems, and the critical pedagogy movement has not collapsed from its own shortcomings. As technology has progressed, and the world with it, the critical pedagogy movement has simply become less and less relevant.

We now live in a postdigital age, where human destinies cannot be thought of without technologies. In a way, this was always the case—*homo sapiens* has survived because of technologies such as fire, clothing, and agriculture. But in our world, technologies permeate all aspects of our being. 'The postdigital is hard to define; messy; unpredictable; digital and analog; technological and non-technological; biological and informational. The postdigital is both a rupture in our existing theories and their continuation' (Jandrić et al., 2018, p. 895).

In the early twenty-first century, postdigital (educational) research has strongly refocused to technologies—but critical pedagogy has barely budged. Admittedly, there were some movements such as Networked Learning which actively implemented principles of critical pedagogy in their work (Networked Learning Editorial Collective, 2021; Networked Learning Editorial Collective et al., 2021). However, the majority of mainstream research, found under various names such as e-learning, digital learning, and Technology Enhanced Learning, was strongly focused on an efficiency of instruction at the expense of emancipation and social justice. This is evidenced in patterns of rational, deterministic, and repetitive policy discourse over more than two decades (Hayes, 2015, 2019; Hayes & Bartholomew, 2015; Hayes & Jandrić, 2014). Twenty years later, the marriage of digital technology and education has produced a huge body of research and has become more mainstreamed than critical pedagogy at its heyday. While some of us have actively worked on connections between critical pedagogy and technology, we have been seriously outnumbered: tech people did not care about critical pedagogy, and critical pedagogy did not care about tech. This ship has sailed—critical pedagogy has missed its historical opportunity to make a deep impact on digital learning.

But the wheel of development never stops, and each turn presents a new opportunity. These days, relationships between technology and education are rapidly moving from endless discussions about the mutual impacts of online and offline spaces, 'physical and virtual' realities, and so on. In our postdigital condition, they have become widely understood as equal and different. In the meantime, natural sciences have moved from physics to biology; burning questions of today are about mutual interaction between information systems and biological systems. While educational theory and practice still grapples with important questions of digital learning, especially with the recent Covid-19 global turn to online education (see Jandrić, Hayes, et al., 2020), our focus in this chapter is on the biodigital-postdigital configuration.

THE BIODIGITAL CHALLENGE OF CRITICAL PEDAGOGY

During the past 30 or so years, the ecopedagogy movement has done tremendously important work with regard to the environmental challenge of critical pedagogy.[1] Understood as 'reinventions of Paulo Freire's work and the topic of an unfinished book due to his untimely death,' these efforts have centered 'environmental teaching on critically understanding the connections between social and environmental violence' (Misiaszek, 2020a, p. 748). This brought about Richard Kahn's unofficial (but highly influential) program of contemporary ecopedagogy movement aiming to:

1. provide openings for the radicalization and proliferation of ecoliteracy programs both within schools and society;
2. create liberatory opportunities for building alliances of praxis between scholars and the public (especially activists) on ecopedagogical interests; and
3. foment critical dialogue and self-reflective solidarity across the multitude of groups that make up the educational left during an extraordinary time of extremely dangerous planetary crisis (Kahn, 2010, pp. 27–28).

So far so good—the importance of these goals, and their elusiveness as moving targets, justifies all efforts and we can only regret that the ecopedagogy movement has not attracted wider attention.

But then, as the Covid-19 pandemic, Great Thunberg's efforts, and recent educational research clearly point out, educational programs, various alliances, dialogue, and solidarity are now rapidly changing through biodigital aspects of the postdigital condition. Michael Peters, Petar Jandrić, Sarah Hayes, and Derek Ford have recently written several papers and started several edited projects[2] which explore the biodigital-postdigital configuration in relation to critical pedagogy (Jandrić & Ford, 2020), biodigital philosophy and new postdigital knowledge ecologies (Peters et al., 2021a), biodigital technologies and the bioeconomy (Peters et al., 2021b), emerging biodigital-postdigital configurations (Peters et al., 2021c), and their reflections to academic publishing (Peters et al., 2021d).

We are not the only ones in these efforts. During the past few years, Ben Williamson has written several important articles which advance the concept of 'precision education,' which 'is an emerging combination of psychological, neuroscientific and genetic expertise, with a particular emphasis on using advanced computational technologies to produce "intimate data" about students' bodies and biological associations with learning' (Williamson, 2019a). Martyn Pickersgill (2020), Johnson et al. (2020), and others, are studying relationships between heritable changes in gene expression, or epigenetics, and education. Jessica Pykett (2015), and again Ben Williamson (2019b), are investigating neurotechnology, neuroeducation, and brain-based teaching models. These considerations are now entering funding schemes, so aforementioned researchers have just started a project 'The rise of data-intensive biology in education' funded by the Leverhulme Trust (Williamson, 2020). These considerations are now also raised in policy documents by countries and organizations such as UNESCO (for a detailed overview, see Peters et al., 2021b).

These rapidly developing research and policy efforts reach way beyond ecopedagogy's traditional focus to ecoliteracy programs, alliances of praxis, and critical dialogues (Kahn, 2010). Yet they also intersect, and in a dialectical manner. Applications of neurotechnology cannot be thought of without critical dialogues between everyone who may be affected by them. Dialogues need to be informed, so we all need to educate ourselves about these developments. And policy, politics, and (educational) praxis require development of strong alliances; to make an impact, individual voices need to come together. This is where new biodigital studies of education urgently need critical pedagogy; and this is where critical pedagogy, in order to keep up with the times, urgently needs biodigital studies of education.

Postdigital Convergences

It is easy to claim that the two fields need to come together in articulation. It is much more difficult to justify why they need to come together, address resistance to coming together, and point toward ways in which this coming together could be productive. In this section we will support our claim for the new marriage between critical pedagogy and biodigital studies of education in two ways. First, we will look at philosophy and applications of recent techno-scientific convergences. Second, we will explore ways in which these convergences play out in various crises identified in the Introduction.

Toward a Meta-Convergence

Since the 2000s, reports about various convergences have started to pop up in academic literature. In their book, *Managing Nano-Bio-Info-Cogno Innovations: Converging Technologies in Society*, Bainbridge and Sims (2006) claimed that '[t]remendous human progress is becoming possible through the development of converging technologies stimulated by advances in four core fields: Nanotechnology, Biotechnology, Information technology, and new technologies based in Cognitive science (NBIC).' Here, we can see the emergence of a new transdisciplinary 'nano-bio-info-cogno' paradigm which encompasses traditional disciplines in the natural sciences such as biology, chemistry, and physics.

This convergence between disciplines is only one part of the story. Practically, and also epistemically, they are enabled by an (older) emergence of techno-science, techno-politics, and even techno-nationalism, which has been explored by philosophers such as Michael Peters (1989), Bernard Stiegler (2019), and many others. Two aspects of techno-science are especially relevant for our discussion (Peters et al., 2021a). First, today's experimental science is enabled by technics. When we study elementary particles in a physics accelerator such as the Large Hadron Collider at CERN, we do not see the actual particles—our eyes see marks on our screens, and their numerical representations, made by the computer. When we map the human genome, we do not really see the DNA spiral—again, our eyes also see only various computer-made representations. In this way, technology gains a lot of its own agency in laboratory research, because a different representation may take us to different conclusions. Since the late twentieth century, this brings about vivid discussions about the changing agency of human and non-human researchers, usually represented as a kind of symmetry (Fuller & Jandrić, 2019; Jones, 2018); philosophically, it results in a 'posthumanist shift from using computers to collaborating with computers' (Peters et al., 2021a).

Second, techno-science also allows a lot more agency to researchers. Traditional science was about discovering nature's workings; these days, technology provides 'up to recently unimaginable opportunities for tinkering with and actively transforming living organisms' (Peters et al., 2021a). Examples include cloning, germline gene therapy, and many other applications. Which scientist, and indeed which human being, can resist the siren call of trying to change their own bodily setup and destiny? But these attempts, as we discussed elsewhere (Peters & Jandrić, 2019), need careful ethical guidance—and this guidance, being a social construct, requires a lot of theoretical and practical work.

These convergences may have originated from the natural sciences, but they have soon poured over to the humanities (e.g., digital humanities), the social sciences (see Williamson's 2019a notion of digital policy sociology), and of course economy. Peters et al. (2021b) provide a detailed study of bioeconomy-related policy documents recently published by institutions such as UNESCO, OECD, and several national governments. In another paper, Peters et al. (2021c) link these convergences with aforementioned studies in the field of education (Johnson et al., 2020; Pickersgill, 2020; Pykett, 2015; Williamson, 2019a, 2019b; and others). 'This signals that our neatly divided convergences (biology-bioinformation, science-technology, etc.) require a meta-convergence. We, thus, arrive to the postdigital convergence of information, biology, science, technology, politics, society and various other phenomena that remain unmentioned' (Peters et al., 2021a).

This postdigital meta-convergence 'simultaneously leads to convergence and divergence of research activities. Convergence: this unified ecosystem allows us to answer questions, resolve problems and build things that isolated disciplinary capabilities cannot. Divergence: this creates new pathways, opportunities, competencies, knowledge, technologies and applications' (Peters et al., 2021a). Research activities are inextricably linked to social conditions—politics, policy, discourse, and economy. They also require ethical guidance. This is why Peters and Besley, in their recent article, call for urgent development of a critical philosophy of the postdigital (Peters & Besley, 2019).

Postdigital Crises

In the introduction we outlined various crises of today. The environmental crisis, which has been humanity's constant companion since the arrival of the age of the Anthropocene. Natural crises, such as earthquakes, which do not seem to directly stem from human activities. Social crises, such as lockdowns and school closures resulting from the Covid-19 pandemic. The case of Covid-19 is a particularly good example of simultaneous convergence and divergence of these (types of) crises.

Covid-19 is a natural crisis, not unlike earthquakes, floods, and fires. Viruses constantly mutate and move between animals and humans; these mutations and movements periodically produce nasty virus strains which seriously affect human beings. SARS-CoV-2 seems to have emerged from bats or similar animals, mutated, and transmitted to humans at a wet market in Wuhan, China. This assumption already has a social character, as virus transfer is obviously linked to storage, transport, and preparation of human food. This also has an environmental character, because it is a clear outcome of consuming wildlife (O'Sullivan, 2020).

Once the virus has arrived in the human population, its spread depends on a combination of natural factors (infectivity) and social factors (human contact). Immediately after the emergence of Covid-19, both factors have been addressed—the first through the development of vaccines, and the latter through various social isolation measures. These measures have caused social crises in all areas of human life, including work and education. Interestingly enough, lockdown measures have simultaneously caused some positive environmental impacts such as reduction of pollution caused by traffic and production (Lewis, 2020). Some suggest that the virus could act as a 'portal,' a gateway between one world and the next (Roy, 2020) or even 'predict the imminent demise of neoliberalism' (Matthewman & Huppatz, 2020). At the moment of writing this article, there are more publications on the Covid-19 crisis than any individual can read. However, it is abundantly clear that Covid-19 is simultaneously a natural, environmental, and social crisis.

In our postdigital age, all types of crises converge. Convergence of information and biology has enabled scientists to develop and register the first Covid-19 vaccine less than one year after its outbreak, thus showing the power of open science (Peters et al., 2020). Its flip side of the coin, divergence, has created new classes of winners and new classes of losers. As such, 'it will provide opportunities for "disaster capitalists" to profit, it will enhance certain forms of surveillance, and it will impact some constituencies far more negatively than others' (Matthewman & Huppatz, 2020). Some sectors of the economy such as tourism are on their knees, while others, such as online delivery, are on a strong rise. This reconfigures social relationships built in previous ages such as finance capitalism and algorithmic capitalism, and it gives rise to new inequality lines characteristic for our age of bioinformational capitalism.

TIME TO JOIN THE GREAT CONVERGENCE

Critical pedagogy has always been about justice, equality, emancipation, and freedom. Its important trajectory, ecopedagogy, has focused on environmental justice, environmental equality, environmental emancipation, and environmental freedom. However, our age of convergences does now allow for such specialization anymore, so we again repeat our recent claim that all of critical pedagogy needs to become ecopedagogy (Jandrić & Ford, 2020). Critical pedagogy's anti-capitalism now acquires a distinct form of anti-bioinformational-capitalism and related discourse. Critical pedagogy's concern with emancipation and equality now needs to take the environmental turn. Critical pedagogy's understanding of human agency needs to take into account the agency of non-human entities. Critical pedagogy's utopia, which has always been a constantly moving target, has just become even more elusive.

Joining the great convergence deeply transforms critical pedagogy. Only very recently, critical educators working on emancipation and social justice could hold their Freirean *circulos de cultura* and safely ignore computers—save for emails and social networks for distributing invitations, and perhaps photocopiers for multiplying workshop materials. Over the years, we have met many critical pedagogues who stubbornly insisted on using digital technology very sparingly, and only in a very instrumentalist way outlined above. The Covid-19 pandemic has already changed this through various lockdown and social isolation measures, causing outbursts of sadness and anger (see Sapon-Shevin & Soo-Hoo, 2020). However, the continuum between the digital and the analog is just one of many aspects of our postdigital reality. *Circulos de cultura* cannot ignore that participants of one skin color have much more chance of dying of Covid-19 than those of other skin colors, demonstrating the diversity of 'postdigital positionalities' as each of us encounters the pandemic as individuals (Hayes, 2021). Those organizing *circulos de cultura* cannot ignore that information about one's participation may be automatically collected and fed into life-decisive algorithms such as credit scores. Critical pedagogues cannot ignore new forms of ableism, sexism, and various other discriminating -isms as they reconfigure old lines of discrimination and create new ones. For a surprisingly long time, critical pedagogy has managed to ignore digital technologies; now it needs to urgently accept and critique them in a bigger package containing biotechnologies.

Some important attempts in this direction have already been made in the context of the Covid-19 pandemic. In his recent article, 'Will We Learn from COVID-19? Ecopedagogical Calling (Un)heard,' Greg Misiaszek asks: '(Un)heard' in the title questions if we will learn from experiencing COVID-19 to counter unrestrained environmental devastation occurring, or will we remain largely untaught? In response, Misiaszek argues for 'the need for transformative, Freirean-based ecopedagogy for praxis through, in part, problematizing and then countering dehumanizing, deplanetarizing pandemic responses to "wake" us in recognizing the need of socio-environmental justice and sustainability' (Misiaszek, 2020b, p. 28). Blending the pandemic challenge with socio-environmental justice and sustainability, this is a prime example of convergence between critical ecopedagogy old and new, fit for our historical moment.

Looking beyond the pandemic, which reformations does critical pedagogy require? In a recent article, Jandrić and Ford identified some directions for development of new ecopedagogies:

> Critical Philosophy of Technology and Studies of Science and Technology (STS), Big Data, Algorithms, Artificial Intelligences, and New Capitalisms, Bioinformational Capitalism and Viral Modernity, Anti-imperialist, Anti-colonial, and Decolonization Studies/Movements, Postdigital Feminisms, Intersectionality and Identity Politics as Ecologies of Collective Resistance, (Critical) Posthumanism and Transhumanism, Critical Disability Studies, Queer Theories, Postdigital Aesthetics, (Science) Fiction and Future Studies, Myth, Religion, and Belief. (Jandrić & Ford, 2020)

Toward the end of their article, Ford and Jandrić (2020) reflect on the perspectives and write: 'Some of these perspectives are not fully commensurable, while others significantly overlap and use different paths to arrive to similar conclusions. We are at the very brink of the postdigital age; at this stage, this messy and sometimes paradoxical nature of our knowledge is just a part of the game.' Linked to these ideas, in her recent book, *Postdigital Positionality*, Hayes has connected the nature of being 'postdigital' to extend how 'positionality' might be understood in this context: 'Positionality theory, where identity is fluid, dynamic and contextual, is one way to examine individual experiences in postdigital society and to discuss implications for assumptions about inclusivity' (Hayes, 2021). Authors who write about positionality in the context of critical pedagogy suggest that '[p]ositionality acknowledges complex differentials of power and privilege while simultaneously identifying the value of multiple ways of knowing and being that arise from our multiple identities' (Acevedo et al., 2015).

In the light of these acknowledgments, it is no longer possible to take a critical pedagogical position to identify 'multiple ways of knowing and being that arise from our multiple identities' without connecting culture and technology with such ideals concerning citizenship:

> Postdigital positionality offers a powerful route towards re-engaging the separate terrains of culture and technology with citizenship in an ongoing, inclusive, 'postdigital dialogue' (Jandrić, Ryberg, Knox, Lacković, Hayes, Suoranta, Smith, Steketee, Peters, McLaren, Ford, Asher, McGregor, Stewart, Williamson and Gibbons, 2018). This is a community dialogue which universities can and should take a lead on, in collaboration with schools, human rights agencies, charities, legal and technical experts and individuals (UPP Foundation, 2018, Hambleton, 2020, Hayes, et. al, 2020). This is not least because an innocent sounding term like 'data' now brings acute risks to those most vulnerable in society (The State of Data 2020: 5). (Hayes, 2021)

If in postdigital we acknowledge convergence, then in positionality, we acknowledge divergence. Critical pedagogy now needs to adopt a more inclusive critique of these factors, together, so that it takes into account digital technologies, data, algorithmic culture, and biodigital aspects of the postdigital condition that diverse individuals now experience differently.

As such, we do need deep postdigital feminists; from Donna Haraway onwards, feminist critique has been indispensable for our understandings of postdigital humans (Savin-Baden, 2021). We also need deep critics of all shapes and hues in areas such as bioinformational capitalism and others. While these rapidly developing areas are complex enough in their own right, they now need to find a new level of functioning that extends our thinking beyond traditional disciplines.

At this moment, reaching this level is burdened with numerous methodological questions (Jandrić, 2021), and perhaps it is indeed necessary that most researchers work like hedgehogs and dig their own holes deeper and deeper. However, the transformation required by today's critical pedagogy is much deeper than turning our attention to this or that problem or problematic area. We need to develop these and other problems and fields, and this development should not take place in isolation, but using the fox approach—in convergence with other problems and fields (see Jandrić, 2017, Chapter 6 for a detailed overview of the hedgehog and the fox approach). To combine these approaches, we need to engineer a new species of critical pedagogue, the hedgefox, which combines properties attributed to proverbial hedges and foxes. Amazingly, Google returns 131,000³ results for the word hedgefox, indicating that the idea is far from new. 'Hedgefoxes combine the best properties of their two mammalian relatives. Like the hedgehog, the hedgefox is a synthesizer; but like the fox, the hedgefox cares about, and advances theories that take account of, and make sense of, the complexities of reality' (Loewenstein et al., 2007, p. 3).

Hedgefox Critical Pedagogy

While contemplating some amusing descriptions of the party animal behavioral characteristics of hedgehogs and foxes, we are reminded that parties, due to social distancing measures, are in themselves becoming a distant memory. Yet, recalling such gatherings where there are usually those who 'take outrageous positions and push their arguments to the limit, generating heated debate' (hedgehogs) and those that 'stand on the sidelines shaking their heads and rolling their eyes at the naivety of the hedgehogs' wild speculations' (foxes), those who advance 'theories that take account of, and make sense of, the complexities of reality' (hedgefoxes) (Loewenstein et al., 2007, p. 3) can be particularly compelling. Absorbing too is the question concerning whether hedgefoxes are 'born' or 'made' and perhaps also whether foxes or hedgehogs are more likely to become hedgefoxes? While it may take time and reflexive interaction, this can lead to:

> emergence of a hedgefox period with a common language, a shared understanding of a number of issues, and, most characteristically of hedgefoxism, a nuanced theoretical perspective that made sense of, and in fact eliminated, what had previously appeared to be disagreements and contradictions. (Loewenstein et al., 2007, p. 5)

To engineer a new species of critical pedagogue, that resembles the analogy of the hedgefox in their reflexive interaction with converging perspectives, similar stages of party animal debate may be required. This seems to us a good starting point, to bring cross-disciplinary hedgehogs and foxes together at the point of live, provocative online postdigital debate (Hayes et al., 2021) and also via collective writing that challenges and revises rigid structures for edited collections (Peters et al., 2021d).

However, there are other matters of environmental justice too that hedgefox critical pedagogy might engage with and theorize more broadly in the light of recent techno-scientific convergences, crises, and reconfigurations of critical pedagogy fit for our historical moment. These include routes of activism such as NonViolent Direct Action (NVDA), for example tunneling, that might appeal to those hedgehogs that like to dig deep. Protest tunneling has quite a history, as illustrated by the well-known environmentalist Daniel Hooper, better known as 'Swampy' and one of the Newbury campaigners who 'dug deep' during the 1990s to occupy 'a network of tunnels in protest against a planned leisure complex development in Crystal Palace' (Taylor, 2021a). Now in 2021, at the height of the pandemic, we can notice HS2 protestors who 'have secretly built a tunnel under a busy square by London's Euston station' (Taylor, 2021b). Such an example demonstrates both postdigital convergence (as engineering, politics, economy, law, environment, digital technology, and media coverage) meet with the positionality of each protestor (Larch Maxey, 48, Blue Sandford, 18, and another activist called Scotty) and we can acknowledge their divergence in their 'stronghold built from pallets, complete with towers nicknamed "Buckingham Pallets"' (Taylor, 2021a).

As debate on this topic gets underway at the Hedgefox Critical Pedagogy party, a good place to start might concern the critical stances that ecopedagogies could take across the postdigital disciplinary convergences mentioned above. The legal possession of space and land by HS2 and the burrowing into this by protestors in quite a feat of engineering has complex dimensions that a fox could lay out for discussion. From the body cameras worn by the security and police who will be required to remove protestors, to the use of force on NVDA citizens, from the additional strain on emergency services during a pandemic and economic costs, to the climate and environmental emergency that humanity now faces, and what it means to get up close with the earth to engage 'with another dimension of nature in a physical, visceral and intimate way' (Taylor, 2021b).

Though we have raised many challenges that the critical pedagogy movement has faced we have proposed new and exciting tunnels of exploration for the most focused of hedgehogs and most skeptical of foxes. We invite others to contribute to a discussion only just beginning, as we explore a forthcoming postdigital 'hedgefox period' and develop a new species of critical pedagogue in the process.

Notes

1. In this place it would be commonplace academic practice to try and delineate similarities and differences between critical pedagogy and ecopedagogy. Yet, based on our recent work, we deliberately refuse to engage in this type of analysis. In our experience of working with recent attempts to define the field of Networked Learning (Networked Learning Editorial Collective, 2021; Networked Learning Editorial Collective et al., 2021), we came to realize that any attempt at definition always excludes someone and includes someone else. Any attempt at definition either unnecessarily narrows down the field or becomes so wide that it also becomes pointless. And so on… A good overview of arguments in favour of our refusal can be found in Bayne's contribution to (Networked Learning Editorial Collective et al., 2021).
2. See Peters, M. A., Jandrić, P., & Hayes, S. (2022). *Bioinformational Philosophy and Postdigital Knowledge Ecologies*. Cham: Springer, and Jandrić, P., & Ford, D. R. (2022). *Postdigital Ecopedagogies: Genealogies, Contradictions, and Possible Futures*. Cham: Springer.
3. Simple Google search conducted on 22 January 2021.

References

Acevedo, S. M., Aho, M., Cela, E., Chao, J. C., Garcia-Gonzales, I., MacLeod, A., Moutray, C., & Olague, C. (2015). Positionality as knowledge: From pedagogy to praxis. *Integral Review: A Transdisciplinary & Transcultural Journal for New Thought, Research, & Praxis, 11*(1), 28–46.

Bainbridge, W. S., & Sims, W. (Eds.). (2006). *Managing nano-bio-info-cogno innovations: In converging technologies in society*. Springer. https://doi.org/10.1007/1-4020-4107-1

Ellsworth, E. (1989). Why doesn't this feel empowering? Working through the repressive myths of critical pedagogy. *Harvard Educational Review, 59*(3), 297–325.

Freire, P. (1972). *Pedagogy of the oppressed*. Penguin.

Fuller, S., & Jandrić, P. (2019). The postdigital human: Making the history of the future. *Postdigital Science and Education, 1*(1), 190–217. https://doi.org/10.1007/s42438-018-0003-x

Hayes, S. (2015). Counting on the use of technology to enhance learning. In P. Jandrić & D. Boras (Eds.), *Critical learning in digital networks* (pp. 15–36). Springer.

Hayes, S. (2019). *The labour of words in higher education: Is it time to reoccupy policy?* Brill.

Hayes, S. (2021). *Postdigital positionality: Developing powerful inclusive narratives for learning, teaching, research and policy in Higher Education*. Brill.

Hayes, S., & Bartholomew, P. (2015). Where's the humanity? Challenging the policy discourse of technology enhanced learning. In J. Branch, P. Bartholomew, & C. Nygaard (Eds.), *Technology enhanced learning in higher education*. Libri.

Hayes, S., & Jandrić, P. (2014). Who is really in charge of contemporary education? People and technologies in, against and beyond the neoliberal university. *Open Review of Educational Research, 1*(1), 193–210. https://doi.org/10.1080/23265507.2014.989899

Hayes, S., Jopling, M., Hayes, D., Westwood, A., Tuckett, A., & Barnett, R. (2021). Raising regional academic voices (alongside data) in Higher Education (HE) debate. *Postdigital Science and Education, 3*(1), 242–260. https://doi.org/10.1007/s42438-020-00131-6

Jandrić, P. (2017). *Learning in the age of digital reason*. Rotterdam: Sense.

Jandrić, P. (2020). Corona-party at the ruins of an earthquake. *Social Epistemology Review and Reply Collective, 9*(5), 34–39.

Jandrić, P. (2021). The postdigital challenge of critical educational research. In C. Mathias (Ed.), *The handbook of critical theoretical research methods in education* (pp. 31–48). Routledge.

Jandrić, P., & Ford, D. (2020). Postdigital ecopedagogies: Genealogies, contradictions, and possible futures. *Postdigital Science and Education*. https://doi.org/10.1007/s42438-020-00207-3

Jandrić, P., & Ford, D. R. (2022). *Postdigital ecopedagogies: Genealogies, contradictions, and possible futures*. Cham: Springer.

Jandrić, P., Hayes, D., Truelove, I., Levinson, P., Mayo, P., Ryberg, T., et al. (2020). Teaching in the age of Covid-19. *Postdigital Science and Education, 2*(3), 1069–1230. https://doi.org/10.1007/s42438-020-00169-6

Jandrić, P., Jaldemark. J., Hurley, Z., Bartram, B., Matthews, A., Jopling, M., et al. (2020). Philosophy of education in a new key: Who remembers Greta Thunberg? Education and environment after the coronavirus. *Educational Philosophy and Theory*. https://doi.org/10.1080/00131857.2020.1811678

Jandrić, P., Knox, J., Besley, T., Ryberg, T., Suoranta, J., & Hayes, S. (2018). Postdigital Science and Education. *Educational Philosophy and Theory, 50*(10), 893–899. https://doi.org/10.1080/00131857.2018.1454000

Johnson, M. W., Maitland, E., & Torday, J. (2020). Covid-19 and the epigenetics of learning. *Postdigital Science and Education*. https://doi.org/10.1007/s42438-020-00190-9

Jones, C. (2018). Experience and networked learning. In N. Bonderup Dohn, S. Cranmer, J. A. Sime, M. de Laat, & T. Ryberg (Eds.), *Networked learning: Reflections and challenges* (pp. 39–56). Springer International. https://doi.org/10.1007/978-3-319-74857-3_3

Kahn, R. (2010). *Critical pedagogy, ecoliteracy, & planetary crisis: The ecopedagogy movement*. Peter Lang.

Lewis, T. (2020). Cities gone wild. *Postdigital Science and Education, 2*(3), 597–600. https://doi.org/10.1007/s42438-020-00120-9

Loewenstein, G., Vohs, K. D., & Baumeister, R. F. (2007). Introduction: The Hedgefox. In K. D. Vohs, R. F. Baumeister, & G. Loewenstein (Eds.), *Do emotions help or hurt decision making? A hedgefoxian perspective* (pp. 3–9). Russell Sage.

Matthewman, S., & Goode, L. (2020). City of quakes: Excavating the future in Christchurch. *New Zealand Sociology, 35*(2), 77.

Matthewman, S., & Huppatz, K. (2020). A sociology of Covid-19. *Journal of Sociology, 56*(4), 675–683. https://doi.org/10.1177/1440783320939416

McLaren, P., & Jandrić, P. (2020). *Postdigital dialogues on critical pedagogy, liberation theology and information technology*. Bloomsbury.

Misiaszek, G. W. (2020a). Countering post-truths through ecopedagogical literacies: Teaching to critically read 'development' and 'sustainable development.' *Educational Philosophy and Theory, 52*(7), 747–758. https://doi.org/10.1080/00131857.2019.1680362

Misiaszek, G. W. (2020b). Will we learn from COVID-19? Ecopedagogical calling (un)heard. *Knowledge Cultures, 8*(3), 28–33. https://doi.org/10.22381/KC8320204

Misiaszek, G. W., & Torres, C. A. (2019). Ecopedagogy: The missing chapter of pedagogy of the oppressed. In C. A. Torres (Ed.), *Wiley handbook of Paulo Freire* (pp. 463–488). Wiley-Blackwell. https://doi.org/10.1002/9781119236788.ch25

Networked Learning Editorial Collective. (2021). Networked learning: Inviting redefinition. *Postdigital Science and Education*. https://doi.org/10.1007/s42438-020-00167-8

Networked Learning Editorial Collective et al. (2021). Networked learning in 2021: A community definition. *Postdigital Science and Education*. https://doi.org/10.1007/s42438-021-00222-y

O'Sullivan, V. (2020). Non-human animal trauma during the pandemic. *Postdigital Science and Education, 2*(3), 558–596. https://doi.org/10.1007/s42438-020-00143-2

Peters, M. A. (1989). Techno-science, rationality and the university: Lyotard on the 'postmodern condition.' *Educational Theory, 39*(2), 93–105. https://doi.org/10.1111/j.1741-5446.1989.40000.x

Peters, M. A., & Jandrić, P. (2019). AI, human evolution, and the speed of learning. In J. Knox, Y. Wang, & M. Gallagher (Eds.), *Artificial Intelligence and inclusive education: Speculative futures and emerging practices* (pp. 195–206). Springer Nature. https://doi.org/10.1007/978-981-13-8161-4_12

Peters, M. A., Jandrić, P., & Hayes, S. (2021a). Biodigital philosophy, technological convergence, and new knowledge ecologies. *Postdigital Science and Education*. https://doi.org/10.1007/s42438-020-00211-7

Peters, M. A., Jandrić, P., & Hayes, S. (2021b). Biodigital technologies and the bioeconomy: The global new green deal? *Educational Philosophy and Theory*. https://doi.org/10.1080/00131857.2020.1861938

Peters, M. A., Jandrić, P., & Hayes, S. (2021c). Postdigital-biodigital: An emerging configuration. *Educational Philosophy and Theory*. https://doi.org/10.1080/00131857.2020.1867108

Peters, M. A., Jandrić, P., & Hayes, S. (2021d). Revisiting the concept of the 'edited collection': Bioinformation philosophy and postdigital knowledge ecologies. *Postdigital Science and Education, 3*(2), 283–293.

Peters, M. A., Jandrić, P., & Hayes, S. (2022). *Bioinformational philosophy and postdigital knowledge ecologies*. Springer.

Peters, M. A., Jandrić, P., & McLaren, P. (2020). Viral modernity? Epidemics, infodemics, and the 'bioinformational' paradigm. *Educational Philosophy and Theory*. https://doi.org/10.1080/00131857.2020.1744226

Peters, M. A., & Besley, T. (2019). Critical philosophy of the postdigital. *Postdigital Science and Education, 1*(1), 29–42. https://doi.org/10.1007/s42438-018-0004-9

Pickersgill, M. (2020). Epigenetics, education, and the plastic body: Changing concepts and new engagements. *Research in Education, 107*(1), 72–83. https://doi.org/10.1177/0034523719867102

Pykett, J. (2015). *Brain culture: Shaping policy through neuroscience*. Policy Press.

Roy, A. (2020, April 3). The pandemic is a portal. *Financial Times*. https://www.ft.com/content/10d8f5e8-74eb-11ea-95fe-fcd274e920ca. Accessed 29 Jan 2021.

Sapon-Shevin, M., & SooHoo, S. (2020). Embodied social justice pedagogy in a time of 'no touch.' *Postdigital Science and Education, 2*(3), 675–680. https://doi.org/10.1007/s42438-020-00177-6

Savin-Baden, M. (Ed.). (2021). *Postdigital humans: Transitions, transformations and transcendence*. Springer.

Stiegler, B. (2019). *The age of disruption: Technology and madness in computational capitalism*. Polity Press.

Taylor, D. (2021a, January 27). On Swampy ground: A brief history of protest tunnelling in the UK. *The Guardian*. https://www.theguardian.com/environment/2021/jan/27/on-swampy-ground-brief-history-protest-tunnelling-tunnels-uk-hs2. Accessed 29 Jan 2021.

Taylor, D. (2021b, January 27). HS2 protesters hope to occupy Euston tunnel for weeks. *The Guardian*. https://www.theguardian.com/environment/2021/jan/27/hs2-protesters-hope-to-occupy-euston-tunnel-for-weeks. Accessed 29 Jan 2021.

Williamson, B. (2019a). Digital policy sociology: Software and science in data-intensive precision education. *Critical Studies in Education*. https://doi.org/10.1080/17508487.2019.1691030

Williamson, B. (2019b). Brain data: Scanning, scraping and sculpting the plastic learning brain through neurotechnology. *Postdigital Science and Education, 1*(1), 65–86. https://doi.org/10.1007/s42438-018-0008-5

Williamson, B. (2020). *The rise of data-intensive biology in education—A new project!* https://codeactsineducation.wordpress.com/2020/12/08/data-intensive-biology-education/. Accessed 29 Jan 2021.

CHAPTER 19

Contemporary Critical Library and Information Studies: Ethos and Ethics

Toni Samek

"The future is already here – it's just not evenly distributed" by William S. Gibson.

INTRODUCTION

In the call for submissions to the fall 2021 volume of the *Journal of Academic Freedom* for the American Association of University Professors (AAUP), libraries and librarians was a topic sought alongside academic freedom and freedom struggles, sanctuary campuses, pedagogy and affect, the material means of mental production, and international practices. On libraries and librarians, the call stated:

> In the struggle for academic freedom, libraries are essential sites and librarians are essential workers. How can libraries be spaces for the expansion of academic and other freedoms? How do issues around collections, catalogs, access, reference, and information literacy affect academic freedom? How have librarians expanded academic freedom in fights against austerity budgets, profit-driven publishers, and surveillance, and in fights for open access, privacy, and freedom from harassment? (AAUP, 2021, Libraries and Librarians, para 9)

T. Samek (✉)
University of Alberta, Edmonton, AB, Canada
e-mail: toni.samek@ualberta.ca

© The Author(s), under exclusive license to Springer Nature Switzerland AG 2022
A. A. Abdi and G. W. Misiaszek (eds.), *The Palgrave Handbook on Critical Theories of Education*, https://doi.org/10.1007/978-3-030-86343-2_19

This call squarely places library and information concerns in higher education and educational studies more broadly. And it sets a stage on which to showcase the multi-scale area of library and information studies (LIS) as it pertains to critical, liberatory, and ethical library and information efforts and their inherent interplay with the global education enterprise. For the purposes of this chapter, the spotlight is on critical library and information studies (CLIS), an umbrella phrase used to encompass a variety of movements through time and across geography, including but not limited to progressive librarianship, socially responsible librarianship, radical librarianship, activist librarianship, and critical librarianship, and reflective of allied efforts in sister information-based fields that reflect librarians and other information workers (e.g., archivists, museum professionals) who participate in political movements and discourses that exceed but affect their profession. In so doing, CLIS contributes to transdisciplinary interrogations of conventional education and the advancement of social justice involving informational, cultural, and cultural heritage brokers. The recent edited collection entitled *Re-making the Library Makerspace: Critical Theories, Reflections, and Practices* for example, effectively demonstrates how hands-on librarians and educators together re-think, interrupt, and re-work makerspaces as a counter to the confines of prevailing maker culture (Melo & Nichols, 2020).

In the twenty-first century, CLIS has established traction, in part secured by the emergence of the *Journal of Radical Librarianship* in 2014 and the *Journal of Critical Library and Information Studies* in 2017. The *Journal of Radical Librarianship* formed following discussions at the Radical Librarians Collective (2013–) meetings in London, UK. The journal's scope is "any work that contributes to a discourse around critical library and information theory and practice" (*Journal of Radical Librarianship*, About the Journal, n.d., para 1) and the following subject areas are considered "indicative rather than exhaustive" of these interests: politics and social justice; information literacy; digital rights; anti-racist theory, critical race analysis, anti-colonial studies; scholarly communication; equity, diversity, and inclusion; gender variance, queer theory, and phenomenology; political economy of information and knowledge; cataloging and metadata; technology and data; critical pedagogy; and, sustainability and environmentalism (*Journal of Radical Librarianship*, About the Journal, n.d., para 2).

The *Journal of Critical Library and Information Studies* is published by Litwin Books, a US independent academic publisher, which through its Library Juice Press imprint publishes "books that examine theoretical and practical issues in librarianship from a critical perspective, for an audience of professional librarians and students of library science" (Litwin Books, 2021, para 2). The mission of the journal is to "serve as a peer-reviewed platform for critical discourse in and around library and information studies from across the disciplines. This includes but is not limited to research on the political economy of information, information institutions such as libraries, archives, and museums, reflections on professional contexts and practices, questioning current paradigms and academic trends, questioning the terms of information science, exploring methodological issues in the context of the field, and otherwise enriching and broadening the scope of library and information studies by applying diverse critical and trans-disciplinary perspectives" (*Journal of Critical Library and Information Studies*, Mission, n.d., para 2). As asserted in the inaugural issue by co-editors Andrew J. Lau, Alycia Sellie, and Ronald E. Day, the journal reflects a response to "increasingly commoditized, monetized, and 'productized' scholarship" and was "envisioned as both intervention and resistance to its commercialization and rarefication, as well as narrow definitions and conceptions of library and information studies that privilege or cast the field in the terms and methods of positivist or empiricist paradigms and dominant epistemological and ontological constructs, and the normative tendencies of the field to center such paradigms. Moreover, JCLIS seeks to publish essays and reviews that are explicit and unabashed in their commitments to social justice, ethics, and intellectual freedom" (Lau et al., 2017). The dual aims of intervention and resistance suggest endeavors in the territory of critical social justice. And bring to mind the importance of exploring different views of social justice, of which there are many, including the critique "We Need Liberal Social Justice, not "Critical Social Justice" by liberal humanist Helen Pluckrose.

This chapter grounds CLIS in its historical roots and main concerns, and offers concrete examples of broad contemporary CLIS efforts, as well as a summary of CLIS in the Canadian context. Special attention is given to a core aspect of librarianship, knowledge organization. Artificial intelligence (AI) is addressed at the close of the chapter to position CLIS within broader calls for literacy in all its forms (e.g., print, information, data, digital, algorithmic), social justice, and just readings of educational technology as we look to the future. The conclusion reinforces intellectual freedom as a central concern for future study, as a condition of human rights, whistleblowing, witnessing, and justice, as well as contested in explorations of injustice and harm.

BACKGROUND AND CONTEXT

Today's CLIS literature is part of a long narrative arc within LIS literature more broadly. In a chronology of the early "progressive" print-based library literature and the more recent resources that began to proliferate online, Toni Samek (2004) situates the US title, the *Progressive Librarians' Council Bulletin*, launched in 1939, as the forerunner to contemporary CLIS literature. Unfortunately, there is but a small pool of retro-focused CLIS scholarship. Al Kagan's (2015) monograph entitled *Progressive Library Organizations: A Worldwide History* stands as a rare entrée to "the history and impact of the seven most important progressive library organizations worldwide–in Austria, Germany, South Africa, Sweden, United Kingdom, and two in the United States" (McFarland, n.d., para 1). The sparse status of CLIS historical scholarship, at least in the English language, is in part explained by an already small collection of history produced in the context of LIS, a dearth of historical scholars in LIS programs, and the erosion of history courses in the LIS curriculum.

In its welcome statement, the international Association for Information Science and Technology (ASIS&T), identifies its membership as "thousands of researchers, developers, practitioners, students, and professors in the field of information science and technology from 50 countries around the world" (ASIS&T, About, n.d., para 1). The association is home to a special interest group for the history and foundations of information science, which "encourages and supports work on the history and theoretical development of information science," and its chair "serves as a representative on the editorial board of *Information & Culture: A Journal of History* (ASIS&T, Special Interest Group, n.d., para 1). However, for context, ASIS&T members "represent the fields of information science, computer science, linguistics, management, librarianship, engineering, data science, information architecture, law, medicine, chemistry, education, and related technology" (ASIS&T, Welcome, n.d., para 1), and is not a concentrated source for CLIS contribution, including its history. In a tighter frame, the Association for Library and Information Science Education (ALISE), described as a "non-profit organization that serves as the intellectual home of faculty, staff, and students in library and information science, and allied disciplines" (ALISE, Welcome, n.d., para 2), is a hub for LIS educators in the US and Canada who teach in Master of Library and Information Studies programs (or equivalents), programs (including in Canada) that fall under the assessment purview of the American Library Association's (ALA) Committee on Accreditation. Of the approximately 50 ALA-accredited programs, eight of them are located in Canada. An "Historical Perspectives" special interest group is part of the ALISE bureaucratic structure, but tellingly the *ALISE Research Taxonomy* is devoid of the key words: "history," "historical," and "historical method." This taxonomy "provides an overview of research areas of interest to ALISE members. The taxonomy was created by examining research areas of ALA-accredited programs in North America to find patterns and was last updated in 2016 ... [and] is used by ALISE members to select their areas of research and teaching interests as well as to provide keywords for ALISE conference proposals" (ALISE, Research Taxonomy, 2016, para 1). This chapter purposefully infuses historical perspective specific to CLIS, because it is inextricably tied to the history of librarianship. And this is a knowledge base and literature not stewarded intensively by the above-noted communities of scholars. It is important to note that well beyond the memberships of these associations, staff, and students at colleges and universities with diploma programs contribute to CLIS, as do practitioner librarians and other information workers more broadly. For example, academic librarian Emily Drabinski (Interim Chief Librarian at the Mina Rees Library at the Graduate Center, CUNY), a practitioner and scholar immersed in critical pedagogy, is scheduled to teach a new offering Critical Librarianship in Praxis, in August 2021 for the UCLA

California Rare Book School (Critical Librarianship in Praxis, Upcoming Courses, UCLA California Rare Book School, n.d.). The School is tied to the Department of Information Studies in the Graduate School of Education and Information Studies at UCLA.

A pattern of discourse revealing pushes and pulls in the development of library ideology has been ongoing since the 1930s progressive library movement. It is tied up with the *Library Bill of Rights*, the inaugural ideological assertion of the profession, of intellectual freedom, and adopted by the world's oldest and largest library association, the ALA (1876–) in the late 1930s. *The Library Bill of Rights* notably affirmed intellectual freedom externally for the library's public.

> First drafted by library director Forrest Spaulding in 1938, the bill was designed to speak out against the "growing intolerance, suppression of free speech and censorship affecting the rights of minorities and individuals." One year later, the revised document was adopted by the American Library Association. It has since evolved to include topics such as book banning, race and gender discrimination, and exhibit spaces. Based on the First Amendment, the Library Bill of Rights guides librarians in serving their communities and protecting the rights of all patrons. (ALA, Office for Intellectual Freedom, n.d., para 2)

Importantly, from its emergence, the historical trajectory of CLIS is bound up with information ethics, intellectual freedom, and human rights more broadly, because it did not solely focus its gaze outward from the library to broader society, but also inward to library culture itself. Samek notes

> Progressive library discourse is rooted in the 1930s progressive library movement in the U.S., when library activists of the 1930s pressured the ALA to be more responsive to issues put forth by young members involved in such issues as peace, segregation, library unions, and intellectual freedom. By 1940, a new group called the Progressive Librarians' Council emerged in order to provide a united voice for librarians who sought change in the association. By the end of its first year, the Progressive Librarians' Council had 235 members. Many were involved with ALA's Staff Organizations Round Table, formed in 1936, and Library Unions Round Table, formed in 1940. In addition, the *Progressive Librarians' Council Bulletin* provided a forum for activities on behalf of freedom of expression. The Bulletin printed outspoken opinions "not tolerated" by the traditional communication organs - *Library Journal*, *Wilson Library Bulletin* and *ALA Bulletin*. Eventually, after ALA's Staff Organizations Round Table and Library Unions Round Table gained momentum and the number of round tables in general increased, the Progressive Librarians' Council disbanded.

Increased ALA responsiveness to its membership was a central issue for activist librarians in the 1930s and again in the 1960s. While comparing radical librarians of the 1930s with the rebels of the 1960s, library educator and scholar Jesse Shera noted that "the actors are different, but the script is much the same." The nature of library activism of the 1930s mirrors the 1960s in a number of ways:

(1) activists called for ALA to operate democratically; (2) criticized the homogeneity of the professional discourse; and (3) paid attention to the needs of the librarian, not just of the institution.

Like progressive library discourse, American library rhetoric on intellectual freedom also dates back to the 1930s. Starting in the late 1960s, however, advocates of an alternative library culture based on the concept of library social responsibility, that included the librarian's right to freedom of expression, lobbied the ALA to extend the concept of intellectual freedom to include library practitioners as well as library users. For example, these alternative library culture advocates believed that while, as professionals, librarians have "the responsibility for the development and maintenance of intellectual freedom," as citizens, librarians have the fundamental right to freedom of expression (e.g., library employee freedom of speech in the workplace on professional and policy issues and freedom of the library press). Progressive librarianship is inextricably linked to the concept of intellectual freedom and the more "universal" concept of human rights. (Samek, 2004, pp. 3–4)

With the fresh perspective of 2021, it is worth noting a heightened period of debate has occurred approximately every thirty years from the 1930s and extending into: (1) the late 1960s and early 1970s social responsibility library movement in a tightly bound matrix with exploration of intellectual freedom and rejection of library neutrality; (2) the rise of the Internet in the 1990s characterized by controversies around access to information (including digital information) and concomitant attacks on school and public library Internet access policies, opposition to the commodification of information, promotion of cultural diversity, prioritization of people over capital, and defense of democratic values; and, (3) contemporary understandings of neoliberalism, neutrality, expressive freedom, justice, diversity, equity, inclusion, anti-racism, and cancel culture. If the thirty-year cycle continues, we can expect another intense period of debate, inclusive of intellectual freedom, by 2050, because it is the thread that binds the periods together.

INTELLECTUAL FREEDOM

The International Federation of Library Associations and Institutions (IFLA), formed in 1927 and based in the Hague, acknowledged the precarious roles played by library and information workers in its 1983 adoption at the General Conference in Munich of the *Resolution on Behalf of Librarians Who are Victims of Violation of Human Rights*. It states: "In the name of human rights, librarians must, as a profession, express their solidarity with those of their colleagues who are persecuted for their opinions, wherever they may be. The Council mandated the President of IFLA, when informed of specific cases, after due considerations to intervene when appropriate with competent authorities on behalf of these colleagues" (IFLA, 1983, para 2). In 1989 in Paris, IFLA recalled the 1983 Munich resolution and put forth the *Resolution on Freedom of Expression, Censorship and Libraries*. It was not until 2005 that ALA Council, on behalf of a national association, led in the adoption of its Resolution on Workplace Speech. The resolution cements the significance of free expression inside library work culture, as opposed to intellectual freedom as a core library value exclusively intended for the public served by the library institution. The resolution affirms:

> WHEREAS, The American Library Association is firmly committed to freedom of expression (Policy 53.1.12); and WHEREAS, The library is an institution that welcomes and promotes the expression of all points of view; and WHEREAS, Library staff are uniquely positioned to provide guidance on library policy issues that is informed by their experience and education; now, therefore, be it RESOLVED, That ALA Council amends Policy 54 (Library Personnel Practices) by adding: 54.21 Workplace Speech Libraries should encourage discussion among library workers, including library administrators, of non-confidential professional and policy matters about the operation of the library and matters of public concern within the framework of applicable laws. (ALA, 2005, paras 1–4)

In 2012, ethos and ethics momentum picked up speed when the IFLA's Governing Board endorsed the *Code of Ethics for Library and Other Information Workers*. It is organized around six critical themes: "(1) access to information; (2) responsibilities toward individuals and society; (3) privacy, secrecy and transparency; (4) open access and intellectual property; (5) neutrality, personal integrity and professional skills; (6) colleague and employer/employee relationship" (IFLA, 2016, Preamble, para 1). IFLA gives attention in the code to urgent labor topics within contemporary library and information workplace culture (e.g., whistleblowing, workplace speech, and gender pay equity) conditional to closing the gap between rhetoric and reality in the global library and information environment.

The IFLA code reveals the real need for intercultural understandings of complex and often competing contexts that influence work on the ground. Most notably, though, it includes the important disclaimer that IFLA has no enforcement authority over library administrations. Not just at IFLA, but in most instances, the association rhetoric is persuasion and consensus building and aspirational. Only a handful of national library associations have included actual sanctions for librarians who violate their code of ethics. Thus, for example, ALA's Resolution on Workplace Speech does not trump the need for the LeRoy C. Merritt Humanitarian Fund in the US, which exists to support, maintenance, medical care, and welfare of librarians

> Denied employment rights or discriminated against on the basis of gender, sexual orientation, race, color, creed, religion, age, disability, or place of national origin; or

Denied employment rights because of defense of intellectual freedom; that is, threatened with loss of employment or discharged because of their stand for the cause of intellectual freedom, including promotion of freedom of the press, freedom of speech, the freedom of librarians to select items for their collections from all the world's written and recorded information, and defense of privacy rights. (LeRoy C. Merritt Humanitarian Fund, n.d. para 1)

As Samek notes in IFLA's inaugural *SpeakUp!* Blog

Actualization of any code of ethics in our field rests on multiple conditions, including: employment terms in any given library administration; labour law and related legislation in any given legal jurisdiction; influence and consensus making within the library and information community and society more broadly; and ultimately, individual conflicting obligations to ourselves, to our profession, to our employer, to our community, and to the law.

Despite clear core values, it is not easy to reconcile these various considerations. Of course, some librarians and other information professionals have been known to suffer personally and professionally in the process. (Samek, 2018, paras 5–6)

Given the monolithic nature of libraries, archives, and museums, it is important never to lose sight of the actual people who work within their walls (physical and virtual).

Librarianship in North America is essentially an unregulated profession. Ultimately, professional association-based ethics statements do not trump employer rights, collective agreements, employee and customer codes of conduct, institutional policies with consequences if violated, human resources policies, employer's accountability to human rights codes, and labor law. At play within this dynamic matrix, is debate about what is and is not a library issue. This debate has endured through generations and it is alive and well in contemporary CLIS, where current calls for defining, redefining, and even confining intellectual freedom in the context of harm appear widely in academic and professional literature, conference programs, social media postings, and more. A highly publicized example, globally, is the charged debate over controversial speakers (e.g., Megan Murphy) in publicly funded spaces, including in public and academic libraries. LIS and CLIS therein, reflecting society at large, is widely and deeply exploring the mix of opinion, perspective, and experience. Indeed, the 2021 Elements of Empowerment conference included a full day of bystander intervention in the workplace to stop race-based harassment education offered by Hollaback! trainers, and is described below.

The last several years have not only seen an uptick in exciting diversity and social justice work and scholarship in libraries and related organizations, but also in the negative comments and opposing opinions that have been registered as a result. Free speech is certainly something that we embrace, but harassment, bullying, trolling, doxxing, and other mentally and physically harmful behaviors go well beyond free speech and cannot be tolerated. In 2019 we began these important conversations and linked these phenomena to library and information science, and now in 2021, we will continue this work by strategizing ways to *combat* bullying and trolling. On March 23-24, 2021, we will hear from experts on cyberbullying, LIS mental health, intellectual freedom, and being an active bystander/up-stander. (Elements of Empowerment, n.d., para 3)

Freedom of expression exemplified by the core library value of intellectual freedom is a central concern sewn into the fabric of LIS discourse from the 1930s through to CLIS today. Of course, it reflects broader societal explorations in global information ethics, philosophy, ideology, law, human rights, social justice, labor, and so on, including in Canada.

Contemporary Activity

Today on a global level, critical librarians and other information workers are engaged with critical theory and pedagogy, grassroots organizing, decolonization of institutions, justice, diversity, equity, respect, anti-racism and expressive freedom, and literacy in all its forms (e.g., print, information, data, digital, alogrithmic). From freedom of opinion and the right to know to the more recent right to be forgotten, human rights are conditional subject matter alongside information ethics and related concerns in the informational, cultural, and cultural heritage network. Carolin Huang's (2020) lead contribution to *The Journal of Contemporary Issues in Education* special issue on Critical Library and Information Studies: Educational Opportunities presents an unprecedented snapshot of the presence of CLIS in Canada today and in what Huang perceives to be its radical expression. Huang, who undertook the article as an online graduate LIS student at the University of Alberta, cast fresh eyes on the terrain from Montreal, finding it attending to

> increased cuts to library and archives, neoliberal discourse in library associations and policies, unionization at academic libraries, decolonization of library education and practice, the absence of Indigenous and people of colour librarians, librarianship as a feminist profession, the effects of postmodernism on archives, archiving of marginalized histories, social exclusion perpetuated by the profession, intellectual freedom for the library profession, advocacy for diversity in hiring and collections, and community-led librarianship. Two major events that have shaped contemporary radical librarianship in Canada are the cuts to Library and Archives Canada and the release of the Truth and Reconciliation Commission (TRC) Report. Other shaping factors include the broader structures of neoliberalism, racism, and homo/transphobia, in addition to the debates on homelessness, Internet censorship, and technological innovation that has preoccupied the entire field of librarianship. (Huang, 2020, p. 11)

While there is clear evidence critical librarians and other information workers in Canada share compassion and conviction for critical advances through research and practice that encourage transformations, these well-intentioned efforts reveal troubling limits. Huang finds

> what arises as gaps include: the early history of radical librarianship in Canada; geographic contexts outside major English-speaking cities; theoretical perspectives using critical theory; perspectives from Indigenous and racialized librarians and archivists; critical LIAS [library, information and archival studies] education and information literacy; social exclusion based on gender identity; critical work on homelessness and poverty; considerations of disability; and ties between librarianship, grassroots organizing and social movements in Canada. These silences are indicative of the persisting power relations that affect the library, archival and information setting. (Huang, 2020, p. 14)

Huang's (2020) recommended remedy includes: more theoretical works to complement the plethora of "practice-driven focus" and "attention to action-driven" knowledge (p. 14); understanding CLIS is not straightforward and does not "entail a teleological direction toward justice or progress, and instead, encompasses the many ways librarianship both contributes to and subverts power" (p. 4); nurturing "pockets of dissent" (p. 4); ongoing "self-reflection, and conceptual rethinking" (p. 4) to strengthen CLIS scholarship and ensure library and other information workers are "always aware of the dominant ideologies that pervade" our spaces (p. 4); and, conceiving thought as a "form of labour in and of itself for its ability to transform dominant epistemological paradigms and forms of knowledge production" (p. 14). These constructive suggestions align with others voiced earlier in Canada. For example, they echo David J. Hudson's articulation of how CLIS can perpetuate "the primacy of practicality as a pedagogical method" and the need for new "LIS spaces that go beyond solution-oriented scholarship and ordinary language" (Hudson, 2017, p. 27 as cited in Huang, 2020). As witnessed in person by Samek, Hudson's voice stood out loud and clear in October 2012 in Ottawa on the floor of the Canadian Association of University Teachers Librarians' Conference on the theme defending academic librarianship. Hudson spoke at a microphone set up for Q&A, accounting he was the only identifiable person of color in the room of approximately one hundred academic librarians drawn from academic libraries across Canada. By no coincidence, Hudson is a co-founder of the Canadian Association of Professional Academic Librarians, founded in 2012. Of note,

> CAPAL is a national membership association representing the interests of professional academic librarians in relation to the areas of education, standards, professional practice, ethics, and core principles. CAPAL differs from other library associations in that it is an advocacy group focused on the individual

and the profession. Like other academic associations, we aim to work collaboratively with local, provincial and national organizations currently working on behalf of librarians and libraries.

CAPAL has evolved in response to the challenges academic librarians have faced in recent years. A pivotal catalyst for forming this association was the national response organizers received to the symposium "Academic Librarianship: A Crisis or Opportunity" held at the University of Toronto on November 18, 2011. The response was overwhelming and the message clear: the concerns of academic librarians were not being addressed. (Canadian Association of Professional Academic Librarians, About, History, 2021, paras 1–2)

Further afield, Ian Beilin (2017, p. 195) reinforces Samek's characterization of critical librarianship as a risk-based endeavor involving "an international movement of library and information workers that considers the human condition and human rights over other professional concerns" (Critical Librarianship, 2007, para 3, as cited in Beilin). Beilin (2017, p. 208) offers "Critical librarianship can and should embrace academic theory, in all its variety, while at the same time remain true to the visions articulated by Samek … This is precisely what a theoretically informed critical librarianship is capable of doing" (Samek, 2007, p. 204 as cited in Beilin). This check and balance protects against the danger of an elitist, academic centric critical librarianship that "will exclude many if not all librarians and LIS scholars outside academia [and academic librarianship in particular] who consider themselves 'critical' or committed to social justice" (Beilin, 2017, p. 196). This requires intensive individual and collective effort, given, for example, the urgent scholarship by Beth Patin, Melinda Sebastian, Jieun Yeon, and Danielle Bertolini that advances the subject of epistemic injustices, including information injustices. They find epistemic injustice in LIS in at least four forms (testimonial, hermeneutical, participatory, and curriculum) and call for acknowledgment of the harm done, and the need for actual interruptions to reduce the harm and to achieve justice (Patin et al., 2020). Hermeneutical harm is picked up below.

KNOWLEDGE ORGANIZATION

Hermeneutical harm is heavily evident in the core of LIS, in knowledge organization, because information seekers, such as teachers and learners, rely on knowledge organizing systems to access information. And this often occurs through rear-view mirror systems in libraries (and archives, and elsewhere). For example, through information seeking using Library of Congress Classification, Dewey Decimal Classification, and Universal Decimal Classification In "Mind the Metadata," Samek observes, "Several generations of librarians, including: Sanford Berman; Frank Exner, Little Bear; Hope Olson; and, K.R. Roberto, have raised awareness about the power of naming, descriptive vs. prejudicial labelling, and calls for cataloguing reform" (Samek, 2016, para 3).

Samek provides coverage of a 2015 letter written by Berman that he sent to the *American Libraries* magazine. It reads, in part,

> Dear Colleagues: Mass incarceration. Stop-and-frisk. "Broken windows" policing. War profiteering. Science denialism. AIDS denialism. Climate change denialism. Anti-vaccine movement. Micro aggression. Stereotype threat. Native American Holocaust. Armenian Genocide denialism. Wage theft.
>
> These topics appear frequently in the media. And libraries have materials on them. But they cannot be found by subject-searching catalogs because the Library of Congress [LC] has failed to create and assign appropriate subject headings, even though they've been formally recommended. If you agree that such rubrics would contribute to public debate and policy-making, please contact LC's Cataloging Policy & Support Office (Washington, DC 20540-4305). (Berman, 2015, p. 1)

Kenny Garcia observes, "Information is not neutral, thus the way that information is presented by librarians adds meaning and context for students. There is power and privilege in the ways in which information is presented and processed by instructors and students. The dialectical relationship between students who can access the information and those without access is separated by pay walls, skewed algorithms, and hegemonic authority controlled vocabulary" (Garcia, 2015, para 3). Continuing the discourse, Litwin Books and Library Juice Press seek book proposals and manuscripts for an ongoing series entitled "Critical Information Organization in Library and Information Science" described below.

> The introduction of new cataloging standards (RDA) and a greater recognition of the place of cataloging data in a linked data environment have brought major changes to library cataloging. Critical librarianship has also influenced conversations around ethics in cataloging and cataloging theory by shifting the discussion away from the idea that catalogers can work towards an ideal catalog in efforts of inclusion towards a recognition that standards cannot serve conflicting worldviews and are limited by the implicit bias of their creators. (Litwin Books & Library Juice Press, Series on, 2021, para 2)

This line of inquiry builds naturally on other pioneering works in CLIS, such as Safiya Umoja Noble's Algorithms of Oppression: How Search Engines Reinforce Racism and Sarah T. Roberts' Behind the Screen: Content Moderation in the Shadows of Social Media. These contributions blend with critical digital media studies and technology, and encourage our attention to AI.

AI AND ETHICS

AI has become dominant across both public and private sectors in corporations, media, academia, and public institutions including libraries, and makes a strong case for leveraging the influence of CLIS in service of education. In December 2020, educational associations within the library and information community adopted a statement on AI ethics and the contributions of diverse voices in the discussion which affirms "ASIS&T, ALISE and the i[information]Schools support the work of researchers, such as Timnit Gebru and others, who seek to identify potential flaws and biases in the algorithms used by AI that may disproportionately impact diverse populations" (ASIS&T, Statement on AI ethics, 2021, para 1). That said, statements don't guarantee action and can consciously and unconsciously feed problematic ethics washing. Huang, Samek, and Ali Shiri argue because "of the essential position of librarianship in the information economy, how librarianship approaches the major technological changes affecting higher education today will help shape the trajectory of AI in learning and teaching" (Huang et al., 2021). They assert

> The unquestioned celebration of ethics across AI industries requires careful examination as the phenomenon of ethics washing is rising. What librarians must remember is that an ethics grounded in an analysis of social inequality must be formed beyond professional codes and in the social spaces they occupy, within and beyond the library setting. In many instances, LIS scholars are optimally positioned to leverage their knowledge, expertise and networks to foster and contribute to major education priorities around AI for higher education. The combination of information ethics, information science and educational technologies built into LIS programs and now, the fluid impact of COVID-19 on higher education is all the more reason to identify and explore AI, ethics, and educational perspectives in LIS for the benefit of all with the aim to realize a closing of the gap between rhetoric and reality. It is recommended LIS programs broadly take a proactive, holistic and direct interest in artificial intelligence (and machine learning or data science) alongside offerings and contributions in information ethics, while closely examining their own evolving local labour practices, policies, and processes, which are ever evolving.

CLIS contributes to important explorations into information science and educational technology. The following excerpt from a January 2021 call for chapter proposals for a book project with the working title *Ethics in Linked Data* helps to illustrate the point for just about anyone who is invested in teaching and learning, and research and scholarship today, especially given how diverse communities across the world have been propelled into remote learning systems during the COVID-19 pandemic.

> By recognizing the current and historical use of technologies as control mechanisms among people and communities (for example, the intertwining of utilitarian and imperialist data generation in the 19th century to the use of data in genocides, algorithmic bias, and surveillance capitalism today), and

acknowledging that design and use of technology does not happen in a vacuum, proposals should speak to a variety of ongoing conversations on how linked data expands or counteracts many issues often discussed in critical information organization such as those listed below, among others. This book aims to collect the voices of practitioners, technologists, and developers working on linked data initiatives; scholars working at the intersection of ethics, cultural heritage, and technology; and workers in GLAMS [galleries, libraries, archives, museums, special collections], among others in order to explore emerging and changing technical and ethical landscapes. (Burlingame et al., 2021, paras 3–4)

Conclusion and Future Study

Garcia (2015) reminds us in 2007 Berman proposed to the Cataloging Policy and Support Office of the Library of Congress a new subject heading termed "CRITICAL LIBRARIANSHIP," a label Berman argued for on the basis of Samek's use of the term in print in the 2007 monograph entitled *Librarianship and Human Rights: A Twenty-first Century Guide*. The subject heading has not been adopted as yet. Nor have Berman's subsequent requests in 2008 for "CRITICAL CATALOGING" and in 2020 for "WOKE CATALOGING" (S. Berman, personal communication, January 2021). Important tasks ahead are to read, view, listen, and play with information to realize the hard work of learning, unlearning, and relearning necessary to knowledge development, and to participate in defining and redefining education in the effort to not confine it. CLIS plays an important role in agitating for the role of librarians and other information workers in these efforts.

CLIS has a history. Undoubtedly it also has a future. It is our collective responsibility to distribute that future evenly. Historical perspectives and the Canadian base are under-documented in CLIS. Its health relies on differing voices, and many more of them need to be expressed and heard. Intellectual freedom endures as a thread binding past to future, as a condition of human rights, whistleblowing, witnessing, and justice, as well as contested in explorations of injustice and harm. As the future of CLIS unfolds, there will be profound implications for the global academic enterprise with respect to freedom of expression, including impacts of the status of intellectual freedom, workplace speech, and academic freedom. As witnessed virtually by Samek, at the outset of the keynote Learning and Engaging with Indigenous Ways of Knowing at the BC Library Conference, keynote speaker Sierra Tasi Baker requested the virtual audience not record and not take notes, but just listen. The request was profound given librarian and information workers' deep historical relationship with manuscripts, documents, and records.

REFERENCES

American Association of University Teachers. (2021). *Journal of Academic. Freedom Call for Papers*. Retrieved January 30, 2021, from https://www.aaup.org/reports-publications/journal-academic-freedom/call-papers?link_id=3&can_id=5e3c5301d81f6dc4bb18fbe03d884628&source=email-article-submissions-due-february-8-2&email_referrer=email_1054580&email_subject=article-submissions-due-february-8

American Library Association. (2005). *Resolution on Workplace Speech*. Retrieved January 30, 2021, from http://www.ala.org/advocacy/sites/ala.org.advocacy/files/content/intfreedom/statementspols/ifresolutions/Resolution%20on%20Workpl.pdf

American Library Association, Office for Intellectual Freedom. (n.d.). *The library bill of rights and the freedom to read statement*. Retrieved January 30, 2021 from, http://www.ala.org/aboutala/offices/oif/LBOR-FTR-statement-pamphlet

Association for Information Science and Technology. (n.d.). *About ASIS&T*. Retrieved January 30, 2021, from https://www.asist.org/about/

Association for Information Science and Technology. (n.d.). *Special interest group on the history and foundations of information science*. Retrieved January 30, 2021, from https://www.asist.org/sig/sighfis/

Association for Information Science and Technology. (n.d.). *Welcome to ASIS&T*. Retrieved January 30, 2021, from https://www.asist.org/

Association for Information Science and Technology. (2021). *Statement on AI ethics and the contributions of diverse voices in the discussion*. Retrieved January 30, 2021, from https://www.asist.org/2020/12/21/ethics-in-ai-statement/

Association for Library and Information Science Education. (n.d.). *Welcome to ALISE!* Retrieved January 30, 2021, from https://www.alise.org/

Association for Library and Information Science Education. (2016). *ALISE research taxonomy*. Retrieved January 30, 2021, from https://www.alise.org/research-tax onomy-

Beilin, I. (2017). Critical librarianship as an academic pursuit. In K. P. Nicholson & M. Seale (Eds.), *The politics of theory and the practice of critical librarianship* (pp. 195–210). Library Juice Press.

Berman S. (2015, 19 May). Letter on the subject "Comment Enabled" sent from Sanford Berman (4400 Morningside Road, Edina, Minnesota 55416) to *American Libraries* (50. E Huron Street, Chicago, Illinois 60611).

Burlingame, K., Provo, A., & Watson, B. M. (2021, January 11). *Call for chapter proposals: Ethics in linked data*. Litwin Books & Library Juice Press. Retrieved January 30, 2021, from https://litwinbooks.com/call-for-chapter-proposals-ethics-in-linked-data/

Canadian Association of Professional Academic Librarians. About. History. Retrieved May 6, 2021, from https://capalibrarians.org/about/history/

"Critical Librarianship: An Interview with Toni Samek," *the (unofficial) BCLA intellectual freedom committee blog*. November 13, 2007. https://bclaifc.wordpress.com/2007/11/13/critical-librarianship-an-interview-with-toni-samek/

Critical Librarianship in Praxis. Upcoming Courses. UCLA California Rare Book School. Retrieved May 7, 2020 from https://www.calrbs.org/courses/upcoming-courses/

Elements of Empowerment: Defeating the Bullies and the Trolls in the Library. (n.d.). Retrieved January 30, 2021, from https://sites.google.com/view/elementsofempowerment/home

Garcia, K. (2015, 22 June). Keeping up with ... critical librarianship. *Association of College and Research Libraries*. Retrieved January 30, 2021, from http://www.ala.org/acrl/publications/keeping_up_with/critlib

Huang, C. (2020). On the importance of theory in LIAS: A review of literature on radical librarianship in Canada. *The Journal of Contemporary Issues in Education*, 15(1), 4–21.

Huang, C., Samek, T., & Shiri, A. (2021). AI and ethics in higher education: An LIS perspective. *Journal of Education for Library and Information Science*, 62(4), 351–365.

Hudson, D. J. (2017). On "diversity" as anti-racism in library and information studies: A critique. *Journal of Critical Library and Information Studies*, 1(1), 1–36. https://doi.org/10.24242/jclis.v1i1.6

International Federation of Library Associations and Institutions. (1983). *Resolution on behalf of librarians who are victims of violation of human rights*. Retrieved January 30, 2021, from https://www.ifla.org/files/assets/faife/publications/policy-documents/munich.pdf

International Federation of Library Associations and Institutions. (2012). *Code of ethics for librarians and other information workers*. Retrieved January 30, 2021, from https://www.ifla.org/publications/node/11092

Journal of Critical Library and Information Studies. (2017). About the Journal. Mission. Retrieved January 30, 2021, from https://journals.litwinbooks.com/index.php/jclis/about

Journal of Radical Librarianship. About the Journal. (n.d.). Retrieved January 30, 2021 from, https://journal.radicallibrarianship.org/index.php/journal/about

Lau, A., Sellie, A., & Day, R. E. (2017). Editors' Note. Why is the journal of critical library and information studies needed today? *Journal of Critical Library and Information Studies*, 1(1), 1–6. https://doi.org/10.24242/jclis.v1i1.48

LeRoy C. Merritt Humanitarian Fund. (n.d.). American Library Association. Retrieved January 30, 2021, from http://www.ala.org/aboutala/affiliates/relatedgroups/merrittfund/merritthumanitarian

Litwin Books & Library Juice Press. (2021). Retrieved January 30, 2021, from https://litwinbooks.com/

Litwin Books & Library Juice Press. (2021, January 11). *Call for chapter proposals on ethics in linked data*. Retrieved January 30, 2021, from https://litwinbooks.com/call-for-chapter-proposals-ethics-in-linked-data/

Litwin Books & Library Juice Press. (2021). Series on Critical Information Organization in LIS. Retrieved January 30, 2021, from https://litwinbooks.com/series-on-critical-information-organization-in-lis/

McFarland. (n.d.). About the Book *Progressive library organizations: A worldwide history*. Retrieved January 30, 2021, from https://mcfarlandbooks.com/product/progressive-library-organizations/

Melo, M., & Nichols J. (2020). *Re-making the library makerspace: Critical theories, reflections, and practices*. Library Juice Press.

Noble, S. U. (2018). *Algorithms of oppression: How search engines reinforce racism*. NYU Press.

Patin, B., Sebastian, M., Yeon, J., & Bertolini, D. (2020). Toward epistemic justice: An approach for conceptualizing epistemicide in the information professions. *Proceedings of the Association for Information Science and Technology, 57*(1). https://doi.org/10.1002/pra2.242

Pluckrose, H. (2021, April 15). We need social justice, not "critical social justice". *Symposium*, No. 1. Retrieved May 6, 2021, from https://mail.google.com/mail/u/0/#label/Publishing%2FAli+Abdi+Book+Chapter/WhctKJWQntcngbGXKgBdkNSSzjxPZQTbhCnjvfPKmrGwDsSVwsbKvBgnVgzkFdPhQsjbhmG

Samek, T. (2004). Internet and intention: An infrastructure for progressive librarianship. *International Journal of Information Ethics, 2*, 1–18. https://doi.org/10.7939/R3XP6VH1Z

Samek, T. (2007). *Librarianship and human rights: A twenty-first century guide.* Chandos Publishing.

Samek, T. (2016, September 14). Mind the Metadata. Centre for Free Expression Blog. Retrieved January 30, 2021, from https://cfe.ryerson.ca/blog/2016/09/mind-metadata

Samek, T. (2018, January 12). First Loyalty. International Federation of Library Associations and Institutions SpeakUp! Blog. Retrieved January 30, 2021, from https://blogs.ifla.org/faife/2018/01/12/first-loyalty-by-toni-samek/

CHAPTER 20

Critical Methodologies and an Art-Based Method of Research in Higher Education Institutions

Janna M. Popoff

INTRODUCTION

Critical methodologies through art, specifically photography, can help to holistically understand the educational and social experiences of students in higher education institutions. Visual research methods such as photography help to mitigate the pressure on language, specifically English, and aims to lessen the hegemonic linguistic hierarchies of the English language and its colonial footprints. Photography acts as the data collection method that invites participants to reflect on their lives as well as represent their experiences to an audience. On the one hand the researcher/audience has access to a hidden world, but on the other hand participants have control over what they want to reveal. In essence, one is invited in, invited to participate in the experiences of another. Songtag (1977) poignantly reflected that "photographed images do not seem to be statements about the world so much as pieces of it, miniatures of reality that anyone can make or acquire" (p. 2). The data collection tool, photography, is in the hands of the participants of a study, and in turn, the visual image relays what is important to the participants. Utilizing critical methodologies that employ the method of photography, this chapter: (a) explores how inclusive, democratic, and participatory research benefits international student participants, (b) explores an alternative method of data collection, and (c) contributes to a growing body of critical visual methodologies. Further,

---

J. M. Popoff (✉)
Thompson Rivers University, Kamloops, BC, Canada
e-mail: jpopoff@tru.ca

© The Author(s), under exclusive license to Springer Nature Switzerland AG 2022
A. A. Abdi and G. W. Misiaszek (eds.), *The Palgrave Handbook on Critical Theories of Education*, https://doi.org/10.1007/978-3-030-86343-2_20

Sontag elaborated that the camera is an extension of one's consciousness in that an experience is captured in a photograph and there is proof that an event occurred. A photograph can be used as a powerful tool that offers evidence that something happened, that in essence, "I was here," "I did this," and "This happened to me."

Exploring critical methodologies reflexively is an important part in changing research processes and reshaping elements of research in order to address how methodologies should be reconstructed and reintroduced. Shaping methodologies to contexts and to utilize conceptual frameworks which include liberating, democratic, participatory structures can help achieve holistic research (West et al., 2012). A critical methodology is not simply prescribed to one's research techniques but "denotes a contextual and evolving theory of inquiry within a research program that includes assumptions about the target subject matter and its rigorous investigation, as well as practical research strategies that follow from those assumptions" (Yanchar et al., 2005, p. 35). Therefore, developing, altering, and applying research approaches that engage and enhance the researchers' and the participants' understanding of the questions posed by the research are essential components of critical methodologies. Subsequently, the intention and thought in selecting a methodological framework or strategy, along with a method that reflects and actualizes the inclusive, participatory, and democratic nature of the study becomes a very conscious act.

Methodology and Method

How one does research and the methodological tools the researcher chooses indicates the epistemological positionality of the researcher and reflects deeply on their academic values and the contribution to expanding progressive and alternative methodologies. Smith (1999) put forth:

> Method is important because it is regarded as the way in which knowledge is acquired or discovered and as a way in which we can "know" what is real. Each academic discipline is attached not just to a set of ideas about knowledge, but also to methodologies. (p. 164)

Historically, there has been a strong influence of positivist research methods in which data are collected, measured, and quantified in "rational" and "scientific" frameworks. However, positivist methodologies do not consider the contextual, historical, and humanistic sides of participants in studies. Crotty (1998) stated that "Articulating scientific knowledge is one thing; claiming that scientific knowledge is utterly objective and that only scientific knowledge is valid, certain and accurate is another" (p. 29). In the past, and persisting into the present, some research continues to be prescriptive, hegemonic, and hierarchical. Freire (2005) stated that:

Any situation in which "A" objectively exploits "B" or hinders his and her pursuit of self-affirmation as a responsible person is one of oppression. Such a situation in itself constitutes violence, even when sweetened by false generosity, because it interferes with the individual's ontological and historical vocation to be more fully human. (p. 55)

Therefore, when research is done to participants instead of with participants, the researcher is acting as an oppressive force, and one that could be causing violence to a population.

Defining the differences between method and methodology can help clarify the tools (method) used in research versus the construction of the theoretical design (methodology). Crotty (1998) defined research methods as "the techniques or procedures used to gather or analyze data related to some research question or hypothesis" (p. 3). Further, methodology is "the strategy, plan of action, process or design lying behind the choice and use of particular methods and linking the choice and use of the methods to the desired outcomes" (Crotty, 1998, p. 3). Therefore, presently embedded in some institutions' ideas of what constitutes "serious research" are methodologies and methods that lack the critical self-awareness of the researchers who actualize them and consideration of the individuals who participate in the data collection. For instance, questionnaires can be prescriptive and leading in their line of inquiry which can limit research participants' answers because of constricted questions that are skewed toward mis/guided hypotheses and interpretations. Therefore, data can be filtered and partial depending on how questions are created, stated, and delivered. Furthermore, remnants of colonial methods are visible and invisible depending on who is using them and to whom they are being done to. Subsequently, reflexivity on methodologies and data collection is needed for research projects. Reflexivity allows the researcher to reflect critically on their own methods and consider the groups with which they are engaging in research and the methodology that would best suit the participants as well as the goals of the research. Moreover, critical reflection on methodologies would allow the implementation of equitable and egalitarian methodologies that may result in the most pliability for praxis in developing new ways of researching.

Smith (1999) has advocated for the decolonization of methodologies which encompasses utilizing alternative methods and methodologies. In addition, Smith has advocated for communities outside of academia to have access to information gained from research, specifically from indigenous groups that have often had research done to them and not with them. Decolonization of research can and should be applied to critically reflexive research in all disciplines of research projects in order to change the overall practices of, at times, an invasive research landscape. How research is conducted should never be something that is done to a group but in the spirit of social justice and democracy should be carried out in a way that is a beneficial activity for a group. For example, the methodology of photovoice is a visual, democratic, and participatory methodology that aims to recognize participants as co-creators of knowledge. In photovoice, participants use the method of photography to communicate what is important to them through visual representations of their lives. Songtag (1977) postulated that "the ultimate wisdom of the photographic image is to say, 'There is the surface. Now think-or rather feel, intuit-what is beyond it, what the reality must be like if it looks this way'" (p. 17). The photograph acts as a focal point for dialog with the participants, the researcher, and the audience who sees the photographs in public exhibitions in a variety of community settings. Moreover, the power that comes with knowledge should be accessible to a variety of communities, and these communities include the participants who are part of the research, academic communities, and the general public. Research needs to be ethical, equitable, and accessible to communities inside and outside of higher educational institutions in order to deconstruct constructs of power and control.

When a methodological position is formed and a method is selected, it should stand that "investigators begin with a theoretical and historical sense of the subject matter and questions worth studying, the appropriate strategies for investigating those questions, and the most effective ways of handling problems that arise in the course of research" (Yanchar et al., 2005, p. 35). Additionally, critical methodology first begins with asking the question of whether there is theoretical consistency within the research plan. Further, does the method consider the subject matter, the participants, and the theoretical strategies of the research? In short, methodologies frame how the questions are being asked and how they are going to be answered. Moreover, the state of what critical methodologies includes is a "continued reflection on and revision of old methods, along with innovation and development of new ones, based on the exigencies of theoretical exploration and critical disciplinary self-examination" (Yanchar et al., 2005, p. 28). Therefore, critical researchers seek methodologies that reflect and consider the ways in which data are created with participants in a study. It is imperative to ask how the research will benefit the participants, their community, and the larger global community. Traces of the colonial past have left indelible footprints across the academic landscape, and to move into inclusive research, methodologies need to supersede the oppressive, hierarchical, restrictive, and prescriptive methodologies of the past. Precedented practices in methodologies have harnessed both the participants and researchers to a yoke of antiquity, but moving forward academics and researchers must insist on methodologies that are equable, democratic, and inclusive, and that contribute to a variety of communities both inside and outside of academic institutions.

A Case Study

I included myself in the research as a participant as well as the researcher. My purpose for including myself in the study had four main positions. The first is that at the time I was also an international student studying in higher education in Beijing. The second is that I did not want to ask the participants in the study to be vulnerable and open if I was not also vulnerable and open, and as hooks (1994) emphasized in her writing on the emotionally vulnerable classroom, the teacher needs to take the same risks they ask of their students. As well, recognizing that one could view participation in a study as contamination of data, Rodriguez (2010) stated "although disclosing oneself may be viewed as 'contaminating the data,' one could argue that it further encourages the participant to elaborate on their experiences. Demonstrating empathy to the respondent gives the message that they are capable and deserving participant" (p. 494). The third main position, following the philosophy of Harding (1995), who questioned whether there is really ever objective research at all considering the standpoint of the researcher, which renders research to be subjective, is that I embraced the subjectivity of the framework of the project and included myself. Furthermore, participating in the study allowed me to negotiate hierarchies of power between the researcher and the researched. In turn, I was able to mitigate power dynamics and thus able to actualize a democratic research methodology in line with feminist ideologies and practices of participatory research.

Additionally, Smith (1999) asserted:

> Most research methodologies assume that the researcher is an outsider able to observe without being implicated in the scene. This is related to positivism and notions of objectivity and neutrality. Feminist research and other more critical approaches have made the insider methodology much more acceptable in qualitative research. (p. 137)

Therefore, the idea that objective and neutral research can be conducted is a fallacy that is upheld by positivist epistemologies that are a disservice to progressive, inclusive, and heuristic research. Further, aside from me acting as a participant/researcher, the strongest tool for deconstructing hierarchies of power lay in the methodology of photovoice and the method of photography by putting the data collection device (taking photographs) into the hands of the participants. The real source of power came from the co-creation of knowledge from the participants. In the next section I will explain the origin of the photovoice methodology, how and why it is used, the theoretical concepts, and the actualization of this democratic and participatory methodology.

The Photovoice Methodology

Photovoice is a methodology developed by American scholars Wang and Burris (1994) to understand the lives and needs of disadvantaged Chinese women living in Yunnan province. Photography is the method, and acts as the data collection device used in the photovoice methodology. Wang and Burris developed and employed the photovoice methodology in order to visually see the needs of the women in Yunnan province and to mitigate the pressure of relying on language or facing language barriers to communicate. Subsequently, photovoice has been used in social work, hospitals and health care, and education to name some of the areas where this methodology has been applied in order to visually understand the experiences of participants in a variety of studies. Not only is the visual aspect of photography communicative, but the methodology asks the participants of the study to be actively involved in showing what is important to them instead of using assumptive questions that may not be in line with the participants' situations, needs, and concerns.

Feminist Epistemologies

This next section starts with a reflection on Virginia Woolf's quote from her essay on Joyce from the journal *Modern Fiction* (McNeille, 1984) where she wrote:

> Let us record the atoms as they fall upon the mind in the order in which they fall, let us trace the pattern, however disconnected and incoherent in appearance, which each sight or incident scores upon the consciousness. Let us not take it for granted that life exists more fully in what is commonly thought big than in what is commonly thought small. (p. 161)

For me, this quote is an important introduction to the significance of the small occurrences in day-to-day life that make up the important things that affect each of us and imprint on our consciousness. No matter how small, or in fact because of the smallness, the moment/s matter more. For example, small moments of life that are captured through photographs are the important moments that make up the whole of an experience. Things that are commonly thought small are perhaps more important than what is commonly thought big to the lives of the participants in this study because it is these small needs, that often have big consequences, and are often overlooked by the institution. However, utilizing feminist epistemologies that seek to understand and record the smaller things in the participants lives, we can see how small moments reflect larger issues for international students studying in Beijing.

Feminist epistemologies make use of methodologies which utilize storytelling, parables, poetry, photovoice, video, and revisionist history to name a few. Representing and learning from the lives of participants can be actualized by means of participation in the research itself. This means that the tools of meaning-making and data production should be placed in the hands of the participants in order to try to achieve social transformation, community engagement, and personal and communal emancipation. Therefore, for the research that I conducted at a higher education institution in Beijing I used feminist methodologies as part of photovoice. These methodologies were employed because they engaged the participants of the study in a participatory, inclusive, and democratic research using the method of photography and group discussions based on participants' photographs.

The photovoice methodology has three theoretical frameworks that include feminist theory, documentary photography, and participatory research (Wang & Burris, 1994). The methodology of photovoice relies on these three frameworks, and documentary photography acts as a tool in the hands of the participants to document and represent their daily lives living and studying in Beijing. Berger (1976) commented that to capture a moment in time in a photograph is a very reflective and thoughtful process; that this moment meant something more than all the other moments that came before is nothing short of monumental.

CRITICAL CONSCIOUSNESS AND PARTICIPATORY THEORIES

Critical consciousness and participatory research seek to lessen the hierarchical systems of the researcher and participants by incorporating research participants into the process of making their own meaning. Freire (2005) said that people who find themselves in certain situations will reflect on their own "situationality" when they are challenged by it, and "Human beings *are* because they *are in* a situation. And they *will be more* the more they not only critically reflect upon their existence but critically act upon it" (p. 109). What Freire stated applies to both the research participants and the researcher, where both critically reflected on their situationality in this study's research process, and were able to critically act in the form of offering solutions to institutional and personal problems. Freire's empowerment education theory focuses on encouraging individuals to become active in addressing the needs of their community. In the research study as a goal, empowerment education started with the data collection, and participants delved into their own communities and photographed their concerns and reflections. Once completed, the participants moved into facilitated group discussions, sharing with one another what the photographs meant to them. Group dialog allowed the participants to build upon each other's concerns, helping to shape and identify the needs of their community (Wang & Burris, 1994).

For Freire (2005), it was imperative that the relationship between the researcher and the community of participants was not one of objectification and that members of the community are authorities of their experience and critical investigation. Freire's theories included the belief that research is not neutral and needs to be participatory in its investigations. The goals of research also need to work toward emancipation and social justice, and research that asks participants to reflect on and challenge their roles within their own communities can start to achieve these goals.

Furthermore, oppressed people who become aware of their situations could transform their environments through praxis (Rahman, 1991). The photographs and the dialogs that were generated were sources of information that came from the sometimes emotional situations in the photographs. Through group dialogue, we were able to transform consciousness and praxis as we collectively reflected on how international students can improve their situations in Beijing both personally and institutionally (Freire, 2005). The aim of dialog was to create change which was a process that required participants to engage, interact, and reflect on their actions to achieve social change and justice (Mayfield-Johnson & Butler, 2017).

THE PHOTOVOICE PROCESS

The photovoice methodology was implemented in two groups of six and seven student participants. Each participant was asked to take photographs of their lives—their day-to-day lives, what engaged them, their struggles and triumphs, a reflection of their lives as international students. The participants shared five to six of their selected photographs with the group and discussed what the photographs meant to them. The groups practiced the SHOWeD method of talking about the photographs. SHOWeD is an acronym developed by Wang and Burris (1994) inclusive to the photovoice methodology. SHOWeD is explained as: What do you **S**ee here? What is really **H**appening here? How does this relate to **O**ur lives? **W**hy does this condition **E**xist? What can we **D**o about it?

Most often, the narrative descriptions of the photographs in the group meetings resulted in conversations regarding how other participants were affected by the same concerns. Questions were posed for more information and clarification on the situations being presented and this resulted in deep discussions. In this way, through discussion of the images in the photographs, and observations of the content of the photographs, generative themes emerged. These generative themes are important because they show how the participants were thinking and feeling about their reality, both visually and verbally. More concisely, Freire (2005) stated:

> To investigate the generative theme is to investigate the people's thinking about reality and people's action upon reality, which is their praxis. For precisely this reason, the methodology proposed requires that the investigators and the people (who would normally be considered objects of that investigation) should act as *co-investigators*. The more active an attitude men and women take in regard to the exploration of their thematics, the more they deepen their critical awareness of reality and, in spelling out those thematics, take possession of that reality. (p. 106)

The important generative themes that emerged from the participants' photographs and discussions could be used as essential information in changing and developing institutional protocols and policy regarding international student experiences—academically, emotionally, and socially—within higher educational institutions on their road to internationalization. Not only did important generative themes emerge from the photographs, but from what I observed of the participants, a supportive community formed, and from that community bonds of friendship, alliance, and understanding were constructed organically. From my perspective, and as well from my participation in the group meetings, that life as an international student became a lot less lonely and isolating when vulnerabilities were shared and solutions were offered.

At the end of the data collection, as part of the last component of the photovoice methodology, an exhibition of students' photographs was held in a public space with participants' permission. This was an exhibition space where the international students, faculty, and the Beijing public could view the photographs of the students in the study. In this third space, the exhibition space and the photographs provided and an environment where the uniqueness of each person was seen as a complex individual who occupied more than just the role of an international student (Bhabha, 1994).

The Power of Photography

Art, and specifically in this case, photography, has the power to act as a springboard for dialog, a spark for a memory, a cathartic emotional release, and in some cases, transparency. Photography can be revelatory in how power is normalized, and the exposure of voices, interests, and concerns that may not otherwise be known from nondominant international student populations, such as queer students, women, and families, who have now had a space to communicate their concerns. For example, one of the participants, a Bangladeshi mother of two young boys, revealed in her photographs how busy an average day is for her. Without family housing on campus and access to schools or daycare on or close to the university campus, she needs to live in the suburbs of Beijing, far from campus. The morning includes waking up very early to get her children ready for school, and then she travels in to the university. Through this participatory research the students learned that their concerns were not superfluous, that their needs were important, and most importantly that they were not alone in their struggles.

Feminist theory provided one of the theoretical frameworks for photovoice and offered an alternative data collection tool that aimed to involve and recognize women as participants instead of subjects. In some traditional patriarchal research women can be viewed as research subjects, something that is *done* to women. In contrast, photovoice empowered women to control their own research experience by having total control of the photographs they took, the images they captured, to communicate their experiences and have their voices heard as international students in Beijing (Smith, 1987; Weiler, 1988).

Women who come from countries where traditional forms of patriarchy control society often find themselves subjugated within that society. Therefore, through photovoice, women have a tool (the photograph) in which to express themselves freely with their own agency because they completely control the content they want to communicate. In research, it is sometimes the case that those who have control of knowledge production are those who are seen as experts—the ones who have the social and academic power to decide what is useful knowledge. However, in using egalitarian participatory research methods, the research participants were in control of their knowledge production, and groups that once may have been seen as powerless have the ability to participate in their knowledge production and decide what is useful information (Darroch & Giles, 2014).

Another example of a theme that surfaced through photographs was from a woman of color who was an English as a second language speaker. She took some photographs inside the university classroom with other classmates. In one photograph she showed herself giving a presentation, and in another she showed herself in class working with a group of other classmates. When she spoke about the photographs to the research group she spoke of how she noticed the professor favored those with native English speaking abilities and how she felt that her halting spoken English was a perceived disadvantage to her representation of her academic abilities during presentations. For international students who are teachers in their home countries in their native language(s), this experience of language hierarchies can be daunting and jolting. To be proficient in one or many other languages besides English, and then be evaluated for your intellectual ability based on language, is humbling to say the least.

The topic of discrimination was communicated when the photographs of the classroom situation were discussed. Discriminatory language hierarchies, from a few professors, were perceived by some of the international students, and for example native English speakers are favored, followed by fluent nonnative speakers (Tsuda, 1998). It was revealed through group discussions, based on the photographs, that international students have no recourse to complain of prejudice because a complaints procedure within the university was absent. Therefore, without an institutional history of complaints there is no record of discord, and as a result no growth or change within the university (Ahmed, 2019). Through exploring the themes that surfaced from the photographs, problems on campus surfaced and recognition that support was needed became evident. Therefore, what was learned from the participants experiences can directly influence, change, or build new policies on campus to benefit international students' experiences.

Documentary Photography

The role of documentary photography is to communicate a moment or moments in the lives of groups of people to illustrate an emotional representation of their experiences. Photographs can tell a story that express humanistic, emotional, and compassionate events, and reflect politics and the effects of political systems (Wu & Yun, 2007). Documentary photography has been used as a tool to help vulnerable populations of people tell their stories to the world. Often, these groups have been women, children, victims of war, the impoverished, and the elderly but also, people in the healthcare system, and people in educational institutions. Photovoice is a tool that gives people who are oppressed or underrepresented a means to control their decision in what they want to communicate and how they want to be represented. Often, it is the members of the community who are most succinct and poignant about what needs to be said or known about their experiences (Goo et al., 2011; Wang & Burris, 1994).

Traditionally, photovoice has been used to give voice to vulnerable groups, but photovoice is an adaptable data collection tool and Wang et al. (1996) stated that it should be and can be used in a variety of research situations. Photovoice is able to collect data in a way that captures emotions and feelings that words are not able to. Additionally, photographs add deeper expressions and thoughts from participants who may believe that it is challenging to express themselves with accurate nuance through language, and perhaps even more so, through a foreign language, such as English (Wang & Hannes, 2014).

Feminist researchers seek to produce collaborative environments where everyone participating is a co-creator of knowledge. Therefore, in the photovoice methodology stories emerge from the photographs, and stories can be a powerful way to communicate the intricacies of the dominate themes that emerge in the lives of international students studying in Beijing. In China, quantitatively in numbers, the data provide statistical information on international students. However, the questions of "how" and "why" cannot be answered in numbers, and rarely does one *see* the lives of international students studying in China. Photovoice allows themes to unfold and emerge from the photographs. In the data collection process participants are co-creators of knowledge and bring their awareness to their own situatedness as an international student. Their participation in the study is reflected in the photographs they took which drew attention to the extraordinary visual reflections on their lives as expats and international students for a moment of time in Beijing.

Using photography, it was easy to see how traditional methods, for example positivist research, could have limited or even negated the holistic and heuristic methods of data collection in this study. If quantitative positivist forms were employed, the fertile revelations of the lived experiences of international students studying in a Beijing higher educational institution would have been lost (Rodriguez, 2010). The photovoice methodology included each person contributing to meaning-making, and from the participants photographs important generative themes emerged that reflected the lives of international students' concerns, triumphs, and frailties of living and studying abroad as expats for a time. As Freire (2005) put forth, "Thematic investigation thus becomes a common striving towards awareness of reality and towards self-awareness, which makes this investigation a starting point for the educational process or for cultural action of a liberating character" (p. 107). Critical and reflexive methodologies that employ alternative methods answer the questions of "why" and "how?" that quantitative research leave us to posit. Further, Smith (1999) emphasized the importance of knowledge as not only acquired but shared and dispersed from communities to other communities outside of institutions. Knowledge is power, and Smith theorized that knowledge needs to be spread as part of a continual sharing practice as an extension of research practices. The photography exhibition at the end of the research project in Beijing with international students succeeded in bridging communities and thus was able to spread knowledge outside of the university into the greater Beijing community.

The Photography Exhibition

The knowledge learned from this study conducted in Beijing was shared with the larger Beijing community in the form of a photography exhibition in the hopes of creating knowledge bridges. It was important to the study to take the photographs—the co-creation of knowledge—into a public space to reach people who would not normally interact with international students. The goal of a public exhibition was to share the worlds of international students living in Beijing with a larger community, both foreigners and locals alike. The exhibition of the participants' photographs created a reflexive and productive (praxis) third space. Homi Bhabha (1994) stated that a third space is one in which an in-between space occurs, where cultural structures are seen and negotiated, and new possibilities can be produced. Bhabha's theory on cultural difference provides the concept of hybridity and calls to question preconceived notions of culture and identity. This hybridity acts as an alternative to essentialism, and this third space acts as "These 'in-between' spaces [that] provide the terrain for elaborating strategies of selfhood – singular or communal – that initiate new signs of identity, and innovative sites of collaboration, and contestation, in the act of defining the idea of society itself" (Bhabha, 1994, p. 1).

Engagement with this third space asks for interactions between and with the international student/s and the audiences/communities who see these visual representations of international students' lives in a foreign country. Art, and specifically in this case, photography, has the power to act as a springboard for dialog, a spark for a memory, and a cathartic emotional release. Photographs can create transparency, and they can be revelatory in how power is normalized. Photographs can create space for voices and themes, interests, and concerns that may not otherwise be known from nondominant international student populations such as queer students, women, and families.

Exhibiting photographs of international students functioned as a knowledge-sharing device. Smith (1999) reminded us that to assume that differing parties would not be interested in understanding and learning about the deeper issues would be to make assumptions about who and what interests people. Therefore, photographs displayed in an exhibition to the general public is with the hope that dialog is sparked. The reflexive and critical researcher should always be aware that it is imperative to ensure that research is done ethically and has mutual benefits to all parties involved in research studies and beyond. Sharing knowledge inside and outside of communities means moving academic knowledge into larger communities, and equitable access to knowledge is made possible and seriously considered as an extension of critical methodologies (Smith, 1999). Moreover, a public photography exhibition, with the participants permission, is one way to share knowledge with larger communities outside of the university when employing photovoice.

> There are diverse ways of disseminating knowledge and of ensuring that research reaches the people who have helped make it. Two important ways not always addressed by scientific research are to do with "reporting back" to the people and "sharing knowledge." Both ways assume a principle of reciprocity and feedback. (Smith, 1999, p. 15)

A photography exhibition is one way of sharing knowledge outside of an academic setting. Not only does a public exhibition connect communities, it creates dialog with diverse groups and allows people to learn about the international students who are living and learning in their city.

The next section explores the ability to be flexible in methodologies, and the importance of adjusting methodological procedures that work with the participants.

Critical Methodology

Critical methodology is the rigorous and precise evaluation and reevaluation of methodological self-examination. When a researcher reflects on their methodology and methods they should, according to Yanchar et al. (2005):

> [...]focus on the creative processes of theory formation and problem solving, which would be aided by various methodological procedures. In this sense, methods become practice-oriented, or practical extensions of the researchers' theories and assumptions through their use as perspectival research strategies. (p. 35)

Photovoice is a methodology that utilizes the action- and practice-based data collection tool of photography, which the participants control. This means that participants communicate what is important to them, and the data collection becomes a democratic method instead of a prescriptive method as seen in positivist research.

In addition, a researcher using critical methodologies should be able to accommodate, change, and develop certain strategies that consider the unique, significant, and particular situations of the participants (Yanchar et al., 2005). For instance, often a researcher is overly concerned with adhering to a methodological frameworks and fails to adapt processes and procedures to the participants, situation, location, etc. in a study. For example, in my study on international students in a HEI in Beijing, students who were motherscholars believed that they could not devote time to the research because they could not always attend the group meetings. Moreover, some motherscholars would return to their home countries to see their children when national holidays or breaks in their timetable allowed travel, which meant they were not always present on campus to participate in the research project. Because of my perceived need to adhere to the protocols and structures of the photovoice methodology, important information regarding the lives of mothers who were students was lost. The methodology should have been adjusted to suit the mother-scholars. The adjustment to include motherscholars could have meant forgoing the in-person group meetings, to meeting with the women on-line for one-to-one interviews and discussions about their photographs. Photovoice was developed to be a flexible methodology, and in this instance utilizing the adaptability of photovoice was a critical opportunity to change procedures and to contribute to the growth of this critical research methodology. Recognizing the limitations and the assumptions attached to the methodology and being open to challenging or changing methodological assumptions in order to better suit the participants are essential in conducting inclusive and humanistic research (Yanchar et al., 2005).

Adjusting methodology to accommodate different kinds of participants is imperative when researchers think critically about their methodologies. Therefore, methodological reflection is not simply a one-off, and critical reflection needs to be consistent throughout the research process. Accommodating and adjusting methods and methodology to suit the in/consistencies and changes of the participants is a process of critical reflection that is a key dynamic of the critically present researcher. Without this consistent reflexive practice, the evolution of methodologies can become stagnant, and the praxis of research will not be transformed (Freire, 2005). The role of the critical researcher and critical methodologies is to constantly reflect on and strive to acknowledge "that its [methodology] underlying assumptions are historically situated, temporary and continually subject to critical examination and revision" (Yanchar et al., 2005, p. 36).

CONCLUSION

Utilizing critical methodology, and a visual method data collection using photography, this writing explored how inclusive, democratic, and participatory research benefited international students studying in China. Additionally, the information learned from international student experiences can inform policy changes on an institutional level that can improve the lives of international students studying in Beijing. Although this study was conducted in Beijing with this specific group of participants, this writing highlights the importance of critical and reflective methodologies that can be applied beyond this specific location and research group. Visual research methods such as photography help to mitigate the pressure on language barriers, English, and aim to lessen the hegemonic linguistic hierarchies of the English language and its imperialistic legacies (Tsuda, 1998). Furthermore, in line with Freirean philosophy (2005), emancipatory and participatory methodology/methods are needed in order for people to free themselves from oppression, which means that participants need to be active in their own education (and research) at all levels. Therefore, change in communities comes from empowering participants through the research processes, ensuring that participants are not simply the subjects of data collection but co-creators of knowledge who actively make meaning from their lived experiences (West et al., 2012).

Knowledge gained from communities and data that is co-created with participants need to support participants in applying, distributing, and utilizing information that was gained from research. For too long researchers have used methods that benefit them and the institution but not the participants and communities. Exploitation of minority groups, people of color, and the economically disadvantaged, to name a few, have not always been the benefactors of research and the data collection that was *done to them* in the guise of what was *good for them* (Rodriguez, 2010). Applying critical methodologies in theory, in practice, and in principle can alleviate the colonial residue that has been left behind and garner new and evolving conversations. Exploring and questioning the role of methodology should be part of the critical researchers practice in order to adapt methodologies and methods that consider the human beings that research purports to understand and represent.

REFERENCES

Ahmed, S. (2019). *What's the use?: On the uses of use*. Duke University Press.
Berger, J. (1976). Drawn to that moment. *New Society*, 41–44. https://www.spokesmanbooks.com/Spokesman/PDF/90Berger.pdf
Bhabha, H. K. (1994). *The location of culture*. Routledge.
Crotty, M. (1998). *The foundations of social research: Meaning and perspective in the research process*. London: Sage Publications.
Darroch, F. E., & Giles, A. R. (2014). Decolonizing health research: Community-based participatory research and postcolonial feminist theory. *Canadian Journal of Action Research*, 15(3), 22–36. https://doi.org/10.33524/cjar.v15i3.155

Freire, P. (2005). *Pedagogy of the oppressed*. New York: Continuum.
Goo, D. L., Lai, E., & Lai, K. (2011). *Photovoice literature review*. Team Lab, 1–15. https://fliphtml5.com/bsxh/waqn/basic
Harding, S. (1995). "Strong objectivity": A response to the new objectivity question. *Feminism and Science, 104*(3), 331–349. http://www.jstor.org/stable/20117437
Hooks, b. (1994). *Teaching to transgress: Education as the practice of freedom*. Routledge.
Mayfield-Johnson, S., & Butler, J. (2017). Moving from pictures to social action: An introduction to photovoice as a participatory action tool. *New Directions for Adults & Continuing Education, 2017*(154), 49–59. https://doi.org/10.1002/ace.20230
McNeille, A. (Ed.). (1984). *The essays of Virginia Woolf: Vol. 4: 1925 to 1928*. The Hogarth Press.
Rahman, M. A. (1991). Action and knowledge: Breaking the monopoly with participatory action research. In O. Fals-Borda & M. A. Rahman (Eds.), *The theoretical standpoint of PAR* (pp. 13–24). Apex Press.
Rodriguez, D. (2010). Storytelling in the field: Race, method, and the empowerment of Latina college students. *Cultural Studies Critical Methodologies, 10*(6), 491–507. https://doi.org/10.1177/1532708610365481
Smith, D. E. (1987). *The everyday world as problematic*. Northeastern University Press.
Smith, L. T. (1999). *Decolonizing methodologies: Research and indigenous peoples*. London: Zed Books.
Songtag, S. (1977). *On photography*. Farrar.
Tsuda, Y. (1998). Critical studies on the dominance of English and the implications for international communication. *Japan Review, 10*, 219–236. http://www.jstor.org/stable/25791026
Wang, C., & Burris, M. A. (1994). Empowerment through photo novella: Portraits of participation. *Health Education Quarterly, 21*(2), 171–186. https://doi.org/10.1177/109019819402100204
Wang, C., Burris, M. A., & Ping, X. Y. (1996). Chinese village women as visual anthropologists: A participatory approach to reaching policymakers. *Social Science Medicine, 42*(10), 1391–1400. https://doi.org/10.1016/0277-9536(95)00287-1
Wang, Q., & Hannes, K. (2014). Academic and socio-cultural adjustment among Asian international students in the Flemish community of Belgium: A photovoice project. *International Journal of Intercultural Relations, 39*, 66–81. https://doi.org/10.1016/j.ijintrel.2013.09.013
Weiler, K. (1988). *Women teaching for change: Gender, class, and power*. Bergin.
West, R., Stewart, L., Foster, K., & Usher, K. (2012). Through a critical lens. *Qualitative Health Research, 22*(11), 1582–1590. https://doi.org/10.1177/1049732312457596
Wu, J., & Yun, G. (2007). Beyond propaganda, aestheticism and commercialism: The coming of age documentary photography in China. *Javnost—The Public, 14*(3), 31–48. https://doi.org/10.1080/13183222.2007.11008945
Yanchar, S. C., Gantt, E. E., & Clay, S. L. (2005). On the nature of a critical methodology. *Theory & Psychology, 15*(1), 27–50. https://doi.org/10.1177/0959354305049743

CHAPTER 21

Rise of a "Managerial Demiurge": Critical Analysis of the Digitalization of Education

Juha Suoranta, Marko Teräs, and Hanna Teräs

False clarity is only another name for myth. Myth was always obscure and luminous at once. It has always been distinguished by its familiarity and its exemption from the work of concepts. (Horkheimer & Adorno, 2002, p. xvii)

INTRODUCTION

This chapter reflects on the seemingly self-evident reified phantasmagoria of the digitalized future of education, which frequently appears in influential educational policy documents. We study selected policy documents in the light of the Frankfurt School critical theory to analyze and criticize modernity's culture and social existence.[1] In what follows, we explore two main questions. Firstly, we examine how the future and digitalization of education are reified. Secondly, we explore what certain concepts of critical theory, such as instrumental reason, language universe, power, and alienation, reveal from the

---

J. Suoranta (✉) · M. Teräs
Tampere University, Tampere, Finland
e-mail: juha.suoranta@tuni.fi

M. Teräs
e-mail: marko.teras@tuni.fi

H. Teräs
Tampere University of Applied Sciences, Tampere, Finland
e-mail: hanna.teras@tuni.fi

© The Author(s), under exclusive license to Springer Nature
Switzerland AG 2022
A. A. Abdi and G. W. Misiaszek (eds.), *The Palgrave Handbook on Critical Theories of Education*, https://doi.org/10.1007/978-3-030-86343-2_21

official education policy discourses and futures materialized in the educational policy and vision documents.

We argue that these documents are cultural and ideological artifacts, objects of power, that in fact operationalize the future they claim to merely forecast. The ultimate message of our analysis is that the mythical future these policy documents and their grand narrative speak about is the future they are textually constructing, creating the social reality in their own image.

The future of digitalized education appears progressive, rational, and inevitable. Under its trendy clothes of scientific rationality, calculability, and certainty, with an added twist of silicon chic giving the digitalized future the current unquestioned and uncriticized popular-boy-of-the-school status, is still just another *human* endeavor with old utopias and myths. The eighteenth century Enlightenment vision was to liberate humanity from mythical thinking and replace the myth with reason, even if it originated from the mythical thought (Horkheimer & Adorno, 2002). This chapter claims that the mythical never disappeared, but indeed presents itself again in the cloak of digitalization of education that claims to ensure us "a future."

We are writing our chapter amid the digitalization of higher education, the current megatrend of international higher education worldwide. Digitalization highlights entrepreneurial ideas in higher education, promises mythical acceleration of fluid learning processes, and boosts the economy. As such, digitalization of higher education can be considered as part of academic capitalism, "a tendency toward overruling the genuine rules of scientific practice by the rules of capitalist competition" (Münch, 2020, p. 12; see also Cantwell & Kauppinen, 2014; Musselin, 2018; Poutanen et al., 2020; Slaughter & Rhoades, 2004).

Finnish higher education, our operational context, is an active partaker of the digitalization megatrend. The Finnish educational system is publicly funded and, in an international comparison, relatively centralized with national educational legislation. As such, it has been an easy target to top-down management and goal steering. However, "the market-based rhetoric and practices have not been able to take root in the core areas of the traditional Nordic welfare state – education, social services, and health – as easily as in other areas of society" (Rinne et al., 2002, p. 655). All compulsory schools follow the core national curriculum, and higher education is steered from the Ministry of Education with economic sticks and carrots. Although schools and higher education institutions have relative decision power and autonomy, the Finnish national authorities have the upper hand in educational decision making and future planning.

In Finland, as in most other European countries, business sector lobbyists along with the doctrine of New Public Management have for years expressed worries that the country's current higher education model lacks future orientation in terms of skills, competencies, and mindsets needed in the future work life. Therefore, the business sector has lobbied business-oriented agendas to the Finnish education system (see Kauppinen & Moisio, 2008). Key themes in this have been the marketization of education, international competitiveness, and entrepreneurship education (Poutanen et al., 2020).

Simultaneously, Finnish national administration of education began to demand more efficiency, calculability, predictability, and controllability—all the McDonaldization thesis's general features (see Ritzer, 1998, p. 5; Rinne, 1999). Finnish sociologists of education have characterized the development from the 1990s as a shift from a relatively autonomous and democratic higher education toward a top-down governed managerial university (Rinne, 2014). The neoliberal business logic and de-democratization of higher education have been driven by changes in legislation, which in turn was motivated and advised by reports and vision documents emphasizing the necessity of such measures in order to ensure economic competitiveness in the globalizing market (Poutanen et al., 2020). Furthermore, the recent developments suggest the rise of "fast policy" in educational policymaking (Hardy et al., 2020). The latest catchphrase in this business-driven, the winner-takes-it-all educational discourse has been the digitalization of education, which, according to business-oriented spokespeople, catapults Finland's economic success.

The Myth of the Digitalization of Education: Managerial Demiurge at Work

We have used the Finnish Ministry of Education and Culture policy paper *Higher Education and Research for the 2030s Vision Roadmap* (the topic: digitalization of education) (Ministry of Education and Culture, 2019a) and its background material (Ministry of Education and Culture, 2019b) for the critical analysis of the myth of digitalization of education. From 2017 to 2019 Finnish Ministry of Education and Culture formulated a vision for higher education and research for 2030 (Ministry of Education and Culture, 2019a), which describes future challenges for all sectors of life:

> Digitalization, artificial intelligence and robotization are changing society, working life, the logic of making a living, and also people's general living and competence needs. Competence is the best protection amidst changes in work, technology, and the world. If the labour market and the competence of the population are functioning well, the society can adapt to forces such as automation that change the society and work. (Ministry of Education and Culture, 2019a, p. 5; translated by the authors)

The roadmap also outlines a seemingly dire present where success appears to be slipping away from our grasp and where parts of Finnish knowledge and skills base are crumbling. Improving quality, productivity, and effectiveness are considered national challenges. Higher Education Institutes' Digivision, 2030 is a new national project that aims to operationalize the education roadmap vision. All Finnish higher education institutions have signed the preliminary agreement for the development. The objective is to create a "national digital service platform" with "guidance based on digital pedagogics, the learner's path and shared data," "AI solution as an aid in guidance," and "support for change management for higher education institutions" (Higher Education Institutes' Digivision 2030, 2019, p. 3).

We argue that such vision documents and roadmaps are primary tools in creating a specific and powerful discourse of the digitalization of education. After Mills (2000), we describe these documents with the metaphor *managerial demiurge* since they control higher education's material resources and public development. As Mills suggested, at first glance, they appear as rational but soon become fetishized, and in the end, manipulate discussion and development. We have applied document analysis (Bowen, 2009; Gross, 2018) and the Foucauldian idea of "eventualization" in a close reading of the documents (Foucault, 1996; Miller & Rose, 2008). A primary function of 'eventualization' is simply to problematize the self-evident, to question "those self-evidences on which our knowledges, acquiescences and practices rest" (Foucault, 1996, p. 277).[2] Using this methodological idea, as Miller and Rose (2008) have suggested, we move from *why* to *how*, that is, how the myth of digitalization of education is constructed.

In what follows, we analyze the aforementioned policy documents of digitalization of education in the light of four concepts from critical theory: instrumental rationality, a closed discourse universe, power, and alienation. In reading the following analysis, one should keep in mind that the documents are part of the "educational–digital industrial complex," by which we mean an informal alliance between the educational administration and business sector: especially a partnership between the public education, intergovernmental organizations and ed-tech companies.[3] Their combination affects national educational policies and practices. Our interest is to understand how these powers are discursively constructing the myth of the digitalization of education.

Policy Document as Manifestations of Instrumental Rationality

As tools to achieve the goals, the *Higher Education and Research for the 2030s Vision Roadmap* introduces development programs. Two of them ('Higher education reform and the environment for digital services' and 'A higher education community with the skills to deliver the best learning outcomes and settings in the world') refer to the digitalization of education. They suggest that digitalization is a major force changing society and will impose new operating methods and educational content. In the future, higher education should leverage digitalization for new pedagogical thinking and create a service environment that will improve accessibility, flexibility, continuous learning, and international collaboration in the university sector. The aim is to introduce new pedagogical approaches, counseling services, digital content, and modularity. The vision document argues that these changes lead to increased numbers of degrees and international students and improve the overall access to education.

Themes that spur from these developments are *demand-* and *anticipation-led education*. *Continuous learning* is seen as a cornerstone of the new learning products (Ministry of Education and Culture, 2019a, p. 17).

In a critical look, these sorts of policy documents fulfill the fundamental characteristics of *instrumental rationality*. As Brookfield (2005) points out, referring mainly to Max Horkheimer's thinking: "[t]his form of thought is seen in the belief that life can be ordered and organized into mutually exclusive, yet interlocking, categories." Furthermore, instrumental rationality "is applied to solve problems of how to attain certain short-term social and economic objectives. In the scramble to achieve short-term ends, the application of reason to abstract universals such as justice, equality, and tolerance becomes increasingly impossible." At the same time, thinking is objectified and fetishized, and it achieves an existence of its own, separated from the thinker (pp. 70–71; Horkheimer, 2002, 2004).

Furthermore, the vision report refers heavily to the OECD's working paper "Collaboration, Alliance, and Merger Among Higher Education Institutions," written by a consultant who has also worked for the World Bank. The report states that the recommendations are only its author's views. However, in the vision document, the consultant's opinions and rhetoric are taken as indisputable facts. Thus, the OECD's ideas are brought to national educational debate by interpreting the recommendations as factual statements. In this "domestication" process, local educational administrators and bureaucrats tend to be active agents who put a new element as part of an existing field of specific activities (Alasuutari & Alasuutari, 2012).

In our case, "to be an active agent" means to interpret suggestions as facts. It is essential to note this connection since the OECD is among the most powerful international players in education policymaking (see Ball, 2012; Lingard & Sellars, 2016; Prytz, 2020; Sellar & Lingard, 2013; Verger, 2013). As Miettinen (2019) has pointed out, the OECD's data formation and presentation of results differ from the scientific practices. The organization's reports do not usually refer to scientific studies but their own previous publications. However, the OECD has left its mark on the *Higher Education and Research for the 2030s Vision Roadmap* in that the Finnish document resembles the OECD's standard rhetoric. The seemingly concrete language makes the vision roadmap appear reasonable and logical while its concreteness hides the vagueness of the used concepts and the assumptions these concepts are based on (see also Miettinen, 2019). The overall approach of the OECD and the like seems to be that a range of global firms "who will benefit hugely from any business that might come their way as a result of changing pedagogical practices, learning materials, testing material, ongoing professional development" (Ball, 2012; Robertson, 2016, p. 281).

Closing the Discourse Universe

Intergovernmental and governmental organizations' reports and general communication on e.g., news sites and technology company blogs describe a future disrupted by an uncertain labor market and fueled by digitalization and automation. Future jobs are seen as something we do not know about yet, but despite the obscurity, it is firmly believed that new competencies and skills such as entrepreneurship and teamwork will be needed in "the future." This argumentative logic also often emphasizes the need to change teaching and learning practices as "the traditional forms" of education cannot prepare "the learners" for the future. Thus, the education sector is destined to employ new ways of teaching and learning driven by digitalization. According to this logic, digitalization is affecting the future of competence requirements and work, therefore we should leverage digitalization to create future employment. In sum, due to a different kind of a future where digitalization and automation have "disrupted" most jobs, education needs to change in order to serve such a future better, and digitalization should be the driver of such change in education.

The contemporary language that permeates the future of education and society is deterministic, but more importantly, a type that already constructs and normalizes "a future." Marcuse describes a *closed discourse universe* where "[m]agical, authoritarian and ritual elements permeate speech and language" (Marcuse, 2007, p. 89). Through continuous repetition, specific meanings of a concept are hammered in. Or, as Marcuse (2007) describes it on grammatical level: "A specific noun is almost always coupled with the same "explicatory" adjectives and attributes makes the sentence into a hypnotic formula which, endlessly repeated, fixes the meaning in the recipient's mind. He does not think of essentially different (and possibly true) explications of the noun" (p. 94). How the noun is used in public policy documents and opinions, its analytical structure becomes insulated and governed by disruptions against it (Marcuse, 2007, pp. 91–92).

Digitalization is usually described with surprisingly univocal sentences in various sources, primarily through its *positive potential* to disrupt and transform education. Still, when following the path to these arguments, all too often there lies not much else behind them than other sources that argue the same. Marcuse (2007) writes:

> The concept tends to be absorbed by the word. The former has no other content than that designated by the word in the publicized and standardized usage, and the word is expected to have no other response than the publicized and standardized behavior (reaction). The word becomes *cliché* and, as cliché, governs the speech or the writing. (p. 90)

Digitalization has become a vague but solidified and presupposed concept in public debate, a cliché. As Marcuse (2007) emphasizes, "communication thus precludes genuine development of meaning" (p. 90). As digitalization is continuously described through its positive potential, its meaning becomes taken for granted, and further development of its other potential meanings becomes more difficult or ceases altogether. Therefore, the claim that *digitalization can transform education*, "has lost all cognitive value and serves merely for recognition of an unquestionable fact" (Marcuse, 2007, p. 98). Even if not concretely present in the message, this message's positivity is already taken for granted.

Furthermore, the cliché begins to hide under itself that which actually takes place. Even if contradictions appear between the truth of the noun and the truth of everyday experience, these can be ignored or even turned into positive explanations. This can take place because, as Marcuse (2007) writes, "[t]he ritualized concept is made immune against contradiction" (p. 92). Even more, authoritarian, standardized language solidifies a concept and makes contradictions, such as "war is peace" seem reasonable, logical, and perfectly natural (Marcuse, 2007, p. 92). Similarly, the claim that digitalization has the potential to transform education is increasingly presupposed as something positive, which also affects the ways it is studied. Still, there are many accounts that reveal the mismatch between the grand narrative of the potential of digitalization and the actualization of that potential in education (e.g. Mertala, 2020), be it technology-enhanced learning in general (Bayne, 2015), tablets (Mertala, 2020), datafication (MacGilchrist, 2019) or student information systems (Heimo et al., 2016). However, it has been noted that such critical accounts have largely been ignored (see Selwyn, 2011, 2016). This can easily take place due to the presupposition of positivity and progress of technological development; as always, "the next version of the software will be better".

A closed deterministic language universe is an example of structural violence in education. Administrators' and experts' reports affect directly governmental policies and teachers and students who have to live up to often unrealistic expectations and acknowledge with regret that they cannot actualize the "potentials" demanded in the digitalization of education documents. As Marcuse (2007) writes, the use of functional language suppresses society's history, but more importantly, also its future. The development of digitalization ignores the long unrealized history of overly positive technological determinism while deterministic language closes the creation of broader meanings. In the case of digitalization, the prevailing meaning—the "truth" of the increasingly fixed and presupposed noun "digitalization"—is the meaning assigned by ed-tech companies, "technology enthusiasts" and administrative demiurges, not necessarily the meaning teachers and students could make. Veering beyond this public truth, "beyond the closed analytical structure is incorrect or propaganda" (Marcuse, 2007, p. 91). As Marcuse (2007) aptly summarizes.

> In exhibiting its contradictions as the token of its truth, this universe of discourse closes itself against any other discourse which is not on its own terms. And, by its capacity to assimilate all other terms to its own, it offers the prospect

of combining the greatest possible tolerance with the greatest possible unity. Nevertheless, its language testifies to the repressive character of this unity. This language speaks in constructions which impose upon the recipient the slanted and abridged meaning, the blocked development of content, the acceptance of that which is offered in the form in which it is offered. (p. 94)

Operationalizing and Legitimizing the Future Through Exercising Power and Violence

The Roadmap for Implementing Vision 2030 document's background material, "Where we are now" (the literal meaning in the Finnish version is closer to "a shared situation picture"), narrates a dire future where automation and digitalization have taken or changed jobs and created an unstable labor market. To tackle this, a certain set of competencies are needed, together with efficient ways to construct these competencies (i.e., digitalization of education). Hence, the call for action (five development programs to rule them all, of which Digivisio 2030 is one materialized project), otherwise we must bear the consequences, which are only generally described (missing out in the global competition), but indeed, ominously implied.

Digitalization of education and competencies are intended to operationalize the vision and make the desired future more certain. The means receive their legitimization through the described future challenges which is a narrative built from the now and the suggested future. In short: this story of the future is a certain kind of power and violence (Benjamin, 2002). As no one can really know what the future brings, the described future is a narrative myth, which is used to operationalize technocratic faith. This operationalization takes place through reacting to a myth, something that does not exist (the future), and thus bringing it into existence through those reactions. The following presents how it is glued into a seemingly democratic co-creation process.

Both "Higher education and research vision 2030" and "Digivisio 2030" proudly emphasize that stakeholders have been involved in constructing the future, in addition to developing the ways to get there. This claim of "involving stakeholders" further legitimizes the vision and the means, as it dresses the process in democratic clothing—now, to question the vision and the means would be to go against *a shared* vision and means. But in fact, the stakeholders who have been "involved" are not given a proactive role in imagining and shaping the future, instead, they are assigned the task to negotiate *a reaction* to a future that has already been determined, although it not yet exists. Now the parties, the Ministry of Higher Education and the Digivision 2030 working group who drive the technocratic future, are able to speak with the voice of the involved stakeholders (i.e., everyone who is important). Still, what is left unspoken is, for example, in what ways exactly the stakeholders were involved (e.g., in the workshops described in the vision background documents), whose voices were heard, but more importantly, how the future was already prescribed at the moment the stakeholders were involved. Luckily, the background document that summarizes the workshops is freely available (Ministry of Education & Culture, 2017). It describes them as follows:

> The aim of the workshops and the Foresight Friday event was to discuss 2030 objectives, *enframed by the large megatrends*. The workshop began from futures that rule out each other and *together set objectives that best fit the world of the digital global economy*. (p. 9; translated from Finnish by the authors, italics added)

The document presents several predesigned workshop canvases, one of which themed as *Quality and contemporary education and competence*, with questions such as: "Think about how the drivers of change and megatrends (such as digitalization) affect" and "What kind of competence is needed?" As such, the conditions of "global megatrends" and "digital global economy" have power over imagination in the workshop, and thus, the outcomes are already violently submitted under their rule. Therefore, it is unsurprising that the general outcome of the workshop can be described as to ensure employment in a precarious global labor market with ever-matching competencies and continuous learning, supported by digitalization, as these were the preselected ingredients given to the stakeholders to use for forming the future vision.

According to Benjamin (2002), there is no "power" or "violence" as such, but concepts are always temporal, receiving their meaning as part of historical situations (see also Lindroos, 2014). This means that each era should redefine their meanings that transform during historical and political events (ibid.). Operationalizing and legitimizing the future through such governmental development programs which are justified with international and intergovernmental organizations' reports, presents a global flow of power and surprisingly homogeneous ideas. When following this flow deeper, for example, by a critical examination of the sources used in such reports, one finds not *futures* but *a future*. It is often driven and justified by technology companies, enthusiasts, and futurists in their terms. This is exemplified in a recent report by the Finnish National Agency for Education (Nyyssölä & Kumpulainen, 2020) that describes the future of primary education in Finland and backs up its claims of digital future and its potential with several unscholarly and commercial technology blogs, often written by vendors in whose direct interests it is for readers to buy the future vision they portray. All of this raises a question: if no one really knows the future, how can it be globally so homogeneously univocal?—unless it is set and constructed now in the present. Hence, once again, this constructed myth of the "future" is sovereignly exercising power over how other potential *futures* of education might come forth.

Digitalization Policy Documents as Sources of Alienation

Higher Education and Research for the 2030s Vision Roadmap and related documentations are textualities constructing an objectified and alienating reality of the already planned and designed world. As such, as general discursive templates of the educational–digital industrial complex, they form a fundamental part of governmentality as a set of diverse combinations of governing mechanisms and technologies of power executed by governmentalized states or state unions (Lemke, 2000; Rantala & Suoranta, 2008).

In understanding the vicious effects of policy documents on digitalization in higher education as sources of students' and teachers' alienation, we need to refer to Marx's early writings on political economy. The concept of alienation originally derives from philosopher G.W.F. Hegel, but it was Marx who made it famous in the nineteenth-century social sciences. In Marx, alienation means that the majority of people have lost control of their lives. In a capitalist class society, they cannot reach their full potential. Their relations with each other are distorted. They work for someone else's benefit and feel that they cannot associate with or be an integral part of society. In his *Economic and Philosophical Manuscripts of 1844*, Marx writes bluntly about the logic of capitalism:

> Worker sinks to the level of a commodity and becomes indeed the most wretched of commodities; that the wretchedness of the worker is in inverse proportion to the power and magnitude of his production; that the necessary result of competition is the accumulation of capital in a few hands, and thus the restoration of monopoly in a more terrible form; and that finally the distinction between capitalist and land rentier, like that between the tiller of the soil and the factory worker, disappears and that the whole of society must fall apart into the two classes—*property owners* and propertyless *workers*. (Marx, 1932, p. 28)

As Marx further notes, the more wealth the worker produces, the poorer she or he becomes: "The worker becomes an ever cheaper commodity the more commodities he (*sic*) creates. The *devaluation* of the world of men is in direct proportion to the *increasing value* of the world of things. Labor produces not only commodities; it produces itself and the worker as a *commodity*—and this at the same rate at which it produces commodities in general" (ibid.). Policy documents on digitalization are products of labor which Fuchs (2014) describes as digital labor and, as such, in Marx' view, "*something alien*" (Marx, 1932, pp. 28–29).

However, workers are not to blame for their alienation and general position in the dominant hierarchy. Based on private ownership, capitalism forces people to submit to the working-class in the division of labor which turns them into objects (or mere commodities) causing political, social, and individual alienation. In other words, in a class society, people's minority, or "a dominant class controls human minds, bodies, social relations, the work process, the economy and the whole of society" (Fuchs, 2014, p. 349). Furthermore, as Marx points out, in capitalism, "work is value-generating abstract labour" abstracted from human needs. It serves "the structural needs of capital as self-valorizing value through the exploitation of labour" (Fuchs, 2016, p. 17).

In capitalism's exploitation of labor, work is commodified, and in Marx's thinking, the commodity-form becomes capitalism's primary social relation characterizing all aspects of human endeavor. Policy documents on digitalization of higher education (including digitalization programs and digital visions) are parade examples of a capitalist commodity-form and the general tendency of the educational sphere's alienation at least in three ways.

First, they represent commodified forms of human labor and rationality. In Marx's terms, they are abstract labor and, as such, part and parcel of capitalism as a "system that strives to turn everything into commodities (commodification) so that it is an object of abstract labour and can be exchanged with money in order to create profit" (Fuchs, 2014, p. 348). Commodity-form and alienation are evident in the documents' general view of the educational world, e.g., when future universities are labeled as "datafied universities" and defined as "service organizations" instead of critical teaching and learning institutions. "Service organizations" also imply that students (or their future employers?) are customers and teachers are mere service providers. In this spirit, it is possible to proclaim the following grandiose goal: "A digital service environment development program will be launched, which will create a set of digital services consisting of universities' own and common solutions that serve degree studies and continuous learning."

Second, the alienation concerns the producers who write these documents. They are often bureaucrats in public administration or well-paid consultants, to whom the profession has become a paycheck, and who have subsumed themselves as demoralized tools or servants in the service of power, bureaucracy, and ed-tech business. Nevertheless, they are part of commodified labor. Their work is separated from its results and the means of production and their identities and life. Writing a policy document is another job to be done, more or less irrelevant to them—their misery grows, as Marx notes, "with the power and volume of their production" (ibid.). Their work is a real example of capitalism's functioning as dead labor and surplus-value creation. In Marx words, "capital is dead labour, that, vampire-like, only lives by sucking living labour, and lives the more, the more labour it sucks" (Marx, 1887, p. 163).

Third, alienation does not concern only human beings as capitalism's dead labor but also the language used in the policy documents. New mechanistic rhetoric derives primarily from the engineering sciences and their jargon of project management. Features of the digital rhetoric without human beings' meaning-making and pedagogical interaction include such buzzwords as "datafication," "learning analytics," "interoperability of teaching and studying information," "service channel," "smooth knowledge flow," "modular study supply," "study path," "digital service environment of higher education," "joint action plan," and "content production collaboration." At the core of this new rhetoric is one magic verb: to develop. Everything must be developed for development's sake as if there was nothing valuable in the current higher education. In an incessant development, there seems to be a means but no ends. In this sense, the datafication and digitalization rhetoric have no meaning over themselves, as the following quotes demonstrate.

> The goal is to implement a digital services ecosystem that serves degree programs as well as continuous learning. The ecosystem will consist of in-house and shared solutions and a service channel to connect these. Compatibility of data sets, smooth national data flow and shared policy are essential. (…) Modularity in curricula and study programs is required in order to enable personalized and flexible study paths and to develop the recognition of previously acquired competences. (Ministry of Education and Culture, 2019a, p. 21, translated by the authors)

The document's clause, "unification of contents through datafication and learning analytics," means that higher education and its "contents" must follow the same-size-fits-all -principle (while at the same time in other parts, claiming 'personalization'). In other words, in the digitalized future there is even less face-to-face dialog in the universities, so crucial in developing critical consciousness. "Modular knowledge and curricula" mean that teaching is provided in easily chewed pieces, learning will be passed to learner-consumers as sliced into easy-to-follow parts, and knowledge served in containers, in ready-made packages that can be exchanged for other packages. Above all, the documents emphasize developing work-life competencies, "fluid learning," and cost savings.

> The combination of digital courses and classroom-based teaching requires new types of content that enhance employability skills and enables flexible degree programs and continuous learning. Cooperation and division of labor will diversify students' study paths and skills, support the quality of education, and achieve cost savings. (Ministry of Education and Culture, 2019a, p. 21, translated by the authors)

The student-centered rhetorics employed in the documents may at the first glance look like an emancipatory turn in the delivery of higher education. Using digital technologies such as artificial intelligence and algorithms for the *personalization of learning* and *diversification of learning paths* indeed sound like it. However, a closer look reveals a different reality behind the words. Students are, in fact, less and less able to fulfill their potential as the study paths that used to be open-ended and messy are now predetermined and directed by "tireless and fearless AI tutors" (Ministry of Education and Culture, 2019b, p. 22) whose recommendations are based on computer-readable behavioral data rather than the unique personal interests, motivations and talents of human beings. After all, the documents do not talk about personalization in the humanistic sense of the word, as the result of these algorithm-driven processes will always be bulk, always predetermined, always aiming at the same desired outcome: a more efficient acquisition of competencies that serve the needs of the marketplace and the economy. A humanistic personalization of learning may lead to the flourishing of the individual. In contrast, the personalization described in these documents most probably leads to the alienation of the individual and the thriving of markets.

Marx believed that alienation reached its peak in the position of the nineteenth-century factory worker who was merely a cog in the machine. In the factory, the worker was separated from the product of labor, from the means of production, and, of course, from the profits. However, as Fromm (2004, p. 45) has noted, Marx could not foresee that there will be alienated classes other than the working-class, namely the middle and upper-middle class. He did not realize that "alienation was to become the fate of the vast majority of people, especially of the ever-increasing segment of the population which manipulate symbols and men (*sic*), rather than machines" (ibid., p. 45). Thus, Fromm argues that the middle class can be even "more alienated today than the skilled manual worker," for they need to sell not only their labor power but also their personalities in order to maintain their living standards. In a more recent study, part of the middle class in the office and administrative jobs (who call themselves "flunkies," "goons," and "duck tapers") say that their work is not at all useful to anyone. They also state that they are unhappy in their jobs, and work is actually a bullshit job (Graeber, 2018).

These middle class "symbol manipulators" worship corporations and the capitalist system, false gods in Fromm's view. However, Fromm clarifies that "as far as consumption is concerned, there is no difference between manual workers and the members of the bureaucracy," and notes that nowadays both have more to lose than their chains: a well-paid job and a consumerist lifestyle. They "are not related to the world productively, grasping it in its full reality and in this process becoming one with it." In contemporary society, people are—perhaps even without realizing it—ready to "worship things, the machines which produce things—and in this alienated world they feel as strangers and quite alone" (Fromm, 2004, p. 57).

Conclusion

We have suggested in this chapter, based on our empirical analysis of the Finnish national educational policy documents, that digitalization of education is a part of managerial demiurge's administrative apparatus in the mythmaking. First, the documents are ultimate manifestations of instrumental rationality. Second, the documents form a closed discourse universe that determines the totality of an educational realm. They are distant from the teachers' and students' reality and leave no space for teachers' and students' agency. Third, they use discursive power by constructing a narrative myth of the educational-technological future, which cements the general technocratic faith. Last, the documents represent a capitalist commodity-form and partake in creating an estranged and alienated higher education sphere. As such, these documents are powerful objects of transnational educational bureaucratic apparatus which constructs social reality as its own image. As Lefebvre (2002) points out:

> *Bureaucracy* tends to operate for and by itself. By establishing itself as a 'system', it becomes its own goal and its own end; at the same time, in a given society, it has real functions, which it executes more or less effectively. Thus it modifies the everyday, and this too is its goal and its aim. However, it never succeeds in 'organizing' the everyday completely; something always escapes it, as bureaucrats themselves ruefully admit. The everyday protests; it rebels in the name of innumerable particular cases and unforeseen situations. (p. 300)

As a result, students and teachers are losing their possibility to act as active agents, transformative intellectuals, and dissidents in their field of expertise. Instead, they are in danger of becoming objects of an alien world created over and against them. More often than not, the policy documents on the digitalization of education seem to ridicule the students' and teachers' intellect as moral agents of future education and history-making in general. They do not encourage students and teachers to "understand the everyday life from the perspective of those who are the most powerless in our society so that society can be transformed in the interest of a more humane and just existence" (McLaren, 2015, p. 141). Instead, they form their own discursive universe without other reference points than themselves and the monetary necessities beneath the discursive surface. Thus, they act as myth provoking demiurges to fulfill Marx's (1932) prophecy: "the *alienation* of the worker in his (or her) product means not only that his (or her) labor becomes an object, an *external* existence, but that it exists *outside him* (or her), independently, as something alien to him (or her), and that it becomes a power on its own confronting him (or her). It means that the life which he (or she) has conferred on the object confronts him (or her) as something hostile and alien" (p. 29).

Digitalization of education receives its justification from what is not yet here—as if it was almost already here, but yet to be realized "in the future." This future is often constructed by intergovernmental organizations and technology corporations, together with consulting firms (see also Mirrlees & Alvi, 2020; Williamson, 2021). Governmental organizations use their visions in their reports and their future workshops, which are already enframed within and geared toward an already decided digital future. Perhaps, in the final analysis, digitalization of education is a project for *certainties,* drawing our attention away from the fact that people—us as educators—are constructing the always undetermined future. Digitalization shows itself as progress, but it bears kinship with old history myths, especially with Enlightenment: to seek means to make the world more predictable and more manageable with knowledge, the myth of Enlightenment has now the face of digitalization. And, as Fromm puts it, the fear is that a new specter is stalking in our midst:

A completely mechanized society, devoted to maximal material output and consumption, directed by computers; and in this social process, man himself [sic] is being transformed into a part of the total machine, well fed and entertained, yet passive, unalive, and with little feeling. (…) Perhaps its most ominous aspect at present is that we seem to lose control over our own system. We execute the decisions which our computer calculations make for us. We as human beings have no aims except producing and consuming more and more. We will nothing, nor do we not-will anything. (Fromm, 1968, p. 1)

The ideological base of the myth-making discursive apparatus of education's digitalization is the will to fight and abolish *uncertainties* with administrative control and the managerial demiurge's operations (see also Timcke, 2020). For those who have faith, the chosen ones, in the digitalization of education, such working machinery appears as an effective and reliable assembly line for the future. Furthermore, due to the suggested precariat future job market, continuous and lifelong learning is needed, with a system that unites the education sector and the industry together as one machinery. Thus, the certainty of a positive future of work is determined and ensured. Managerial demiurge works, as described, "to benefit the learner" and "the learner in mind", but only to the extent where it stays within the frame of digitalization, competencies, and the determined future. The individual is involved and attached in the machinery by appealing to the narrative of *benefits*, for who would dare to say they do not wish for a better future? The presuppositions of the future of digitalized education and its alternatives remain unquestioned.

Notes

1. By no means the critical theory is a solid framework and that all members of the Frankfurt school would have accepted it as such and interpreted it as an all-encompassing explanation of the social reality. Instead, different Frankfurt school theorists interpret it differently at different times, not to mention those who have labeled their intellectual works as a critical theory at other times and places. It is altogether questionable if there ever was a conventional idea or essential interpretation of the critical theory, only various interpretations (see Jeffreys, 2016; Peters et al., 2003; Wiggershaus, 1994). We are inclined to think that critical theory as a critical reflexive and self-reflexive project, means that "prior to the acquisition of knowledge we must first inquire into and establish what may or may not count as knowledge" (Peters et al., 2003, p. 17). Furthermore, self-reflexivity includes an understanding that we as researchers are always in the same world as our study objects and that we need to take our positionalities into account in our interpretations. Thus, like Peters, Olssen, and Lankshear (2003, p. 18) state, "'critical' as it occurs in 'critical theory,' was used to refer to social theory that was genuinely self-reflexive: that is, theory that could account for their own conditions of possibility and for their potentially transformative effects. The other features of critical theory have been seen to include its explanatory, normative, and practical dimensions: it must provide empirical and testable accounts of social conditions (focusing on the causes of oppression); it must aim

toward change for the better, an alleviation of the human condition or 'emancipation'; and it must do so by providing a better self-understanding of the social agents who aim at transformation."

2. "What do I mean by this term? First of all, a breach of self-evidence. It means making visible a singularity at places where there is a temptation to invoke a historical constant, an immediate anthropological trait, or an obviousness which imposes itself uniformly on all. To show that things "weren't as necessary as all that". it wasn't as a matter of course that mad people came to be regarded as mentally ill; it wasn't self-evident that the only thing to be done with a criminal was to lock him up; it wasn't self-evident that the causes of illness were to be sought through the individual examination of bodies; and so on. A breach of self-evidence, of those self-evidences on which our knowledges, acquiescences and practices rest. This is the first theoretico-political function of 'eventualization'" (Foucault, 1996, p. 277).

3. The concept of the educational–digitally industrial complex stems from C. Wright Mills's influential works on the rise of the administrative class and the power elite (Mills, 2000). Mills defined the power elite's core as the men who move in and between three circles: the industrial, the military, and the political (Mills, 2000, p. 289). The concept has its origin also in US President Dwight D. Eisenhower's speech in 1961, where he used the expression to express his worry about the balance of power in making military decisions in the US; who had the power to make decisions: democratically elected politicians or business executives? Later, e.g., Picciano (1994) and Brightman and Gutmore (2002) have used the concept "educational-industrial complex" in referring to the decision-making processes in the use of information technologies in education.

References

Alasuutari, P., & Alasuutari, M. (2012). The domestication of early childhood education plans in Finland. *Global Social Policy, 12*(2), 129–148. https://doi.org/10.1177/1468018112443684

Ball, S. (2012). *Global Education Inc.: New policy networks and the neoliberal imaginary*. Routledge.

Bayne, S. (2015). What's the matter with 'technology-enhanced learning'? *Learning, Media and Technology, 40*(1), 5–20. https://doi.org/10.1080/17439884.2014.915851

Benjamin, W. (2002). In M. Bullock & M. W. Jennings (Eds.), *Walter Benjamin: Selected writings* (Vol. 1, pp. 1913–1926). Belknap Press of Harvard University Press.

Bowen, G. A. (2009). Document analysis as a qualitative research method. *Qualitative Research Journal, 9*(2), 27–40.

Brightman, H., & Gutmore, D. (2002). The educational-industrial complex. *The Educational Forum, 66*(4), 302–308. https://doi.org/10.1080/00131720208984848

Brookfield, S. (2005). *The power of critical theory for adult learning and teaching*. Open University Press.

Cantwell, B., & Kauppinen, I. (Eds.). (2014). *Academic capitalism in the age of globalisation*. Johns Hopkins University Press.

Foucault, M. (1996). *Foucault live: Collected interviews, 1961–1984*. Semiotext(e).
Fromm, E. (1968). *The revolution of hope: Toward a humanized technology*. Bantam Books.
Fromm, E. (2004). *Marx's concept of man*. Continuum.
Fuchs, C. (2014). *Digital Labor and Karl Marx*. Routledge.
Fuchs, C. (2016). *Critical theory of communication: New readings of Lukács, Adorno, Marcuse, Honneth and Habermas in the age of the Internet*. University of Westminster Press.
Graeber, D. (2018). *Bullshit jobs: A theory*. Allen Lane.
Gross, J. (2018). Document analysis. In B. Frey (Ed.), *The sage encyclopedia of educational research, measurement, and evaluation* (pp. 545–548). Sage.
Hardy, I., Heikkinen, H., Pennanen, M., Salo, P., & Kiilakoski, T. (2020). The 'spirit of the times': Fast policy for educational reform in Finland. *Policy Futures in Education, 19*(7), 770–791. https://doi.org/10.1177/1478210320971530
Heimo, O., Rantanen, M., & Kimppa, K. (2016). Wilma ruined my life: How an educational system became the criminal record for the adolescents. *ACM SIGCAS Computers and Society, 45*(3), 138–146. https://doi.org/10.1145/2874239.2874259
Higher Education Institutes' Digivision 2030. Finland as a model country for flexible learning. (2020). Arene & Unifi. https://digivisio2030.fi/wp-content/uploads/HEI-Digivision-2030.pdf
Horkheimer, M. (2002). *Critical theory: Selected essays*. Continuum.
Horkheimer, M. (2004). *Eclipse of reason*. Continuum.
Horkheimer, M., & Adorno, T. W. (2002). *Dialectic of enlightenment: Philosophical fragments*. Stanford University Press.
Jeffreys, S. (2016). *Grand hotel abyss. The lives of Frankfurt School*. Verso.
Kauppinen, I., & Moisio, O.-P. (2008). Taloudellisista intresseistä ja vanhoista kauneista kumpuava korkeakoulupolitiikkamme. *Tiedepolitiikka, 3*, 7–22.
Lefebvre, H. (2002). *Critique of Everyday Life*. Verso.
Lemke, T. (2000, September 21–24). *Foucault, governmentality and critique*. Paper presented at the Rethinking Marxism Conference, University of Amherst (MA).
Lindroos, K. (2014). Valta, kritiikki ja Walter Benjamin. In A. Laitinen, J. Saarinen, H. Ikäheimo, P. Lyyra, & P. Niemi (Eds.), *Sisäisyys & Suunnistautuminen* (pp. 411–427). Jyväskylän yliopistopaino.
Lingard, B., & Sellar, S. (2016). The changing organizational and global significance of the OECD's education work. In K. Mundy, A. Green, B. Lingard, & A. Verger (Eds.), *The handbook of global education policy* (pp. 357–373). Wiley.
Macgilchrist, F. (2019). Cruel optimism in edtech: When the digital data practices of educational technology providers inadvertently hinder educational equity. *Learning, Media and Technology, 44*(1), 77–86. https://doi.org/10.1080/17439884.2018.1556217
Marcuse, H. (2007). *One-dimensional man: Studies in the ideology of advanced industrial society* (2nd ed.). Routledge.
Marx, K. (1887). *Capital: A critique of political economy* (Vol. 1). Retrieved from https://www.marxists.org/archive/marx/works/download/pdf/Capital-Volume-I.pdf
Marx, K. (1932). *Economic and philosophical manuscripts of 1844*. Retrieved from https://www.marxists.org/archive/marx/works/1844/manuscripts/preface.htm
McLaren, P. (2015). *Pedagogy of insurrection*. Peter Lang.

Mertala, P. (2020). Paradoxes of participation in the digitalization of education: A narrative account. *Learning, Media and Technology, 45*(2), 179–192. https://doi.org/10.1080/17439884.2020.1696362

Miettinen, R. (2019). 21. vuosisadan kompetenssit – OECD kasvatuksen kielen uudistajana [12st Century competencies: OECD as a reformer of the language of education]. *Kasvatus, 50*(3), 203–215.

Miller, P., & Rose, N. (2008). *Governing the present: Administering economic, social, and personal life*. Polity Press.

Mills, C. W. (2000). *The power elite*. Oxford University Press.

Ministry of Education and Culture. (2017). *Korkeakoulutus ja tutkimus 2030 -visiotyö: Yhteenveto Demos Helsingin yhteiskehittämisprosessista visiotyössä* [Higher education and research 2030 vision: Summary of the vision co-creation process facilitated by Demos Helsinki]. https://minedu.fi/documents/1410845/4177242/OKM+visiotyö%2C+Demoksen+yhteiskehittämisprosessi.pdf/c14c31fd-8bfa-485c-9cc5-e92174f902e4/OKM+visiotyö%2C+Demoksen+yhteiskehittämisprosessi.pdf

Ministry of Education and Culture. (2019a). *Korkeakoulutus ja tutkimus 2030 -luvulle: vision tiekartta* [Roadmap for implementing vision 2030]. https://minedu.fi/documents/1410845/12021888/Korkeakoulutus+ja+tutkimus+2030-luvulle+VISION+TIEKARTTA_V2.pdf/43792c1e-602a-4776-c3f9-91dd66ba9574/Korkeakoulutus+ja+tutkimus+2030-luvulle+VISION+TIEKARTTA_V2.pdf

Ministry of Education and Culture. (2019b). *Visio 2030 Työryhmien raportit* [Vision 2030 Working Group Reports']. https://minedu.fi/documents/1410845/12021888/Visiotyo%CC%88ryhmien+yhteinen+taustaraportti_v2.pdf/d69fc279-d6a9-626d-deac-712662738972/Visiotyo%CC%88ryhmien+yhteinen+taustaraportti_v2.pdf

Mirrlees, T., & Alvi, S. (2020). *EdTech Inc. Selling, automating and globalizing higher education in the digital age*. Routledge.

Münch, R. (2020). Academic capitalism. *Oxford Research Encyclopedia of Politics*. Retrieved December 18, 2020, from https://oxfordre.com/politics/view/10.1093/acrefore/9780190228637.001.0001/acrefore-9780190228637-e-15

Musselin, C. (2018). New forms of competition in higher education. *Socio-Economic Review, 16*(3), 657–683.

Nyyssölä, K., & Kumpulainen, T. (2020). *Perusopetuksen ja kouluverkon tulevaisuudennäkymiä: Raportit ja selvitykset 2020:25*. Finnish National Agency for Education. Retrieved January 17, 2021, from https://www.oph.fi/fi/tilastot-ja-julkaisut/julkaisut/perusopetuksen-ja-kouluverkon-tulevaisuudennakymia

Peters, M., Olssen, M., & Lankshear, C. (2003). Introduction: Futures of critical theory—Dreams of difference. In M. Peters, M. Olssen, & C. Lankshear (Eds.), *Futures of critical theory—Dreams of difference* (pp. 1–21). Rowman & Littlefield.

Picciano, A. (1994). Technology and the evolving educational-industrial complex. *Computers in the Schools, 11*(2), 85–102. https://doi.org/10.1300/J025v11n02_08

Poutanen, M., Tomperi, T., Kuusela, H., Kaleva, V., & Tervasmäki, T. (2020). From democracy to managerialism: Foundation universities as the embodiment of Finnish university policies. *Journal of Education Policy*. https://doi.org/10.1080/02680939.2020.1846080

Prytz, J. (2020). The OECD as a Booster of National School Governance. The case of New Math in Sweden, 1950–1975. *Foro de Educación, 18*(2), 109–126. https://doi.org/10.14516/fde.824

Rantala, L., & Suoranta, J. (2008). Digital literacy policies in the EU—Inclusive partnership as the final stage of governmentality? In C. Lankshear & M. Knobel (Eds.), *Digital literacies: Concepts, policies and practices* (pp. 91–117). Peter Lang.

Rinne, R. (1999). The rise of the McUniversity. In I. Fägerlind, I. Holmesland, & G. Strömqvist (Eds.), *Higher education at the crossroads*. Studies in Comparative and International Education 48 (pp. 157–169). Stockholm University, Institute of International Education.

Rinne, R. (2014). Surviving in the Ruins of the University—Lost autonomy and collapsed dreams in the Finnish transition of university policies. *Nordic Studies in Education, 34*(3), 213–232.

Rinne, R., Kivirauma, J., & Simola, H. (2002). Shoots of revisionist or just slow readjustment? The Finnish case of educational reconstruction. *Journal of Educational Policy, 17*(6), 643–658.

Ritzer, G. (1998). *The McDonaldization thesis*. Sage.

Robertson, S. (2016). The global governance of teachers' work. In K. Mundy, A. Green, B. Lingard, & A. Verger (Eds.), *The handbook of global education policy* (pp. 275–290). Wiley.

Sellar, S., & Lingard, B. (2013). The OECD and global governance in education. *Journal of Education Policy, 28*(5), 710–725. https://doi.org/10.1080/02680939.2013.779791

Selwyn, N. (2011). Editorial: In praise of pessimism-the need for negativity in educational technology. *British Journal of Educational Technology, 42*(5), 713–718. https://doi.org/10.1111/j.1467-8535.2011.01215.x

Selwyn, N. (2016). Minding our language: Why education and technology is full of bullshit … and what might be done about it. *Learning, Media and Technology, 41*(3), 437–443. https://doi.org/10.1080/17439884.2015.1012523

Slaughter, S., & Rhoades, G. (2004). *Academic capitalism and the new economy*. Johns Hopkins University Press.

Timcke, S. (2020). The one-dimensionality of econometric data: The Frankfurt School and the Critique of Quantification. *TripleC, 18*(1), 429–443. https://doi.org/10.31269/triplec.v18i1.1121

Verger, A. (2013). *WTO/GATS and the global politics of higher education*. Routledge.

Wiggershaus, R. (1994). *The Frankfurt School*. Polity Press.

Williamson, B. (2021). Meta-edtech. *Learning, Media and Technology*. https://doi.org/10.1080/17439884.2021.1876089

PART VI

Critical Community-Engaged Learning/Research

CHAPTER 22

Critical Comprehensive Peace Education: Finding a Pedagogical Nexus for Personal, Structural, and Cultural Change

Tony Jenkins

Had peace educators been better students of history, we might have understood from the outset of our work that significant change in human behaviors and human institutions cannot be achieved without change in the cultures which give rise to and are shaped by the behaviors and institutions.—Betty Reardon (2000, p. 416)

[Most social] movements…have of necessity for the most part taken an oppositional stance to policy establishments rather than a transformational stance toward systems and the culture which produce them.—Betty Reardon (2000, p. 417)

Peace education is rooted in traditions of critical theory. While the field is broad and dynamic, most theorists and practitioners share the conviction that peace education should support learners in developing a critical consciousness of the world as it is and should be. Furthermore, peace education is overtly and intentionally political, seeking to foster the human agency necessary for social and political transformation. Inquiry into violence, in its myriad of direct and indirect forms (Galtung, 1969), including especially epistemic violence, is the focal point from which peace education provides its diagnosis and prognosis. Some, if not most institutionalized forms and approaches to peace education are politically benign; in an effort to be adopted into schools many take

T. Jenkins (✉)
Georgetown University, Washington, DC, USA
e-mail: jenkins@i-i-p-e.org

the path of least resistance, opting to forsake the critical social dimensions in favor of more politically acceptable interventions. The hope, for some, is that this strategy affords an opportunity to change the institution from within. Programs such as social emotional learning and conflict resolution programs tend to emphasize psycho-social approaches to change, accentuating behavioral and social changes among students. While such programs foster social emotional intelligence and may capacitate learners for constructive conflict management, they generally fall short in capacitating the critical thinking, imaginative, futures oriented, and political competencies are seen as necessary for pursuing socio-political change. At the same time, many critical theorist-practitioners fail to see the essential interdependencies between psycho-social and socio-political approaches to educational change. Fostering human agency for social and political action, one of the central pillars of peace education, requires a holistic, comprehensive pedagogical approach. Having cognition of a social problem, even when accompanied by a vision of a preferred social alternative, is generally insufficient if the internal conviction to take external action is not also generated. Given this challenge, this chapter will explore the possibilities for developing a critical, comprehensive pedagogical approach to peace education that exists at the nexus of personal, structural, and cultural change.

Peace Education: A Field in and of Praxis

Peace education is a field in and of praxis; its parameters and guiding principles are consistently evolving through the reflective learning of its practitioners and theorists (Bajaj, 2008b; Haavelsrud, 1996; Haavelsrud & Cabezudo, 2013; Harris & Morrison, 2013; Jenkins, 2019; Reardon, 2000, 2015b; Wintersteiner, 2009; Zembylas & Bekerman, 2013). As the field developed more formally over the past half century, there have been many debates as to its social purposes, goals, and approaches. These disputes have provided opportunities for critical reflection and interrogation, opening the doors for new evolutions. The debates that shape these evolutionary developments, similar to other transdisciplinary social and educational sciences (Boulding, 1956; Jenkins, 2013a), are reflective of the varying contexts and conditions of those who were, and are actively engaged in peace education. In Freirean terms, these contexts represent the elicited, generative themes of the learning of the field (Freire, 1970). While there is near-universal agreement that the central problématique of peace education is violence in all its various forms and manifestations (Reardon, 1988), there are many, wide-ranging discussions as to the most efficacious, ethical, and contextually relevant educational strategies, methods, pedagogies, and approaches for nurturing and sustaining personal, social, and political change and transformation. Werner Wintersteiner (2009) contests that "there is no concept that explains sufficiently how education fits into the process of political change. We have to be aware of this theoretical gap of peace research rather than to blame peace education for it" (p. 52).

These contested theories of change illuminate the need for increased dialogue among practitioners and theorists to learn and appreciate the contextual milieus shaping preferred approaches. They also call for a renewed emphasis on rigorous evaluation and research (Wisler et al., 2015), as well as training in research methods consistent with social justice pedagogies. When evaluating formal educational interventions, the external myriad of direct and indirect social, cultural, and political educational influences, which comprise the contextual conditions (Haavelsrud, 1996; Haavelsrud & Cabezudo, 2013) of a given population, require researchers to make intuitive judgments. These intuitions constitute a critical and valid form of knowledge (Hajir & Kester, 2020), yet they foster uncertainties and anxieties among those who generally hold positivist renderings of the world (Walzer, 1993).

One of the prominent discussions currently influencing the field weighs psycho-social against socio-political approaches to educational change (Bar-Tal, 2002; Hajir & Kester, 2020; Zembylas & Bekerman, 2013). In generalized terms, psycho-social approaches are individual-centered, oriented toward worldview change of the learner, and emphasizing the development of inner moral resources and social emotional competencies. Such approaches have a tendency to fixate on the individual as the locus of the problem that is to be fixed, accompanied by a linear view of social change captured by the refrain often attributed to Gandhi: "If you want to change the world, start with yourself." Zembylas and Bekerman (2013) challenge the assumption "that lack of peace, tolerance, justice, equality, and recognition is primarily considered a product of 'ignorance'" (p. 201) and bring attention to the importance of centering education on the social, historical, political, and structural contexts that give rise to such "ignorance" (see also: Bajaj & Brantmeier, 2011). From this viewpoint, many significant scholarly calls for reclaiming critical peace education have been made over the past two decades. Critical peace education theorists bring attention to socio-political approaches that center institutions and structural violence as that which must be transformed. Juxtaposed with the psycho-social, socio-political approaches tend to overlook psychological barriers and motivators for political engagement, and may have a pedagogical leaning toward rationalism (which many theorists consider a contested terrain of structural violence). The scholarly propensity to see these two approaches as polarities may be owed, in part, to those "paradigmatic dichotomies set by Western epistemologies" (Zembylas & Bekerman, 2013, p. 1999), which ignore their essential interdependencies. To advance the transformative potential of peace education, a conscious effort should be made to shift academic energy from debate to dialogical encounter. How are the psycho-social and socio-political approaches to educational change related? What are the interdependencies between personal and political change? Arguably, human agency may be the crucial point of pedagogical convergence that may help us render a more comprehensive and holistic view of critical peace education. An examination of some of the historical developments of the field that have shaped these different views will be explored before diving into these specific inquiries.

A Brief History of Peace Education Developments

The history of peace education comprises formal, non-formal, and informal developments, with the still contested formalization of the academic field emerging in the latter half of the twentieth century. Harris and Morrison (2013) trace the earliest origins of peace education to informal, cultural practices and community-based peace education strategies. They also point to the influence of activist movements, suggesting that modern peace education may have emerged in Europe during the Napoleonic Wars via progressive intellectuals. Throughout much of the twentieth century, the rise of peace education has been largely considered a response to global issues, particularly violent conflicts, and wars (Bajaj, 2008b; Harris & Morrison, 2013; Pervical, 1989; Reardon, 1988, 2000; Wulf, 1974). Arising from these contexts, early approaches to peace education focused on the achievement of negative peace (Galtung, 1969), which emphasizes the elimination and reduction of direct forms of violence.

It is generally recognized that peace education emerged as a more formal academic pursuit with the formation of the Peace Education Commission (PEC) of the International Peace Research Association in 1973. In *An Intellectual History of the Peace Education Commission of the International Peace Research Association* Mindy Pervical (1989) examines the complex conditions that gave rise to the development of the field and the field's relationship to other realms of peace knowledge, particularly peace research:

> Peace education, and the formation of PEC as a major expression of that field, is a manifestation of a complicated variety of social, academic, political and psychological trends. It is the culmination of interests spawned from religion, politics, education, philosophy, economics and history. Peace researchers were responsible for introducing to educators a consistently *critical approach* to the problems of war and violence which allowed them to retain a theoretical framework independent of the popular peace philosophy of the day. (pp. 45–46)

The critical approaches referred to by Percival probe the possibilities of peace education contributing to "positive peace," which is characterized by the absence of both direct and indirect violence, and the presence of social justice and human rights (Galtung, 1969). Indirect violence, as coined by Johan Galtung (1969) refers to forms of harm (social, cultural, political, and economic) that are not physical in nature, yet are obviously intimately related to physical violence and often give rise to it. Indirect violence can be conceptualized as any form of harm that prevents the achievement of one's full human potential—or violates one's human dignity. Johan Galtung further delineated two forms of indirect violence: structural and cultural. Structural violence is systemic and institutionalized: it's violence that harms a specific group of people by either denying them certain basic rights or preventing them from equitable access to resources. It is exemplified by policies and practices of discrimination based on age, gender, sex preference, race, ethnicity, class, and religion. Magnus Haavelsrud (Haavelsrud, 1996), a contemporary to Galtung, observes that "structural violence also has other more subtle consequences. It kills the imagination of powerless people, it alienates marginalized boys and girls, men and women, to the extent that they become passive acceptors of oppressive reality" (p. 67). Cultural violence is more symbolic and insidious; it is rooted in social and political assumptions and beliefs used to justify direct and structural violence that are passed on and reproduced culturally—often via formal education. The lenses of structural and cultural violence broadened the scope of peace education's inquiry and learning goals. From this vantage, the problématique of violence requires critical investigation of the full array of human inventions, institutions, and cultural practices. With this critical awareness, the knowledge, skills, and values that peace education seeks to inculcate and nurture become much more context-dependent. The influences of structures and institutions must be examined for their contextual impacts on social and political relations.

Perhaps even more important, the critical lens requires inquiry into how structures, institutions, and cultures may be sources of epistemological and/or pedagogical violence. Many critical peace education scholars acknowledge that how we come to know, what it is that we think that we know, significantly impacts how we will come to use and act upon that knowledge in the world (Jenkins, 2008). For example, the cognitive imperialism of colonialist pedagogies is an impediment to critical and reflective thinking, social imagination, and the possibilities of peace and social justice. The emphasis on knowledge production and reproduction of Eurocentric/Western pedagogies, adopted by most systems of formal education, inherently imposes a finite set of deterministic social and political values that serve to maintain the world as it is. Such pedagogies mold individual epistemic assumptions of both teachers and students to conform to a narrow view of acceptable forms of knowledge and thought. Hajir and Kester (2020) argue that certain epistemic assumptions "value reason and rational dialogue as a means toward transformation and emancipation while failing to attend to unequal power relations operating in the background, such as the subjugation of non-rational ways of knowing/being" (p. 518). This epistemological violence produces cognitive biases, and is an obstacle to the development of a learner's full human potential, well-being, and flourishing. This enduring legacy of colonialist pedagogies is a fundamental source of cultural, structural, and direct violence that the current generation of peace education scholars seeks to bring renewed attention to.

The influence of feminist perspectives is also critical to the evolution of peace education, likely having the most significant and maturing impact on the field, and to peace knowledge in general. Feminists, largely through the PEC, introduced women's perspectives and feminist analysis to peace research. Women's concerns were largely ignored within the IPRA archipelago and considered peripheral to the issues of war, disarmament, and traditional peace and security. The feminists countered this false logic through critical structural analysis, showing the interconnections between women's issues and quotidian experiences of violence and the war system. With a particular focus on the multiple forms of sexist violence suffered by women in most societies and the effects of armed conflict on women, came the recognition that these multiple forms of violence, both in times of apparent peace as well as in times of war, were interconnected in a global culture of violence. These trends illuminated and brought wider attention to gender inequality—war interconnections. Understanding these interconnections in turn led more feminist scholars, researchers, and peace activists, to adopt as a working premise the assertion that gender violence is one component of an essentially violent patriarchal international system (Jenkins & Reardon, 2007).

Patriarchy established a new lens through which the war system could be analyzed. It also forced, albeit uneasily and slow, a gendered structural analysis of IPRA and the guiding principles, goals, and values of peace research in general. While these substantive contributions have been significant, the influence of feminist perspectives on comprehensive peace education and transformative pedagogy are perhaps even more foundational. Pervical (1989) observed that "structural change, feminists argued, would be unsuccessful without attention to personal, inner change, and changes in human relationships, as authentic transformation can occur only when people change their values, behaviors, and their worldviews" (p. 103). The affective, intuitive, creative, psychological, emotional, care, and relational dimensions—largely considered inferior women's concerns—had a significant impact on broadening the scope of peace education. There was a call for the person to be given as much attention as the political. The feminist perspective was relational rather than conflict centered, recognizing that the resolution of conflicts was meaningless if the underlying relationship was not also addressed and made whole. Percival's interviews with PEC members revealed the basis of a feminist peace education framework built upon three essential principles:

> (1) An interconnectedness between the personal and the political, (2) a restoration of the values of 'insight and imagination' and (3) inclusion of the sentimental and emotional in the study of peace and education for peace. The primary goal of education for peace is, therefore, to reveal and develop talents and characteristics conducive to a meaningful and life-enhancing existence. (p. 103)

The goals and purposes derived from this perspective intimate a positive peace orientation, emphasizing building and establishing the conditions necessary for peace to flourish. This emphasis is not at the expense of the pursuit of negative peace (Ragland, 2012) or the resistance to violence and the dismantling of war, rather, the feminists thought it essential to pursue both, viewing holism, and interconnectedness as vital to the process of educating for a culture of peace. This thinking presupposes the violent alignment of the gender order as an overarching concern for both women and men. With the emergence of masculinities studies in the 1990s, men's negative experiences of the patriarchal gender order emerged from the shadows, finally giving credence to the long-overlooked structural analysis brought into the discussion by feminists some 20 years earlier (Jenkins & Reardon, 2007).

As this critical gender analysis reveals, it's also important to observe the historical development of peace education in relationship to other fields of peace knowledge. Betty Reardon (2000) asserts peace knowledge as the "various learning, research and action practices related to peace" (p. 420). Peace knowledge is a spectrum, comprising knowledge about the substance of peace, violence, conflict, and world order; knowledge necessary for analyzing and interpreting violence, conflict, and peace; as well as the knowledge, skills, and capacities necessary for building just, peaceful relationships, institutions, and world order. Reardon orders peace knowledge into four interdependent categories: peace studies, peace research, peace education, and peace action. Peace research outlines much of the substance and methods of the peace knowledge field and prepares learners with the analytic and interpretive skills essential to future research. Reardon historically situates peace research within academic traditions of irenology and polemology (as well as other social and political science disciplines), which emerged largely in Europe in the 1950s, and was more officially adopted as peace research with the founding of IPRA in 1964. In Reardon's framing of peace knowledge, peace studies are the realm that emphasizes the transfer of peace-related knowledge and issues. Peace studies are now well situated within the academic system. Peace action refers to knowledge and skills essential to nonviolent strategy and action, civil resistance, conflict transformation, peacebuilding, conflict management, and future thinking. Most knowledge related to peace action is pursued outside the university system through non-formal training programs conducted by non-governmental and civil society organizations. Peace education, based upon the substance of all the other realms, is especially concerned with the role of education (formal, non-formal, informal) in contributing to a culture of peace and emphasizes methodological and pedagogical processes and modes of education that are essential for transformative learning and nurturing attitudes and capacities for pursuing peace personally, interpersonally, socially, and politically. In this regard, peace education is holistic, intentionally transformative, and politically and action-oriented.

In delimiting these spheres of peace knowledge, Reardon provides historical context and examines the interrelationships among the typologies. In Reardon's observation, the spheres are not dichotomous, rather they reciprocally inform and shape each other. This holism is rarely pursued in academia where the relationship between knowledge, learning, research, and action remains relatively contentious (Boulding, 1956; Jenkins, 2008, 2013a). For example, "traditional peace knowledge, such as that taught in many university programs, draws from positivist research traditions, where objectivity outweighs subjectivity" (Jenkins, 2013b, p. 174). Fortunately, the evolution in academic peace knowledge fields has gradually moved toward the subjective (Charmaz, 2005), recognizing that the social justice researcher "no matter how objective – is an active participant in the creation of meaning at all stages of their research or practice: the design, the hypothesis, the questioning, and the analysis" (Jenkins, 2013b, p. 175). Recognizing this relationship could spur a transformation in the academic discourse toward transdisciplinarity. Further, it implies the emergence of an ethical disposition for all fields of peace knowledge: that all research, knowledge generation, learning, and action should be directed toward positive social purposes. Increased exchanges and collaborative knowledge creation between the spheres are essential. Returning to the previous reflections on epistemological violence, there is a need as well to take up the task of analyzing education systems and pedagogies to assess their positive and negative impacts toward a culture of peace.

In *Peace Education: A Review and Projection*, Betty Reardon (2000) reflects further upon "the conceptual evolution of the pedagogical purposes and the historical conditions in which they evolved" (p. 417). Reardon's reflections mirror aspects of Percival's investigation of the developments of the field within the PEC. Reardon begins by describing what she terms "traditional peace education," a broad categorization that she stipulates as "planned and guided learning that attempts to comprehend and reduce multiple forms of violence (physical, structural, institutional and cultural) used as instruments for the advancement or maintenance of cultural, social or religious beliefs and practices or of political, economic or ideological institutions or practices" (p. 401). This definition is consistent with recent theorists' views on critical peace education, albeit with a few nuanced distinctions. Reardon suggests the traditionalist approach focuses on the transmission of knowledge and development of skills of peacemaking without necessarily taking into consideration the personal, inner or transformative dimensions and development of supportive attitude and capacities called forth by other approaches. She also refers to traditional peace education somewhat interchangeably as "essential" peace education, and education that only focuses on the transmission of knowledge (minus the skills) as "supportive" peace education. Reardon also specifies several general approaches to education that have their basis in the traditional approach: international, multicultural, and environmental education. These traditional approaches are grouped with human rights education and conflict resolution as "essential peace education," recognizing "the substance it addresses is about what peace is, its essence, and assumes that without knowledge of what comprises it, peace cannot be pursued, much less achieved. Certain knowledge is essential to peace" (p. 404). She suggests that elements of these traditional approaches have deep historical roots connected to social and political movements, and thus pre-date much of the theory and curricula of more modern peace education.

Comprehensive peace education, another of Reardon's (2000) conceptions rooted in the feminist tradition, is put forward as an essential evolutionary step in the field:

> The approach... seeks to integrate relevant aspects of education for and education about peace into a common conceptual framework with its foundation in the purposes of essential and traditional peace education and its pedagogies derived from a developmental concept of learning for social change. It was to some degree a response to the problem of fragmentation and proliferation of approaches to peace education... It owes much to the emergence of holism as a general principle of learning and curriculum development that gained more advocates among educators during the 1980s. (p. 412)

Comprehensive peace education differs from traditional peace education in that it advocates for intentional system change as well as the transformation of human consciousness and human society. For Reardon, developing critical and reflective consciousness is seen as an essential basis for the possibility of social action and engagement as well as the pursuit of a good and meaningful life.

Another present phase of peace education development is rooted in the vision of a culture of peace (Jenkins, 2013b; Reardon, 2000; Wintersteiner, 2009). This vision, articulated in the 1999 UN Declaration and Program of Action on a Culture of Peace is based upon "a set of values, attitudes, traditions and modes of behavior and ways of life" (United Nations General Assembly, 1999) that flow from several interrelated principles including respect for life, human rights, the peaceful settlement of conflicts, sustainable development and ecological integrity, gender equity, and human dignity. Betty Reardon (2000) observed that:

> Given the particular nature of the current problems of violence and the unprecedented opportunities presented by the growing attention to the concept of a culture of peace, in particular, questions of the development of consciousness, and human capacities to intentionally participate in the evolution of the species and the reconceptualization of culture should inform the next phase of peace education which might now address the "heart of the problem." A culture of peace perspective promises the possibility to probe these depths, the "heart", the self-concept and identity of the human species and the cosmologies from which these concepts and the dominant modes of thinking of a culture of violence arise. Now, as never before, all of education needs to be concerned about the questions of what it is to be human and how formal curriculum can facilitate the exploration of that question so as to prepare learners to participate in social change, political-economic reconstruction, transformation of culture and consciousness. Clearly, this requires profound changes throughout all educational systems, but most especially it demands equally significant developments in peace education, a new concept of purpose, a more fully developed pedagogy, broader dimensions than even comprehensive, feminist or ecological and cooperative education have envisioned. (p. 415)

Reardon's vision calls for nothing short of a prophetic shift in culture and in the educational institutions and pedagogies that give rise to, support, and sustain dominant worldviews and ways of being.

Historical Reflections

The preceding review of the historical developments of the field, while far from complete, helps illuminate the praxis at the heart of peace education that reflects the contextual realities from which various orientations and approaches to peace education have emerged. Elements of critical peace education, of varying approach and quality, have been foundational to the field throughout its development. Early efforts, centered primarily on deconstructing the conditions of direct violence and creating the conditions for a negative peace, fall somewhat short of the holism called for by present-day critical peace education thinking. Many such efforts fail to discern the critical interdependence between forms of direct, structural, and cultural violence. Raising such linkages is key to the pursuit of transformative socio-political change. Feminists helped bring further attention to structural and cultural violence by observing the quotidian impacts of war and conflict. From this perspective, feminists also perceived and theorized change holistically, observing an integral interrelationship between structural change and personal change. While some feminists might hold the view that change in values, behaviors, and worldviews should precede structural change (and thus a presumed preference for psycho-social approaches), there is a clear symbiosis between the two approaches. By further applying a lens of epistemological violence (as rooted in colonialist pedagogies, for example), structural and cultural violence can be seen as having a direct relationship to individual attitudes and worldviews. In general terms, how we perceive the world is shaped by structural, cultural and other contextual conditions; and our perceptions of the world in turn shape how we interact with the world. Thus, as feminists have long avowed, the personal and the political are essentially inseparable. Therefore, critical peace education should seek to be holistic, while contextually specific, in its approach to nurturing learners to be agents of change.

Political & Contextual Patterns

Patterns and preferences for the policy adoption of psycho-social vs socio-political approaches can certainly be observed under some generalized contextual conditions. Peace education policy that emerges from above is more likely to be psycho-social in nature. For example, states experiencing and emerging from direct, violent conflict are prone to adopt psycho-social approaches. One reason for this is that it diverts attention away from the failings of the state (i.e., structural failures), and puts the locus on the individual citizen as the broken link in the system. From a more benevolent view, a psycho-social emphasis may be seen as essential to peacebuilding efforts confronting long-standing ethnic and political identity conflicts. In Western democracies, particularly in the USA, there is also a tendency to adopt psycho-social programs in schools in the form of interventions such as social emotional learning (SEL), peer mediation, and conflict resolution programs. Such programs center student behavior as the problem and generally avoid the institutional and structural analysis that might threaten the political establishment and status-quo. While such programs undoubtedly have an individual and social benefit, they commonly fail to address the contextual conditions from which the perceived negative student behaviors originate. Restorative justice programs are somewhat caught in the middle of this milieu. When applied critically, restorative justice brings an intentional focus to structural and relational patterns. Unfortunately, in many cases, restorative justice is applied unceremoniously as little more than an alternative form of school discipline (Winn, 2018; Zehr, 2002).

In contrast, educational projects adopting a socio-political lens is more likely to originate from civil society. Such approaches, consistent with the feminist view, originate from more intimate and direct experiences with structural violence. These projects, typically undertaken by NGOs and community organizations, mostly operate in non-formal spaces. These efforts take roots in community spaces, where their values and learning goals become culturally embraced. As a result of this cultural acceptance, social and political authorities have little recourse but to consider these changes for formal curricular adoption (Jenkins & Segal de la Garza, 2021). In the view of many educational researchers, this bottom-up approach may be the most probable pathway toward policy implementation in formal education.

Pedagogical Pathways to Human Agency

> Acquiring peace knowledge rarely results in peace activism due to apathy, privilege, and the normalization of violence…—Rita Verma (2017, p. 8)

> What we are about, on a day-to-day basis, is actually how we change paradigms. We must change ourselves and our immediate realities and relationships if we are to change our social structures and our patterns of thought.—Betty Reardon (2015c, p. 112)

> The most influential factor in transformative learning is the conscious, reflective experience of the learner.—Betty Reardon (2015a, p. 159)

Integrating peace education into formal schools has long been championed by peace educators as an essential peacebuilding strategy (Bajaj, 2015), recognizing that formal schooling is perhaps the most influential site of cultural production and reproduction in society. Schools not only provide knowledge and skills, but also shape social and cultural values, norms, attitudes, and dispositions. However, as previously acknowledged, educational policy is generally established from the worldview of a relative few social and political elites who seek to maintain their power and privilege through the maintenance of the status quo. From the lens of critical peace education, this policy influence can itself be considered a form of structural violence, which, by design, establishes and maintains an inequitable distribution of power in society. Thus, advocating for critical peace education, which by its nature invites critical interrogation of institutionalized learning as a potential source of structural violence, presents many strategic challenges. As Zembylas and Bekerman (2013) observe, "what education is asked to correct has little to do with education and a lot to do with the world in which schools exist, the very world they are asked to support" (p. 202). In response to the hopelessness this view may generate, Zembylas and Bekerman suggest that efforts may be better focused on the "struggle to change pedagogical practices and strategies" (p. 203). Pedagogical adaptation, integration, and curricular infusion are short-term strategic work-arounds, with potential indirect long-term benefits to these policy challenges.

How then might critical comprehensive peace education be approached pedagogically and utilized as a counter-hegemonic force for knowledge decolonization and a source of personal and social liberation accompanied by structural change? Pedagogical holism is the starting point. The learning must provide opportunities for reflection on the interdependence between personal and political realities (Bajaj & Brantmeier, 2011). The learning must also be meaningful; it must center and draw from the learner's experience of the world and should be pursued through various modes of critical self-reflection (Freire, 1970; Hajir & Kester, 2020; Jenkins, 2016, 2019; Mezirow, 1991; Reardon & Snauwaert, 2011; Verma, 2017) Social transformation is dependent upon human agency (Bajaj, 2008a), which is the keystone in the bridge that spans the personal and the political dimensions of one's subjective reality. For Jack Mezirow (Mezirow, 1991), one of the founding fathers of transformative learning theory, human agency is the outcome of a transformative learning process. Mezirow suggests that worldview transformation is pursued through four stages (see Fig. 22.1), which are guided by accompanying pedagogical principles: (1) the centrality of experience (it is the learner's experience that is the starting point and the basis of the subject matter), (2) critical self-reflection (the internalized processes of meaning making), (3) rational discourse as a form of social validation in the process of meaning transformation, and (4) responsive action. Mezirow's view is consistent with Freirean praxis (see Fig. 22.2), a learner-centered cycle of "reflection and action upon the world in order to transform it" (Freire, 1970).

For both Mezirow and Freire, if the learning is to be meaningful it must center the learner's experience, drawing forth cognitive, affective, and intuitive interpretations of their subjective reality and aiding them in finding ways and means to express and articulate their experience. By centering inquiry and reflection on the student's experience, and making the student's experience the subject matter of the learning, learners are invited to theorize an understanding of their reality. Reflection is the soul of all transformative peace pedagogy, raising critical consciousness by bringing attention to experience and questioning worldview assumptions. Action is then the process of seeking to live one's truth through experimentation in new ways being and acting, both personally and politically. Perhaps overlooked in the Freirean model is

Fig. 22.1 Mezirow's stages of worldview transformation (a pathway to human agency)

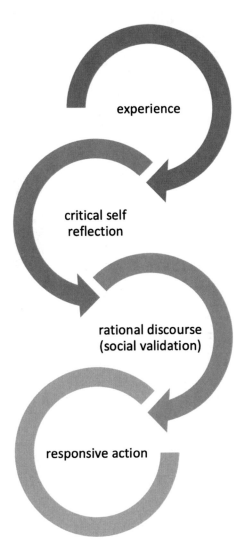

the importance of social learning in worldview transformation (stage 3 of Mezirow). For Mezirow (1991), this is a process of social validation in which personal reflection is corroborated with others, where "the personal meanings that we attribute to our experience are acquired and validated through human interaction and communication" (p. xiv). Reardon adds to this a political dimension: "while it is possible for the [reflective] process to remain inward and still be productive of learning, the practice of reflective inquiry as peace education - learning toward social and political change – must become outwardly dialogic…" (Reardon & Snauwaert, 2011, p. 7). Reardon's reflection illuminates the importance of integrating a community-centered political

Fig. 22.2 Paulo Freire's praxis

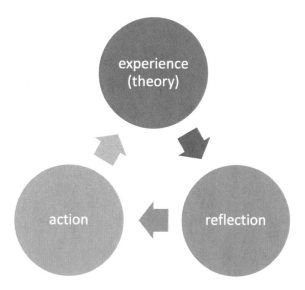

praxis, as a process of shared meaning-making, into transformative pedagogical practice.

The action dimension of the learning praxis establishes human agency as one of the central goals and a guiding social purpose of all transformative peace learning. Human agency is fostered via a holistic, comprehensive critical pedagogy that is guided by an awareness of the interdependencies between psycho-social and socio-political change. In other words, transformative critical pedagogies are premised upon a holistic theory of change in which personal, structural, and cultural change are in a symbiotic relationship. Further, as implied by Reardon, Freire, and Mezirow, learning for personal, structural, and cultural change is both relational and learner-centered. I've previously described this holistic, transformative framework as a *pedagogy of relationships* (illustrated in Fig. 22.3). The pedagogy of relationships introduces four intentional, learner-centered dimensions of reflective inquiry focused on examining the learner's interdependent relationships to the present, past, future, and others. (Previous iterations of this framework included additional dimensions, with a strong emphasis on examining the relationship of the teacher to the student [Jenkins, 2013b, 2019]. It is beyond the scope of this short chapter to illuminate these additional dimensions.)

In applying this pedagogical framework, peace education necessitates a critical reflection on each of these dimensions. As Rita Verma (2017) observes, "openings are created when unlimited questioning is encouraged of the past, present and future and when the three are understood to be in continual embrace and tension" (p. 10). One's relationship to the past might be examined via inquiries supporting reflection upon historically relevant social, cultural, political, and economic foundations of society and their influences

Fig. 22.3 A pedagogy of relationships

upon perceived reality. Such critical reflection upon the past can foster critical self-reflection and double-loop learning (Marsick & Saugeut, 2000) that supports questioning of epistemological assumptions. Critical reflection upon one's experience of the present (a form of reflection-in-action) supports affective and intuitive awareness, which, when connected to critical reflection of past assumptions, can foster critical consciousness. Holistically reflecting on our relationship to the past and present may free the self from assumptions of the past as well as foster worldview transformation. On a more pragmatic level, psycho-social reflection supports the development of emotional intelligence and capacitates learners to constructively deal with conflict and to respond to violence with nonviolence. The learner's relationship to the future must also be considered. This requires imaginative, ruminative, and contemplative reflection (Reardon, 2013). Elise Boulding reminded us that the images we hold of the future are rooted in our present experience of the world and in our interpretations of the past (Boulding, 1988, 2000; Morrison, 2013). Warren Ziegler adds that "the future is nothing more and nothing less than a grand act of the human imagination" (Ziegler, 1982). Humans construct reality in their minds before acting on it externally, "thus how we think about the future also shapes the actions we take in the present" (Jenkins, 2020). Further, "to open ourselves up to thinking about preferred futures requires, at least temporarily, that we step away from rational thought and embrace our intuitive and affective ways of thinking, knowing and being" (Jenkins, 2020). Constructive and transformative human agency is dependent upon our ability to envision a preferred world, and further, to believe that a new world is even possible. For the learning to become socially and politically transformative, it must also invite reflection on our relationship to others that comprise our moral universe. Transformative learning for political and structural change is a form of community praxis. Through collective reflection on action, social and cultural assumptions are challenged, and new expressions of reality are validated. As a form of political learning, Reardon observed that if reflective learning were to be "left at the inward without the communal sharing, it might become meditative rather than ruminative, remaining personal, not becoming a social learning process, preparatory to the public political discourse for change" (Reardon & Snauwaert, 2011, p. 8). Human agency, from Reardon's perspective, is fostered through both personal and social reflection.

Conclusion

> Critical peace education is oriented towards the particularistic, seeking to enhance transformative agency and participatory citizenship, and open to resonating in distinct ways with the diverse chords of peace that exist across fields and cultures.—Monisha Bajaj (2015, p. 4)

> [Pedagogy is the] determinant of human relationships in the educational process. It is itself the medium of communication between teacher and learner, and that aspect of the educational process which most affects what learners receive from their teachers.—Betty Reardon (1993)

At the heart of this essay has been a spirited attempt to address Wintersteiner's (2009) distressed concern that "there is no concept that explains sufficiently how education fits into the process of political change" (p. 52). It is easy to see how top-down, strategic efforts to institutionalize peace education in schools rarely succeed, particularly as critical approaches to peace education challenge the very structures and ways of thinking that schools have been designed to uphold—and schools are but an extension of a given society. Although this conclusion seems to present an insurmountable challenge, pursuing the integration of critical peace education into schools should remain a priority. However, we may wish to approach the task of transforming formal education as critical pedagogues, and not as politicians. Institutions learn in similar ways to humans: they are more likely to transform when the learning is elicited from within, rather than imposed by an authority from above. Generating transformative institutional agency is a process of learning as much as it is a process of politics.

I've put forward that the answer to how we pedagogically generate human agency might be the missing piece to the puzzle of how education can contribute to political and structural change. Political agency is particularly goal directed and assumes an individual is acting with intention toward applying their individual power to effect change on the structures of society. Of course, human agency can be hampered by the presence of conditions of enduring structural violence and oppression. Nonetheless, cultivating the human agency necessary for intentionally pursuing personal, structural, and cultural transformation can be approached through elicitive and reflective learning that fosters recognition of the intimately intertwined relationships between present structural conditions, social and political histories, individual psychological dispositions, and the epistemic conditioning that shapes one's orientation to the world. The potential for human agency is further enhanced when the inward reflective learning becomes a social, dialogic process of communal meaning-making and potential political action.

Critical, comprehensive peace education contributes to the process of political/structural change in many ways. As a desired formal curricular intervention, it may serve to disrupt the production and reproduction of legacies of epistemic violence. Pursued as a holistic pedagogical intervention, educators emerge as the locus of the political mediation, facilitating transformative learning opportunities that may lead to cultivating human agency that is the fountain of personal, structural, and cultural change. Zembylas and Bekerman (2013) caution that "educators cannot do it all, they cannot change the world, but they should do the most they can in changing, a bit, their immediate contexts" (p. 203). Most important, as I've observed elsewhere, we must be aware that "the disposition that we take as educators in the classroom is political. It is the modeling of a political relationship that is extended outside of the classroom. As such, we need to be ever mindful of how our teaching praxis informs and shapes political externalities" (Jenkins, 2019, p. 204). This responsibility placed upon educators as agents of structural change is a tremendous burden, but it is not all that dissimilar to the strains and struggles experienced by those living under, and seeking to change, the day-to-day oppressions of systems of structural violence. If we accept the strategic proposal put forward here that peace pedagogues are the key link in the chain of social and political change pursued through education, we might begin by prioritizing the development of transformative teacher training programs to foster the human agency of critical, reflective peace educators.

REFERENCES

Bajaj, M. (2008a). "Critical" peace education. In M. Bajaj (Ed.), *Encyclopedia of peace education* (pp. 135–146). Information Age Publishing.

Bajaj, M. (2008b). *Encyclopedia of peace education*. Information Age Publishing.

Bajaj, M. (2015). 'Pedagogies of resistance' and critical peace education praxis. *Journal of Peace Education, 12*(2), 154–166. https://doi.org/10.1080/17400201.2014.991914

Bajaj, M., & Brantmeier, E. J. (2011). The politics, praxis, and possibilities of critical peace education. *Journal of Peace Education, 8*(3), 221–224. https://doi.org/10.1080/17400201.2011.621356

Bar-Tal, D. (2002). The elusive nature of peace education. In *Peace education: The concept, principles, and practices around the world* (pp. 27–36). Lawrence Earlbaum.

Boulding, K. (1956). *The image: Knowledge in life and society*. University of Michigan Press.
Boulding, E. (1988). *Building a global civic culture: Education for an interdependent world*. Syracuse University Press.
Boulding, E. (2000). *Cultures of peace: The hidden side of history*. Syracuse University Press.
Charmaz, K. (2005). Grounded theory in the 21st century: Applications for advancing social justice studies. In N. K. Denzin & Y. S. Lincoln (Eds.), *In the Sage handbook of qualitative research* (3rd ed.). Sage.
Freire, P. (1970). *Pedagogy of the oppressed*. Herder and Herder.
Galtung, J. (1969). Violence, peace, and peace research. *Journal of Peace Research*, 6(3), 167–191.
Haavelsrud, M. (1996). *Education in developments* (Vol. 1). Arena.
Haavelsrud, M., & Cabezudo, A. (2013). Rethinking peace education. *Journal of Conflictology*, 4(1), 3–13. Retrieved from http://journal-of-conflictology.uoc.edu
Hajir, B., & Kester, K. (2020). Toward a decolonial praxis in critical peace education: Postcolonial insights and pedagogic possibilities. *Studies in Philosophy and Education*, 39(5), 515–532. https://doi.org/10.1007/s11217-020-09707-y
Harris, I., & Morrison, M. L. (2013). *Peace education: 3rd edition*. McFarland.
Jenkins, T. (2008). A peace education response to modernism: Reclaiming the social and pedagogical purposes of academia. In J. Lin, E. Brantmeier, & C. Bruhn (Eds.), *Transforming education for peace*. Information Age Press.
Jenkins, T. (2013a). Reflections on Kenneth E. Boulding's the image: Glimpsing the roots of peace education pedagogy. *In Factis Pax*, 7(1), 27–37. Retrieved from http://www.infactispax.org/journal/
Jenkins, T. (2013b). The transformative imperative: The National Peace Academy as an emergent framework for comprehensive peace education. *Journal of Peace Education*, 10(2), 172–196. https://doi.org/10.1080/17400201.2013.790251
Jenkins, T. (2016). Transformative peace pedagogy: Fostering a reflective, critical, and inclusive praxis for peace studies. *In Factis Pax*, 10(1), 1–7. Retrieved from http://www.infactispax.org/journal
Jenkins, T. (2019). Reardon's edu-learner praxis: Educating for political efficacy and social transformation. In D. Snauwaert (Ed.), *Exploring Betty A. Reardon's perspective on peace education: Looking back, looking forward* (pp. 199–205). Springer. https://doi.org/10.1007/978-3-030-18387-5_15
Jenkins, T. (2020, August 27). *The future is now: A pedagogical imperative for peace education*. Retrieved March 23, 2021, from https://www.peace-ed-campaign.org/the-future-is-now-a-pedagogical-imperative-for-peace-education/
Jenkins, T., & Reardon, B. (2007). Gender and peace: Towards a gender inclusive, holistic perspective. In C. Webel & J. Galtung (Eds.), *Handbook of peace and conflict studies* (pp. 209–231). Taylor & Francis.
Jenkins, T., & Segal de la Garza, M. (2021). *Mapping peace education*. Retrieved March 23, 2021, from https://map.peace-ed-campaign.org/
Marsick, V., & Saugeut, A. (2000). Learning through reflection. In M. Deustch & P. Coleman (Eds.), *The handbook of conflict resolution*. Jossey-Bass.
Mezirow, J. (1991). *Transformative dimensions of adult learning*. Jossey-Bass.
Morrison, M. L. (2013, February 15). *What the future Holds: Trends in peace education*. Retrieved March 23, 2021, from https://www.peace-ed-campaign.org/what-the-future-holds-trends-in-peace-education/

Pervical, M. (1989). *An intellectual history of the Peace Education Commission of the International Peace Research Association*. Teachers College Press.

Ragland, D. (2012). *Theorizing justice in Betty Reardon's philosophy of peace education*. Doctoral dissertation, The University of Toledo.

Reardon, B. (1988). *Comprehensive peace education: Educating for global responsibility*. Teachers College Press.

Reardon, B. (1993). Pedagogy as purpose: Peace education in the context of violence. In P. Cremin (Ed.), *Education for peace* (pp. 101–113). Educational Studies Association of Ireland and Irish Peace Institute.

Reardon, B. (2013). Meditating on the barricades: Concerns, cautions, and possibilities for peace education for political efficacy. In P. P. Trifonas & B. Wright (Eds.), *Critical peace education: Difficult dialogues* (pp. 1–28). Springer. https://doi.org/10.1007/978-90-481-3945-3_1

Reardon, B. (2015a). Human rights learning: Pedagogies and politics of peace. In D. Snauwaert & B. Reardon (Eds.), *Betty A. Reardon: A pioneer in education for peace and human rights* (pp. 145–164). Springer.

Reardon, B. (2015b). The fundamental purposes of a pedagogy of peace. In D. Snauwaert & B. Reardon (Eds.), *Betty A. Reardon: A pioneer in education for peace and human rights* (pp. 93–108). Springer.

Reardon, B. (2015c). Toward a paradigm of peace. In D. Snauwaert & B. Reardon (Eds.), *Betty A. Reardon: A pioneer in education for peace and human rights* (pp. 109–120). Springer.

Reardon, B. A. (2000). Peace education: A review and projection. In B. Moon, S. Brown, & M. Ben Peretz (Eds.), *International companion to education*. Routledge.

Reardon, B., & Snauwaert, D. T. (2011). Reflective pedagogy, cosmopolitanism, and critical peace education for political efficacy: A discussion of Betty A. Reardon's assessment of the field. *In Factis Pax, 5*(1), 1–14. Retrieved from http://www.infactispax.org/volume5dot1/Reardon_Snauwaert.pdf

United Nations General Assembly. (1999). *Declaration and programme of action on a culture of peace*.

Verma, R. (2017). *Critical peace education and global citizenship: Narratives from the unofficial curriculum*. Routledge.

Walzer, M. (1993). *Interpretation and social criticism*. Harvard University Press.

Winn, M. T. (2018). *Justice on both sides: Transforming education through restorative justice*. Harvard Education Press.

Wintersteiner, W. (2009). Educational sciences and peace education: Mainstreaming peace education into (Western) academia? In G. Salomon & E. Cairns (Eds.), *Handbook on peace education* (pp. 45–59). Psychology Press.

Wisler, A., del Felice, C., & Karako, A. (Eds.). (2015). *Peace education evaluation: Learning from experience and exploring prospects*. Information Age Publishing.

Wulf, C. (1974). *Handbook of peace education*. International Peace Research Association.

Zehr, H. (2002). *The little book of restorative justice*. Good Books.

Zembylas, M., & Bekerman, Z. (2013). Peace education in the present: Dismantling and reconstructing some fundamental theoretical premises. *Journal of Peace Education, 10*(2), 197–214. https://doi.org/10.1080/17400201.2013.790253

Ziegler, W. (1982). *A mindbook of exercises for futures-invention*. Futures-Inventions Associates.

CHAPTER 23

Showing Up for the Rat Race: Beyond Human Capital Models of Higher Education

Alison Taylor

INTRODUCTION

This chapter addresses questions around the relationship between higher education and graduate work. In particular, it examines how the purposes of higher education are framed in terms of preparing graduates for work in a knowledge economy. In Part 1, I argue that although social democratic promises of the postwar period for upward mobility, job security, and political and social equality have been shown to be empty, they still influence higher education in problematic ways. Most notably, students are encouraged to pursue an ideal of the "good life" that is impossible for many to attain through no fault of their own.

In Part 2, I draw on the capabilities approach and provocative ideas about rethinking work as alternatives to traditional human capital models in higher education. Such alternatives widen the lens beyond learning for paid work by giving equal priority to education for citizenship, public good professionalism, and social justice through strong state support for human development.

A. Taylor (✉)
University of British Columbia, Vancouver, Canada
e-mail: alison.taylor@ubc.ca

PART 1: PROBLEMS WITH NEOLIBERAL HUMAN CAPITAL MODELS OF HIGHER EDUCATION

Neoliberalism and Its Effects on the Public Sphere and Democracy

Since 2008, capitalist accumulation has involved the commodification of public services, facilitated by neoliberal trade policies, and the continuing development of information communication technologies (Huws, 2014). As a result, it has become easier to relocate economic activities and manage them remotely, including the outsourcing of public services. The commodification of welfare systems has caused growing labor insecurity in the public sector (Doogan, 2009), which affects both public sector workers and citizens more generally. Concurrently, there has been an increase around the world in nonstandard work arrangements including the "on-demand," "platform," or "gig" economy (Brown et al., 2020). Trends toward more insecure and routinized work are likely to continue with productivity improvements from digital technologies eliminating many jobs and routinizing others.

In the realm of politics, Wendy Brown (2019) argues that three decades of neoliberal policies constitute an assault on democracy and conceptions of the common good. The violence that accompanied the transfer of power from President Trump to President Biden in January 2021 is only one example, which resonates with the rise of authoritarian populism internationally. In Canada too, decades of neoliberal policies have taken a toll. Neoliberal attacks on the society have meant the disappearance of "the space of civic equality and concern with the common good that democracy requires" (cf. Brown, 2019, p. 183).

Neoliberal policies encourage a discourse of free, responsibilized individuals who self-invest in order to maintain or enhance their human capital. According to Feher (2009), human capital discourse has shifted over time with the growth of globalized and unregulated financial markets that are more concerned with maximizing the distribution of dividends in the short term than with optimizing long-run returns on investment. Accordingly, he argues that human capital investments have become less about maximizing the returns on one's investments (monetary or psychic) than with increasing the stock value of the capital with which one is identified. This broader conception of human capital maps on to what we hear from working undergraduates.

THE PROBLEM OF PRESSURE AND BURNOUT

> For undergraduate students today, juggling multiple commitments is the norm. What feminist writers in the 1980s referred to as the second shift–i.e., the unpaid domestic labour that compounded women's paid work–has become a "triple" or even "quadruple" shift for students who are balancing paid work, academic work, domestic labour and/or volunteer work. (Taylor, 2020)

Brown et al. (2020) suggest that "rather than education being a source of individual and economic freedom, there is increasing psychological pressure on students, resulting in rising numbers suffering from mental health problems" (p. 2). Our interviews with working university students in Canada confirm that many are struggling with the perceived pressure to prepare themselves during their program for post-graduation work. This pressure is often described in terms of becoming the "super student" who invests appropriately in their own human capital in the hopes of future rewards. This is the student who moves seamlessly across multiple activities: attending classes, acing exams, demonstrating leadership in extra-curricular activities, volunteering to demonstrate their suitability for professional programs, and working in career-related areas to secure their future. As one undergraduate reflects, "even if it's not a job, [it's] a rat race to get to the next thing, Because I know in undergrad once you're in fourth year in the honors program, then it was 'how are you getting to grad school, are you applying for [funding], are you doing this?' It's just like *go, go, go*, how are you getting to the next thing?" She concludes, it's tough "to have to be here plus be five years into your future, ten years into your future."

The feeling of pressure is expressed even more poignantly by those who feel they're not succeeding in the "rat race." For example, another student comments:

> It's really discouraging to see myself do poorly in things that I'm really invested in. You know, like when I put off some work or something, it's not out of laziness, it's out of like the inability to be in like the emotional state to tackle it right now. And that's definitely hard because like [pause] there is so much competition on the [university] campus and there are so many people that do so well, if not flawlessly. … So, you know, trying to compete with people who may not have the same obstacles as I do.

Obstacles for students include learning disabilities and mental health challenges as well as financial pressures. International students face additional pressures if they wish to pursue permanent residence in Canada after graduation. A great deal of invisible work is required for students to feel they are competitive (Taylor & Taylor-Neu, forthcoming). The predominance of the human capital model of subjectivity—for students as well as for other groups (cf. Feher, 2009)—often translates into self-blame, when one struggles to "invest" adequately.

Another student, who works throughout the year because she has to finance her own studies, worries that her combined labor will take a toll later:

> I have a fear that in working and going to school, I'm gonna burn myself [laughs] out and that when I graduate, I'm just not gonna want to do anything … So, that's why I kind of am thinking I won't do grad school right after. I might go into the work field for a few years. And then hopefully, that will allow me to pay down my student loans, get some work experience and then

hopefully travel a little bit … just find a healthier balance before I decide to do grad school or more research. But yeah, I'm scared that I'm gonna graduate, like even with the passion and like the direction I have, I'd just be tired.

These quotes from students raise questions about what the work of being a student and employee involves, why they're working so hard, and whether their efforts are likely to be rewarded by attaining the kind of work they desire. The studies referenced in the next section make it clear that the workplaces we are preparing students for are changing and the promises about returns on investments in education look increasingly hollow.

The Problems of Job Scarcity and Quality

Although it is common in policy circles to hear employers and governments talk about the need for knowledge workers with higher education credentials, there are good reasons to be skeptical about the discourse of labor scarcity as well as assumptions about the economic returns on investments in education. Recent research that examines international trends highlights the failure of orthodox human capital promises. For example, Brown et al. (2020) suggest rates of return on education in American and Britain over a forty-year period seriously challenge the learning-earning equation. Data suggest that there is a scarcity of good jobs rather than a scarcity of labor. Livingstone (2019) adds that although the Canadian labor force has "the highest level of general post-secondary education completion in the world" (p. 156), the underutilization of professional employees' qualifications has become a significant problem. Together, these studies suggest that although an "educational arms race" (Livingstone et al., 2021) has been a common response to "credential hyperinflation" (Brown et al., 2020, p. 2), the relationship between learning and earning is more complicated.

Brown et al.'s (2020) analysis draws on census and labor force data in the United States and United Kingdom between 1970 and 2010 to look at wages and earnings over time. Interestingly, wages were higher in real terms for most workers in 1970 than in 2010. These authors also compared the incomes of college graduates and high school graduates over this period, but instead of focusing on averages (which hide a great deal of variation within groups), they also examined the bottom and top segments of the distribution. This approach revealed "increasing segmentation, stratification, and in some cases polarization within and between occupations" (Brown et al., 2020, pp. 59–60). In spite of the rise in educational attainment over time, "investment in a college education has not resulted in parallel income growth" (p. 54). Overall, the median earnings of graduates have not been commensurate with the rise in technical, managerial, and professional employment. Further, outcomes are stratified by type of education and institution as well as by class, gender, race, ethnicity, industry, and occupation. In sum, authors describe the problem as a shortage of quality jobs and differences in labor market power—not a scarcity of qualified labor, as suggested by orthodox human capital models.

Like Brown and his co-authors, Livingstone et al. (2021) suggest that there is no necessary correspondence between formal educational qualifications and the actual skills required for jobs. In fact, a greater supply of qualified applicants is likely to result in less bargaining power. Canadian data confirm this—while about a quarter of the employed labor force had completed a post-secondary credential in 1982, this proportion had grown to around two-thirds by 2016 (Livingstone et al., 2021). Survey data also confirm an increase over this period in both *credential underemployment* (those reporting a credential greater than required for their job) and *subjective underemployment* (the extent to which respondents perceive themselves to be overqualified for their jobs). For post-secondary graduates, credential underemployment increased from 34 to 45% between 1982 and 2016, while subjective underemployment increased from 22 to 38% (Livingstone et al., 2021). The proportion of professional employees reporting underemployment also grew significantly over this period. Younger workers and racialized youth tend to have higher rates of underemployment (De Jong & Madamba, 2001). Underemployed workers report declining task autonomy, and diminished participation in organizational decision-making. Thus, professional employees appear to have become "proletarianized" over time in Canada as well as in the United States (Pulskamp, 2006).

In sum, the research conducted by Brown et al. (2020) and Livingstone et al. (2021) provides counter-narratives to the discourse of "learning for earning" in higher education. These authors argue for a closer examination of changes in labor markets, work processes, and the trends that are likely to impact future work. Following such an examination, Brown et al. argue for a new human capital model in higher education that places individual growth throughout life at the center. They acknowledge that rethinking higher education is insufficient without also rethinking work and the current distribution of opportunities in society. Ensuring that all employees are able to apply their skills in workplaces through collective action is important, as is addressing growing economic polarization in society.

The Problem of Value and the Imperative to Rethink Work

> That action of getting what one can because the other people are getting theirs, that action of thinking that "fairness" in democracy equals no one having a cushion (and so claims on economic justice become special-interest claims rather than the claims any member of the body politic might make)—this kind of dark relationality comes out of political depression and an incapacity to think otherwise. (Berlant, 2012)

My discussion to this point has focused on the hollow promises of human capital models in higher education that are highlighted in analyses of the changing relationship between education and work (Brown et al., 2020) and the proletarianization of some forms of professional work (Livingstone et al., 2021). Further, human capital promises are troubling insofar as they are rooted in a system of value and values that opposes the public good that is necessary for human flourishing. In her book "Cruel Optimism," Berlant (2011) asks, "Why do people hold on to fantasies of the good life, meritocracy, the family, or the political" when these optimistic attachments are detrimental to their wellbeing? Through the lens of affect theory, Berlant explores the techniques people adapt to navigate the "exhaustive terrain of neoliberal capitalism" (Lippert, 2013, p. 143).

David Graeber's (2018) book about contemporary work supports Berlant's claim that work and pleasure need reinvention. Graeber traces shifting ideas about the value of work over time: most notably, the shift from the notion that labor produces value to the belief that capital produces value; the economic value of paid (over unpaid) work; the contradictory nature of attitudes toward work; and the inverse relationship between the economic value and the social value of many jobs.

Dominant ideology holds that capitalists are the drivers of wealth and prosperity, in contradistinction to a labor theory of value. Economists have long equated value with paid work, despite the fact that unpaid work—including household work, charitable works, political volunteering, and many artistic activities—have value that is more difficult to quantify. Brown et al. (2020) and Livingstone et al. (2021) also problematize the invisible nature of gendered reproductive work in the home, including care work, that is essential to sustaining society. As Brown et al. (2020) affirm, "it is only when social activities get bundled and formalized in labor contracts that they are judged to constitute part of labor demand because they are defined to have market value" (p. 175). This vision of value also omits the growing range of nonstandard paid work (including gig and platform work), which fails to conform to the standard employment relationship of full time, year-round work with one employer.

Graeber (2020) refers to the moral value placed on work historically to explain the contradictory reality evident in sociology of work literature: the fact that although people find their sense of self-worth in work, most people also claim to hate their jobs. He traces this back to the Puritan tradition, which perpetuates the idea that people gain their self-worth from their work *because* they hate their jobs. The "work-as-an-end-in-itself" morality is described in terms of an ethic that "if you're not destroying your mind and body via work, you're not living right" (Graeber, 2018, p. 216). He further observes that a perversion of values has developed as a result, whereby those who are doing pointless or even harmful work are paid more than those who know their work is socially valuable and useful. He elaborates his ideas as follows:

> Bullshit jobs proliferate today in large part because of the peculiar nature of managerial feudalism that has come to dominate wealthy economies—but to an increasing degree, all economies. They cause misery because human happiness is always caught up in a sense of having effects on the world; a feeling which most people, when they speak of their work, express through a language of social value. Yet at the same time they are aware that the greater the social value produced by a job, the less one is likely to be paid to do it. (Graeber, 2018, p. 243)

In the context of Covid-19, this argument became more compelling, as it became obvious that low-paid "front line" service workers including grocery store workers, bus drivers, and laundry workers in hospitals are essential workers, unlike hedge fund managers, political consultants, and marketing executives. The inverse relationship between the economic value and social value of jobs helps to explain why people may hold onto visions of the good life that impedes their flourishing (Berlant, 2011). In what follows, I consider ways of disrupting the narrow value system that has developed over time.

Part 2: Alternatives to Neoliberal Human Capital Thinking

In Part 1, I discussed how changes in work over time challenge simplistic ideas about the financial returns to higher education. I further argued that the problematic valuation of work in society calls for a reinvention of work, which attends to the inequitable distribution of and valuation of labor. So, what does this mean for higher education? In Part 2, I suggest that universities could do more to disrupt the influence of traditional human capital models by playing a greater role in challenging social inequities, including those related to how different kinds of work are valued. The capabilities approach provides a partial direction for this kind of change as do Marxian-inspired ideas.

Paid Work vs. Community-Engaged Learning and Unpaid Work

How do universities perpetuate a discourse of learning for earning? The concept of work-integrated learning (WIL) has become very popular in Canadian universities and internationally as a way of enhancing graduates' employability in a competitive labor market as well as enhancing their learning (Jackson, 2015; Taylor et al., 2020). WIL includes short-term work placements, cooperative education programs, internships, practicums, project-based learning, and community-based learning (Drysdale et al., 2016).

However, access to WIL opportunities (especially more prestigious ones) is inequitable. For example, research suggests that first-generation students (students whose parents did not complete post-secondary education) in Canada (Sattler & Peters, 2013) and international students in Australia

(Gribble et al., 2015) have less access to WIL. While Sattler and Peters (2013) do not explain the lower rate of participation of first-generation students in Canada, our research suggests that such students often lack information about opportunities as well as forms of social and cultural capital that would help them secure positions. International students in Australia were also found to face barriers related to their lack of social networks and English language proficiency, as well as less willingness on the part of employers to invest in them (Gribble et al., 2015). Relatedly, a European study found that ethnic minority students worked more hours and perceived more work–study conflict than others (Meeuvwise et al., 2017).

Although community-engaged learning (CEL) is usually included under the umbrella of WIL, the aims of CEL go beyond employability. Further, CEL programs tend to lack parity of esteem vis-à-vis other WIL activities. Such programming:

> [U]sually includes a 'course-based, credit-bearing, educational experience in which students participate in an organized service activity that meets identified community needs and reflect on the service activity in such a way as to gain further understanding of course content, a broader appreciation of the discipline, and an enhanced sense of civic responsibility' (Bringle & Hatcher, 1996, p. 222). It can be distinguished from work-integrated learning programs in the type of community partners involved (usually not-for-profit sector) and the aims of learning (e.g., learning for citizenship as well as employment). (Raykov & Taylor, 2018)

Both in the United States and Canada, CEL is often marginalized within higher education in terms of core funding for programs, the extent to which faculty are provided with support and recognition for this work, and as a result, the number of faculty and students who participate (Butin, 2006; Taylor, 2017). Especially when CEL programs are housed within student services offices at universities (including career centers), staff feel pressured to justify their work in terms of graduate employability. While our interviews with students who participated in CEL during their undergraduate programs at a small eastern Canadian university suggest that such experiences often play a significant role in their further education and career decisions (Taylor et al., 2021), a narrow employability focus tends to reduce such experiences to their economic utility and misses their broader potential for collective human flourishing and active citizenship. Our research on service learning identifies features that are more expansive. In particular, what Butin (2007) describes as "anti-foundational service learning" encourages students to question common-sense social categories and welcomes tensions and dilemmas in student learning as opportunities for reflection. Through thoughtfully constructed CEL opportunities and dialogue about their boundary-crossing experiences between classrooms and communities, students can participate in socially valuable work and reflect on their place in the world in relation to others.

Our 2019 survey of undergraduates at a research-intensive university in western Canada indicates that around half (49%) engaged in a wide range of unpaid work for an average of six hours per week, including student clubs and associations, curricular or co-curricular volunteer work in the community, and internships (Raykov et al., 2020). Common motivations for such participation included making a social contribution as well as socializing with others. Interestingly, unpaid work was reported by students to be more influential than paid work for developing career-related skills, deciding on future education plans, and for career plans. Our interviews with students indicate further that they often felt more freedom, less sense of hierarchy, and greater ability to control what they did in unpaid compared to paid work. At the same time, low-income students reported an inability to participate in unpaid work because of their requirement to work for pay. Other writers also acknowledge that the costs of unpaid opportunities are prohibitive for many students (Bassett et al., 2019; Grenfell & Koch, 2019). Our interviews with students support survey findings about the value students place on "meaningful" work as well as differences in access to opportunities.

The Aspiration for Socially Valuable Work

As suggested in Part 1, many students in our study felt pressured to succeed "the way that they [universities] want us to." At the same time, when asked how they perceive meaningful work, most students responded in ways that go beyond learning for earning. For example, an international student replied:

> [A] big thing for me is [work] has to give back to the community. If I don't see myself giving back then I don't think there is a purpose. And … some of the classes you take are just requirements. And I tend not to do well in those because I don't think they're important to the community for me or when I go back, how is it going to help my community or my place.

Another student shared that she wants to help others develop, as well as to grow personally:

> I find my job meaningful [when] … I am given an ability to grow as a person and change as a person and realize things as a person. … and when you're collaborating with other people, you are allowing them to grow as a person because they're learning things from you and … [One wants] work that you feel is self-fulfilling and you're not leaving it feeling like empty as a person, right? You're feeling more satisfied with your life, if that makes sense.

A third student expressed a desire to be involved in social change:

> I want to be able to make some sort of small-scale difference in individual lives. … I want to have both parts of the career where it's meaningful on a day-to-day level with people, and then eventually meaningful on like a policy, changing some of the things about how we approach law in this country, make it better.

These comments are typical of student responses to questions about what they want from work, and suggest that their aspirations are more expansive than is assumed by traditional human capital models.

Our research findings regarding CEL and students' unpaid work more generally can be productively put in dialogue with the human capabilities approach (CA). Brown et al. (2020) and others advocate for such an approach as an alternative to traditional human capital models in higher education in order to place human development at the center. I argue further that to effectively disrupt the problematic valuation of contemporary jobs (Graeber, 2018) as well as to address the external conditions that enable or limit opportunities (Sayer, 2012), CA should be informed by other critical theories, most notably Marxian thinking. The next section explores this approach to economy and education.

HIGHER EDUCATION AND THE CAPABILITIES APPROACH

> [Amartya] Sen carefully distinguishes between the accumulation of human capital and the expansion of human capability (Sen, 1997, 1999). While the former aims at enhancing productivity or production possibilities, the latter focuses on the ability to lead a life one has reason to value, thereby implying that valuable lives may include aspects beyond mere participation in productive activities. (Bonvin, 2019, p. 275)

The capabilities approach was developed by the economist and philosopher Amartya Sen (1992) as a way of rethinking the meaning of human development; it builds on ideas from humanist social philosophy and humanist economics (Boni & Walker, 2013). In its challenge to traditional economics, CA is reminiscent of work by feminist economists. For example, Marilyn Waring (1990) also raised important questions about the limitations of economic measures like GDP (Gross Domestic Product), including a disregard for the invisible work of women and the costs of environmental degradation. CA proposes that assessing people's quality of life involves examining what opportunities they have to lead the lives they value. Debates within CA center on how it is applied—notably, the selection of relevant capabilities and the relative priority or weighting given to each capacity. While Sen argues that any list of capabilities is context-dependent, Nussbaum (2000) argues for a general list that can be translated into different contexts. The political impact of CA is evident in the United Nations Development Programme's Human Development Report, which focuses each year on a theme related to development, understood as the expansion of people's capabilities. The CA has also been used to assess gender inequality in advanced economies, and to empirically assess policies (Robeyns, 2006).

CA relies on two key concepts of capabilities and functionings. While "functionings" refer to what a person actually is or does, "capabilities" refer to what a person can be or can do (Bonvin, 2012, p. 11). Following Sen, CA proponents recognize that because different groups face distinct challenges (e.g., persons with disabilities), what is required for them to convert resources into capabilities or real freedoms to lead a valuable life differs. In addition to material resources, Sens' work suggests that the development of capabilities requires the possibility to voice one's preferences and expectations and for these to count in decision-making processes; in other words, there is a requirement for democratic governance (Bonvin, 2012). Sen's concept of conversion recalls Bourdieu's ideas about how the conversion of different forms of capital affects social inequalities, and in fact, some writers have drawn on these ideas to examine how conversion factors help or hinder the development of capabilities (cf., Hart, 2019).

Hart's (2019) Sen-Bourdieu framework raises an important point about the strengths and weaknesses of CA. While Robeyns (2003, p. 66) describes the strengths of CA as its attention to "people's beings and doings" in non-market as well as market settings and its recognition of human diversity, she acknowledges that it is "underspecified" and requires additional social theories. Sayer (2012) argues further that the radical potential of CA is missed because of "attempts to use its normative theory without an adequate account of the social structures that enable or limit human capabilities in particular situations" (p. 580). Sayer and other authors attempt to address the gaps in CA. For example, Walker (2010) argues for bringing Sen's CA together with ideas from critical pedagogy to inform undergraduate university education with social justice aims, and Robeyns (2003) presents a feminist capability perspective on gender inequality. Sayer (2012) draws on the theory of contributive justice to ask questions about what kinds of paid and unpaid work people are allowed or expected to contribute, as key to understanding the external constraints on the development of capabilities.

In Part 1, I highlighted the importance of bringing Marxian perspectives to the discussion of CA. This could offer insights into the reproduction of inequalities within new modes of capital accumulation. More encompassing theories of value in society further complement these approaches. A brief look at how CA has been taken up in higher education confirms the need for such theoretical dialogues.

The Capabilities Approach in Education

The CA approach has been taken up by writers focused on gender equity in South African schools (Walker, 2006); the vision of public good professionalism in universities (Walker & McLean, 2013); and a more expansive vision for vocational education and training (VET) (Bonvin, 2019; Powell &

McGrath, 2019). The education system is seen as having a crucial role to play in developing students' capabilities and developing professionals who advocate for social change. In the latter case, writers believe that a critical interpretation of the capabilities approach can provide an ethical framework for professional education (Walker, 2010; Walker et al., 2009). This perspective advocates for universities as places that contribute to more equitable and democratic societies by challenging the current distribution of opportunities as well as developing students' capabilities. Professionals are seen as elites who must play a role in social change (Walker et al., 2009). I argue elsewhere (Taylor, 2021) that while this perspective is morally compelling, it does not take into account the changes that have occurred in professional work. Thus, while it makes sense to see university students in professional faculties as privileged vis-à-vis students who lack access to higher education, they can also be seen as caught up in the pursuit of visions of a "good life" that are not realizable and workplace structures that are far from equitable.

Some of the writings on vocational education and training are more attentive to what is required for CA to critically address the complex relationship between higher education and work, and the ways in which the social organization of work and existing power relations can restrict capabilities. For example, Powell and McGrath (2019) suggest that human capital models in the VET system in South Africa fail to support the aspirations of unemployed youth. Like the Canadian university students cited above, their interviews with youth suggest that they desire work that produces what is needed, promotes recognition and self-worth, provides a livelihood, and contributes to their communities—aspirations that are "more broadly human and collective" than is suggested by "productivist" discourse (p. 388). Bonvin (2019) adds that a CA approach considers the intrinsic value of education and its non-economic contributions to collective as well as individual human and social development.

A capability-friendly economy and society would consider the availability of jobs, job quality, working conditions, labor regulations, workplace relations, and collective agreements (Bonvin, 2012). It would also view the social welfare system as key to people's ability to refuse "valueless" work and to balance work and family life (Bonvin, 2012, p. 15). Such an approach asks important questions like Who is able to develop different kinds of competencies? Who benefits from this development? How are different work opportunities distributed? What levels of worker discretion are provided in different jobs? And, most importantly, how are inequities in the ability to live a life that one values addressed?

This last question gestures toward the discussion raised in Part 1 regarding how to reinvent work. Graeber's (2018) historical analysis suggests that the validation of "bullshit jobs" is deeply rooted, and democratic governance will require significant struggle. As Sayer (2012) observes, "democracy usually stops at the workplace door" (p. 585). As a partial solution, Graeber, like Brown et al. (2020), advocates for a universal basic income (UBI) as a way of detaching work from compensation—detaching the domain of economic value from the domain of social values. A government program in which every adult receives a minimum income would establish the principle that everyone deserves the material resources to live. It establishes the "right of material existence for all people" (Graeber, 2018, p. 279).

Bringing this discussion back to the student voices cited above, our interviews point to students' yearning for meaningful work. During their undergraduate programs, many students are engaged in "survivalist" work rather than "opportunity" work (Powell & McGrath, 2019, p. 387). Further, many cannot consider the possibility of unpaid work because of mounting student debt. Movement toward a vision for higher education that embraces a critical CA approach requires wider access to opportunity work, for example, through a more generous student finance system or universal basic income. For example, Nordic countries like Finland and Norway offer more generous support for students, including free tuition as well as generous public subsidies (Garritzmann, 2016; Välimaa, 2015). An alternative vision also requires a shift from the narrow focus on graduate employability toward a focus on graduate capabilities directed toward participation in families, communities, politics, and society, as well as the labor market.

Concluding Comments

Higher education enrolments have become more skewed toward practical or applied programs over time in North America (Brint et al., 2005). There is no question that students are concerned about their future work prospects. However, changes over time in work mean that this future is more uncertain and quality work is scarce. It is also problematic that socially valuable work is often least valued. In such a context, I believe higher education has at least three roles to play.

The first role involves expanding the ways we think about "preparing" undergraduate students to include opportunities focused on developing capabilities beyond qualifications for specific professions. Our research on community-engaged learning and students' unpaid work suggests that work is more consequential in positive ways when students are able to choose it, when workplace relations are less hierarchical, and when that work is seen to have social value. More opportunities of this kind could be built into programs and made accessible to a wider range of students. Second, universities could promote critical analysis of work. It is unfair to task students with being public good professionals if they're likely to experience work that is proletarianized within a system that promotes winners and losers. As workplace technologies proliferate, including artificial intelligence, it is clear that a rethinking of work is urgently needed. Finally, increasing access to higher education must be accompanied by greater attention to how pedagogical practices privilege some students and disadvantage others. The capabilities approach's commitment to equal valuing of diversity based on gender and sexuality, race, ethnicity, social class, and disability reinforces the critical role of education in human and social development.

REFERENCES

Bassett, A. M., Brosnan, C., Southgate, E., & Lempp, H. (2019). The experiences of medical students from First-in-Family (FiF) university backgrounds: A Bourdieusian perspective from one English medical school. *Research in Post-Compulsory Education, 24*(4), 331–355. https://doi.org/10.1080/13596748.2018.1526909

Berlant, L. (2011). *Cruel optimism*. Duke University Press. https://doi.org/10.1215/9780822394716

Berlant, L. (2012). Affect in the end times: A conversation with Lauren Berlant. *Qui Parle, 20*(2), 71–89. Retrieved from http://read.dukeupress.edu/qui-parle/article-pdf/20/2/71/339725/71Berlant.pdf

Boni, A., & Walker, M. (Eds.). (2013). *Human development and capabilities: Reimagining the university of the twenty-first century*. Routledge. https://doi.org/10.1080/19452829.2014.906198

Bonvin, J. M. (2019). Vocational education and training beyond human capital: A capability approach. In S. McGrath, M. Mulder, J. Papier, & R. Suart (Eds.), *Handbook of vocational education and training: Developments in the changing world of work* (pp. 1–17). Springer. https://doi.org/10.1007/978-3-319-94532-3_5

Bonvin, J. M. (2012). Individual working lives and collective action: An introduction to capability for work and capability for voice. *Transfer, 18*(1), 9–18. https://doi.org/10.1177/1024258911431046

Bringle, R., & Hatcher, J. (1996). Implementing service-learning in higher education. *Journal of Higher Education, 67*(2), 221–239. https://doi.org/10.1080/00221546.1996.11780257

Brint, S., Riddle, M., Turk-Bicakci, L., & Levy, C. (2005). From the liberal to the practical arts in American colleges and universities: Organizational analysis and curriculum change. *The Journal of Higher Education, 76*(2), 151–180. https://doi.org/10.1080/00221546.2005.11778909

Brown, W. (2019). *In the ruins of neoliberalism: The rise of antidemocratic politics in the west*. Columbia University Press. https://doi.org/10.1080/1462317X.2019.1659943

Brown, P., Lauder, H., & Cheung, S. (2020). *The death of human capital?* Oxford University Press. https://doi.org/10.1093/oso/9780190644307.001.0001

Butin, D. (2006). The limits of service-learning in higher education. *Review of Higher Education, 29*(4), 473–498. https://doi.org/10.1353/rhe.2006.0025

Butin, D. (2007). Justice-learning: Service-learning as justice-oriented education. *Equity and Excellence in Education, 40*(2), 177–183. https://doi.org/10.1080/10665680701246492

De Jong, G. F., & Madamba, A. B. (2001). A double disadvantage? Minority group, immigrant status, and underemployment in the United States. *Social Science Quarterly, 82*, 117–130. https://www.jstor.org/stable/42955706

Doogan, K. (2009). *New capitalism? The transformation of work*. Polity. https://doi.org/10.1177/13684310100130021102

Drysdale, M., McBeath, M., Johansson, K., Dressler, S., & Zaitseva, E. (2016). Psychological attributes and work-integrated learning: An international study. *Higher*

Education: Skills and Work-Based Learning, 6(1), 20–34. Retrieved from https://doi.org/10.1108/HESWBL-02-2015-0004

Feher, M. (2009). Self appreciation; or, the aspirations of human capital. *Public Culture, 21*(1), 21–41. https://doi.org/10.1215/08992363-2008-019

Garritzmann, J. (2016). *The political economy of higher education finance: The politics of tuition fees and subsidies in OECD countries: 1945–2015*. Palgrave Macmillan. https://doi.org/10.1007/978-3-319-29913-6

Graeber, D. (2018). *Bullshit jobs: A theory*. Penguin Random House. https://doi.org/10.1177/0486613419870319

Graeber, D. (2020). Policy for the future of work. In R. Skidelsky & N. Craig (Eds.), *Work in the future: The automation revolution* (pp. 157–173). Palgrave Macmillan. https://doi.org/10.1007/978-3-030-21134-9

Green, F., & Henseke, G. (2016). Should governments of OECD countries worry about graduate underemployment? *Oxford Review of Economic Policy, 32*(4), 514–537. https://doi.org/10.1093/oxrep/grw024

Grenfell, L., & Koch, C. (2019). Internship courses for all? Supporting students undertaking unpaid university-run legal internships. *Alternative Law Journal, 44*(3), 226–231. https://doi.org/10.1177/1037969X19845688

Gribble, C., Blackmore, J., & Rahimi, M. (2015). Challenges to providing work integrated learning to international business students at Australian universities. *Higher Education, Skills and Work-Based Learning, 5*(4), 401–416. Retrieved from https://doi.org/10.1108/HESWBL-04-2015-0015

Hart, C. S. (2019). Education, inequality and social justice: A critical analysis applying the Sen-Bourdieu Analytical Framework. *Policy Futures in Education, 17*(5), 582–598. https://doi.org/10.1177/1478210318809758

Huws, U. (2014). *Labor in the global digital economy*. Monthly Review Press. https://www.jstor.org/stable/j.ctt1287j8b

Jackson, D. (2015). Career choice status among undergraduates and the influence of work-integrated learning. *Australian Journal of Career Development, 24*(1), 3–14. Retrieved from https://journals.sagepub.com/doi/10.1177/1038416215570043

Lippert, L. (2013). Review of Berlant, Lauren: Cruel optimism. *Kritikon Litterarum, 40*(1–2), 116–119. https://doi.org/10.1515/kl-2013-0021

Livingstone, D. W. (2019). Proletarianization of professional employees and underemployment of general intellect in a 'knowledge economy': Canada 1982–2016. *Labour/Travail, 84*, 141–166. https://doi.org/10.1353/llt.2019.0035

Livingstone, D. W., Adams, T., & Sawchuk, P. (2021). *Professional power and skill use in the 'knowledge economy': A class analysis*. Brill Publishers.

Meeuvwise, M., de Meijer, L., Born, M., & Severiens, S. (2017). The work-study interface: Similarities and differences between ethnic minority and ethnic majority students. *Higher Education, 73*(2), 261–280. https://doi.org/10.1007/s10734-016-0012-1

Nussbaum, M. (2000). *Women and human development: The capabilities approach*. Cambridge University Press. https://doi.org/10.1080/713659331

Powell, L., & McGrath, S. (2019). Capability or employability: Orientating VET toward "real work". In S. McGrath, M. Mulder, J. Papier, & R. Suart (Eds.), *Handbook of vocational education and training: Developments in the changing world of work* (pp. 1–25). Springer. https://doi.org/10.1007/978-3-319-94532-3_12

Pulskamp, J. (2006). Proletarianization of professional work and changed workplace relationships. In P. Durrenberger & J. Marti (Eds.), *Labor in cross-cultural perspective* (pp. 175–192). Altamira Press.

Raykov, M., & Taylor, A. (2018). *Beyond learning for earning: The long-term outcomes of course-based and immersion service learning*. Report for St. Francis Xavier University. Retrieve from cIRcle http://hdl.handle.net/2429/66995

Raykov, M., Taylor, A., Jamal, S., & Wu, S. (2020, December). *Student volunteer work and learning: Undergraduates' experiences and self-reported outcomes* (37 pp.). Retrieve from cIRcle http://hdl.handle.net/2429/76610

Robeyns, I. (2003). Sen's capability approach and gender inequality: Selecting relevant capabilities. *Feminist Economics, 9*(2–3), 61–92. https://doi.org/10.1080/1354570022000078024

Robeyns, I. (2006). The capability approach in practice. *The Journal of Political Philosophy, 14*(3), 351–376. https://doi.org/10.1111/j.1467-9760.2006.00263.x

Sattler, P., & Peters, J. (2013). *Work-integrated learning in Ontario's postsecondary sector: The experience of Ontario graduates*. Higher Education Quality Council of Ontario.

Sayer, A. (2012). Capabilities, contributive injustice and unequal divisions of labour. *Journal of Human Development and Capabilities, 13*(4), 580–596. https://doi.org/10.1080/19452829.2012.693069

Sen, A. (1992). *Inequality reexamined*. Oxford University Press. https://doi.org/10.1093/0198289286.001.0001

Sen, A. (1997). Editorial: Human capital and human capability. *World Development, 25*(12),1951–1961. https://doi.org/10.1016/S0305-750X(97)10014-6

Sen, A. (1999). *Development as freedom*. Alfred A. Knopf.

Taylor, A. (2017). Service-learning programs and the knowledge economy: Exploring the tensions. *Vocations and Learning, 10*(3), 253–273. https://doi.org/10.1007/s12186-016-9170-7

Taylor, A. (2020, August 6). Drop tuition fees: University students face a precarious future amid Covid-19. *The Conversation*. Retrieve from https://theconversation.com/drop-tuition-fees-university-students-face-a-precarious-future-amid-covid-19-129285

Taylor, A. (2021). Professional education, professional work, and their connections: A conversation. In M. Malloch, L. Cairns, K. Evans, & B. O'Connor, (Eds.), *Sage handbook of learning and work* (pp. 421–434). Sage.

Taylor, A., Corrigan, J., & Peikazadi, N. (2021). Community service learning: Possibilities for critical vocationalism in higher education. In S. Brigham, R. McGray, & K. Jubas (Eds.), *Adult education and lifelong learning in Canada: Advancing a critical legacy* (pp. 136–147). Thompson Educational Publishing.

Taylor, A., Raykov, M., & Sweet, R. (2020, January). *Hard working students: Report of 2018 and 2019 survey findings*. Access on cIRcle http://hdl.handle.net/2429/73374

Taylor, A., & Taylor-Neu, R. (forthcoming). Post-secondary education's chronic problem (OR, It's about time). In A. Abdi (Ed.), *Equity and social justice education perspectives in Canada*. Canadian Scholars Press.

Välimaa, J. (2015, February 17). Why Finland and Norway still shun university fees—Even for international students. *The Conversation*. https://theconversation.com/why-finland-and-norway-still-shun-university-tuition-fees-even-for-international-students-36922

Walker, M. (2006). Towards a capability-based theory of social justice for education policy-making. *Journal of Education Policy, 21*(2), 163–185. https://doi.org/10.1080/02680930500500245

Walker, M. (2010). Critical capability pedagogies and university education. *Educational Philosophy and Theory, 42*(8), 898–917. https://doi.org/10.1111/j.1469-5812.2007.00379.x

Walker, M., & McLean, M. (2013). *Professional education, capabilities, and the public good*. Routledge. https://doi.org/10.4324/9780203083895

Walker, M., McLean, M., Dison, A., & Peppin-Vaughan, R. (2009). South African universities and human development: Towards a theorisation and operationalisation of professional capabilities for poverty reduction. *International Journal of Educational Development, 29*(6), 565–572. https://doi.org/10.1016/j.ijedudev.2009.03.002

Waring, M. (1990). *If women counted: A new feminist economics*. Harper Collins Publishers.

CHAPTER 24

The Challenges of Doing Radical Pedagogy in Social Movements in South Africa

Salma Ismail

INTRODUCTION

The article will examine the complexity of doing radical pedagogy in social movements in South Africa. Radical pedagogy is used to conscientize people about discriminatory practices in society. The reasons for such a discussion arose from my empirical research in two social movements (Victoria Mxenge Project and the Treatment Action Campaign and one non-governmental organization—Research and Alternative Education in South Africa) over a sustained period of more than 20 years. One example to illustrate this complexity from my research shows that there appears to be a dilemma with how facilitators engage with indigenous knowledge practices (IK) and often at times facilitators are hesitant to contradict or challenge IK even when IK is harmful to women. The findings here note the limitations of doing radical pedagogy in social movements for social justice in neo-liberal times.

At a theoretical level, I will argue, that there has not been significant attention to theorize the synergies or contradictions between radical pedagogy, indigenous knowledge, and decoloniality in the informal context in South Africa and to shed light on the above.

The significance of the research is to recover radical pedagogies and experiment with a decolonial lens for social change.

S. Ismail (✉)
University of Cape Town, Cape Town, South Africa
e-mail: Salma.Ismail@uct.ac.za

CRITICAL CONCEPTS THAT WILL GUIDE THE STUDY

Antonio Gramsci (1971) and subsequently Paulo Freire (1983) were amongst the first philosophers to consider learning theories which start with the oppressed, to formulate tools for a radical pedagogy formed and owned by the oppressed and suggested that learning was a social process. Gramsci (1971) viewed civil society as an oppositional space in which the dominant ideology can be challenged in which counter hegemonic action is directed against the state.

Freire (1973) endorses peoples' ability to think critically about their education situation; this way of thinking allows them to recognize connections between their individual problems and experiences and the social contexts in which they are embedded which is defined as the power and know-how to take action against oppression.

Radical pedagogy is strongly associated with informal learning which is largely learning not acquired through formal institutionalized education. Newman's (2005) has classified informal learning into three categories as incidental, interpersonal, and instrumental. His classification has relevance for this study as he outlines how people learn instrumental skills such as: the ability to write a pamphlet and to use information and knowledge as resources in the fight against capitalism; interpretive skills to understand what people are like and to make sense of peoples' actions and behavior; and critical skills such as challenging power relationships.

Radical Pedagogy has important links with Indigenous knowledge (IK) and practices as it reaffirms the knowledge of those communities which was destroyed during colonialism and in South Africa under apartheid. Indigenous Knowledge Systems (IKS) have been defined as "… the combination of knowledge systems encompassing technology, philosophy, social, economic, learning/educational, legal and governance systems" (Odora Hoppers, 2001, p. 76). Surrounding the IKS have been polarizing scholarly debates regarding the validity of indigenous knowledge since much of it was destroyed under colonialism and within the realms of "science," when in South Africa traditional medicine was put forward above approved drugs by HIV/AIDS denialists. This example highlights that IKS is not always progressive.

CONNECTING RADICAL PEDAGOGY WITH IKS AND DECOLONIAL THEORY

Steve Biko (1987) and Franz Fanon (1961) often quoted in the decolonial literature stressed the importance of the oppressed freeing themselves from the dehumanizing psychological oppression of colonialism and neo-colonialism. This philosophy was for many black educators an introduction to People's Education which used a Freirian methodology to conscientize people in the Black Consciousness Movement to take pride in being black and to unify the oppressed in the struggle against apartheid in SA.

In South Africa today there is a strong call from students and some academic staff for a decolonized curriculum and pedagogy, originating from the #Rhodes MUST Fall student movement in 2015. These calls link with the views of Maldonado-Torres (2007, p. 263) who argues that "the decolonial turn involves interventions at the level of power and knowledge" which implies a shift away from a reliance on the Western canon and production of knowledge and to restore indigenous knowledge systems. Andreotti (2011) another decolonial scholar connects knowledge to action, affirming the view that knowledge is political, and allowing for critique and challenges to the normative project. These ideas are in sync with radical pedagogy.

Research Design and Methodology

A qualitative research design was used in all three organizations. In all three studies, data was gathered in focus group and individual interviews, by observations, document analysis, and informal visits, to present three in-depth case studies.

The sites of research were in poor African communities and aimed at broad transformation in these communities. Permission was sought beforehand from the Ethics Committee of the University and negotiated in organizational meetings and with each person interviewed. All the usual ethical procedures were followed such as signed consent forms giving permission for the research on the understanding that participation was voluntary and that no real benefit would come to interviewees apart from having a reflective discussion on what they have learnt informally and how, permission to record interviews, participant checking of their transcripts, use of documents and photographs.

In the Victoria Mxenge (VM) project the women requested to be named as they felt very proud of their achievements and wished to use the publications to advocate for their model of low-cost housing. In the other two projects (Treatment Action Campaign and PRAESA), I made it clear to participants that although I would not name them but that their organizations were very specific to the causes and had charismatic and popular leaderships so they may be identified through the naming of the organization. However, I made sure that no direct quotes could be attributed to any one person in both organizations.

In all three projects, I have worked in a principled way with great respect for the community throughout the research process and mindful of Spivak's not to speak for the subaltern and that my representation of them is a partial story and not a description of their entire lives. The research in VM was a longitudinal study over a period of 20 years and in the other two organizations the research was over a period of two years.

In VM, poor women are concerned with building low-cost housing, individual and focus group interviews were held with leaders, members, and facilitators of VM and selected leaders in the housing movement. I observed many workshops and meetings to get a sense of the pedagogy and general commitment to the philosophy of the organizations.

In the Treatment Action Campaign (TAC) involved in HIV/AIDS education, people interviewed were the Manager of the Treatment Literacy Programme, two counselors, two facilitators, two people living with HIV/AIDS, and one program officer and observations were in a public health clinic in Khayelitsha.

In the Programme for Research and Alternative Education in South Africa (PRAESA) involved in creating a reading culture through the Nal'ibali project, the Director was interviewed, one researcher who is no longer working at PRAESA, one program officer, two literacy specialists, one facilitator, and two participants. Observations were of a workshop with reading club leaders to model to them how to make the reading enjoyable and creative and another observation in a primary school in Khayelitsha to observe a teacher facilitating a reading club.

Two of my Masters students assisted with the fieldwork in TAC and PRAESA.

Presentation of Findings

I will briefly describe each case, shifts in the pedagogy as the context changed and then challenges popular educators faced in each one.

The Victoria Mxenge (VM) Project

The VM project, is an affiliate of the South African Homeless People's Federation (Federation) and was linked to international social movements such as Indian Slum Dwellers International (SDI). The VM story highlights the creative and critical role that radical adult education played in a development context in South Africa post-1994, after the election of a democratic government. The VM women were poor homeless women, had migrated from rural areas to live on the outskirts of Cape Town. Some of them came in search of their husbands who were working in Cape Town and living in single sex hostels, others in search of employment to escape the poverty in the rural areas. Most of them had some schooling and they lived under customary African law in which the male is the head of the household.

They successfully combined popular education and a people-centered development philosophy to save, secure land, state finance (subsidies), land, built more than 5000 houses, and a VM community. Their rallying slogan was "We build houses and communities." They became the leaders in the Federation. They believed very strongly that learning needed to be supported; therefore, training was done in a collective. Learning was a social process and included knowledge which became a communal asset.

In the VM project, learning happened within a framework of Popular Education, strongly echoed feminist pedagogy, and was positioned to support the struggles of women in oppressed communities (Walters & Manicom, 1996). The pedagogy worked toward consciousness-raising, and valued working with women's experiences, local/indigenous knowledge, collective decision-making, and participation at all levels of the program. The VM women learned informally in many different ways. They learned individually, in collectives, in social activities, and in learning networks. The learning was technical and cognitive, knowledge was socially constructed and the members in the movement took ownership of the knowledge. For example, in a workshop on design and planning, a professional architect acting as an advisor would ask the women to dream their imaginary houses, then there was a discussion about what a house should offer. These ideas were then brought to life by modeling houses using cardboard. "After designing the cardboard houses, we cost them and look at how much concrete would be needed, in terms of dividing the house everybody had a say where we should have the kitchen, bedrooms and lounge" (focus group interview, 2001) (Ismail, 2015, p. 31).

In a strong oral culture, participation was demonstrated by the high attendance at meetings. The membership saw meetings as important forums in which to express their ideas, obtain information and knowledge, and build links with people. The members' high levels of participation indicated their material stake in their savings and government subsidies, in the organizations, and also that members held their leaders accountable, valued transparency, and wanted clarity about developments within the organization and within housing.

Problem-solving through dialogue was another valued practice, which the women traced back to African traditions and women's ways of finding solutions. The women said "If there is an eviction in one community we will assist them in solving their problems" focus group interview) (Ismail, 2015, p. 35). In these situations, the members learned through listening, observing, questioning, looking at alternatives, and evaluating other savings groups' experiences to explore solutions to their troubles. Some members could articulate the knowledge and ideas they picked up through the discussions, whereas for others, just being part of the process and the group was enriching and gave them a sense of belonging. Through this methodology learning was widespread. Generally, problem-solving was a collective responsibility and consensus was sought from the majority before decisions were taken. The culture in the organization was sufficiently secure so women were confident and effective. These methods of learning—through problem-solving, dialogue, and intensive listening—held seeds of feminist pedagogy and Freire's action and reflection cycle.

The ways in which the Federation members learned, changed as the institutional arrangements shifted from advocating for development to providing houses. For the VM women, from 1992 to 2001, when learning was in tandem with development and mobilizing poor communities, the philosophy and practice of participatory methodologies formed the key strategies to learning and empowerment. This changed during 2001–2003, when demands for housing escalated and VM formed a partnership with the state to scale up delivery and then learning was directed at leaders of savings groups.

During this period, not everybody was taken through the entire process of learning to obtain housing subsidies to drawing plans and building houses, the knowledge spread was uneven, and this led to a loss of confidence in the peoples housing process. The VM leaders were seen as service providers and blamed for the ineffective delivery of housing, of a lack of transparency and authoritarianism. In 2006, the Federation split into two organizations; one remained The South African Homeless People's Federation and the other became the Federation for the Upliftment for the Poor (FEDUP) signaling a more radical approach.

The Treatment Action Campaign (TAC)

This is one of the outstanding examples of solidarity in rights-based social movements in post-apartheid South Africa. It is a movement which campaigns for affordable treatment for people living with HIV and AIDS. In 2004, the TAC achieved success in overturning government policy and won the right to free treatment and medicine for poor people living with HIV/AIDS. The right was won through using radical pedagogy which challenged state and corporate power.

In the TAC, the lessons start from the experiences of the oppressed and underline the connections between individual problems and the social context highlighting a strong relationship between education and politics. A few examples of how this was achieved in 1999 when TAC printed HIV-positive T-shirts, the T-shorts brandished the words "HIV positive," as a tool to break the secrecy, shame, and stigma surrounding HIV/AIDS. From 2001 onward TAC used popular media which played a critical role in explaining the science and treatment such as the multilingual TV series—Beat it! which used volunteers, untrained actors, to raise issues and fight stigma in a soapy style; as did the free magazine Equal Treatment, published in several languages, which explained the science and treatment in clear terms and carried photos and stories of ordinary people living openly with HIV before treatment became available and afterward (Low et al., 2010).

Alongside these methods TAC had on the ground volunteers who first learnt from doctors in the organization, Medicines Sans Frontiers (Doctors without Borders) and other activists and then educated others, going from door to door in communities explaining to people the science of the medicines and treatment. It was a time of denialism by the South African President and his Health Minister, so TAC members were central to countering the myths being spread by government in the period from 1996 to 2008.

When mobilizing for its court challenges TAC used education interventions such as posters and pamphlets and its campaign built solidarities across race, class, different genders and linked with civil society organizations both nationally and globally. For example, the civil disobedience campaign "Dying for Treatment" built on past histories of civil disobedience and was initiated when the TAC took court action against government and after receiving overwhelming support laid a charge of culpable homicide against the former minister of health, Manto Tshabalala—Msimang and minister of trade and industry Alec Erwin (Low et al., 2010). The continuous, contentious collective action of TAC produced solidarity, and the kind of actions reported above served as the basis for social movement solidarity with ordinary people against a hostile government (Adapted from Tarrow, 2011).

The TAC won the right to have free treatment and medicines for poor people living with HIV/AIDS in 2004. This human rights health issue was won by mass protests, court action, and creating powerful partnerships, with lawyers and service providers, with researchers and advocacy groups, locally, nationally, and internationally (Klugman, 2015, p. 10). Included in this mobilization was an undertaking that grass roots activists had to be able to interact with experts and be able to challenge both local and national government myths. Therefore, the TAC ran a sustained education campaign to counter state supported AIDS denialism and critical in this fight was winning the court case to provide free drug and to implement a national program for HIV treatment (Low et al., 2010).

Subsequent to the court victory to have free treatment TAC's engagement with the government changed from mainly adversarial to winning government support to implement treatment in the state clinics. Since its success, the pedagogy has become more "mainstream" as is illustrated by its Treatment Literacy Programme. This program is now the key focus and involves a transfer of knowledge and resources. This includes information about HIV and AIDS, medicines, how to take these correctly, including importance of adherence, healthy diets, and the side effects of the drugs, safe sex practices and volunteers distributing pamphlets and condoms (Ismail, 2017).

The TAC staff also act as counselors especially for women who know that they are HIV positive but have not told their husbands as the women say that their husbands do not test "so we don't know their status" (patient at clinic, 2014). In these situations, culture is invoked as an explanation, as this quote from a facilitator illustrates: "So its cultural beliefs that is a challenge, men don't want to get tested, they wait for the female partners to disclose and if their partner says I am positive then the man will say, Ok its coming from you" (Interview March, 2014) (Ismail, 2017, p. 164).

My investigations on tracing the changes in radical pedagogy from the community to the clinics illustrated that the facilitators show that teaching involves respect, concern for others and to build a community with a lively, social spirit and measure of solidarity. The findings also indicate that the education work is based on the concerns of the learner and giving information and knowledge in a sincere way in the hope that person will act on it.

The Project for the Study of Alternative Education in South Africa (PRAESA)

This project researched language policy in a newly democratic South Africa in 1994.

Education and particularly language policy during apartheid denied Africans equal opportunity, a livelihood, and access to higher education. The key purpose underlying PRAESA's work is to help to reverse this injustice. Mother tongue teaching is stigmatized because it was used during the apartheid period to divide people and to denigrate African languages. However, it is used here, to signify the language that a young child uses at home and is competent in. PRAESA's policy was based on a "radical critique of the previous racist education that belittled African languages and prepared black people for an oppressive and exploited position in society" (adapted from Trimbur, 2009, p. 86).

The key purpose underlying PRAESA's work is to help to reverse this injustice. Language policy is a contentious issue, and the 1976 black student revolt was ignited when the apartheid state wanted to impose Afrikaans—which was seen as the language of the oppressor—as a compulsory language in black schools. More recently, in September 2015, black students in the established Afrikaner universities protested against language policy, demanding that the primary medium of instruction be changed from Afrikaans to English (Ismail, 2016).

The government's language policy is to switch to teaching in the English medium after 3 years of schooling in the learner's home language. PRAESA's language policy envisaged teaching in the learner's mother tongue during the first five years of schooling and then for learners and teachers to switch in the following year to English as the medium of instruction. This challenge to the hegemonic view led to advocacy work at many levels: government, schools, parents, and universities.

PRAESA's attempts to convince the Department of Education (DOE) to have teaching for the first five years in the mother tongue failed. Parents, teachers, and principals remained unconvinced, and although in some pilot projects it has been successfully implemented, it has never become mainstream policy in any school. Therefore, PRAESA re-focused their energy and attention away from introducing mother tongue education in schools to work instead within the community. This development led PRAESA to look at other ways of fostering mother tongue education and this was the start of the *Nal'bali* project. Nal'ibali (in isiXhosa means "here is the story") reading for enjoyment campaign, which is a national campaign to promote a reading culture specifically among young children in poor African communities (Ismail, 2016).

The practice of bilingual language learning went slowly into the reading clubs, first at school level, then into homes, and the community. The aims of the reading clubs were to compensate for failures in the school system and the lack of a reading culture in the homes as well as a need to encourage the community to participate in education (Pluddemann, 2015). One of the literacy specialists expressed the purpose of her work as, "Well first of all if you have been to observe schools, you would've seen how children are being robbed of a good education and watched the outdated methods teachers use, then you wish you can show that there are alternative ways of doing things" (Interview, 2014) (Ismail, 2016, p. 7).

A reading club can be started anywhere, and the person who starts it is the "story sparker" who may register the club with *Nal'ibali*. This organization then assists them with training and resources (books, posters) and workshops which provide methods on how to make reading fun and enjoyable so that the readers will continue reading outside the workshops. The facilitators also try and advise on how to choose relevant books for particular age groups and publicize stories which they hope will become popular favorites among the children. The Nali'ibali project has become a national campaign and PRAESA is also reformulating its campaign in the language of human rights and has just released a Charter which explains children's rights to education.

The renewed focus of pedagogy in PRAESA is intended to contribute to the development of a literate society which may encourage the community to take responsibility for building a reading culture and to empower those who come into contact with it (Pluddemann, 2015). It does so by focusing on building relationships through informal learning and engaging communities in the struggle for their right to a sound education. Reading clubs provide a space for discussion about the significance of indigenous languages and related issues of identity, and they enable people to talk about education as a human right, thus highlighting the possibilities of community-centered pedagogy. On reflection, this research confirmed that pedagogies can help to change things for the better. There may be no clear transformative agenda, but we were inspired and impressed by the passion and commitment of the *Nal'ibali* educators and it was wonderful to witness their successes (Ismail, 2016).

CHALLENGES WITH RADICAL PEDAGOGY IN THE 3 CASE STUDIES

The findings are presented thematically and highlight key challenges facing radical educators.

Connection to IKS

In VM, women consciously formed a woman-led organization and since they won the right to own their own homes, they were in a more powerful position to challenge men with regard to their reproductive rights, and able to discuss the use of contraception with their husbands. As this quote from Nokhangelani demonstrates, "Men must know that we are their left-partners because they stay in the house built by us and Xoliswa says so now it is not easy for them to kick you out" (Interviews, 1996; Ismail, 2015, p. 52). However, they did not challenge broader patriarchal relations in the home and community. So later when the state declared that there would be joint ownership of subsidized housing, many of the women did not fight back. Another example where retrogressive IK practices won out, was when women did not interrogate the practice of lobola (bride payment). The process entails that the woman's family negotiate a bride price which can be in the form of cattle or cash. A practice which diminishes woman's power in the marriage as it reduces her role to a minor in the marriage.

In the TAC, the facilitators were eager to transfer knowledge and change behaviors as their campaign for free anti-retroviral was also a campaign to disprove the state's previous notion that HIV/AIDS had no scientific basis and could be cured by traditional medicines and by ending poverty. But transfer of knowledge is not sufficient to challenge power relations in the home and community as shown in this example. When TAC facilitators at a clinic held a session on treatment literacy and inquired from women why their husbands have not tested when the women have tested positive for HIV, the women invoked culture to explain their husband's refusal to be tested or to practice safe sex. In the women's testimony IK was used to explain some husbands continued refusal to be tested or use safe sex practices. Generally, the male is assumed to be the dominant sexual partner and has to initiate condom usage.

The women showed their vulnerability and they spoke without fear, this is valued in feminist practice. The facilitators in turn showed respect for them and their knowledge but I think the facilitators must find the courage to challenge oppressive IK. They could use women's experiences as a building block to reflect and be critical of these practices and for women to act in solidarity and invoke the African cultural belief in Ubuntu in order to persuade their partners to go for testing thereby recovering IK concepts which can give rise to knowledge and actions that are transformative (Ismail, 2017). Ubuntu which in the African language means "humanity" but more literally translated into *"I am what I am because of who we are" is a philosophy that could reconcile the dominance of destructive sexual practices.*

In PRAESA, one critique made by a reading club volunteer from the black township of Khayelitsha was that many of the books did not contain African role models or African stories. The lack of African role models and stories can be traced back to apartheid when the absence of African languages in educational materials was deliberate and used to undermine IK (Ismail, 2016).

Challenges to the State

In South Africa, some social movements do partner with the state to realize their goals and often this relationship is in favor of the state. The state is often a reluctant partner and the social movement has to ensure that the government fulfills its promises. The response of the VM women to the housing crises has gone through many iterations with the state: from critical engagement to partnership to becoming an independent housing contractor, and they have shown time and time again that they can learn and build capacity to carry out development. The state, however, has fragmented the housing movement and betrayed its promises to the poor. The state's policy and the framing of the development paradigm has forced social movements into competing for resources, and to not seek more inclusionary approaches. In thinking about future resistances, solidarity action to raise consciousness against housing commodification holds the possibility of a new vision for both the social movements in the informal settlements and current urban housing social movements (Ismail, 2019, pp. 18–19).

The activist history of TAC which is present in the minds of HIV patients is that TAC won the struggle for medicines for treatment in public health facilities. Now that this treatment and medicines are available, TAC has taken on a role in ensuring state compliance and monitoring the state to have stocks of the medicine in all the clinics (Stocks campaign) as well as HIV/AIDS patients' keeping to the medicine regime hence the Treatment Literacy Programme in clinics. There are often clashes with the state about the supply of medicines and during the COVID 19 pandemic people are fearful that the state will not secure sufficient vaccines to ensure herd immunity.

PRAESA had a different trajectory of working with the state in comparison to the two examples above, PRAESA started its work with the state but no longer actively seeks engagement with the state, but they will work with government when requested to do so. Their frustrating experiences when trying to implement language policy in the schools have made them opt to work in the informal context. Here they experience less bureaucratic control and are free to experiment and engage children and adults in a reading campaign which also grows into a love of indigenous languages. Most importantly, its strategy is to work with communities and use learning in an informal context to organize people and to guide communities to knowledge that will contribute toward social change—however gradual and incremental this may be. As one *Nal'ibali* facilitator put it, "Our benefits are not immediate, it's a process...a journey. So, we try and ensure that the reading clubs also understand it in that way" (Ismail, 2016, p. 6).

The attempts of PRAESA to influence language policy by piloting mother tongue instruction in schools demonstrate that the state does not privilege African languages. Under the African National Congress (ANC) government, even with its policy of promoting IKS, the dominance of English has been sustained and IKS has been shifted to the periphery (Ismail, 2016). All three case studies suggest that in the context of increased neo-liberalism there is a decline in challenging power relations which is an important facet of radical pedagogy and of their previous work when challenging the state.

The leadership in VM and TAC had become "organic intellectuals" and their activism although not against the state was based on rights-based approaches to human rights. However, their activism could not be sustained in particular when the pedagogy changed to provide information, training and counseling, and engagement with issues of power is restricted to ensuring that social goods can be secured. These shifts are difficult to challenge in the movements particularly in a context wherein there is greater uncertainty, decreased funding, increased poverty as well as a revival of indigenous knowledge to allow people to connect with their histories which was destroyed first under colonialism and then under apartheid.

Exclusionary Practices

In VM, hierarchies and authoritarianism started to emerge in 2001 and the leadership was said to "act like bosses" (Interview with member, 2001) (Ismail, 2015, p. 75) A possible explanation for this is that VM women were at a different phase in their personal life histories to when they had started in 1992. To some degree VM women's personal needs were out of sync with the aims of the Federation which was to rotate leadership and spread skills and expertise. In 2003 the VM women were older and may have had different and conflicting interests and needs. VM women's material conditions had changed; they needed regular incomes as they had loans to repay, houses to maintain, and their children had grown up. These life changes illustrate that individuals and groups have different goals and interests in adult learning and these need to be understood as contested activities around which there is conflict.

Likewise, in TAC and PRAESA, where facilitators (are often volunteers) depend on stipends for an income and often the expectation is that they will become employed and progress up the organization's hierarchy. However, with decreased funding, increased bureaucratization, a renewed emphasis on efficiency and reporting and to employ formally qualified personnel, the facilitators feel unsupported in these hard economic times. So, dependency on external funding has become a constraint and presently hope in the two organizations is kept alive by a supportive network and building solidarity between activists and the community.

CONCLUSION

My findings from the three case studies point out the limitations of popular education in social movements as Liam Kane (2005) argued in his study with the Brazilian Landless Movements that although the education work was powerful and led to the attainment of social goods as in the case of VM and TAC—however later there was no clear-cut opposition to the state as no continuous analysis was made on the structural nature of poverty or reflection on the pedagogical models. The literature on social movements suggests that movements generally lose momentum and may dissolve once the issues under protest are resolved. These movements may not be concerned with the capture of state power and revolutions.

In challenging patriarchy—Alvarez's (1999) concludes from her case study of Brazilian women's organizations that there was no automatic relationship between consciousness raising, empowerment, and political change, and illustrates that consciousness raising is not linear. This is a critical issue where poor black women have been most heavily affected by the lack of housing and the HIV/AIDs epidemic. These social movements have empowered many urban and rural women and women have been in key leadership positions who put forward alternate visions.

However, it is time to question IK practices which are not radical and harmful to women and learn from decolonial pedagogies. Gramsci (1971) argued that past histories infuse everyday consciousness and Freire put forth that learnt worldviews often continue even after the structural relationship has been severed (quoted in Motta & Esteves, 2014).

The decolonial feminists (Cusicanqui, 2012; Lugones, 2010) argue that revealing the layers of subjugation is an important epistemic development of decolonialism/decolonial feminism. Lugones (2010, p. 756) argues for the construction of a new subject of a new feminist geopolitics of knowing and loving. A decolonizing pedagogy is about developing a critical consciousness of internal neo-colonial conditions and its possible transformation and to remember that the integrity of the indigenous body and mind is central to social analysis and knowledge production (Tejeda et al., 2005). For example, the women of Standing Rock said "we are not protestors but water protectors"—in line with their ancient traditions. https://www.resilience.org/stories/2019-04-30/standingrock-three-years-and-still-fighting/ bell hooks (1990, p. 15) quoted by Motta & Esteves (2014, p. 3) advises "[that] after one has resisted there is the necessity to become- to make oneself anew…That process emerges as one comes to understand how structures of domination work in one's own life, as one invents alternative habits of being and resists from marginal space of difference inwardly defined." This learning and unlearning can occur in the formal education, in the informal spheres of everyday life and centrally, in the pedagogical practices (formal and informal) of social movements.

These findings from critical community-engaged research can be viewed as a basis for constructive change and open a discussion for ideas for other social movements beyond these case studies. Ideas on pedagogical interventions in these times of great unpredictability that will seek to form links with decolonial pedagogies and build solidarity across social movements.

References

Alvarez, S. E. (1999). Learning in Brazilian Women's Organisations. In G. Foley (Ed.), *Learning in social action: A contribution to understanding informal education*. Zed Books.

Andreotti, V. (2011). *Actional postcolonial theory in education*. Palgrave Macmillan.

Biko, S. (1987). *I write what I like -a selection of his writings*. Heinemann.

Cusicanqui, S. R. (2012). Ch'ixinakax utxiwa: A reflection on the practices and discourses of decolonization. *The South African Quarterly, 111*(1), 95–109.

Fanon, F. (1961). *The wretched of the earth*. Oxford Online Books.
Freire, P. (1973). *Cultural action for freedom*. Penguin.
Friedman, S., & Mottiar, S. (2004). *Rewarding engagement? The Treatment Action Campaign and the politics of HIV/AIDS*. University of Kwa Zulu-Natal Press.
Freire, P. (1983). *Pedagogy of the oppressed*. Continuum.
Gramsci, A. (1971). *Selections from the prison notebook* (Edited and translated by Q. Hoare & G. Nowell-Smith). Lawrence and Wishart.
hooks, b. (1990). *Yearning: Race, gender and cultural politics*. South End Press.
Ismail, S. (2015). *The Victoria Mxenge Housing Project: Women building communities through social action and informal learning*. UCT Press/Juta.
Ismail, S. (2016). Possibilities of a community centred pedagogy: A snapshot of a reading project in Cape Town. *Concept: The Journal of Contemporary Community Education Practice Theory, 7*(3), 30–41.
Ismail, S. (2017). Contours of radical pedagogy: Saving lives and building solidarity. In A. Von Kotze & S. Walters (Eds.), *Forging Solidarity-popular education at work* (pp. 159–170). Sense Publishers.
Ismail, S. (2019). 'Imali Nolwazi (we need money and knowledge)'—A rallying cry from the South African Homeless People's Federation. *Radical Housing Journal, 1*(1), 151–169.
Kane, L. (2005). Ideology matters. In J. Crowther, V. Galloway, & I. Martin (Eds.), *Popular education: Engaging the academy: International perspectives*. NIACE.
Klugman, B. (2015). Employee volunteering and monitoring and evaluation. Presentation at the 2015 Beyond Painting Classroom Conference.
Low, M., Tomlinson, C., Kardas-Nelson, M., Kim, K., Geffen, N., & Filani, F. (2010). *Fighting for our lives: The history of the Treatment Action Campaign 1998–2010*. Treatment Action Campaign.
Lugones, M. (2010). Toward a decolonial feminism. *Hypatia, 25*(4), 742–759.
Maldonado-Torres, N. (2007). On the coloniality of being. *Cultural Studies, 21*(2–3), 240–270. https://doi.org/10.1080/09502380601162548
Motta, S. C., & Esteves, A. M. (2014). Reinventing emancipation in the 21st century: The pedagogical practices of social movements. *Interface: A Journal for and About Social Movements Editorial Volume, 6*(1), 1–24.
Newman, M. (2005). Popular teaching, popular learning and popular action. In J. Crowther, V. Galloway, & I. Martin (Eds.), *Popular education: Engaging the academy: International perspectives* (pp. 22–31). NIACE.
Odora Hoppers, C. (2001). Indigenous knowledge systems and academic institutions in South Africa. *Perspectives in Education, 19*(1), 74–85.
Pluddemann, P. (2015). *Imagining community reading clubs as a Third Space for literacy*. Paper presented to the 9th Pan-African Literacy for All Conference and 10th RASA National Literacy Conference, 2nd-5th September in Cape Town.
Spivak, G. (1994). Can the subaltern speak? In P. Williams & L. Chrisman (Eds.), *Colonial discourse/post-colonial theory: A reader*. Columbia University Press.
Tarrow, S. (2011). *Power in movement—Social movements and contentious politics*. Cambridge University Press.
Tejeda, C., Espinoza, M., & Gutieerrez, K. (2005). Towards a decolonising pedagogy: Social justice reconsidered. In P. P. Trifonas (Ed.), *Pedagogies of difference-rethinking education for social change* (pp. 1–9). Routledge.

Trimbur, J. (2009). Popular literacy and the resources of print culture: The South African Committee for Higher Education. *College Composition and Communication, 61*(1), 85–108.

Walters, S., & Manicom, L. (Eds.). (1996). *Gender in popular education: Methods for empowerment.* Zed Books.

PART VII

Critical Perspectives on Science and Mathematics Education

CHAPTER 25

Decolonizing Science Education in Africa: Curriculum and Pedagogy

Samson Madera Nashon

INTRODUCTION

Science curriculum and pedagogy in Africa are often overly exam-driven, teacher-centered with colonial as well as foreign-leaning characterizations. This apparent static nature of curriculum and pedagogy is due in part to emphasis on passing examinations and the perception that innovative pedagogies such as those attuning to contemporary issues such as understanding science through local African contexts is considered time wasting (Sifuna & Otiende, 2006). Moreover, initially those in Africa and in the diaspora who may be positioned to influence change are often trained abroad, or trained locally by foreign experts, thus lacking the skills needed to reform curriculum and pedagogy to reflect the local context (Sifuna & Otiende, 2006). In addition, they often tend to borrow from foreign instructional models not suited for the African learner. This has made students less inclined to contextualize what they learn and especially with regard to understanding the scientific phenomena embedded in their local contexts. As well, the students are less welcoming to decolonizing pedagogies that place context as central to meaningful and relevant learning of science. Instead, they focus more on how to pass their examinations. The need to understand science contextually, which is a central tenet in decolonizing science education, is regarded as superfluous to examination performance and, at best, perpetuates the traditional culture where science is

S. M. Nashon (✉)
University of British Columbia, Vancouver, Canada
e-mail: samson.nashon@ubc.ca

understood as an encapsulated system that has no relevance in terms of their local contexts and everyday lives (Tsuma, 1998). This chapter will highlight ongoing research by the author where specific local contexts in an African setting have been successfully used to develop curricular units that engage students in unpacking and understanding scientific phenomena embedded in their local context as a way of decolonizing science curriculum and pedagogy. Using examples of contextualized curricula in investigating student science learning and its effect on teachers' teaching, the author will draw upon the research studies he has been doing in Kenya for the last 15 years where national curriculum is interpreted and implemented through a series of contextualized lessons with student learning and teachers' teaching analyzed. But first, it is important to provide the historical foundations on which Kenyan curriculum has evolved.

Background

Kenya, like many developing countries, faces many significant environmental challenges, particularly around local manufacturing and degradation of the natural environment (Ce'car et al., 2014), which are given little prominence or attention in the school science curriculum. Although there have been attempts through numerous educational reforms to make school science relevant in post-independence Kenya (Gachathi, 1976; Kamunge, 1988; Koech, 2000; Mackay, 1981; Ominde, 1964a, 1964b), the question of relevance and impact has continued to persist. These attempts to reform education have included linking science learning to production activities and products in Kenya's ubiquitous *Jua Kali sector* (Nyerere, 2009; Swift, 1987; Waddington, 1987). "*Jua Kali*" is a small-scale manufacturing and technology-based service sector (UNESCO/UNEVOC, 1998). The name is derived from the conditions (scorching sun) under which the artisans who manufacture equipment and provide related services to other small-scale producers operate.

This question of relevance is still a key part of the ongoing discussion about the reform agenda including two previous major Social Science and Humanities Research Council (SSHRC) of Canada funded studies (2006 & 2010) from which important insights into the ways science is taught and understood contextually were generated. It was the view of the investigators of which I was a principal investigator that making science relevant through local contexts is a key decolonizing strategy for science education. When students are judged to understand science through the lens of their local environment and explain events in real life in terms of the science they learn, then we can reasonably claim a degree of meaningful learning from relevant contexts and hence a decolonized curriculum and instruction. Here, students tend to own the learning process and indeed take responsibility for their own learning.

Further analysis of the current discourse among stakeholders (e.g., the *National Council for Science and Technology* [NCTS], the *Kenya Ministry of Education*, and the *Kenya Science Teachers Association* [KSTA] and the *UN*

Environmental Program [UNEP]) about how to make science relevant still indicates a collective desire to understand science contextually. And, in particular, there is ongoing desire to develop and implement curriculum that enables students to investigate and understand the science embedded in effects of manufacturing activities and products on local environmental sustainability. This is especially important to Kenya given its vision of attaining industrialized nation status by 2030 (Government of Kenya, 2007). Furthermore, there is strong evidence that there is value in understanding the science embedded in local environmental issues (Hodson, 1994; Nashon, 2013).

The team that I led in implementing the studies has extensive understanding about the Kenyan learner in particular, including (a) how students struggle to learn in Western-modeled classrooms (Nashon & Anderson, 2008a); (b) the need for meaningful assistance to change from cultural worldviews to canonical science (border crossing) (Aikenhead, 1996); (c) the desire for a moral obligation to assist others—collaborative classroom culture. In other words, there was a desire among the students and teachers who participated in the studies to not leave their peers behind, and hence, the "walking together," a practice that is resonant with local socio-cultural practices (Gitari, 2006); (d) a respect for cultural knowledge as well as canonical science, and the ability to hold both worldviews and use them relevantly (collateral learning) (Jegede, 1995); and (e) the importance of relevance in science learning (Knamiller, 1984). These understandings are vitally important for teachers to embed in their pedagogies the learners' local settings with a view to making science learning relevant to Kenyan students. Moreover, these insights are key to designing effective, learning experiences for contemporary classrooms in Kenya and in other developing countries. However, in today's Kenya, like in many other African countries, these insights are still not fully harnessed by the education system (Anderson et al., 2015; Nashon, 2013; Tsuma, 1998). But clearly, all these learner attributes can be effectively mediated through contextualizing science learning. For example, this can in part involve students in understanding the science embedded in the effects of the ubiquitous local Kenyan *Jua Kali* activities on their local environmental sustainability.

CURRICULUM AND PEDAGOGY IN KENYAN CLASSROOMS

In Kenya today, as already highlighted above, science curriculum and pedagogy are often overly exam-driven and teacher-centered with colonial, as well as foreign-leaning characterizations (Ooko et al., 2017; Sifuna & Otiende, 2006). This apparent static nature of curriculum and pedagogy is due in part to a pedantic emphasis on passing examinations and the perception that innovative pedagogies such as those attuning to contemporary issues, such as environmental sustainability and learning in the local contexts, is a waste of time (Nashon, 2013; Sifuna & Otiende, 2006). The pressure of passing exams often has many Kenyan students less sensitive to environmental discourses, but rather they focus more on how to pass exams. The need to understand science contextually, is regarded by both teachers and students as being superfluous to examination performance, and at best, perpetuates the traditional teaching culture where science is understood as an encapsulated system that has no relevance in terms of local environmental sustainability or the local context (Julius & Wachanga, 2013; Tsuma, 1998; Wachanga & Mwangi, 2004). Any attempts to integrate into curriculum visits to authentic science learning environments, such as *Jua Kali* or local forests where they can engage with the science embedded in the effects of *Jua Kali* production activities on the local environmental sustainability are seen as a "waste of time." But for most Kenyans, the question of relevance is very important as eloquently expressed by Tsuma (1998): "no Nation can develop in any sense of the term, with a population which has not received a thorough and relevant education" (p. i). And, although there have been attempts to demonstrate the richness of *Jua Kali* in scientific phenomena (Anderson et al., 2015; Nashon, 2013; Nashon & Anderson, 2008a, 2008b, 2010, 2013a, 2013b; Nashon & Madera, 2013; Nashon et al., 2015; Ooko et al., 2017), there has not been extension of these reforms in school curriculum to investigate how students understand the science embedded in the effects of *Jua Kali* production activities and products on local Kenyan environmental sustainability. Hence, there is a need to have students in Kenya engage in the more contemporary global question of environmental sustainability. Importantly, there is the need to have students unpack the science embedded in the effects of *Jua Kali* production activities and products on their local environmental sustainability as a more relevant and meaningful science learning strategy. This is what I consider an important motive toward decolonizing science education in Kenya and for that matter in Africa This approach holds the potential to lead to a more scientifically and environmental sustainability oriented and prosperous society. Moreover, it will lead to the betterment of the natural physical environment of the nation through environmental stewardship of informed citizens.

Learning from Ongoing Research

Insights from previous SSHRC-funded studies (2006 & 2010) that I facilitated caused my team to raise questions about students' understanding of the science embedded in the effects of *Jua Kali* production activities and products on their local environmental sustainability. Noteworthy, among the many *Jua Kali* production activities and products from which scientific phenomena and local environmental sustainability can be investigated, the *charcoal stove* stands out to be of significant importance because: (a) it is ubiquitous and used daily by students in most households across Kenya; (b) it uses natural resources including charcoal, although varieties are being produced that use sawdust, kindlers, or agricultural residues—all of which are in limited sustainable supply; (c) there are vigorous innovations in the *Jua Kali* regarding production of the most efficient charcoal or agricultural residue stoves—so as to improve efficiency and cook most food using minimum fuel resources;

and (d) its use has very significant implications on degradation of forests and other rare plant and tree species sustainability. According to Beru et al. (2014), the connection between sustainability and the production of such stoves has profound implications on Kenya's wood fuel sources—the forests. Despite such obvious connections between real world issues, school science discourses do not include understandings of science embedded in the effects of *Jua Kali* production activities and products on local environmental sustainability. These issues have been evoked by insights from the 2006 SSHRC funded study and engagement with students in Kenya where: (1) students understood science better in a canonical sense when instruction used local contexts to mediate curriculum; (2) students were provoked and inspired to make critical assessment of their prior learning strategies and habits by fascinating and contextualized experiences; and (3) students became acutely aware that the learning strategies they used were a consequence of the nature of the prevailing curriculum and lack of pedagogical models that make science relevant (Nashon, 2013; Nashon & Anderson, 2008a, 2008b, 2013a, 2013b; Nashon & Madera, 2013; Nashon et al., 2015). Also, the latter 2010 study revealed how the Kenyan teachers' teaching was impacted by this way of student learning including: (1) the teachers' literal and rigid interpretations and strict adherence to the official curriculum conflicted with the students' desires to understand scientific phenomena embedded within their local environment; (2) the science teachers' inability or ability to sustain students' motivation to understand science through local contexts in part depended on their initial teacher training; and (3) implementation of the contextualized science reduced the gulf that often hindered free student–teacher dialogue due to the teachers' endeavors to maintain science and teacher statuses (Anderson et al., 2015; Nashon, 2013; Nashon & Anderson, 2013b). With this knowledge platform, the investigation has been extended to include high school students' learning and understanding of the science embedded in the effects of *Jua Kali* production activities and products (local manufacturing) on their local environmental sustainability in Kenya.

Significantly, the outcomes of the 2006 study led to a deeper appreciation for the notion that natural *modes* of learning are uniquely culturally mediated and harnessing this understanding can profoundly transform science curriculum and pedagogy in Kenya, Africa and elsewhere. Although the study, which focused on Kenya, has given us deeper understandings about Kenyan learners' modes of learning and the kinds of experiences that evoke as well as provoke these natural modes of learning, and which transformed the students' perceptions of the nature of science and science learning, very little was understood about the collateral impact the transformations had on the science teachers' pedagogy and school culture. And, given the demonstrated effectiveness of the study's innovative contextualized curricular and pedagogical experiences on student science learning, it became imperative to frame a study that documented, interpreted, and understood transformations in (1) science teachers' professional and social cultural values surrounding educational practices, and (2) school culture.

The 2006 SSHRC funded *Canadian-East African Collaborative for the Study of Ways of Knowing* (CEACSWOK), which investigated and elucidated East African (EA) students' ways of knowing (WOK) that were invoked and engaged as the students experienced integrated classroom-*Jua Kali* science curriculum activities, now became the *Canadian-East African Collaborative for the Study of Student Learning and Pedagogy* (CEACSSLAP) as a way of extending the investigation into the collateral impact of successful transformations in student learning had on their science teachers' teaching practices and socio-cultural values and school culture in the reformed science curriculum and pedagogy. As a team, we investigated transformations in East African science teachers' socio-cultural values surrounding their professional practices as well as collective changes in school-culture as they journeyed through changes in both curricular and pedagogical reforms. The outcomes of the study had implications on our current understandings of culturally based pedagogies and their application to curriculum and instruction beyond the traditional Western models. Moreover, these extended understandings about the African and for that matter indigenous learner as demonstrated in Jegede's (1995) notion of collateral learning; Aikenhead's (1996) notion of border crossing; Gitari's (2006) notions of moral obligation and knowledge guarding; and Anderson and Nashon's (2009) notion of natural *harmonics* of the African learner. These understandings are key to designing effective, inclusive learning experiences for our contemporary multicultural primary, secondary and post secondary classrooms. As already highlighted above the 2010 study about the effect of student learning on the teachers' teaching practices and school culture was inspired by the outcomes of the 2006 SSHRC funded research study that generated important insights about curricular and instructional experiences that are in harmony with the students' natural (cultural) modes of learning (Anderson & Nashon, 2007; Nashon & Anderson, 2008a, 2008b; Nashon & Madera, 2013). The outcomes led to a deeper appreciation for the notion that natural *modes* of learning are uniquely culturally mediated and harnessing this understanding could profoundly transform science curriculum and pedagogy in EA and elsewhere.

Although the study focused on Kenya, it offered deeper understandings about the Kenyan learners' modes of learning and the kinds of experiences that evoke as well as provoke these natural modes of learning, and which transformed the students' perceptions of the nature of science and science learning. Hence the questions: What transformations are notable in science teachers' socio-cultural values and collective school-culture surrounding professional practices as they journey through both curricular and pedagogical reforms? What theoretical and practical insights can be gained from the teachers' and schools' professional transformations as they navigate through curricular and pedagogical reforms? These kinds of questions were considered suitable for investigation using a socio-cultural framework (Kozulin, 2003; Rogoff, 1990) due to its emphasis on the importance of human interactivity within social settings, and an interpretive methodology (Schwandt, 2003) that employed case studies (Stake, 1995) to generate rich descriptions of transformations in the teachers' pedagogical knowledge (Shulman, 1986) and school culture (Goodlad, 1984).

The outcomes of the study included development of new theoretical understandings about collateral impact of students' successful learning on teachers' teaching practices and socio-cultural values as they journeyed through and experienced their students' success in reformed science curriculum and pedagogy.

As already argued, there still continues to be no strong curriculum link between activities in the *Jua Kali* that have come to characterize the common socio-cultural environment of many young Kenyans and for that matter many East Africans, their school science (classroom knowledge) and the ways in which they learn, which are culturally shaped (Cobern & Aikenhead, 1998). *Jua Kali* (a Kiswahili word derived from conditions under which artisans operate—*scotching sun*) has products such as charcoal stoves, kerosene lamps, and chicken brooders, all of which are prevalent household items ubiquitous in everyday Kenyan culture and rich in scientific phenomena. But, any attempt to link classroom science to the real world of *Jua Kali* activities cannot be effective if there is no understanding of students' natural ways of learning embedded in their worldviews of science learning, which are shaped by their socio-cultural environment. Moreover, even with such an understanding, the link may not be effective without also understanding how teachers' teaching practices and socio-cultural values, and collective school culture are impacted as they journey through and experience their students' successful learning resulting from their engagement of their natural modes of learning evoked by the context in which the teaching and learning take place. All of this is situated against the contextual backdrop of school curriculum and pedagogy that are based on traditional western models, exam-driven, and highly teacher-centered.

Moreover, this being situated in the larger body of literature on indigenous peoples' ways of learning attempted to fill the void that existed in this body of literature about the EA learner, under the inescapable influence of the socio-cultural environment in which the learner resides. Studies in the 1970s and 80s documented different WOK and how what students bring to science classrooms, a product of their WOK, impacted classroom learning and teaching. These ideas were referred to variously as children's science or alternative frameworks (Driver et al., 1997), lay science (Furnham, 1992), plain common sense (Hills, 1989), naïve science (Nickerson, 1986). According to Hodson (1998), these ideas are formed in many ways including talking with others, interaction with media, visits to other settings such as zoos, museums, amusement parks, etc. Moreover, Hodson adds, everyday language use influences their understanding of phenomena experienced in life. There have been attempts to explain how these ideas are constructed. For instance, Cajete (1999) reveals how Native science as a way of life is derived from lived experiences and practice within Native communities. He adds: "Native life in community is a primal pathway to knowledge of relationship with the natural world" (p. 99) (see also Beck & Walters, 1980). Other studies have been conducted among the Chinese, African American, etc., and most point to the fact that there is WOK that goes beyond the traditional Western thought. Thus, the argument in this chapter is that tapping into these ways of knowing through local contexts is a great way to decolonizing science education and pedagogy and enhancing canonical science to be relevant and meaningful to this learner.

A study by Guerts (2002) revealed pointers to the uniqueness of some of the ways Africans construct knowledge. She has challenged the commonly held assumption in the Western thought that "all humans possess identical sensory capabilities and that any cultural differences we might find would be inconsequential" (p. 3). For example, one outcome of her ethnographic study of a community in Ghana, West Africa identifies bodily ways of gathering information as profoundly involved in society's epistemology and the development of cultural identity. What this demonstrates is how framing science within local cultural contexts is critical to moving toward decolonizing our curriculum and instruction. Similarly the work of Jegede (1995), Aikenhead (1996), and Aikenhead and Jegede (1999) in Canada and Africa shows how cultural practices profoundly influence the way students *collaterally make sense* (hold multiple worldviews) of the world (see also Baker et al., 1996; Cobern & Aikenhead, 1998). The equivalent in Western cultures is what some scholars call cognitive apartheid (Cobern, 1996; Cobern & Aikenhead, 1998; Young, 1992). According to Cobern (1996), the students simply wall off the concepts that do not fit their natural worldviews and instead create a compartment for scientific knowledge from which it can be retrieved on special occasions, such as school exams. Moreover, as Young (1992) notes: "…this is likely to be more common if the new challenges the old. Under such circumstances, it is difficult for the new knowledge to be really made the pupil's own, a part of reality. It gets learned in a shallow way and … easily forgotten after the last examination, if it was ever really understood in the first place…" (p. 23). In other words, colonization is the fodder for shallow understanding of the world around the African learner as Western thought presents science as if it is delinked from the learner. But contextualizing the learning process is the methodology for decolonizing science education.

For East Africans (EAs), *Jua Kali* forms an important part of their construct of cultural identity, and, hence, is a key locus to understanding their way of learning science. But what the 2006 SSHRC funded study on students' ways of knowing in science discourses revealed is that if instruction is organized in ways that are in accord with the students' natural modes of learning, the learning process changes dramatically as the students start to see and appreciate the relevance of the science concepts to their local cultural contexts generating in them a motivation to understand the science embedded in their local environment or understand science in terms of their local environment (Nashon & Anderson, 2008a).

Whereas this study was largely situated in constructivist literature that focuses on students' preconceptions, the emergent analyses have moved it more into the literature on socio-cultural frameworks, with the realization that the students have natural (cultural) modes of learning that are culturally shaped and that harnessing these modes of learning to organize science instruction might be more fruitful in terms of learning canonical science in a more relevant and meaningful manner. This is what I consider to be a key step in decolonizing science learning. Studies such as these are better framed when they take into account emergent literature on pedagogical content knowledge (Shulman, 1986). Moreover, an assumption that is commonly made, indeed a fundamental premise of teacher ethnography, is that teachers' life experiences influence the kind of teachers they become, our views on teaching, and ultimately the way they teach. It is this understanding that motivates an investigation into how teachers are impacted by their students' learning experiences, hence making the project more holistic by studying student learning and pedagogy as an intertwined enterprise. What such an investigation aimed to demonstrate was how decolonized or contextualized science learning can impact the teachers' subsequent teaching. It is the influence of children's success that is most important, as it is central to curriculum decolonization.

Shulman (1986) introduced the term pedagogical content knowledge (PCK) as "the ways of representing and formulating the subject that make it comprehensible to others" (p. 9). Schulman's version of PCK refers to teachers' interpretations and transformations of subject matter knowledge in the context of facilitating student learning. Following Shulman's work, numerous studies have been conducted on teachers using a variety of interpretations of PCK. According to Abd-El-Khalick (2000), the construct has been studied among teachers including science teachers. Emerging from these studies is the assumption that the view that PCK is a separate domain of knowledge and that teachers' knowledge of subject matter directly translates into their teaching practices. But as Abd-El-Khalik (2000) notes the assumption has come under challenge by empirical research (e.g., Gess-Newsome, 1999) and that there is no emerging literature base that illuminates the re-conceptualization of the originally vague construct of PCK (e.g., Gess-Newsome, 1999).

However, there seem to have emerged a consensus on the nature of PCK as the experiential knowledge and skills acquired through classroom experience (Gess-Newsome, 1999), and as the integrated set of knowledge, concepts, beliefs, and values which teachers develop in the context of the teaching situation (Gess-Newsome, 1999). Thus, experienced teachers possess an integrated and developed understanding of teaching.

This perspective is consistent with Gess-Newsome's (1999) integrative and transformative models of PCK. The integrative model which comprises knowledge domains of content (subject matter), pedagogy, and context is considered to exist as separate entities, similar to a mixture of rice, sorghum, and wheat grains. Adherents (Fernández-Balboa & Stiehl, 1995) of this type of PCK argue that proficiency at any of the components of the mixture would enhance the whole PCK. Moreover, they argue, having knowledge about the components of PCK independently determines a teacher's ability to integrate these components. On the other hand, adherents (Marks, 1990) of the transformative model consider PCK as a synthesized knowledge, where content and pedagogy are integrated and transformed into classroom practice. And that it is impossible to distinguish PCK from either subject matter knowledge or general pedagogical knowledge. Yet many studies have continued to show that a majority of beginning teachers tend to rely more heavily on one domain of knowledge rather than drawing simultaneously from all domains, as is the case with an expert teacher (Ball & Bass, 2000; Davis, 2003; Grossman, 1990), which indeed was noted in the CEACSWOK study. Therefore, the integrative model may likely portray the PCK of beginning teachers, while the transformative model is more suitable to represent the PCK of experienced teachers. But it is not just as simple as that—to lay this only on beginning teachers. To the contrary, the blame for the case of East Africa, and Kenya for that matter can be attributed to an overly exam and teacher-centered curriculum where "objective" content is assessed. Otherwise pedagogic content knowledge may depend on complex interactions between discipline knowledge, pedagogic knowledge, and the teacher's experiences in teaching that knowledge. In one of my numerous studies with teachers, the study about the status of Physics 12 in BC, the physics teacher, and teaching styles were prominently mentioned as impacting students' decisions about Physics 12 (Nashon, 2003; Nashon & Nielsen, 2007). In the same vein literature indicates that quite often science teachers conform to instructional models they were exposed to as high school students (Blanton, 2003).

Thus in an attempt to contextualize science learning and teaching, which basically was about decolonizing pedagogy, the team I worked with on the Kenyan study, co-developed and implemented the reformed science curriculum units with the science teachers. In this way my co-principal investigator, David Anderson and I hoped for a high possibility that the teachers' pedagogy got impacted, especially given the successful learning experienced by their students. The knowledge and practice of a teacher to provide the most useful teaching situation is to make a topic comprehensible to learners (Shulman, 1986). Although there are several models, Gess-Newsome's (1999) integrated and transformative model complemented by the socio-cultural theory is very important in interpreting this kind of teaching and learning. Although Gess-Newsome (1999) uses the venn diagram to illustrate integrative view of PCK, when distinct parts of a mixture are visible and can be picked out easily, one can also see in the same diagram a transformative view, where the analogy of white light (Green + Red + Blue) is applied to signify transformative PCK—parts not easily seen or white light seen as a whole but components not visible (Fig. 25.1).

The study with Kenyan science teachers adopted the two models for the purpose of understanding the East African teachers' PCK in terms of overall transformation and the integrative model to understand where deficits or credits might exist in their PCK, and in particular to locate which aspects of PCK were impacted. Whereas, the two models as conveyed in literature seem to show one as better than the other, the Kenyan research team applied both complementarily in terms of understanding teachers' professional practices. These models are best complemented by the socio-cultural theory because

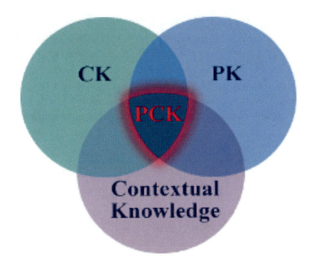

Fig. 25.1 Integrated and Transformative Model, Gess-Newsome, 1999

I consider teaching to be a social as well as a cultural act, enacted in a cultural environment.

According to Lantolf (2006), sociocultural theory considers human psychological development as being mediated by physical and symbolic tools, and that these evolve over time as cultural representations including language (Wertsch, 1998; Vygotsky, 1986). It further premises that practical and intellectual activities do not occur in isolation. Thus, there exists a strong and essential relationship between learning processes and their cultural, historical, and institutional settings (Wertsch, 1998). Wertsch further adds that learning cannot be separated from the influence of an individual's social and cultural worlds. In a similar vein teaching cannot be separated from the influence of the social and cultural worlds where it is enacted.

Inspiration

The interest in WOK stems, in part, from another study (Nashon & Anderson, 2004) that investigated students' metacognition across learning contexts, which revealed interesting insights into the role students' socio-cultural background plays in how they make sense of classroom and out-of-school experiences in Canada and Japan. For example, the study revealed cultural differences in the way Japanese students verify their views with references to peer groups in specific ways the Canadian students do not (Hisasaka et al., 2005). Moreover, Nashon's (2003) work on the nature of analogies that Kenyan teachers and students use in the teaching and learning of physics concepts revealed that the analogies were largely anthropomorphic and environmental—that is, culturally constructed (Nashon, 2003, 2004). A similar study, conducted in Nigeria, West Africa by Lagoke et al. (1997), revealed how biology instruction, which employed the use of environmental and anthropomorphic analogies, led to a reduction in the gender gulf in performance. In addition, Nashon's study in Uganda, which examined students' conceptions of HIV/AIDS, showed that most students understood HIV/AIDS in anthropomorphic and environmental terms (Mutonyi et al., 2010). This reiterates the argument that contextualizing science curriculum and instruction is a critical aspect of decolonizing science pedagogy in Kenya and for Africa and elsewhere.

Conclusion and Ontological Position

In advocating for the decolonization of curriculum and pedagogy in Kenya and Africa for that matter, I espouse and am guided by ontological and epistemological commitments that consider learning to be occurring holistically and not in isolated contexts as well as a dynamic process developed through experiences that are interpreted in the light of the learners' prior knowledge, attitudes, and personal background. Furthermore, I consider the socio-cultural identity of the individuals and the group to which they belong as determining the cultural tools (Ways of Knowing) that they use to make sense of the world. Also, I believe that, students' Ways of Knowing (WOK) rarely develop instantaneously, but rather, through catalytic events that connect classroom science to the real world and these have the potential to gradually affect WOK over a period of time. I also believe that although there are diverse WOK, some of the WOK can propagate misconceptions. I acknowledge the unique ways in which science differs from other ways of understanding and interpreting nature. But if the learning discourse is framed in the learners' local environment with a focus on interpreting the embedded science, then I consider such learning to be relevant and meaningful. This in essence, forms the background on which I advocate for decolonizing pedagogy through contextualization as a way of making science relevant and meaningful to the African learner.

References

Abd-El-Khalik, F. (2006). Preservice and experienced biology teachers' global and specific subject matter structures: Implications for conceptions of pedagogical content knowledge. *Eurasia Journal Mathematics, Science and Technology Education, 2*(1), 1–29.

Aikenhead, G. S. (1996). Science education: Border crossing into the subculture of science. *Studies in Science Education, 27,* 1–52.

Aikenhead, G. S., & Jegede, O. J. (1999). Cross-cultural science education: A cognitive explanation of a cultural phenomenon. *Journal of Research in Science Teaching, 36*(2), 269–289.

Anderson, D., & Nashon, S. (2007). Predators of knowledge construction: Interpreting students' metacognition in an amusement park physics program. *Science Education, 91*(2), 298–320.

Anderson, D., Nashon, S., & Thomas, G. (2009). Evolution of research methods for probing and understanding metacognition. *Research In Science Education, 39*(2), 181–195.

Anderson, D., Nashon, S., Namazzi, E., Okemwa, P., Ombogo, P., Ooko, S., & Beru, F. (2015). East African science teachers' pedagogical transformations during and after enacting and experiencing student learning in a reformed contextualized science curriculum. *Journal of Science Teacher Education, 26*(7), 599–617.

Baker, D., Clay, J., & Fox, C. (1996). Introduction. In D. Baker, J. Clay, & C. Fox (Eds.), *Challenging ways of knowing: In English, maths and science* (pp. 1–9). Falmer Press.

Ball, D. L., & Bass, H. (2000). Making believe: The collective construction of public mathematical knowledge in the elementary classroom. In D. C. Phillips (Ed.), *Constructivism in education: Opinions and second opinions on controversial issues. Yearbook of the national society for the study of education* (pp. 193–224). Chicago: University of Chicago Press.

Beck, P. V., & Walters, A. L. (1980). *The sacred ways of knowledge sources of life*. Navajo Community College Press.

Beru, F., Nashon, S., Anderson, D., Opata, P., Ooko, S., Okemwa, P., & Wafula, S. (2014). *An exploratory study on the impact of wood fuel use and planning strategies for its sustainability in Western Kenya*. Paper presented at 2nd Biannual International Conference, University of British Columbia, Vancouver, BC, Canada, July 12–15.

Bingle, W. H., & Gaskell, P. J. (1994). Scientific literacy for decision making and the social construction of scientific knowledge. *Science Education, 78*(2), 185–201.

Blanton, P. (Ed). (2005). Constructing knowledge. *The Physics Teacher, 41*(2), 12.

Cajete, G. (1999). *Native science: Natural laws of interdependence*. Clear Light Publishers.

Ce'car, E., Ekbom, A., & Nyangena, W. (2014). *Environmental and climate change policy brief Kenya*. Sida's Helpdesk for Environment and Climate Change.

Cobern, W. W. (1996). Worldview theory and conceptual change. *Science Education, 80*, 574–610.

Cobern, W. W., & Aikenhead, G. S. (1998). Cultural aspects of learning science. In B. Fraser & K. Tobin (Eds.), *International handbook of science education*. Kluwer Academic Publishers.

Driver, R., Leach, J., Millar, R., & Scott, P. (1997). Perspectives on the *nature of science*. In *Young people's images of science* (pp. 24–45). Open University Press.

Davis, H. A. (2003). Conceptualizing the role and influence of student-teacher relationships on children's social and cognitive development. *Educational Psychologist, 38*(4), 207–234.

Emerton, L. (1997). *The national economy and environmental degradation in Kenya*. African Wildlife Foundation Discussion Papers Series: Applied Conservation Economics Discussion Paper No. 3, ACE-DP-3 (pp. 1–14). Nairobi, Kenya: African Wildlife Foundation.

Erickson, F. (1986). Qualitative research methods on teaching. In M. C. Wittrock (Ed.), *Handbook on research on teaching* (pp. 119–161). Macmillan.

Fernández-Balboa, J. M., & Stiehl, J. (1995). The generic nature of pedagogical content knowledge among college professors. *Teaching and Teacher Education, 11*(3), 293–306.

Furnham, A. (1992). Lay understanding of science: Young people and adults' ideas of scientific concepts. *Studies in Science Education, 20*, 29–64.

Gachathi, F. (1976). *Report of the national committee on educational objectives and policies*. Government Printer.

Gess-Newsome, J. (1999). Pedagogical content knowledge: An introduction and orientation. In J. Gess-Newsome & N. G. Lederman (Eds.), *Examining pedagogical content knowledge: PCK and science education* (pp. 3–17). Kluwer.

Gitari, W. (2006). Everyday objects of learning about health and healing and w for science education. *Journal of Research in Science Teaching, 43*(2), 172–193.

Goodlad, J. (1984). *A place called school*. McGraw-Hill.

Grossman, P. L. (1990). *The making of a teacher: Teacher knowledge and teacher education*. Teachers College Press.

Guerts, K. L. (2002). *Culture and senses*. University of California Press.

Hills, G. L. (1989). Students' untutored beliefs about natural phenomena: Primitive science or common sense? *Science Education, 73*, 155–186.

Hisasaka, T., Anderson, D., & Nashon, S., & Yagi, I. (2005). Research regarding children's metacognition in physics learning environments: Using cognitive psychology to improve physics education. *Physics Education in Tohoku, 14*, 69–74.

Hodson, D. (1986). The nature of scientific observation. *School Science Review*, 17–29.

Hodson, D. (1994). Seeking directions for change: The personalisation and politicisation of science education. *Curriculum Studies, 2*, 71–98.

Hodson, D. (1998). *Teaching and learning science*. Open University Press.

Jegede, O. J. (1995). Collateral learning and the eco-cultural paradigm in science and mathematics in Africa. *Studies in Science Education, 25*, 97–137.

Julius, J. K., & Wachanga, S. W. (2013). Effect of experiential concept mapping teaching strategy on students' achievement in chemistry in Imenti South District, Kenya. *International Journal of Social Science & Interdisciplinary Research, 2*(8), 1–9.

Kamunge, J. (1988). *Report of the presidential working party on education and manpower development for the next decade and beyond*. Government Printer.

Knamiller, G. W. (1984). The struggle for relevance: Education in developing countries. *Studies in Education, 11*, 60–96.

Koech, D. (2000). *The commission of inquiry into the education system of Kenya*. Government Printer.

Kozulin, A. (2003). Psychological tools and mediated learning. In A. Kozulin, B. Gindis, V. S. Ageyev, & S. Miller (Eds.), *Vygotsky's educational theory in cultural context* (pp. 15–38). Cambridge University Press.

Lagoke, B. A., Jegede, O. J., & Oyebanji, P. K. (1997). Towards an elimination of the gender gulf in science concept attainment through the use of environmental analogues. *International Journal of Science Education, 19*(4), 365–380.

Lantolf, J. P. (2006). Sociocultural Theory and L2: State of the Art. *Studies in Second Language Acquisition, 28*(1), 67–109.

Lantoff, J. P. (2006). Conceptual knowledge and instructed second language learning: A sociocultural perspective. In. S. Fotos & H. Nassaji (Eds.), Form focused instruction and teacher education: Studies in honour of Rod Ellis (pp. 35–54). Oxford University Press.

Lasky, S. (2005). A socio-cultural approach to understanding teacher identity, agency and professional vulnerability in a context of secondary school reform. *Teaching and Teacher Education, 21*, 899–916.

Lederman, N. G. (1992). Students' and teachers' conceptions of nature of science: A review of the research. *Journal of Research in Science Teaching, 29*(4), 331–359.

Lederman, N. G., & Niess, M. L. (1997). The *nature of science*: Naturally? *School Science and Mathematics, 97*(1), 1–2.

Lederman, N. G., Abd-El-khalick, F., Bell, R. L., & Schwartz, R. S. (2002). *Nature of science* questionnaire: Toward valid and meaningful assessment of learners' conceptions of *Nature of science*. *Journal of Research in Science Teaching, 39*(6), 497–521.

Mackay. (1981). *Second university in Kenya—Report of presidential working party*. Government Printers.

Marks, R. (1990). *Pedagogical content knowledge in elementary mathematics*. Unpublished doctoral dissertation, Stanford University.

Mutonyi, H., Nashon, S., & Nielsen, W. S. (2010). Perceptual influence of Ugandan students' understanding of HIV/AIDS. *Research in Science Education, 40,* 573–588.

Nashon, S. M. (2003). Teaching and learning high school physics through analogies in Kenyan classrooms. *Canadian Journal of Science, Mathematics, and Technology Education* (CJSMTE), *3*(3), 33–345.

Nashon, S. M. (2004a). The nature of analogical explanations high school physics teachers use in Kenya. *Research in Science Education, 34*(3), TBA.

Nashon, S. M. (2004b). The nature of analogical explanations high school physics teachers use in Kenya. *Research in Science Education, 34,* 475–502.

Nashon, S. M. (2013). Interpreting Kenyan science teachers' views about effect of student learning experiences on their teaching. *Canadian Journal of Science, Mathematics and Technology Education, 13*(3), 213–231.

Nashon, S. M., & Anderson, D. (2004). Obsession with 'g': A metacognitive reflection of a laboratory episode. *Alberta Journal of Science Education, 36*(2), 39–44.

Nashon, S. M., & Anderson, D. (2008a). Interpreting student learning through integrated classroom-field trip science discourses in Kenya. CD of Conference In *Proceedings for NARST Annual International Conference* (p. 13). Baltimore, Maryland, USA, March 30–April 2, 2008.

Nashon, S. M., & Anderson, D. (2008b). *Using integrated classroom-field trip science discourses to understand student learning in Kenya*. Paper presented at CSSE-SCÉÉ 2008, Vancouver, BC, Canada (pp. 1–14). Ottawa: CSSE.

Nashon, S. M.,& Anderson, D. (2010). Profiling and interpreting East African students' science learning worldviews. In *CD of Conference Proceedings for NARST Annual International Conference*. Philadelphia, PA, USA, March 21–24.

Nashon, S. M., & Anderson, D. (2013a). Interpreting student views of learning experiences in a contextualized science discourse in Kenya. *Journal of Research in Science Teaching, 50*(4), 381–407.

Nashon, S. M., & Anderson, D. (2013b). Teacher change: The effect of student learning on science teachers' teaching in Kenya. *International Journal of Engineering Education, 29*(4), 1–7.

Nashon, S. M., & Madera, E. (2013). *Instrument for assessing disposition for contextual learning of science of students in East Africa*. Sage. https://doi.org/10.1177/2158244013494862

Nashon, S. M., & Nielsen, W. (2007). Participation rates in Physics 12 in BC: Science teachers' and students' views. *Canadian Journal of Science, Mathematics and Technology Education, 7*(2/3), 93–106.

Nashon, S. M., Anderson, A., Okemwa, P., Kelonye, F., Ooko, S., & Ombogo, P. (2015). Student learning impact on science teachers' teaching: The case of a Form 3 science class in Kenya. *Journal of Technology & Socio-Economic Development, 4,* 32–38.

Nashon, S. M., Anderson, D., & Nielsen, W. S. (2009). An instructional challenge through problem solving for physics teacher candidates. *Asia–Pacific Forum on Science Learning and Teaching, 10*(1), 1–21.

Nickerson, R. S. (1986). Reasoning. In R. F. Dilton, & R. J. Sternberg (Eds.), *Cognition and instruction*. Academic Press.

Nyerere, J. (2009). *Technical and vocational education and training (TVET) sector mapping in Kenya*. Edukans Foundation.

Ominde, S. H. (1964a). *Kenya Education committee report, Part I*. Government Printer.

Ominde, S. H. (1964b). *Kenya Education committee report, Part II*. Government Printer.

Ooko, S., Beru, F., Nashon, S., Anderson, D., & Namazzi, E. (2017). Contextualized science teaching and student performance: The case of a Kenyan girls' science class. *International Journal of Engineering Education, 33*(3), 1110–1116.

Ooko, S., Festus, B., Nashon, S., & Anderson, D. (2018). *Contextualized learning and transition from Secondary School to University: The Case of a Day Secondary School in Kenya*. Paper published in the proceedings of the International Conference on Future of Education, Colombo, Sri Lanka, Vol. 1, pp. 63–73.

Rogoff, B. (1990). *Apprenticeship in thinking*. Oxford University.

Rogoff, B. (2003). Firsthand learning through intent participation. *Annual Review of Psychology, 54*, 175–203.

Schwandt, T. (2003). Three epistemological stances for qualitative inquiry: Interpretive, hermeneutics, and social constructivism. In N. Denzin & Y. Lincoln (Eds.), *The landscape of qualitative research: Theories and issues* (pp. 292–327). Sage.

Shulman, L. S. (1986). Those who understand: Knowledge growth in teaching. *Educational Researcher, 15*(2), 4–14.

Sifuna, D. N., & Otiende, J. E. (2006). *An introductory history of education*. University of Nairobi Press.

Stake, R. (1995). *The art of case study research*. Sage.

Swift, D. J. (1987). School physics and rural technology. In D. J. Waddington (Ed.), *Education, industry and technology* (pp. 53–59). Pergamon Press.

The Republic of Kenya Master Plan on Education and Training (MPET), 1997–2010, September 1998.

Tsuma, O. G. K. (1998). *Science education in the African context*. Jomo Kenyatta Foundation, ISBN 9966-22-145-X.

UNESCO. (1997). "Under the Sun or in the Shade? Jua Kali in African Countries". National Policy Definition in Technical and Vocational Education Beyond the Formal Sector. A Sub-regional Seminar for Eastern and Southern African Countries, Nairobi, Kenya, September 15–19.

UNESCO/UNEVOC. (1998). "Under the Sun or in the Shade? Jua Kali in African Countries". National Policy Definition in Technical and Vocational Education: Beyond the Formal Sector. A Subregional Seminar for Eastern and Southern African Countries, Nairobi, Kenya, 15–19 September, 1997, Document Nr ED/IUG/014.

Valerie, L. A., Abd-El-Khalick, F., & Lederman, N. G. (2000). Influence of a reflective explicit activity-based approach on elementary teachers' conceptions of *Nature of Science*. *Journal of Research in Science Teaching, 37*(4), 295–317.

Vygotsky, L. S. (1986). *Thought and language* (A. Kozulin, Trans.). MIT Press.

Wachanga, S. W., & Mwangi, J. G. (2004). Effects of cooperative class experiment teaching method on secondary School Students Chemistry Achievement in Kenya's Nakuru District. *International Education Journal, 5*(1), 26, 36.

Waddington, D. J. (Ed.). (1987). *Education, industry and technology*. Pergamon Press.

Wertsch, J. V. (1998). *Mind as action*. Oxford University Press.

Young, R. (1992). *Critical theory and classroom talk*. Multi-lingual Matters.

CHAPTER 26

Indigenous Epistemologies and Decolonized Sustainable Livelihoods in Africa

Edward Shizha

Introduction

Knowledge constructions are important to peoples' sustainable livelihoods. How people perceive their socio-cultural well-being and how they determine the course of their livelihoods depend on the available knowledge resources. Each society is surrounded by different webs and networks of knowledges that exist in their ecological settings, whether "traditional" or "modern." The use of the plural "knowledges" in this chapter is deliberate to indicate the diversity of African Indigenous peoples (IPs), the focus of this chapter. How these knowledges are exploited contribute to the peoples' or communities' well-being, and these are a matter of how they are constructed, defined and the purpose for which they are constructed. This chapter re-considers mainstream accounts of what is science, and how the subject matter seems to represent a colonized conception of science that is Western and hegemonic. The chapter is also a theoretical review of contexts that define Indigenous epistemologies and their role in people's sustainable livelihoods. Livelihood in this chapter refers to how communal/rural or Indigenous African people manage their lives through the application of Indigenous knowledges (IKs) to promote their welfare. The chapter also focuses on livelihoods that Sati et al. (2014) describe as increased well-being, reduced vulnerability, improved food security and more sustainable use of natural resources base. The chapter applies an analysis

E. Shizha (✉)
Wilfrid Laurier University, Brantford, ON, Canada
e-mail: eshizha@wlu.ca

that critiques the old colonial hegemonic ways of viewing Indigenous epistemologies and imposed practices for sustainable livelihoods in Africa. Deploying this critical analysis of decolonizing knowledge/epistemologies as seeking improvements of contemporary life contexts is basically the foundations of critical educational and epistemological perspectives.

What is Epistemology?

Philosophically, epistemology is about knowledge construction and what counts as knowledge. To cite Cunningham and Fitzgerald (1996), "Epistemology is ... what can be counted as knowledge, where knowledge is located, and how knowledge increases" (p. 36). In other words, it involves questions and arguments about what knowledge consists of and what it is based on. Knowledge is what our lives are based on, how we interpret and make sense of our world, our worldviews and how we construct meaning out of our everyday experiences. Therefore, epistemology could be explained in terms of how we socially construct our way of life and, in turn, socially construct our sociocultural environment as well as how we exploit our ecological systems for our sustenance. This argument echoes early Greek philosopher Plato's view that epistemology is an attempt to understand what it is to know, and how knowledge is good for the knower (Steup & Neta, 2020). In addition, the English philosopher John Locke viewed epistemology as an attempt to understand the operations of human understanding, while to Immanuel Kant it is an attempt to understand the conditions of the possibility of human understanding (Steup & Neta, 2020). Human understanding and conditions of understanding are controlled by the cultural conditions and the socio-cultural environment of the people. Therefore, the social and cultural beliefs and experiences of the people have an influence on their epistemology, i.e., the way they know their world. The way knowledge is defined is "very problematic and subjective as it is perceived from the perspective of the knower(s), those individuals who construct bodies of ideas that they make use of in their everyday lives" (Shizha, 2017, p. 268). In Africa, different cultural and social conditions may influence how knowledge is constructed and understood. Knowledge construction has no universal procedures but following the views of constructivism and phenomenology, it is a construct that exists within the confines of particular social groups (Kapoor & Shizha, 2010; Kimble, 2013; Shizha & Abdi, 2014) as the groups navigate their ecosystem and biocultural diversity, and their cosmological universe.

African Indigenous Epistemologies and Science

African Indigenous epistemologies, in general, and the construction of Indigenous scientific knowledge have been historically ignored in research and development, including in educational institutions, which prefer to advance hegemonic colonial Eurocentric epistemological knowledge foundations. Whereas

African ways of knowing have previously been misunderstood, misinterpreted, ridiculed and ignored in colonial knowledge discourses (Ngara, 2013), IK systems have resisted this marginalization and are having an impact in education and in international development (Shizha, 2015). The subject on what entails IKs has been covered in many debates and analytical discussions (Dei, 2019; Khumalo & Baloyi, 2017; Shizha, 2019, 2020). Khumalo and Baloyi (2017) describe IKs as knowledges that sustained communities for years prior to colonialism which downplayed their value. They were knowledges that contributed to sustainable livelihoods for people and communities, mainly in food production and sustainable health systems. On defining IKs, Dei (2019) believes that they encapsulate the common-good-sense ideas and cultural knowledges of local peoples concerning the everyday realities of living. These knowledges are part of the totality and holistic cultural heritage and histories of IPs. They define how people exploit their natural environment, how they read their cosmological universe and interacted with their ecological systems and utilized their biocultural diversity. IPs have their scientific knowledges that explain the complexity and totality of their existence and the evolution of their physical universe. The knowledges are a result of their lived experiences, and as Matsika (2012) elaborates, the knowledges exist and are developed through the experiences of the local communities in the process of managing the conditions or context that challenge their everyday life. Lived experiences are the basis of Indigenous epistemologies that encompass experiential knowledges constructed through experimentation with the natural environment and observing the changes in their ecological and cosmological universes.

Indigenous epistemologies, therefore, refer to the totality of Indigenous ways of constructing and understanding their existence. They are situationally based knowledge systems that are socially created and collectively produced and transmitted (Shizha, 2019). They are not individualistic or individually patented and copy righted because they are peoples' epistemologies which are communally owned (see Shizha, 2017). Epistemologically, the knowledges are living embodiments of the continuously changing lives of IPs, which are influenced by their interactions of different community knowledges, which are shared by different communities. The epistemologies are neither universal nor homogeneous to African people. Each community has its own forms of knowledges that depend on its cultural and social foundations. However, there are common principles shared by IPs when it comes to knowledge construction and utilization. For example, the value on the respect for one another (*Ubuntu*) and respect for the elders as well as respect for the village teachings and beliefs are universal to IPs. Further, it is the Indigenous spiritual belief that the creator brought the rules and regulations to be followed in personal and ecological interactions for sustainable livelihoods. Thus, traditional knowledges belong to the community and not to individuals. The promotion of communalism rather than individualism is pervasive in Indigenous cultures. Berkes (2012) describes IKs as culturally adaptable intergenerational ecological knowledges about the relationship of living beings with their environment. Therefore, Indigenous epistemologies are based on the interaction that peoples have with their natural environments and how they exploit the environments. Knowledge creation and the meanings attached to the knowledge are determined by life experiences and the exploitation of the biocultural and ecological systems to sustain livelihoods. The knowledges are considered as cultural capital relied on for food and livelihood security. Reading the ecological and cosmological universe requires a cultural and spiritual understanding of the interconnectedness of the people and their universe (Shizha, 2020). It is a scientific understanding that defines IKs as science. IKs as science emerge from the belief, and evidence, that they can contribute solutions to the unprecedented threats that humanity faces (Thompson et al., 2020) and that the knowledges are linked to local practices that are important in offering theoretical advancement and practical approaches for the sustainable use and management of natural resources (Tengö et al., 2014), as well as contributing to biodiversity conservation and other sustainability challenges (Cockburn et al., 2019). They are an alternative science and challenge western science which define Indigenous epistemologies as unverifiable and unscientific.

African Indigenous scholars are challenging the negative perceptions that were promoted by colonial Eurocentric views of Indigenous sciences (Dei, 2019; Khumalo & Baloyi, 2017; Shizha, 2017, 2020). Eurocentric epistemologies tend to demote and undermine Indigenous sciences as lacking positivism and scientism (defined from a Eurocentric paradigm). However, all forms of knowledges are embedded in the culture of the knowledge producers. Today's scientific knowledge constructions are phenomena of the post-positivist philosophy of science, a thinking after positivism that challenges the traditional notion of the absolute truth of knowledge (Phillips & Burbules, 2000) and recognizing that there is nothing "positive" about claims of knowledge arising from the behavior and actions of humans (Creswell, 2008). Positivism is a Eurocentric hegemonic cultural construct that imposes definitions on other cultures in what Popper (2000 [1963]) describes as falsificationism—a problem of meaningfulness or significance, a problem of truth or acceptability. Hence what is knowledge in western societies may not be universalized and considered knowledge in other societies. Every society or community, western or non-western, has a culture and science that is particular to it (Shizha, 2013). Consequently, Cajete (2018) concludes that the culture of western science is equally foreign to western and non-western societies. Despite all the attempts by hegemonic positivist western sciences at de-epistemologizing and de-referencing other forms of sciences, African Indigenous epistemologies have maintained their place in African-defined realities. Every culture owns a science that exists in its specific socio-cultural, political, ecological and cosmological contexts. Several post-positivist philosophers of science reject positivism and offer views that emphasize the relativity of scientific knowledge (Lather & St. Pierre, 2013; Leavy, 2015; Phillips & Burbules, 2000) and share the view that science is a social construction of reality and that knowledge and its validation and legitimation are contextual. These contexts shape what defines knowledge and what defines science. Positivist approaches, which determine "acceptable standards of knowledge", marginalize IKs, and lack of codification is seen as an excuse to relegate them to the periphery (Shizha, 2017). The knowledges are misclassified as non-empirical ontological bodies that exist outside the scientific jurisdictions of verifiable, reliable and patentable inventions and discoveries. However, IKs do not need to be discovered and they do not need external validation because they already exist and are used by their owners. The question of ownership and intellectual property rights is held as an important aspect of the knowledge politics. But, given the importance of social communities to the construction of knowledges, the issue of IK production and ownership becomes a collective process.

The collectivist and constructionist nature of IKs and sciences are relative to any community's science. Science is an epistemological relativism (Siegel, 2011) and a cultural construct (Shizha, 2013), and there are many "cultural scientific communities" (Ogawa, 1995) that are not exclusive to Western societies. There are many cultural ways of understanding and giving meaning to nature. Siegel (2011) acknowledges that knowledge is relative because different cultures and societies accept different sets of principles, criteria and standards of evaluating knowledge claims, and there is no neutral way of choosing between these alternative sets of standards. Arguably, the differences between western science and Indigenous sciences exist not so much in the content, but in the normative ways of knowing and the interpretative framework that underpins such knowledge. Sankey (2009, p. 3) defines epistemic relativism as "a view about epistemic norms" and defines an epistemic norm as "a criterion or rule that may be employed to justify a belief." In Sankey's view in epistemic relativism there are no universal epistemic norms. Epistemic norms operate in different cultural contexts, where these contexts are defined by systems of different beliefs and different sets of norms (Sankey, 2012). For Sankey's relativism, whether a belief is justified, or counts as knowledge, depends on epistemic norms, and so, given that different epistemic norms can operate in different contexts, the same belief might be rational and justified knowledge relative to one context, and not to another. As Siegel (2011) further clarifies "the doctrine of knowledge relativism emanates from Plato's idea that humans are the measure of all things ("*homo mensura*")," and that any given thing "is to me such as it appears to me and is to you such as it appears to you" (p. 42). Thus, in both philosophical and sociological terms humans are the creators of their world and determine the processes through which sets of knowledges are generated, processed, legitimated, accepted and protected to support sustainable livelihoods.

African Epistemologies and Sustainable Livelihoods

Knowledges, how they are constructed, understood and utilized, are vital to peoples' livelihoods. The foundations of a people's welfare (socially, mentally and physical health) are in the production and use of their knowledges. IPs have drawn on their own sources of knowledges and experiences about biocultural diversity and ecological environment, featuring its diversity and adaptation, in mediating their relationship with the local environment and ecosystems (Jianchu & Mikesell, 2003). The ecological system in the form of biodiversity and local environment contributes to sustainable livelihoods among IPs. However, their knowledges and their lived experiences have received sparce attention by African researchers and educational institutions. Education has contributed to the negativities and misconception about IKs, which were colonially defined as illogical and irrelevant to socio-economic development (Dei, 2019; Ogawa, 1995; Shizha, 2020), hence its marginalization. However, both Indigenous and western scientific knowledges are imperfect and incomplete on their own and using one does not necessarily reject the other. However, due to the vulnerability of Indigenous sciences, they need protection from being assimilated into the western sciences.

Protection of Indigenous biodiversity and ecosystems is the foundation for sustainable livelihoods. IPs use their knowledges to interpret their relationship with the local environment using a holistic approach of management of natural resources with conservation and sustainability as the core values (Soh & Omar, 2012). Soh and Omar (2012) describe a sustainable livelihood approach as comprising the capabilities, assets, including both material and social resources and activities required as the means of living, and an approach that identifies poverty as a condition of insecurity or vulnerability. This approach also believes that one should maintain, protect or enhance capabilities and assets both now and in the future, while not undermining the natural resource base (Meikle & Bannister, 2003). Sustainability is also based on evolving thinking about the way the vulnerable live their lives and the importance of policies and institutions (Serrat, 2017). Institutions like education in Africa should increasingly be involved in investigating ways and designing programs that help Indigenous people develop sustainable livelihoods. Working together with Indigenous communities and engaging them in their socio-cultural practices and ways of knowing in terms of protecting and using resources sustainably should be their goal. The sustainable livelihoods approach facilitates the identification of practical priorities for actions that are based on the views and interests of those concerned (Serrat, 2017). It is a process of knowledge construction and co-construction that makes the connection between people and the overall enabling environment that influences the outcomes of livelihood strategies thus improving community livelihoods. It brings attention to bear on the potentials people have in terms of their skills, social networks, cultural knowledges, and the ability to influence their socio-cultural, physical and health development. Connectivity between

Indigenous people, their cosmological universe and their ecosystem demonstrates the linkage between cultural and biocultural diversity and the natural environment as means to promote people and community livelihood interactions. The success of individual/personal livelihoods depends on the success of community livelihoods—they depend on each other.

Land-use practices as a resource for both individual and community livelihoods connect people to their ecological system and access to biodiversity, and this is a product of a long history of creative adaptation to local environments and ecological conditions such as climate, terrain, soil, water, air, plants and animals (Dei, 2019). From their analysis of land-use by Indigenous people, Jianchu and Mikesell (2003) concluded that these adaptive practices have given rise to the knowledge that enables the people to live well and with confidence in diverse and sometimes harsh environments, as well as to develop their livelihoods, such as fishing, hunting and gathering, shifting cultivation, nomadic pastoralism and terraced agriculture, as well as trade in natural and cultural products through social networks. These practices are important in promoting and enhancing their livelihoods. One of the most important aspects of IPs' livelihoods is reading the weather patterns and following climatic changes. This scientific knowledge helps them to determine their agricultural productivity, which in turn affects food security for their communities. For Indigenous people, the climatic conditions are the backbone for sustainable livelihoods. Reading weather patterns and changes in the movements of the winds and clouds, reading changes in the seasons is/was scientific knowledge that assisted them to prepare and manage their agricultural activities (Shizha, 2014). Today, the world is faced by global warming and environmental and weather-related disasters and while these disasters could be classified as natural, the human factor in the causes cannot be overruled. Climate variability and change affect the ability of rural communities to satisfy needs that are inherent to the environment (Bate et al., 2019) such as sufficient rain for farming, and adequate pastures for animals that provide food for IPs. Nonetheless, valuable local knowledges relevant to climate change and adaptation are held by rural societies and these knowledge systems are transmitted and renewed by each succeeding generation, ensuring the well-being of people by providing food security, environmental conservation, and early warning systems for disaster risk management (Mafongoya & Ajayi, 2017).

African Indigenous Knowledges and Security

Food security or insecurity determines sustainable livelihoods. The extent food is available or not available determines the health state of individuals and communities. Food security depends on the application of knowledge and how the resources that assist in food production are maintained and sustainably used. In this regard, IK systems can contribute to the achievement of food security. As reported by Ngara (2013), local people have accumulated vast experiences through informal experiments and intimate understanding of the environment especially in relationship to land and its use. Africans like other Indigenous people have generated agricultural systems over the years (Tirivangasi & Tayengwa, 2017) that have been sidelined to the subsistence level of food production and have been interfered with by western modes of food production which focus on mass production at the expense of land protection and resource maintenance. Agricultural education in schools promotes commoditization of land and food production (Ntsebeza & Hall, 2007). Commoditization takes land away from Indigenous farmers and impacts land and IPs' food security whereby production is dictated by the demands of the market, which by its capitalist nature disempowers local people by dispossessing them of land ownership, thus disrupting the sustainability of their Indigenous food security systems. In other words, commoditization and marketization of land and food production has marginalized IKs and farming systems. The commodity farming replaces the Indigenous agricultural systems which are not geared for the market (Ntsebeza & Hall, 2007) since historically and traditionally, IPs did not produce food for the capitalist markets, but for their communities and their survival.

Eurocentric systems of education have modeled young people who perceive farming in commercial and capitalist perspectives rather than in sustainable ways (Kapoor & Shizha, 2010). The commercialization and market economy introduced to Indigenous communities have divided the elder and young generations due to different values and production expectations placed on the land. Whereas adults might have a sustainability perspective, young people who have gone through the western agricultural education system are likely to have a capitalist and market-driven liberalist perspective—maximizing profits from the land. The rapid and often coerced divorcement of Indigenous people from dependence upon and rights to their immediate environment for their livelihoods has been set in motion by the differences between Indigenous elders' thinking, and the young people's market-driven perspectives which is supported by both the government (policy makers) and educational institutions, which undervalue IK systems. As Jianchu and Mikesell (2003) argue, "One of the first aspects of Indigenous culture to fall before the onslaught of outside commercial and chemically civilization is knowledge, its use of biological resources for medicine, food and shelters, land-use practices and customary institutions for governing access to natural resources" (p. 4). Commercialization, commoditization and marketization are antithesis to sustainable food security and introduce individualism that takes away communal custodianship of the Indigenous resources.

Eurocentric Epistemological Foundations in Higher Education in Africa

The extent to which IKs and sciences are applied in higher education institutions in Africa leaves a lot to be desired. While IK scholars advocate for the protection of IKs, they do not advocate for its marginalization in educational institutions but its promotion (Cajete, 2018; Dei, 2019; Shizha, 2014, 2017). Higher education in Africa cannot be distanced from its colonial past. Institutions and structures of higher education (both universities and colleges) mirror colonial hegemonic structural and institutional authority that favored and valorized Eurocentric knowledges, values and normative standards (Cajete, 2018; Dei, 2019) at the expense of Indigenous epistemologies. However, when introduced to the education system, IK systems bring a cognitive diversity to the scientific learning process. Just as biodiversity is essential to nature and invaluable for human beings, so too is cognitive diversity (Harding, 1998) and yet, Africa's higher education is still concerned by the continuing dominance of Western/Northern epistemologies, economic and political theory in its intellectual academic discourses (Nirmal & Rocheleau, 2019). Education in Africa should be decolonized and delivered in contexts that foster productive alliances with multiple perspectives that are Indigenous, post-development and pluriversal in thought and design (Escobar, 2018). Pluriversality rather than universality should be the central paradigm shift to higher education science and knowledge discourses. Education should focus on engaging students in political struggles against capitalist economics, neoliberal and imperial political regimes, extractivism and environmental pillage (Brownhill et al., 2012). For sustainable livelihoods, environmental protection and Indigenous ideologies on protecting Indigenous landscapes, their ecological systems and biodiversity should be foundational to the epistemologies that are presented for debate in educational institutions.

Viewing higher education in Africa as the space for advancing Eurocentric epistemologies plays in the hands of those who want to perpetuate the dependence of Africans on foreign and alien ideologies on survival and development strategies. Kallis (2017) states that decolonization requires a commitment to "create an alternative social-ecology and a fundamentally different basis for action" (p. 25), positioning it as "a call to free the social imaginary from the ideology of a one-way future consisting only of growth" (p. 99) based on colonial Eurocentrism. Decolonizing colonized thought engages new ways of processing knowledge and critical reflections on the relativism of knowledge. It entails the realization that it may be incorrect to assume that "if only the traditional education system inherited from colonialism were to be strengthened, it would prepare people effectively for a competitive global economy, thus magically ensuring outcomes such as material sufficiency, harmony and social cohesion" (Hickling-Hudson, 2002, p. 576). What African educators should realize is that Eurocentric knowledge and practices have disempowered IPs from achieving sustainable livelihoods using their cultural knowledges and sciences. In traditional society, they were able to mitigate against droughts by protecting wetlands and growing crops that were resistant to droughts, and they were also knowledgeable about reading the weather and the movements of winds to prepare for farming. With the advent of colonialism, some of this knowledge gradually vanished as they were introduced to "better" ways of farming that included the use of chemicals like fertilizers and pesticides that damaged the soil and disrupted biodiversity and the ecosystem.

Sustainable livelihoods in Africa can be achieved by going back to the basics, in Amilcar Cabral's (1973) terms, 'a return to the source,' to revitalize Indigenous sciences and epistemologies and reclaim their role in socio-cultural and economic development. The role of education cannot be overruled for this process to succeed. Incorporation and integration of Indigenous epistemologies will go a long way in promoting successful sustainable livelihoods. Among the many things we can learn from IKs and IPs is how to shift from a reductionist to a systemic view of the world, which leads to a shift from expert-based environmental management to a participatory-based ecosystem stewardship (Jianchu & Mikesell, 2003). The participation of Indigenous elders in formal education systems, such as having an elder-in residence in higher education institutions will build trust and promote collaboration in knowledge production. Collaborating with Indigenous elders and communities will not only help in archiving IKs but will also promote science as a living and ever-changing knowledge system that is co-created for the benefit of different communities. For sustainable livelihoods to be achieved in Africa, communities should be involved in participatory knowledge institutionalization in education to solve existing and future problems.

Community-based applications are likely to succeed more than applications that are determined by outsiders. For example, Indigenous farmers' knowledges and perceptions of climate and ecological change is a function of traditions and customs that could be shared with other institutions and disseminated collaboratively. For example, in the Bui Plateau of the Bamenda Highlands of Cameroon, Indigenous scientific climate and ecological change perceptions are institutionalized to enable local people to plan and cope with the impact of environmental change in agriculture and other sectors (Tume et al., 2019). Perceptions of these changes by rural communities are concentrated on observations of variations in temperature, rainfall and vegetation patterns, which are often backed by blending such perceptions with institutional scientific evidence (Tume et al., 2019). The importance of institutionalizing IKs was reported by Grenier (1998), who mentioned that villagers in Indonesia were able to identify 146 tree types whereas western trained biologists from a nearby university had identified only 16. Moreover, Indigenous people live in harmony with nature and are therefore highly knowledgeable about their ecosystems and changes that may upset the equilibrium within nature (Nawrotzki, & Kadatska, 2010) an experience that university scientists may not have access to. Using the collaborative community participatory approach makes local people actors in analyzing their living conditions for positive sustainable outcomes. In West Africa, an initiative bringing together the forecasting knowledge of M'bororo pastoralists with scientific long-term and seasonal weather information was piloted by the Association for Indigenous Women and Peoples of Chad, the IPs of Africa Coordinating Committee (IPCC) and UNESCO (Mafongoya & Ajayi, 2017) and the IPCC's assessment report concluded that IKs are an invaluable basis for developing adaptation and natural resource management strategies in respect to environment and other forms of change that should be recognized in education and be part of institutional knowledge.

Indigenous Peoples' Survival Under COVID-19 and Research

The world is experiencing a pandemic that requires all forms of knowledges and sciences to be explored to come up with a cure or vaccine. The Corona Virus (COVID-19) that started in China in November 2019 resulted in lockdowns that brought the world to a halt. Indigenous sciences can contribute to the discovery of a cure if Indigenous epistemologies and ways of knowing are taken seriously. According to the Food and Agricultural Organization (FAO, 2020), IPs are the living proof of humankind's resilience shown by how they have survived pandemics, invasions and outbreaks for centuries. Their resilience is manifested in how they continue to rely on community practices and traditional knowledges to cope with diseases. FAO's observation seems to support that IPs' sustainable health livelihoods are supported and maintained by their Indigenous epistemologies and their interaction with their ecological systems and biodiversity. It should be noted that IPs in Africa and globally are equally affected by COVID, and a successful adaptation or integration of Indigenous approaches to public health in Africa must be anchored in the principles of self-determination for IPs to determine their own paths to healing and to health (Richardson & Crawford, 2020). What this means is that IPs should be consulted when determining their healing and how the healing process should be conducted (Shizha & Charema, 2011).

In Africa, decolonization of science requires Indigenous people to fully participate and contribute to research that seeks medicines and remedies for new diseases such as COVID. While we might not know fully what is happening in Indigenous communities in Africa, they would like to be included in the search for a COVID cure relying on their traditional knowledges and practices (UN Inter-Agency Support Group, 2020). The role of elders in Indigenous communities is particularly significant as they play a key role in keeping and transmitting Indigenous traditional knowledge and culture and practices that can contribute to their health, well-being and the protection and recovery of their people. Currently, there is no specific antiviral drug developed in Africa to treat this new respiratory disease. Most treatment strategies focus on managing symptoms and supportive therapy such as supplementary oxygen and mechanical ventilation (Richardson & Crawford, 2020). However, Dwarka (2020) reports that in South Africa, efforts are underway to bring IKs into researching how to mitigate against COVID. A first "scientific" study of African medicinal plants for bioactive compounds to determine the possibility of detecting a cure for COVID is being planned by the University of KwaZulu Natal in South Africa highlighting the acceptance of Indigenous healing plants and their role in discovering cures for pandemics and other diseases thus decolonizing the dominance of Western "scientific" healing hegemonies (Shizha & Charema, 2011). A few African countries, such as Madagascar, have experimented with traditional herbal remedies to find a cure. Madagascar used a traditional herbal plant *artemisia annua* to come up with Covid-Organics (CVO), herbal supplements that are used as immune boosters and health tonics (Barker, 2020). While WHO and the African Union have not conclusively supported its use because of the lack of a rigorous testing protocol, Madagascar has highlighted the need for Africans to start exploring and experimenting with Indigenous healing practices and integrating such practices with western medical practices. South Africa has a long tradition of using plants for medicinal purposes with some, such as *Aloe ferox*, *Sutherlandia frutescens* and *Kiggelaria africana*, having been studied as sources of useful compounds (Dwarka, 2020). In Botswana, Kenya, South Africa and Zimbabwe, *lippia javanica* is used for a wide variety of traditional uses, the most important traditional applications include its uses as herbal tea and ethnomedicinal applications for colds, cough, fever or malaria, wounds, repelling mosquitos, diarrhea, chest pains, bronchitis, and asthma (Chigora et al., 2007; Semenya et al., 2013). However, there are no studies to determine the efficacy of these herbs in treating COVID. Governments, universities and biochemical research centers in Africa should collaborate with Indigenous traditional healers to carry out studies and trials that determine whether there are available traditional herbs that alleviate the effects of the Corona virus. Africa has many traditional healing procedures that use plants and herbal remedies that could help in coping with diseases and pandemics such as COVID to promote sustainable health.

Conclusion

Postcolonial Africa has continued to depend on colonial Eurocentric epistemological practices to determine their livelihoods. These practices have been driven by the education system, which changed the way that Africans used to believe in themselves and the way they experienced the world. While western education has brought new thinking and ways of understanding the world, there is paucity of research, development and dissemination (RDD) on Indigenous epistemologies, and the extent to which they promote and support human livelihoods. Africa is endowed with plants that can be processed to research on possible healing efficacies for different diseases including COVID-19. While in some continents, such as Europe and Asia, researchers have discovered vaccines for COVID, in Africa there is no evidence that research is in progress. Even the earlier reported University of KwaZulu Natal expected research on Indigenous plants has not begun. The development of scientific research and knowledge production is not the absolute domain of Western researchers and scholars but all including IKs stakeholders. African Indigenous researchers and scholars should aim to decolonize and disrupt the false superiority of Western science and become visible in the science world and raise their voices and participation in the production of scientific knowledge. Universities and higher education in general should respect the contribution of Indigenous sciences by providing space for conducting Indigenous sciences research. They should avoid knowledge trivialization by deeming IKs and sciences inconsequential to social development and sustainable livelihoods. Universities and researchers should collaborate with Indigenous communities, elders and traditional healers in an atmosphere of trust, equality and genuine participatory involvement while protecting the cultural knowledge of the communities.

References

Barker, A. (2020). Could it work as a cure? Maybe: A herbal remedy for coronavirus is a hit in Africa, but experts have their doubts. *Time*. Retrieved January 6, 2021, from https://time.com/5840148/coronavirus-cure-covid-organic-madagascar/

Bate, G. B., Kimengsi, J. N., & Amawa, S. G. (2019). Determinants and policy implications of farmers' climate adaptation choices in rural Cameroon. *Sustainability, 11*(7), 1–14.

Berkes, F. (2012). Implementing ecosystem-based management: Evolution or revolution? *Fish and Fisheries, 13*(4), 465–476.

Brownhill, L., Turner, T. E., & Kaara, W. (2012). Degrowth? How about some "de-alienation"? *Capitalism Nature Socialism, 23*(1), 93–104.

Cabral, A. (1973). *Return to the source: Selected speeches of Amilcar Cabral*. Monthly Review Press.

Cajete, G. A. (2018). Envisioning indigenous education: Applying insights from indigenous views of teaching and learning. In E. McKinley & L. Smith (Eds.), *Handbook of indigenous education* (pp. 823–845). Springer.

Chigora, P., Masocha, R., & Mutenheri, F. (2007). The role of indigenous medicinal knowledge (IMK) in the treatment of ailments in rural Zimbabwe: The case of Mutirikwi communal lands. *Journal of Sustainable Development in Africa, 9*(2), 26–43.

Cockburn, J., Cundill, G., Shackleton, S., & Rouget, M. (2019). The meaning and practice of stewardship in South Africa. *South African. Journal of Science, 115*(5/6), 1–13.

Creswell, J. W. (2008). *Educational research: Planning, conducting, and evaluating quantitative and qualitative research* (3rd ed.). Pearson Education Inc.

Cunningham, J., & Fitzgerald, J. (1996). Epistemology and reading. *Reading Research Quarterly, 31*(1), 36–60.

Dei, G. J. (2019). Indigenous governance for Africentric school success. In E. McKinley & L. Smith (Eds.), *Handbook of Indigenous education* (pp. 169–186). Springer.

Dwarka, D. (2020). SA researchers looking at medicinal plants for possible COVID-19 treatments. *ENCA News*. Retrieved December 14, 2020, from https://www.enca.com/analysis/sa-researchers-looking-medicinal-plants-possible-covid-19-treatments

Escobar, A. (2018). *Designs for the pluriverse: Radical interdependence, autonomy, and the making of worlds*. Duke University Press.

Food and Agricultural Organization (FAO). (2020). *COVID-19 and IPs*. United Nations.

Grenier, L. (1998). *Working with indigenous knowledge: A guide for researchers*. IDRC.

Harding, S. (1998). *Is science multicultural? Postcolonialisms, feminisms, and epistemologies*. Indiana University Press.

Hickling-Hudson, A. (2002). Re-visioning from the inside: Getting under the skin of the World Bank's education sector strategy. *International Journal of Educational Development, 22*(6), 565–577.

Jianchu, X., & Mikesell, S. (2003). Indigenous knowledge for sustainable livelihoods and resources governance in the MMSEA region. In *Proceedings of the III Symposium on MMSEA* 25–28 August 2002. Lijiang, China.

Kallis, G. (2017). *In defense of degrowth: Opinions and minifestos*. Creative Commons.

Kapoor, D., & Shizha, E. (Eds.). (2010). *Indigenous knowledge and learning in Asia/Pacific and Africa: Perspectives on development, education and culture*. Palgrave Macmillan.

Khumalo, N., & Baloyi, B. C. (2017). African indigenous knowledge: An under-utilised and neglected resource for development. *Library Philosophy and Practice*, 1663. Retrieved January 4, 2021, from https://digitalcommons.unl.edu/libphilprac/1663/

Kimble, C. (2013). Knowledge management, codification and tacit knowledge. *Information Research, 18*(2), 1–15.

Lather, P., & St. Pierre, E. (2013). Post-qualitative research. *International Journal of Qualitative Studies in Education, 26*(6), 629–633.

Leavy, P. (2015). *Method meets art: Arts-based research practice*. The Guilford Press.

Mafongoya, P. L., & Ajayi, O. C. (2017). *Indigenous knowledge systems and climate change management in Africa*. CTA.

Matsika, C. (2012). *Traditional African education: Its significance to current education practices with special reference to Zimbabwe*. Mambo Press.

Meikle, S., & Bannister, A. (2003). *Energy, poverty and sustainable urban livelihoods: Concepts and implications for policy* (Working Paper No. 126). Development Planning Unit, University College, London.

Nawrotzki, R. J., & Kadatska, P. (2010). Addressing climate change with indigenous knowledge. *International Journal of Climate Change, 2*(1), 33–47.

Ngara, R. (2013). Shangwe music for spiritual rituals: A symbolical enactment. *Studies of Tribes and Tribals, 11*(2), 127–133.

Nirmal, P., & Rocheleau, D. (2019). Decolonizing degrowth in the post-development convergence: Questions, experiences and proposals from two indigenous territories. *Environment and Planning: Nature and Space, 2*(3), 465–492.

Ntsebeza, L., & Hall, R. (2007). *The land question in South Africa: The challenge of transformation and redistribution.* HSRC Press.

Ogawa, M. (1995). Science education in a multiscience perspective. *Science Education, 79*(5), 583–593.

Phillips, D., & Burbules, N. (2000). *Postpositivism and educational research.* Rowman & Littlefield.

Popper, K. (2000 [1963]). Conjectures and refutations. In T. Schick (Ed.), *Readings in the philosophy of science* (pp. 9–13). Mayfield Publishing.

Richardson, L., & Crawford, A. (2020). COVID-19 and the decolonization of indigenous public health. *CMAJ, 192*(38), E1098–E1100.

Sankey, H. (2009). Witchcraft, relativism and the problem of the criterion. *Erkenn Erkenntnis, 72*(1), 1–16.

Sankey, H. (2012). Scepticism, relativism and the argument from the criterion. *Studies in History and Philosophy of Science, 43*(1), 182–190.

Sati, V. P., Wei, D., & Xue-Qian, S. (2014). *Sustainable livelihood strategies and options: A case study of the Upper Minjiang River Basin, China.* Lambert Academic Publishing.

Semenya, S. S., Potgieter, M. J., & Tshisikhawe, M. P. (2013). Use, conservation and present availability status of ethnomedicinal plants of Matabele-Village in the Limpopo Province, South Africa. *African Journal of Biotechnology, 12*(18), 2392–2405.

Serrat, O. (2017). *The sustainable livelihoods approach: Knowledge solutions.* Springer.

Shizha, E., & Charema, J. (2011). Health and wellness in Southern Africa: Incorporating indigenous and western healing practices. *International Journal of Psychology and Counselling, 3*(9), 167–175.

Shizha, E. (2013). Reclaiming our indigenous voices: The problem with postcolonial Sub-Saharan African school curriculum. *Journal of Indigenous Social Development, 2*(1), 1–18.

Shizha, E. (2014). Counter-visioning contemporary African education: Indigenous science as a tool for African development. In E. Shizha & A. A. Abdi (Eds.), *Indigenous discourses on knowledge and development in Africa* (pp. 78–93). Taylor & Francis/Routledge.

Shizha, E. (2015). Reclaiming Indigenous cultures in African education. In W. J. Jacobs, S. Y. Cheng, & M. K. Porter (Eds.), *Indigenous education: Language, culture, and identity* (pp. 301–317). Springer.

Shizha, E. (2017). Indigenous knowledges and knowledge codification in the knowledge economy. In P. Ngulube (Ed.), *Handbook of research on theoretical perspectives on indigenous knowledge systems in developing countries* (pp. 267–288). IGI Global.

Shizha, E. (2019). Building capacity for indigenous people: Engaging indigenous philosophies in school governance. In E. A. McKinley & L. T. Smith (Eds.), *Handbook of indigenous education* (pp. 187–205). Springer.

Shizha, E. (2020). African indigenous agricultural technologies: Decolonizing and indigenizing technology education. In M. T. Gumbo (Ed.), *Decolonization of technology education: African indigenous perspectives* (pp. 149–169). Peter Lang.

Shizha, E., & Abdi, A. A. (Eds.). (2014). *Indigenous discourses on knowledge and development in Africa.* Taylor & Francis/Routledge.

Siegel, H. (2011). Epistemological relativism: Arguments pro and con. In S. D. Hales (Ed.), *A companion to relativism* (pp. 201–218). Blackwell.

Soh, M. B. C., & Omar, S. K. (2012). Small is big: The charms of indigenous knowledge for sustainable livelihood. *Procedia-Social and Behavioral Sciences, 36*, 602–610.

Steup, M., & Neta, R. (2020). Epistemology. *The Stanford Encyclopedia of Philosophy* (Fall 2020 Edition). https://plato.stanford.edu/archives/fall2020/entries/epistemology/

Tengö, M., Brondizio, E. S., Elmqvist, T., Malmer, P., & Spierenburg, M. (2014). Connecting diverse knowledge systems for enhanced ecosystem governance: The multiple evidence base approach. *Ambio, 43*, 579–591.

Thompson, K., Lantz, T., & Ban, N. (2020). A review of indigenous knowledge and participation in environmental monitoring. *Ecology and Society, 25*(2), 1–27.

Tirivangasi, H. M., & Tayengwa, D. (2017). Indigenous knowledge systems (IKS) and food security in South Africa: Is land reform a prerequisite? *Journal of Human Ecology, 57*(3), 118–124.

Tume, S. J. P., Kimengsi, J. N., & Fogwe, Z. N. (2019). Indigenous knowledge and farmer perceptions of climate and ecological changes in the Bamenda Highlands of Cameroon: Insights from the Bui Plateau. *Climate, 7*(138), 1–18.

UN Inter-Agency Support Group. (2020). *Guidance note for the UN system on indigenous issues*. https://www.un.org/development/desa/Indigenouspeoples/covid-19.html

CHAPTER 27

Centering Race, Racism, and Black Learners in Mathematics Education: A Critical Race Theory Perspective

Julius Davis

INTRODUCTION

Science, technology, engineering, and mathematics (STEM) knowledge plays a significant role in promoting and advancing global capitalism, gentrification, and international warfare to protect and promote whiteness (Morales-Doyle & Gutstein, 2019). The global impact of racism, anti-Blackness, and Eurocentrism in STEM education has primarily gone uncontested and unchallenged (Davis, 2018; Martin, 2019; Martin et al., 2019). STEM education fields are viewed and operated as race-neutral, culture-free, and objective disciplines, but they are not. Critical examinations of STEM fields and Black students are confined to two main disciplines: mathematics and science education (Martin, 2003, 2009; Mutegi, 2011). Most critical examinations of STEM education have occurred in mathematics education, the gatekeeper to the STEM enterprise (Martin et al., 2010).

Black scholars have been leading the way in establishing new paradigms and theories to offer critical perspectives of mathematics education, especially for Black learners (Davis & Jett, 2019; Davis & Martin, 2008; Leonard & Martin, 2013; Martin, 2009). Scholars have offered critical perspectives of mathematics education policies, research, curriculum, mathematics standards, pedagogy, courses, standardized testing, racialized achievement gaps, research approaches, and how they impact Black students (Davis, 2018; Davis & Jett,

J. Davis (✉)
Bowie State University, Bowie, MD, USA
e-mail: jldavis@bowiestate.edu

2019; Martin, 2009). These critiques have ushered in a liberatory paradigm to advocate for Black learners and challenge the Eurocentric paradigm in mathematics education (Martin, 2010; Martin et al., 2019). Scholars have centered Black students' mathematical experiences in the liberatory paradigm to address race, racism, and the impact of whiteness.

Critical race theory (CRT) has emerged as a framework to address race, racism, classism, and gender in mathematics education. CRT also advocates for liberatory outcomes for Black learners in mathematics education. In this chapter, I continue to illustrate CRT's usefulness as a framework for identifying, analyzing, and beginning to address the impact of race and racism for Black learners in mathematics education. By employing the lessons learned from the use of CRT in critical examinations of mathematics education, liberatory outcomes—such as reframing mathematics standards, discourses, pedagogy, and classroom settings—may be attainable for Black learners.

CRITICAL RACE THEORY IN MATHEMATICS EDUCATION

Researchers have traced the genealogy of critical race theory in mathematics education (CRT(ME)) to William F. Tate's scholarship (Davis & Jett, 2019). In the twentieth century, Tate (1993) published the first CRT(ME) article entitled, "Advocacy versus Economics: A Critical Race Analysis of the Proposed National Assessment in Mathematics" in *Thresholds in Education*. In the same year, Tate collaboratively published another article merging the law, CRT, education, and mathematics education (Tate et al., 1993). A few scholars have considered Tate to be the chief architect of CRT in education because of his early scholarship (Davis & Jett, 2019; Lynn & Adams, 2002). Most scholars in the space employ Ladson-Billings' and Tate's (1995) seminal article, "Toward a Critical Race Theory of Education," in *Teachers College Record* to introduce this framework in the field. However, Tate considers Derrick Bell (1976) to be the first savant to introduce CRT to the educational community with the article, "Serving Two Masters: Integration Ideals and Client Interests in School Desegregation Litigation" in *The Yale Law Journal*. Tate developed into one of the leading CRT in education scholars, earning him his reputation as the Father of CRT(ME).

CRT(ME) is a pedagogical, theoretical, methodological, and analytical framework that attempts to understand and critique race, racism, classism, sexism, and other forms of oppression. Davis (2019) asserts that scholars who seek to use CRT(ME) must have an operationalized definition of race and racism, a critical view of Black adults and students' lived experiences in urban areas, a sociohistorical context to analyze race and racism, and developed sociopolitical consciousness. The foundational components of CRT(ME) involve :

a. Accepting racism as an endemic and permanent feature of American society, including schools, mathematics spaces, and structures;
b. Challenging the dominant ideology, paradigms, research, theories, and texts about Black adults and students used to blame them for the conditions of their communities, families, schooling, and mathematics education;
c. Centralizing the racialized, gendered, classed, and mathematical experiences of Black adults and students;
d. Using an interdisciplinary approach and knowledge to better understand race, racism, sexism, classism, life, and mathematical experiences of Black adults and students in and out of mathematics spaces; and
e. A commitment to achieving liberatory and social justice outcomes for Black adults and students in society, schools, and mathematics spaces (Davis, 2019, p. 192).

Applying these essential elements of CRT (ME) facilitates the identification of race-specific factors that have a negative impact on learning outcomes for students of color—in this case, Black students—within both institutional and individual mathematics paradigms. By accepting the widespread and pervasive presence of racism in the discipline's very foundation but simultaneously challenging the dominant ideology and centralizing Black mathematical experiences in the discourse, CRT offers a means of redressing the historically monochromatic mathematics education of the West.

While CRT is by no means restricted to the examination of racism against African Americans and Black people more broadly, some scholars have argued that CRT's foundational elements in law and education are rooted in a focus on Blackness and have accordingly called for BlackCrit in education to engage in a deeper understanding of Black identities, needs, aspirations, and hopes (Dumas & Ross, 2016). Early articulations of CRT in the law and education indicate that Black people's experiences have been privileged and that Blackness has been conflated with the concept of race, writ large (Phillips, 1998). Many of the key critical race scholars in law and education are Black and have grounded their scholarship in the Black experience, which is significant to the framework. Non-Black scholars have critiqued them in education and the law for centering the experiences, histories, and present conditions of Black people (Phillips, 1998), but most of the CRT critiques in the law and education from the Black experience are about the Black/white binary or paradigm.

I have centered the Black/white binary in mathematics education scholarship and do not view it as a problematic choice, but rather as one that is essential to understanding how racism (white supremacy, in particular) impacts Black people (Davis, 2019). Black scholars should use CRT in law, education, and mathematics education to center Black experiences, cultures, histories, and present conditions without focusing on all racial and ethnic groups. In mathematics education, CRT(ME) has been primarily advanced by critical Black scholars for use with Black populations who have centered Blackness in explicit and implicit ways. My analysis of Black history has illustrated how Black people's needs often get lost if Blackness is not centered, particularly when all other racial and ethnic groups' needs are prioritized at the exclusion of Blackness. Black scholars have acted with a sense of urgency to conceptualize, analyze, and deploy this justice-seeking as counter-oppressive critical scholarship committed to challenging and undermining knowledge, learning, and pedagogical racism foremostly weaponized against Black people.

Scholars have argued that CRT in education is not equipped to address anti-Blackness because it is a theory intended to focus on racism and not Blackness's specificity (Dumas & Ross, 2016). I agree with the need to explicate the specificity of Blackness and the need for "language to richly capture how anti-[B]lackness constructs Black subjects, and positions them in and against the law, policy, [education], and every day (civic) life" (Dumas & Ross, 2016, p. 417). Scholars recognize that anti-Blackness and white supremacy are different and that CRT in education does not fundamentally possess the language needed to fully express Blackness or anti-Blackness (Dumas & Ross, 2016). Anti-Blackness is a social construct that highlights how Blackness is despised and embedded in the lived experiences of Black people and in opposition to whiteness, which is perceived as pure and humane (Dumas & Ross, 2016). White supremacy "informs and facilitates racist ideology and institutional practice" (Dumas & Ross, 2016, p. 417) that is connected to whiteness.

Dumas and Ross (2016) used Ladson-Billings' and Tate's (1995) proclamation that Blackness needs to be communicated in detailed ways to articulate BlackCrit in education. While I appreciate how Dumas and Ross (2016) expressed the need for BlackCrit in education to centralize discourses and experiences of Blackness and anti-Blackness, most of their arguments have used CRT in education to create this space, which suggests that the framework is fundamentally equipped to address the specificity of Blackness, anti-Blackness, and racism. Scholars in mathematics education have begun to use BlackCrit in education to poignantly address Blackness and anti-Blackness in the field (Martin et al., 2019).

A CRITICAL RACE ANALYSIS OF MATHEMATICS EDUCATION

Critical race theory provides the components necessary to critically examine STEM education through theoretical, methodological, pedagogical, and analytical lenses. Education policies, funding, mathematics standards, standardized testing, racialized achievement gaps, curriculum, instruction, assessment, and courses are sources of anti-Blackness, whiteness, racism, and white supremacy. These education areas illuminate how race and racism impact Black learners in STEM, but for the purposes of this chapter, I focus on mathematics education.

The Impact of Educational Laws and Policies on Mathematics Education

To fully understand the experiences of and challenges for Black adults and children in mathematics education, it is necessary to reach an understanding of race, laws, policies, education, and social customs in America. Mathematics education is a microcosm of a larger educational and social system predicated on race, law, and the exclusion of Black people that still exists in the present day. The Father of CRT, Derrick Bell, developed the concept of revisionist history to "reexamine America's historical record, replacing comforting majoritarian interpretations of events with ones that square more accurately with" Black peoples' experiences—in this case, mathematics education (Delgado & Stefancic, 2001, p. 20). It is important to note that racism and racialized issues impacting society and the larger field of education also impact what transpires in mathematics education.

One of the main ways that institutional, structural, and systemic racism continues to persist in schools and mathematics settings is through federal, national, state, and local laws and policies (Martin, 2003, 2007, 2009; Snipes & Waters, 2005; Tate, 1993, 1997). The federal, state, and local governments have a long history of institutionalizing laws and policies that renew and rejuvenate social constructions of race and racism in education and mathematics education—legislative and policymaking contexts that significantly impact and exclude Black people. For instance, Jim Crow Laws of the late eighteenth- and early-to-mid-nineteenth-century—a subject to which this chapter will return in the next section—upheld school segregation based upon the principles of scientific racism.

Historically and presently, most legislative and policymaking bodies in education, mathematics education, and other societal contexts are mainly composed of white people. A significant reason for pervasive whiteness in legislative and policy contexts stems from efforts to maintain white power structures and exclude and dehumanize Black people, thereby creating institutionalized anti-Blackness. From my analysis, there is no period in American historical or contemporary records when anti-Blackness was critically examined and addressed in the legal, social, educational, and mathematical records for the betterment of Black people. Ladson-Billings (2006) argued that Black communities had little to no legislative representation in or access to the educational franchise that whites occupied with social, legal, and economic power.

Legal, social, and racial segregation of Black people from white people in educational and policymaking arenas has a long history in the United States of America. During the eighteenth and nineteenth centuries, many Black people were enslaved, legally and socially separated from white people, and forbidden to be educated, especially in arithmetic. The prevailing thoughts about Black people were that they were inferior, subhuman, and lacked the intelligence to overturn slavery and their inhumane treatment (Tate, 1997). Most Black people did not have any of the legal or political rights afforded to white people.

Therefore, they had no legal rights to oppose them or advocate for themselves in legal or policymaking arenas and social settings (Ladson-Billings, 2006). This line of thinking and related legal and social practices represents some of the foundational anti-Blackness embedded in society and educational and mathematical spaces through legal, political, and social actions. After abolishing slavery, Black codes and social practices maintained racial segregation and inhumane treatment in educational areas and, by default, mathematics learning spaces.

Racialized Legal, Educational, and Mathematical Developments in the Nineteenth Century

During the nineteenth century, the institutionalization of race in American society significantly impacted the role of education and law. The federal government's role in education became more formalized, with efforts focused on vocational training and land grants. It created the Office of Education in 1867. The government sought to collect information about schools and teaching that would lead to effective school systems. Given the racial temperament of the time in the federal government, justice, and legislative bodies, it was evident that Black people were not considered in the development of effective education. White interests and white power were the focal points of the development of school systems. America's economic growth and its white power structure were the driving forces behind the federal government's educational investments.

In the late nineteenth century, the U.S. Supreme Court upheld racial segregation through the *Plessy v. Ferguson* (1896) ruling, establishing a law for a legal distinction between Black and white people. As a result, the "separate but equal" doctrine was birthed to maintain legal segregation under the false guise of equality in public spaces, including educational and mathematical spaces. From the *Plessy v. Ferguson* ruling, restrictive Jim Crow laws became commonplace to enforce racial segregation and the unfounded belief in the superiority of white people and inferiority of Black people.

In Georgia, *Cumming v. Richmond County Board of Education* (1899) was a class-action suit and another landmark U.S. Supreme Court case that further sanctioned the de jure segregation of races in American schools. The plaintiffs, J.W. Cumming, James S. Harper, and John C. Ladeveze, claimed that a $45,000 tax levied against the elementary, middle, and high schools was illegal given that Black people were excluded from high schools and these educational spaces were exclusively for white students. The plaintiffs in the class-action suit sought an injunction to bar the money collection because it was earmarked for the white-only high school system. The Supreme Court justices indicated that they had no jurisdiction, ruling to allow the city to determine the allocation of taxes unless it utterly disregarded Black people's constitutional rights.

Throughout the nineteenth century, there were several developments in mathematics teaching that coincided with the federal government's efforts to shape education and school systems. White men were the primary leaders in shaping the mathematics education landscape in both K-12 and higher education settings. Teaching arithmetic and numbers, calculator usage, logic and the utility of mathematics, teaching methods, and principles of psychology—including how psychology impacts teaching and learning—were the focal points of the development of mathematics education (Bidwell & Clason, 1970). During this period, national education organizations and committees were formed to shape the mathematics education organization (Bidwell & Clason, 1970). Given the racialized nature of the law, society, and education, Black adults and children were not central to these mathematics education developments. These developments represent the foundational white power structure. Whiteness was the ultimate property right, and exclusion of Blackness was central in mathematics education.

Pre and Post *Brown* Mathematics Education Developments

National education organizations and the federal government's legal and economic role in education and mathematics education expanded in the twenty-first century under continued racial turmoil in the larger society and the educational sphere. In the early part of the twenty-first century, education organizations and committees were commissioned to shape the teaching of elementary and secondary arithmetic and mathematics in private and public schools. Mathematics organizations emerged to defend and shape the mathematical landscape in K-12 and college settings.

The Mathematical Association of America (MAA) and the National Council of Teachers of Mathematics (NCTM) were founded in 1915 and 1920, respectively, as two predominately white organizations that have shaped mathematics education. White men were the primary founders and leaders of these organizations, which were historically derived from white institutions of higher education. The MAA focused on collegiate and secondary mathematics. Klein (2003) noted that NCTM was created at the behest of the MAA. NCTM and MAA are organizations that have played a significant role in shaping school mathematics, mathematics content, pedagogy, learning, assessment, research, and the future direction of mathematics education. The 1923 Report, also known as the Reorganization of Mathematics in Secondary Education, was an influential group report designed to shape the discipline. These organizations and committee members shaping mathematics education were primarily white mathematics teachers, professors, researchers, and policymakers.

The early formation of these organizations and committees represents Harris's (1993) arguments about whiteness as property and the exclusion of Blackness in mathematics education. These entities were responsible for providing leadership in mathematics education for the country when Black adults and children were overtly treated as second-class citizens, and racial conflict and racial segregation defined American society and schools. It would be unreasonable to assume that the racial tensions of American society and schools did not affect these organizations and Black adults' and children's mathematics education. Before the landmark *Brown v. Board of Education of Topeka* decision, several mathematics and mathematics education developments excluded Black people altogether.

In the twentieth century, the *Brown* case overruled the *Cumming* and *Plessy* Supreme Court decisions. The justices in the *Brown* decision unanimously ruled that racial segregation in public schools was unconstitutional. The decision helped establish that the "separate but equal" doctrine in education and other places was not equal. The court ruling was instrumental in efforts to desegregate American public schools. *Brown* represents a legal remedy to a social problem (Tate et al., 1993). It also connotes that the decision to desegregate schools was not one that white people willingly conceded to, but one that they were forced to accept through protests, the courts, executive orders, and the military.

Many critical race theorists have offered a critical analysis of the *Brown* decision in the larger field of education and mathematics education (Bell, 1976; Bullock, 2019; Tate et al., 1993). Central to these critiques is the loss of scores of Black educators and administrators, the closure of Black schools, and the integration of Black children into hostile white schools with white educators, students, and stakeholders who did not want them in their spaces and possessed low expectations of them connected to racist assumptions and beliefs about Black people. In those ways, CRT also allows scholars to explore the educational losses that came with desegregation. Integrating schools also inaugurated a period during which Black students were being pushed into lower-level mathematics courses, and gifted education, advanced placement, and honors programs and courses were developing for white educators and students in mathematics as a form of racial segregation based on the idea of white superiority.

FEDERAL LEGISLATION, STANDARDS, STANDARDIZED TESTS, AND RACIALIZED ACHIEVEMENT GAPS

The federal government enacted the ESEA, requiring schools to use standardized tests that ultimately renew and rejuvenate racism in mathematics education. The ESEA required schools to use standardized tests to measure students' performance in mathematics and other subject areas. The federal government's legislative branches have played a significant role in ensuring that standardized tests and standards-based reform shape national, state, and local legislation and policies. The laws and policies enacted fail to take issues of race and racism, past and current inequities, and injustices against Black people—which continue to shape how these legal documents impact Black students' education, in general, and specifically in mathematics education—into consideration (Ladson-Billings, 2006; Martin, 2003). These legal materials maintain and sustain racism (white supremacy) in schools, mathematics settings, and society.

The *No Child Left Behind (NCLB) Act* was one of the policies aimed at shaping Black students' mathematics education, specifically through high-stakes testing. Initially, the ESEA required schools to use standardized tests, and later, NCLB reauthorized and repositioned standardized testing. The policy repositioned standardized testing by seeking "to close the so-called racial achievement gap ... that is to move students who are socially identified as African American [and other marginalized students] from their perceived positions of mathematical illiteracy to new positions of mathematical literacy occupied by Whites" (Martin, 2009, p. 316). The federal government created NCLB based on the premise that white students were mathematically literate and Black students were mathematically illiterate (Davis & Martin, 2008). Embedded in this policy were racist assumptions and beliefs about Black and white students' intellectual abilities in mathematics. Black students unable to earn test scores at the level of their white counterparts were characterized through inferior labels associated with racist beliefs and assumptions about them, their school systems, schools, and mathematics performance (Davis & Martin, 2008; Lattimore, 2001, 2003, 2005).

In 2015, the *Every Student Succeeds* (ESSA) *Act* reauthorized ESEA and replaced the NCLB Act to expand the federal government's role in public education. The Act redirected responsibility for standardized testing and academic standards in mathematics to the states. The ESSA did not require states to adopt Common Core State Standards (CCSS) Initiatives in mathematics (which were developed and sponsored by the National Governors' Association and Council of Chief State School Officers). States could withdraw. Although the legislation prohibited the federal government from influencing states to adopt the standards, the Race to the Top federal grant funds required states who received the funds to adopt the CCSS in mathematics.

Tate's (1995) scholarship is mainly responsible for critically examining mathematics standards on behalf of Black students in urban areas. Tate (1995) and Apple (1993) contend that mathematics standards are a slogan system that led to the illusion that everyone's interests are being met while really representing the interests of those in power (i.e., Whites). Critical race theory's interest convergence principle addresses how whites-only support efforts that converge with their interests. In his critique of CCSS, Gutstein (2010) further states that:

> The lives and voices of people and scholars of color are "conspicuously absent." There is also no mention of class or gender. It is as if one could develop a common core of standards and ignore these issues. Yet institutional and structural racism and political economy loom large in the experiences of urban youth, both within and outside the mathematics classroom. (p. 16)

CCSS lacks a discussion of race, racialization, racism, and equity as if Blacks do not exist, underscoring the disregard for issues of race and inequality that permeates many white mathematics organizations, as well as government boards and committees.

Standardized tests were designed to continue the tradition of upholding racist beliefs and assumptions and subordinating Black students under the idiom of "scientific" theories (Gould, 1981; Ladson-Billings, 1999; Tate, 1993). According to Ladson-Billings (1999), "throughout U.S. history, the subordination of Blacks has been built on "scientific" theories (e.g., intelligence testing), each of which depends on racial stereotypes about Blacks that makes the conditions appear appropriate" (p. 23). Conditions such as low-test scores and high rates of remedial class participation give the appearance that the situation in schools serving large numbers of Black students was appropriate. Tate (1993) made the case that institutional and structural racism has placed standardized testing measures in a position to maintain white privilege and advantages in education, economics, and other human activities. He argued that standardized tests were "scientifically" constructed to reproduce Black students' lived realities socially. He declared that standardized tests were designed to prepare poor Black students to replicate their parents in the labor division by providing them with instruction in mathematics suitable for this purpose.

The tax base supporting predominantly Black schools continues to be insufficient to implement mathematics standards and assessments. Most schools serving large Black student populations operate from an inadequate tax base. While taxes must be given the appearance of neutrality (Tate, 1993), the current school funding system was like the past funding system. Essentially, relying on taxes derived from poor Black communities creates the same funding disparities historically experienced by Black people. The school funding structure makes Black students victims of systemic and structural racism, even if they never experience individual acts of racism (Ladson-Billings, 1999). Black students were generally in schools that were drastically underfunded compared to those serving white students (Kozol, 2012; Ladson-Billings, 1999). Schools serving Black students lack the funding to implement (mathematics) education policies and other costs associated with educating them. Tate (1993) argued that Black students were put in a subordinate position by continually disenfranchising educational and economic policies.

In the twentieth century, the importance of mathematics shifted as science and technology placed new demands on mathematics because of World War II (Moses & Cobb, 2002). International warfare and capitalism are two important pillars of white power that rely on mathematics education to maintain and expand white supremacy. World War II and the Cold War were instrumental to the federal government's increased investment in education and mathematics education. Mathematics was viewed and positioned as the key discipline to advance America's international standing in warfare, economics, and STEM education. A critical race analysis underscores the role that whiteness plays in creating (mathematics) education policies at the national/federal, state, and local levels. Martin (2008) has critiqued mathematics education policy arenas, specifically, the National Math Advisory Panel, as a white institutional space. The panel was mainly composed of white mathematics educators, and "no African American, Latino, or Native American mathematics education researchers were members of the Panel" (Martin, 2008, p. 390). Black mathematics education researchers' exclusion from these policymaking spaces helps to manifest anti-Blackness in decision-making that impacts Black learners, educators, and researchers.

A Critical Race Analysis of Mathematics Curriculum, Pedagogy, and Courses

CRT(ME) exposes Eurocentrism and whiteness in the mathematics education curriculum, pedagogical approaches, and courses. Anderson (1990) asserts that the presence of Eurocentrism and whiteness and the exclusion of Blackness have been institutionalized in the mathematics curriculum. Ladson-Billings (1999) argued that efforts to challenge white supremacy—the dominant culture of power and authority in the educational setting—was muted and erased by the master script. She described Swartz's (1992) notion of the master script as the,

> silenc[ings of] multiple voices and perspectives, primarily legitimizing dominant, White, upper-class, male voicing as the "standard" knowledge students need to know. All other accounts and perspectives are omitted from the master script unless they can be disempowered through misrepresentation. Thus, content that does not reflect the dominant voice must be brought under control, mastered, and then reshaped before it can become a part of the master script. (p. 341)

She continues to note that the mathematics curriculum used in U.S. schools, generation after generation for centuries, "has been reproduced in the objective and subjective pursuit of justifying racism and imperial rule" (p. 350).

White men have been centered in the mathematics curriculum as the intellectual proprietors of knowledge without any consideration of Black people's contributions to mathematics in Africa and the U.S. Anderson (1990) states, "The dominant [mathematics] curriculum in use today throughout the United States is explicit in asserting that mathematics originated among men in Greece and was further developed by European men and their North American descendants" (pp. 349–350). Black mathematicians are seldom mentioned in textbooks or other curricula materials, and are often "relegated to passing sentences, paragraphs, or, on rare occasions, a non sequitur chapter" (p. 350). The dominant mathematics curriculum used in U.S. society reinforces anti-Blackness, as well as racist perceptions of Black people's inferiority (Anderson, 1990) and white people's superiority (Martin, 2009). Davis (2018) argued that the dominant curriculum does not include Black people's contributions and represents a taken-for-granted power structure.

The pedagogical strategies used to teach Black students frequently start from the premise that they are deficient (Ladson-Billings, 1999). Ladson-Billings argues that the instructional approaches used for Black students mainly revolve around some aspect of remediation. Black students' mathematics instruction emphasizes drill, repetition, and convergent, right-answer thinking (Ladson-Billings, 1997). These students rarely receive instruction that encourages them to challenge mathematics rules or to use their prior knowledge and experiences to support and challenge their school mathematics. The masses of Black students, more so those students who were poor, were typically overrepresented in lower-level mathematics courses (Oakes, 1990). Generally, schools serving Black students provide less challenging, intellectually rigorous mathematics instruction and curriculum (Brand et al., 2006; Ladson-Billings, 1997). Taken separately, these acts may appear normal, but taken together, they perform to systematically exclude others—a strategy that was typically associated with the pedagogy in schools serving Black learners.

Moreover, school desegregation gave birth to tracking, a practice used to re-segregate Black and white students in mathematics classrooms (Oakes, 1990). Tracking practices were used to track the masses of Black students into lower-level schooling and mathematics tracks, while advanced programs were used to benefit and protect white students' privileges in mathematics settings (Snipes & Waters, 2005; Tate et al., 1993). The masses of Black students continue to be exposed to lower-level mathematics content, lower-level instruction by inexperienced, less qualified, and less prepared teachers (Oakes, 1990). White students were more often exposed to what was perceived as a better-quality curriculum, higher-level content, and more challenging and rigorous instruction by more qualified, experienced, and prepared teachers in mathematics (Martin, 2007). White students were most often provided access to "gifted" programs, honors programs, and advanced placement programs within "desegregated" schools. Martin (2007) argues

> ...tracking is... one component of a societal sorting system that sets students up for different positions in a social hierarchy that benefits some and marginalizes or disempowers others. Although White students are tracked as well, the larger reward systems in which tracking occurs often afford White students' important opportunities to recover and rebound from these experiences. (p. 17)

In essence, tracking maintains the benefits and advantages conferred to whites without threatening their economic and social advantages (Ladson-Billings, 1999). In addition, the curriculum, instruction, assessment, school funding, and desegregation efforts used to configure the educational system were never designed to provide Black students with the education, particularly in mathematics, that would (a) allow them to infringe on the white monopoly of intellectual, material, physical, and fiscal resources, (b) improve the lived realities of the masses of Black people, and (c) allow them to be self-sufficient. The school system was designed and intended to ensure that the only way Blacks would change their social conditions would be through education to a white standard that would not threaten whites' social, economic, educational, and mathematical interests.

THE LIBERATORY PARADIGM IN MATHEMATICS EDUCATION

Over the last ten years, a paradigm shift has focused on Black learners, providing them with a liberatory mathematics education (Martin, 2010; Martin & McGee, 2009). The paradigm shift has been led by critical Black scholars who seek to challenge the deficit discourse, inadequate conceptualizations of race and racism, privileged perspectives of mathematics, substandard instruction, and mistreatment of Black students in mathematics education research, policy, classrooms, and out of school spaces (Martin, 2008, 2009; Martin et al., 2010). The mathematics education liberatory paradigm has mainly focused on pedagogy and research related to Black students (Martin, 2010). Martin and McGee (2009) argue, "any relevant framing of mathematics education for African Americans must address both the historical oppression that they face and the social realities that they continue to face in contemporary times" (p. 210). As the situation is now, mathematics education is the leading STEM field challenging racism and advancing a liberatory paradigm for Black learners.

Success and high achievement in mathematics education for Black students are mainly based on their grade point average, standardized test scores, and college-level course participation. I have challenged the high achievement and successful Black learners' paradigm in my scholarship because success based on grades, grade point average, standardized test scores, and college-level course participation is grounded in the Eurocentric paradigm and not the liberatory paradigm (Davis, 2018). Successful and high-achieving Black students in mathematics education have a responsibility to give back to their communities as a means of ensuring that others are supported and liberated.

In Martin's (2010) edited book, *Mathematics Teaching, Learning and Liberation in the Lives of Black Children*, he assembled critical Black scholars committed to Black students with a meaningful liberatory mathematics education to "change the direction of research on Black children and mathematics" (p.vi). Scholars have examined and explained Black learners' achievement, learning, experiences, socialization, and identity development through the lens of Black liberation. In my view, Black learners in a liberatory paradigm are instrumental in advancing the Black liberation struggle in and out of mathematics education. Black adults and students in mathematics education must develop a collective agenda that uses their intellect, as well as their economic and political resources, to achieve liberatory outcomes for their people and communities. Such a liberatory mathematical paradigm, as advanced by Black scholars for Black learners, is critically informed (undergirded) by interactively connected conceptual, theoretical, and practical perspectives of CRT(ME).

REFERENCES

Anderson, S. E. (1990). Worldmath curriculum: Fighting Eurocentrism in Mathematics. *The Journal of Negro Education, 59*(3), 348–359.

Apple, M. W. (1993). The politics of official knowledge: Does a national curriculum make sense? *Discourse, 14*(1), 1–16.

Bell, D. (1976). Serving two masters: Integration ideals and client interests in school desegregation litigation. *The Yale Law Journal, 85*(4), 470–516.

Bidwell, J. K., & Clason, R. G. (1970). *Readings in the history of Mathematics education*. National Council of Teachers of Mathematics.

Bullock, E. (2019). Mathematics curriculum reform as racial remediation: A historical counterstory. In J. Davis & C. C. Jett (Eds.), *Critical race theory in Mathematics education* (pp. 32–55). Routledge.

Brand, B. R., Glasson, G. E., & Green, A. M. (2006). Sociocultural factors influencing students' learning in science and Mathematics: An analysis of the perspectives of African American students. *School Science and Mathematics, 106*(5), 228–236.

Davis, J. (2018). Redefining Black students' success and high achievement in Mathematics education: Toward a liberatory paradigm. *Journal of Urban Mathematics Education, 11*, 69–77.

Davis, J. (2019). Using critical race theory as a pedagogical, theoretical, methodological, and analytical tool in mathematics education for Black students in urban areas. In J. Davis & C. C. Jett (Eds.), *Critical race theory in Mathematics education* (pp. 32–55). Routledge.

Davis, J., & Jett, C. C. (Eds.). (2019). *Critical race theory in Mathematics education*. Routledge.

Davis, J., & Martin, D. B. (2008). Racism, assessment, and instructional practices: Implications for mathematics teachers of African American students. *Journal of Urban Mathematics Education, 1*(1), 10–34.

Delgado, R., & Stefancic, J. (2001). *Critical race theory: An introduction*. New York Press.

Dumas, M. J., & Ross, K. M. (2016). "Be real black for me" imagining BlackCrit in education. *Urban Education, 51*(4), 415–442.

Gould, S. J. (1981). *The mismeasure of man*. Norton.

Gutstein, E. (2010). The common core state standards initiative: A critical response. *Journal of Urban Mathematics Education, 3*(1), 9–18.

Harris, C. I. (1993). Whiteness as property. *Harvard Law Review*, 1707–1791.

Jett, C. C. (2019). Mathematical persistence among four African American male graduate students: A critical race analysis of their experiences. *Journal for Research in Mathematics Education, 50*(3), 311–340.

Klein, D. (2003). A brief history of American K-12 Mathematics education in the 20th century. *Mathematical Cognition*, 175–225.

Kozol, J. (2012). *Savage inequalities: Children in America's schools*. Broadway Books.

Ladson-Billings, G. (1997). It doesn't add up: African American students' mathematics achievement. *Journal for Research in Mathematics Education, 28*(6), 697–708.

Ladson-Billings, G. (1999). Chapter 7: Preparing teachers for diverse student populations: A critical race theory perspective. *Review of Research in Education, 24*(1), 211–247.

Ladson-Billings, G. (2006). From the achievement gap to the education debt: Understanding achievement in US schools. *Educational Researcher, 35*(7), 3–12.

Ladson-Billings, G., & Tate, W. F. (1995). Towards a critical race theory of education. *Teachers College Record, 97*(1), 47–68.

Lattimore, R. (2001). The wrath of high-stakes tests. *The Urban Review, 33*(1), 57–67.

Lattimore, R. (2003). African-American students struggle on Ohio's high-stakes test. *Western Journal of Black Studies, 27*(2).

Lattimore, R. (2005). African American students' perceptions of their preparation for a high-stakes mathematics test. *Negro Educational Review, 56*(2/3), 135.

Leonard, J., & Martin, D. B. (Eds.). (2013). *The brilliance of Black children in Mathematics.* Information Age.

Lynn, M., & Adams, M. (2002). Introductory overview to the special issue critical race theory and education: Recent developments in the field. *Equity & Excellence in Education, 35*(2), 87–92.

Martin, D. B. (2003). Hidden assumptions and unaddressed questions in Mathematics for all rhetoric. *The Mathematics Educator, 13*(2).

Martin, D. B. (2007). Beyond missionaries or cannibals: Who should teach mathematics to African American children? *The High School Journal, 91*(1), 6–28.

Martin, D. B. (2008). E(race)ing race from a national conversation on Mathematics teaching and learning: The national Mathematics advisory panel as white institutional space. *The Mathematics Enthusiast, 5*(2), 387–398.

Martin, D. B. (2009). Researching race in Mathematics education. *Teachers College Record, 111*(2), 295–338.

Martin, D. B. (Ed.). (2010). *Mathematics teaching, learning, and liberation in the lives of Black children.* Routledge.

Martin, D. B. (2019). Equity, inclusion, and antiblackness in Mathematics education. *Race Ethnicity and Education, 22*(4), 459–478.

Martin, D. B., Price, P. G., & Moore, R. (2019). Refusing systemic violence against Black children: Toward a Black liberatory Mathematics education. In J. Davis & C. C. Jett (Eds.), *Critical race theory in Mathematics education* (pp. 32–55). Routledge.

Martin, D. B., Gholson, M. L., & Leonard, J. (2010). Mathematics as gatekeeper: Power and privilege in the production of knowledge. *Journal of Urban Mathematics Education, 3*(2), 12–24.

Martin, D. B., & McGee, E. (2009). Mathematics literacy for liberation: Reframing mathematics education for African-American children. In B. Greer, S. Mukhophadhay, S. Nelson-Barber, & A. Powell (Eds.), *Culturally responsive Mathematics education* (pp. 207–238). Routledge.

Morales-Doyle, D., & Gutstein, E. R. (2019). Racial capitalism and STEM education in Chicago public schools. *Race Ethnicity and Education, 22*(4), 525–544.

Moses, R., & Cobb, C. E. (2002). *Radical equations: Civil rights from Mississippi to the algebra project.* Beacon Press.

Mutegi, J. W. (2011). The inadequacies of "science for all" and the necessity and nature of a socially transformative curriculum approach for African American science education. *Journal of Research in Science Teaching, 48*, 301–316.

Oakes, J. (1990). *Multiplying inequalities: The effects of race, social class, and tracking on opportunities to learn mathematics and science*. The RAND Corporation.

Phillips, S. L. (1998). Convergence of the critical race theory workshop with LatCrit theory: A history. *University of Miami Law Review, 53*(4), 1247–1256.

Snipes, V. T., & Waters, R. D. (2005). The Mathematics education of African Americans in North Carolina: From the brown decision to no child left behind. *Negro Educational Review, 56*(2/3), 107.

Swartz, E. (1992). Emancipatory narratives: Rewriting the master script in the school curriculum. *The Journal of Negro Education, 61*(3), 341–355.

Tate IV, W. F. (1993). Advocacy versus economics: A critical race analysis of the proposed national assessment in Mathematics. *Thresholds in Education, 19*(1–2), 16–22.

Tate IV, W. F. (1995). School mathematics and African American students: Thinking seriously about opportunity-to-learn standards. *Educational Administration Quarterly, 31*(3), 424–448.

Tate IV, W. F. (1997). Critical race theory and education: History, theory and implications. In M. Apple (Ed.), *Review of research in education* (pp. 195–247). American Educational Research Association.

Tate IV, W. F., Ladson-Billings, G., & Grant, C. A. (1993). The Brown decision revisited: Mathematizing social problems. *Educational Policy, 7*(3), 255–275.

CHAPTER 28

Mobility of Syrian–Canadian Students and Continuity of Math Education: A Comparative Curriculum Mapping Approach

Dania Wattar and Emmanuelle Le Pichon

INTRODUCTION

The increased mobility of students in education poses new challenges to our schools (Herzog-Punzenberger et al., 2017; Le Pichon, Siarova, & Szonyi, 2020). How can we welcome these students taking into account their previous learning? Typically, the school integration of newcomer students is based primarily on the expectations of the host country's system. The expectations of the host school systems are not only expectations related to the language of the school but also the curriculum. Each country and each Canadian province defines learning objectives according to the age of the students. What we too often forget is that school curricula vary considerably from country to country and, in Canada, from province to province. If the above reasoning is accurate, then teachers cannot expect the same from a student coming from Syria, China, or even Alberta to Ontario. The curricula of the countries in which the students have studied need to be considered in order to understand what these same students have already learned and how they learned it. Therefore, we propose that a constructive strategy in this regard should include a thorough exploration of the curriculum of the country in which the students have been

---

D. Wattar (✉) · E. Le Pichon
University of Toronto, Toronto, ON, Canada
e-mail: dania.wattar@utoronto.ca

E. Le Pichon
e-mail: e.lepichon@utoronto.ca

© The Author(s), under exclusive license to Springer Nature Switzerland AG 2022
A. A. Abdi and G. W. Misiaszek (eds.), *The Palgrave Handbook on Critical Theories of Education*, https://doi.org/10.1007/978-3-030-86343-2_28

schooled. In this study, funded by a SSHRC Institutional Grant (Le Pichon, 2018–2019), we explored the extent to which the identification of curriculum similarities and differences between home and host countries can be used to support the educational mobility of the students. The expected benefit from developing a comparative curriculum mapping of math education in Syria and Ontario (Canada) was that it could help teachers gain a clearer picture of previously acquired academic skills, as well as potential areas requiring extra attention.

In our explorative study, we examined this strategy as applied to the mathematics curriculum at the junior and intermediate levels. First, we compared the Ontario and Syrian mathematics (Grades 4–8) curricula in terms of content, language, and approach to teaching mathematics. The goal was to identify differences and similarities between the programs. Once the expectations of the Ontario and Syrian programs were matched, we developed a comprehensive resource for teachers and parents and posted it on a bilingual website. The ultimate aim was to use this study to inform teachers of these differences, help them adjust their expectations to the newcomer population from Syria, and provide them with a clearer picture of previously acquired academic skills and potential areas requiring attention.

Overview of the Curricula

The Province of Ontario

Education in Canada is a provincial responsibility. Therefore, curriculum documents are issued by the Ministry of Education in each province. In Ontario, the Ministry of Education sets overall and specific expectations that teachers must teach in their program at a particular grade. The mathematics curriculum outlines a set of expectations in different strands, including number sense and numeration, measurement, geometry and spatial sense, patterning and algebra, and data management and probability. The curriculum also outlines basic considerations to accommodate the needs of language learners, such as language learning strategies, and a discussion of antidiscrimination in Math education. It includes recommendations to accommodate language learners, whether in English or French (Ontario Ministry of Education, 2005).

It is interesting to note that increasing attention is being paid to the language learners of the school in the curricula. In 2020, the curriculum was revised, and considerations for language learners included additional recommendations such as an emphasis on the orientation toward language as a resource (Ruiz, 1984): "Translingual practice is creative and strategic, and allows students to communicate, interact, and connect with peers and teachers for a variety of purposes" (Ontario Ministry of Education, 2020, p. 96). The document also emphasized the importance of building on students' strengths, social and cultural background, and acknowledging the need to provide tasks that are accessible and mathematically challenging. Finally, the ministry recommends representing concepts in different languages and to work with families and community members to support student learning (Ontario Ministry of Education, 2020).

The Context in Syria

Education in Syria is centralized. The Syrian Ministry of Education issues curriculum textbooks that are taught across the country. These textbooks include a student copy and a teacher guide for each subject. Mathematics textbooks include different units, with each unit consisting of different lessons that teachers are expected to teach throughout the year. A lesson includes learning objectives, concepts, descriptions, rules, properties, and activities. Each unit includes a set of problems to be solved by students.

Teachers across Syria are expected to go through the textbooks, teach content, and students work on the problems that are in the textbook. Some teachers use additional questions, visuals, or manipulatives to support teaching, but teaching is primarily based on the ministry-issued textbooks. These textbooks can be accessed online (see Syrian Ministry of Education, 2021). The language of instruction in Syria is Arabic with some English and French concepts included in some subjects such as math and science (Wattar, 2014).

CURRICULUM MAPPING

We analyzed the documents identified as official curriculum. With respect to the Ontario curriculum, we examined the mathematics curriculum for Grades 1–8 (Ontario Ministry of Education, 2005), with a focus on the junior and intermediate levels (Grades 4–8), which are critical in the transition to secondary school. This document defines general and specific expectations for each grade level. With respect to the Syrian curriculum, we considered the official textbooks issued by the Ministry of Education from Grades 4 to 8 (Syrian Ministry of Education,). The analyses include the repertoire of topics taught for each grade level and the different characteristics of the text, including the language of instruction, numbers used, and teaching strategies. The identification of the topics studied at each level is based on the identification of more general strands that are taught throughout the years. To illustrate the flow of topics for Grades 4 to 8 in the Syrian math curriculum and facilitate curriculum mapping, we followed the model established by the Ontario Ministry of Education on its resource website for teachers (Edugains, n.d) (see Table 28.1).

Table 28.1: This chart is a summary of the topics taught in mathematics in Ontario from Grades 1–8 on the Ministry of Education website (Edugains, n.d.). This document is often used by Ontario teachers to understand how each topic (e.g., addition and subtraction) is taught progressively over the years

Table 28.1 Reproduction of the synthesis of the Ontarian Curriculum in math, Grades 1–8 (Edugains, n.d.)

Grade 1	Grade 2	Grade 3	Grade 4	Grade 5	Grade 6	Grade 7	Grade 8
Addition and Subtraction Problems with Sums to 10 • Add, subtract and identify strategies • Solve a variety of problems that involve addition and/or subtraction	**Addition and Subtraction Problems with Sums to 20** • Add, subtract and identify strategies • Solve a variety of problems that involve addition and/or subtraction	**Addition and Subtraction Problems with Sums to 100** • Add, subtract and identify strategies • Solve a variety of problems that involve addition and/or subtraction	**Operations Involving Numbers 0 to 10 000** • Add and subtract four-digit whole numbers • Multiply and divide 2-digit by 1-digit whole numbers • Investigate and apply the commutative and distributive properties	**Operations Involving Numbers 0.01 to 10 000** • Multiply 2-digit by 2-digit whole numbers • Divide 3-digit by 1-digit whole numbers • Solve whole number multiplication and division problems	**Operations Involving Numbers 0.01 to 1 000 000** • Solve problems involving addition and subtraction of whole and decimal numbers • Multiply and divide 4-digit by 2-digit whole numbers • Solve problems involving multiplication and division up to 4-digit by 2-digit whole numbers	**Represent, Compare, Order and Operate Using Decimal Numbers** • Represent, compare, and order decimal numbers to hundredths • Add and subtract decimal numbers • Multiply and divide to thousandths by whole numbers	**Multi-Step Problems Involving Whole and Decimal Numbers** • Add, subtract, multiply, and divide whole and decimal numbers • Solve multi-step problems involving whole and decimal numbers

Grade 1	Grade 2	Grade 3	Grade 4	Grade 5	Grade 6	Grade 7	Grade 8
			• Connect between student-generated and standard algorithms for multiplication and division • Solve problems involving addition, subtraction, and multiplication	• Add and subtract decimal numbers to hundredths • Solve problems involving addition and subtraction of decimal numbers	• Solve problems involving multiplication and division that involve decimal tenths with whole numbers	• Apply order of operations to evaluate numerical expressions involving whole and decimal numbers • Solve single- and-multi-step problems involving operations with whole and decimal numbers Convert between first degree metric units Solve real-life problems that require conversions	

(continued)

Table 28.1 (continued)

Grade 1	Grade 2	Grade 3	Grade 4	Grade 5	Grade 6	Grade 7	Grade 8
Compare and Order Numbers to 20 • Estimate quantities • Compare and order numbers to 20 based on quantity • Compare and order numbers to 20 using a number line	**Multiplication and Division with Products to 20** • Decompose numbers into groups of equal size • Investigate combining equal groups (multiplication) • Investigate partitioning into equal groups (division) • Investigate division as equal sharing: – find the number of items in a group – find the number of groups for a set of items	**Multiplication up to 7 × 7 and Division to 49 ÷ 7** • Multiply and divide using a variety of mental strategies					

This table allows teachers to understand what is essential for the academic progress of the students and in the introduction of new subjects. For instance, a teacher who welcomes a twelve-year-old student will refer to the chart to determine the essential learning expectations for further learning. Diagnostic assessment is done in reverse order, starting with the expected knowledge corresponding to a particular age and working backwards to the essential knowledge of previous years if the expectations are not met. This allows teachers to understand what is essential to progress and what is not.

Since the topics are organized differently in the Syrian curriculum, the classification of topics in Arabic was done in three steps. The first step was to identify the themes common to both curricula (Syria and Ontario). This was followed by identifying the organization of these topics over the years of elementary school in Syria. The final list of themes, organized by grade level, allowed the creation of summary tables (see Table 28.2) similar to those developed by the Ministry of Education in Ontario.

Figure 28.1: This image includes four Syrian mathematics textbooks. Each textbook was incorporated in the analyses. The different strands were identified and organized into units categorized by grade level. This classification allowed the elaboration of a table in Arabic (see Table 28.2), later translated into English. The table includes each of the strands and the details of the content by grade level (see Tables 28.2 and 28.3)

Table 28.2: This table represents the organization of topics in the Syrian math curriculum from Grades 4 to 8. Thus, the table provides an overview of how each topic (e.g., operations) is taught progressively over the years.

Table 28.2 Synthesis in Arabic of the Syrian curriculum grades 4–8

الصف الثامن Grade 8	الصف السابع Grade 7	الصف السادس Grade 6	الصف الخامس Grade 5	الصف الرابع Grade 4	
الأعداد العادية والعمليات عليها الجمع والطرح الضرب القسمة تمرينات ومسائل	الأعداد الطبيعية الأعداد الصحيحة الجمع والطرح الضرب القسمة الأعداد العادية العمليات على الأعداد العادية الأعداد العادية ومعلم المستوي	الأعداد الطبيعية جمع الأعداد الطبيعية وطرحها ضرب الأعداد الطبيعية قسمة الأعداد الطبيعية	الأعداد الطبيعية قراءة وكتابة الأعداد الطبيعية بالملايين(الآن تستعمل الأرقام الإنكليزية) كتابة العدد بالصيغة العددية والصيغة اللفظية استخدام جدول الخانات تقريب الأعداد الطبيعية تقريب العدد إلى منزلة محددة جمع الأعداد الطبيعية و طرحها: جمع الأعداد ضمن الملايين طرح عدد من عدد آخر مقارنة الأعداد الطبيعية حتى الملايين ترتيب الأعداد الطبيعية حتى الملايين ضرب الأعداد الطبيعية	- أعداد حتى ٩٩٩٩٩ تمثيل العدد في جدول المنازل كتابة العدد بالصيغة التفصيلية والصيغة اللفظية موازنة الأعداد (مقارنة) من خمس منازل وترتيبها التقريب إلى أقرب عشرة التقريب إلى أقرب مئة جمع أعداد مؤلفة من خمس منازل طرح أعداد مكونة من خمس منازل معنى القسمة كتابة عبارة القسمة وتحديد المقسوم و المقسوم عليه والناتج (ناتج القسمة) حساب ناتج القسمة الربط بين الضرب والقسمة	الأعداد العمليات الحسابية مقارنة الأعداد (موازنة الأعداد) الكسور والأعداد العشرية
قوى الأعداد العادية قوى العدد ١٠ قواعد على العدد ١٠ قوى صحيحة لعدد نسبي الجذور التربيعية وخواصها					

Fig. 28.1 Syrian maths books and mapping

Table 28.3 Synthesis in English of the Syrian curriculum Grades 4–8

Topic	Grade 4	Grade 5	Grade 6	Grade 7	Grade 8
Numbers	• Numbers to 99999 *Note: The book for this grade uses the numbers ١, ٢, ٣, ٤ • representing numbers in place value table • writing numbers in details (using place value) and words • comparing and ordering numbers from five digits • even and odd numbers	• Natural numbers • reading and writing numbers in millions *note: numbers are written the same as in English (1, 2, 3) • comparing natural numbers (millions) • ordering natural numbers (millions)	• Natural numbers • adding, subtracting and multiplying natural numbers	• Natural numbers • writing numbers using digits and words • using place value table	Rational numbers • operations on large numbers
Operations	adding numbers from five digits division writing a division sentence and	adding and subtracting natural numbers adding and subtracting numbers (in millions)	Addition and subtraction of natural numbers Multiplication of natural numbers	Integers (addition and subtraction) Multiplication Division Rational numbers Operations on Rational numbers	(Addition and Subtraction Multiplication solving World problem

The table shows the progress made in each theme in Grades 4–8 based on each strand. For example, in the table above, the first row shows the topics related to the number strand. As can be seen, in Grade 4, Syrian students are expected to learn numbers up to 99,999, to represent numbers in a place value chart, and to write them. The expectations for the year are also to learn to compare, order numbers up to five digits, and even and odd numbers.

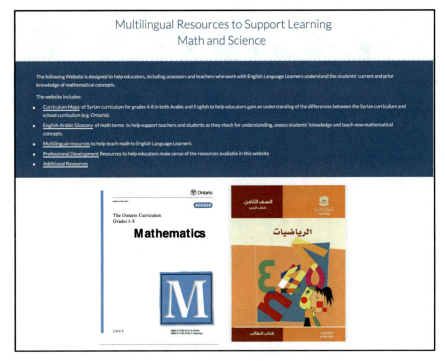

Fig. 28.2 The website features the multilingual resources as well as the curriculum mapping and the comparative analysis of the programs

In Grade 5, concepts are expanded and students are expected to learn to order, compare, and write numbers up to one million. In Grade 8, rational numbers are introduced and students are expected to apply operations on large numbers.

Table 28.3: This table shows the progress made in each topic in Grades 4–8 based on each strand in the Syrian curriculum

First Results

The Syrian Curriculum

One of the first observations when analyzing the Syrian curriculum is the change in the spelling of the numbers in the fifth grade. The first author of this chapter, having grown up in Syria, noted this discovery which represented a change in the 2000s in mathematics education in Syria. In Grades 1–4 textbooks, the Hindu–Arabic script of the numerals (i.e., ١،٢،٣،٤،٥،٦،٧،٨،٩،١٠) was used. In the 5th grade, the Arabic numerals used in Canada were introduced (i.e., 1,2,3,4,5,6,7,8,9,10). In addition, Arabic symbols (i.e., س، ع، ص) were replaced in 5th grade by the symbols of the Latin alphabet (i.e., x, y, z) in equations. One must be aware of these important changes when receiving a student from Syria in Canada. Indeed, assessing mathematical knowledge without taking this aspect into account could lead to thinking that students cannot read or count if they are presented with exercises containing the Arabic numerals in Grade 5, when in fact they have simply not learned to read the numbers in this script yet, which does not affect their ability to calculate but implies learning this new script.

To this difficulty is added the orientation of the mathematical writing. Indeed, the direction of writing equations in the textbooks from right-to-left is replaced in Grade 5 by equations written from left-to-right. On the other hand, the text explaining the equations is always written in Arabic and is read from right-to-left. Again, this observation is crucial because it means that Syrian students have to adapt to this new difficulty in fifth grade.

These initial observations, while seeming innocuous at first glance, greatly complicate the diagnostic evaluation of these students if they are ignored. However, if they are considered, they can allow teachers to adapt the right measures and to evaluate students at their proper level.

Analyses of the Differences and Similarities

The in-depth analysis of the curricula allowed for the perspective of differences in terms of program content and pedagogical approach to mathematics teaching.

Grade Expectations and Extent of Learning for Each Grade Level

Although by the end of Grade 12, Syrian and Ontario students have achieved roughly the same academic level in equivalent areas, including calculus and algebra, the levels at which topics are introduced differ across programs. For example, exponents appear in Grade 6 in Syria, while, in Ontario, exponential notation and area measurement are linked (e.g., cm^2), but the explicit introduction of exponents with repeated multiplication occurs only in Grade 8. Similar observations were noted for theoretical probability.

Theoretical probability is introduced in Grade 7 in Syria. Students are expected to learn how to calculate theoretical probabilities as well as events and complementary events (Syrian Ministry of Education, 2018, 2019c). In Ontario, complementary events appear in Grade 8, but the concept of theoretical probability is gradually introduced from Grade 6 as follows: in Grade 6, students are asked to predict the outcome of an experiment and to represent their prediction as a ratio, that is, the number of favorable outcomes to the total number of possible outcomes. Students are then expected to relate this ratio to theoretical probability. In Grade 7, they learn how to perform experiments involving two independent events and compare experimental and theoretical probability (Edugains., n.d.; Ontario Ministry of Education, 2005). These examples provide insights into the differences in the introduction of concepts in the two curricula and how these differences affect the expectations of teachers in both countries.

One might conclude that, in principle, Syrian students newly arrived in Ontario would be at a relative advantage in terms of content as students in Syria are often expected to apply theoretical concepts earlier than in Ontario. However, this does not mean that students in Ontario are learning less mathematics than in Syria. In fact, as we have seen in the preceding comparison, Ontario students are gradually introduced to the subject of probability and theoretical probability. Additionally, they are taught to conduct experiments, compare experimental and theoretical concepts, and apply the rules of theoretical probability to learn about complementary events.

Moreover, the comparison showed how both curricula differ in terms of process and pedagogy. In Syria, concepts are condensed into one grade and students are expected to learn different concepts in a short period of time. In Ontario, concepts are spread over three school years. While at first glance, the approach may seem diluted, one quickly realizes that the purpose of spreading a concept over three years is to develop a gradual and deeper knowledge of that same concept. This observation is reflected in the topic of data management.

In Ontario, students are expected to collect, organize, and represent data beginning in Grade 4. They learn to create and conduct a survey, and to organize and represent data in a simple manner. Each year, students are introduced to new types of graphs and build on what they have learned in previous years by going further. In Grade 5, students learn about pictographs, bar graphs, stem and leaf plots. Continuous line graphs are introduced in Grade 6, a variety of graphs to represent discrete and continuous data in Grade 7, and, in Grade 8, histograms are taught. Creating and conducting surveys develops throughout the year. Students begin by creating simple surveys and continue to learn important elements of survey creation, such as identifying bias (Grade 7) and creating a survey or experiment involving numerical data (Grade 8). In contrast, Syrian textbooks emphasize reading, interpreting, and constructing graphs. In Grade 7, the emphasis is on representing and reading different types of graphs, such as bar graphs, double bar graphs, histograms, and pie charts. They do not include designing surveys, experiments, and learning about bias.

Differences also appear in numeracy: while number comparison and rounding appear in Grade 6 in both the Syrian and Ontarian curricula, the range of numbers used in Ontario is up to one million while in Syria it is one thousand million. The explanation of this difference is often attributed to socio-economic circumstances: the value of the Syrian currency is much lower and fluctuating than the Canadian dollar. As a result, Syrian students have to learn how to manage higher numbers than their Canadian counterparts.

In the previous examples, we discussed how topics are presented and taught differently in Ontario and Syria. We focused on examples that illustrate different approaches to teaching content. In Syria, the approach is abstract, and knowledge is condensed. In Ontario, topics are introduced gradually and reinvested in an experiential learning perspective. However, this approach means that Ontario students access some topics later than their Syrian counterparts. The different approaches to teaching the subjects are also evident in the way the subjects are organized and presented over the years. In the next section, we will look at how subjects are organized differently in each program.

Strands and Organization of Topics

In Ontario, the curriculum includes five strands (number sense and numeration, data management, patterning and algebra, measurement, and geometry) (Ontario Ministry of Education, 2005). In 2020, the Ministry of Education introduced the strand of social emotional learning. With this change, a new name was introduced for each strand, the result being: number, algebra, data, spatial sense, and financial literacy (Ontario Ministry of Education, 2021). These strands are the same in Grades 1–8.

The organization of the Syrian school program differs greatly. The number of units and topics vary by grade. Units do not always have a "general" title, but often include a more specific title. For example, Grade 4 math includes 9 units. Unlike Ontario's general strands, the units vary: while some encompass many subtopics like geometry, other units address specific subtopics such as multiplication and division levels 1 and 2. For instance, Grade 6 includes six units, and each unit includes more than one topic or strand. Unit 1 includes representing graphs, natural numbers, lines, angles, and triangles. Grade 7 includes eight units: numbers and operations, algebraic expressions and equations, rate and ratios, symmetry, parallelogram, triangle and circle, 3-D shapes, statistics, and probability. While some topics such as number sense appear at each grade, other topics such as data management and probability are highlighted differently for each grade. In addition, in Grade 8, mathematics is grouped into two main strands: algebra and geometry.

Pedagogical Considerations

In addition to differences in the organization of subjects and in the extent of learning per topic and grade level, the curricula differ in the pedagogical approach to teaching mathematics. Syria generally follows a deductive approach: students learn a concept, memorize it, and then apply it by solving problems. Therefore, each lesson begins with the concept and its definition, a mathematical procedure, followed by examples and activities to learn how to solve such a problem. As an example, consider how the topic of events and probability is presented in Grade 7. The following structure appears: a connection to previous learning is presented in a short paragraph, followed by an example introducing the topic, the explanation of the results, and finally the rule of theoretical probability. The textbooks then include examples of how to use the rule, before another rule is introduced about the probability of events happening. Another concept is then introduced and the lesson concludes with problems.

The Ontario curriculum emphasizes exploration, the use of a variety of strategies to solve problems, and the approach to teaching. This represents a more inductive and explorative approach to learning. Using the example of probability, we see how the concept is gradually introduced: with the objectives of Grades 6–8 in mind, students from Grade 1 are introduced to experiments, the prediction of outcomes, their representations, the outcomes as a ratio, followed by the comparison of the results of their experiments to theoretical probability. Students are expected to represent the probability as a value between 0 and 1. Grade 7 includes research, prediction skills, and applications of the terms as well as experiments involving two independent events. Then, again a comparison between experimental and theoretical probability is added to the program.

Lastly, in Grade 8, students study the discrepancy between theoretical and experimental probability, making connections, complementary probability. Finally solving problems involving experimental and theoretical probability as well as complementary events are discussed.

This brief presentation of the comparison of curricula highlighted differences not only in terms of content or programming but also in terms of pedagogical approach. All of these aspects put together particularly complicate the diagnostic evaluation of newly arrived Syrian students in Ontario and the organization of the continuity of their education beyond the language difference.

With this in mind, we set out to understand the effects of our results on different groups: as both authors of this chapter are instructors at the Ontario Institute for Studies in Education, the first group was made up of Teacher Candidates (TCs) and graduate students. The goal was to help these future teachers develop an understanding of the challenges imposed by the mobility of newly arrived Syrian students in learning mathematics. The second group was composed more casually by Syrian parents whom the first author met through her work with a non-governmental organization and a private Islamic school. In the following paragraph, we report on our preliminary reflections on these presentations and how they led to the development of new research questions, which are the basis of our current projects on mathematics and science education in Canada.

Dissemination of the Results

After the curriculum mapping and glossary layout, we created a website and uploaded the curriculum mapping and glossary. As stated at the beginning of this chapter, the ultimate goal was to enable teachers to better assess their Arabic-speaking students from this country. In doing so, we realized that not only were we making the resources accessible to teachers but that these resources could also be useful to parents and communities.

Reflections Based on Teacher Candidates' Feedback

Workshops, discussions, and one-on-one sessions were conducted with teacher candidates in two courses on supporting language learners and students from refugee backgrounds in 2019 and 2020. During these sessions, students were provided with the results of the research presented above, summarized in a visual overview of both curricula. The goal was to help teachers understand their students' backgrounds in order to make a smoother transition from one school system to another. In addition, we wanted to ensure that teachers give students opportunities to develop their prior knowledge of mathematics and demonstrate their learning, and, in doing so, challenge them to succeed. Both similarities and differences between curricula were exemplified as well as some examples of teaching approaches in both systems. An activity invited TCs to solve some mathematical problems and shared their insights on the activity and its potential to help them support their students' learning.

Organization of the Sessions

A series of mathematical questions that addressed issues related to linguistic and cultural understanding were developed based on the results of the curriculum mapping. The levels of complexity increased as the tasks unfolded. The idea was to put TCs in a situation of linguistic and cultural insecurity by offering them mathematical texts as they are presented in the Syrian program. However, they were also presented with the key to solve the difficulties. For example, the operations were presented in the Hindu–Arabic script with their correspondence in the Arabic script; the mathematical sentences from right-to-left and not from left-to-right; and some of the problems to be solved required specific cultural knowledge which complicated the mathematical solution. Teachers would discover quickly that in order to solve the problems, they would have to use metacognitive strategies (inference, deduction, comparisons, ask for assistance, collaboration …). Additionally, the mapping of topics allowed teachers to make informed understanding of topics that were explored in different grades as well as how topics are taught over the years.

Effects of Training Sessions on Teacher Candidates

The first set of comments from the teachers crystallized around their feelings during these activities. By trying to solve mathematical problems in a different language and context, not being the creators of the activities themselves, they had to constantly check their work to solve problems that they usually solve with ease and became more self-aware. They declared spending more time than they were used to decoding, translating, and answering simple arithmetic questions.

A second set of comments from teachers about this experience was that this workshop gave them a better understanding of the many facets of mathematical learning. Some teachers explained that prior to this session, they wondered how students came up with certain answers in their classes. By confronting these difficulties themselves, they understood the possible errors induced by the context and not by the degree of mathematical difficulty. For example, a translation chart helped them decode numbers in arithmetic tasks. However, when they had to solve right-to-left problems, they were left with questions such as if the place value (e.g., the place of ones, tens, and hundreds) in a number was the same in Arabic and English. During the workshop, they understood the complexity that students face in their educational mobility and the importance of recognizing both the students' efforts and their backgrounds.

Third, teachers have been led to revisit the importance of metacognitive strategies. In one session, a teacher privately asked the presenter what place value was and how to understand the value of each digit in a number in Arabic. Another asked the question in the group. In another workshop, no one asked about place value and one teacher ended up guessing while trying different solutions. This experience opened up discussions about the importance of supporting students, presenting them with a welcoming environment, and encouraging them to collaborate. Even though collaboration is encouraged in Ontario, pairwise collaboration is not traditional in teaching and learning mathematics. Each student must learn to solve a problem on their own. Yet, a collaboration between these teachers was paramount in accomplishing this task. It is important to understand that students rarely use asking for assistance as a strategy (Le Pichon et al., 2009).

Fourth, these activities sparked discussions around the role of cultures in the construction of knowledge. Teachers were interested in learning about different number systems, an interest that led to talking about the contributions of Arab mathematicians to mathematics, or mathematicians from around the world. Students then raised the possibility of inviting their own students to explore the history of mathematics to engage the school community in recognizing the contributions of different civilizations to the development of this science. Some TCs subsequently sent follow-up messages in which they shared resources on number systems, the contributions of different civilizations to mathematics, or resources such as the 1001 Muslim Contributions to Learning (National Geographic Kids, 2012).

The sessions ended with discussions of the implications of this work for the teaching practices of the teachers in question. These discussions provided TCs with an understanding of the importance of building on students' linguistic and cultural funds of knowledge (Moll et al., 1992). Among the topics discussed in the different sessions were the need to build on students' prior knowledge and the possibility of using translanguaging practices (Vogel & García, 2017). These sessions allowed students to consider languages in a different light. Languages had become tools for transmission rather than an end in itself, allowing students to access academic content. Pedagogical practice involving clear instructions and the leverage of the languages present to convey information appeared essential. In this context, the legitimacy of monoglossic practices (one class, one language, see also Blommaert, 2009) was largely questioned. Finally, these exercises in cultural decentration allowed candidates to become aware of the possibility of providing a relevant and rewarding context for students to increase their motivation, through, e.g., historical research on the origin of a spelling or a concept and its discovery. In sum, TCs were able to challenge the assumption that learning of mathematics is neutral, and replace it with a linguistically and culturally situated science. They experienced firsthand the crucial role of language and culture in learning mathematics.

Although the project was primarily aimed at developing tools for teachers, the mapping and resources developed have proven to be particularly useful for parents and community inclusion.

Effect of Training Sessions on Parents

During the year of the project's development, the first author had the opportunity to disseminate the results through workshops, group discussions, and one-on-one sessions with parents involved in various associations. Despite the differences in socio-economic status, educational backgrounds, and length of stay in Canada of the parent communities, the reaction was unanimous: all were eager to better understand the Canadian school system and our approach proved to be particularly fruitful for this understanding.

Many parents expressed both (1) their dissatisfaction with the Canadian curriculum and (2) their sense of disempowerment.

(1) Dissatisfaction: As we saw earlier, the differences between the curricula are numerous and the density of the Syrian program was compared to the spread of the same subjects over three years in Canada. The parents' reactions to discovering the similarities and differences between the Syrian and Ontario curricula were invaluable. For them, it was also an opening to a new perspective: those who tended to think that their children were not learning because they did not have to memorize rules, spent their days experimenting, and took three years to learn a concept that they could have learned in one year, felt dissatisfied. They particularly appreciated the opportunity to discuss the advantages and disadvantages of both programs.

(2) Disempowerment: While feeling dissatisfied with the Canadian program, parents also felt incompetent and disempowered in their ability to help their children progress and learn. There was a disconnection between the children who were educated in a system inherent to their Canadian life and the parents who did not understand the system in which their children were being educated. Based on the

recognition of parents' experiences, their knowledge, and a partnership approach, parents felt legitimized in their primary role as educators of their children. Importantly, the resources we developed made the Ontario curriculum accessible to them and gave them the opportunity to act upon the situation. We often repeat that students learn from what is familiar to them, forgetting that the same is true for parents. In this case, using the Syrian curriculum to help them understand the Ontario curriculum allowed them to feel connected to their children's education and to regain confidence in their abilities as educators of their children. Introducing them to these tools allowed us to consider their concerns in collective discussions and to value their own funds of knowledge.

Although the goal of our work was not to involve parents, circumstances have shown us that the simple act of comparing programs allowed us to influence both parents' satisfaction with the Ontario school system and their ability to take action in their children's education, regardless of their academic level.

Collaboration Between Schools and Parents Based on Reciprocal Understanding

While significant efforts have been made to provide resources on mathematics education in many languages (e.g., Ontario Ministry of Education, 2021), our project revealed significant gaps in the inclusion of families of newly arrived students, and in our case, Syrian families in particular. The recent shift to an asset-based pedagogy is challenging existing monoglossic approaches to the current curricula and evaluation practices. This expression used by Blommaert does not refer to the use of a single language but more broadly to the narrow perspective of a focus on a single culture and the separation of knowledge (Blommaert, 2009).

The research we undertook did not seek to solve the problem of the integration of language learners in the school system by addressing their individual needs but rather to better understand the different perspectives through the mapping of curricula in different countries. This research has revealed differences and similarities in content (curriculum content), script and syntax of mathematics (e.g., in the way mathematics is written), pedagogy (inductive versus deductive), and grade distribution. In spite of all these differences, an important aspect was that both programs allowed students to complete their schooling with broadly the same learning outcomes. This aspect allowed us to reassure the parents about the content of the Ontario curriculum.

Thus, an essential outcome of this preliminary research is that our approach reinforced this asset-based pedagogy by re-considering the linguistic and cultural richness that newcomers bring with them (see for instance Seals & Peyton, 2017; Guo, 2012). The sessions allowed teacher candidates to deepen their understanding of the many factors that influence the transition from one school program to another. Through an intercultural lens, they were invited to think beyond the curriculum that they teach and know. They became aware of the diverse ways of knowing, teaching, and learning. The workshops often allowed teachers to think about their students in new ways, rethink how they teach math to language learners and learn new insights about the contribution of different societies to mathematics learning throughout history (see also Le Pichon et al., 2020).

Additionally, and in contrast to previous work, which often focuses on the education of teachers and on language and translation issues, the comparative curriculum approach seems to have put parents back at the heart of their children's education. The enthusiasm of the parents toward the discovery of the differences and similarities of the systems seemed to restore their sense of empowerment. The transformation of parents' attitudes and willingness to support their children brought about by the workshops is both consistent with and goes beyond the emerging work on the inclusion of family languages in education (Piccardo, 2013). It involves in-depth work on our own system of teaching the school systems and curricula of the populations that join the Canadian school system. It also helps educators to work toward recognitive justice in their practice (Gale & Densmore, 2000). This finding allows us to assume that outreach to parent communities, which would include a comparison of home and target country knowledge, would pave the way for a strong partnership between parents and schools (as also suggested by Antony-Newman, 2020). This intercultural framework invites parents to become true partners in supporting their children's learning. It involves a consultative step of evaluating their contribution, which can lead to emancipation.

Similar to the study of Attar et al. (2020), one essential aspect to the success of our work with Syrian communities is the first author's membership in that community. She was raised in Syria and was able to conduct the workshops in Arabic. She was therefore a role model for the parents' community and the shared language and culture helped build trust within the mutual recognition. This aspect is an essential element of mediation between the parties represented by the school institution and the newly arrived families. The training of mediators from the communities in question, also called settlement workers in Ontario, could perhaps open the door to a policy of inclusion based on reciprocal understanding rather than a policy of integration that seeks to fill the individual gaps of newcomers to the target society.

While our project has been very beneficial from both TCs and parents' standpoints, it has not yet allowed us to reach out to the in-service teaching community. The resources developed were used as a basis to conduct workshops with TCs to develop intercultural understanding and metacognitive awareness. The question, then, is the following: how can we act to bring about sustainable change? What are their specific needs and expectations? The projects we are currently working on explore these questions more closely, seeking new opportunities for dialog. We believe that they represent a step toward emancipating the decolonization of curricula by broadening through the perspectives of newcomers in education.

REFERENCES

Antony-Newman, M. (2020). Curriculum orientations and their role in parental involvement among immigrant parents. *Curriculum Journal, 31*(3), 340–356. https://doi.org/10.1002/curj.10

Attar, Z., Blom, E., & Le Pichon, E. (2020). Towards more multilingual practices in the Mathematics assessment of young refugee students: Effects of testing language and validity of parental assessment. *International Journal of Bilingual Education and Bilingualism,* ahead-of-print (ahead-of-print), 1–16. https://doi.org/10.1080/13670050.2020.1779648

Blommaert, J. (2009). Language, asylum, and the national order. *Current Anthropology, 50*(4), 415–441.

Edugains. (n.d.). *Targeted implementation planning supports for math: Grades 1 to 8 summary.* http://www.edugains.ca/resourcesMath/CE/TIPS4Math/Grades1to8Summary_AODA.pdf

Gale, T., & Densmore, K. (2000). *Just schooling: Explorations in the cultural politics of teaching.* Open University Press.

Guo, Y. (2012). Diversity in public education: Acknowledging immigrant parent knowledge. *Canadian Journal of Education / Revue Canadienne De L'éducation, 35*(2), 120–140.

Herzog-Punzenberger, B., Le Pichon-Vorstman, E., & Siarova, H. (2017). *Multilingual education in the light of diversity: Lessons learned. NESET II report.* Publications Office of the European Union.

Le Pichon, E., Cole, D., Baauw, S., Steffens, M., van den Brink, M., Dekker, S. (2020). Transcultural itineraries and new literacies: How migration memories could reshape school systems, In L. Passerini, M. Proglio, G. Trakilović (Eds.), *The mobility of memory: Migrations and diasporas across European borders.*

Le Pichon, E., Siarova, H., & Szonyi, E. (2020). *The future of language education in Europe: Case-studies of innovative practices.* NESET II report, Publications Office of the European Union.

Le Pichon, E. (2018). *Comparative curriculum mapping approach to bridging mathematical skills of Syrian newcomer students.* SSHRC Institutional Grant (SIG)— Explore Grant.

Le Pichon, E., de Swart, H., Ceginskas, V., & van den Bergh, H. (2009). Language learning experience in school context and metacognitive awareness of multilingual children. *International Journal of Multilingualism, 6*(3), 256–280.

Moll, L. C., Amanti, C., Neff, D., & Gonzalez, N. (1992). Funds of knowledge for teaching: Using a qualitative approach to connect homes and classrooms. *Theory Into Practice, 31*(2), 132–141.

National Geographic Kids. (2012). *1001 Inventions and awesome facts from Muslim civilization: Official children's companion to the 1001 inventions exhibition.* National Geographic Kids.

Ontario Ministry of Education. (2021). *Important information in many languages.* http://www.edu.gov.on.ca/eng/parents/multilanguages.html

Ontario Ministry of Education. (2020). *The Ontario curriculum, grades 1–8: Mathematics 2020.* Queen's Printer for Ontario. https://assets-us-01.kc-usercontent.com/fbd574c4-da36-0066-a0c5-849ffb2de96e/90439c6e-f40c-4b58-840c-557ed88a9345/The%20Ontario%20Curriculum%20Grades%201%E2%80%938%20-%20Mathematics,%202020%20(January%202021).pdf

Ontario Ministry of Education. (2005). *Mathematics: The Ontario curriculum grades 1–8*. Queen's Printer for Ontario. http://www.edu.gov.on.ca/eng/curriculum/elementary/math18curr.pdf

Piccardo, E. (2013). Plurilingualism and curriculum design: Toward a synergic vision. *TESOL Quarterly, 47*(3), 600–614. https://doi.org/10.1002/tesq.110

Ruiz, R. (1984). Orientations in language planning. *NABE: The Journal for the National Association for Bilingual Education, 8*(2), 15–34.

Seals, C. A., & Peyton, J. K. (2017). Heritage language education: Valuing the languages, literacies, and cultural competencies of immigrant youth. *Current Issues in Language Planning, 18*(1), 87–101.

Syrian Ministry of Education. (2021). *Curriculum: Grade 4*. http://moed.gov.sy/site/cur/04

Syrian Ministry of Education. (2018–2019a). *Mathematics: Grade 4, student book*. General Printing Corporation.

Syrian Ministry of Education. (2018–2019b). *Mathematics: Grade 7, student book*. General Printing Corporation.

Syrian Ministry of Education. (2018–2019c). *Mathematics: Grade 5, student book*. General Printing Corporation.

Syrian Ministry of Education. (2018–2019d). *Mathematics: Grade 8, algebra, student book*. General Printing Corporation.

Syrian Ministry of Education. (2018–2019e). *Mathematics: Grade 8, geometry, student book*. General Printing Corporation.

Syrian Ministry of Education. (2017–2018). *Mathematics: Grade 6, student book*. General Printing Corporation.

Vogel, S., & García, O. (2017). Translanguaging. In G. Noblit (Ed.), *Oxford research encyclopedia of education*. Oxford University Press. https://doi.org/10.1093/acrefore/9780190264093.013.181

Wattar, D. (2014). *Globalization, curriculum reform and teacher professional development in Syria*. PhD thesis, University of Alberta.

PART VIII

Critical Gender/Feminist Studies in Education

CHAPTER 29

Transforming Sub-Saharan African Universities—Transnational Collaborations at the Intersections of Gender as a Viable Pathway?

Philomina Okeke-Ihejirika

INTRODUCTION

I present this commentary, bearing in mind, two crucial realities among others that Sub-Saharan Africa's (henceforth referred to as Africa) universities wrestle with, as they strive to respond to twenty-first-century development challenges. First, public funding will neither lend itself to nor be sufficient for, the bold moves needed to fully support academic endeavors revamp and transform academic institutions (Amin & Ntembe, 2021; Oketch, 2016; Swartz, 2006). It is therefore important to explore avenues for diversify their institutional funding base—with the understanding that meaningful structural transformations at the macro level will require new support strategies to muster the level of independence necessary to enable them to assert system-wide radical agendas. Second, the world of teaching and research in the academy is increasingly becoming an internationalized and communal endeavor, connecting local and global networks of actors (Adanu et al., 2015; Cherney et al., 2015; Woolley et al., 2014). It is equally pertinent that African institutions give more serious thought than before to building relevant and meaningful institutional linkages to expand capacity in research and student training, and in turn, contribute to the local as well as the global knowledge bank. The need for transnational collaboration is also vividly expressed by the continent's poor representation among other higher education systems, despite an overall

P. Okeke-Ihejirika (✉)
University of Alberta, Edmonton, AB, Canada
e-mail: pokeke@ualberta.ca

© The Author(s), under exclusive license to Springer Nature Switzerland AG 2022
A. A. Abdi and G. W. Misiaszek (eds.), *The Palgrave Handbook on Critical Theories of Education*, https://doi.org/10.1007/978-3-030-86343-2_29

rapidly rising enrolments in the post-independence era. As Zeleza (2021) noted,

> In 1959, on the verge of Africa's 'year of independence' in 1960, when seventeen countries achieved their freedom from colonial rule, there were only seventy-six universities across Africa mostly concentrated in South Africa, Egypt, and parts of West Africa. The number rose to 170 in 1970, 294 in 1980, 446 in 1990, 784 in 2000, 1,431 in 2010, and 1,682 in 2018. Enrolments rose from 0.74 million in 1970 to 1.7 million in 1980, 2.8 million in 1990, 6.1 million in 2000, 11.4 million in 2010, and 14.7 million in 2017…[Yet] Africa remained with the lowest levels of higher education institutions and tertiary enrolments. (p. 2)

It is therefore safe to say that African universities stand to gain substantially from transnational collaborations that are geared toward addressing key structural challenges that could propel the continent on a faster, stable and steady growth path. In this regard, scholars and other professionals within the new African diaspora—who are well equipped and strategically placed to participate in this project of assistance could make a huge difference. Senior scholars, in particular, are usually well positioned to pursue initiatives on the continent, given their professional expertise and experience, considerable independence within Western institutional bases, as well as broad networks and linkages with relevant agents of tertiary education (Akalu, 2016; Teferra, 2021; Foulds & Zeleza, 2014). Where and how gender is situated in this project matter. The centrality of gender to this project, I argue, would be evident if positioned as a set of critical lenses for much needed scrutiny: our investigations into the social statuses, identities and structures that mediate how men and women are treated in society as well as the multiple social intersections (class, race, ethnicity, religion, language, etc.) that mediate this treatment (Crenshaw, 1991, p. 2) Women's role and statuses as knowers and actors that are often neglected in how the academy is constituted as institutions with diversely situated persons and collectives. A feminist perspective compels that we capture, as much as possible, how the reproduction of power and power relations across gender and its multiple social intersections mediate academic cultures and practices for various groups (Johnson, 2015; Okeke-Ihejirika et al., 2019).

I wish to state, however, that this commentary is by no means a comprehensive response to discourses that decry the marginalization of feminist scholarship in Africa's universities. It is also not designed to confront the full barrage of practices of exclusion in Africa's universities that marginalize women's role as agents of change (Mama, 2003; Odejidi et al., 2006; Okeke-Ihejirika, 2017), trivialize gender and its intersectionalities as a crucial entry point to social research and continually sideline the production of feminist knowledge as a scholarly endeavor that could significantly transform academia and society (Ampofo, 2016; Feminist Africa, 2007). I also do not intend to take on the controversies fueled by an apparent division between discourses that are considered *feminist scholarship* and those perceived as simply discourses on *gender* or *gender and development* (Cornwall et al., 2007). On the contrary, my commentary is meant to spur more debates and, in particular, enlarge the existing pockets of conversations in order to make room for graduate students and emerging scholars across Africa, male and female alike, who, from the little they have been exposed to, are excited about scholarship that originated from gender, but have little or no access to explore its ever-broadening contours, dynamics and dimensions. For many of them, the beginning point is gaining an understanding of gender (including its embedded social intersections) as a useful category of analysis. Most importantly, I wish to state that my analysis explores the building of meaningful collaborations with this entry point rather than its comprehensive interrogation—which remains an unfinished project well beyond the scope of my work.

Context

The neglect suffered by Africa's universities since the 1980s along with the need to diversify knowledge sources in an increasingly globalizing world provide a strong impetus for building collaborative research networks. Many scholars in the field deplore the dismal state of research and teaching in Africa, insufficient infrastructure facilities, poor staffing and inadequate funding (Tafida et al., 2015). Budget limitations, others argue, hamper the building of research communities, by dampening the potential and motivation for capacity building (Illing, 2012). Indeed, over the past two decades, a good number of international funding agencies have made sizable investments, human and material, all in a bid to revamp Africa's universities, particularly the various research traditions within its diverse intellectual communities. Among these entities is Fulbright, one of the most prominent exchange programs, which has provided scholars in six global regions, including Sub-African Africa, for over seven decades. Named after one of the United States' highly esteemed political figures, William J. Fulbright, the program supports scholarly exchanges for teaching and research to and from African countries (Fulbright Scholar Program, n.d.). Similarly, the Carnegie African Diaspora Fellowship Program (CADFP, 2013), launched in 2013, deploys the expertise of African-borne scholars who reside in the United States and Canada to enhance research collaboration, curriculum co-development and graduate training in universities located in Ghana, Kenya, Nigeria, South Africa, Tanzania and Uganda.

Similarly, several promising bilateral educational initiatives have emerged such as the Sweden-Uganda 5-year agreement (OpenAid, n.d.) and the Academic Model Providing Access to Healthcare (AMPATH), which began as a modest partnership between Indiana University-Purdue University Indianapolis (IUPUI) and Kenya's Moi University. AMPATH now flourishes as a robust "North–South, US-Kenya medical partnership that provides opportunities for faculty members from both institutions in education, research, and clinical service health and social services to a wide swath of residents in western Kenya" (Tobenkin, 2016, p. 18).

South African universities have benefited tremendously from a large number of international research collaborations and capacity-building programs funded by agencies like The Ford, Carnegie and Mellon Foundation, and Erasmus Mundus Programs. These new interventions have played a major role in expanding graduate student enrolment, and research and supervision support structures (Luescher-Mamashela et al., 2015). Undoubtedly, the resulting linkages for international collaboration and funding complemented broader strategic measures that moved forward a minimum of five South African universities in global university rankings (CWUR, 2017).

These emerging collaborations underscore the increasing interest and differing agendas of stakeholders, who make decisions about, fund or manage universities in Africa. Nonetheless, there appears to be an acute dearth of literature on scholarly collaborations in Africa, even though the handful of studies on the experiences and outcomes of research collaborations in Africa do suggest a positive outlook. International research collaboration, a recent study notes, facilitates "intra- and inter-disciplinary partnerships that resulted in maximizing the capacity-building efforts. The exposure to this collaboration improved both individual and institutional research capacity in the south" (Frantz et al., 2014, p. 1228). Ronel Callaghan's evaluation of collaborative initiatives in South Africa equally highlighted the importance of interdisciplinary approaches for transforming teaching challenges into learning opportunities (Callaghan, 2015).

Although the importance of these partnerships has long been recognized and the positive outcomes celebrated, the potential that gender holds—as an entry point in terms of transforming, expanding and sustaining the visions that propel these collaborations—has remained largely under-explored. This brief commentary seeks to provoke more discussion into what could be, at least, one viable pathway to re-invigorating the African academy. My contextual exploration of research collaboration at the intersections of gender is based on two decades of experience as a transnational feminist scholar who has been actively engaged in various academic ventures both in Africa and across several Western countries. Below, I will explore the potential that gender holds as (a) a strategic point of entry into collaborative research initiatives that might engender meaningful interdisciplinary interactions, (b) to open up critical sites for the production of feminist knowledge and (c) to enhance graduate training. I pay particular attention to contemporary social problems that could lend themselves to new forms of research collaborations that might be better informed by feminist scholarship on gender, and its intersections. Most importantly, my conclusive commentary draws attention to the various ways that women, as a significant but largely marginalized constituency in Africa's university systems, can be strategically situated in such collaborations as scholars, subjects of study and stakeholders. Through these roles they will become actively involved in the transformation of Africa'sExploring Transnational Collaborations at universities.

REVIEW OF LITERATURE

A number of scholars have emphasized the importance of scholarly collaborations for graduate training in an era of diminishing public funding. The funding crises, another recent study notes, have "serious implications...not only for research output in the form of publications but also for the training of graduate students in the country" (Illing, 2012, p. 5). International networks and partnerships that support local institutions, students and faculty, and value and account for local imperatives and contexts, can create platforms for knowledge building and sharing that serve transformational ends in the global South, in particular (Klopp et al., 2014). This study also notes that such initiatives should aim to "both stimulate trans-cultural, multi-directional global knowledge flows and strengthen local institutions, research, and pedagogy ...[to effect] more equitable participation in constructing and leveraging global, as well as local, urban knowledge" (Klopp et al., 2014, p. 207).

Similarly, a 2015 study of doctoral nursing programs in South Africa emphasized the need to develop sustainable strategies that could reinforce supportive frameworks of multi-tier collaborations of stakeholders, funders, institutions and student cohorts. In the face of the acute decline of institutional funding, the study argues, such collaborations, "would need to be supported systemically, administratively and academically though the remit of the educational trust and/or other like-minded organizations" (Comiskey et al., 2015, p. 651). Many scholars, policymakers and funding partners view these emerging collaborative initiatives for graduate training among a number of universities in Sweden, South Africa and Uganda as potential models for North–South collaboration, given the creative forms of blended learning and digital pedagogy embedded (Protsiv et al., 2016). This model, however, may not thrive given the paucity of high-level local research capacity.

The literature also suggests that collaborative research could help improve student writing skills and competencies: It could be employed to create intellectual communities where students, their peers, and their tutors share constructive feedback (Dowse & Howie, 2013). Other scholars and stakeholders in tertiary education have also discussed the significance of research collaborations across national and international borders. Some examine how a common teaching platform acts as a collaborative model, one that is aimed at enhancing undergraduate nursing education in South Africa's universities (Daniels & Khanyile, 2013). Other scholars consider the collaborative capacity building that is targeted to graduate health science students between low-and middle-income countries (LMICs) in Africa, Asia and Europe (Atkins et al., 2016). As well, researchers have investigated partnerships between US-based

Nigerian physicians and their local partners, particularly in developing and boosting modern healthcare systems in Nigeria (Nwadiuko et al., 2016).

Some researchers look at scientific co-authorship among African scholars as a mode of research collaboration; they consider the ways in which over-emphasis on collaborations in natural and applied sciences excluded other knowledge disciplines (Pouris & Ho, 2014). The expectations and challenges of multi-institutional partnerships between universities in Africa and the United States aimed at facilitating necessary educational reforms and transformation have been explored (Semali et al., 2013). Finally, intra-continental collaborations between the Mauritian and South African university system, as they seek to develop human resources capacity for Ph.D. education and programs have also been studied (Samuel & Mariaye, 2014).

All these studies unearth crucial insights into potential pitfalls and important considerations for building viable collaborative initiatives. However, they do not provide a comprehensive critical assessment of the scope, quality and outcomes of these collaborations. Much of the literature focuses on South African universities, and mainly on collaborative initiatives in the natural and applied science disciplines, often among local universities. More importantly, what are largely absent as objects of study are gender and its intersections, both as constitutive social categories that define the agents and nature of inquiry, as well as being critical entry points to epistemologies that could disrupt systemic inequities in society.

Transforming the African Academy: Gender as Subject and as a Constitutive Category

From a general feminist standpoint, gender is a crucial basis for constituting and transforming social relations of power (Acker, 1992; Budgeon, 2013; Metcalfe & Rees, 2010). Gender relations refer to "a complex system of personal and social relations of domination and power through which women and men are socially created and maintained and through which they gain access to power and material resources or are allocated status within society" (IFAD, 2000, p. 4; Johnson, 2015; Okeke-Ihejirika, 2017). From a general feminist standpoint, gender is a crucial basis for constituting and transforming social relations of power (Berger & Guidroz, 2010; Laube, 2021).

The experiences of Western colonization have "gendered" and "racialized" African women and men in different ways, but it is safe to say that the transition into postcolonial societies has, for the most part, benefited men (Chadya, 2003). Africa's universities reflect the resultant systemic gender inequities, which are replicated in a diversity of administrative structures as well as institutional cultures (Mama, 2003; Okeke-Ihejirika, 2004). It is, however, important to note that women within and outside the academy are not entirely vulnerable to these postcolonial circumstances. Overtly and covertly, they do resist their subordinate status in various social arrangements, including the university, thereby creating a diversity of resilient platforms to negotiate or navigate the "concrete constraints" that contemporary social arrangements have thrown in their path (Kandioti, 2010, p. 81).

In making a case for gender inclusivity in academic structures, relations and processes within African universities, it is also important to clearly differentiate between (a) the conventional line of advocacy that emphasizes the need to make room for women and (b) a viable argument for placing gender issues at the center of deliberations for transforming African universities. Arguing for research at the intersections of gender should be premised on existing evidence that strongly supports the position that diversity and social inclusiveness of any sort ultimately serve the society well. The current state of knowledge in the field recognizes that men and women are equal partners in nation building and social progress. Existing literature clearly shows that, on average, societies and economies that attend to gender inequalities have better prospects for growth and robustness (GGGR, 2014; Mercer Report, 2014).

In light of this knowledge, questions regarding the feminization of poverty, intimate partner violence and participation in public decisions cannot be removed from the development challenges of contemporary Africa (Bamiwuye & Odimegwu, 2014; Idoko et al., 2015; Uthman et al., 2010). In the African context, women's strategic position in the family, their role in food production, and their grip on the informal economy, among other instances, certainly suggest that empowering them is not a matter of charity but, rather, of self-preservation. Women's role in development becomes even more critical and inevitable, particularly in an era in which the supply of human capital in Africa is highly deficient. The diversity and depth of gender inequality on the continent thus compels the African academy to forge the necessary multidisciplinary linkages to probe the socio-cultural, economic and political histories that undergird contemporary life. This stance is both intellectual and political; it is also strongly linked to fundamental questions about voice, power and responsibility in the content and management of African universities (Mama, 2003, 2011; Morley, 2006; Okeke-Ihejirika, 2004).

Exploring Transnational Collaborations at the Intersections of Gender: A Viable Pathway to Transforming the African Academy

Local and global actors who pursue development initiatives increasingly recognize the importance of integrating gender and its intersections into the analysis of complex social problems. Over the past two decades, many Western humanitarian organizations, research funding agencies (Bill & Melinda Gates Foundation, 2016) and governments (The Government of Canada, 2017; USAID, 2012) have made significant policy changes that respond to documented evidence and emerging social trends about the many ways gender is implicated in persistent social inequalities, especially in developing regions like Africa. This wind of change is also evident in the rising profile that gender has gained in major development organizations in Africa—at least in principle. Still, the search for viable pathways to social progress continues to present problematic complexities at every turn (African Development Forum, 2008; UNECA, 2017). Indeed, the scant available data with which to address Africa's social problems is succinctly expressed in a 2013 publication by the United Nation's Economic Commission for Africa:

> Over the last decade, the centrality of gender equality in the achievement of socio-economic and cultural development in society has been widely documented and proven....Considering this situation, there is a need for improving national capacity of African countries to collect, compile and disseminate gender statistics, by strengthening ongoing initiatives and activities in the region and by undertaking new initiatives that might invigorate the availability and improvement of gender indicators. (UNECA, 2016)

The urgency to cast a "gender lens" on existing measures that are aimed at addressing social problems also resonates in emerging trends that are increasingly changing social expectations of the ivory tower. African governments, universities and scholars cannot afford to ignore these trends. Such trends include the following, although this is merely a selection:

1. A shift away from what I refer to as "scholarship for its own sake," to research that recognizes that social problems are complex and may call for a team approach rather than individual isolated inquiries (Carr et al., 2018).
2. A push toward what I call the 5th space, which encourages meaningful, multidisciplinary interactions among global intellectuals who nurture academic networks that significantly undercut the challenges of collaboration across various geophysical location (Grand Challenges n.d.; Bill and Melinda Gates Foundation n.d.).
3. Recent directives from global decision makers, particularly the United Nations as well funding agencies that operate in Africa, which suggest substantive social transformation cannot occur without a robust infusion of gender considerations into university culture, decision making, curriculum, research and graduate training (Unmillennium Project n.d.; Sustainable Development n.d.; UNIDO n.d.). These entities increasingly demand research collaboration among scholars, decision makers and community stakeholders, and closer ties between academia and industry—with gender considerations as a central component.

The quest for a collaborative network of knowledge production and sharing among scholars from the sciences, humanities, social sciences, law and so forth creates a web of cross-disciplinary spaces for broadening knowledge production. These spaces are not confined to the conventional interdisciplinary intersections in the social science and humanities that feminist scholarship has so far gained entry into. Academic knowledge can be "gendered" through the intersecting activities of multiple agents from a multiplicity of knowledge bases as they negotiate and transform transnational and postcolonial contexts of mobility and development (Bailey, 2010). Gendering research spaces also entails tapping into the network of transnational African female feminist scholars; their research, knowledge production and continual scrutiny of the policies and practices of Africa's universities have propelled many of the interventions made by Western stakeholders.

Integrating understandings of gender and its intersections into scholarly collaborations also has crucial implications for graduate student training. At this level, students should wrestle with the "whys" and "hows" of critical inquiry. Furthermore, their training should be rooted in an intellectual tradition that exposes them to the complexity of social problems. It is also crucial to guide students toward innovative research approaches that embed multidisciplinary lenses into their research methods. Institutional collaborations, driven by diaspora engagement, may not only enhance graduate training but could also hasten the building of Indigenous communities of scholars and researchers. Such a development is likely to foster viable platforms for nurturing broader research agendas that could respond to today's complex social problems. As noted earlier, research and scholarship in the twenty-first century are increasingly collaborative endeavors, requiring the mobilization of teams, resources and infrastructure across disciplines, institutions and global regions.[1]

Working as a multidisciplinary team improves the quality of proposals, viability of research projects and the learning experiences of scholars, students, practitioners and policymakers. Collaborating in the 5th space not only increases the potential for acquiring more research funding, it also provides diverse sets of expertise and methodologies for robust graduate training in research skills. The vision is to equip emerging scholars with the relevant skills to align research programs to real-life problems. As their expertise grows, these emerging scholars become what may be referred to as global intellectuals. It will not matter where they are located; they will be sought after because they have what it takes to compete and contribute significantly to the world community. Moreover, they can easily be identified as important players in a knowledge economy where information, rather than money, is the major currency.

It is also important to stress that the process of building Africa's knowledge economy calls for culturally located agents well attuned to local conditions and well aware of the stakes involved in protecting a people's knowledge base and civilization. These agents must be located in a research tradition that not only challenges them to take on social problems but also rewards them with appropriate incentives. International collaboration, if properly situated, may not only facilitate the training of a new generation of scholars, it could also provide the framework for setting up a broader research agenda for the continent. Moving in this direction requires the expertise of African scholars at home and in diaspora who could assist in rebuilding organizational structures as well as managing process and performance. As resource persons with institutional networks locally, internationally and transnationally, senior scholars in diaspora could assist new universities to set up centers and programs that respond to local knowledge demand, engage in capacity building with respect to co-curricular development and expand research and funding bases through collaboration with African-based scholars. Such an arrangement could nurture stronger networks of stakeholders working toward desired goals and a greater sense of community that gives ownership and direction to Africans (Zeleza, 2013; Foulds & Zeleza, 2014).

The envisioned transformation in Africa's universities will also hinge on the reach of transnational partnerships that these universities are able to forge and leverage. Moreover, the success of collaborative research depends on what robust frameworks the policymakers and academia are willing to put in place. Knowledge synthesis rarely happens in a vacuum; it requires structures that will evolve according to local demands and dynamics. The goal is not to adopt a provisional approach, but to create frameworks of stakeholders, funders, institutions and student cohorts that will sustain these multi-tiered international linkages over time—until they become not only self-sustaining, but also institutionalized. In this twenty-first century, the impact of successful research collaborations on graduate training and human capacity development will depend largely on an aggregation of teams, resources and infrastructure across disciplines, cultures, institutions and global regions. These factors certainly cannot be over-emphasized.

While transnational research collaborations have great potential for Africa's universities, they also currently have their drawbacks, which must not be overlooked. It is safe to say that most ongoing collaborations are largely organized and executed according to the dictates of Western funding agencies. Hence, their sustainability also depends more on the flow of funding, rather than on the capacity of African diaspora scholars and their partners on the continent, to mobilize time and expertise toward significant structural change. The ongoing unstable funding climate could undermine the current seeds of transformation planted by strategically placed global scholars who have invested tremendously in Africa's universities (Mbeiki, 2003).

The quest for research collaborations at the intersections of gender, especially the transnational dimension, must also consider the possible impacts of the migration of human expertise. The largest proportion of poorest countries in the world today is found in Africa. This condition has led to the flight of human capital, otherwise known as "the brain-drain." This entails knowledge loss, whereby highly skilled professionals, including doctors, engineers and university lecturers, immigrate abroad for greener pastures. Africa migrants voluntarily take advantage of various immigration policies in Europe, Australia, and North American countries that aim to attract qualified international students and skilled workers from across the globe to boost their economic growth and development.[2] This brain drain, an emerging discourse explores (Olutayo, 2016), could in some respects, translate into a brain gain in the long run (Geber, 2013).

Conclusion

The need for African universities to collaborate with their counterparts in the global North to address development challenges of the twenty-first century and beyond remains a recurring concern among academics, university administrators, government officials and funding organizations. I have argued in this paper that much literature discusses research collaboration and its benefits to graduate students. However, a good deal of this work has focused on South African universities, looking at collaborations in the natural and applied science disciplines. It has also targeted collaborations between universities in the same regions or localities. All this literature suggests that experiences and outcomes of research collaborations in Africa are positive. Nevertheless, I have shown that the recommendations so far articulated scholars have not significantly addressed the gaps in these collaborations; nor have they translated to lasting transformation-driven outcomes. If anything, research collaborations are still patchy and poorly executed. I have also shown that the existing literature has not paid much attention to work that emphasizes what I call "transnational scholarly collaborations at the intersections of gender." Indeed, one cannot help but notice that there has been very little attention paid to gender as both a central and strategic entry point in research collaborations.

Despite the contributions of women to various aspects of human endeavors in Africa, gender still remains largely absent from many conversations about transforming Africa's universities, as if to suggest that the female contribution can be only marginal at best. It is in this context that I argued for the importance of gender and its intersections—if we, as scholars and stakeholders, hope to contribute toward the transformation of our universities. It is a fact that bridging gender disparities will boost the productive capacities of not only the education sector but also the economy on the whole.

Although I am extremely concerned about the poor state of research collaboration and the seeming apathy of the authorities in some of the African universities, one of the most reassuring findings of my study is that research collaboration has great potential to transform Africa's universities and position our continent on a path of transformational development. Certainly, more research collaborations and partnerships across the globe are urgently needed. This study thus envisages that the establishment of such frameworks will facilitate four key developments, which are critical to sustaining a viable research collaboration across transnational borders:

- mutual understanding among all the stakeholders
- collective commitment to achieving prioritized developmental goals
- creative strategies directed at capacity-building outcomes

- measurable feedback via monitoring, evaluation and reassessments of results.

These seemingly giant steps are possible. Unfortunately, they will remain simply visions yet to be acted upon, unless the political will can be generated to infuse gender concerns into the policy and practice of education in Africa, particularly in universities. Beyond making gender central to academic endeavors on the continent, it is also crucial to center feminist scholarship as a site for institutional transformation. This is not simply in terms of knowledge produced but also through institutional policies and practices. Part of this political resolve, embedded in institutional structures, will depend on administrators and faculties that create spaces where women's voices are recognized and appreciated. Further, it will require that transparency and ethical imperatives underscore practices and processes, and that commitments to knowledge production, synthesis and dissemination inform graduate training and research collaboration policies.

Research has continued to underscore that gender inequality serves as a major barrier to the transformation of African universities and the economic growth of Africa more generally (UNECA, 2011). As I highlighted earlier, including gender and its intersections as constitutive social categories and as critical entry points to epistemologies is essential in African universities; this strategy has great potential to transform African society. Any contemporary discourse on Africa's future must factor in the role of women because they are also primary stakeholders in the transformation and development we all envisage; moreover, they can readily mobilize individual and collective resources toward the realization of a future that is both inclusive and empowering for everyone on the continent. Therefore, the government, university administrators and scholars must work together to create a gender-affirming space in academia, one that is conducive to the inclusion and participation of women. Such a space would acknowledge that women, intrinsically, are formidable agents of change.

I conclude this commentary with an emphatic note on the need to explore all avenues possible in order to attract new voices into our discourses on feminist or gender scholarship. As I mentioned earlier, forums for feminist debates remain an elusive space for many graduate students and emerging scholars in Africa. These debates, regardless of their level of sophistication, are not likely to achieve much if they remain little enclaves for scholars who are privileged in one way or the other to participate. We also run a risk of marginalizing feminist scholarship further in the future if the simple notion of gender as a useful category of analysis does not inform the worldview of a sizeable proportion of emerging cohorts of scholars in the continent.

Notes

1. In addition to Foulds and Zeleza (2014), analyses of exchange programs offered by western universities provide a critical lens here. See, for instance, Shayo, R. 2014. Prospects and challenges of international academic exchange programmes between universities in northern and southern countries: reflections from a visiting scholar from an African university. *Nokoko* (4)109–144.
2. For instance, the United States, Germany, France, Australia and Canada Immigration system seeks to attract competent individuals who have distinguished themselves in their field.

References

Acker, J. (1992). Gendered institutions: From sex roles to gendered institutions. *Contemporary Sociology, 21*(5), 565–569.

Adanu, R., Mbizvo, M. T., Baguiya, A., Adam, V., Ademe, B. W., Ankomah, A., Aja, G. N., Ajuwon, A. J., Esimai, O. A., Ibrahim, T., & Mogobe, D. K. (2015). Sexual and reproductive health research and research capacity strengthening in Africa: perspectives from the region. *Reproductive Sealth, 12*(1), 1–3.

African Development Forum. (2008). *Achieving gender equality and women's empowerment in Africa progress report*. http://www1.uneca.org/Portals/ngm/CrossArticle/1/Documents/ADFVI_Progress_Report_ENG.pdf

Akalu, G. A. (2016). Revitalising higher education in the age of globalisation: The African dilemma. In E. Shiza & L. Diallo (Eds.), *Africa in the age of globalisation: Perceptions, misperceptions and realities*. Ashgate.

Amin, A., & Ntembe, A. (2021). Sub-Sahara Africa's higher education: Financing, growth, and employment. *International Journal of Higher Education, 10*(1), 14–23.

Ampofo, A. (2016). Re-viewing studies on Africa, #Black Lives Matter, and envisioning the future of African studies. *African Studies Review, 59*(2). https://doi.org/10.1017/asr.2016.34

Atkins, S., Marsden, S., Diwan, V., Zwarenstein, M., & ARCADE consortium. (2016). North-South collaboration and capacity development in global health research in low-and middle-income countries–the ARCADE projects. *Global Health Action, 9*(1), 30524.

Bailey, A. J. (2010). Population geographies, gender, and the migration-development Nexus. *Progress in Human Geography, 34*(3), 375–386.

Bamiwuye, S. O., & Odimegwu, C. (2014). Spousal violence in sub-Saharan Africa: Does household poverty-wealth matter? *Reproductive Health, 11*(1): 2–10.

Berger, M., & Guidroz, K. (Eds.). (2010). *The intersectional approach: Transforming the academy through race, class and gender*. University of North Carolina Press.

Bill & Melinda Gates Foundation. (n.d.). *Our work in Africa*. http://www.gatesfoundation.org/Where-We-Work/Africa-Office

Bill & Melinda Gates Foundation. (2016). *A conceptual model of women and girls*. https://docs.gatesfoundation.org/Documents/BMGF_EmpowermentModel.pdf

Budgeon, S. (2013). The dynamics of gender hegemony: Femininities, masculinities and social change. *Sociology, 48*(2), 317–334. https://doi.org/10.1177/0038038513490358

Callaghan, R. (2015). Transforming teaching challenges into learning opportunities: Interdisciplinary reflective collaboration. *Africa Education Review, 12*(4), 599–617.

Carnegie Corporation. (2013). *Carnegie African diaspora fellowship program.* https://www.iie.org/Programs/Carnegie-African-Diaspora-Fellowship-Program

Carr, G., Loucks, D. P., & Bloschl, G. (2018). Gaining insight into interdisciplinary research and education programmes: A framework for evaluation. *Research Policy, 47*(1), 35–48.

Chadya, J. M. (2003). Mother politics: Anti-colonial nationalism and the woman question in Africa. *Journal of Women's History, 15*(3), 153–157.

Cherney, A., Head, B., Povey, J., Boreham, P., & Ferguson, M. (2015). The utilisation of social science research: The perspectives of academic researchers in Australia. *Journal of Sociology, 51*(2): 252–270.

Comiskey, C. M., Matthews, A., Williamson, C., Bruce, J., Mulaudzi, M., & Klopper, H. (2015). Scaling up nurse education: An evaluation of a national PhD capacity development programme in South Africa, in the context of the global shortage of nursing graduates. *Nurse Education Today, 35*(5), 647–652.

Cornwall, A., Harrison, E., & Whitehead, A. (2007). Gender myths and feminist fables: The struggle for interpretive power in gender and development. *Development and Change, 38*(1), 1–20.

Council for International Exchange of Scholars (CIES). (n.d). *Fullbright scholar program.* https://www.cies.org/about-us

Crenshaw, K. (1991). Mapping the margins: Intersectionality, identity politics, and violence against women of color. *Stanford Law Review, 43*(6), 1241–1299.

CWUR. (2017). *Shanghai normal university ranking.* https://cwur.org/2017/Shanghai-Normal-University.php

Daniels, F. M., & Khanyile, T. D. (2013). A framework for effective collaboration: A case study of collaboration in nursing education in the Western Cape, South Africa. *Nurse Education Today, 33*(9), 956–961.

Dowse, C., & Howie, S. (2013). Promoting academic research writing with South African Master's students in the field of education. In T. Plomp & N. Nieveen (Eds.), *Educational design research–Part B: Illustrative cases* (pp. 851–879). SLO.

Feminist Africa. (2007). *Rethinking universities.* http://www.agi.ac.za/sites/default/files/image_tool/images/429/feminist_africa_journals/archive/09/fa_9_entire_journal.pdf

Foulds, K., & Zeleza, P. T. (2014). The African academic diaspora and African higher education. *International Higher Education, 76*, 16–17.

Frantz, J. M., Leach, L., Pharaoh, H., Bassett, S. H., Roman, N. V., Smith, M. R., & Travill, A. (2014). Research capacity development in a South African higher education institution through a North-South collaboration. *South African Journal of Higher Education, 28*(4), 1216–1229.

Geber, H. (2013). Can mentoring decrease the brain drain of academics from Africa? *Procedia-Social and Behavioral Sciences, 93*, 215–220.

GGGR. (2014). *The global gender gap report.* http://www3.weforum.org/docs/GGGR14/GGGR_CompleteReport_2014.pdf

Grand Challenges (n.d.). *Funding opportunities.* http://www.grandchallenges.ca/funding-opportunities/

Idoko, P., Ogbe, E., Jallow, O., & Ocheke, A. (2015). Burden of intimate partner violence in The Gambia: A cross sectional study of pregnant women. *Reproductive Health, 2*, 2–6.

IFAD. (2000). *An IFAD approach to: Gender mainstreaming: The experience of the Latin America and the Caribbean division.* International Fund for Agricultural Development (IFAD).

Ikejiani, O. (1960). *Nigerian education.* Longmans.

Illing, N. (2012). Funding drought hits experimentally based South African researchers and their graduate students. *South African Journal of Science, 108*(3–4), 1–5.

Johnson, A. T. (2015). Performing and defying gender: An exploration of the lived experiences of women higher education administrators in sub-Saharan Africa. *Educational Management Administration and Leadership, 42*(6), 835–850.

Kandioti, D. (2010). Bargaining with patriarchy. In C. McCann & S. K. Kim (Eds.), *Feminist theory reader: Local and global perspectives* (pp. 80–81). Routledge.

Klopp, J., Chanin, J., Ngau, P., & Sclar, E. (2014). Globalisation and the urban studio: Evaluating an inter-university studio collaboration in Nairobi. *International Development Planning Review, 36*(2), 205–226.

Laube, H. (2021). Outsiders within transforming the academy: The unique positionality of feminist sociologists. *Gender and Society, 35*(3), 476–500. https://doi.org/10.1177/08912432211000329

Luescher-Mamashela, T. M., Ssembatya, V., Brooks, E., Lange, R. S., Mugume, T., & Richmond, S. (2015). Student engagement and citizenship competences in African universities. In N. Cloete, P. Maassen, & T. Bailey (Eds.), *Knowledge production and contradictory functions in African higher education* (pp. 230–259). African Minds.

Mama, A. (2003). Restore, reform but do not transform: The gender politics of higher education in Africa. *JHESA/RESA, 1*(1), 101–125.

Mama, A. (2011). The challenges of feminism: Gender, ethics and responsible academic freedom in African universities. *Journal of Higher Education in Africa, 9*(1&2), 1–23.

Mbeiki, T. (2003, July). *Address to the University of West Indies, Jamaica* . http://appablog.wordpress.com/2007/11/16/african-union-african-diaspora-ministerial-conf

Mercer Report. (2014). *When Women thrive—Mercer's global gender diversity research.* http://www.mercer.com/content/dam/mercer/attachments/global/webcasts/mercer-global-gender-research-findings-when-women-thrive-businesses-thrive.pdf

Metcalfe, B., & Rees, C. (2010). Gender, globalization and organization: Exploring power, relations and intersections (Guest Editorial). *Emerald Insight, 29*(1), 5–22.

Morley, L. (2006). Hidden transcripts: The micropolitics of gender in commonwealth universities. *Women's Studies International Forum, 29*(6), 543–551.

Nwadiuko, J., James, K., Switzer, G. E., & Stern, J. (2016). Giving back: A mixed methods study of the contributions of US-based Nigerian physicians to home country health systems. *Globalization and Health, 12*(1), 33.

Odejidi, A., Akanji, B., & Odekunle, K. (2006). Does expansion mean inclusion in Nigerian higher education? *Women's Studies International Forum, 29*(6), 552–561.

Okeke-Ihejirika, P. (2004a). Higher education for Africa's women: Partners with or cheerleaders for men? In P. Zeleza & Olukoshi A. Dakar (Eds.), *African universities in the twenty-first century: Volume II knowledge and society.*

Okeke-Ihejirika, P. (2004b). *Negotiating power and privilege: Igbo career women in contemporary Nigeria.* Ohio University Press.

Okeke-Ihejirika, P. (2017). Asserting agency by negotiating patriarchy: Nigerian women's experiences within university administrative structures. *Journal of Global South Studies, 34*(1), 1–21.

Okeke-Ihejirika, P., Moyo, S., & Van Den Berg, H. (2019). Exploring the experiences of female graduate students in African universities: Questions about voice, power, and responsibility. *Gender and Women's Studies, 2*(3)1, 1–14.

Oketch, M. (2016). Financing higher education in sub-Saharan Africa: Some reflections and implications for sustainable development. *Higher Education, 72*, 525–539.

Olutayo, A. O. (2016). Democracy, funding of higher education and students' 'brain drain' in Nigeria: Development implications for now and the future. *Journal of Management and Social Sciences, 5*(2), 1–14.

Openaid. (n.d.). *Bilateral research cooperation Uganda 2015–2020—11 Swedish universities through ISP.* https://openaid.se/activity/SE-0-SE-6-5118006002-UGA-43082/

Pouris, A., & Ho, Y. S. (2014). Research emphasis and collaboration in Africa. *Scientometrics, 98*(3), 2169–2184.

Protsiv, M., Rosales-Klintz, S., Bwanga, F., Zwarenstein, M., & Atkins, S. (2016). Blended learning across universities in a South–North–South collaboration: A case study. *Health Research Policy and Systems, 14*(67), 1–12.

Samuel, M. A., & Mariaye, H. (2014). De-colonising International collaboration: The University of Kwazulu-Natal-Mauritius institute of education Cohort PhD programme. *Compare: A Journal of Comparative and International Education, 44*(4), 501–521.

Semali, L. M., Baker, R., & Freer, R. (2013). Multi-institutional partnerships for higher education in Africa: A case study of assumptions of international academic collaboration. *International Journal of Higher Education, 2*(2), 53–66.

Shayo, R. (2014). Prospects and challenges of international academic exchange programmes between universities in northern and southern countries: Reflections from a visiting scholar from an African university. *Nokoko, 4*, 109–143.

Swartz, D. (2006). New pathways to sustainability—African universities in a globalizing world. In M. O. Nkomo, D. Swartz, & B. Maja (Eds.), *Within the realm of possibility: From disadvantage to development at the University of Fort Hare and the University of the North* (pp. 127–166). HSRC Press

Tafida, A., Kasim, U., & Chima, P. (2015). Analysis of factors enhancing pitfall in research and teaching of the Nigerian University system. *International Journal of Higher Education, 4*(3), 82–89.

Teferra, D. (2021). Editorial: The role of the African intellectual diaspora in advancing higher education. *International Journal of African Higher Education, 8*(2), 1–9. https://ejournals.bc.edu/index.php/ijahe/article/view/13469

The Government of Canada. (2017). *Policy on gender equity.* http://international.gc.ca/world-monde/funding-financement/policy-politique.aspx?lang=eng

Tobenkin, D. (2016). Collaborating with Africa. *International Educator, 25*(5), 18.

United Nations Economic Commission for Africa (UNECA). (2011). *The African gender development index 2011: Promoting gender equality in Africa.* https://www.uneca.org/sites/default/files/PublicationFiles/agdi_2011_eng_fin.pdf

United Nations Economic Commission for Africa (UNECA). (2016). *Compendium of gender statistics in Africa.* https://ecastats.uneca.org/acsweb/Portals/0/ACSVirtualSpaces/Compendium%20of%20Gender%20Statistics%20in%20Africa_ENG.pdf

United Nations Economic Commission for Africa (UNECA). (2017). *The African gender and development index—Technical note.* https://www.uneca.org/sites/default/files/PublicationFiles/agdi_technical-note_en.pdf

United Nations Industrial Development Organization (UNIDO). (n.d.). *Africa.* http://www.unido.org/africa.html (Date required because link is now broken).

United Nations. (n.d.-a). *Millennium development goals.* https://www.un.org/millenniumgoals/

United Nations. (n.d.-b). *Sustainable development goals.* https://sustainabledevelopment.un.org/?menu=1300

USAID: From the American People. (2012). *Gender equality and female empowerment policy.* https://www.usaid.gov/sites/default/files/documents/1865/GenderEqualityPolicy_0.pdf

Uthman, O. A., Lawoko, S., & Moradi, T. (2010). Sex disparities in attitudes towards intimate partner violence against women in sub-Saharan Africa: A socio-ecological analysis. *BMC Public Health, 10*(1), 2–8.

Woolley, R., Sánchez-Barrioluengo, M., Turpin, T., & Marceau, J. (2014). Research collaboration in the social sciences: What factors are associated with disciplinary and interdisciplinary collaboration? *Science and Public Policy, 42*(4), 567–582.

Zeleza, P. (2013). *Engagements between African diaspora academics in the US and Canada and African institutions of higher education: Perspectives from North America and Africa* (p. 234). Carnegie Corporation of New York.

Zeleza, P. (2021). Higher education in a post-covid-19 world: Challenges and opportunities for African universities. *CODESRIA Bulletin Online, 1*, 1–10.

CHAPTER 30

Revisiting Francophone Sub-Saharan Africa's Eurocentric Education System Through a Decolonial Feminist's Lens

Gertrude Mianda

Introduction

Focusing specifically on the education system in francophone Sub-Saharan African countries, this chapter brings to light the gender inequality embodied in the colonial education system. Education here should be understood as the transmission of skills and knowledge in formal school settings around organized activities within that space. The outcomes are also related to the organization of the society as whole (Abdi & Cleghorn, 2005).

Most African countries have been independent for a half century or more, yet the contemporary education system in Sub-Saharan Africa still reflects the colonial legacy (Falola, 2020; Hima, 2020; Mianda, 2002, 2019, 2020). That this education system perpetuates gender inequality, marginalizing African women, can, in particular, be seen in francophone Sub-Sharan African countries (Mianda, 2002, 2019). The relevance of analyzing such systems in this Sub-Saharan African region is based on the common language that this entity called francophone Sub-Saharan Africa shares. Notwithstanding the fact that these francophone countries are in different sub-regions, they are bound by a common language—French—which stemmed from colonization by France as well as Belgium, the latter in central Africa specifically (Manning, 2008). It is worth noting that the introduction of the French language preceded official colonization in the seventeenth century (Baghana et al., 2020, p. 55). While

G. Mianda (✉)
Glendon Campus, York University, Toronto, ON, Canada
e-mail: mianda@yorku.ca

the formal French model of education reflects inheritance from the former colonizing European countries, it is often overlooked that, prior to colonization, Africa had developed formal education to a high degree. University education in Timbuktu existed in the thirteenth century (Kane, 2016). Formal education existed in Ancient Egypt and in Nubia (Troche, 2020, pp. 39–46).

Scholars have pointed out that the French language in Sub-Saharan Africa is characterized by diversity manifested through the inclusion of different mother tongues (Baghana et al., 2020). This multiplicity of French colored with local African languages does not influence the education curriculum, which is still given in standard French and was, most often, designed and implemented by the colonial order.

The call for decolonization in education is concerned with the curriculum (Adebisi, 2016) because in many countries the curriculum still reproduces the colonial legacy or has not changed it significantly (Falola, 2020, p. 7).

Ngugi wa Thiongo (1987) promotes the use of African languages as a way of decolonizing education. Questioning the hegemony of the colonial language in education also entails resisting the Eurocentric gender model which is inherent in the curriculum and emanates from the coloniality of gender (Lugones, 2007, 2010). This heteronormative Eurocentric binary gender system is constitutive of and interconnected with the coloniality of power that classifies the world population based on race and control of labor (Quijano, 2007; Quijano & Ennis, 2000). The coloniality of gender sheds light on the intersectionality of race, gender, class, and sexuality constitutive of the coloniality of power (Lugones, 2007, 2010). I argue for the decolonization of the education system through the lens of an African feminist decolonial perspective which rejects Eurocentric gender coloniality from which the Eurocentric model of education emanates.

This chapter brings to light how the coloniality of gender established gender discrimination which, through the colonial education system in francophone Sub-Saharan Africa, depreciates women (Berger, 2016; Martin, 2009; Mianda, 2002, 2009, 2019). The effect of that legacy continues to be manifested in the gender gap which leaves women behind men at all educational levels in post-colonial Africa (Berger, 2016; UNESCO, 2015). The first section of this chapter briefly describes the colonial education system in francophone Sub-Saharan countries and sheds light on differences between colonial and Indigenous education. Its intention is to provide insight into holistic Indigenous education which, by transmitting African values, did not necessarily exclude women. Using the African feminist decolonial lens, section two discusses the decolonization of education.

The Colonial Education System and the Marginalization of Women in Francophone Sub-Saharan Africa

In most francophone Sub-Saharan African countries, the colonial system of education was under the responsibility of the missionaries (Martin, 2009;

Mianda, 2002, 2007). Because they were among those who penetrated Africa before colonization was established officially, it is not trivial that, at the Berlin conference in 1885, the missionaries were designated as the best colonizers (*The Colonial Misunderstanding*, 2004). Nor is it surprising that they were entrusted with responsibility for the education system throughout most of Francophone Sub-Saharan African.

This ownership of education by missionaries was not an innocent act. In contrast, rather, it shows how colonization operated through the coloniality of power (Quijano, 2007) to imbue its domination over the colonized populations. The way in which the colonizing structure illuminates the process of colonization is instructive. Indeed, the colonizing structure had three interlocking elements—the domination of physical space, the reformation of native minds, and the integration of local economic histories into the Western perspective (Mudimbe, 1988, p. 2) which "completely embraces the physical, human, and spiritual aspects of the colonizing experience" (Mudimbe, 1988, p. 2).

Moreover, to ensure the functioning of the colonial order, colonization relied on three interconnected pillars—administrative, economic, and missionary—each of which was enshrined in the colonizing structure and constituted a support mechanism through which the colonial order operated. The colonial system of education illustrates the interconnectedness of these three pillars in ways that benefitted the colonial order.

Colonial Gender Education in Francophone Sub-Saharan Africa

In many francophone Sub-Sharan African countries, the missionaries were entrusted to lead the colonial education system based on an agreement between the European colonial government and the Holy Ghost Fathers (Martin, 2009; Mianda, 2002, 2007). The education system they established aimed to train Africans to work in the modern activity sector to benefit the European imperialist economy. For that purpose, the education system they imposed encoded the gender division that was central to the Eurocentric colonial gender system (Lugones, 2007).

The heteronormative binary system characteristic of the European gender system is constitutive of and interconnected with the coloniality of power they used to classify the world's populations based on race and the control of labor (Quijano, 2007). Thus, the coloniality of gender reveals the interconnection of race, gender, class, and sexuality (Lugones, 2007, 2010).

To understand the gender division in the colonial education system that was implemented in francophone Sub-Saharan Africa by France and Belgium, two important aspects must be noted. First, the gender division stems from the western vision of the separation between the spheres of production and reproduction which is rooted in Ancient Greek culture (Mudimbe, 1994a, 2006, pp. 162, 164; Okin, 2000, pp. 345–351). Second, the gender division in colonial education had to be brought into line with the three pillars of the colonizing structure that made colonization function effectively.

In Greco-Roman antiquity, the Athenian model established the separation of the family and public spheres by associating "woman" with the first and "man" with the second.

The Greek paradigm demanded that girls be respectable daughters of citizens and become the mother of citizens. This rule was based on the opposition between *oikos* and *polis* with *oikos* representing the interior, femininity—the condition and the possibility of the continuity of the *politeia*. The *polis*, on the other hand, referred to the exterior, the masculine, the paradigm of the preservation of the *politeia* (Mudimbe, 1994a, 1994b, p. 83).

The *politikonis* is the place of knowledge (Mudimbe, 1994a, 1994b, p. 90). It is a city which constitutes (educates, creates, fulfills) a man (Mudimbe, 1994a, 1994b, p. 90). Thus, in the city of Athena, men were associated with the *polis*, the space of Power and Knowledge exclusively for men from which women were excluded (Mudimbe, 1994a, 1994b, pp. 82–90). Women were considered inferior to men. In a well-known statement in his *Poetics*, Aristotle notes that: "(…) a woman and a slave, both can be equally good; but a woman is an inferior being and a slave is worthless" (quoted in Mudimbe, 1994a, 1994b, p. 90).

This division of gender roles that confines women to the interior—the domestic sphere—and reserves ownership of knowledge to men has stood the test of time and marked the education system in Europe through the nineteenth century (de Keukeleire, 2020; Dinet, 2011; Picco, 2018). Its sequel persists in the contemporary period manifesting itself in the opposition between male and female spheres (Okin, 2000).

In France as well as Belgium, girls were admitted to the school system later than boys. Before the seventeenth century, education was a privilege for girls of the bourgeois class and the curriculum was limited to socializing them to Christian values and teaching skills to organize the domestic sphere. For boys, the purpose of school was training to occupy public space. For the popular class, up to the nineteenth-century school generally remained accessible only to boys (de Keukeleire, 2020; Dinet, 2011; Picco, 2018).

Girls' schools were initially in the hands of religious congregations and girls were taught Christian values and housework (Dinet, 2011; Picco, 2018). Throughout the eighteenth and nineteenth centuries in Europe, education was based on the ideology that it should train women to become good wives devoted to their husband and children (Dinet, 2011).

Women were admitted to secondary schools as well as universities later than men and they were subjected to a different curriculum. Women were first admitted to the university in Belgium about 1880. Nevertheless, prior to 1921, women could not be educated in professions such as law, medicine, or pharmacy because these professions were characterized as being incompatible with women's roles as mothers and wives. The law adopted in 1921 authorized women's access to these professions (Jamin & Loriaux, 2001). In France, it was not until 1902 that universities began to admit women to medical and pharmacy schools (Dinet, 2011). Thus, with its so-called "civilizing" mission, colonization introduced its Eurocentric system of education, which vehicles the patriarchal ideology inherited from the ancient Greek and Roman gender model, into Africa.

As was the case in Europe, the colonial education system in Sub-Saharan Africa was initially in the hands of missionaries (Martin, 2009; Mianda, 2002, p. 144; 2009) who had no interest in incorporating African knowledge through education so that students would be equipped to compete with Europeans (Barnes, 2020, p. 151). The gendered education system that they established is indicative of the missionaries' will to serve the interests of the colonial order by collaborating closely with its economic and administrative pillars. The way in which the system of education designed its curriculum reveals the nested relationship between various colonial administrations and the mining and agricultural companies.

The colonial ideology was that women in Africa, like those in Europe, should be relegated to the domestic sphere. With such a mindset, the curriculum created by missionaries, as well the organization of agriculture imposed by the colonial order, seemed to agree in their functioning. In fact, both the way the colonial missionaries framed the curriculum and the ways the colonial administration reshaped the division of labor in the agricultural sector resulted in marginalizing women by alienating their labor to their husband and family.

The purpose of the curriculum in colonial education was to train boys to acquire technical skills to become artisans, craftsmen, and other auxiliaries, positions which were subordinate to those of the colonial settlers. In most colonies, this boys' education was introduced prior to that for girls (Dianzinga, 2015; Martin, 2009, p. 76; Mianda, 2002, p. 146). The initial focus of girl's education was on a curriculum that emphasized home making skills such as laundering, ironing, serving, fieldwork, cooking. As in Europe, the colonial curriculum was designed to prepare girls to become Christian wives and mothers who would be trained in domestic skills and be attentive to nurturing their husband and children (Martin, 2009, pp. 76–77; Mianda, 2007, p. 146). With its intention to bind women to the household and limit their knowledge, the colonial education system subjugated African women by alienating control over them to men.

Given the interlocking nature of the colonizing structure, the subordination of women through the colonial education system was also strengthened by the colonial administration. In agriculture, laws were introduced that transformed collectively held land into private property and designated the husband as the sole household head. Thus, husbands were provided a legal basis for their wives' economic dependence (Coquery-Vidrovitch, 1997, p. 65). The colonizers' bias against women as cash crop producers resulted in women being overlooked with respect to cash crop agricultural production and confined to subsistence crop production for family consumption and cultivate of foodstuffs for the market (Coquery-Vidrovitch, 1997, pp. 59–64).

In this way, the gender pattern that prevailed in Europe was replicated in the francophone Sub-Saharan African colonies. Hence, the colonizers overlooked the gender division that existed in Indigenous education which did not put women aside in the process of training or limit their scope of learning. The colonial education system, therefore, introduced a process that distanced Africans from their environment for the purpose of making them closer to the West (wa Thiong'o, 1987). It served as a channel to decolonize the minds of the colonized.

Indigenous Education and Gender in Sub-Saharan Africa

Education is defined as a process through which one generation transmits to the next "the accumulated wisdom and knowledge of society and prepare young people for their future membership of the society and their active participation in its maintenance and development" (Abdi, 2006, p. 15). Prior to colonization, Africa had Indigenous knowledge of its own. This Indigenous knowledge is characterized by the "connections with spirit, and metaphysical realms of existence of a place (Dei, 2014, p. 167). Indigenous knowledge is, therefore, a system that expresses the holistic natural and environmental views of individuals belonging to a community and their relationship to their environment (Semali, 1999; Zulu, 2006). Despite the diversity characteristic of Sub-Saharan African countries, including those identified as francophone, they share a common core of cultural traits with respect to Indigenous knowledge (Paré-Kaboré, 2013; Zulu, 2006).

Through African education, Indigenous knowledge was passed from the older to the younger generation in an informal manner through oral traditions (Abdi, 2006; Brock-Utne, 2000, p. 112; Nwafor & Ozioko, 2018; Omolewa, 2007). Youth learned by imitating their elders and by practice (Adeyemi & Adeyinka, 2002; Brock-Utne, 2000, p. 17; Emeagwali & Dei, 2014; Nwafor & Ozioko, 2018; Pourchez, 2014).

Given its method of communicating knowledge, African Indigenous education is to be distinguished from Western education. African Indigenous education was mainly based on participatory ways of knowing and learning, allowing individuals to learn by imitation through ceremonies, work, and oral literature. The community and the family and/or parents were responsible for passing knowledge on to the young generation through stories, proverbs, riddles, and by live examples (Kumbu, 2012; Omolewa, 2007). Indigenous education was based on principles of preparation, functionalism, communalism, perennialism, and holisticism (Adeyemi & Adeyinka, 2002; Brock-Utne, 2000). The ways in which it integrated many activities such as rituals and skills (Omolewa, 2007; Owuor, 2007) through activities such as games, dancing, music, sports, the teaching of ethical values, and other practices which it also incorporated, reveals its holistic character (Brock-Utne, 2000, p. 112).

Indigenous knowledge was also transmitted through well-structured institutions such as initiation rituals, a type of formal institution shared throughout most of francophone Sub-Saharan Africa. Initiation rituals were carried out by community members chosen for their mastery of knowledge as well as their wisdom (Mosweunyane, 2013). The rituals were to prepare youth—both girls and boys—at the time of their transition to adulthood for the roles they would occupy in society throughout their adult social lives (Kumbu, 2012; Obasi, 2018, p. 154; Omolewa, 2007). Indigenous education taught skills according to gender roles (Nwafor & Ozioko, 2018). Gender-based separation was thus central to the initiation rituals whose curriculum incorporates specific content for boys and girls. Each gender was taught so that they acquired the skills they needed to fulfill their distinctive adult gendered social roles. For their part, boys were prepared to fill socially defined masculine roles by learning specific skills necessary to becoming farmers, warriors, and blacksmiths (Obasi, 2018, p. 154). Indigenous education taught girls to become good mother, wives, and homemakers (Adeyemi & Adeyinka, 2002; Nwafor & Ozioko, 2018; Obasi, 2018). From this perspective, Indigenous education is comparable to Western education.

However, despite the gender inequality in it that contributed to women's inferior status related to sexuality (Mianda, 2020), Indigenous education did not intend to bind women exclusively to the household or distance girls from learning necessary skills for living. While skills were taught in accordance to gender roles, girls enjoyed equal status in learning which was rooted in Indigenous knowledge that "extolled motherhood and spirituality especially for women as illustrated in the case of Nnobi and Nsukka women in pre-colonial time" (Obasi, 2018, p. 154). "(I)t is through initiation ritual that girls received training in medicinal and religious knowledge" (Obasi, 2018 p. 157). Based on its holistic quality, Indigenous African education content is material, physical, and social, as well as spiritual and promotes moral and intellectual values (Adeyemi & Adeyinka, 2002; Brock-Utne, 2000). Hence, the Indigenous knowledge transmitted to girls also reflects its spiritual dimension. Girls were trained to acquire female mysteries, herbal and indigenous medicine, and religious values related to motherhood (Obasi, 2018). Through imitation and practice, girls gained skills related to childbirth, obstetrical technics, and healing strategies using herbal remedies for various treatments (Pourchez, 2014). They were taught by women elders in the community or family (Nwafor & Ozioko, 2018; Obasi, 2018; Pourchez, 2014). The Indigenous knowledge that women received was not uniquely focused on medicinal aspects. According to the gender division of labor, in agriculture women were responsible for planting crops. They learned knowledge about the use of local pesticides and other indigenous methods of plant preservation transmitted through generations.

Igbo women's use of their local knowledge to preserve crops is a testimony to the gendered curriculum in Indigenous education. From that curriculum women mastered specific knowledge about how to produce soap with local raw materials, palm oil, kernel oil, and a variety of other products (Nwafor & Ozioko, 2018).

As primary family health care providers, African women received knowledge about healing. Through their holistic African indigenous education, women also learned to master technics related to the production and conservation of crops and to produce materials according to their gender role. Despite the gendered nature of the Indigenous education system's curriculum, women were not set aside in the process of acquiring knowledge in the way that the colonial system of education marginalized them. In contradiction to the holistic nature of the Indigenous education system, the colonial education system intended to bind women to the domestic sphere where they were to be housekeepers. In fact, the missionaries responsible for education wanted to reproduce in Africa their own Eurocentric gender model with its patriarchal values which consolidate women's inferiority.

Decolonizing Education in Francophone Sub-Saharan Africa

Decolonizing the education system can be defined as a process that:

> includes, but is not limited to reclaiming, rethinking, reconstituting, rewriting, and validating the indigenous knowledges and language, and repositioning them as integral parts of the academy in universities where teaching and learning reinforce hegemonic and oppressive paradigms which allocate differential social locations to Western and indigenous knowledges. (Shizha, 2010, pp. 115–116)

Given that, discussion of decolonizing the system of education in Africa fosters passionate debate among scholars because, even since independence, the education system in most Sub-Saharan African countries has continued to carry the colonial legacy (Falola, 2020). To Africanize the current curriculum, numerous scholars advocate for the inclusion of Indigenous knowledge values (Abdi, 2006; Dei & Asgharzadeh, 2006; Semali & Stambach, 1997; Shizha, 2010, 2014). Decolonizing formal education or its curriculum does mean replacing it by Indigenous knowledge. It is a process of "moving forwards, not backwards" (Adebisi, 2016, p. 437). Asserting gender equity, some scholars also focus on the right to education for girls, meaning claiming representation in the education system for them (Okeke, 2006, p. 81).

The argument in favor of decolonizing the colonial education system targets the effect colonial education has had on African people's minds. Therefore, the classroom is approached as a site of psychological violence which has left its permanent imprint on the minds of Africans (wa Thiong'o, 1987, p. 9). In that sense, the colonial language learned in classroom has played a critical role as a tool that served to disconnect Africans from their culture (wa Thiong'o, 1987, pp. 16–17). Further, mastering the colonial language was a way in which to be "civilized" and be distinguished from the "non-civilized." To mention one illustration, as the language of education in colonized francophone countries, the French language established a new criterion of stratification dividing "civilized" from "non-civilized" Africans (Mudimbe, 1994b).

Language, as pointed out by wa Thiong'o, was "the most important vehicle through which that [colonial] power fascinated and held the soul prisoner." "Language was the means of the spiritual subjugation" (Garnier, 2011; wa Thiong'o, 1987, p. 9). Similarly, Mudimbe (1988) noted the roles that missionaries and ethnologists played in reforming Africans' minds. As mentioned, the missionaries oversaw the administration of colonial education in most francophone Sub-Saharan African countries. In this regard, they were in control of the production of knowledge in the education system which reproduced Eurocentric gender values in the curriculum.

Little attention had been given to decolonizing the curriculum regarding the Eurocentric gender model that was imposed through the colonial education system in the hands of missionaries. The Eurocentric gender model implemented through the curriculum similarly affected the minds of African men and women. To illustrate this transformation of minds by colonial education, one should refer to the cliché that situates the primary place of women as "the kitchen." The coloniality of being which resulted from the Eurocentric gender curriculum introduced by missionaries is that women should be bound to the house and men be providers of the household. While men were trained to be subaltern to the white colonizer, women were taught only how to manage the household. In the formal education system introduced by the colonial order, they were marginalized. This gender division affected women's status, making them economically dependent on men. The status imposed on women by the colonial order is in contradiction with the role women played in pre-colonial Africa.

African feminists have criticized the eurocentrism of the coloniality of gender, denouncing its racist characteristics, classism, and its representation of African women's roles (Amadiume, 1997; Mianda, 2002, 2009; Ogundipe, 1994; Oyewumi, 1997, 2003; Thiam, 1986). In that regard, African feminism is, by essence, decolonial as it rejects the Eurocentric coloniality of gender. It highlights the difference from the African gender system with its own patriarchal values while recognizing the multiplicity of women's experiences in intersectional ways (AFF, 2007).

Given African feminists' intersectional analysis based on race, gender, class, and sexuality, African decolonial feminism is inclusive in the sense that it takes into consideration the situation of all individuals in the African context. It also resists and questions the effects of the global capitalist system and its impact on African women as well as men.

Consideration of the African decolonial feminist lens which rejects the Eurocentric curriculum with is its focus on coloniality of gender is essential to decolonizing the African education system to include Indigenous knowledge. From this perspective, it is not mainly aimed at claiming only the right **to** education for girls but also to claiming the right in education for them.

The right to education for girls is a response to the politics of mainstreaming that came in the aftermath of the first United Nation's decade for women which continues to be carried on through sustainable development goals. It has resulted in progressively reducing gender disparities in the education system in Africa (Berger, 2016; Mianda, 2019) but it has not resolved the question of power in the education system in terms of who is entitled to be the knowledge producer. Some scholars also advocate the right to education for women by promoting and claiming their integration in science, technology, engineering, and mathematics fields (Falola, 2020, pp. 20–21).

On the other hand, girls' backwardness in education is commonly attributed to early pregnancy and marriage (Fredriksen & Fossberg, 2014). Pointing out these factors, which relate to African customs and traditions, is a way of ignoring the effect of the Eurocentric gender system imbedded in colonial education which framed the curriculum that marginalized women in the science disciplines. Indigenous knowledge was not designed to exclude women from the practice of science because women mastered certain healing techniques using herbs and developed numerous skills to practice agriculture in a holistic way that promoted the continuing well-being of their ecosystem.

African decolonial feminists oppose the Eurocentric coloniality of gender which served as a basis for the colonial education system. By advocating the decolonization of education, African decolonial feminists bring the Indigenous knowledge system to the center of the curriculum. In addition to rejecting the Eurocentric binary gender system with its racism, classism, and sexism, doing this entails going backward to learn from the past when women were included as knowledge producers. Excavating the past does not imply replicating it in the present context. Rather, we need to dig into the past to learn from and put lessons from that past experience in conversation with the present to adapt so that we can move forward toward our aim of more social justice for women as well as men.

Hence, decolonizing education should make use of the African decolonial feminist lens through all disciplines in the education system for students as well as in education administration. African decolonial feminists seek to decenter the biased Eurocentric male view of the world and to introduce the holistic African view knowing that it has its own gender inequity that need to be challenged in pursuing the quest for social justice for all.

Conclusion

By questioning the Eurocentric coloniality of gender model missionaries used as the basis for framing the curriculum in the colonial education system in francophone Sub-Saharan Africa, African decolonial feminists are well positioned to claim for the decolonization of education. African feminists seek to re-insert African women as well as men in the mainstream as producers of knowledge adapted in the present context. In consideration of the fact that although Indigenous knowledge was divided by gender and characterized by its own gender inequalities, it did not exclude any individual based on gender, African decolonial feminists advocate not only for girls' right to education but for girls' right in education. African decolonial feminism is against the Eurocentric gender binary model based on inequalities generated at the intersection of gender, race, class, and sexuality. By critiquing both gender inequalities in Africa and those imposed by the Eurocentric coloniality of gender, African decolonial feminists seek social justice.

REFERENCES

Abdi, A. A. (2006). Culture of education, social development and globalization. In A. A. Abdi, K. P. Puplampu, & G. J. S. Dei (Eds.), *African education and globalization: Critical perspectives* (pp. 13–30). Lexington Books.

Abdi, A. A., & Cleghorn, A. (2005). Sociology of education: Theoretical and conceptual perspectives. In A. A. Abdi & A. Cleghorn (Eds.), *Issues in African education: Sociological perspectives* (pp. 3–23). Palgrave Macmillan.

Adebisi, F. I. (2016). Decolonising education in Africa: Implementating the right to education by re-appropriating culture and indigeneity. *NILQ, 67*(4), 433–451.

Adeyemi, M. B., & Adeyinka, A. A. (2002). Some key issues in Africa traditional education. *McGill Journal of Education, 37*(2), 223–240.

African Feminist Forum Working Group (AFF). (2007). *The preamble of the Charter for feminist principles for Africa African feminist forum working group (2007). Charter of feminist principles for African feminists.* African Women Development Fund. Retrieved from https://awdf.org/wp-content/uploads/AFF-Feminist-Charter-Digital-%C3%A2%C2%80%C2%93-English.pdf

Amadiume, I. (1997). *Re-inventing Africa: Matriarchy, religion and culture.* Zed Books.

Baghana, J., Slobodova, N. K., & Birova, J. (2020). The French language in sub-Saharan Africa: Revisited. Research result. *Theoretical Applied Linguistics, 6*(1), 54–64.

Barnes, A. E. (2020). Christianity and vocational education in Africa. In M. Abidogun & T. Falola (Eds.), *The Palgrave handbook of African education and indigenous knowledge.* Retrieved from https://doi.org/10.1007/978-3-030-38277-3_7

Berger, I. (2016). *Women in twentieth century Africa: New approaches to African history.* Cambridge University Press.

Brock-Utne, B. (2000). *Whose education for all? The recolonization of the African mind.* Falmer Press.

Coquery-Vidrovitch, C. (1997). *African women: A modern history.* Westview Press.

de Keukeleire, M. (2020, June). L'accès pour les femmes à l'éducation: prémices à leur émancipation? *Le GRAIN.* Retrieved from https://www.legrainasbl.org/index.php?option=com_content&view=article&id=629:l-acces-a-l-education-pour-les-femmes-premices-a-leur-emancipation&catid=9&Itemid=103#_ftn13

Dei, G. J. S. (2014). Indigenizing the school curriculum: The case of the African university. In G. Emeagwali & G. J. S. Dei (Eds.), *African indigenous knowledge and disciplines* (pp. 165–180). Sense Publisher.

Dei, G. J. S., & Asgharzadeh, A. (2006). Indigenous knowledge and globalization: An African perspective. In A. A. Abdi, K. P. Puplampu, & G. J. S. Dei (Eds.), *African education and globalization: Critical perspectives* (pp. 53–78). Lexington Books.

Dianzinga, S. (2015). Parcours des femmes dans l'histoire du Congo (1892–1985). *Revue Cames, 1*(5).

Dinet, D. (2011). L'éducation des filles de la fin du 18è siècle jusqu'en 1918. *Revue Des Sciences Religieuses, 85*(4), 47–49.

Emeagwali, G., & Dei, G. J. S. (Eds.). (2014). *African indigenous knowledge and disciplines*. Sense Publisher.

Falola, T. (2020). Introduction to Africa's educational wealth. In J. M. Abidogun & T. Falola (Eds.), *The Palgrave handbook of African education and indigenous knowledge*. Palgrave Macmillan. Retrieved from https://doi.org/10.1007/978-3-030-38277-3_7

Fredriksen, B., & Fossberg, C. H. (2014). The case for investing in secondary education in Sub-Sahara Africa (SSA): challenges and opportunities. *International Review of Education, 60*(2), 235–259.

Garnier, X. (2011). Ngugi wa Thiong'o et la d/colonisation par la langue. *Littératures noires, 3*. Retrieved from https://doi.org/10.4000/actesbranly.488

Hima, H. (2020). Francophone education intersectionalities: Gender, language, and religion. In J. Abidogun & T. Falola(Eds.), *The Palgrave handbook of African education and indigenous knowledge*. Palgrave Macmillan. Retrieved from https://doi.org/10.1007/978-3-030-38277-3_7

Jamin, T., & Loriaux, F. (2001). Les femmes et le droit à l'instruction. *Évolution des mentalités entre le XVII siècle et t aujourd'hui*. Retrieved from https://perso.helmo.be/jamin/euxaussi/femme/femecole.html

Kane, O. O. (2016). *Beyond Timbuktu: An intellectual history of Muslim West Africa*. Harvard University Press.

Kumbu, P. M. (2012). *Du Mariage à la Famille de Base en Milieu Yonbe. Jalons pour un projet éducatif* (Thèse de doctorat). Faculté de théologie.

Lugones, M. (2007). Heterosexualism and the colonial/Modern gender system. *Hypatia, 22*(1), Winter. *Hypatia, 22*(1), Special issue: Writing against heterosexism (pp. 186–219). https://doi.org/10.1111/j.1527-2001.2007.tb01156.x

Lugones, M. (2010). Toward a decolonial feminism. *Hypatia, 25*(4, Fall). Retrieved from http://pds25.egloos.com/pds/201211/27/71/Toward_a_Decolonial_Feminism.pdf

Manning, P. (2008). *Francophone Sub-Saharan Africa, 1880–1995* (2nd ed.). Cambridge University Press.

Martin, P. M. (2009). *Catholic women of Congo-Brazzaville, mothers and sisters in troubled times*. Indiana University Press.

Mianda, G. (2002). Colonialism, education, and gender relations in the Belgian Congo: The Evolué case. In J. Allman, S. Geiger, & N. Musisi (Eds.), *Women in African colonial histories* (pp. 144–163). Indiana University Press.

Mianda, G. (2007). Du Congo des évolués au Congo des universitaires. In I. Ndaywel (Ed.), *L'Université dans le devenir de l'Afrique. Un demi-siècle de présence au Congo-Zaïre*. L'Harmattan.

Mianda, G. (2009). L'État, le genre et l'iconographie: l'image de la femme au Congo belge. In I. Ndaywel è Nziem & E. Mudimbe-Boyi (Eds.), *Images, mémoires et savoirs. Une histoire en partage avec Bogumil Koss Jewsiewicki*. Karthala.

Mianda, G. (2019). Women in Central African history. In *Oxford research encyclopedia of African history*. Oxford University. Retrieved from http://oxfordre.com/africanhistory

Mianda, G. (2020). Central African education: Indigenous to western. In J. M. Abidogun & T. Falola (Eds.), *The Palgrave handbook of African education and indigenous knowledge*. Palgrave Macmillan. Retrieved from https://doi.org/10.1007/978-3-030-38277-3_7

Mosweunyane, D. (2013). The African education evolution: From traditional training to formal education. *Higher Education Studies, 3*, 50–59.

Mudimbe, V. Y. (1988). *The invention of Africa: Gnosis, philosophy, and the order of knowledge*. Indiana University Press.

Mudimbe, V. Y. (1994a). *The idea of Africa*. Indiana University Press.

Mudimbe, V. Y. (1994b). Les Corps Glorieux des Mots et des Êtres. *Esquisse d'un Jardin Africain à la Bénédictine*. Présence Africaine.

Mudimbe, V. Y. (2006). *Cheminements. Carnets de Berlin (Avril–Juin 1999)*. Humanitas.

Nwafor, F. I., & Ozioko, A. O. (2018). Igbo indigenous science: An ethnobiologist perspective. In J. Abidogun (Ed.), *African science education: Gendering indigenous knowledge in Nigeria*. Taylor & Francis.

Obasi, W. N. (2018). Creating gender parity. Igbo women's indigenous science knowledge practice. In J. Abidogun (Ed.), *African science education: Gendering indigenous knowledge in Nigeria* (pp. 153–178). Taylor & Francis.

Ogundipe, L. (1994). Stiwanism: Feminism in the African context. *Re-creating ourselves; African women & critical transformations* (pp. 207–232). Africa World Press.

Okeke, P. E. (2006). Higher education for Africa's women: Prospects and challenges. In A. A. Abdi, K. P. Puplampu, & G. J. S. Dei (Eds.), *African education and globalization: Critical perspectives* (pp. 79–92). Lexington Books.

Okin, S. M. (2000). Le genre, le public et le privé. In Collectif (Eds.), *Genre et politique. Débats et perspectives*. Mesnil-sur-l'Estrée, Gallimard.

Omolewa, M. (2007). Traditional African modes of education: Their relevance in the modern world. *International Review of Education, 53*, 593–612.

Owuor, J. A. (2007). Integrating African indigenous knowledge in Kenya's formal education system: The potential for sustainable development. *Journal of Contemporary Issues in Education, 2*(2), 21–37.

Oyewumi, O. (1997). *The invention of women: Making an African sense of western gender discourses*. University of Minnesota press.

Oyewumi, O. (2003). *African women and feminism: Reflecting on the politics of sisterhood*. Africa World Press.

Paré-Kaboré, A. (2013). L'éducation Traditionelle et la Vie Communautaire en Afrique. Repères et Leçons d'Expériences pour l'Education au Vivre Ensemble. *McGill Journal of Education/Revue des Sciences de l'éducation de McGill, 48*(1), 15–33.

Picco, D. (2018). La monarchie française et l'éducation des filles nobles (XVIè-XVII siècles). *Encounters in Theory and History of Education, 19*, 35–51.

Pourchez, L. (2014). Savoir des femmes. Médecine tradtionnelle et nature (Maurice, Rodrigues, La reunion), Presses de science Po. *Les Tribunes de santé, 3*(44), 51–71. Retrieved from https://www.cairn.info/revue-les-tribunes-de-la-sante1-2014-3-page-

Quijano, A. (2007). Coloniality and modernity/rationality. *Cultural Studies, 21*(2), 168–178. Retrieved from https://doi.org/10.1080/09502380601164353

Quijano, A., & Ennis, M. (2000). Coloniality of power, eurocentrism, and Latin America. *Nepantla: Vieux from South, 1*(3), 533–558.

Semali, L. (1999). Community as classroom: Dilemmas of valuing African indigenous literacy in education. *International Review of Education, 45*(93–40), 305–319.

Semali, L., & Stambach, A. (1997). Cultural identity in an African context: Indigenous education and curriculum. *Folklore Forum, 28*(1), 3–27.

Shizha, E. (2010). Rethinking and reconstituting indigenous knowledge and voices in the academy in Zimbabwe: A decolonization process. In D. Kapoor & E. Shizha (Eds.), *Indigenous knowledge and learning in Asia/Pacific and Africa: Perspectives on development, education, and culture*. Palgrave Macmillan.

Shizha, E. (2014). Indigenous knowledge systems and the curriculum. In G. Emeagwali & G. J. S. Dei (Eds.), *African indigenous knowledge and the disciplines* (pp. 113–129). Sense Publisher.

Teno, Jean-Marie (Producer & Director), with Mauch, B. (2004). *The colonial misunderstanding/Le Malendentu Colonial*. Motion Picture. Les Films du Raphia.

Thiam, Awa. (1986). *Speak out, black Sisters: Feminism and oppression in Black Africa* (Dorothy S. Blair, Trans.). Pluto Press.

Troche, Julia. (2020). Ancient Africa education: Egypt and Nubia. In J. M. Abidogun & T. Falola (Eds.), *The Palgrave handbook of African education and indigenous knowledge*. Retrieved from https://link.springer.com/book/10.1007/978-3-030-38277-3

UNESCO. (2015). *Education for all 2000–2015: Achievements and challenges*. Retrieved from https://www.gcedclearinghouse.org/sites/default/files/resources/232565e_0.pdf

wa Thiong'o, N. (1987). *Decolonising the mind: The politics of language in African literature*. James Currey; Heinemann Kenya; Heinemann; and Zimbabwe Publishing House.

Zulu, I. M. (2006). Critical indigenous African education and knowledge. *The Journal of Pan African Studies, 1*(3), 32–49.

PART IX

Critical Indigenous and Southern Epistemologies of Education

CHAPTER 31

Critical Theory as Lived Meaning: Exploring Anti-Racist Practice in Post-Secondary Education

Derek Tannis

Reflecting

I greet her and walk with her to the office we are meeting in, making small talk. I slide open the glass door to a fluorescently lighted, nondescriptly furnished space. She puts down her bag and sits on the edge of a chair, looking down at the floor. I move to the desk and, from my satchel, pull out an envelope. I sit down, place my clasped hands on the desk and explain the purpose of the meeting, elaborating on our earlier phone conversation, asking her again if she wants to have someone else present. She says, in a tight voice, "I will see if I need someone after this meeting". I assure her of my focus on her wellbeing and success and as I talk, my shoulders release, my hands unclasp. In the ensuing silence, I sense my foreignness to this space, swooping in from another campus miles away, my privilege and institutional position palpable. The student leans back and I explain that I have a letter for her that we can discuss together. She glances at me skeptically and then reaches over and takes the envelope. She removes and unfolds the letter slowly and holds it with both hands close to her face, covering everything but her eyes. When she comes to the first sentence of the allegation, she abruptly presses the letter into her lap. She shifts as if to stand up, then speaks in a quickening voice, "It says here that I raised my voice. That I was threatening". She shakes her head, "Well…What do you expect? I've learned to fight for myself. I was in prison. I am a strong, Indigenous woman.

D. Tannis (✉)
School of Continuing Studies, McGill University, Montreal, QC, Canada
e-mail: derek.tannis@mcgill.ca

© The Author(s), under exclusive license to Springer Nature Switzerland AG 2022
A. A. Abdi and G. W. Misiaszek (eds.), *The Palgrave Handbook on Critical Theories of Education*, https://doi.org/10.1007/978-3-030-86343-2_31

A mother. If someone sees me as threatening, well, I am protecting myself. My family". We sit looking at one another in silence, and then, she says, as if to herself, "But...maybe I could have done it different. I am learning to be proud without being angry".

INTRODUCTION

In this reflection, I recall the contours of a critical moment, as the Director overseeing my institution's student conduct office in the province of Saskatchewan (Canada), with an Indigenous student facing charges of non-academic misconduct. In that meeting, institutional power and policy are omnipresent. The procedures of student non-academic conduct policy are not abstractions; they are experienced through our interactions, embodied in the presentation of a letter. From a critical perspective, underlying societal racism and the legacies and contemporary realities of colonization in our Canadian context are palpable, evidenced by disproportionately low Indigenous post-secondary participation and completion rates, and disproportionately high incarceration rates (Battiste, 2013; Daschuk, 2014; Stonechild, 2006). Saying this is not to judge the student's conduct, but rather to investigate my own context as a Settler-Canadian, committed to advancing anti-racist practices in post-secondary education (Mackey, 2016; Regan, 2010; Denis, 2007).

This chapter draws upon my study of the co-creation of transformative Indigenization and internationalization in post-secondary education (Tannis, 2019). In this research, which included conversational interviews with 23 faculty, staff and students, anti-racism emerged as a central, underlying aspect of the participants' approach to their practices as leaders, teachers and help providers. Following Kendi's definition of anti-racism (2019), my participants' anti-racist practices surfaced through their experiences "supporting an antiracist policy through their actions or expressing an anti-racist idea" (p. 13). Their actions and expressions reflected assertions that "racial groups are equals in all their apparent differences – that there is nothing right or wrong with any racial group" and that "racist policies are the cause of racial inequities" (p. 20). As with my experience in student conduct, the participants in my study recognized that, as anti-racist practitioners, we are "surrounded by racial inequity, as visible as the law, as hidden as our private thoughts" (p. 22). In this sense, this chapter opens to the question of what it means to "knowingly strive to be an antiracist" in our post-secondary institutions, a practice that demands "persistent self-awareness, constant self-criticism, and regular self-examination" (p. 23).

Using this as a case study, I thus attempt, in the following pages, to show how critical phenomenology offers a unique and valuable addition to critical policy analyses of anti-racism. In the first section of this chapter, I situate myself and my research approach. In the second and third sections, I engage a critical phenomenological analysis of my research participants' descriptions of their anti-racist practices. In the last section, I conclude by linking this case study with the central argument of this chapter—that critical approaches to phenomenology can bring lived meaning to critical theories of education. In this chapter, I follow aspects of a phenomenological writing style that include "methods of tone, lived-thoroughness, nearness, intensification, appeal, and answerability" (van Manen, 2014, p. 241). Thus, I will be using first-person and, at times, will speak of "we" and "our", when reflecting on lived anti-racist practice. This approach is not meant to be presumptuous, nor exclusionary, but is rather a stylistic approach that aims to "reflect on life while reflecting life" (p. 296).

Seeking

It may go without saying that the relationship between phenomenology and critical theory is fraught with distrust (Marder, 2014; O'Neill, 1972). The underlying disagreements are many: phenomenology is questioned on the basis of the extent to which subjective interpretations of phenomena can be *bracketed*, or suspended; empirical limitations of early claims of phenomenology are questioned in terms of uncovering universal essences of lived experiences; and subsequently, critics argue that phenomenology is not an appropriate methodology to explore social, cultural and economic structures of power (Marder, 2014). According to Marder (2014), these critiques have, however, also been part of ongoing reformulations of phenomenology as critical turns toward empiricism, being, ethics and interpretation itself. In the words of Salamon (2018), what makes phenomenology critical is that "it is following an imperative that is both critical in its reflexivity and phenomenological in its taking-up of the imperative to describe what it sees in order to see it anew" (Salamon, 2018, p. 12).

The application of phenomenology to the human sciences is therefore diverse and contentious in its range, scope and methods (van Manen, 2014). For the study that forms the basis of this chapter, I drew upon the approach and methods outlined by van Manen (1997, 2014) and Vagle (2014). The interviewing technique of van Manen (1997) focuses on recalling lived experiences related to the topic of inquiry. For both van Manen and Vagle, the researcher sees the process as a conversation, consolidating and sharing back lived experience descriptions that participants have offered, exploring together their potential lived meanings. Vagle, applying phenomenology to political philosophy, adds a further layer, employing the term *lines of flight*.

> [T]he concept, *lines of flight*, does not assume that any thing, idea, belief, goal, phenomenon, person, animal, object, etc., can be thought of as stable, singular, and final. Instead, all things are connected and interconnected in all sorts of unstable, changing, partial and fleeting ways. This is important to post-intentional phenomenology as a political philosophy as the connective nature of social, ethical, and political relations does not lend itself to simplicities and essences. It does lend itself to complexities and tentative understandings. (Vagle, 2014, p. 118)

A fundamental aspect of critical phenomenology is a commitment to remain as open as possible to the "complexities and understandings" of lived experience, as it relates to other disciplinary knowledges, including critical sociological and political theories (Vagle, 2014, p. 18). Vagle draws from Dahlberg (2006) in employing the term, *bridling*, as a way to ensure "we do not understand too quick, too carelessly" such that we "do not make definite what is indefinite" (p. 16). This indefinite approach to research analysis is grounded upon "the problem and promise of openness" which "may still be the source from which phenomenology's richest possibilities spring forth, even in these dark times" (Salamon, 2018, p. 16).

While there remain philosophical differences between critical theories of education, including Critical Race Theory, and critical phenomenology, there is also, as Salamon (2018) wrote, a potential for tapping their "richest possibilities" by drawing from their commonalities (p. 16). These commonalities are grounded in three interconnected ways. First, they view what we term reality as being socially constructed, including "relationships of inequality and privilege" (Diem et al., 2019, p. 6), such that we experience "racism [as being] embedded in the structure of society" (Bonilla-Silva, 2015). In this sense, to explore our realities through these approaches, "attention is given to the differences between policy rhetoric and practiced reality" (Diem et al., 2014, p. 1072). As Husserl (1970/2002) wrote, we live our social realities in "a realm of original self-evidences […] in immediate presence, or, in memory […] arising out of particular activities" that are rooted in "the concreteness of the lifeworld" (p. 167). As Henry and Tator (2009), explained, the *concreteness* of everyday racism in the lifeworld of our post-secondary institutions opens to the exigency of critical analyses of anti-racist policy and practice.

> Everyday racism in the academy, as well as across a wide range of interlocking institutional and discursive spaces, involves the many and sometimes small ways in which racism is experienced by racialized people in their interactions with the members of the dominant White culture. It expresses itself in behaviours; anecdotes; sexualized, ethnicized, and racialized jokes; inappropriate glares and glances; gestures; and forms of speech. Often it is not consciously experienced by its perpetrators, but it is immediately and painfully felt by its victims. The everyday racism in the academy heightens one's sense of vulnerability and affects one's sense of self-esteem and personal self-confidence. (Henry & Tator, 2009, p. 27)

Given that critical theories of education and critical phenomenology pay particular attention to everyday practice, they also place emphasis on narratives that critique or counter dominant, or taken-for-granted, discourses (Bonilla-Silva, 2015; Diem et al., 2019; Vagle, 2014). As Bell (2016) wrote, narratives create potential openness, whereby others "will often suspend their beliefs, listen to the story, and then compare their views, not with mine, but with those expressed in the story" (p. 36). For van Manen (2014), the impact of "stories or anecdotes" can be attributed to the fact "that they can explain things that resist straightforward explanation or conceptualization" through "the vividness and presence of an experience" (p. 251). The underlying tension, however, with individual accounts of racism and anti-racism is that they may perpetuate the perception that racism is fundamentally an individual experience, rather than being ideologically and structurally framed (Bonilla-Silva, 2015). Addressing such ideological framing is arguably central to the context of education (Cueto & Rios, 2016; Dua, 2009; Ladson-Billings, 1999; Parker, 2020) and educational research (Harper, 2012). For, while phenomenological traditions place "value" on "how the human being experiences the world" (van Manen, 2014, p. 58), critical approaches to a phenomenology of anti-racist practice in post-secondary education must also take, as its starting point, that our experiences and ways of interpreting them, even in the moment of their being experienced, are deeply conditioned by socio-economic, socio-historical and socio-cultural factors (Marder, 2014; O'Neill, 1972; Vagle, 2014). Such a starting point must necessarily recognize ongoing racist and colonial policies and practices as they are lived (Kendi, 2020; Russell, 2020; Tuck & Wayne, 2012). This recognition thus includes the contextual, inter-subjective knowledges and experiences that shape our interpretation of anti-racist policy through lived practice (Schwartz-Shea & Yanow, 2012). In the words of Schwartz-Shea and Yanow (2012),

> Admitting the possibility (and legitimacy, from a scientific perspective) of local knowledge in the search for understanding contextualized concepts and actor meaning-making of events, etc. opens the door to knowledge generated by others than the scientist alone. Sense-making by the researcher depends, in this view, on sense-making by those actors, who are called upon to explain them to the researcher (whether literally, in interviews, or in the common conversations of everyday living, or less directly, in written or other records that constitute the material traces of acts, things, and words). (Schwartz-Shea & Yanow, 2012, p. 80)

To argue that anti-racist policy, as embodied practice, involves shared sense-making, thus demanding that my positionality not be overlooked. I come to the topic and practice of anti-racism as someone who has been working in the post-secondary sector for over 25 years, largely in the international education and student services areas. I am a cisgender male, Settler-Canadian with Scottish-Irish and Lebanese-Syrian roots, born and raised in Ottawa, Canada. As a post-secondary practitioner, dedicated to anti-racism, my understandings of my own identity and privilege have shifted and continue to shift considerably. In the words of Nancy (2015), I have come to understand identity as "the landing point – or the point of inscription, one might say – when a path can begin to be traced out [...] A point and a labyrinth, such is the secret of an identity" (p. 22). I recognize that one of my central *landing points* is that I have been brought up within a family and society that has been, and continues to be, shaped by the labyrinthine webs and layers of colonization and structural racism.

My "privileged status" in being able to take the time to research and write on the topic of anti-racism requires my commitment to "formulating a meaningful purpose and being the measure for the ultimate efficacy" of what I write (Fenton, 2020). Writing about lived experience of anti-racist practices within "post-secondary communities [that] face special challenges when it comes to policy engagement on divisive issues" (Remocker et al., 2020, p. 187) requires that I must, as a non-racialized student services practitioner, continuously "engage in self-disclosure of how it [racism] lives within me" (Brookefield, 2014, p. 91). In such self-disclosure, I recognize the limits of my own philosophical traditions and understandings that I have drawn upon in this chapter. In this spirit, these next pages are, using Rocha's (2015) words, akin to dipping a sponge into the ocean of our lifeworld(s), saturated with legacies and structures of racism and colonialism:

> Being is the sea, and we are within it, pulled by the subsistent tides and forces, existing as an embodied sponge, always gushing with excess — saturated with and within Being, alive with energy and spirit. [...] Unlike the methods of science, phenomenological method is not intended to simply address the cup of existence as fully as possible. The phenomenologist tries – and always must fail – to explore the very horizon of saturation and gain insight into the ontological excess that eludes our particular ways of being-within, subsisting, existing, and thereby extending potentiality, the saturation-point of the imaginable, the possible, and the real. (Rocha, 2015, p. 26)

Saying

Exploring the prevalence and impacts of racism in post-secondary education is a context where "the stakes are indeed high: to talk about racism is to occupy a space saturated with tension" (Ahmed, 2012, p. 162). The tendency in research and practice is to reframe racism in terms that are more palatable, less discomforting for those who are non-racialized (Ahmed, 2012; Harper, 2012). In my research, I experienced this tendency, both in how I framed my research questions and in my participants' responses. However, through building trust and engaging in multiple conversational interviews, my participants' lived experiences of racism surfaced.

> I facilitate a seminar where I'm not responsible for curriculum. I have no power, no authority, no control in terms of lecture content...But I do have that learning space within the seminar in which to foster a positive and safe learning environment. In every class I facilitate, I want to provide the opportunity that allows for the student to come forward and say, "I grew up in a racist household. I only know negative stereotypes or I know nothing at all. I grew up in a household

where people said bad things about Aboriginal people". I facilitate an environment that allows for the students to explore and discover that for themselves. There's an awareness and they're young. They don't want to be ugly, right? They want to be better than that, right? They aspire to be better.

In this reflection, Elsie, an Indigenous scholar, cultural practitioner and teacher, speaks of how she navigates her intentional, transformative role within the constraints, and pervasive racism, of a predominantly White post-secondary environment. Elsie endeavors to make her classroom a space where students can come to see their own racism and express their learning and growth, each in their own developing understandings of the anti-Indigenous racism that permeates their lifeworlds. She acknowledges the youth of her students, and of her own position as an experienced Indigenous educator, where she "sits back a bit more" having "already been through all of these things". Elsie's approach may seem, in some sense, antithetical to anti-racist practice; however, Dominic, in reflecting on a human rights disclosure meeting with a colleague, also speaks to this seemingly acquiescent approach.

> I can't get her to verbalize what I think might be going on, and I sense it as a failure of our climate. What is it about our environment here that won't allow her to say that to me? What is it about her work environment that has damaged her to the point where she can't even say the words? If she doesn't want to identify as having been subjected to racism, I'm okay with that. I don't want to put her into a victim box. I look at it as, "What's wrong with this system? Why can't we have these conversations?". Even the idea of saying the word "racism". If you accuse someone of being racist, that's pretty heavy. If she doesn't want to talk about racism, okay. We can we talk about conversation coaching, about how to avoid those conversations. We can talk about how to make her more equipped to stand up for herself. I'll do what I can within where she's prepared to go.

For Dominic, acknowledging that a colleague is experiencing racism involves listening and responding to his colleague in a way that respects how she describes her experience. He does not interject his interpretation, but reflects, internally, on what her experience says about the environment they work in together and how he might be able to assist over time, to a point where his colleague may be able to name the racism she may likely be experiencing. Leonardo and Porter (2020) described what may be at the heart of the approach that Elsie and Dominic, and the participants in my study spoke of, in some way or another:

> When paired with clarity in purpose and solidarity with the other, where judgement is practiced but one is never judged, discomfort can be liberating because it enables whites and people of color to remove the mask. They may end up knowing each other more fully as human beings rather than the shell of one:

whites assumed to be more superior than they are, people of color more inferior than they are. After many years in the university setting, we have learned that this apostasy – of creating risk as the antidote to safety – leads to more transformative learning opportunities. (Leonardo & Porter, 2020, p. 203)

Acknowledgements of students' and colleagues' lived experiences with racism may be integrated into one's depth of awareness of the context in which they disclose their experiences. The potentially weakening label of victimhood, re-victimizing repercussions from accusing another of racism, or the defensive withdrawal of engagement in the face of being accused of racism all loom heavily. Even if our students and colleagues do not name racism, by entering into our anti-racist offices and classrooms, we might presume they are seeking the means to refuse the racist treatment they are facing, or that they may, under the right conditions, be capable of refusing underlying aspects and ideologies that frame their own racist identities. As we may intuitively grasp, or as we may have directly experienced ourselves, such refusal takes on a different tenor than acknowledgment. Sophie describes such an experience.

> A professor makes an Islamophobic comment. I am sitting next to a friend who wears a hijab. She looks at me and I am thinking, "She can't speak. She's much more vulnerable than I am. She's not born here." I say, "What you just said was very essentializing and smacks of Islamophobia, and I really don't appreciate you speaking that way about my community". I have a lot of good friends in the class, but no one acts as an ally. The professor responds, "I'm just telling the truth and it makes you uncomfortable."

Sophie reflects upon an interaction from her university studies that has shaped her understanding of how racist behavior can be enacted within a university context. Sophie's experience reveals the impact of inappropriate faculty-student interaction and opens to tensions that are often just beneath the surface of the post-secondary institutions in which we work. As a graduate student, she underscores the risks and vulnerabilities of refusing to be the object and subject of racism, of sensing (self-) protectiveness, alienation and disapprobation, even when surrounded by friends. She determines to speak out, in the face of a faculty member, who, exerting his power differential, seeks to "disrupt [her] practical relation to self by denying [her] recognition for particular claims to identity" (Honneth, 1995, p. 132). Melinda speaks to such refusal in defending what she terms the "honour" of international students at an institution-wide meeting on internationalization strategy.

> Students, Deans, people have been elected to serve on this committee. People get going on how international students can't speak English, why are we letting them in, it's too much work. A faculty member is sitting in front of me, waving her hands around and complaining about the Chinese students in her class. I feel I'm going to take it on. I look around. I like to see if someone's going to take it on and, if they're not going to, then I do. As long as I know enough or

am reasonably sure I can make a rational argument. Because if you're a woman in administration, you don't get lots of chances to make a significant point. I'm frustrated and get indignant. It's full of falsehoods. It doubly annoys me when I'm in a meeting with academics who will never let their students get away with an assertion without evidence. All of those emotions get to me and my heart starts to pound. I start speaking and then I'm mad at myself because I'm not putting it in a very eloquent way. I'm just mad and adversarial. I haven't made a friend but at least those words are floating out there in the air.

Refusal for Melinda, as a white female Dean, includes a calculated risk. Before interjecting, Melinda scans the group to see if there is anyone who might contest what is being said. As she goes to speak, she senses a change in her emotional and physical state and her words become less articulate. She is deeply aware of her relational connection with her colleagues, of the adversarial tone that can invariably come with addressing racism.

Along these lines, many participants described refraining from using terms like White privilege loosely, too early on in their courses or workshops, or without advance context or consideration of the potential effect, knowing how quickly such a term can shut down their students and colleagues. From DiAngelo's (2018) perspective, such an approach might be sidestepping what she terms *white fragility* in the face of being called to task for racist microaggressions, or using Kendi's terms (2020), *racist abuse*. However, it may also be said that, from a phenomenology of practice perspective, Elsie, for example, nurtures an "emancipatory biographical praxis" which, in being "usefully explored and enhanced", she feels helps her students transform their understanding of the racism that Indigenous peoples face and their role in its perpetuation (Hoggan et al., 2017, p. 58). In a sense, it may be that anti-racist practice, spoken as acknowledgment and refusal of our institutional policies, invites or challenges us to assume our responsibility in creating *braver anti-racist spaces* of engagement (Arao & Clemens, 2013).

Following Levinas (1998/1974), in such spaces, we may experience more than what is and isn't "said" (Levinas, 1998/1974, p. 5). We may experience a signifying beyond what is said, and in that sense, in the lived relationality of our anti-racist practice, "saying is not a [language] game" (Levinas, 1998/1974, p. 5). Levinas (1998/1974) wrote:

Responsibility for the other, in its antecedence to my freedom, its antecedence to the present and to representation, is a passivity more passive than all passivity, an exposure to the other without this exposure being assumed, an exposure without holding back, exposure of exposedness, expression, saying. This exposure is the frankness, sincerity, veracity of saying. Not saying dissimulating itself and protecting itself in the said, just giving out words in the face of the other, but saying uncovering itself, that is, denuding itself of its skin, sensibility on the surface of the skin, at the edge of the nerves, offering itself even in suffering. (Levinas, 1998/1974, p. 15)

In our day-to-day work, we may indeed sense that we are involved in some kind of game, navigating the politics and demands of our institution, where we "protect" ourselves, by "giving out words in the face of the other" (Levinas, 1998/1974, p. 15). And yet also, at the same and at other moments in time, we may be involved in work that, in taking us beyond our zones of comfort and into unknown horizons, "uncovers" who we are in communion with, that opens us to the sensibility of saying itself, to the "vulnerability, exposure to outrage, wounding" in the exposure of our "saying" in our anti-racist practices (Levinas, 1998/1974, p. 15).

DOING

> I am with one of my friends at a restaurant downtown. Two guys walk by and one calls me the "N-word". They walk away, then loop back. We're standing in a circle talking. There is tension, as if they are thinking, "What are you going to do?" I am thinking, "It's one in the morning. I'm tired. Some guy just called me the 'N-word'. I might try to fight him, but that's not something that will reflect good on anything I'm doing." So instead, I decide, "If they have a conversation with me, I'll try to speak to them like a person."

In this reflection, Terrence, a student leader at his institution, describes being a target of racist aggression. Terrence's reaction reaches deep into his identity and past experience, having been in similar situations before and not having restrained his response. In this moment, he suppresses his initial impulse to fight back, knowing that his actions would also reflect on his role as a student leader. The alienation and racism that Terrence describes cannot be compartmentalized. Terrence brings such (recent) experiences of racist abuse with him into his post-secondary environment, into the work he is doing as a student leader. In this line of explicit racism, Cassandra reflects on a moment, when in the midst of her day, she finds herself speaking with a man who proclaims his support for a terrorist organization, demanding a ticket to a sold-out panel on the Syrian refugee crisis.

> A person scares the bejesus out of our receptionist and is transferred to me. He rants on the phone, "Why are you holding this panel? Why do you care about refugees? I support ISIS." I basically say, "This is my role and what I can tell you. If you have other concerns, these are your options." He hangs up. I'm in shock. I tell my supervisor and he calls the police. They come, take a statement, and undercover police attend the event.

Cassandra reacts resolutely, and yet, once she has time to reflect, realizes just how serious the situation is, not just for her, but for her colleagues and for her institution as a whole. Like Terrence, she does not engage in a verbal altercation, but redirects him and, ultimately, ensures the safety of the event that she is hosting. In the face of racist threats or support of violence, Cassandra and

Terrence do not engage with their self-disclosed antagonists with reciprocated violence, verbal or otherwise. Knowing their own relationship to anti-racist practice, they exert a level of self-awareness that extends beyond the moment, into their relationships with the communities they are part of and in which they work. It may be said that they refuse to be drawn into the webs of antagonism and the logic of violence, yet also acknowledge the inherent "agonistic confrontation" at the heart of anti-racist practice (Mouffe, 1999, p. 756). In a relatable context, Chris says:

> When an adversary is strong and belligerent and is doing so in order to have the outcome they want, I'm not very good at even staying in the conversation. I just get angry and I shut down. I go red, my headache will start to throb even more and I will stew on it for days. This is the individual's interpretation of the institution. Because of where they interact in the institution, they may or may not have got that right. It's my struggle to find more spaces of interaction that counter that perspective, that allows me to develop my own understanding of "Is that really likely to happen? Is that threat based on just a pattern of how you get things done? Is that a true reading of the politic and the environment at the level you operate in? Is that just your own individual perspective?"

In this reflection, Chris describes his struggle to keep international student issues on the institutional agenda's hierarchical, decision-making process. He describes such experiences as being fundamentally adversarial, similar to Melinda's earlier reflection about what she described as defending the "honour" of Chinese, international students. As an adversary, for Chris and many of the participants in my study, persistence in pursuing a particular policy goal or related shift in institutional culture, requires them to attenuate themselves to the perspectives, influences and privileges of power in the face of conflicting issue-framing and/or decisions on policy instruments (Stone, 2002). They seem to speak to the "mixed game" of "pluralist politics", which is "in part collaborative and in part conflictual and not as a wholly co-operative game as most liberal pluralists would have it" (Mouffe, 1999, p. 756).

As we enter into adversarial positionalities as anti-racist practitioners, sensing that we are becoming unfriendly, potentially experiencing changes in our physical states, with rising heart rates, a quickening voice, a headache, we may be experiencing our deviation from the dominant pattern of liberal consensus that currently pervades the social and political sphere (Mouffe, 2005). Such struggle against the "deep seated internal contradictions" and "structure and power relationships" delimits radical, transformative institutional change (Burrell & Morgan, 1979, p. 34). We may sense that we should, by the dominant, normative standards of our institutions, remain (questionably) objective, cool, unemotional, and yet find that the situations we face require us to act with firmness and clarity that, from that same standard, positions anti-racist practice as threatening (Ahmed, 2012). It may be said that anti-racist practitioners will necessarily experience "disagreement concerning the way social justice should be integrated into [their] institutions", in ways that are more or less "considered as legitimate and indeed welcome" (Mouffe, 2005, p. 113). Henry and Tator (2009) speak to this underlying agonism, applying the term *democratic racism*:

> Democratic racism is an ideology in which two conflicting sets of values are made congruent to each other. Commitments to democratic principles such as equality, fairness, and justice *conflict* with, but also *coexist* with, negative feelings about racialized individuals and groups and discrimination against them. One of the consequences of this conflict is a lack of support for policies and practices that might improve the relatively low status of racialized communities. (Henry & Tator, 2009)

As practitioners, we may be engaging multiply in the spheres of policymaking, teaching, helping and leading, depending on our role(s) within our institutions. In that sense, at any point in the day, we may be simultaneously engaged in pursuing anti-racist policy within our division, helping racialized students through difficult situations, and teaching students, drawing from anti-racist methods and content. From the perspective of critical phenomenology, anti-racist practice may be understood, in this sense, as policy embodiment, whereby "policy discourses […] are always and inevitably mediated for individuals through their material (flesh and blood, sentient, thinking and feeling) bodies" and the "actions" of our colleagues and students (Evans & Davies, 2012, p. 624). Sophie speaks to such policy embodiment, as anti-racist practice, in visceral terms:

> Students in my workshops or my university classes make Islamophobic comments. Everybody wants to talk about terrorism all the time. You just scratch the surface. It's just waiting. I offer my own body as a site of study that interrupts these notions of what this identity group is and to begin to complexify, demystify this exoticized trope that circulates through society. I can do that with my students because that's what I'm there for. I'm not there to be in battle.

Sophie's observations on the "offering of her body" reveals her non-combative approach to engage her students in exploring their prejudices, ignorance, concerns, and questions. In so doing, she enacts what it means to be spoken of, demanding her students to try to see her more clearly in their (mis)understandings of Islam and what it means to be Muslim. Sophie takes up with her students how it is that, in the context of post-secondary education and the broader society in which they live, "bodies that signify religiosity" can often be "suspected of being biased" (Douglass, 2016, p. 111). In recounting the racism that she experiences, it is as if Sophie becomes a "liminal pathway" for her students' evolving certainties about Muslim women (Sehdev, 2010, p. 117). Sehdev (2010) poetically and forcefully depicts such embodied liminality, using an analogy of "bridging" for the difficult work of intercultural learning (p. 117):

> The bridge is liminal because the crosser is surrounded with its absence, and with the knowledge of that liminality is necessary for any sort of political or cultural connection. The subjectivities of women of colour comprise the anchoring posts of the bridge, and their stretching bodies, the planks. This is not an apparently warm embrace or a chokehold, though it is bodily, dangerous and often painful. The bridge is a gruesome structure dependent on the labour of those stretching to create the passageway *upon the backs* of those who are liminal and so implicates the crosses in the threat of the pain of those who are crossed upon. (Sehdev, 2010, p. 117)

When a colleague offers herself, like Sophie, to bridge differences, increase understanding or address inequity and prejudice, there is a risk taken that not all of us might be able to comprehend. Sehdev's (2010) analogy evokes hooks' (2010) description of the physical, emotional and inter-subjective, lived meaning of critical thinking. For hooks (2010), critical thinking is a relational, public offering of our personhood in spaces that, in the act of offering, help our students and colleagues to develop "empathy for others, an understanding of the circumstances that influence and inform their thoughts and behaviours" (hooks, 2010, p. 186). As Sophie demonstrates, this offering, or "labour", of "bridging" (Sehdev, 2010, p. 117) as a teacher and trainer requires her to "anchor her subjectivity" such that her students and colleagues can "cross" her own "body" as a site of resilience, wisdom, courage and compassion (Sehdev, 2010, p. 117). In recognizing the tension and potentiality of her intersectional positionality, Sophie, like many of the participants in my research, describes herself as pushing against the limits of the certainties we hold in the "bright light of the public realm" of our institutions in what we do and say (Arendt, 1958, p. 51). In the words of Ahmed (2012):

> The body who is "going the wrong way" is the one experienced as "in the way" of a will that is acquired as momentum. For some, mere persistence, "to continue steadfastly," requires great effort, an effort that might appear to others as stubbornness, willfulness, or obstinacy. […] Diversity work thus requires insistence. You have to become insistent to go against the flow, and you are judged to be going against the flow because you are insistent. A life paradox: you have to become what you are judged as being. (Ahmed, 2012, p. 186)

Being

Andreotti (2015) once described *going upriver* in addressing the sources of social injustices, shrouded in the "shine" of the "modern colonial imaginary" (p. 227). She argued that, in our day-to-day lives, we become distracted with the work of attending to the tangible effects of social injustices. For Andreotti, such "upriver work", however, requires "essential, difficult and often disturbing begged questions that may implicate rescuers in the reproduction of harm" (p. 227). Andreotti (2015) and Ahmed (2012) reflect, in each their own ways, the *paradox of anti-racist practice*: as we seek to say and do things that we hope might (radically) transform our institutions, we do so in a social, cultural, political and economic environment that is steeped in multiple forms of racism (Kendi, 2020).

At the outset of this chapter, I included a reflection on an experience I had in my role in student conduct at my current institution. Coming into that experience, I was rethinking our approach to student conduct, recognizing that something was not working, and in fact, was, in some ways, creating more conflict than resolving it. In that moment with the student, I sensed I was part of a "relational nexus" that was "accompanied by a vast array of other modes of relation" (p. 11) that extended far beyond the institution, reaching into the "liminal space that accounts for both the political and racialized natures" of Indigenous identities (Russell, 2020, p. 217). Leading up to, during and following that meeting, I sought guidance and support from Indigenous and non-Indigenous colleagues to engage, respectfully and holistically, in restorative approaches to working through the allegations of non-academic misconduct. Throughout, my intention was to help find resolution in ways that addressed the needs and wellbeing of all involved. We didn't know at the time that by taking this approach, we had begun our path toward a renewal of our student conduct approach. Months later, at campus-wide gathering, involving an Indigenous Elder, faculty, student services colleagues and students, we laid the foundation for working toward integrating restorative, culturally enriched and responsive approaches to student conduct. I have come to understand the kind of process we undertook as a form of attempting "treaty-making as a verb" (Mackey, 2016, p. 141). Mackey (2016) wrote:

> [W]e need to think about how "we treaty," and how to behave responsibly if "we treaty together" or "make treaty" together. It is a relationship we *build over time*. Like all good relationships, there are rules of respect and autonomy, but there can be no pre-planned and decided trajectory because a treaty is relational and interactive. Relationships are by their nature *uncertain*: they require seeing, listening and responding creatively to an "other" who is autonomous and also connected to us. (Mackey, 2016, p. 141)

Following the intention of this chapter, it may be that through reflecting upon, and engaging a concept such as lived, ongoing treaty-making, we may be also opening to how critical theory is lived, as practice. Exploring such lived experience may open critical theory to new pathways yet to be explored, or re-open, and question established meanings of older pathways previously taken. To approach critical theory in this manner may be a means to engage the "legacy of critical theory" as a "critique of the present" by which "the past is constantly transformed" (Claussen & Maiso, 2019, p. 63). Applying critical phenomenology to the exploration of lived, anti-racist practice may also be a means to reinvent critical theory from this inside (Allen, 2016). For Allen (2016), such a reinvention requires attention to lived social relations and the practice of reasoning, not as a universally normative set of standards, but as being a set of standards that are constantly in a state of (re)negotiation among diverse peoples and perspectives. This reinvention, Allen argued, is necessary because "critical theory runs the risk of becoming overly utopian unless it identifies normative potentials that are present in existing social reality" (p. 227).

As anti-racist practice, approaching critical theory as lived meaning requires decentering the "modern/colonial imaginary" in order to reconsider "what is intelligible, the range of questions that can be formulated, and the appropriateness of responses: what is possible to think and to identify with" (Andreotti, 2015, p. 225). In critical phenomenological terms, such decentering is not only about what we say and do. As Mackey (2006) described, such a decentering requires us to open to other ways of being with others. To do so, we need to be curious, to reposition ourselves and relook at things we may have stopped seeing, or to open ourselves to sense what we may have overlooked or chosen to ignore (Morgan, 2016). In relation to anti-racist practice, such an approach may open us to new ways of reflecting, seeking, saying and doing that may take us further upriver in ways that can, as much as possible, avoid "the reproduction of harm" (Andreotti, 2015, p. 227). Along the way, and even at the destination or "landing point from where our path may be traced out" (Nancy, 2015, p. 22), we may find that agonism and liminality may be the only constant we can be sure of. In the words of Sophie,

> There's a collective in the city that put on a day around decolonization. These two amazing young scholars are giving a panel on decolonial practices and cultural appropriation. There is no remnant, no shred of the weight of European modernity in this room. I am almost lightheaded. I have a question about the appropriation by White middle class Americans of hip hop. I am a bit emotional because I am thinking of Palestinian hip hop and how important that form has been to them as a revolutionary form in a space where there are limited forms of resistance. I don't feel particularly comfortable. It is a slightly dangerous space. I feel myself being decentered. I have never been so excited. It is beautiful. I just want to sit there for the rest of my life.

REFERENCES

Ahmed, S. (2012). *On being included: Racism and diversity in institutional life*. Duke University Press.

Allen, A. (2016). *The end of progress: Decolonizing the normative foundations of critical theory*. Columbia University Press.

Andreotti, V. (2015). Global citizenship education otherwise. In A. Abdi, L. Shultz, & T. Pillay (Eds.), *Decolonizing global citizenship education* (pp. 221–236). Sense Publishers.

Arao, B., & Clemens, K. (2013). From safe spaces to brave spaces: A new way to frame dialogue around diversity and social justice. In L. Lendreman (Ed.), *The art of effective facilitation* (pp. 135–150). Stylus Press.

Arendt, H. (1958). *The human condition*. University of Chicago Press.
Battiste, M. (2013). *Decolonizing education: Nourishing the learning spirit*. Purich Publishing.
Bell, D. (2016). Who's afraid of critical race theory. In E. Taylor, D. Gillborn, & G. Ladson-Billings (Eds.), *Foundations of critical race theory in education* (pp. 31–42). Routledge.
Bonilla-Silva, E. (2015). More than prejudice. *Sociology of Race and Ethnicity, 1*(1), 73–87. https://doi.org/10.1177/2332649214557042
Brookefield, S. (2014). Teaching our own racism: Incorporating personal narratives of whiteness into anti-racist practice. *Adult Learning, 25*(3), 89–95.
Burrell, G., & Morgan, G. (1979). *Sociological paradigms and organisational analysis: Elements of the sociology of corporate life*. Ashgate Publishing.
Claussen, D., & Maiso, J. (2019). Critical theory and lived experience. *Radical Philosophy, 2*(06), 68.
Cueto, D., & Rios, F. (2016). Multicultural education and critical race theory in the academy. In V. Farmer & E. Farmer (Eds.), *Critical race theory in the academy* (pp. 43–60). Information Age Publishing.
Dahlberg, K. (2006). The essence of essences—The search for meaning structures in phenomenological analysis of lifeworld phenomena. *International Journal of Qualitative Studies on Health and Wellbeing, 1*, 11–19.
Daschuk, J. (2014). *Clearing the plains*. University of Regina Press.
Denis, V. S. (2007). Aboriginal education and anti-racist education: Building alliances across cultural and racial identity. *Canadian Journal of Education/Revue canadienne de l'éducation*, 1068–1092.
DiAngelo, R. (2018). *White fragility: Why it's so hard for white people to talk about racism*. Beacon Press.
Diem, S., Young, M., & Sampson, C. (2019). Where critical policy meets the politics of education: An introduction. *Educational Policy, 33*(1), 3–15.
Diem, S., Young, M., Welton, A., Cumings, M., & Lee, P.-L. (2014). The intellectual landscape of critical policy analysis. *International Journal of Qualitative Studies in Education, 27*(9), 1068–1090.
Douglass, L. (2016). Embodying authenticity in higher education. In J. Cohen, J. Gammel, & A. Riley (Eds.), *New directions for teaching and learning, 147*, 107–115.
Dua, K. (2009). On the effectiveness of anti-racist policies in Canadian universities: Issues of implementation of policies by senior administration. In F. Henry & C. Tator (Eds.), *Racism in the Canadian university: Demanding social justice, inclusion, and equity* (pp. 160–196). University of Toronto Press.
Evans, J., & Davies, B. (2012). Embodying policy concepts. *Discourse: Studies in Cultural Politics of Education, 33*(5), 617–634.
Fenton, Z. (2020). On becoming a critical race scholar. In V. Farmer & E. Farmer (Eds.), *Critical race theory in the academy* (pp. 325–338). Information Age Publishing.
Harper, S. (2012). Race without racism: How higher education researchers minimize racist institutional norms. *The Review of Higher Education, 36*(1), 9–29.
Henry, F., & Tator, C. (2009). Theoretical perspectives and manifestations of racism in the academy. In F. Henry & C. Tator (Eds.), *Racism in the Canadian university: Demanding social justice, inclusion, and equity* (pp. 22–59). University of Toronto Press.

Hoggan, C. Mälkki, K., & Finnegan, F. (2017). Developing the theory of perspective transformation: Continuity, intersubjectivity, and emancipatory praxis. *Adult Education Quarterly, 67*(1), 48–64.

Honneth, A. (1995). *The struggle for recognition: The moral grammar of social conflicts.* The MIT Press.

hooks, b. (2010). *Teaching critical thinking: Practical wisdom.* Routledge.

Husserl, E. (2002). The way into phenomenological transcendental philosophy by inquiring back the pregiven life-world. In D. Moran & T. Mooney (Eds.), *The phenomenology reader* (pp. 151–174). Routledge. (Reprinted from The crisis of European sciences and transcendental phenomenology: An introduction to phenomenological philosophy, D. Carr, Trans., (pp. 103–137), 1970).

Kendi, I. X. (2019). *How to be an antiracist.* One World.

Ladson-Billings, G. (1999). Just what is critical race theory, and what's it doing in a *nice* field like education? In L. Parker, D. Deyhle, & S. Villenas (Eds.), *Race is…race isn't: Critical race theory and qualitative studies in education* (pp. 7–30). Westview Press.

Leonardo, D., & Porter, R. (2020). Pedagogy of fear: Toward a Fanonian theory of "safety" in race dialogue. In L. Parker & D. Gillborn (Eds.), *Critical race theory in education* (pp. 189–207). Routledge.

Levinas, E. (1998/1974). *Otherwise than being or beyond essence* (A. Lingis, Trans.). Duquesne University Press.

Mackey, E. (2016). *Unsettled expectations: Uncertainty, land and settler decolonization.* Fernwood Publishing.

Marder, M. (2014). *Phenomena-critique-logos: The project of critical phenomenology.* Rowman & Littlefield International.

Morgan, M. (2016). *Levinas's ethical politics.* Indiana University Press.

Mouffe, C. (1999). Deliberative democracy or agonistic pluralism. *Social Research, 66*(3), 745–758.

Mouffe, M. (2005). *The democratic paradox.* Verso.

Nancy, J.-L. (2015). *Identity: Fragments, frankness.* Fordham University Press.

O'Neill, J. (1972). Can phenomenology be critical? *Philosophy of Social Sciences, 2*(1), 1–13.

Parker, L. (2020). "Race is…race ain't": An exploration of the utility of critical race theory in education. In L. Parker & D. Gillborn (Eds.), *Critical race theory in education* (pp. 27–39). Routledge.

Regan, P. (2010). *Unsettling the settler within: Indian residential schools, truth telling, and reconciliation in Canada.* UBC Press.

Remocker, C., Dyck, T., & Reist, D. (2020). Engaging the "heart and mind": Building community capacity for culturally grounded approached to substance use on post-secondary campuses. In L. Levac & S. Wiebe (Eds.), *Creating spaces of engagement: Policy justice and the political crat of deliberative democracy* (pp. 187–207). University of Toronto Press.

Rocha, S. (2015). *Folk phenomenology: Education, study and the human person.* Pickwick Publications.

Russell, C. (2020). Critical race theory in Indigenous contexts. In V. Farmer & E. Farmer (Eds.), *Critical race theory in the academy* (pp. 215–226). Information Age Publishing.

Salamon, G. (2018). What's critical about phenomenology? *Pucta: Journal of Critical Phenomenology, 1*(1), 8–17.

Schwartz-Shea, P., & Yanow, D. (2012). *Interpretive research design: Concepts and processes*. Routledge.
Sehdev, R. (2010). Lessons from the bridge: On the possibilities of anti-racist feminist alliances in Indigenous spaces. In L. Simpson & K. Ladner (Eds.), *This is an honour song: Twenty years since the blockades* (pp. 105–124). Arbeiter Ring Publishing.
Stone, D. (2002). *Policy paradox: The art of decision-making*. W. W. Norton.
Stonechild, B. (2006). *The new buffalo: The struggle for aboriginal post-secondary education in Canada*. University of Manitoba Press.
Tannis, D. (2019). *Horizons of belonging: Co-creating transformative Indigenization and internationalization in higher education*. Doctoral dissertation, University of Alberta. Education and Research Archive.
Tuck, E., & Wayne, W. (2012). Decolonization is not a metaphor. *Decolonization: Indigeneity, Education & Society, 1*(1), 1–40.
Vagle, M. (2014). *Crafting phenomenological research*. Left Coast Press.
van Manen, M. (1997). *Researching lived experience: Human science for an action sensitive pedagogy*. The Althouse Press.
van Manen, M. (2014). *Phenomenology of practice: Meaning giving methods in phenomenological research and writing*. Left Coast Press.

CHAPTER 32

Critical Adult Education in the (Neo)colonies: Racial/Colonial Capitalist and Social Movement Ontologies of Land

Dip Kapoor

INTRODUCTION

Critical theories of society and education seek to advance the pursuit of a new world without dogmatic anticipation and through a relentless "criticism of existing conditions", "not afraid of its findings and just a little afraid of the powers that be" (Marx, 1967, p. 212). Education in any space, when informed by critical theory, seeks to unveil these ontological possibilities (existing conditions), while actively addressing them through the development of a "revolutionary/transformative praxis" which generates a "critical dialectical understanding of our present conditions" (Allman, 1999, p. 58). To this end, critical theory is a normative reflection that is historically and socially contextualized, clarifying the meaning of concepts and issues, describing and explaining social relations and articulating and defending ideals and principles. Unlike positivist social theory, which purportedly separates social facts from value (claim of value neutrality), critical theory with a practical interest in emancipation relies on critical description and explanation. The *given* is evaluated in normative terms so that questions about what occurs in a society

---

Dedication: Dr. Abdul Aziz Choudry (1966–2021)—friend, activist and social movement educator/intellectual par excellence.

D. Kapoor (✉)
University of Alberta, Edmonton, AB, Canada
e-mail: dkapoor@ualberta.ca

© The Author(s), under exclusive license to Springer Nature Switzerland AG 2022
A. A. Abdi and G. W. Misiaszek (eds.), *The Palgrave Handbook on Critical Theories of Education*, https://doi.org/10.1007/978-3-030-86343-2_32

and why, who benefits and who is harmed are asked and social theory is then unlikely to reify the *given* social reality of domination and exploitation. Critical theories of society and education universalize the capacity for critical inquiry of oppositional and autonomous thought and education and are constitutive of learning, activism and social movement pedagogy (Choudry, 2015).

A radical education is one which links pedagogic processes and practices to a project of social transformation. Euroamerican Marxist critical theory or socialist praxis (Allman, 1999) understands "existing conditions" (the *given*) and related revolutionary praxis in terms of the labor-capital (relations) dialectic and the disruption of the reproduction of capitalist class/social relations of production (and society) including hegemonic capitalist/liberal education as a moment within the process of the social reproduction of labor power in/for capitalism. Marxism grounds the project of radical education in the interests of establishing socialist relations.

Indigenous and anti/decolonial critical theories germinating from European settler colonies (Canada, US, Australia, New Zealand) (Alfred, 2005; Coulthard, 2014; Grande, 2004, 2015) and the (neo)colonies or colonies of exploitation (Veracini, 2015) in Africa, Asia and the Americas/Caribbean (Fanon, 1967; Freire, 1970; Guha, 1997; Nkrumah, 1965; Quijano, 2000, 2005; Rodney, 1982) understand existing and recurring conditions in terms of the land-based settler/neocolonial-anti/decolonial (relations) dialectic, respectively, and a related anti/decolonial revolutionary praxis vis-à-vis racial/colonial capitalist relations. Anti/decolonial projects ground radical education in the interests of (Indigenous) sovereignty and/or self-determination/autonomy, working toward socio-cultural, political-economic and subjective transformations.

This chapter stretches critical adult education, which is predominantly associated with western Marxist and/or post-structural variants, by engaging an anti/decolonial critique (critical theories) of Euroamerican racial/colonial capitalist ontologies of land, wherein land is construed as being vacant and therefore available for enclosure as private property and treated as a tradeable market commodity. The main proposition thereof is that a materialist ontology of land as private property and a (fictitious) commodity for accumulation at the expense of a resident population (racial/colonial relations) enables Euroamerican settler colonialism and recursive (neo)colonization in the colonies of exploitation (Veracini, 2015) to the present day. Construed on onto-axiological assumptions from the Papal *Doctrine of Discovery* and the instrumental philosophical ruminations of John Locke in *The Two Treatises of Government*, the current land grab has been described as being unprecedented since the time of Euroamerican colonization (fifteenth–twentieth century) (Araghi & Karides, 2012). These colonial dynamics warrant continued critical consideration in terms of their neocolonial structural specificities (Nkrumah, 1965; Trask, 1999) given Patrick Wolfe's assertion pertaining to the settler colonies—"invasion is a structure, not an event" (2016, p. 33) and for informing and learning from Indigenous-peasant anti/decolonial social movement land ontologies.

Anti/decolonial critiques of this racial/colonial capitalist ontology of land for accumulation predicated on recursive dispossession inform the onto-epistemological grounds for anti/dispossession social movement pedagogies addressing food/land sovereignty and popular indigenous, forest-dweller, pastoralist, fisher and small/landless peasant movements in the (neo)colonies. Contrary to Euroamerican racial/colonial capitalist ontologies of land (Dunbar-Ortiz, 2014; Nichols, 2020; Wolfe, 2016; Wright, 2015), land in these contexts of subaltern social action is generally not understood in anthropocentric terms as a possession or property form, except where racial/colonial capitalist hegemony has been reproduced. Nor is land an object of control but one of (historical) relationships with territory and place, including the responsibility to ensure against *Victorian holocausts* (Davis, 2001/2017) and (neo)colonial projects of racialized dispossession and attempts at Indigenous eradication (Fanon, 1967; Galeano, 1972; Rodney, 1982; Wolfe, 2016).

Racial/Colonial Capitalist Ontologies of Land: Discovery and Property

> The discovery of gold and silver in America, the extirpation, enslavement and entombment in mines of the aboriginal population, the beginning of the conquest of the looting of the East Indies, the turning of Africa into a warren for the commercial hunting of black-skins, signaled the rosy dawn of the era of capitalist production. (Marx, 2007, p. 823)

The Papal *Doctrine of Discovery*, initially formulated in response to the conquest of the Americas, came to be known as the law of nations and later, international law whereby European sovereignty was first asserted over the lands and inhabitants of the New World. While establishing European sovereignty over these dominions, the Native right of occupancy entitled Natives to use a territory that Europeans had (ostensibly) discovered (Wolfe, 2016, p. 141). The "culture of conquest—violence, expropriation, destruction and dehumanization" in the Americas, however, began in the 11th to the thirteenth century when Europeans conducted the Crusades to conquer North Africa and the Middle East, well before the Atlantic crossing and Columbus' departure for the Americas. That is, the institutions of colonialism and methods for relocation, deportation and expropriation of land had been practiced and perfected by the end of the fifteenth century within Europe (enclosures) and during the crusades (Dunbar-Ortiz, 2014, pp. 32–34; Robinson, 2000). The process of colonial capitalist accumulation and organization under the profit motive by European states expanded overseas thereafter encompassing the Caribbean, Central America, Mexico and the

Andes followed by West and South Africa, North America, and the rest of South America. Then came all of Africa, the Pacific and Asia. As Dunbar-Ortiz goes on to note, the only difference between these western European voyages and prior seafaring ventures by the Inuit (Eskimos), Norse, Arabs, South Asian, Chinese, Japanese, Peruvian and Melanesian and Polynesian fishing peoples of the Pacific is that "they had developed the bases for colonial domination and exploitation of labor in those colonies that led to the capture and enslavement of millions of Africans for transport to the American colonies" (2014, p. 34).

The Papal Bulls of Discovery (*Doctrine of Discovery*) Romanus Pontifex (1455) issued by Pope Nicholas V and *Inter Caetera* (1493) pronounced by Pope Alexander VI provided the framework for colonization by Spain, Portugal and England and for the Atlantic slave trade. King Alfonso of Portugal, for instance, was exhorted in Romanus Pontifex to invade, search out, capture, vanquish and subdue all Saracens and pagans whatsoever, and other enemies of Christ wheresoever placed, and the kingdom and all goods whatsoever held and possessed by them and to reduce their persons to perpetual slavery and to convert them to his and their use and profit (Wright, 2015). From the mid 15th to the mid-twentieth century most of the non-European world was colonized under the *Doctrine of Discovery*, one of the first principles of international law Christian European monarchies promulgated to legitimize claiming the land of non-Europeans (Wolfe, 2016; Wright, 2015), initially dividing the globe between the two Iberian monarchies of Spain and Portugal. The Pope gave the Americas to the former and West Africa to the latter under the Treaty of Tordesillas (1494) (Dunbar-Ortiz, 2014, p. 199).

The *Doctrine*, as Robert Miller (2006, pp. 3–5) describes it, is constituted by 10 elements which define international law then and to date (Wolfe, 2016) to varying degrees in different colonial contexts (and especially in British colonies),[1] including the following:

(1) **First Discovery** (the first European country to "discover" new lands unknown to other Europeans gained property and sovereign rights over the lands);
(2) **Actual occupancy/possession** (first discovery claims could only be made into title via actual occupancy);
(3) **Preemption** (the discovering European country had sole right to buy the land);
(4) **Terra nullius** (lands actually owned, occupied and/or utilized were considered "vacant" and available for "discovery claims" if they were not being "properly used" according to European and American law and culture);
(5) **Christianity** (only Christians had the right to land, sovereignty and self-determination);

(6) **Civilization** (God had directed Europeans to bring civilized ways and education and religion and to exercise guardianship powers over the uncivilized); and
(7) **Conquest** (military victory over and a "term of art" when used in relation to the element of "discovery").

Unsurprisingly, Frantz Fanon (1967/1963, p. 32) subsequently concluded that "When you examine at close quarters the colonial context, it is evident that what parcels out the world is to begin with the fact of belonging to or not belonging to a given race, a given species. In the colonies, the economic sub-structure is also a superstructure and the cause are the consequence"; an observation subsequently taken up by the Black Radical Tradition and the development of a critical theorization of "racial capitalism" (Robinson, 2000).

Referring to settler colonization in the US, Patrick Wolfe elaborates by noting that the White man's discourse of property was "color coded on the colonial ground" wherein "Black people's labor and Red people's land produced the White man's property—a primitive accumulation if ever there was one. Native and enslaved were of antithetical but complementary value to White society" (2016, p. 3). While Black slaves were valuable commodities (labor) and hence demographically fostered, Natives obstructed the expansion of settlement (land) and no effort was spared to eliminate them. While for Durkheim, religion was society speaking, for Wolfe, "race is colonialism speaking, in idioms whose diversity reflects the variety of unequal relationships into which Europeans have co-opted conquered populations" (p. 5).

This racial/colonial Anglo-European system of "land ownership" subsequently worked as a tool of "legalized theft", in the apprehension of Indigenous territory whereby in the nineteenth century alone, 9.89 million square miles of land or 6% of the land on the earth's surface had been colonized by Anglo-settlers (Nichols, 2020, p. 51; Weaver, 2006). The colonial empires of the west—Portugal, Spain, France, Great Britain, the Netherlands/Dutch, Belgium, Germany, Italy and the United States—eventually claimed possession at one time or another to all of the Americas and Australia, 99% of Polynesia, 90% of Africa and nearly 50% of Asia (Townsend, 1941), i.e., by the 1930s, ex-colonies and colonies under formal European government included 85% of the earth's land surface (Fieldhouse, 1989, p. 373). Europe is "literally the creation of the Third World, an opulence that has been fueled by the sweat and the dead bodies of Negroes, Arabs, Indians and the yellow races" (Fanon, 1967/1963, p. 76). Alternately and in keeping with the Lockean (John Locke, 1632–1704) narrative and the wider discourse of the *Doctrine of Discovery* which the British philosopher and Oxford academic provided in the *Two Treatises of Government* (1698), one that would profoundly influence Euroamerican colonial ideology, private property accrued from the admixture of (Black) labor and (Red) land (Wolfe, 2016).

John Locke was deeply enmeshed in the administrative webs of racial/colonial capitalism and the ideational texture of this political-economic vision as Secretary of the Council of Trade and Plantations (1673–1674) and later via membership to the Board of Trade and Plantations (1696–1700). The Earl of Shaftesbury involved him in his designs to found a colony in Carolina (America) and Locke helped draft its Fundamental Constitutions (1669). Locke invested in colonialism as he held shares in the Royal African Company that traded in slaves, was a merchant adventurer of the Bahamas (1672–1676) and engaged in stock-jobbing in East India Company bonds. According to Herman Lebovics, Locke was the wise organic intellectual of the seventeenth-century British elite and future generations of British ruling classes and a great philosopher of the developing world system which linked the old world with the new with ties of domination and subordination. This Atlantic economy, as incubator of global capitalist relations, conceived, justified and defended by Locke, hinged upon the "slave plantation complex" that was developed on land taken from Native Americans, was run by slave labor imported from Africa and existed for the sole purpose of producing a cash crop for export. Those at the helm of the state knew that there would be no English Empire without the Caribbean (sugar), slaves and demand for mainland staples and English manufactures (Ince, 2015, pp. 5–8).

The first theoretical move of the Lockean *Treatises* and the defense of colonial appropriation of land was to assert the Christian theological declaration that the earth is an open common, i.e., the common inheritance of "mankind" (*res nullius*). Locke inverted the meaning of this (the commons) to a negative sense re-describing "common inheritance = inappropriable" to "common = not yet appropriated" (Nichols, 2020, p. 156). "God gave the World to Men in Common but since he gave it to them for his benefit and the greatest conveniences in life they were capable to draw from it, it cannot be supposed he meant it should always remain common and uncultivated" (Locke quoted in Ince, 2011, p. 40). The fulcrum of Locke's theory of (land as) property thereof then becomes the basis of the theoretical assault on Indigenous (and subsequently, in the neocolonies) land/territory wherein he proposed that enclosing and improving land by "mixing labor" (superior productivity/utilization) yields private property or entitlement to land, thereby disqualifying Amerindian hunting and gathering practices. The Devonshire farmer described in the *Second Treatises* is the only legitimate proprietor and citizen, i.e., the "industrious and rational" being to whom, Locke claims, God gave the world (Arneil, 1994, p. 609).

He then proceeds to establish the (alleged) "universal benefits" (including for the dispossessed/colonized) of enclosure for improvement (moral rationale for private appropriation) via the notion of production for the "common stock of mankind" along with the restrictive (limiting) moral provisions pertaining to the "proscription of spoilage" (waste) and leaving to others "enough and as good" of the common. The introduction of his concept of *money* (presented as a universal with tacit consent) thereafter, however, by unmooring (land) appropriation and value creation from the limits of a subsistence economy (while overcoming the spoilage limitation), unleashes the power of obligatory labor to increase the "common stock of mankind"/maximalization (economic growth), potentially circumventing these restrictive provisions, for (alleged) universal benefit (Arneil, 1994, 1996; Ince, 2011, 2015). In James Tully's words (in Ince, 2015), "the Aboriginal peoples are better off as a result of the commercial system of private property" thanks to "not only finished products but also the opportunities to labor"; in short "they are more than compensated for their loss" (of land/territories); a justification for appropriation based on "universal benefit" and the Catholic principle of non-exclusion (Ince, 2015, p. 12).

> Layers of conceptual ambivalence generated by these theoretical maneuvers enable Locke to configure inclusionary and exclusionary provisions in ways that authorize the dispossession of Native Americans at the same time it captures them in myths of natural equality and mutual consent and a global vision of prosperity. Locke's theory of property subtly co-articulates socio-spatial displacement and exclusion on the one hand and liberal values and the promise of development on the other. It thereby recasts in a liberal mold the fulcrum of 17th century Atlantic capitalism, namely, colonial land appropriations and indigenous dispossession. (Ince, 2015, p. 17)

These metaphysical and practical assumptions are compounded by Locke's assertion that Native Americans do not live under institutionalized governments and absence of proper political societies and sovereign authority renders America vacant territory (*terra nullius*) and therefore open to colonial appropriation (Ince, 2015, p. 10). Locke is skeptical of violent conquest however and in chapter sixteen of the Second Treatise, he establishes his preference for appropriating land by industry rather than force wherein English colonization, as per his theory of property is concerned, is justified "not just by the command of God and natural law but because each colonist has a natural right within himself, through his labor, to appropriate land" (Arneil, 1996, p. 74) as private property. But as Robert Nichols elaborates, property is normally/logically prior to theft but in the colonial (Lockean) context, "theft is the means by which property is generated" or "dispossession is effectively a form of property-generating theft" (2020, p. 9).

Discovery and Lockean notions of land and property while providing the ideational basis for the transatlantic process of enclosure authored a global vision of material and historical progress underpinned by a universalist liberal ideology of improvement and prosperity beyond America, repainting colonial capitalist land appropriations as peaceful, commercial and universally beneficial acts of settlement and development (Arneil, 1996; Galeano, 1972; Ince, 2011, 2015; Rodney, 1982). Mike Davis (2001/2017), in *Late Victorian Holocausts: El Nino Famines and the Making of the Third World*, to consider but one illustrative application, demonstrates the implications of the Lockean liberal capitalist (including Smith, Bentham and Mills) ontological and axiological position on land/property and production (labor-capital) for the exploitation colonies by elaborating on the connection between colonialism, capitalism and global climate patterns (and ecological racism) in the golden (colonial) age of liberal capitalism. He links the impositions of colonial capitalist development to climate change and the spread of famine in the late nineteenth/early twentieth century (in India, China, Brazil, Ethiopia, Korea, Vietnam, Philippines and New Caledonia) wherein millions of Indians, according to Davis, were murdered by the theological application of the sacred principles of these Anglo-European philosophers; a genocide wherein 30–60 million died worldwide while being forcibly incorporated into the political and economic structures of this modern world system.

Given the five-hundred-year history of Euroamerican colonization and colonial structuration, North–South relations were marked by what the Peruvian sociologist Anibal Quijano references as a continuous "global coloniality of power" (2000; 2005, pp. 56–57) defined by:

(a) a new system of social domination built around the idea/foundation of 'race' (a modern European mental construct bearing no relation to previous reality) and racialization of relations between European colonizers and the colonized in order to normalize the social relations of domination created by conquest and the new system of capitalist exploitation;

(b) the formation of a new system of exploitation (capitalism) which connects in a single combined structure all the historical forms of control of work and exploitation (slavery, servitude, simple commodity production, reciprocity, capital) to produce for the capitalist world market—a system with a racialized division of labor and control of resources of production is foundational; and

(c) a new system of collective authority centered around the hegemony of the state or a system of states with populations classified in racial terms as "inferior" being excluded from the formation and control of the system.

Euroamerican colonialism, however, was dialectically imbricated with anticolonial struggles in the colonies of exploitation or (neo)colonies which included: (1) the defense of, and by, pre-existing states of their polities against western expansion; (2) popular and often violent nativist uprisings and reactions to western interference and imposition of institutions and customs via militant or missionary Christianity; (3) slave revolts (e.g. African and Creole) against plantation owners and masters; (4) issue-specific ameliorative uprisings exposing a colonial injustice in the interests of reform/concessions; and (5) organized movements and violence against colonial regimes for national independence (Benjamin & Hidalgo, 2007, p. 59). Subsequently, between 1940 and 1980, more than eighty colonies achieved their independence and were eventually recognized as sovereign nation-states.

Racial/Colonial Capitalist Ontologies of Land: Post Independence Development and Neocolonialism

Considering the "global coloniality of power" (Quijano, 2000), as soon as the colonies of exploitation gained their legal independence, they found themselves tethered to the imperial powers by the post-war UN "development project" (Kamat, 2002; Kothari, 2005; Langan, 2018; Rist, 2014), currently pursued in terms of the MDG/SDG initiatives (2000–2030), prompting Walter Rodney (1982), in *How Europe Underdeveloped Africa*, to urge for an extensive investigation of the phenomenon of neocolonialism in order to formulate the strategy and tactics of African emancipation and development. The essence of neocolonialism, according to the architect of the concept Kwame Nkrumah (1965, p. ix), President of the first Sub-Saharan African state (Ghana) to achieve independence, is that the state which is subject to it is, in theory, independent and has all the outward trappings of international sovereignty but in reality, its economic system and thus its political policy is directed by outside. Through foreign aid for instance, even after formal empire had been dissolved, "the hesitancy of cutting ties from former colonizers is fostered by the sugared water of aid which is the stop-gap between avid hunger and the hoped-for greater nourishment that never comes…imperialism, having quickly adapted its outlook to the loss of direct political control, has retained and extended its economic grip" (p. 33).

In fact, Frantz Fanon (1967) saw neocolonialism as affecting the "Third World" as a whole. The racial/colonial capitalist ontology of land as property and marketable commodity and its neo-Lockean logic found continuity in UN initiatives such as the Millennium Development Goals (MDGs) and related Sustainable Development Goals (SDGs) regimes and the agrarian policies of the World Bank promulgating the corporatization of land and agriculture; a food for profit model. Racial neocolonial capitalist logics in relation to land are reproduced in the post-independence period through a combination of free trade agreements, corporate investment, western aid programs and development aid agents (international development agencies), structural adjustment and the debt mechanism (1980s onwards) and the moral rhetorical imperatives of the MDG/SDGs (Langan, 2018; War on Want, 2012).

"Land grabbing" (Marx, 2007, p. 470) in the name of the post-independence "development project" (see www.grain.org or www.oaklandinstitute.org) from indigenous peoples, small/landless peasants, fishers, nomads and pastoralists in the contemporary period flags "a vast expansion of bourgeois land rights…through a global land grab unprecedented since colonial times…as speculative investors now regard 'food as gold' and are now acquiring millions of hectares of land in the global South (70% of which is in Africa alone—*my addition*)" (Araghi & Karides, 2012, p. 3). An Oxfam study in 2011 suggests that an area in the size of Western Europe (227 million hectares) has been sold or leased since 2001, involving mostly state-corporate investors (125 million have been grabbed by rich countries for outsourcing agricultural production alone in Africa) (Kapoor, 2017). Indigenous scholars recognize this process as an "ongoing colonial relationship between ourselves and those who want to control us and our resources... we are surrounded by other, more powerful nations that desperately want our lands and resources and for whom we pose an irritating problem. This is as true for the Indians of the Americas as it is for the tribal people of India and the aborigines of the Pacific" (Trask, 1999, pp. 102–103). "Once again, such a project exalts white bodies, capitalist investment and private property and while simultaneously condemning brown and black bodies, subsistence production and collective and customary property arrangements (Mollett, 2015, p. 425).

Lorenzo Veracini (2015, p. 26) goes so far as to suggest that "even if colonial and settler colonial formations should be seen as ontologically distinct (antithetical modes of domination), their ultimate complementarity within imperialism should not be minimized", i.e., they could be construed "as compatible yet different forms that routinely interpenetrate and affect in complex ways colonial and postcolonial situations" (p. 53). He goes on to observe that given so-called post colonies engage in settler-colonial projects of their own in relation to their peripheries, this should be seen as confirmation that settler colonialism is a foundational characteristic of a "global settler contemporaneity" (p. 57), i.e., settler-colonial phenomena are "globally constitutive of liberal modernity" and current "international governance" practices (p. 62). For instance, contemporary "land grabbing" in the neo(colonies) by corporations and foreign states who acquire semi-sovereign rights over extensive tracts is still premised on *terra nullius* (aka *Doctrine of Discovery*) and (neo)Lockean notions of land as property for those who maximize utilizations/efficient use (underutilization/inefficient use is a property regime which is fundamentally defective) of land and labor.

> The affinity between resource underutilization and ill-defined private property is organic to neoliberal development thinking. Only a small fraction of African farmers has proof of ownership, giving some the impression of a quintessential Lockean landscape 'owned by all', that is none, and awaiting immanent enclosure. ... More recent allegations that property lacking private title and 'regularization' contributes to under-utilization are widespread in development agencies such as the World Bank (see the latest push in 2018 under the Enabling the Business of Agriculture-EBA- project—*my addition*). In this view, even property that is nominally private but insecure due to weak or unrecorded title amounts to 'dead capital' and is a barrier to the 'highest and best use of land'. (Geisler, 2013, p. 21)

This leads Charles Geisler to conclude that "*terra nullius* remains a viable international legal doctrine and is stirring again as a justificatory logic in north-south land relations. It is neither narrow in scope nor static in application. The line between what is 'cultivated' and 'under-cultivated' is blurring, opening whole continents to new narratives and complex core-periphery interventions" (2013, p. 16). The justificatory claims for land grabs are "a comprehensive rehearsal of *terra nullius* as a doctrine, premised on security concerns, namely food and energy and the threat of war and natural disasters, and treat African land and resources as global commons awaiting legitimate and benevolent enclosure" (p. 16). Low population density is a keystone in enclosure logics in Africa and elsewhere, along with the ascription of underutilized African land and labor, i.e., "African land is abundant but fallow (allegedly) for reasons of mismanagement, corruption, ethnic conflict, indifferent elites, failed land reforms and a plague of social problems" (2013, p. 20).

Settler-colonial logics of *terra nullius* and a global settler-colonial present are also apparent in the post-independence period in green (conservation) grabs wherein programs like REDD+ or Reducing Emissions from Deforestation and Forest Degradation seeking to address climate change via carbon trading deals (green capitalist interventions—see Corporate Watch, A-Z of Green Capitalism) (No REDD in Africa Network, 2015). While the mode of climate legislation itself typifies settler-colonial modes of changing and appropriating land, REDD deals also often bypass indigenous peoples and are negotiated between imperial powers, postcolonial states, speculators and corporations and do not need their involvement to proceed, i.e., settler colonialism persists in the 'sovereign effects' of global financial capital, which has now acquired an unprecedented capacity to dictate policies from above. Thus like settler-colonial discourse in the nineteenth century, the REDD economy is based on notions of 'universal progress' that systematically exclude indigenous constituencies and indeed displace them. No wonder that indigenous organizations have mobilized and tried to coordinate internationally on these issues" (Veracini, 2015, p. 65). The global alliance against REDD+ in its Declaration to Decolonize the Earth and the Sky states:

> After more than 500 years of resistance, we, Indigenous Peoples, local communities, peasant farmers, fisherfolk and civil society are not fooled by the so-called Green Economy and REDD+ because we know colonialism when we see it. Regardless of its' cynical disguises and shameful lies, colonialism always results in the rape and pillaging of Mother Earth, and the slavery, death, destruction and genocide of her peoples. (No REDD in Africa Network, 2015, p. 38)

Terra nullius land-property-enclosure justifications of colonial rule have survived, prompting Lorenzo Veracini to suggest that while land grabbing in the exploitation colonies is typically seen in neocolonial terms, it should also be seen as a settler-colonial phenomenon in certain respects. Alternatively,

> much like our understandings of European conquest in the Americas, contemporary land grabbing is not simply an economic project. We would do well to remember that the myth of empty lands (*terra nullius*) is a racial metaphor marking the racialized dispossession of and genocide of the regions first inhabitants by European powers... understanding land grabbing as a critique of (post-independence-*my addition*) development demands recognition of the spatial and temporal continuities of grabbing as a historical geography of race. (Mollett, 2015, p. 427)

Learning from Indigenous-Peasant Ontologies of Land and Social Movement Activism in the (Neo)colonies

> Some of the most radical critiques and understandings about our societies, our world and its power structures and dominant ideologies and the fragility of the environment—indeed the most powerful visions for social change—emerge from ordinary people coming together and working for such change. (Choudry, 2015, p. 172)

Terra nullius continuities (e.g. land grabbing) have been met with numerous social movements in the (neo)colonies (Third World) in the rural regions and urban periphery (slums) (Caouette & Turner, 2009; Kapoor, 2017; Kapoor & Jordan, 2019; in press; Moyo & Yeros, 2005; Oliver-Smith, 2010). In the Americas alone, the struggles of 210 million indigenous and Afro-descendent peoples over two decades and more pertaining to ancestral territorial claims have by some estimates gained legal recognition to over 200 million hectares of land (Bryan, 2012, p. 215), although such state titling arrangements (especially those involving the World Bank) require continuous struggle in order to ensure that "extra-legal" (land systems that operate outside the state/institutional system) indigenous lands remain inalienable, collective and unindividuated and cannot be sold or used as collateral (Mollett, 2015, p. 422).

Given the critical exploration thus far, the figure is a rudimentary attempt to map out the dialectical relation between racial/colonial capitalism (land as private property/commodity) and its processes, agents/beneficiaries (citizens) and dispossessed/exploited denizens and associated land-based (and other) activisms/resistance (actors and politics) through colonial time and space (Fig. 32.1).

Social movement pedagogies (Choudry, 2015; Foley, 1999) addressing racial/colonial capitalist dispossession informed by ontological and axiological commitments pertaining to land that are often antithetical to *terra nullius* and Lockean property conceptions and colonial capitalist justifications are foundational to the germination, growth and longevity of these movements in the (neo)colonies (Kapoor, 2009; Langdon, 2020; Masalam, 2019; Tarlau, 2019). While there are diverse ontological conceptions of land and related teleology of struggle across the tricontinental, including struggles over rural labor/exploitation and not just land/dispossession, this concluding segment considers some key political learnings from indigenous-peasant anticolonial/decolonial social movement ontologies of land.

The term dispossession, for one, applies to processes of ongoing settler colonization and/or land grabbing in the (neo)colonies as Indigenous Peoples, peasants and land-based social groups are being divested of their lands and the territorial foundations of their societies. The social movement

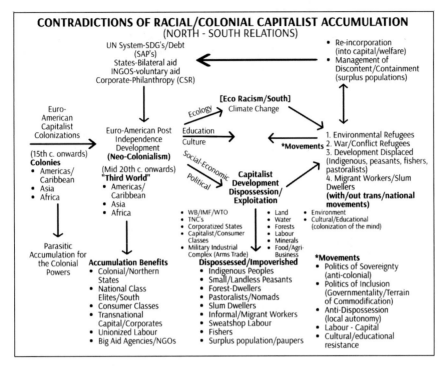

Fig. 32.1 Contradictions of racial/colonial capitalist accummulation (By author)

struggles against dispossession are subsequently sometimes framed (in a discursive politics to undermine anti/decolonial politics) as a struggle for possession which opponents argue is supposed to be contrary to the onto-epistemic and axiological convictions (pertaining to land) of these movements. However, as Mohawk legal scholar Patricia Monture-Angus explains, thereby implying that these struggles are less about dis/possession (anthropocentric land = property implication) than they are about seeking to intervene (responsibility) to prevent desecration of the Earth (which is more than land—biocentric conceptions):

> Although Aboriginal Peoples maintain a close relationship with the land…it is not about control of the land… Earth is mother and she nurtures us all… Sovereignty, when defined as the right to be responsible…requires a relationship with the territory (and not a relationship based on control of that territory)…. What must be understood then is that Aboriginal request to have our sovereignty respected is really a request to be responsible. I do not know of anywhere else in history where a group of people have had to fight so hard just to be responsible. (1999, p. 36)

Alternatively, La Via Campesina (LVC/peasant way), a global indigenous and peasant movement network or movement of movements spanning virtually all continents (including the "Third World") advances an onto-epistemology of land and food sovereignty in a counter and/or parallel project to the land grabbing corporate agro-industrial capitalist agricultural model predicated on materialist ontologies of land and food for profit. LVC is guided by a pedagogy which assumes a cosmic vision of the territories of communities of peasants and landless, indigenous peoples, rural workers, fisherfolk, nomadic pastoralists, tribes, afro-descendants, ethnic minorities and displaced peoples (together referenced as "people of the land"), who base their work on the production of food and who maintain a relationship of respect with Mother Earth and the oceans. LVC is fighting for: food sovereignty; land–water-territories; agro-ecology and peasant's seeds; climate and environmental justice; peasant's rights; dignity for migrants and waged workers; and international solidarity (www.viacampesina.org).

Contrary to the Lockean and Discovery doctrine's exclusionary and racial/colonial capitalist justifications for occupation, private property (tradable commodity) and distributive inequities (monopolies) concerning land, LVC's perspective on land, for what and for whom and why affirms that:

> Land is a good of nature that needs to be used for the welfare of all. Land is not, and cannot be a marketable commodity that can be obtained in whatever quantity by those that have the financial means. We defend the principle of the maximum size of the social ownership of the land per family (patrimony is not just in the name of men) in relation to the reality in each country.
>
> Access to the land by peasants is to be understood as a guarantee for survival and the valorization of their culture, the autonomy of their communities and a new vision on the preservation of natural resources for humanity and future generations. (Desmarais, 2007, p. 36)

Adivasi (original dwellers/India) worldviews suggest that "there is an ontological relationship to land governed by a principal of mutuality where land, river, mountain, animal, plant and spirit are all entwined as an interdependent community of beings. It is this relationship that is at the foundation of resistance against loss of land, not an intrinsic claim to own and use land" (Nirmal, 2016, p. 243). Adivasi resistance to land grabbing in the Western Ghats region is based on an interwoven ontological scheme or synthesis of the ecological, socio-cultural and the political-economic/material (Nirmal, 2016, p. 241), contrary to Lockean approaches which reduce land to a property/commodity form. Adivasi and related ontological politics including that of LVC, by speaking from outside the racial/colonial liberal legal framework, pose fundamental and system destabilizing (counterhegemonic) questions (Kohn & McBride, 2011) including: do the people who inhabit a space have the ability to determine its use in order to fulfill their needs, i.e., are the economic activities in a given area supporting its inhabitants? Is it wrong for foreign corporate capital to occupy/purchase/lease large swaths of land, mechanize production and export food when the inhabitants of that land are going hungry/malnourished?

Frantz Fanon (1967/1963, p. 9) understood that "For a colonized people, the most essential value, because it is the most meaningful, is first and foremost the land: the land which must provide bread and, naturally, dignity". The history of colonization after all, can be read as the hegemonic application of conceptions of property, territory and sovereignty wherein European powers "made maps, drew boundaries, decided which spaces were 'empty' and which were already occupied, introduced different forms of agriculture and even imposed cultural conceptions of how views and landscapes should be perceived" (Kohn & McBride, 2011, p. 100). Furthermore and when all is said and done, the Age of Discovery prescriptions and Lockean colonialism wherein the term colonialism (coming from the Latin word *colere*) means to seek to cultivate-inhabit-guard land, continues to be reserved for Euroamericans and the emergent transnational state-capitalist and consumer classes in the post-independence period.

An aspect of Indigenous-peasant anti/decolonial ontologies of land struggle engaged by these contemporary movements then is to challenge these colonial categories and imposed transformations through colonial space–time, i.e., land provides a materialist basis for revolutionary struggle against ongoing racial/colonial capitalism while an ontological politics pertaining to land forms the basis of an

> *expressive insurgency*: a long term multigenerational struggle that operates under radically asymmetrical power conditions to reorient the very terms of contestation by forcing us to confront the possibility of relating to the earth as something other than an object to be possessed. (Nichols, 2020, pp. 159–160)

Note

1. The Doctrine of Discovery reared its head as recently as 1982 when Spain and the Vatican proposed 1992 as a year of celebration in the United Nations as an "encounter" (where Europe brought civilization and Christianity to Indigenous Peoples) between Europe and the peoples of the Americas (proposal supported by the North Atlantic states, including the US and Canada), wherein the African delegation staged a walk out and returning with a statement condemning the celebration of colonialism in the UN by a body that was ostensibly established for the purpose of ending colonialism. Only 5 years prior, the Indigenous People's Conference of the Americas at the UN's Geneva headquarters had proposed that 1992 be made the UN "year of mourning" for the onset of colonialism, African slavery and genocide against the Indigenous peoples of the Americas (Dunbar-Ortiz, 2014, p. 197).

References

Alfred, T. (2005). *Wasase: Indigenous pathways of action and freedom*. University of Toronto Press.

Allman, P. (1999). *Revolutionary social transformation: Democratic hopes, political possibilities and critical education*. Praeger.

Araghi, F., & Karides, M. (2012). Land dispossession and global crisis: Introduction to the special edition on land rights in the world system. *Journal of World Systems Research, 18*(1), 1–5.

Arneil, B. (1994). Trade, plantations, property: John Locke and the economic defense of colonialism. *Journal of History of Ideas, 55*(4), 591–609.

Arneil, B. (1996). The wild Indian's venison: Locke's theory of property and English colonialism in America. *Political Studies, XLIV*, 60–74.

Benjamin, T., & Hidalgo, D. (2007). Anticolonialism. In T. Benjamin (Ed.), *Encyclopedia of western colonialism since 1450*. Thomson Gale.

Bryan, J. (2012). Re-thinking territory: Social justice and neoliberalism in Latin America's territorial turn. *Geography Compass, 6*(4), 215–226.

Caouette, D., & Turner, S. (Eds.). (2009). *Agrarian angst and rural resistance in contemporary Southeast Asia*. Routledge.

Choudry, A. (2015). *Learning activism: The intellectual life of contemporary social movements*. University of Toronto Press.

Coulthard, G. (2014). *Red skin, White masks: Rejecting the colonial politics of recognition*. University of Minnesota Press.

Davis, M. (2001/2017). *Late Victorian holocausts: El Nino famines and the making of the Third World*. Verso.

Desmarais, A. (2007). *La via Campesina: Globalization and the power of peasants*. Fernwood.

Dunbar-Ortiz, R. (2014). *An indigenous people's history of the United States*. Beacon Press.

Fanon, F. (1967). *Wretched of the earth*. Grove Press (Original work published in 1963).

Fieldhouse, D. (1989). *The colonial empires*. Macmillan.

Foley, G. (1999). *Learning in social action*. Zed Books.

Freire, P. (1970). *Pedagogy of the oppressed*. Herder & Herder.

Galeano, E. (1972). *Open veins of Latin America: Five centuries of pillage of a continent*. Monthly Review Press.

Geisler, C. (2013). New terra nullius narratives and the gentrification of Africa's 'empty lands.' *Journal of World Systems Research, 18*(1), 15–29.

Grande, S. (2004/2015). *Red pedagogy: Native American social and political thought*. Rowman & Littlefield.

Guha, R. (1997). *Dominance without hegemony: History and power in colonial India*. Harvard University Press.

Ince, O. (2011). Enclosing in God's name, accumulating for mankind: Money, morality and accumulation in John Locke's theory of property. *The Review of Politics, 73*(1), 29–54.

Ince, O. (2015). *John Locke and colonial capitalism: Money, possession, and dispossession*. Paper presented at the American Political Science Association (APSA) (33 pages).

Kamat, S. (2002). *Development hegemony: NGOs and the state in India*. Oxford University Press.

Kapoor, D. (2009). Globalization, dispossession and subaltern social movement (SSM) learning in the South. In A. Abdi & D. Kapoor (Eds.), *Global perspectives on adult education* (pp. 71–94). Palgrave Macmillan.

Kapoor, D. (Ed.). (2017). *Against colonization and rural dispossession: Local resistance in South & East Asia, the Pacific and Africa*. Zed Books.

Kapoor, D. & Jordan, S. (2019). *Research, political engagement and dispossession: Indigenous, peasant and urban poor activisms in the Americas and Asia*. Zed Books.

Kapoor, D. (in press). Rural dispossession and resistance in Asia and Africa. In H. Veltmeyer & P. Bowles (Eds.), *Critical development studies: A reader*. Routledge.

Kohn, M., & McBride, K. (2011). *Political theories of decolonization: Postcolonialism and the problem of foundations*. Oxford University Press.

Kothari, U. (2005). *A radical history of development studies*. Zed Books.

Langan, M. (2018). *Neocolonialism and the poverty of development in Africa*. Palgrave Macmillan.

Langdon, J. (2020). *African social movement learning: The case of the Ada Songor salt movement*. BRILL.

Marx, K. (1967). *Writings of the Young Marx on philosophy and society* (L. D. Easton & K. H. Guddat, Eds. and Trans.). Anchor Books.

Marx, K. (2007). *Capital: A critique of political economy-the process of capitalist production*. Cosimo, Inc.

Masalam, H. (2019). Conservation and palm oil dispossession in Sumatra and Sulawesi: Third worldist PAR, indigenous, peasant and small peasant resistance, and organized activisms. In D. Kapoor & S. Jordan (Eds.), *Research, political engagement and dispossession: Indigenous, peasant and urban poor activisms in the Americas and Asia*. Zed Books.

Miller, R. (2006). *Native America, discovered and conquered: Thomas Jefferson, Lewis and Clark, and Manifest Destiny*. Praeger.

Mollett, S. (2015). The power to plunder: Rethinking land grabbing in Latin America. *Antipode, 48*(2), 412–432.

Monture-Angus, P. (1999). *Journeying forward*. Fernwood.

Moyo, S., & Yeros, P. (Eds.). (2005). *Reclaiming the land: The resurgence of rural movements in Africa, Asia and Latin America*. Zed Books.

Nichols, R. (2020). *Theft is property: Dispossession and critical theory*. Duke University Press.

Nirmal, P. (2016). Being and knowing differently in living worlds: Rooted networks and relational webs in indigenous geographies. In W. Harcourt (Ed.), *The Palgrave handbook of gender and development*. Palgrave Macmillan.

Nkrumah, K. (1965). *Neocolonialism, the last stage of imperialism*. Thomas Nelson & Sons Ltd.

No REDD in Africa Network. (2015). *Stopping the continent grab and the REDD-ification of Africa*. NRAN.

Oliver-Smith, A. (2010). *Defying displacement: Grassroots resistance and the critique of development*. University of Texas.

Quijano, A. (2000). Coloniality of power and eurocentrism in Latin America. *International Sociology, 15*(2), 215–232.

Quijano, A. (2005). The challenge of the indigenous movement in Latin America. *Socialism and Democracy, 19*(3), 55–78.

Rist, G. (2014). *The history of development: From western origins to global faith*. Zed Books.

Robinson, C. (2000). *Black Marxism: The making of the Black radical tradition*. University of North Carolina Press.
Rodney, W. (1982). *How Europe underdeveloped Africa*. Howard University Press.
Tarlau, R. (2019). *Occupying schools, occupying land: How the landless worker's movement transformed Brazilian education*. Oxford University Press.
Townsend, M. (1941). *European colonial expansion since 1871*. J.B. Lippincott & Co.
Trask, H.-K. (1999). *From a native daughter: Colonialism and sovereignty in Hawai'i* (Rev. ed.). University of Hawai'i Press (Orginal work published 1993).
Veracini, L. (2015). *The settler colonial present*. Palgrave Macmillan.
War on Want. (2012). *The hunger games: How DFID support for agribusiness is fueling poverty in Africa*.
Weaver, J. (2006). *The great land rush and the making of the modern world, 1650–1900*. McGill-Queen's University Press.
Wolfe, P. (2016). *Traces of history: Elementary structures of race*. Verso Books.
Wright, R. (2015). *Stolen continents: The new world through Indian eyes*. Penguin.

CHAPTER 33

Doing Southern Theory: Shinto, Self-Negation, and Comparative Education

Keita Takayama

INTRODUCING AND DOING SOUTHERN THEORY

Raewyn Connell (2007) coined the term Southern Theory in her book *Southern Theory: The Global Dynamics of Knowledge in Social Science*. The term South is deployed to draw attention to the "periphery-centre relations in the realm of knowledge" (Connell, 2007, p. viii). Her intension is not to "name a sharply bounded category of states or societies, but to emphasize relations—authority, exclusion and inclusion, hegemony, partnership, sponsorship, appropriation—between intellectuals and institutions in the metropole and those in the world periphery" (pp. viii–ix). By recognizing the South as a source of critical theoretical insights, Connell demanded that social sciences address the differential global power relations in knowledge practice, which have left the existing theoretical tools parochial at best. Her work forces us to problematize the kind of relations often implicitly accepted in the process of academic knowledge production and invites us to do research differently, in a way that subverts the prevailing structure of knowledge. Drawing on her work as well as other cognate postcolonial and decolonial scholarship, I have, along with other colleagues, explored what it means to do Southern Theory in the field of comparative and international education (see Takayama, 2015, 2018, 2020a, 2020b, Takayama et al., 2016, 2017).

K. Takayama (✉)
Graduate School of Education, Kyoto University, Kyoto, Japan
e-mail: takayama.keita.7w@kyoto-u.ac.jp

© The Author(s), under exclusive license to Springer Nature Switzerland AG 2022
A. A. Abdi and G. W. Misiaszek (eds.), *The Palgrave Handbook on Critical Theories of Education*, https://doi.org/10.1007/978-3-030-86343-2_33

In my view, doing Southern Theory involves two critical moves. First, it requires us to explicitly recognize the "othered" lands and peoples as a source of intellectual work with global implications. Southern theory departs from the usual relations in social scientific knowledge generation, where the "othered" lands and peoples are treated as "data mine" or "informants." It repositions them as a source of multicentric intellectual work and theoretical insights whose implications extend beyond the original places of generation. That is, it is a call for epistemic justice on the planetary scale. Second, it involves putting those insights and knowledges generated in the othered lands in critical dialogue with the Eurocentric knowledge widely circulated as "universal." It involves provincializing, peculiarizing and then reconstituting the so called "foundational knowledge" or "theories" of a given discipline. It distances itself from postcolonial politics of resentment and nativist essentialism that simply ascribe to and solidify the colonial division of the world (Bhambra, 2014; Chen, 2010). Instead, it calls for a critical engagement with the existing disciplinary knowledge. That is, it recognizes both the indispensability and inadequacy of the existing disciplinary knowledge developed under the strong influence of Western modernity/coloniality (Chakrabarty, 2000). A project could be called Southern Theory, postcolonial or decolonial, depending on the specific intellectual lineages drawn upon, which inform the particular diagnosis of the challenges and the strategies proposed to address them (Alatas, 2006; Bhambra, 2014; Chen, 2010; Connell, 2007; Kurasawa, 2004; Mignolo, 2011).

In pursuing Southern Theory work over the last decade or so, I have attempted to operationalize Connell's notion as an educational project while grounding it in the field of comparative and international education. Firstly, it is an educational project because doing Southern Theory demands that we take up a role as a "teacher" in relation to fellow researchers both in and outside education. It involves inviting others to take the risk of venturing into the unfamiliar intellectual world that sits outside the academic centers of the "West" so as to broaden their epistemic horizons. Assuming the role of teachers means that those who advocate Southern Theory must demonstrate to others how it can be done and what implications, both intended and unintended, it might generate for one's research work. A self-reflective account of the very process of doing this work and its complexities, including this chapter, forms a valuable pedagogic resource.

Secondly, it is an educational project because doing Southern Theory necessarily requires a series of learning and unlearning, or "negations" (Takayama, 2020b). It demands that we question the taken-for-granted premises of disciplinary knowledge and reconstitute it through a set of insights that have been historically excluded from the discussion. But this epistemological shift is incomplete without an equally transformative ontological shift, that is, a shift in how we make sense of our being and relationality to others (Takayama, 2018, 2020b). Taking cues from Keiji Nishitani, Andrea English, and Tim Ingold among others, I have elsewhere situated it at the core of the Southern Theory project to transcend the modern empiricist separation between knowing and being and to embrace the view that a shift in knowing necessarily results in a corresponding shift in being (see Takayama, 2020b).

The proposed ontological shift is what makes Southern Theory an indispensable part of the notion of comparative education as cultural critique, as recently articulated by Rappleye (2020). Drawing on his extended transnational experiences, Rappleye (2020) puts forward the notion of "immigracy of being" as the key disposition that invites "a deep experience of Otherness" to "completely shift the ontological ground" of the researcher self (p. 15). In his view, to compare necessarily involves a cultural critique of self and by extension self-negation. The same cross-cultural critique was at the heart of some of the founding scholars of sociology, including Marx, Weber, and Durkheim (Kurasawa, 2004). Kurasawa (2004) coins the same methodological disposition "ethnological imagination," which he defines as "a critical and cross-cultural hermeneutics of Euro-American modernity whereby engagement with other societies has been essential to the project of self-understanding and self-critique of their own times and places" (p. 4). Practicing ethnological imagination is deeply self-transformative, as "learning about others is not simply an act of cosmopolitan open-mindedness, but an integral part of learning about ourselves and even viewing ourselves as other" (p. 5). What is proposed here is not a call for postmodern relativism, but rather to let "the force of difference" release our imaginations (Geertz, 2000, p. 259). Doing Southern Theory sees disruption and self-negation as central to its educational project. It is necessarily disruptive, as it forces us to particularize and peculiarize the deep-seated assumptions shaping what and how we know and how we exist. It demands that we let go of a secured sense of self, acknowledge the partiality of our knowing and unlearn things that have been embraced as part of what makes us who we are (see Rappleye, 2020; Takayama, 2020b).

Building on the discussion of Southern Theory as a pedagogical project, I am going to deploy my own experience/reflection as a central pedagogical tool. The chapter documents how I have done Southern Theory over the years, with the hope of inviting others to pursue this line of knowledge practice. It is a story of learning through disruption and self-negation, or cross-cultural unlearning, whereby I came to recognize my "home" as the other in an unexpectedly way, and in the course of unlearning, struggled to let go of my secured sense of self. It demonstrates how I learned to embrace the discomfort of having my own subjectivity and "expertise" challenged as a point of departure for renewed understanding of self and others.

Ecofeminist and Decolonial Turns

My latest unlearning journey began when I was introduced to ecofeminist and decolonial literature through a special issue project in Shanghai (see Silova et al., 2020; Takayama, 2020a). In a nutshell, both ecofeminist and decolonial literatures open up space for different epistemologies, ontologies, and cosmologies that have been suppressed by the global spread of Western modernity-coloniality nexus and global capitalism. Ecofeminism recognizes the more-than-human worlds and stresses the need for the coexistence of humans with multispecies communities. Triggered by the human-induced ecological challenges of planetary scale and learning from the Indigenous communities of Australia, Rose (2005), for instance, rejects the human exceptionalism of the Anthropocene era and rearticulates humans as a member of multispecies communities. Rose (2005) draws on her anthropological work with the Australian Indigenous people in Northern Territories to unsettle the human-centric premises of Western philosophy. By describing how the Indigenous concept of "country" operates upon the mutual entanglement of benefits that cut across the human-nature dualism, she puts forward an alternative vision of philosophical ecology that decenters human agency, knowledge, and intentions.

In addition to anthropological studies with Indigenous people, historical studies of the world that once existed is another source of wisdom. To encourage us to remember what has led us to the current epistemological and ontological conditions of modernity and what has been done to those who dare to be different, Stengers (2012) asks us to remember "the smell of burning witches." It is an evocative reminder that there existed social worlds where witches and fairies were embraced as part of the "real" world of humanity and where the distinctions between science and superstition were left opaque and constantly transgressed. The hegemony of scientific rationality and its underside, the eradication of "other" worlds, were not a natural consequence of human progress but of ontological violence. By smelling the burning of witches' flesh, we could develop "our closeness with those who have already been destroyed in the name of rationality, objectivity, and the great divide between nature and culture" (Stengers, 2011, p. 58).

Much of this literature has been taken up in recent "common worlds" educational scholarship, in particular within early childhood education (see Blaise, 2015; Taylor, 2017). These scholars push us to imagine education where humans learn to decenter themselves and reposition themselves as part of multispecies common worlds, and to recognize the agencies of non-human others. They raise important questions about the current articulation of education for sustainability which preserves the central humanistic assumptions, including the logic of human exceptionalism. Taylor (2017), for instance, challenges the positioning of children as environmental stewards, and humans, in general, as the sole agents for solving the current ecological crisis. Furthermore, these post-humanist and ecofeminist studies call upon us to recognize how existing early childhood pedagogic practices already allow for transgressive space where children disrupt the nature-culture binary and where children interact with the more-than-human worlds (Taylor, 2017). Silova (2019) also suggests the tenacity of the "creature communities" today and how social science, including education scholarship, has been blinded to numerous students' encounters with the more-than-human worlds during their schooling.

Decolonial scholarship, represented by Mignolo (2011) and other South American thinkers (e.g., Grosfoguel, 2011), raises a similar set of questions about the powerful genocidal effects of the global spread of Western modernity-coloniality nexus, which began in the late fifteenth-century European colonization of America. The South American decolonial project historicizes with the intention of de-historicizing it, the current structure of knowledge, and recognizes the centuries of Western colonial violence as the constitutive aspect of its "epistemicide," the obliteration of other epistemologies and ontologies from the surface of the planet (Grosfoguel, 2011). It problematizes the modernist, Cartesian premises of science and knowledge that set up the hierarchy of knowing and being and privileged for European countries as the only legitimate source of knowledge and science. On the basis of this historical critique, it calls for the resuscitation of marginalized epistemologies and ontologies in colonized parts of the world that have been pushed to the limits by the Eurocentric geopolitics of knowledge. It is a call toward the world of "pluriversality," where multiple epistemologies and ontologies coexist side by side (Mignolo, 2011).

In a number of places, Mignolo (2011) uses de-westernization and decoloniality to distinguish between different levels of critique of Western modernity/coloniality project. According to Mignolo, de-westernization is a shallower critique of the West in that it rejects the West while maintaining its allegiance to its fundamental logic of modernity. In economy, for instance, de-westernization refers to the rejection of US or World Bank interventions in South America, while still aspiring for a regionally or nationally based model of "development" and "progress" that accepts the same economic rationality and exploitative logic of modernity toward the planet. In the domain of knowledge, de-westernization refers to the rejection of knowledge generated in the West, while still accepting the fundamental philosophical foundations of Western knowledge, namely its epistemology and ontology. Drawing on Mignolo (2011), Silova et al. (2020) recognize that the most penetrating critiques of the modernity/decoloniality nexus are to be found in the decoloniality, not the de-westernization, project, particularly in the realm of spirituality and ontology.

Needless to say, the decolonial critique of Western modernity/coloniality resonates closely with ecofeminist scholarship. Most crucially, both identify the role of culture in constituting the violence of modernity/colonial nexus, more specifically in securing the hyperseparation between adults and children, humans and nature, men and women, civilized and barbaric, and science and myth (see Plumwood, 1993). The Western Enlightenment notion of reason provides the logic of hyperseparation with the former terms defined as the embodiment of reason and the latter terms as "everything that reason excludes" (Plumwood, 1993, p. 20). Both decolonial theory and ecofeminist theory encourage us to engage in cross-cultural critique and practice ethnological imagination: the particularization and peculiarization of now and here. They invite us to imagine different ways of being and knowing that have been suppressed, or even erased, by a set of cultural norms and practices of modernity and imposed through colonial violence.

The above exploration of the ecofeminist and decolonial scholarship led me to one interesting/uncomfortable observation; the critique of modernity/coloniality resonates with what I knew about Shinto, a Japanese animism/religion. Growing up in Japan, I intuitively knew that the nature-centered world view and the rejection of human exceptionalism echoes the core ideas of Shinto animism, despite the fact that I grew up in a non-traditional household where Shinto was not particularly embraced. It was uncomfortable, because I was aware of the tainted history of Shinto, its close link to Japan's imperial aggression during the past wars and its postwar association with nativist politics. Indeed, my previous scholarship was scathingly critical of any attempt to invoke Shinto-informed spiritualities in Japanese education (see Takayama, 2008, 2010). I was not sure how I could possibly reconcile the idea of drawing on Shinto as a potential intellectual resource toward ecologically minded and decolonial education with its unfortunate past. It was with a deep sense of discomfort and uncertainty that I ventured to learn about Shinto.

Shinto's Decolonial Potentials

As Jensen and Blok (2013) point out, "Japan is probably the only major industrialized country in which widespread discussion of animism is still a part of ordinary intellectual discourse" (p. 97). Indeed, the Shinto-inspired, animated worldview pervades all of Japanese society, underpinning mundane aspects of life as well as art forms and cultural practices (Carter, 2013; Nakayama, 2019). Shinto values and practices are so enmeshed in Japanese people's everyday life that they have become their second nature (Kasulis, 2004). According to Nelson (2000), shrine Shinto is "one of the most long-lived of all Japan's institutions, largely because (after nearly fourteen centuries) it continues to help form, orient, and empower a sense of local and ethnic identity" (p. 3).

True to much of animisms in the world, Shinto stresses the greatness of the universe and the relative insignificance of human presence in its entire history. It also recognizes the agencies of the more-than-human worlds and their spiritual impacts on humans. Shinto locates spirits in both humans and non-humans, including stones, rivers, trees, foxes, thunder, ancestors, rice, and waterfalls, that is, radical personalization of the universe (Jensen & Blok, 2013). According to Shinto principles, "gods, men, animals, plants and inanimate objects are mutually permeable entities, appearing as a unified and dynamic field of existence, characterized by particular forms of immanence and vitalism" (Jensen & Blok, 2013, p. 97).

The Shinto cosmology continues to influence the meaning of the term *shizen*, the Japanese translation of nature, the Western concept introduced to Japan in the late nineteenth century. As Nakayama (2019) explains, the Japanese concept of nature does not contain the hierarchical Christian idea, where the creator of the world God exists at the top, then man created in the image of God, with all the other creatures comprising nature at the bottom. Here, "God as a transcendent being does not exist within nature, nor are human beings a part of it" (p. 8). This dichotomy between human beings and nature was central to the emergence of the new science in the seventeenth century, further developed via Bacon and Descartes into the Cartesian worldview and subsequently the conceptualization of nature merely as an object be to controlled by humans (Hickel, 2020; Plumwood, 1993). In contrast, the Shinto animistic view of nature recognizes something sacred in all the creatures who are both physically and spiritually a part of nature. Hence, it defies the usual "opposition …between human subjectivity and natural objectivity" (Nakayama, 2019, p. 9).

The same reverence toward the more-than-human worlds is central to Japanese thought and philosophy, according to Robert Carter (2013). In explaining the central component of the Zen/Shinto philosophy, Carter quotes a Japanese landscape architect/Zen monk, Shunmyo Matsuo:

> I wonder just what kind of spirit a certain stone has and how it would prefer to be set out. This is also true of plants and I always consider how I think the plants would like to be displayed. I always feel at one with the plants, when I am planting them, and with the stones, when I am arranging them. (p. 34)

Carter (2013) refers to Matsuo in his illustration of the key thinkers of the Kyoto School of Philosophy, Kitaro Nishida and Keiji Nishitani, who were likewise influenced immensely by the Zen and Buddhist thought (see Sevilla, 2016). Matsuo's approach to landscaping epitomizes the kind of empathic identification with non-animated objects that transcend the modernist culture-nature, subject-object dualism. Through self-cultivation, one learns to be one with an object (flowers, stones, and trees); it is a state of nothingness where one comes to know a thing not through reason and language but intuitions developed through direct experience. Much of this Shinto-informed sensibilities toward nature permeate various Japanese arts, including traditional garden architecture, calendar pictures, and poetry (see Kato, 2021).

Though Shinto is not explicitly taught in Japanese education due to its principle of secularity (Nakayama, 2019), research has shown that the Japanese curriculum, most notably in the Japanese language textbooks, implicitly teaches children emotional identification with non-human creatures and their worldviews (Gerbert, 1993; Ishihara, 2005). In comparing primary school readers in Japanese and American schools, Gerbert (1993) highlights the nature-centered view of the world and the relative insignificance of humans in Japanese school readers. Her analysis shows that in many of the stories included in Japanese readers, "human protagonists drop out of the picture altogether" (p. 162). In one of the texts that she closely examines, "(t)he self identifies with and merges with nature. It never become a fully constituted 'personality' as often seen in American readers" (p. 164). Japanese children are encouraged to develop "a passive attitude towards nature" (p. 163), "be sensitive to small changes in the environment" (p. 163) and "quietly lose the self in the contemplation of nature" (p. 165). This is contrasted to the American primary school readers where an explicit emphasis is placed on formal reasoning, analytical thinking, and a strongly anthropocentric view of nature.

More recently, the Ministry of Education introduced moral education supplementary texts, arguably to counterbalance the increasing (Western-inspired) emphasis on critical literacy (Ishihara, 2005). What follows is an excerpt from one of the moral education booklets, *Kokoro no nooto* (*Notebook for Heart*):

> Humans are moved by beauty.
> When faced with the magnificence of nature, we feel moved and hold our breath.
> Calm, great ocean that spreads endlessly,
> Vast hills and fields, and towering mountain ranges.
> It feels as though they mercifully embraced us, as though we melted into them.
> But, would this be true?
> When nature bares its fangs,
> it engulfs us with its overwhelming might.
> Thundering noise of crashing waves, the volcanic smoke that shuts out the sky,
> and the massive earthquake that shatters the earth.
> A feeling of awe and respect towards the existence of matters beyond human control springs up. (MEXT, 2002, p. 65)

Similar texts are also found in more recently published moral education readers.

> To feel the greatness
> Rainbows after rain,
> the bright red sun about to set,
> shining aurora,
> drifting ice masses approaching the seashore,
> and splashing waterfalls.
> (Our) heart moves with the overwhelming
> presence of natural phenomena and sceneries.
> When faced with supernatural world beyond
> humans, (we) experience the beauty and

greatness of nature.
They move (us), and (we) appreciate human
Heart. (MEXT, 2014, p. 114)

In these passages, children are to leave behind the modern scientific form of learning where they are to understand, comprehend, and control the awesome. Instead, they are to cultivate "a feeling of awe" (*ikei no nen*) by simply standing "under it, feel themselves to be inherently part of it and it part of themselves" (Kasulis, 2004, p. 167). The MEXT moral education readers, including the ones cited above, are organized around the interconnectedness of self to the broader universe, the environment (nature), family, school, local community, nation, and the global, or an interdependent sense of selfhood (Komatsu et al., 2021). As Japanese children progress with the readers, they learn to position themselves within the broader collectives of expanding scales, but they all stress somewhere in the texts the sense of awe toward the overwhelming presence of nature, insignificance of self, and the existence beyond humans.

According to Thomas Kasulis (2004), the author of *Shinto: The Way Home*, the feeling of awe is central to Shinto. He argues that Shinto, as a contemporary religion in a highly technological society, is striking in its insistence that awe is not to be understood, nor to be comprehended in any systematic way. The point of Shinto practice is "more to make one feel at home with awe rather than try to understand or control it" (p. 167). Kasulis argues that in contemporary modern societies, we have lost this attitude toward the awesome. According to him, "one result of the predominance of scientific thinking is that today our initial response to the awesome is to try to understand it rather than to stand under it. Instead of filling us with a sense of humility before the unknown, awe has come to challenge us as only the not-yet-known. I don't know has become an ego-bruising admission of ignorance instead of a sign of wisdom" (p. 167). Following Shinto, Kasulis invites us to "accept the awesome as part of the world in which we live" (p. 12). Kasulis seems to suggest that the feeling of awe has much to do with letting go of our sense of ego and embracing ignorance as virtue.

It is this rejection of the liberal principle of rationality and critical reason and the restricted sense of self that results from it that are crucial for Bowers' (1987, 1993) articulation of eco-justice pedagogy. In his view, liberal and critical educational thoughts, represented by Dewey, Skinner, and Freire among others, are fundamentally antithetical to the generation of culture that is ecologically sustainable. This is because the liberal theories of education accord the absolute status to reason and rationality as practiced by individuals, and this undermines the authority of traditional patterns of knowledge. As he states, liberal educational thoughts are guided by the Enlightenment notion of rational, autonomous, and self-directing self, and this conceptualization of self as "the epicenter of the social world" (p. 23) has the effect of "relativiz(ing) the communal foundations of a shared sense of moral authority, with the consequence that individual judgement reflects what is perceived as useful, fulfilling, and pleasurable" (Bowers, 1987, p. 25). With "the subjectivism of personal experience" as "the final refuge" (p. 28), it breeds nihilism; it erodes "the sense of being interdependent with the large social and biotic community," which are defined as "an unwelcomed constraint on individual freedom" (Bowers, 1993, p. 27). Hence, the crucial shortcoming of liberal educational theories in light of their potential for an ecologically balanced world is their inability to offer the self-limiting principle, the very cultural condition for the small and interdependent notion of selfhood. As a possible source of the alternatives, Bowers draws attention to indigenous, place-based, and intergenerational knowledges (see also Hickel, 2020).

Most recent education scholarship for a sustainable future reinforces Bowers' conclusion reached more than a few decades ago. For instance, Komatsu et al. (2021) undertook a series of quantitative analyses to identify the possible relationship between what they call ontological individualism, which is opposed to relational, interdependent selfhood, social unsustainability, and student-centered teaching in schools. They establish the empirical foundation for the very assertion made by Bowers more than three decades earlier; student-centered teaching, underpinned by the liberal principle of rational and autonomous self, can accelerate social and ecological unsustainability. Then, they take up the suggestion made by Bowers (1993), to "study other cultures that have evolved in more ecologically balanced ways" (57), and discuss three examples of alternative pedagogic practices designed to promote an interdependent sense of self, namely from Japan, Botswana and minority groups within USA. As an intergenerational body of local knowledge, Shinto can be one of such "othered" cultures that have not only survived the imposition of modernity but is actually thriving today. It can serve as much-needed resources to promote the kind of fundamental cultural shift required toward ecological sustainable, post-growth society (Hickel, 2020).

Politics of Shinto

Endorsing the Shinto animism and its cosmologies in Japanese schooling, however, is a complicated matter. This is because of the highly politicized context within which Shinto has been articulated within Japanese education throughout its postwar history (see Koyasu, 2004). The use of Shinto beliefs in schooling has been intensely contested since the end of the Asia Pacific War. During wartime, Shinto was incorporated into the state apparatus and played a central role in interpellating the people into the wartime imperialist ideology. Public education was the key state mechanism through which the widely accepted Shinto beliefs in nature were mobilized for ideological indoctrination (Hardacre, 2017; Shimazono, 2003). The postwar US-led Occupation ordered the complete removal of Shinto religious elements from state apparatus and put in place constitutional mechanisms to ensure separation of church and state and freedom of religion (Koyasu, 2004). The Occupation blamed Shinto as the ideological source of Japan's wartime ultra-nationalism and imperialism while turning blind eyes to the roles played by other religions (Hardacre, 2017). Its hunt for any remnants of the ostensibly Shinto-informed wartime ideology was so comprehensive that it even banned Japanese martial arts, calligraphies, and other benign cultural artifacts and practices (Shibata, 2004; Tanikawa, 2021).

The US-led Occupation's "demilitarization" of education planted the seed for the postwar political struggles in Japan. Since Japan's formal independence in 1952, those on the political right have consistently demanded the resurrection of the traditional Shinto cosmologies and patriotic values back within formal schooling (see Takayama, 2008, 2010). They call their political agenda the "normalization" of Japanese education, that is, normalizing the "unusual" situation left by the Occupation's imposition of liberal values, which has arguably detached the postwar generations from the nation's cultural "essence." By contrast, the Japanese liberal and left see such a move as a retrogressive desire to reinstate the imperial state and its ideology. They insist on protecting the liberal, democratic, and pacifist principles and constitutional frameworks introduced during the US Occupation. Constitutional arguments were frequently made to prevent Shinto-informed values and any patriotic teaching from entering into education, with liberal critics arguing that they violate the constitutionally guaranteed separation of church and state and freedom of thought (Koyasu, 2004; Miyake, 2003; Nishihara, 2006). The wartime indoctrination through education and the people's general remorse for its consequences were the broader historical backdrop against which the concerns have been expressed by liberals and supported by the broader public (Takayama, 2008, 2010).

Situated within this highly politicized policy context, the seemingly benign Shinto-informed concepts such as "awe and respect towards nature," or "matters beyond humans," and "the insignificance of humans in the whole universe" assume highly contested meanings. Liberals argue that teaching the Shinto-informed worldview reinforces students' passivity toward nature and by extension toward the authority and the state. It is the unquestioned devotion to nature that was then politically appropriated to generate people's allegiance toward the emperor/imperial state and the catastrophic "sacred" war for the imperial household. Instead of teaching children to be passive, hence, the liberal-left critics call for teaching the principles of rationality and critical reason that are central to democratic citizenship (see Irie, 2004; Iwakawa & Funabashi, 2004; Miyake, 2003). To those on the political left, the Shinto-inspired moral education readers, quoted earlier, are nothing but an expression of neo-conservative desire to render people obedient in times of neoliberal economic restructuring. This is exactly the argument that I made in my assessment of the 2006 revision to the Fundamental Law of Education (see Takayama, 2008). As Grosfoguel (2011) points out, nationalism, as a response to the Eurocentric colonial imposition, "reproduces an internal coloniality of power within each nation-state and reifies the nation-state as the privileged location of social change" (p. 23). When Shinto is so tainted with the discriminatory nativist politics of exclusion, could it be "conceptually freed from its historically over-determined connotations of political regression"? (Jensen & Blok, 2013, p. 94).

SALVAGING SHINTO

Would it be possible to salvage "the multivalent ethico-pragmatic character of Shinto" from the nationalistic overtone that has dominated its domestic articulation? (Jensen & Blok, 2013, p. 108). In a sense, Shinto is a placeholder for multiple interests within Japan. The dominant, nationalistic discourse of Shinto, or what Kasulis (2004) calls the highly normative and prescriptive, "essentialist" Shinto spirituality, is certainly with us. But there is also the ad-hoc, flexible, and descriptive form of Shinto as a popular praxis, or what Kasulis (2004) calls the "existentialist" Shinto spirituality, which pervades much of place-based invocations of Shinto cosmologies in festivals, rituals, and mundane life moments. The localized, existentialist Shinto spirituality gives us a way to be radically different today that centers on immanent connectedness of humans and non-humans, hence with considerable implications for reimagining education for sustainable futures. This is the aspect of Shinto that Jensen and Blok (2013) also sees as of great value for science and technology studies, when they argue that Shinto embodies "an alternative politics of the polymorphous enchantments of non-human agency" (p. 108) that can help broaden the theoretical horizon on the entanglements among science, technology, ecology, and cosmos.

However, as Kasulis (2004) reminds us, the two forms of Shinto spiritualities—essentialist and existential—should not be treated as another form of binary. They are "not separate religious traditions but instead overlap in an internal relation with each other" (p. 153). The history of Shinto in Japan has been infused with the tension between these two forms of spirituality, which remains unresolved today (Kasulis, 2004, p. 6). To complicate the matter further, this distinction is not available in the Japanese vocabulary for talking about Shinto, according to Kasulis (2004). Partly because of the nationalist political dominance in the domestic discourse of Shinto, the language of Shinto necessarily implicates essentialist assumptions. This poses immense challenges in terms of "reclaiming" Shinto (Stengers, 2012), that is, teasing out and mobilizing the existential, localized form of Shinto without invoking the essentialist form of Shinto spirituality that has exclusionary effects on the domestic political front. For now, all I can do is sit with the enormity of the conceptual and political challenges and suggest that this conundrum is not necessarily particular to Shinto and Japan. This discussion has wider international implications for education for sustainable futures, given that the political appropriation of nature and the popularized form of animism has been central to the modern formation of nation-state and its physical, epistemic, and ontological violence.

Conclusion with Self-Negation

The purpose of this chapter is educational in that it aims to show what it all means to do Southern Theory in educational research. The narrative exposes the sense of vulnerability one might experience as a result of doing Southern Theory and embracing the disruption that it causes. In my case, it all started with engaging with decolonial and ecofeminist literature and realizing its close relevance to the discussion of Shinto animism. Attempting to embrace Shinto as an alternative source of knowledge, however, forced me to unlearn my well-established views, largely shaped by the postwar political discourse of education in Japan, and let go of the political sensibilities. The whole Japanese domestic debate over the place of Shinto cosmologies in education remains trapped within the discursive legacies of the Occupation and the Cold War. Rethinking the role of Shinto in education is part of what Chen calls the de-cold-war politics, which he argues central to decolonizing imagination in East Asia. It is "to confront the legacies and continuing tensions of the Cold War" so as to "reopen the past for reflection in order to make moments of liberation possible in the future" (Chen, 2010, p. x).

While recognizing the need to rethink the usefulness of postwar binary politics, I remain deeply ambivalent about leaving behind altogether the liberal principles underpinning education. Here I am acutely reminded of the dangers in transferring purely philosophical arguments to the domain of politics that Davis (1998) highlights. In discussing the historical role of Japanese philosophers in promoting Japanese cultural nationalism, Davis makes the following point: "The collapse of subject and object, thought and action—long the aim of Japanese philosophers—may be innocent enough as epistemology or Buddhist soteriology—but it can have a devastating effect when applies to politics" (p. 183). Like Davis, I am worried about the political implications of the Shinto cosmologies in Japanese schools today, when Japanese scholars identify the rise of retrogressive nationalism as well as the depoliticization of education as the major concerns and call for resuscitating the roles of education for democratic politics (see Hirota, 2015; Kodama, 2013).

Foremost scholar of Japanese traditional unlearning and mushin (no mind or nothingness), Nishihira (Nishihira & Rappleye, 2021) makes the following observation about the risk of political appropriation of Japanese traditional concepts of learning for ideological indoctrination:

> For those of us that write about Japanese thought and tradition, we still operate in the shadow of the war, to some extent. We worry that the element of trust and persistence embedded within this model may get co-opted, in a

nationalist context, and transformed into a tool of indoctrination. It is a wariness of getting mistaken for nationalists or apologists for the prewar period, and lingering uncertainties about the possible dangerous potentials of self-negation, that has prevented many Japanese scholars, including myself, from more assertively discussing these models. Future work needs to remain vigilant of this. That said, this 'just trust' call to faith is not unique to this 'Japanese' model, but is a major issue for virtually all forms of tradition– religious, secular, and otherwise. (p. 10)

While Nishihara does not refer to Shinto, the "just trust" call to faith embodies the same rejection of the liberal principle of rationality, reason, and individuality as expressed in Shinto's call for awe. It is notable even some like Nishihara, the foremost expert on the Japanese traditional thoughts in education, express reservation about the possible political appropriation of his work toward nationalistic agenda.

What Nishihara's reflection illuminates is the predicament of reclaiming what is indigenous or tradition in a context where Western liberalism and its associated educational thoughts permeate the political and educational discourse and institutions. In the postwar politics of Japanese education, the rejection of liberal ideas, which is always coupled with the assertion of what is traditional and indigenous, has been so tainted with regressive politics of nativism. As a result, the discourse of Shinto in education has been thoroughly politicized, and its potential for sustainable future has remained largely unexplored. In the face of the planetary ecological crisis, however, there is an urgent need to reassess this mainstream discourse of Japanese postwar education scholarship, "where Japanese-ness is automatically equated with negative distinctness, prewar myths, and an escape from the responsibility of making Japan 'fully modern'" (Rappleye, 2018, p. 17).

This is not at all an endorsement of the nationalist attribution of anything liberal to the postwar US "imposition" and of romanticizing Japan's imperial past. Instead, it is a call for a careful discerning of what is desirable and otherwise toward both ecologically balanced and politically engaged educational thoughts. The outcome of this discerning work is like to be a creative eclecticism of elements that are Indigenous and modern (Western), inviting students to live in multiple worlds simultaneously (Silova, 2019). In this regard, it is encouraging to know that the daily lives of the people in Japan are saturated with both advanced forms of technology and science and the penetrating presence of Shinto animism. It is a country where rocket scientists visit a local shrine for their successful space endeavors (Nelson, 2000, p. 1). And indeed, as amply demonstrated by Gerbert's (1993) study, the strongly nature-centered view of the world has been quietly integrated into Japanese schooling.

It is important to note that Gerbert's insights were only made available to us, as she was willing to look at Japanese primary school readers not through a political lens but cultural ones. This point takes me back to my earlier critique of the English-language comparative education scholarship of

Japanese education and forces me to reflect how much I have shifted over time. About 10 years ago, I published a discursive analysis of the whole scholarship of Japanese schooling and identified the continuing Orientalist logic in this body of research (Takayama, 2011). I rejected its predominantly culturalist framing of Japanese schooling, whereby nation-state was unproblematically conceptualized as a cultural "container" and the assumed existence of "fundamental cultural differences" between Japan and the West (usually USA) remained unquestioned. I maintained that the whole scholarship was deeply apolitical and re-inscribed the nationalistic thesis of cultural homogeneity. The critique included some of the best-known scholarships of Japanese schools, including those by Lewis, Tobin, Cave, and Tsuneyoshi. The argument in this chapter has forced me to reconsider my critical assessment of the scholarship. While I still consider valid much of the critique of the predominantly culturalist framing of Japanese education, I now acknowledge my own blind spot; my critique was strongly shaped by the postwar discourse of Japanese education scholarship whose preoccupation with politics trumps any consideration of culture. After all, I would not have been able to acknowledge the tremendous potentials of Shinto animism for eco-justice pedagogy, had these scholars not offered a culturalist reading of Japanese schools (e.g., Gerbert). Culturalist accounts are problematic, so is a categorical rejection of culture.

Dealing with all these tensions and complexities, involving both intra-national and international politics of difference (Ge, 2015; see also Takayama, 2018, 2020a, 2020b), is part of what doing Southern Theory entails. It demands constant self-critique reflecting on where we have come from and continual search for ways to release ourselves from our habitual modes of thinking and being. Doing all these is a constitutive part of what I consider as doing Southern Theory, and it is one way to make comparative and international education research transformative, meaningful, and politically astute at the same time.

References

Alatas, S. F. (2006). *Alternative discourses in Asian social sciences: Responses to eurocentrism*. Sage.
Bhambra, G. K. (2014). *Connected sociologies*. Bloomsbury.
Blaise, M. (2015). Fabricated childhood: Uncanny encounters with the more-than-human. *Discourse: Studies in the Cultural Politics of Education, 37*(5), 617–626.
Bowers, C. A. (1987). *Elements of a post-liberal theory of education*. Teachers College Press.
Bowers, C. A. (1993). *Education, cultural myths, and the ecological crisis: Toward deep changes*. SUNY Press.
Carter, R. E. (2013). *The Kyoto school: An introduction*. SUNY Press.
Chakrabarty, D. (2000). *Provincializing Europe: Postcolonial thought and historical difference*. Princeton University Press.
Chen, K. (2010). *Asia as method: Toward deimperialization*. Duke University Press.

Connell, R. (2007). *Southern theory: The global dynamics of knowledge in social science.* Crows Nest: Allen & Unwin.

Davis, W. (1998). Religion and national identity in modern and postmodern Japan. In P. Heelas (Ed.), *Religion, modernity and postmodernity* (pp. 169–185). Blackwell.

Ge, S. (2015). *Ajia wo katarukoto no jirenma: chiteki kyoudou kuukan wo motomete* [Dilenma of speaking about Asia: Towards a shared intellectual space]. Iwanami shoten [in Japanese].

Geertz, C. (2000). *Available light: Anthropological reflections on philosophical topics.* Princeton, NJ: Princeton University Press.

Gerbert, E. (1993). Lessons from the "Kokugo" (national language) readers. *Comparative Education Review, 37*(2), 152–180.

Grosfoguel, R. (2011). Decolonizing post-colonial studies and paradigms of political-economy: Transmodernity, decolonial thinking, and global coloniality. *Transmodernity: Journal of Peripheral Cultural Production of the Luso-Hispanic World, 1*(1), 1–38.

Hardacre, H. (2017). *Shinto: A history.* Oxford University Press.

Hickel, J. (2020). *Less is more: How degrowth will save the world.* William Heinemann.

Hirota, T. (2015). *Kyouiku wa nanio subekika: nouryoku, shokugyou, shimin* [What education ought to do: Competency, occupation and citizenship]. Iwanami shoten [in Japanese].

Igarashi, Y. (2000). *Bodies of memory: Narratives of war in postwar Japanese culture, 1945–1970.* Princeton University Press.

Irie, Y. (2004). *Kyoukasho ga abunai: "kokoro no nouto" to koumin/rekishi* [Dangerous textbooks: "Notebook for Heart" and civil/history]. Iwanami shoten [in Japanese].

Ishihara, C. (2005). *Kokugo kyoukasho no shisou* [The philosophy of the national language textbook]. Chikuma shobou [in Japanese].

Iwakawa, N., & Funabashi, K. (Eds.). (2004). *'kokoro no noto' no ho e wa ikanai* [I won't be going towards 'the notebook of heart']. Terakaya Shinsha.

Jensen, C. B., & Blok, A. (2013). Techno-animism in Japan: Shinto cosmorrams, actor-network theory, and the enabling powers of non-human agencies. *Theory, Culture and Society, 30*(2), 84–115.

Kasulis, T. P. (2004). *Shinto: The way home.* University of Hawaii Press.

Kato, M. (2021). The educational function of Japanese arts: An approach to environmental philosophy. *Educational Philosophy and Theory.* https://doi.org/10.1080/00131857.2021.1904396

Kodama, S. (2013). *Gakuryoku gensou* [Illusion of academic achievement]. Chikumashobou [in Japanese].

Komatsu, H., Rappleye, J., & Silova, I. (2021). Student-centered learning and sustainability: Solution or problem? *Comparative Education Review, 65*(1). https://doi.org/10.1086/711829

Koyasu, N. (2004). *Kokka to shisai: Kokka Shintou no genzai* [Nation-state and Shinto ceremonies: The current state of State Shintoism]. Seidosha [in Japanese].

Kurasawa, F. (2004). *The ethnological imagination: A cross-cultural critique of modernity.* University of Minnesota Press.

MEXT. (2002). *Kokoro no no-to, chugakkou* [Notebook for Heart for junior high school]. Akatsuki kyouiku tosho [in Japanese].

MEXT. (2014). *Watashitachi no dotoku, shogakko 5.6 nen* [Our morality, year 5 and 6]. MEXT.

Mignolo, W. (2011). *The dark side of Western modernity: Global futures, decolonial options*. Duke University Press.

Miyake, A. (2003). *"kokoro no no-to" wo kangaeru* [A thought on "The Notebook of Heart"]. Iwanami shoten [in Japanese].

Nakayama, O. (2019). New spirituality in Japan and its place in the teaching of moral education. *Religions, 10*(4), 278. https://doi.org/10.3390/rel10040278

Nelson, J. K. (2000). *Enduring identities: The guise of Shinto in contemporary Japan*. University of Hawaii Press.

Nishihara, H. (2006). *Ryoushin no jiyuu to kodomotachi* [Freedom of conscience and children]. Iwanamishoten.

Nishihira, T., & Rappleye, J. (2021). Unlearning as (Japanese) learning. *Educational Philosophy and Theory*. https://doi.org/10.1080/00131857.2021.1906644

Plumwood, V. (1993). *Feminism and the mastery of nature*. Routledge.

Rappleye, J. (2018). In favor of Japanese-ness: Future directions for educational research. *Educational Studies in Japan: International Yearbook, 12*, 9–21.

Rappleye, J. (2020). Comparative education as cultural critique. *Comparative Education, 56*(1), 39–56.

Rose, D. B. (2005). An indigenous philosophical ecology: Situating the human. *The Australian Journal of Anthropology, 16*(3), 294–305.

Sevilla, A. (2016). Education and empty relationality: Thoughts on education and the Kyoto School of Philosophy. *Journal of Philosophy of Education, 30*(4), 639–654.

Shibata, M. (2004). *Japan and Germany under the U.S. occupation: A comparative analysis of the post-war education reform*. Lexington Books.

Shimazono, S. (2003). State Shinto and the religious structure of modern Japan. *Journal of the American Academy of Religion, 73*(4), 1077–1098.

Silova, I. (2019). Toward a wonderland of comparative education. *Comparative Education, 55*(4), 444–472.

Silova, I., Rappleye, J., & You, Y. (2020). Beyond the Western horizon in educational research: Toward a deeper dialogue about our interdependent futures. *ECNU Review of Education, 3*(1), 46–65.

Stengers, I. (2011). Comparison as a matter of concern. *Common Knowledge, 17*(1), 48–63.

Stengers, I. (2012). Reclaiming animism. *E-flux journal #36*. https://www.e-flux.com/journal/36/61245/reclaiming-animism/

Takayama, K. (2008). Japan's Ministry of Education 'becoming the right': Neoliberal restructuring and the ministry's struggles for political legitimacy. *Globalisation, Societies, and Education, 6*(2), 131–146.

Takayama, K. (2010). From the rightist 'coup' to the new beginning of progressive politics in Japanese education. In M. W. Apple (Ed.), *Global crises, social justice, and education* (pp. 61–111). Routledge.

Takayama, K. (2011). Other Japanese educations and Japanese education otherwise. *Asia Pacific Journal of Education, 31*(3), 345–349.

Takayama, K. (2015). Provincialising the world culture theory debate: Critical insights from a margin. *Globalisation, Societies and Education, 13*(1), 34–57.

Takayama, K. (2018). Towards a new articulation of comparative educations: Cross-culturalising research imaginations. *Comparative Education, 54*(1), 77–93.

Takayama, K. (2020a). Engaging with the more-than-human and decolonial turns in the land of Shinto cosmologies: "Negative" comparative education in practice. *ECNU Review of Education, 3*(1), 46–65.

Takayama, K. (2020b). An invitation to 'negative' comparative education. *Comparative Education, 56*(1), 79–95. https://doi.org/10.1080/03050068.2019.1701250

Takayama, K., Heimans, S., Amazan, R., & Maniam, V. (2016). Doing Southern theory: Towards alternative knowledges and knowledge practices in/for education. *Postcolonial Directions in Education, 5*(1), 1–25.

Takayama, K., Sriprakash, A., & Connell, R. (2017). Toward a postcolonial comparative and international education. *Comparative Education Review, 61*(S1), 1–24.

Tanikawa, T. (2021). *Baseball in occupied Japan: US postwar cultural policy*. Kyoto University Press.

Taylor, A. (2017). Beyond stewardship: Common world pedagogies for the Anthropocene. *Environmental Education Research, 23*(10), 1448–1461.

INDEX

A
Aboriginal studies, 226, 227
adult education, 572
Africa, 64–76, 449, 452, 456
  Kenya, 450–454, 458, 460
  philosophies of education, 63–65, 68, 70–73, 76
agonistic pluralism, 563
alienation, 371, 374, 380, 381, 383
anthropocene, 305, 309, 310, 323, 328
Assessment
  acquired academic skills, 498
  diagnostic assessment, 503
Australia, 225–228, 230, 232, 235–237

B
Bangladesh, 197, 201–203, 208, 209
  peace education, 214
biodigital, 323, 325, 326, 331
British Columbia, 114, 116–118, 120

C
Canada, 131, 132, 136–138, 140–143, 340, 345, 346
  Canadian exceptionalism, 131, 136, 137, 142
  Canadian school system, 512, 514
  Ontario, 497–499, 503, 506–509, 511–514
  peace education, 214

capabilities approach (CA), 413, 419, 422–425
capitalism, 572, 575, 578, 581, 582, 585
China
  citizenship, 182
  democracy, 182, 183, 187–190, 192–194
  histories, 183, 187, 190, 191, 194
citizenship
  China, 182
  global citizenship education (GCE), 12, 148
  lived citizenship, 213
  planetary citizenship education, 311, 312
collaborations, 289
  transnational, 519, 520, 525, 528
coloniality. *See* decoloniality
community
  community-cenetred pedagogy, 439
  community-engaged learning (CEL), 420, 422, 425
  community-engaged research, 443
comparative education, 591, 602
  comparative curriculum mapping, 498
conflict, 394, 396, 398–402, 407
convergence, 326–333
COVID-19, 15, 22, 31, 34, 35, 39, 121, 124, 142, 153, 199, 253, 314, 321, 325, 328–330, 349, 419, 441, 475, 477

credentials, 416
critical consciousness, 148, 151, 152, 155, 157, 158, 361
critical literacy, 291, 596
   ecopedagogical literacy, 301, 303, 306, 307, 309, 310
   media literacy, 43, 205, 322, 333
critical race theory (CRT), v–viii, x, 16, 24, 30, 85, 86, 114, 482–485, 488, 489, 556
cultural reciprocity, 226
culture of schooling, 453–455
curriculum
   curriculum mapping, 498, 499, 505, 509, 510
   internationalization of the curriculum, 132–134, 139, 142
   mathematics curriculum, 498, 499
   sciences curriculum, 290, 293, 449–451, 453–455, 458, 460

D
decoloniality, 15, 16, 18, 63, 234, 262, 266, 268, 270, 273, 277, 309, 310, 431, 538, 545–547, 567, 572, 573, 583, 585, 593
   African decolonial feminism lens, 538, 545, 546
   cognitive colonization, 65, 69
   decolonial social movements, 431
   gender, 538, 545–547
   philosophy, 63
   research methods, 364, 369
   settler colonialism, 263, 264, 267
democracy, 148, 150, 152, 157, 158, 181–189, 192–194
   China, 182, 183, 187–190, 192–194
   democratic education, 181–188, 192–194
   peace education, 197, 198, 200, 205
   social democracy, 255
development, 455, 456, 459, 466, 470, 474, 477
   d/Development, 306–308, 311
   sustainability. *See* sustainability
Dewey, John, 26–29, 32, 38
digitalization. *See* postdigital
disability, 114–116, 118–124

E
ecopedagogy, 9, 14, 301, 302, 304, 305, 307, 308, 313, 314, 325, 330
emotional well-being, 47, 48, 56, 59, 60
employment. *See* work
environmentalism, 248, 301, 302, 310, 313. *See also* Sustainability
   ecofeminism, 592
   ecopedagogy, 301, 302, 304, 313, 314, 325, 329, 330
   Nature, non-anthroposphere, 305
   sustainability. *See* sustainability
epistemologies, 7, 8, 11–13, 16, 456
   feminist epistemologies, 360
   fund of knowledge, 511, 513
   Indigenous epistemologies, 455
   Indigenous knowledge practices, 431
   onto-epistemological, 68, 72
   Ubuntu. *See* Ubuntu
   violence (epistemological), 393, 397, 400, 402, 409
epistemologies of the South/North, v, vii, x, 8–10
   environmentalism, 310
   Indigenous, v, 234
   Southern theory, 591
   Ubuntu. *See* Ubuntu
ethics, 47, 52–56, 58
   environmental, 302, 304, 310
Eurocentricity, 168, 169, 172, 175, 176, 538, 539, 541, 545–547
   credentials, 164–166, 168, 170, 171, 175
   philosophy, 14, 64–66, 76
exceptionalism, 131, 136, 137, 142, 143

F
feminism
   critical feminist theory, 262
   decoloniality, 538, 545, 546
   ecofeminism, 592
   feminist epistemologies, 360
   women scholars, 520, 522, 525, 529, 530
food security, 465, 471–473
Freire, Paulo, 302
futures (*futurities*), 83, 92

G

gender, 520, 521, 522, 524–530. *See also* feminism
  coloniality of gender, 538, 539, 545–547
global citizenship education (GCE), 148–158, 312
globalizations
  environmental pedagogies, 307
  Eurocentric education systems, 170, 171, 541, 545, 546
  knowledges and epistemologies, 169, 175, 305

H

health, 31, 86, 115, 171, 212, 225, 350, 441, 467, 472, 476, 523, 544
  environmental health, 314
Higher Education Institutions (HEIs)
  Aboriginal studies, 227
  African, 519, 522, 524–526, 529, 530
  Australia, 227
  coloniality, 262
  cultural reciprocity, 226
  Indigenous higher education, 226, 227, 262, 267, 271, 273
  internationalization of higher education, 131, 133, 134, 136
  racism, 232, 556
historical analysis, 340
  dehistoricization, 67, 70, 76
  rehistoricization, 70
host country, 497
human capital, 413–419, 422, 424
human rights, 98, 100, 284, 285, 288, 289, 295–297

I

inclusive education, 513
Indigenous, 223–225, 227–233, 236, 454, 538, 542–544, 546, 547
  Aboriginal studies, 227
  higher education, 226, 227, 262–268, 276, 277
  Indigenous epistemologies, 169, 170, 175, 455
  Indigenous knowledge practices, 164, 170, 175, 454
  Indigenous refusal, 262, 271–273, 277
inquiry-based approach, 283
instrumental reason, 371
intellectual freedom, 339, 341–345, 350
internationalization
  internationalization of higher education, 131, 133, 134, 136
  internationalization of the curriculum, 132–134, 139, 142
  internationally educated teachers (IETs), 164–168, 170, 171, 174, 175
  international student, 131–134, 136–143

J

Jua Kali, 450–456

L

land ontologies, 573
language, 284–297
  language learners, 498, 510, 513, 514
  language of instruction, 499
leadership
  critical leadership studies, 263, 267
  managerialism, 266
library and information studies (LIS), 338–340, 344–347, 349
literacy
  critical literacy, 4, 13, 301
  ecopedagogical literacy, 14, 302, 303, 306, 307, 309, 310

M

Marcuse, Herbert, 25, 28, 37, 38, 41
Marxism, 6, 13, 185, 188, 189, 572
math education, 481–485, 487, 488, 490, 491, 493, 498
  Black students, 481, 482, 488–490, 492, 493
  mathematics curriculum, 498, 499
  standardized tests, 488–490
methodologies
  decolonizing research methods, 364, 369

610   INDEX

democratic research, 359, 361
documentary photography, 361, 365
intersectionality, 114–116, 120
participatory research, 355, 359, 361, 363, 364, 369
phenomenology, 555
photovoice, 357, 359–365, 367, 368
Southern Theory, 591
México, 201, 209, 211
  peace education, 214
mobility, 497, 509
  educational mobility, 498, 511
multicentricity, 82, 89, 91

N
negation, 590, 591
neoliberalism, 303, 310, 311, 314, 414

P
parents, 498, 509, 512–514
peace education, 214, 393–403, 405, 406, 408
  comparative study, 214
  comprehensive peace education, 398, 400, 401, 404, 409
  cultural violence, 397, 402
  culture of peace, 398–401
  curricula, 202, 214, 215
philosophies of education, v, 8, 10, 26, 29, 32, 64, 65, 68, 70–73, 76
  African philosophies, 8, 10, 65, 70, 71, 76
  sage philosophers, 72
planetary citizenship education, 311, 312
policy, 114, 116–119, 124
positive psychology, 47, 49–53, 56, 57
post-coloniality. *See* decoloniality
postdigital, 322, 324, 325, 328–333
  biodigital, 323, 325, 326, 331
  higher education, 372, 374, 380–382, 384
praxis, 4–9, 11, 14
psycho-social change, 394, 395, 402, 406
public good, 413, 418, 423, 425
public pedagogy, 28

environmental, 312

Q
qualifications, 164, 170, 416, 417, 425. *See also* Assessment

R
racism, vi, viii, 85–87, 89, 97, 98, 100, 101, 108, 131, 141–143, 578
  critical race theory. *See* critical race theory (CRT)
  ecoracism, 303
  higher education, 232
radical pedagogies, 23, 37, 40, 431–433, 436, 437, 441. *See also* revolutionary pedagogies
research. *See* methodologies
revolutionary pedagogies, 254. *See also* radical pedagogies

S
Santos, Boaventura de Sousa, 309, 310
sciences, 309, 313, 449–458, 460
Shinto [Shintoism], 594, 595, 597–603
socialism, 244, 247, 248
social justice, 47, 59, 60, 100–103, 106, 107, 302, 304, 338, 339, 344, 345, 413, 423
  contributive justice, 423
  socio-environmental justice, 303, 304, 310
  socio-political, 394, 395, 402, 403, 406
social movements, 431, 434, 436, 440–443
  decoloniality, 443
  education, 572
South Korea, 148
STEM and STEAM, 283, 289, 296, 297
  ecopedagogy, 283, 302, 307
sustainability, 301, 304–307, 310, 313, 451–453
  Sustainable Development Goals (SDGs), 546, 579
  sustainable livelihood, 306, 465–467, 469–474, 477
Syrian students, 504, 506, 507, 509

T

technologies, 324, 325, 327, 330, 331. *See also* postdigitalism
  ecopedagogy, 324

U

Ubuntu, 440
Ujamaa, 69
utopia. *See* futures

V

violence
  cultural violence, 397, 402
  culture of peace, 398–401
  epistemological violence, 397, 400, 402
  pedagogical violence, 397
  structural violence, 395–397, 403, 404, 409
virtue ethics, 47, 52–56

W

Westernization, 135, 137
  hegemony, 225
  psychology, 48
work, 413–425
  employability, 419, 420, 425
  learning for earning, 417, 419, 421
  professions, 425
  underemployment, 417
  work-integrated learning (WIL), 419, 420

Printed in the United States
by Baker & Taylor Publisher Services